BEN AND BERTHA BENJAMIN'S
Institute of *West African Spirituality*
Mission Statement
"Fighting for the definition of Black History"
Presents

AFROSACREDSTAR/
THE STORY OF A FAMILY REUNION WITH
OUR
ANCIENT AFRICAN ANCESTORS
Book Four

Grass root Historians
Orchester Benjamin Sr.(Voice)
Linda Benjamin (Heart)
Clovis Benjamin-Dinwiddie (Soul)
Orchester Benjamin Jr. (Mind)

SoulViewWorld LLC/ Publishing
www.SoulViewWorld.com

AFROSACREDSTAR/
The story of a family reunion with Ancient African Ancestors

ISBN 978-0-9773421-9-8

SAN: 257-3326

Book cover star-symbol design © Orchester Benjamin

Photo on back cover taken by Marcus Benjamin

DEDICATION
To the memory of my grandson
Orchester (Rory) Benjamin III
Born February 14, 1986
Died of cancer April 21, 2007

To the memory of my Parents
Ben Jr. and Bertha Benjamin

To the memory of my Grandparents
Thomas, Georgia, and Arnolia Talton
Ben, Julie, and Judy Benjamin

To my sister, brothers, and their families
Clovis R. Brown
Ben Benjamin III
Walter M. Benjamin
To all members of my extended Family, living and dead
And to all of my grandchildren
The Hip-hop generation

ACKNOWLEDGMENTS
Family

I am deeply indebted to my daughter, Clovis Benjamin-Dinwiddie for inspiring me to publish my story in the first place. My son, Orchester Benjamin Jr. who brought me back home, understands what I am doing, why, and helps me keep my head on straight on all levels; and my daughter-in-law, Norma Gooley-Benjamin who gave me invaluable help, especially with the first draft of the manuscript. Finally, my daughter, Linda Benjamin whose assistance with my many rewrites and additions cannot be measured.

However, their help was limited grammar-wise because of my beliefs that in order to be a "honest historian-writer," I insisted on most grammar to remain exactly as I use words in my thinking-understanding process—somewhat Ebonic.

Table of Contents............................Page

BEN and BERTHA BENJAMIN
Institute of West African Spirituality
Mission statement

Fighting for the definition of Black History, by seeking the wisdom and knowledge in West African Spirituality to turn the Black world right-side up, because slavery turned it up-side down. This is found in a family reunion with our Ancient Ancestors among the AfroSacredStars, located in the galaxy that governs West African Spirituality, the system that illuminates, and empowers the Soul of the Game Black people play in life.

Ben and Bertha Benjamin's Institute of West African Spirituality is the gratitude that I have for my Parents for teaching me the two most important things in my life which are to, "Keep an independent mind, and, Learn to do what I want to do." As well as the fulfillment of a vow that I made at their funerals, to institutionalize their spirits to keep them alive. My mother died in 1967, and my father in 1992.

My mother and her father, Grandpa Tom Talton's questions were deeply influenced by Marcus Garvey. While my father and his father, Grandpa Ben Benjamin's questions were deeply influenced by Booker T. Washington. My answers to their questions are found in my, *Grandpa! Tell us a Story/ Drinking from Ancient Wells: Ancient West African Spirituality Series.* In turn, my answers are deeply influenced by John Hope Franklin's, "From slavery to Freedom", along with Alex Haley's "Roots." This includes all Afrocentric writers, especially *Molefi Kete Asante's "The Afrocentric Idea and Afrocentricity,"* although I don't think we took the idea in the same direction.

The following is Ben and Bertha Benjamin's, *"Questions of Black Salvation,"* and my implied answer, *"Black History and African Soul."* On the other hand, some of these questions came from my extended family, especially my Grandparents, Uncles, and Aunts. In the sense that these are some of the questions I heard them talking about back in my childhood, and this made them also my extended family's questions.

PROLOGUE
Kicking the Game around
With my granddaughters about our Ancient Ancestors

Grandpa: "Well Granddaughters, I have kind of moved into the position of taking your minds on adventures, as I have been doing throughout the *"Grandpa! Tell us a Story/ Drinking from Ancient Wells Series."* That means that I can afford to indulge in my favorite pass time of entertaining your brains with something that has been bothering my mind for a long time. I believe that it is time that we have a family reunion with our Ancient African Ancestors.

Although we inherited many things from them, things we used to survive and grow as a people; some where along the line we seem to have forgotten about them. Of the ones that haven't been forgotten about, there seems to be a lot of negative thoughts about them. They don't deserve this kind of treatment. They should be held in high esteem out of respect for their gifts.

This means that we don't know much about them on a conscious level, and therefore, don't show our appreciation for their gifts. That is a shame; after all, they are the roots of the whole Black race, which makes them family. Now tell me, is that any way for family members to act towards each other?

Grandpa personally believes that we should have a special holiday set aside to have communion with our Ancient Ancestors. After all, we have Mother's day, Father's day, some are even talking about a Grandparent's day; so why not an Ancestors day (slave Ancestors), and Ancient Ancestors day (African Ancestors)? They are our ancient grandparents, parents, and cousins. It is time to acknowledge them and their games as members of our family. Isn't that what History of the Game is all about?

I say, lets have a family reunion with our Ancient African Ancestors, get re-acquainted, and then decide what day of the year to honor their memory; create a holiday. What do you think of that as a way to entertain your brain, and maybe learn something about yourself in the process?

Tiffany: "Say, what's up Grandpa? You told us a story of "The Game Black people Play," and that was very interesting. We learned a lot about our history and life. But, and I speak for all of your grandchildren, you talked about human nature and African Traditional Religion throughout *"Grandpa! Tell us a Story/ Series"* like we have a PHD in African theology, and sociology. Is this the way it will be with "Family Reunion with Ancient Ancestors story?" Don't you think we should have some insight into those subjects before we can think about a family reunion? Break it down Grandpa and make it real!"

Rachel: "That's right Grandpa, I have two different races of Ancient Ancestors who are at odds with each other. How does that fit into African theology, sociology, and a family reunion with the Ancient Ones? And, how am I to think about that, like you told your grandsons about *wants, and asking the right questions?* (Mentioned in the prologue of your book, "*Questions of Black Salvation/ Black History and African Soul Story*)." Do granddaughters follow the same thinking process as grandsons?"

Omni: Speaking of thinking, how are we going to understand African Traditional theology and sociology on a deep level without joining their religions, and look at it from the inside?" If not, how are we going to have a family reunion with them?

Nikki: "I have heard all of my life that there is only one true religion, Christianity, and to deal with any other in any way is a sin. How am I going to think about that?"

Grandpa: "Well! Well! Let me see. Grandpa has to come up with a way to explain **theology,** (religious beliefs), and **sociology,** (the way one lives their life according to their religious beliefs) in a way to answer all of your questions. It boils down to **what you want** from the religion one believes in, and **what you get out** of living that lifestyle.

Another way of saying the same thing is that, sociology is how one lives life according to their religious belief; from the point of view of your experience, and *the Game you play in life to get what you want.* I will use your belief and experiences in Christianity as an example.

The theology of sociology is a religion, based on the worship of at least one of the many spiritual aspects of human nature. In the case of Christianity, the spiritual aspect of human nature worshipped, is *Love,* symbolized by Jesus Christ. In your religious beliefs, the power of *Christ is Love, and the power of Love is Christ. They* are one and the same thing.

I know that you hear your Preachers talking about how "Christ's Love can heal the sick and raise the dead," and also how, "God so loved the world that he gave his only begotten son to redeem the world from sin;" and there are thousands of other examples that I could mention to show the central role that Love plays in Christianity.

There can be no doubt about the foundation of love in the Christian religious beliefs, and it is a big part of human nature; especially when we take into consideration the number of Christians in the world. We will have to come to the conclusion that Christians worship Love, and use it as the foundation of the way they live their life.

This means that everything you see Christians doing and saying in their ritualized lifestyle, and the rituals in their church services, is to get Christ' love into their life. The purpose of the way they live their lives; their moral concepts, are designed to keep an ever growing love in their life, as they would say.

Next, take a look at how the Catholic Church worships Ancestors by calling them Saints, and also how all Christian Churches worship Jewish Ancestors as mentioned in the Bible. That to, ritual relationships with Ancestors, is part of human nature. The designed purpose of all of this is directed at getting love into their heart and soul, which is the foundation of theology and sociology of Christianity, and the way they see the world; worldview.

The point is that all of the religious beliefs in the world, past and present, are a Game of life related to one or more aspects of human nature. This is, and was the case with African Traditional Religions before we were brought to America.

In all religions, these aspects of human nature become *original premises for their theological and sociological focus in life*, or to say, the point of departure for their Game of life.

When I speak of original premise as foundations, I mean the things people choose to worship; like the Christians ritual relationship with Love, and how that produced the foundation for the Christian Game of relating to human nature. There is something to be learned in every ancient religious belief.

This means that African religions are the product of Ancient African theology and sociology, based on the aspects of human nature they chose to worship. And the things they worship are the foundation of their Game in life; and their Game traveled down through the generations until it reached African Americans in the 21st Century as gifts to us, and will extend into the future of our unborn as our gifts to them.

So you see **Rachel**, understanding African Traditional Religions, is a way of understanding all religions, and what purpose they serve people, period. It is the study of *universal spirituality*, i.e., human nature. Therefore, to understand your Ancient Ancestors beliefs, in order to understand them, you have to have communion with them as part of studying your history and human nature at the same time. When you understand one path, you understand the nature of all paths. They all lead to wisdom and knowledge. One is not better than another.

As to your question, *do granddaughters follow the same thinking process as grandsons?* That is a very interesting question Rachel; do men and women follow the same thinking process? That tells me that you are successfully entering womanhood. What I mean by that is, you are realizing that your mind's ability to think is the most important thing you have to do, the things you want to do in life; because it is your *responsibility to realize your dreams.*

As Grandpa sees it, men think in terms of, "what I want," and women think in terms of, "what we want;" (we, being her, and the eggs a woman is carrying in her womb.) This means that the two most important right questions a young woman must ask herself is, what do we want, and how much am I going to pay for it? A woman and a man have to keep in mind that what they *want* becomes the *wants of their children; their family's mission (chosen destiny) in life.* So the answer to your question is, *know what you want, and your mind will lead you to it.* So in that respect, men and women follow the same thinking process. The only difference between the two is, "I" want, and "we" want."

Maya: "Stop! Stop! Grandpa, you have ran all kinds of stop signs and red lights in our minds. Back up and let some clarity come into the picture of what you mean by this family reunion with our Ancient African Ancestor thing.

My cousin asked you one simple question, break down African traditional theology and sociology, and you go on some long abstract theatrical explanation. Why don't you just tell us a story about West African Spirituality?

Now I ask you Grandpa, does that fit in with that logic thing you are always talking about leading to an understanding of the wisdom and knowledge of life? Since I reached puberty, I am beginning to wonder about you Antique Gray Heads; but I guess its ok, after all, you have survived long enough to become antique, so I know you can do it once you get on the right track."

Grandpa: "Well Miss Maya, I can see why it would seem like I am side-stepping the issue. So now let me see, how can I make African Traditional theology and sociology *logically* real to my grandchildren, and tell them a story about West African Spirituality?

To really answer Tiffany, Rachel, and Maya's questions will lead us deep into the *Drinking from Ancient Wells* part of the title of "*Grandpa! Tell us a Story Series*"; *and the heart and soul of the physical and spiritual roots of the Game African Americans play. This is what we will "Drink" from those Ancient Wells.*

Now to deal with **Omni's** question, "How are we going to understand African Traditional theology and sociology on a deep level without joining their religions, and look at it from the inside?" Also **Nikki's** question, "I have heard all of my life that there is only one true religion, Christianity, and to deal with any other, in any way is a sin. How am I going to think about that?"

Drinking from Ancient Wells

Since Grandpa is the Chief Detective/ Investigator/Researcher for the Ben and Bertha Institute, the only way I think I can make African theology real, interesting, and educational, is to take my Grandchildren on an adventure of actually having a family reunion with our Ancient Ancestors, We will do this by investigating some of these great Truths in the Ancient Wells of African Traditional religions. This will be the general outline of our family reunion. This doesn't have anything to do with joining their religion, only understanding how it works.

Along with Grandpa, you will be real **Truth** *Detectives, Investigators, and Researchers* working for the Ben and Bertha Benjamin's Institute of West African Spirituality. Your title will be *Junior Truth Investigators*, whose job will be to find African Truths by Drinking from the Ancient African Wells of a family reunion.

We will accomplish our goal by doing some *Detective work* on our Ancient Ancestor's religious beliefs; and you will see the definition and functions of African theology of the Game, and sociology of how to play it. T*his will be the structure of the family reunion.*

We will look at the beliefs of the people on the southern coast of West Africa and the western coast of Central Africa, long before the Europeans came to Africa, to see how they thought about spirituality.

Then we will use those beliefs to understand and write about the roots of African American's history; or to say, look at our history through the eyes of our Ancient Ancestors. T*his is the purpose of the family reunion.*

In addition, to *make it real*, I will use your names (when ever possible) as the names for individual Bush Africans under investigation. In this way, you can visualize and identify with them in your imagination, (*intellectually experience their beliefs*) and better understand what they do, and why. In other words, each one of you will take an active part in the investigation, as well as be characters under investigation. *This will be the way we will participate in the family reunion.*

Grandpa thinks we will have fun being African investigators using African Bush Logic to investigate evidence, and using that evidence to reach conclusions, and using those conclusions to tell the story of our Ancient Ancestor's Game. This will also give you experience in using African Bush Logic.

This should be a fun, and very interesting way of making it *real enough* for you Tiffany, and especially little Miss Maya. This is how we will enjoy the family reunion with our Ancient Ancestor's Games.

Ancient Ancestors

Before we can have a family reunion with our Ancient Ancestors, and make it real as *Detectives/Investigators/Researchers,* we have to research who our Ancient Ancestors are, and where in Africa they were, and, are located, since we call ourselves African Americans.

For the answer to those questions, we will turn to some of my research. I found that Europeans, mostly English in our case, were in the business of buying and capturing Africans, and transporting them to the United States of America to be slaves. Records were kept of most of these transactions, and some of them still exist.

Also, I found that the White people in America buying Africans had concerns about where in Africa we came from; especially rice farmers in South Carolina, and that has been documented.

So first, we will research some researchers, who did original research of those records and documents, beginning with authors Philip D. Curtin's book, *The Atlantic slave trade: a Census*, and Melville J. Herskovits book, *Myth of the Negro Past,* among a lot of others.

These records not only tell us what part of Africa we came from, but also, how many of us from each part, and see how many ideas we can find to use in our investigative research of our Ancient Ancestors.

Below is a compilation showing numbers and places of pick-up and delivery of Africans to the Colony of Virginia between the years 1710 to 1769.

PLACES.............................HOW MANY
Gambia and Senegal 8,793
Ivory Coast, Ghana, Togo...........11,918
Benin and Nigeria....................14,365
Angola and Congo.....................9,001
　　　　　　　　　　　Total 44, 077

Now for those landing in the Colony of South Carolina in the years between 1733 and 1785.

Senegal and Guinea.................13,132
Sierra Leone.............................4,597
Liberia and Ivory Coast................4,542
Ghana, Togo, Benin, Nigeria........18,931
Angola.....................................12,176
Congo and Zaire.......................11,615
　　　　　　　　　　　Total 64,993

When I take a large number of these records, and do our numbers thing, we find that just about an equal number of Africans came to America from each of these areas.

Then, when we investigated this information as foundations on which to build our research, I find that in Virginia between 1710 and 1769, i.e., 59 years, 44,077 Africans came to that state, which equals 747 per year, or about 62 per month. In the case of South Carolina, in 52 years, comes out to be 1249 per year, or about 104 per month.

When we take into consideration that Virginia and South Carolina were by far the biggest importer of slaves, followed by Maryland, Georgia, and later Louisiana, we see that the majority of Blacks were imported into those states. And if we use the same numbers for Maryland, Georgia and Louisiana, as those for Virginia and South Carolina, and allowing for the other much lesser importing states, we estimated that 300,000 to 500,000 Africans were imported into the United States in the 246 years between 1619 and 1865 when the slave trade ended.

In fact, after a close look at the records, we find that 5-10% came between 1619 and 1700. However, the vast majority of Blacks, about 80-90%, came to the United States in the hundred years between 1700 and 1800, and about 5-10% came between 1800 and 1865. Most important, we noticed, that because of the slow rate at which we came, the Africans in the United States always knew what was going on in Africa over our slavery history, 1619-1865.

Meanwhile, when we take into consideration the nature of the wars between European nations over trade with Africa, and the wars between African nations over trade with Europeans, and wars between African and European nations, and where and when they took place, and at the same time, take note that directly and indirectly these wars promoted the slave trade, we can see that all of the Africans who came to America as slaves were warriors captured in war situations.

Also, it is still another way of seeing that the vast majority of Africans that came to the United States were from the above mentioned areas of West and West Central Africa.

This answers the question, Where did our Ancestors come from? The answer is, West and Western Central Africa. The next logical question is, How did our Ancestors come to be in America? Answer, we are captured male and female African warriors brought here as slaves.

Then, we can come to the conclusion that, throughout slavery, it stands to reason that, newly arrived Africans to the United States brought their religious beliefs with them. This kept Africans already in America updated on African Traditional Bush Religion.

Therefore, African Bush Religious Beliefs were a growing and dynamic reality in our slave history in America. More importantly, those beliefs are what guided us through slavery and on into the twenty-first century.

To push our research and analysis even further, when we look on the map and saw this vast area of West and West Central Africa, our research shows us that those areas consisted of seven nations of people. We find that each one of these nations had a name, language, and spiritual beliefs of their own.

They are the *Yoruba-speaking people* of western Nigeria: The *Akan-speaking people* of the southern two-thirds of Ghana, south eastern Ivory Coast, and south western Togo: The *Igbo-speaking people* of south eastern Nigeria: The *Aja-speaking people* of Benin and Togo: The *Secree-speaking people* living in the western half of the Ivory Coast, Liberia, Sierra Leone, and Guinea, some call *The People in the land of Secret Societies:* The Wolof-Serer *Mending-speaking people* in Senegal and Gambia: And seventh, the *Nzere-Bantu speaking* people in the Congo, Zaire, and Angola.

However, we are only going to have a family reunion with five of the seven nations. The reason the other two are not included is that we have already had a reunion, so to speak, with our Ancient **Wolof-Serer-Mending** Ancestors who live in Senegal and Gambia; and our Ancient **Nzere-Bantu** Ancestors who live in the West Central African countries of Congo and Angola in, *Grandpa! Tell us a Story/Drinking from Ancient Wells Series* <u>*The Story of the Game Black people Play-Trilogy-Book Two: The Game's Mind*</u>.

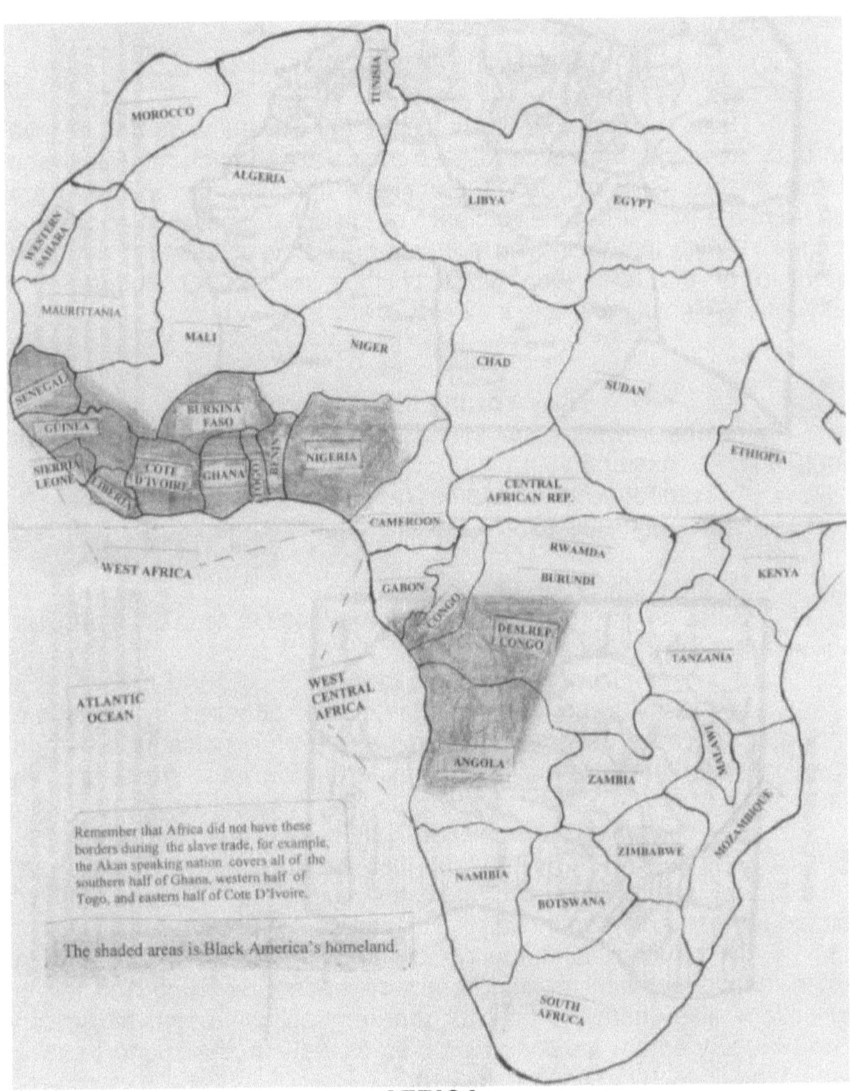

MOROCCO
TUNISIA
ALGERIA
LIBYA
EGYPT
WESTERN SAHARA
MAURITANIA
MALI
NIGER
CHAD
SUDAN
SENEGAL
BURKINA FASO
ETHIOPIA
GUINEA
NIGERIA
SIERRA LEONE
COTE D'IVOIRE
GHANA
TOGO
BENIN
LIBERIA
CENTRAL AFRICAN REP.
CAMEROON
WEST AFRICA
RWANDA
BURUNDI
KENYA
GABON
CONGO
DEM.REP. CONGO
ATLANTIC OCEAN
WEST CENTRAL AFRICA
TANZANIA
ANGOLA
MALAWI
ZAMBIA
MOZAMBIQUE
NAMIBIA
ZIMBABWE
BOTSWANA
SOUTH AFRICA
Remember that Africa did not have these borders during the slave trade, for example, the Akan speaking nation covers all of the southern half of Ghana, western half of Togo, and eastern half of Cote D'Ivoire.
The shaded areas is Black America's homeland.

AFRICA

ANCIENT YORUBA GAME

Using the example of the things that Christians do and believe to bring *Love* into their lives to save their souls through the father-son Gods of their Religion, Jesus Christ and Jehovah; the following are some of the things that the Ancient Yoruba did and believed in order to bring *Creativity* into their lives to become a nation of Artists through the worship of the father-son Gods of their religion, Olodumare and Obatala. Which is the game they play in life.

Key Yoruba terms used

Yoruba vowels have sounds that are familiar in the English language. For example,

A is pronounced as in father (ah).

E has long and short values, pronounced as in gray (ay) and met (eh).

I is generally pronounced (ee).

O has long and short values, pronounced O as in poke and like the A in law (aw).

U is generally pronounced as long oo.

In the following pronunciation guide, stressed syllables are indicated by capital letters. For example, "ah-WO" indicates stress on the second syllable. Where no capitals are shown, the stress is even throughout.

The consonant combination "gh" has no exact equivalent in English. The guttural "g" is sounded just ahead of the "b". The sign "*" next to a syllable ending in "n" indicates nasalization, with the final "n" hinted rather than pronounced.

On the other hand, the Yoruba language is tonal like all African Bush languages, with meaning often dependent on rising and falling inflections, like change o pitch or tone in singing. In fact, all African Bush languages are musical. However, to make it easier and to save time, we will not try to show inflection.

ESU (ay-shoo): The Messenger God, the God of ritual Order; sometimes called the Trickster God.

IFE (ee-FAY: Name of a city, and the Yoruba's cultural center.

OLYA NAL (o-yaw-nla): The Great Earth Goddess, known for her Wisdom of the Womb.

OGUN (O-goon*): God of War and Justice.

OLODUMARE (o-LO-doo-mar-RAY): The Great Creator of the Universe, thought of as the Great Artist.

OLOKUN (o-LO-koon*): Goddess of the Sea.

ON'DODE (awnee-do-day): The Gate Keeper between Heaven and Earth. Also, he who puts the final seal of approval on a person's destiny.

ORI (o-ree): Depending on if it is a man or woman, the God or Goddess that lives inside of a person's head. Generally thought of as the person's Inner Head, or Soul.

(One God with three names)

ORISANLA (o-ree-shah-nla): Chief of the Gods, and Chief Administrator of the World's Affairs.

OLORUN (o-LO-roon*): The Great Creator of the Human Spirit called the Outer Head.

OBATALA: The Great Sculpture God, the Creator of the physical part of Human Beings. The Great Father God.

(One God with two names)

ORUNMILA (o-RUN-mill-LAR): The God of Knowledge.

IFA: The God of IFA Priest and Divination Ritual.

OYA (aw-YAW): The Goddess of the Wind, and Wife of SANGO.

SANGO (shahn-GO): God of Anger and Righteousness.

YORUBA (YO-roo-BAH): Is the name of the people living west of the Niger River in the south western half of Nigeria.

DRINKING FROM ANCIENT WELLS
The Ancient Yoruba

Now GrandKids, the Yoruba are our direct blood-line Ancestors. And it is to them, for reasons to be explained later, that we will turn to begin our first investigative adventure into getting to know something about our influential Ancient Ancestors.

When Grandpa speaks of "the Yoruba," we mean all of the people, some 10,000,000, living in the southwestern fourth of Nigeria West Africa.

All of whom speak the Yoruba language, have the same form of government, social organization, and especially, have the same Ancient Ancestors and religious beliefs.

On the other hand, although the population is divided into Kingdoms, they do not have the same name. The name Yoruba, for the entire group, comes from their Ancient Kingdom by that name, whose ancient cultural capital is the city of Ife. And it is the people of the city of Ife that grew into the many Kingdoms.

It is these Kingdoms that make-up the Nation known as the Yoruba speaking people of South Western Nigeria; named after their Ancient Kingdom.

After saying all of that, the first step we will take is to see just how "ancient" the Yoruba are. We will begin with a short history of the area by doing some investigative work using archaeology data on their ritual art.

With that art evidence, we will show the relationship between a very ancient people's ritual art. The cultural center was located in a place now days called Nok cultural center, and the Ancient-to-present day Yoruba ritual art of ancient Ife cultural center.

From that conclusion, we can get an idea of just how "ancient" Yoruba religious beliefs really are by using African Bush Logic on some scientific evidence.

Archaeology means the scientific study of the life and culture of ancient people. This is accomplished by the digging up of ancient cities, relics, artifacts, etc. etc., and reaching a conclusion based on a combination of facts and theory.

Since we will only create our own theory, we are only interested in the scientific facts which are centered on the method of radiocarbon dating of ancient things.

For example, if a piece of pottery is found, through radiocarbon dating method, its age can be determined, and therefore, the people who made the pottery's age can be known.

In this way, the use of the ritual art can be followed to the present day, and we can safely say that those people lived in those areas and had those religious beliefs since ancient time.

Also if later, we can see what, and how the ritual art is used in the present time, we can get an idea of how the people thought about religion in ancient times. This establishes a historical time-line of their religious beliefs.

For this part of our investigation we will focus on two archaeological sites, Nok and Ife. We will look at the work and findings of three archaeologists, two brothers, William and Bernard Fagg, who worked at the Nok and Ife site; and Frank Willett, who did work at the Ife site.

The cultural area called Nok, is named after a mining village where terracotta sculptures were first found and carbon dated. Terracotta is a term used for sculptures made of pottery.

The name Nok culture, was used by Bernard Fagg, and does not have anything to do with the real name of the ancient people that produced the art. This is an important point to keep in mind.

Most of the Nok sculptures were found in river-beds deposits which were being mined for their tin content. Later, sculptures were found in other parts of the area.

One finding was from a layer of gray-black clay that contained sculpture material, and gave a date of AD 207+/- 50 years (between AD 157 and 257). While another one, worn away by the flow of the river water which was in gravel and sands below the gray-black clay, gave a date of BC 918 +/- 70 years (between BC 988 and BC 848).

One terracotta figurine carries on his head what seems to be a bowl of eggs or fruit, while maybe another seems to be of a domestic cow.

Most of the Nok sculptures are wearing beads, and many stone beads have been found in the archaeological digging, together with quartz cylinders; a grinding stone too has been found which appears to have been used for making these beads.

As to clothes on the sculptures, most wear beaded waistbands from which hangs a small apron, more than likely made of cloth, beadwork, or leather.

Although, one large incomplete originally large sculpture wears a wrapper which hides the feet and carries a grove parallel to the edge which seems to be a hem.

Also a great deal of domestic pottery pots, pans, water vases, food containers etc., have been found with the sculptures. They seemed to have been more or less globular vessels with slightly out-turned rims.

There is also some evidence that shows building material, for, pieces of burnt clay bearing the impression of thin sticks woven together have been found quite frequently, together with more strongly fired clay from furnaces, more than likely bricks.

Beside sculptures, the diggings have also produced large quantities of stone axes, and evidence of iron working, in the form of slags and nozzles of bellows. As well as a small number of iron artifacts, including two iron axes closely resembling stone axes in their form. Three of the sculptures show figures carrying axes over their shoulder.

At the Nok village itself, there are large quantities of carbonized wood in the deposits, and samples have been subject to scientific radiocarbon testing.

For example, a site produced evidence of iron-working and abundant charcoal, a sample of which was dated by radiocarbon dating to BC 280 +/- 280 (between BC 560 and AD 1).

In fact, archaeology sites have produced Nok type terracotta sculptures across central Nigeria in a wide band running diagonally across the country. This tells us that the people of ancient Nok were a part of a very large Ancient Kingdom.

CITY OF IFE SITE

Now we will turn our investigation to the city of Ife, and the archaeologist William and Bernard Fagg, along with the work of Frank Willett.

It is practically impossible to dig a hole in the city of any size without finding the remains of an earlier part of Yoruba culture. Therefore, the archaeologist had lots to work with.

This means that we must come to the conclusion that the city of Ife has been in that spot for many centuries, since the sculptures found are so very numerous and very old.

On the other hand, as far as the religious use of terracotta sculpture heads are concerned, they are used in religious worship in present day Yoruba land. For example, in the annual religious festival in the temple of the God ORISANLA, there is an ancient terra cotta sculpture head still used in worship.

This tells us that this was the use the ancient Noks had for their terracotta heads. The point being, some of these sculptures were used in places of worship.

Sculptures from many of the temples were brought into the King's palace for safe keeping as long ago as 1934, and this process of bringing them together has continued ever since, being helped very much now by the existence of the Ife museum opened in 1953, for, in the holy groves in the forest, these objects are not very safe. Plus there has, since 1956, been an archaeologist resident more or less continuously in Ife.

According to the archaeology data, the Nok sculptures cover a time period from about BC 900, and ended AD 500 +/- 200 years; some 1300 years. On the other hand, sculptures found at the Ife site dated from AD 500 +/- 200 years and 1999; some 1500 years.

And when we take into consideration, the "fact" that nowhere in West or West Central Africa is there a nation of people that produced life-size terracotta sculptures, we must come to the conclusion that the Yoruba nation, as we know it today, was founded by a group that originated in the Nok cultural area about 3,000 years ago.

About 1500 years ago, for some reason or other, the whole group moved their cultural center (capital city) from the Nok area to the present day Yoruba cultural center (capital city) at Ife, and their name has always been Yoruba.

But in any case, now that we have established a Yoruba religious and artistic historical time-line, we will turn our Investigative attention to the Yoruba artist who created the archaeology evidence, to tell us something about the Yoruba culture.

Culture, Art, and the Yoruba Artist

First, as far as our investigation is concerned, we must define the terms Artist, Art, and Culture in Yoruba Society.

The Yoruba word for the power in all spirits is ase (spiritual power), which is given by OLODUMARE (the Great Creator) to every living thing; for instance, Gods, Goddesses, Ancestors, people, animals, and plants. Ase is also contained in the voice with words such as songs, prayers, praises, and curses; including everyday conversations and situations, and group activities such as community rituals. Ase is the major concern of the Artist.

Art is the symbol of the relationship between religious beliefs and culture. By that, we mean that art is the image of the spirit of a culture, and culture is the practice of religious beliefs.

As we use the term, this means that art transforms the spirit of culture into something a person can see, touch, hear, feel, smell, taste, or any combination of the six. Or to say, art displays the spiritual expression of the culture as a pathway to living one's religious beliefs.

What we mean by that is, that an Artist's spirit must possess, and be possessed by the spirit of the subjects of his creation; in this case religious beliefs.

This is accomplished through the process of the Artist first experiencing a communication with a spirit, and uses that experience as the foundation of his conception. This conception transferred to the image of the art piece. And it is the expression of the image that reflects the spirit.

Therefore, the Yoruba artist thinks of him or herself as a priest. He or she is the priest of culture, and deals with the relationship between their culture and religion. Or to say, between beliefs and activities.

As we will see later, there are many art forms to give physical expression to those beliefs. This means that the Artist symbolizes the creative side of the Yoruba people, as well as the God of their religion, OLODUMARE (o-LO-doo-mar-RAY), the Great Creator.

Now from the point of view of our Detective type investigation, this means that the Yoruba's approach to religious sculpture is at least 3,000 years old, or to say very ancient. This is what we mean by the word "Ancient" in the title of this chapter, "Drinking from Yoruba Ancient Wells."

Now with this information as our foundation, we as Detectives can begin to build our own theory about what was going on deep in the Bush of Nigeria over 3,000 years ago.

This brings us to those Ancient Yoruba Artist that produced the sculptured heads and other archaeology evidence, and the question, what else did those Ancient Artist create?

From this and other evidence, we know that 3,000 years ago, the Nok-Yoruba were living in small villages governed by a Chief and a Council of elders. Logic tells us that the Yoruba religion was created long before that time. Doesn't this mean that long before that time, they had institutionalized their religious knowledge?

This lays the foundation for us to tell the story of the Yoruba's Most Ancient Wise Ones, and at the same time, make the case that they created the Yoruba's World View as we know it today. Our story is as follows.

Some time between 3,000 and 4,000 years ago, there was an Ancient Nok-Yoruba Chief and his Council of elders, including his chief Priest and war Chief and the Old Wise Ones of the village, sitting around a fire late in the evening deep in the bush of Ancient Nok Nigeria.

They were faced with the question of how to institutionalize their knowledge as a means of making it useful for generations to come? After many months of thinking about it, their conclusion was to create IFA divination, and a Priest Hood of Knowledge, under their God of Knowledge ORUNMILA (o-RUN-mill-LAR), the God of Knowledge, and his Son, IFA, who became the God of the Priest of knowledge and divination ritual. But what is IFA Divination ritual?

The best way Grandpa can think of to answer that question is to say that it is an institute of Yoruba Ancient Knowledge. Or better still, to say it is a place where their knowledge is stored. For example, the Christian store their religious knowledge in their Bible. In this sense, we can say IFA Divination is a Unique Bible attended to by an organization of Priests.

The logic that the Ancient Wise Ones used, is what Grandpa calls African Bush Intelligence. That is to say, African Bush Intelligence is what the Old Wise Ones used to create IFA Divination as the organizing principle of their Religious Beliefs.

Using our definition of art, this means that the Ancient Wise Ones were Artist, and IFA Divination is their greatest work of art

Divination and Priest' of Knowledge

Well Fellow Investigators, we have laid down the foundation of our investigation. Now we will turn our attention to the organization of IFA Divination priesthood, with a special focus on their education system of teaching knowledge to the younger generation.

For this part of our investigation we have all of the evidence we need, because IFA Divination ritual is still being practiced in Yoruba land today, 2009. The subject is well researched by lots of Scholars.

As Investigators, our goal is two fold, to see the inner working of the IFA ritual, and later we will see the practical application of the process in the lives of the Yoruba people.

By seeing how their Bible is put together, as well as seeing the knowledge it contains, this will give us the opportunity to observe their Ancient Black and Beautiful Mind at Work.

Now when we speak of priesthood, we mean an organization devoted to the teaching of a God or Goddess. Even though we will deal with Yoruba Gods and Goddesses later as a background, we will mention a little something about the God of Divination the IFA priests serve, ORUNMILA.

The Yoruba God of Knowledge, ORUNMILA, is the Great Logician of Heaven who uses that Holy logic to create a divination ritual to demonstrate how that logic works in life.

This is why ORUNMILA is not only called the God of Knowledge, but also is called IFA, the God of Divination; the two go together. The ritual relationship between the two is called IFA Divination ritual.

Now Grandpa knows all of this sounds complicated to my GrandKids, but it will become somewhat clearer when we investigate the IFA priest and divination. Meanwhile, we still have a long way to go.

We will begin with how IFA priesthood is organized, which is organized some what like the Catholic Church; which makes it easier for us to understand.

For example, at the top of the order is Araba (Pope). Who is the supreme High Priest of a very large area; Yoruba land is divided into 16 sections. Meaning, there are 16 Arabas that form the Great Council of IFA priesthood; and this council is its leadership organization.

After the Araba, comes the Oluwo (Archbishop), who is High Priest of a particular city or community of villages. From the Oluwo downwards, there are altogether 16 major High Priest (Bishops) in each section.

Plus, each High Priest (Bishop) has his own set of 16 priests who assist him in administering the ritual in his own area; and these priests are known as Master Priest.

It is the Master Priest who teaches IFA Divination to elemental students; some of which go on to become like college graduates under a Oluwo, and others will go on to be P.H.D students under a Araba. As we mentioned, IFA priesthood and Catholic Priest are organized some what alike.

Now that we see how the Priest is organized into an institution, we can make the next step in our investigation to see how a person is trained to become an IFA Priest. This will give us a good picture of what IFA Divination is all about.

Most IFA Priests start their training under a Master Priest when they first reach puberty, about 12 years old. If he is a normal learner, the training lasts no more than ten to twelve years. This is like going to an American school system from first grade through high school

Meanwhile, to make our investigation more interesting, let's have some fun as Detectives; Grandpa knows his GrandKids love to have fun.

Recall, I mentioned, being as African Bush names are hard to follow; we will one by one use the names of my Cool GrandKids. In this way, as involved characters, you can use your imagination to identify with our Ancient Ancestors.

With this in mind, we will take our minds back in time, say 3,000 years, to a Yoruba village a few generations after the Ancient Wise Ones created the system we call IFA Divination.

This is where we will introduce our first character, Marcus Nok-Yoruba (Marcus) into the picture, and follow him through the process of becoming an IFA Priest.

Marcus is about 12 years old, and has a strong desire to be an IFA Priest, not only because this is a highly respected profession and it will bring honor to his family, but just as important, because he loves knowledge. That is what the priest is all about, Knowledge. Which means this is a big family decision.

When he reaches the age of puberty, his parents make arrangements with a Master Priest, and give him all of the things he will need, and send him to live with the Master Priest; like going away to school.

While his family must pay part of his support for the next 10 to 12 years, he will pay the other part by doing jobs for the Master Priest; like working on his farm, getting firewood and water, and other odd jobs.

Most of his time is spent learning, not from books, but from listening and watching the Master Priest, and he has lots to learn.

First of all, Marcus must learn how to use the tools of the divination ritual; all of which have spiritual aspects. For now we are interested in their "tools" aspect as keys to knowledge.

IFA tools are the means of getting the content of the "Well," as mentioned in the title of this chapter, "Drinking from Ancient Yoruba Wells." It's like using a rope, bucket, and pulley to get water from a regular well.

In this sense, the "tools" consists of sixteen sacred palm-nuts, a divining chain, a flat tray, sacred yellow powder, and an Ibo.

The sixteen sacred palm-nuts are small enough to easily hold in the palm of one hand.

The divining chain is made of cotton string. Four half-nuts of the Opele fruit are attached to each half of the string both on the right and left, for a total of eight half-nuts tied to the string.

Each of these half-nuts have a smooth (outside) surface and a rough (inside) surface.

The basic instruments of Ibo are a pair of cowry shells tied together, and a piece of bone.

The tray of sacred yellow powder is like a serving tray with a thin layer of powder spread on it, for which to make marks during the ritual.

The divining chain and palm nuts are the first instruments in the tools of IFA to be taught to Marcus. He is taught how to recognize the various combinations of the half-nuts of the divination chain, or the palm nuts that symbolize each chapter (Odu) in IFA body of knowledge.

He learns the meaning of the name of one chapter every other day. Which tells us that the Yoruba Bible has chapters, and this is where we will next turn our attention.

We mentioned that the body of knowledge in IFA Divination is like the Christian Bible; not only does it contain all of the Yoruba's sacred knowledge; it is also divided into 256 chapters (Odus), and at least 4,096 verses (stories and poems). The divination tools are the major key to finding chapters and verses, like the table of contents in a book.

There are two categories of chapters. The first category consists of sixteen "major chapters." The second category consists of two hundred and forty "minor chapters," for a total of two hundred and fifty six all together. The name and seniority ranking of the sixteen major chapters is as follows; here we are not concerned with the pronunciation of the following names of chapters, we are more interested in organization structure as related to IFA priesthood organization.

(1) Eji Ogbe	(2) Oyeku Meji
(3) Iwori Meji	(4) Odi Meji
(5) Irosun Meji	(6) Owonrin Meji

(7) Obara Meji   (8) Okanran Meji
(9) OGUNda Meji   (10) Osa Meji
(11) Ika Meji   (12) Oturupon Meji
(13) Otua Meji   (14) Irete Meji
(15) Osse Meji   (16) Ofun Meji

As we mentioned, the sixteen major chapters are more important than the minor ones. The sixteen major chapters contain the most important poems and stories, and are considered as a duty of student IFA priests to know as many poems and stories from this group of chapters.

On the other hand, the two hundred and forty minor chapters are considered the children of the sixteen major chapters. This means the chapters are organized like a family; because each of them has the name of two major chapters.

For example, notice that the first and most important minor chapter is known as "Ogbeyeku," this is a combination of the names of two major chapters, namely, "Ogbe" the first major chapter, and "Oyeku" the second major chapter.

The two hundred and forty minor chapters are arranged in twelve groups, like the twelve clans of a tribe. Each group is known as Apola (section of a tribe). The twelve sections have the names of twelve of the sixteen major chapters, and are arranged as follows;

(1) Apola Ogbe   (2) Apola Oyeku
(3) Apola Iwori   (4) Apola Odi
(5) Apola Irosun   (6) Apola Owonrin
(7) Apola Obara   (8) Apola Okanran
(9) Apola Ogunda   (10) Apola Ika
   (11) Apola Otuurupon   (12) Apola Ose

Each Apola (section) consists of a number of chapters. The first section contains thirty chapters, while the second section contains twenty eight, and so on. However, they add up to two hundred and forty chapters in the minor category.

On the other hand, each one of the two hundred and fifty-six major and minor chapters has its own special "ritual code;" some what like using a computer to retrieve documents from the hard drive. Both the sacred palm nuts and divining chain are used alternatively by the IFA Priest to find the code of each chapter; again like typing a code into a computer.

The sacred palm nuts are used in the following manner. Marcus must learn to put the sixteen palm nuts in the palm of one hand, and try to take all of them out at once with his other hand.

If two palm nuts remain in his hand, he makes one mark on the divination tray dusted with the sacred yellow powder. If one palm nut remains in his hand, he makes two marks. If nothing remains, or if more than two palm nuts remain in his hand, he makes no marks at all.

Each mark or pair of marks is made one below the other, four times. When four marks or pair of marks have been made, the whole pattern thus formed is the "ritual code" of a specific chapter. For example, the ritual codes of the sixteen major chapters are as follows;

(1) Ogbe   (2) Oyeku   (3) Iwori   (4) Odi

```
  1      11      11       1
  1      11       1      11
  1      11       1      11
  1      11      11       1
```

(5) Irosun   (6)Owonrin (7)Obara (8)Okanran

```
  1      11       1      11
  1      11      11      11
 11       1      11      11
 11       1      11       1
```

(9) Ogunda (10) Osa (11) Ika   (12) Otuurupon

```
  1      11      11      11
  1      11       1       1
  1       1      11       1
 11      11      11       1
```

(13) Otua   (14) Irete   (15) Osse (16) Ofun

```
  1       1       1      11
 11       1      11       1
  1      11       1      11
  1       1      11       1
```

When the divining chain is used, Marcus must learn to hold the chain in the middle and throw it on the ground. As we mentioned, the divining chain has four half nuts tied to each side of it.

When the divining chain is thrown forward, all, or some, or none of the half nuts may come to rest with their smooth or rough side facing upwards. The pattern so formed by the half nuts on each throw of the chain is the ritual code of a chapter.

For example, when all of the half nuts present their smooth side, the pattern is regarded as the code of the first chapter (Eji Ogbe). When all of the half nuts present their rough side, the pattern is the code of the second chapter (Oyeku Meji).

When the middle two half nuts on each side of the divining chain present their smooth side, and all the other half nuts present their rough side, the pattern is taken to be the code of the third chapter (Iwori Meji), and so on.

Finally, each of the two hundred and fifty-six chapters has its own positive and, or, negative meaning and Fortitude, which gives them a live spiritual quality. In fact, the Yoruba think of them as low level Gods and Goddesses, who have family type relations with each other. (More on this later).

Learning about divination tools, and how they are used to find the codes of chapters, is as if Marcus has finished "elementary school." Now he is ready for "high school."

Poems

Next we will get into the time consuming part of Marcus' education. He must learn a large number of poems and stories contained in each one of the above-mentioned chapters, (like verses in each chapter of the Christian Bible).

To understand just how time consuming learning IFA poems can be, we will analyze one in detail.

Each poem, with some exceptions, gives out eight pieces of information concerning Yoruba history and Ancestors, as follows;

First piece: Names, or gives the nick-name of the ancient IFA Priest that was performing an IFA ritual when this particular poem became part of a chapter in IFA Divination.

Second piece: Names the ancient person, or God that came to the IFA priest with a problem. If a God or Goddess is named, it means that the poem originated in the time the Gods and Goddess were in the process of creating the world, or living on earth. On the other hand, if a person is named, it means that the poem originated in the time of that particular ancient Ancestor, or not so ancient Ancestor. In any case, it gives information on how old the poem is.

Third piece: Gives the problem that is the focus of the IFA Divination ritual that was preformed at that time.

Forth piece: Gives the instructions that the ancient IFA priest gave to the person, or God. Meaning, what sacrifice he or she was to perform, and to whom.

Fifth piece: Tells if the person, or God followed the instructions of the IFA priest. Meaning, if he or she carried out the sacrifice or not.

Sixth piece: Tells what happened to the person, or God who did or did not follow the IFA priest' instructions.

Seventh piece: Tells of the person, or God's reactions to carrying or not carrying out the IFA priest' instructions.

Finally, the eighth piece: Tells the moral of the poem, as the words of the God of Knowledge spoken through the priest.

There are also short poems that only use the first, second, third, and eighth pieces of information. When beginning study, Marcus must focus on what is called the "long poem" like the following; when he graduates he will be able to shorten them.

The Tall One.........(First priest' nick-name).
The Hefty man........(Second priest' nick-name).
Walk Slowly..........(Third priest' nick-name).
IFA Divination was preformed for Oloofun.....(Name of the ancient person who came to the IFA priest).
When he would take the land of the King to farm upon......(The ancient person's problem).
He was asked to make sacrifice to the Ancestors of his household......(first priest' instructions).
But his sacrifice was not accepted.....(Results).
He was asked to make sacrifice to the Goddess of the Market.....(First priest' second instructions).
He made sacrifice to the Goddess of the Market..........(Followed instruction).
But his sacrifice was not accepted. The Market Goddess refused his sacrifice.....(Results).
He was asked to make sacrifice to his ORI...(Second priest' first instructions).
He made sacrifice to his ORI repeatedly
Until his head became bald...(Followed instructions, no results).
He was asked to make sacrifice to OLYA NAL.......... (Second priest' second instructions).
He made sacrifices to OLYA NAL....(No results)
He was asked to make sacrifice to the Father of Sacrifice. (Third priest' instructions)
He said that he knew that his father is the Ancestor of his household.....(Questioned third priest)
He said that he knew that one's mother is the Goddess of the Market.
He said that he knew ORI to be one's head,
And He knew OLYA NAL to be the Earth Goddess.
But he said that did not know
What was called Father of Sacrifice?
The third priest told him that people's mouths,
People's mouths were referred to as the Father of Sacrifice.
What is it that we worship at Ife?
Their mouths.
I have given to those over there...(Followed instructions).
I have to those over here,
Their mouths.
Their mouths can no longer,
Their mouths cannot work against me.
I have given to those in my household,

I have given to passer-by.
Their mouths cannot,
Their mouths can no longer fight against me.
Fight against me (successful results).

As mentioned, for each poem there is a story; called IFA stories. And maybe if we look at the above poem as a story, which is what the Yoruba do, the poem will become clearer; a short story version goes some thing like the following:

"Once, long ago, a man was trying to get some land from the King on which to make a farm. But his attempts were all unsuccessful because the people in his community were all saying bad things about him to the King. Thus he took his problem to two IFA priests before he found the answer with a third priest. He was the kind of person that was very unfriendly.

But once he began to be friendly, he became successful. The moral of the poem is that in order to "be successful" in life, you must be a friend to your community, otherwise, the whole spiritual world of your religious beliefs cannot help you."

As we can see, another important part of Marcus' education is to learn the meaning of sacrifice as related to each poem. This is a very difficult part of the poetry, since every poem has its own appropriate sacrifice; which sometimes must be improvised upon to serve a special purpose. Like we said, poems are the most time consuming part of Marcus' education.

Grandpa knows that you GrandKids have lots of questions related to the above poem. However, for now we are only interested in an example of how the Ancient Wise Ones packaged their wisdom and knowledge.

We must file in the back of our minds that these poems contain the wisdom and knowledge that gave form and structure to the Yoruba as a people more than 3,000 years ago.

This means that these poems and stories cover the Yoruba's thoughts and actions throughout the whole range of their historical and religious experience. Ranging from the very ancient times until the present day, and deals with all subjects concerning history, religion, music, and their philosophy of life.

In addition, this is why, since ancient times, IFA Priests are known as the guardians, counselors, philosophers, and physicians of the Yoruba people. They are the intellectuals. We can now see the educational value of IFA poems.

The poems are memorized at the rate of one per day, and are memorized with such a great reverence, that not a single word is missed. It is a taboo (sin) for anybody to add or consider subtracting even one word from the body of a poem.

Also, the poems must always be learned in the very form in which it has been preserved and taught from ancient times. In this way, the texts of poems have been kept free from errors. Now to return to Marcus' education.

Marcus would not have a passing grade unless he has learned by heart at least sixteen poems in each of the two hundred and fifty-six chapters. This adds up to a total of 4,096 poems he must learn in "high school."

This means that Marcus would have lots and lots of home work to do each day. He must also learn the story and sacrifice attached to each poem.

On the other hand, as Detectives of history, this means that anything what so ever we want to know about the Yoruba, all we have to do is check out some of the 4,096 poems Marcus must learn. Our job is easy because there are hundreds of books filled with Yoruba poems and stories found in any large library. Now let's get on with our Investigation.

Recall in the introduction in Grandpa's story, I told a little story about my "Highest Valued Beliefs" and the role they play in my life; Grandpa's religion. Now we are going to use IFA poems and stories to take a close look at the "Highest Valued Beliefs" of the Ancient Wise Ones, and the role they play in the lives of the Yoruba People; Yoruba's religion.

This being the direction we are taking to move along with our investigative work, we will analyze some poems and stories. With the goal to find out what they believe about their Great Creator, Gods, Goddesses, Ancient Ancestors, and the creation of the world and mankind; along with their morals and ethics and that kind of stuff.

These were the first poems and stories the Ancient Wise Ones created over 3,000 years ago. For this reason, these are also the first poems and stories Marcus must learn on his spiritual journey to become an IFA Priest.

Meanwhile, Grandpa wants you GrandKids to direct your imagination further back in time, thousands and thousands of years, to the beginning of time even before people were created. Follow with Grandpa analyzing the poems and stories Marcus must learn.

This should be interesting and fun, for we will now focus our attention on the Yoruba's spiritual world of the Great Creator, OLODUMARE, and THE Holy Clan of Gods and Goddesses, and the creation of the Universe.

OLODUMARE

First we will give a kind of overview of a number of poems and stories Grandpa has read.

The Yoruba believe that OLODUMARE (the Great Creator) first created spiritual life, and the means for it to reproduce itself through sex.

This took the form of 7 Gods and 7 Goddesses. Or to say, the Yoruba believe that the first thing created was a family; known as the "Holy Family."

Over time, these Gods and Goddesses multiplied. All of whom were the children, grandchildren, great grandchildren, and so on, until there were 1600 members of OLODUMARE's Holy Family. All of whom are living in OLODUMARE's Palace; a place we will call Heaven.

This was followed by creating the Universe and all therein. The point being that OLODUMARE created Heaven and the Holy Family before the Universe was created.

In the process of creating the Holy Family, some of OLODUMARE's powers were divided between the Gods and Goddesses. After the creation of the Universe, they were given different jobs to do in the Universe.

Meanwhile, each God and Goddess divided their power and responsibilities between their Holy children, and their holy children did the same, until some of OLODUMARE's powers were divided throughout the Holy Family. Thus is an overview of the members of the Yoruba's spiritual world.

Now we will turn to an IFA story to show OLODUMARE's position among the Gods and Goddesses in the Holy Family. At the same time, as Investigators, we can focus on the words and actions of OLODUMARE and the Gods and Goddesses as they functioned in Heaven.

"This IFA story tells of how the Gods and Goddesses, one thousand six hundred strong, got "big-headed" and began to think, since they had all of OLODUMARE's power divided between them, that the position of Chief was unnecessary. They demanded that the Great Creator give up the position of Chief. They in turn would rule the Universe, instead of just being only its managers. OLODUMARE AGREED, but only long enough for them to see what would happen.

OLODUMARE thought that this was a good time to bring Order to the chain of Authority in the Holy Family's thinking, and assure the smooth management of the Universe. To accomplish this, OLODUMARE turned off the Logical Order of the Universe and brought everything to a super big Stop.

Immediately, the Gods and Goddesses had a problem bigger than themselves. They tried every thing they could think of to keep things going, but found that their powers would not work. Even ORUNMILA's advice was consulted, but his IFA Divination tools refused to work.

The daily celebration ceremonies in Heaven between the Gods and Goddesses stopped. Nothing in the Universe moved, all of existence had come to a complete stop.

There was no doubt what so ever, the Gods and Goddesses found themselves in a big mess. There was nothing else they could do but go back to OLODUMARE in shame with drooping heads and confess their mistake.

OLODUMARE forgave them and switched on again the logical order of the Universe, and every thing began to work again. The Gods and Goddesses began to sing;

> Be there one thousand six hundred
> Gods and Goddesses in Heaven
> OLODUMARE is the Chief Unique
> In our recent dispute
> OLODUMARE it is who won
> Yes, OLODUMARE
> Every thing comes from OLODUMARE
> Every thing returns to OLODUMARE.

This IFA story pretty much sums up the Yoruba's beliefs concerning OLODUMARE, the Holy Family, and the organization of Authority in Heaven. At the same time, the story shows that the energy that keeps the world going around comes from OLODUMARE alone.

Still using our Catholic Church example, OLODUMARE would be called "JEHOVAH God." However, the Yoruba think of OLODUMARE as Pure Creative Intelligence, and therefore, he is not thought of as a God (male) or Goddess (female).

On the one hand, the Yoruba Gods and Goddesses are thought of by Catholics as Angels. Although the Yoruba Gods and Goddesses have a much bigger role to play in their religion than the Angels have to play in the Catholic religion.

On the other hand, Yoruba Ancestors, for example, the Ancient Wise Ones, are thought of by Catholic beliefs as Saints. In fact, Yoruba Ancestors have the same role to play as Catholic Saints.

Now Grandpa thinks we will meet some of these Gods and Goddesses, and look at some of their responsibilities as Administrators of the Affairs of the Universe.

We do not have the time or space to check out all of the 1600 Members of the Holy Family. Therefore, we will only meet the ones that will give us the most insight into our investigative question; What is the highest valued Beliefs of the Yoruba religion? For now we will focus on 5 Gods and 2 Goddesses.

The Gods are, and in the order of their creation (1) ORISANLA, (2) ORUNMILA, (3) ESU, (4) OGUN, and (5) SANGO. The Goddesses are (1) OLYA NAL, (2) OYA. Now we will take them in their turn.

ORISANLA

According to IFA poems, ORISANLA is very ancient. He was the first God to be created and receive OLODUMARE's blessing in the form of creative powers. He is OLODUMARE's Chief Administrator. He is the Sculptor God who created mankind.

When ORISANLA had finished the molding of man's body out of clay, OLODUMARE put into him the "breath of life" (in the form of a Chosen Destiny). He takes charge again and sends man on his way into the world, while still keeping an eye on him and guiding him as a Father to his child, as he fulfills his chosen destiny. So the Yoruba sing;

> ORISANLA! The Holy One!
> He who is Greater than Great;
> Clothed in Holy robes
> He sleeps in Holy clothes,
> He wakes in Holy clothes,
> He rises in Holy clothes.
>
> He, who makes eyes, makes nose;
> It is ORISANLA I worship.
> He, who makes ears, makes mouth;
> He who creates as He chooses;
> It is ORISANLA I worship;
> He who created me;
> It is ORISANLA I worship.

Being the creator of mankind, naturally, ORISANLA is the center of Yoruba religious beliefs. He is the Great Father who stands by his children and blesses them. ORISANLA is known as the Great Father God. Just as important, as far as the Yoruba religion is concerned, He is the God of Truth.

ORUNMILA

ORUNMILA, known as IFA, the God of the Divination Priest. Being with OLODUMARE when the Universe was created, he therefore was in a position to know about the nature of most things. Including the nature of the Gods and Goddesses, and of course, mankind. The IFA story that goes with this idea is as follows;

"Once OLODUMARE had a question, and charged the Gods to find the question and answer. All of the other Gods tried and failed to tell OLODUMARE the question and answer. Only ORUNMILA succeeded.

The answer was that OLODUMARE needed someone in the Universe to whom the Gods and Goddesses could turn to for counsel and guidance.

There and then, OLODUMARE appointed ORUNMILA to be the Great Consultant of all in Heaven and on earth; and gave him the title of Chief of Wisdom and Knowledge."

Thus ORUNMILA created the tools of IFA Divination ritual as a means for Gods and Goddesses to consult his knowledge. Later, it was ORUNMILA that gave people a way to consult him through his Divination IFA Priest. He is the God of Wisdom and Knowledge.

ESU

ESU is known the world over as the God of unpredictability, or Trickster God. ESU is a very complicated God, because he does many things at the same time. In some ways he is the key to the function of the Yoruba religion. Grandpa calls him the God of Contradictions. For example, check out the following poem;

ESU turns right into wrong,
Wrong into right.
When he is angry,
He hits a stone until it bleeds.
When he is angry,
He sits on the skin of an ant.
When he is angry,
He weeps tears of blood.
ESU slept in the house,
But the house was too small for him.
ESU slept on the verandah,
But the verandah was too small for him.
ESU slept in a small nut shell,
At last he could stretch himself.
ESU walked through the peanut farm,
The tuft of his hair was just visible.
If it had not been for his Hugh size,
He would not be visible at all.
Lying down,
His head hits the roof.
Standing up,
He cannot look into the cooking pot.

He throws a stone today,
And kills a bird yesterday.
Thus is the nature of ESU

This poem, especially the last three lines, shows the kind of contradicting power that ESU has to work with. He has the ability to distort the reality of the five senses. And this means he has the power to restore reality.

For example, He is the God that has the power to have a positive or negative effect on a person's sense of reality, and therefore, we can say that ESU is a God that deals with Reality. However, as we mentioned, he does many things at the same time.

From what Grandpa gathered from lots of other IFA poems, ESU is primarily a Special Public Relations God between Heaven and Earth, like an Inspector General. He reports directly and regularly to OLODUMARE on the deeds of the Gods, Goddesses, and mankind.

Neglect of proper ritual sacrifices is taken very seriously by ESU; it is his duty to see to it that everybody makes the proper ritual sacrifices, especially as related to IFA Divination.

When a person prays, it is ESU who takes the message to a God or Goddess or Ancestors. In this sense, he serves the same purpose in Yoruba religion as Christ serves in Christianity. He is a Messenger God.

Now we can begin to see just how much power he really has, and the large role he plays in Yoruba religion.

In fact, next to OLODUMARE, ESU is the most powerful God in the governing of the Yoruba religion. In the same sense that next to JEHOVAH, Jesus Christ is the most powerful God in governing Christianity.

ESU is the God of Reality.

OGUN

The IFA story of OGUN is as follows. When the earth had been made, he and a number of other Gods and Goddesses set out from heaven to live on earth where they took up their Manger's Offices and Duties. But on the way to earth, they came to an obstacle called "no road."

Of all of the Gods, it was only OGUN who possessed a machete made of iron, which could get the job done. Therefore, OGUN is the God that "makes a way out of no way."

However, OGUN is best known as the God of War and hunting, both of which calls for killing. It is also said that he is always covered with blood and is "one whose eye balls are like flames of fire. There is an IFA poem that puts it this way;

"Where is OGUN found?
He is found
On the battle field.
He is found
Where there are disagreements.
He is found
Where blood is flowing.
Killing is as satisfying to him
As food to a hungry man.

On the other hand, OGUN is well known as the God of legal oaths and contracts. For example, in Yoruba courts, people taking their oaths to, "speak the truth and nothing but the truth" do so by kissing a piece of iron, mostly a machete.

Anyone who swears falsely by OGUN, or breaks a contract made before him, whether it is related to a business or social or spiritual matter, will be punished.

This means that OGUN is the Yoruba's War God that fights for Justice.

SANGO

It is said that SANGO is the son of a God named JAKUTA. JAKUTA is the only one of the major Gods in the Yoruba religion who never lived on earth. He sent his son SANGO with the Gods and Goddesses who came to earth when it was first created. However, he did visit earth one time, which we will mention later. Nor is he worshipped in shrines.

JAKUTA is the enforcer of the morals and ethics of righteous conduct. But because he is very emotional and has a quick temper, he is thought of as the God of anger.

As the enforcer of morality, he forbids lying, stealing, etc, etc., all of the offenses against Righteousness.

However, JAKUTA gave all of his power to his son SANGO. And for that reason he is worshipped regularly by the priest of his son, for the priest knows they must go through SANGO to get to JAKUTA. For this reason JAKUTA does not have a shrine on earth.

JAKUTA and SANGO have a very close father-son relationship, and like father like son, SANGO is an enforcer of morality, has a quick temper and is very emotional.

SANGO and JAKUTA are known as the Gods of Righteousness.

To continue our investigation, we will now turn our attention to the values associated with a Goddess.

OYA

OYA is a very interesting Goddess because she was married twice, once to OGUN, and then to SANGO. We will begin with OYA and OGUN.

"OYA, the Goddess of the Wind, and OGUN, the God of War got married. Things worked out fine for a while. OGUN, being the God of war, had a blacksmith shop where he made weapons. OYA used her wind, not only to keep things cool, but also to act as a bellow to keep the fire hot enough to heat the iron so that OGUN could design his weapons.

One day OGUN designed two weapons with special powers of justice. He gave one to OYA and said, "When you are in danger, strike with it and the nature of that danger will be destroyed." OGUN kept the other one for himself.

OGUN and OYA were getting along just fine until SANGO came into the picture.

A God by the name of SANGO
Who like so much to be "Cool.'
He plaited his hair like a woman.
And he made holes in his ears
Where he wore gold earrings.
He wore braided gold necklaces.
He wore gold bracelets.
Where you find females,
There you will find SANGO.

SANGO is known as the Playboy of Heaven's society, because of his knowledge about male and female sexual relationships. At the same time, OYA is so sexually attractive, that Gods cannot take their eyes off her. She too, loves to play the games in male-female relations.

One day SANGO came to OGUN's shop to have some work done, and with his arrival came trouble in the paradise of OGUN and OYA's relationship.

So when SANGO and OYA laid eyes on each other, the attraction was so strong that they disappeared together. Meanwhile, OGUN did not know what happened, and sent some young Gods to look for OYA. However, they returned singing;

We went to the east for OYA
Where she used to sing,
But we did not find OYA.
We went to the west in search of OYA

Where she used to dance
But we did not find OYA.
We searched for her in the north
Where she used to eat
But we did not find OYA
We search for her in the south
Where she use to play
But we did not find OYA
We searched and searched,
But could not find OYA

To OGUN this was injustice, and being the God of War that fights for justice, rushes to track down SANGO and OYA. Finally he saw their love nest far deep in the forest.

SANGO and OYA could see OGUN coming in the far distance. SANGO realized, although OGUN was his older brother, he is a War God, and if it came to a fight, he would lose. But OYA told him she could take care of the situation, and rushed out to meet OGUN.

They came closer and closer, both had their weapon of justice in their hands, and finally coming into contact with both striking at the same time, all danger to both disappeared.

Which meant that OGUN's reason to fight disappeared. He realized that females have the right to choose. If OYA would fight to defend SANGO, he had nothing to fight for. OYA belonged to SANGO by right of female choice. After which OGUN moved into the hills and remained a bachelor to this very day."

Following this, SANGO and OYA got married. Now SANGO is known to be the sexiest God in Heaven, a master in the game of male-female relationships, and dominates his wives. This was proven by the many wives he had under his control, and none could become Chief wife.

However, this changed when he married OYA. On the other hand, OYA is known as the sexiest Goddesses in Heaven's community.

On the day they got married, ORUNMILA performed Divination for SANGO, and the following IFA poems tell how OYA became Chief Wife;

What is it we call "OYA?"
Goddess of the rushing wind,
That tears down trees from the top.
One who causes heavy dark clouds
But brings no rain.
Now we shall praise OYA.

Which ORUNMILA says is called
Determination, the Wind.
Meaning "swept clean."
IFA, I say, let her blow!
Twist! Tear! They ask where?
It tore up the place of our friend SANGO.
Child of established wealth,
Tore his house to shreds as he sat peaceful.
Swept up all his money, all his clothes, everything.
So that his many wives wept.
What sort of thing is that?
We looked around.
Nothing to be seen.
What sort of an invisible housecleaning?
OYA!

SANGO had finally met his match, OYA cleaned up his situation, organized it to please herself. She became Chief Wife, and there was nothing SANGO could do about it."

As we mentioned, OYA is a very interesting Goddess, she could be as calm as a cool wind on a hot summer day. Or she could be as destructive as a hurricane.

Now before we can get any insight into the nature of OYA, first we have to take a look at the nature of 5 of the Gods we mentioned.

Each God represents a "value." For example, ORISANLA represents "Truth," ORUNMILA represents "Knowledge," OGUN represents "Justice," ESU represents "Reality," and SANGO represents "Righteousness."

We can come to the conclusion that the Yoruba believe that these are the "values" they should use to govern their lives as a people, and they take their beliefs in these values to the point of worshipping them as Gods.

Now as we mentioned, there are 1600 Gods and Goddesses in Heaven, which means that there are 1600 values governing the Universe. Which gives us some insight into the nature of OLODUMARE and the Universe. However as Detectives, we are only interested in the highest valued of these values in the spiritual world of the Yoruba religion.

Recall in the introduction, and Grandpa's lil story about my highest valued beliefs, and the role they played in my life. Thus is the nature of what we are looking for in the Yoruba religion.

Even though we have a long way to go before we get the full picture of Yoruba religion, this gives some understanding of the direction we are taking as Detectives. As well as getting some insight into what Marcus must learn to become an IFA Divination Priest.

On the other hand, this pretty much sums up an example of the kinds of things that the Yoruba's Ancient Wise Ones were thinking about their religion over 3,000 years ago. As well as the things they wanted to pass down the generations in the form of IFA poems and stories.

Next we will return to the division of OLODUMARE's powers between the Goddesses and Gods. You see, each of OLODUMARE's creative powers has a male and female side, and it is the two sides together that make the power complete.

For example, we will take the case of SANGO and OYO, and the values in OLODUMARE's emotions. Of which anger is symbolized by a storm. Now for a storm to be a storm; there must be thunder, lightning, and strong winds. This means that SANGO and OYO together symbolize the Great Storm of OLODUMARE's anger. This is the meaning of marriage between the Gods and Goddesses.

From this point of view, OYA symbolizes the power of female sexuality, and SANGO symbolizes the power of male sexuality.

On the one hand, the same is true of the original 14 Gods and Goddesses who receive creative powers. This also means that the Gods and Goddesses have equal power, and one cannot dominate the other.

On the other hand, this means that OYA is unique in that she symbolizes two values, female Justice and Righteousness.

IFA CREATION STORY

As we mentioned a number of times, IFA poems and stories serve the purpose of the Yoruba's bible. As a bible, it too has a creation story. The story gives the details of what was happening in heaven between the Gods and Goddesses just before, during, and after the creation of human beings. The Yoruba's Adam and Eve story so to speak. The story is as follows:

"In ancient days, at the beginning of time, but after OLODUMARE created the Gods, Goddesses, and the universe; there was no solid land on earth where people now live. There was only outer space, heaven, and down below. It was the Goddess OLOKUN, who ruled over the vast expanses of water, known as earth.

Meanwhile, living in heaven, were 1600 Gods and Goddesses, each having creative powers of their own, but none of whom had the creative knowledge and powers equal to those of OLODUMARE. This is how it was, and all was satisfied.

That is, all except ORISANLA, king of the White Cloth, meaning, he is OLODUMARE's Executive Officer. Who was thinking, "I have all of this power, but there is nothing for me to do."

Finally, he begins to think of a way to create images of Gods and Goddesses as a living work of art, called Human Beings. Looking around for a place to begin, he saw the wet earth, and got a great idea. After thinking about it a long time, he took the great idea to OLODUMARE.

ORISANLA: "The place ruled by Goddess OLOKUN is nothing but a great wet mess, and serves no purpose. If there were solid land in her kingdom, like forests, hills, and valleys, surely it could be populated by Gods and Goddesses and living things."

OLODUMARE, seeing that ORISANLA really wanted to create a heaven called earth, and Gods and Goddesses called Human Beings, answered; "That would be a good thing, but to cover water with land is a complicated job, can you do it?"

ORISANLA replied: "Goddess OLYA NAL and I can get the job done."

ORISANLA left OLODUMARE and went to the place of ORUNMILA, who understood the secrets of existence. He said to him, "OLODUMARE has instructed me to go down below and make land where there is nothing but water, so that living things can have a place to live. You, ORUNMILA, who can divine the meaning of all things can instruct me further on how to get the job done."

ORUNMILA gathered his Divination tools. (sixteen palm nuts, a tray, and yellow powder) He threw sixteen palm nuts, and read their meaning by the way they fell. He gathered them up and threw them again, again reading their meaning. After repeating the process a number of times, adding meaning to meaning, he said, "This is what you must do. Descend to the water on a gold chain, taking with you a snail shell full of sand, a five toed hen to scatter the sand, and a palm nut."

ORISANLA went next to OGUN's blacksmith shop and asked him to make a gold chain long enough to reach from heaven to the surface of the water below.

OGUN asked, "Do you have gold to make such a chain."

ORISANLA answered, "Don't worry about that, just begin the work."

ORISANLA then went to SANGO who loved to wear gold jewelry, and asked for his gold. Then he went to ESU, and asked for his gold, and took it to OGUN. OGUN said, "This is not enough gold."

So ORISANLA continued looking for gold. He asked all of the other Gods and Goddesses, asking each of them for all of the gold they had. Some gave gold dust, and some gave rings, bracelets and pendants.

He returned again to OGUN saying, "Here is more gold for the chain."

OGUN answered, "This is not enough gold."

ORISANLA replied, "This is all of the gold in heaven."

OGUN said, "This will not make the chain long enough to reach the water."

ORISANLA answered, "No matter, make the chain anyway."

OGUN went to work on the chain. When he finished, he took it to ORISANLA.

ORISANLA said, "It must have a hook on one end."

OGUN replied, "There is no more gold."

ORISANLA answered, "No matter, it must have a hook, melt down a few links."

OGUN took a few links of chain, and made a hook and fastened it to one end of the chain. When he finished, he took the chain to ORISANLA.

Give me! I will give you.
The tether does not enter ground easily
ORUNMILA.
He performed IFA divination for ORISANLA
On the day he and OLYA NAL
Was to enter the world.
On that day they went to OLODUMARE
To receive the basket of good character.
OLODUMARE gave it to them.

On the way to the edge of the sky, ORISANLA became thirsty. They met a Goddess carrying palm wine. He drank until he could not control his senses. (This shows how ORISANLA was using the basket of good character).

OLYA NAL took the basket of good character back to OLODUARE. When she got there, OLODUMARE told her, "I give you this calabash to use."

When ORISANLA's eyes opened, he returned to OLODUMARE annoyed, and said, "Why has the basket of good character disappeared?"

OLODUMARE replied; "So."

Then ORISANLA said that he would never again drink palm wine. ORISANLA lost the right to his idea to create dry land, this became OLYA NAL's job, but being OLODUMARE's Chief administrator, ORISANLA was allowed to keep his idea of creating living things.

OLYA NAL, now the Goddess of Fortitude, fastened the hook of the gold chain to the edge of the sky, and lowered the chain. ORUNMILA gave her the things that were needed; a snail shell of sand, a five toed hen, and a palm nut.

Then OLYA NAL gripped the chain with her hands and began the journey down to the watery world, followed by ORISANLA. Half way down, she encountered darkness. Further down she could hear the wash of the waves, and felt the damp mist rising from OLOKUN's kingdom of the sea.

She reached the end of the golden chain, but she was not yet at the bottom, and she just hung there thinking, "If I let go of the chain I will fall into the sea." Then she heard ORUNMILA's voice from far above saying, "The sand."

So OLYA NAL took the snail shell and poured out the sand. Again, she heard ORUNMILA call to her, saying this time, "The hen."

OLYA NAL dropped the hen where she had poured the sand. The hen began to scatter the sand unevenly, forming hills and valleys.

After accomplishing this, OLYA NAL and ORISANLA let go of the chain, and came down and walked on the solid earth that was created.

OLODUMARE wanted to know how OLYA NAL and ORISANLA were progressing, and told Agemo the chameleon to visit the earth. Agemo went down the chain and found OLYA NAL. He said, "OLODUMARE instructed me to "go down and find out how things are going."

OLYA NAL answered, "As you can see, land has been created, but there is too much darkness and coldness, the land should have light and heat."

Agemo returned to heaven, then reported what he had heard. OLODUMARE agreed that there should be light down below, and made the sun, and set it in motion in the sky. After that, there was warmth and light in the world.

OLYA NAL named the place where she had come down "Ife" (the future Yoruba's cultural city). She built a house, and planted her palm nut, and a palm tree sprang out of the land. It matured and dropped its palm seeds. More palm trees came into being. Thus, there was vegetation life in Ife.

One day ORISANLA thought, "Now it is time to create human life." He dug clay from the ground; from the clay he shaped human figures in the image of Gods and Goddesses, with special emphasis on their heads.

He worked without resting, and became tired and thirsty. He said, "There should be palm wine in this place to help in going on working." So he stopped working, and turned his attention to the palm trees, where he drew their inner fluids to make palm wine.

When the palm juices were fermented, ORISANLA began to drink and drink and drink, until he was real mellow. Then he put his drinking cup aside and went back to making human beings. (This shows again, that the lack of Fortitude is a problem in getting things done).

But because he was so high on palm wine, his mind was going further and further away from his original design. Some were humpbacked, club footed; some had six fingers, or two fingers grown together; all of the things that we think of as birth defects.

However, like OLODUMARE did with the Gods and Goddesses, ORISANLA gave humans some of his creative intelligence, called their Outer Head; finally, being so high, he went to sleep.

Meanwhile, OLYA NAL was watching what was going on, and when ORISANLA went to sleep, she thought, "Each of these figures are truly a work of art, but there is something missing," so, she bestowed upon them good character.

When ORISANLA awoke with a big hangover, still not noticing what he had done with the clay figures, he called out to OLODUMARE saying, "I have created human beings, but only you can give them the Spiritual Breath of Live. OLODUMARE heard ORISANLA's request, and gave each figure a Purpose in Life, a Personal Destiny.

Now that people were living on the earth, ORISANLA gave them the Tools of Survival, called Outer Head. (Outer Head means that he gave them a creative mind to use, to deal with living in the world). ORISANLA saw all that he had created, he was pleased, but said, "Never again will I drink palm wine."

The people planted, and began growing food plants, and like the palm tree, they matured and dropped their seeds. Over time, Ife became a growing city, and OLYA NAL became its Goddess Queen.

But a time came when ORISANLA grew lonesome for Heaven. So he ascended by the golden chain, and there was a great festival on the occasion of his return.

The Gods and Goddesses heard him describe the land, and 401 of them decided to go down and live among the newly created humans.

Thus, many Gods and Goddesses departed from heaven, but not before ORISANLA instructed them on their obligations; "When you settle on earth, never forget your duties to humans. Whenever you are approached for help, listen to what is being asked of you. You are the protector of human kind, but OLYA NAL and her descendants will rule."

With ORISANLA now living in heaven full time, he created an Outer Head (creative mind) shop in heaven which is ran by his chief assistant and craftsman, Ajala.

Although ORISANLA is OLODUMARE's Chief Administrator in the management of the world affairs, he seems to not have it all together. There was always something missing in his work, and this was definitely the case when Ajala became his assistant.

Nobody knows why ORISANLA picked Ajala for his assistant. Maybe he is his son, or a palm-wine addict, for he operates just like ORISANLA, only, Ajala's weakness is in his memory.

For example, he never remembered to pay his debts and always had creditors looking for him. And never having much money, he was always hiding out.

But this is not the problem, as ORISANLA's Chief Craftsman, he sometimes forgot to put the necessary finishing touches to some of the outer-heads made by him.

For instance, he might forget to bake some of them in fire, or he might over bake them. This makes the Outer Heads weak, and unable to bear the strains of the long journey through life.

If a man or woman makes the mistake of picking one of these bad heads, he or she is doomed to failure in life. All of his or her time and energy is spent fixing mistakes made by their bad heads (bad minds).

If a man or woman is lucky to choose one of the really goods heads made by Ajala, that person can spend all of their time and energy fulfilling their chosen destiny, and therefore have a successful life.

Now Fellow Detectives, lets take a look at where we have come so far investigating the Yoruba religious Beliefs. We have OLODUMARE, who created the Universe and Gods and Goddesses. And we have ORISANLA who Created Human Beings, and OLYA NAL who created the land on which human beings live.

Next we will turn our attention on the relationship between OLODUMARE and Human Beings. Recall, after ORISANLA created people, he asked OLODUMARE to give them the Spiritual Breath of Life. But what is that?

OLODUMARE, Mankind, and ORI

According to Yoruba beliefs, the reason a person exists, and the things that happen to him or her in life, are already planned before they are born; this is the meaning of Destiny.

At the same time, they also believe that it is the person, him or herself, that chooses what is to happen to him or her in life before they are born; this is the meaning of Chosen Destiny.

IFA poems and stories indicate that the major thing OLODUMARE does to get enjoyment out of existence, is the creation of Spirits to be born on earth as people; being as the Gods and Goddesses do all of the work of managing the affairs of the world.

It is this Spirit and its Chosen Destiny that the Yoruba call ORI, or the Spirit of Chosen Destiny. And the Christians call, the breath of life. The Yoruba also believe that after a person is born, ORI makes its home in their Inner Head.

Now let's take a close look at ORI. And, naturally there is an IFA story of how ORI comes into reality. Only in this story, Grandpa is going to be the Spirit of Chosen Destiny.

The story tells of how, once OLODUMARE has created a Spirit, that Spirit kneels before OLODUMARE, and the questions and answers goes as follows:

OLODUMARE: "What are you going to do in life?"

Grandpa Spirit: "I am going to be born an Afro-American, to a man named Ben, and a woman named Bertha in the village of Flora, Louisiana.

I will grow up to be handsome and popular with the women, but be a loner by nature, and will live my life more or less like an outlaw.

The first 52 years of my life will be divided between raising a family of two girls and one boy, traveling, going in and out of penitentiaries, dealing with a lot of different women, and playing around with philosophical thoughts.

When I reach the age of 52, I will begin to research and write a book about Afro-American history for my grandchildren. Later will establish and run a memorial institute of African Intelligence, dedicated to my mother and father until I get old and die."

OLODUMARE: "To! It is sealed!"

At this point, still using myself as an example, Grandpa would leave the presence of OLODUMARE on the long journey from heaven to earth. On the way, I would meet ON'DODE, the Gate Keeper, to whom I must repeat what I was going to do, and the gate Keeper also sealed my Chosen Destiny.

The IFA poem that goes with the above story is as follows;
"That which is chosen kneeling,
Is that which one seeks
On being born into the world;
We knelt down and chose a destiny,
Then, the world makes us forget."

Of all of the heads Ajala made, though some had good memory, none had a good enough memory to recall making a choice of destiny in heaven. This is why when people are born, they forget their chosen destiny. For this reason, people sometimes spend a lifetime trying to find out what their destiny is.

Thus is the nature of the relationship between OLODUMARE and mankind.

ORI

Grandpa thinks as this point we should take a closer look at the idea of ORI. This is really what we call Soul. If this be the case, then SOUL means, that a Spirit with a Chosen Destiny that has a God-like-quality, being as it comes from the holy of holy, OLODUMARE.

Now let's look at the next poem that shows ORI as a guide in life, and how the Yoruba's Ancient Wise Ones related to its God-like-qualities; as seen below.

He who is wise,
Is made wise by his ORI.
He who is not wise,
Is made foolish by his ORI.
Other people don't like to see
A man relieved of his burdens in life.
ORI is the guide,
Who can lead me on the journey
Of my destiny?
With out turning back.
It is my ORI whom I praise.
My ORI, I salute you.
If I have wealth,
It is ORI whom I praise.
My ORI, I salute you.
If I have children on earth,
It is ORI whom I praise.
My ORI, I salute you.
All good things that I have in life,
It is ORI whom I praise.
My ORI, I salute you.
You who will never leave me,
Who blesses me more
Quicker than other Gods.
No God blesses a man
Without the consent of his ORI.
My ORI, I hail you.
A person whose sacrifice is accepted

By his ORI is greatly blessed.

There is no doubt, according to this IFA poem, that the Yoruba Ancient Wise Ones believed that ORI is a God quality within every person, a quality we call Soul. This Soul is their guardian in life.

Well Fellow Detectives, it is time to kind of sum up what Marcus has learned up to this point. The Ancient Yoruba Wise Ones believed that OLODUMARE created Gods and Goddess, and ORISANLA created human beings (mini-Gods and Goddesses).

They also believed that, as far as people are concerned, there is a permanent path-way between heaven and the womb, which has four stops on the journey.

First stop is OLODUMARE, where a destiny is chosen and approved.

Second stop is at the Gateway, where ON'DODE gives the second seal of approval to the destiny.

Third stop, just outside of the gateway, but still in heaven, is at ORISANLA's Outer Head shop. Where one must be very careful in choosing a head.

Finally, the fourth stop is in his or her mother's womb, from which he or she is to be born into the world.

Finally, the Ancient Wise Ones believed that OLODUMARE gave them the moral right to do what they decided they wanted to do. And their highest valued beliefs, Truth (ORISANLA), Justice (OGUN), Righteousness (SANGO), Knowledge (ORUNMILA), Reality (ESU), Fortitude (OLYA NAL), and Determination (OYO) are the driving forces in people fulfilling their Chosen Destiny. This also shows the value of highest valued beliefs.

Another important point must be made about ORI, it never dies. After death of the physical body, ORI returns to heaven, where OLODUMARE makes judgment as to how well ORI did in fulfilling the destiny it chose. In other words, did ORI live the life he or she personally chose for him or her self, and OLODUMARE gave the seal of approval?

The Yoruba do not believe in a heaven or hell in the Christian sense. They believe that if a person does not fulfill his or her destiny, they must be reincarnated as grand and great grand children in his or her family.

For example, when Grandpa dies, and if I have not finished writing this book, and established an Institute of African Bush Intelligence, I must be reincarnated as one of my great grandchildren, and continue working on it until I finish the job.

Then, and only then, can I settle down in Ancestor land with my Ancestors for eternity. The point being, every one must finish their destiny, whether it takes one lifetime, or many lifetimes. But in any case, there is no kind of punishment like burning in hell forever.

This would show, that the nature of mankind, is to be a spiritual part of OLODUMARE's creativity, with a Purpose in life. The purpose is to fulfill a Chosen Destiny. Thus, is the center core of Yoruba religion. And like all religions, the Yoruba also have a moral code related to their center core.

Now we will turn our investigative attention to how evil entered the world.

Jealousy and Greed

In the beginning, when ORISANLA created people, it was only the city of Ife that was populated. Life was good for the people, and what ever the people needed, it was provided by ORISANLA.

Every family had its fields, and every field produced good crops of food. If there was something lacking, the people sent the Messenger, ESU, to ORISANLA to ask for it.

No person had less than enough, and no one had more than any other person in Ife.

All shared equally in the things provided to them by ORISANLA, and all was satisfied, until the Evil of Jealousy and Greed turned the world upside down. As shown in the following IFA story:

"There came into the crowded marketplace one day, a certain man of Ife, who looked around him and said, "Why is it that all men look the same? All men have the same amount of everything. No man has more or less than the next one. There is sameness among men. There is no variety. Is this living in a state of creativity?"

A great discussion began. Men in the marketplace argued. One man said, "Yes, it is true. Why must I have no more than other people?" Another man said, "There is no denying it. The sameness among men is boring." Another said, "The Gods are different from one another. We too should be different."

Some men argued against it, saying, "No, there was wisdom in the way all men were made alike and given equal portions of things. Let us be satisfied with the way things are." But most of the men of Ife became infected with the idea that to be equal with others, was to be deprived of creativity.

The people called for help from ORISANLA, but he did not hear them, (maybe he was drunk on palm wine, the story does not say. But in any case, this also shows a lack of Fortitude).

So they went to ESU, who now lived on earth, and begged him to carry to ORISANLA, the information about the state of affairs developing between people. ESU said to them, "Where is the sacrifice that should accompany the message?"

They brought a goat and sacrificed it, saying, "This is the food for ORISANLA."

But ESU did not move. He said, "Where is the rest?"

The people said, "We do not understand you. Have we not brought a sacrifice for ORISANLA?"

ESU answered, "You asked me to make a great journey. You asked me to be your interpreter. Does not a person make a gift to the lowest messenger? Give me my part, and then I will go." (This is why, forever after, ESU must get paid first, the first sacrifice always belongs to ESU).

So the people gave a sacrifice to ESU. After which, first one man, then another, sought out ESU and asked for something that other people did not have.

One wanted more money. Another asked for servants and slaves to do his work for him. Some objected to the color of their skin; some wanted brown skin, some wanted yellow skin, some wanted black skin, and some wanted white skin.

Then ESU left them and went up to heaven to tell ORISANLA what was happening to the land and the people over which OLYA NAL ruled. ORISANLA was very concerned. He sent ESU back to earth so that he would better understand the people's complaints.

ESU went back to Ife, and day by day he heard people ask for this or that. Again and again he reported to ORISANLA what the people were saying. In the beginning, ORISANLA listened patiently, but at last he said, "These men are becoming unbearable. Tell them to stop their complaints. They should be satisfied with the way things are."

Again ESU went to Ife. He said to the people who were complaining, "I have reported everything to ORISANLA. I have told him what you want. He has considered your requests. He says, "The men are ungrateful and unreasonable."

In the beginning, he arranged the world so that you would all be equal in appearance, and in the things you own. This is the way of harmony.

The people did not like what they heard from ESU. They insisted on having the things they wanted. So the Messenger reported once more to ORISANLA. This time, ORISANLA said impatiently, "Very well, give them what they want."

The next time ESU appeared in Ife, he began distributing things among the men; different colors for different men, more land, gold, servants and slaves, and the list goes on and on.

After every thing had been given out, ESU returned to heaven and reported to ORISANLA.

However, men began to quarrel about who had received the better gifts from ORISANLA. Some complained that they deserved more. Men of different colors became proud. They looked at one another with suspicion.

Those who owned more, looked down on those who owned less, and people who had less, tried to get something from the ones who had more."

There is a short IFA poem that goes with the above story, which is as follows:

"If you meet Jealousy,
Run from Jealousy.
If you meet Greed,
Run from Greed.
The primitive monkey was black,
This jealousy it is that soaked the monkey's
Clothes in palm oil, and turned him red.
This greed it is that killed the leopard,
Leopard, the master of the wilderness.
If you meet jealousy and greed,
Run, Run, Run."

This poem means that in the Yoruba religion, Jealousy and Greed are thought of as the root of all evil, or in Christian religion, as a sin. This is the meaning of the Yoruba saying, "Jealousy and Greed turned the world upside down.

However, more important, if a person chooses his or her destiny, the things he or she wants from life, and it is approved by OLODUMARE, and they want to go in another direction, then they have lied to the Great Creator.

Jealousy and Greed had a major impact on the Yoruba's religious thoughts. It caused people to lose the knowledge of "right conduct," and replace it with "wrong conduct," and in turn, robbed the people of their Chosen Destiny, and this did not sit well with OLODUMARE, ORISANLA, or OLYA NAL. Thus is how Jealousy and Greed gave birth to Wari, on an individual level.

OLYA NAL and the Origin of Kingship

On the other hand, when OLYA NAL earned the right to create dry land, she also earned the right to rule the land as a Queen. This meant that she created and organized the Yoruba society. OLYA NAL was a good Queen, and ruled the people with compassion and understanding.

However, when the Gods and Goddesses were living among the people on earth, they married and began families with humans, and this was the case with OLYA NAL, who became the mother of 16 sons by a human father.

This means, being as OLYA NAL was a Queen and a Goddess, her sons were divine Princes'. This is the meaning of divine, half God or Goddess, and half human.

After thinking about it for a long time, OLYA NAL created sixteen bags of cowries, sixteen bags of beads and other jewelry, sixteen pieces of royal cloth, and she made sixteen crowns with a Vail to cover the face.

In the process, she made her sons Princes', and vowed that when she stepped down from the thrown, her sons would rule as Kings. In this sense, she created an institute of Kingship, and her sons became the Royal Family, and at the same time, she created how the Yoruba society was to be organized, with Kingship. OLYA NAL ruled over the city of Ife for many more years, and an Ifa story goes on to explain:

"One day, without any warning, OLYA NAL became blind. Ifa divination was performed for OLYA NAL, and it was found that the Sea Goddess, OLOKUN was the cause of her problem, and as a sacrifice, she should wash her eyes in salty sea water; that was Ifa's answer.

In turns, she sent each of her sixteen sons to the sea for the salt water. Each returned bringing only fresh water because they were busy taking advantage of her blindness and stealing OLYA NAL's treasures. Until ORANMILYAN, the youngest, finally succeeded, because he was the only one that was not consumed by Jealousy and Greed.

OLYA NAL washed her eyes in the salt water, and could see again. Then she learned that all of her sons, except ORANMIYAN, had stolen her treasures and all of her crowns, except the one she wore herself.

In gratitude to ORANMIYAN, she gave him a sword. ORANMIYAN took it and cut some of the beaded fringes from OLYA NAL's crown, and because of this, he is not permitted to wear a crown which covers his face as other Yoruba Kings do.

The fifteen older brothers took the cowries, beads, cloth, food, and every thing they thought precious, and left their younger brother nothing. They left the city of Ife, each with his own followers, to start kingdoms of their own in other parts of what is now known as Yoruba land.

OLYA NAL then made ORANMIYAN, King of Ife as his inheritance. And the earth opened to receive her, and she gravitated down into the earth, and it closed behind her. This is how it came to be that OLYA NAL became known as the Great Earth Goddess.

Things were peaceful for many years. Meanwhile, the fifteen kingdoms scattered across the land ruled by ORANMIYAN's brothers grew rich and powerful.

However, the kingdom of Ife, ruled by ORANMIYAN, became the riches, wisest, and most powerful of them all, in the minds of all the people in the world.

Because of this, his brothers became jealous and greedy, and sought to defeat Ife, and take ORANMIYAN's last inheritance, the Kingdom of Ife. Thus is how warfare (Wari) between kingdoms was born.

Just as Ife's name was famous, the name ORANMIYAN became famous, as a warrior King. He was ferocious and triumphant as a warrior. Whenever Ife was under attack, it was always ORANMIYAN, with the magic sword given to him by his mother, who led Ife warriors into battle.

His brothers had lots and lots of good warriors, but ORANMIYAN was the best of the best. His long sword struck terror into the hearts of those who sought to defeat Ife.

He was first on the battle field and the last to leave, and his path would be seen by the dead bodies left behind by his weapon. Great warriors came face to face with ORANMIYAN and were defeated.

Soon he saw that it was no good just sitting and waiting for his brothers and their army of warriors to attack Ife, and decided to lead a war expedition to the land of each one of his brothers to teach them a lesson. Upon leaving, he left his son Odudua in charge of the city during his absence.

ORANMIYAN went to the Kingdoms of his brothers, and after defeating them, said, "This earth belongs to me, given to me by OLYA NAL, our mother.

His brothers begged for mercy, crying, "You are master." They bowed down before ORANMIYAN, and he pardoned them. However, there was one condition, his brother Kings, and their descendants, should always be under him and his descendants. And every year, they would come to his capital Ife, and pay homage and tribute.

Meanwhile, ORANMIYAN was away for such a long time that it was thought that he and his warriors must have been killed, and at last, the people of Ife made his son, Odudua King. For some time ORANMIYAN's son ruled them wisely and they prospered, and the people were happy.

But ORANMIYAN and his warriors were not dead, and as he approached Ife, he could hear the notes of the Royal trumpet, which is sounded only for the King. Knowing that nobody could be aware of his return, he asked a man working on a farm, "For whom the Royal trumpet was being sounded?"

"For the King," said the man.

"Yes, but which King?" asked ORANMIYAN.

The man said, "Don't you know that the son of ORANMIYAN, Odudua, is King, and rules over us wisely and well? His father was killed in battle many months ago."

ORANMIYAN knew that it was time to join his mother, OLYA NAL. He called the people together. He said, "Soon I must go. When I am no longer here, continue to live as great people. Do not let our enemies make the city of Ife small in the minds of men. Continue to be courageous, so that Ife will go on living. I will give my sword to my son Odudua, and he will protect you."

Then he stamped his foot on the ground. The earth opened. He descended into the earth, and it closed behind him as it had for his mother, OLYA NAL. This was how ORANMIYAN departed from his people.

The Yoruba think of Jealousy and Greed as male and female spiritual forces, and they gave birth to war. In other words, the first major impact of Jealousy and Greed on the world was warfare between the Kingdoms.

OLYA NAL, WISDOM OF THE WOMB

Creativity is the ancient knowledge of ORISANLA.
Fortitude is the ancient wisdom of OLYA NAL
IFA divination was performed for ORUNMILA,
Who was going into the mysteries of women.
He was told to put on an image (mask),
Head ties, and leg rattles.
He obeyed, he put them on.
He arrived into the wisdom of the womb,
And survived.
He rejoiced in dancing and singing.
I have covenanted with wisdom of the womb
I am blessed.

Recall, in the Yoruba's creation story, OLODUMARE first gave the basket of good character to ORISANLA who got drunk, then the basket of good character was given to OLYA NAL, and she gave it to women.

This means, to become immoral is a sin against OLYA NAL, and through her, against OLODUMARE.

Therefore, Yoruba religion teaches that Fortitude should be the dominant feature of a person's life, or to say, to the Yoruba, Fortitude is next in value to ORI. The value of Fortitude is stated in the following poem;

The world of women is mysterious; governed by wisdom of the womb, Fortitude. Naturally, there is an IFA poem along this line;

Fortitude is which enables the rope of life
To stay unbroken in one's hand.
So declares Priest ORUNMILA.
Who by means of Fortitude,
Was going to win the rope of life
From the four hundred Gods and Goddesses.
Fortitude is all that is required
There is no unhappy destinies in Ife city.
Fortitude is all that is required.
Come; count the many blessings of Fortitude.
Fortitude carries blessings in her arms,
Fortitude carries blessings on her back.
Come; behold the many blessings of Fortitude.

There is also a short poem stating the effects of weak Fortitude, which goes as follows;

Leave her along, let her run
It is her Fortitude that chases her about.
So declares Priest ORUNMILA
To a woman who fears un-seen enemies.
Will you but practice Fortitude?
And stop running about like a coward.

Wisdom of the womb is dangerous, because its power can be in witchcraft. The best way Grandpa can think of to define witches, according to the way Africans think, is to think of them as ritual priestess of the wisdom of the womb. They used their knowledge of this power of rituals to reach negative ends in society. However, we will deal with witchcraft in another place and time.

Ancestors

As the IFA story goes, one day, ORUNMILA invited his sons to celebrate an important festival with him. And as each one arrived, they bowed down and saluted their father with the words "May the sacrifice be accepted and blessed" as a sign of their respect and obedience to him; all but the last born, Olowo.

When ORUNMILA demanded that Olowo give the salute as the others had done, he refused, saying he was as important as

ORUNMILA was, and therefore would bow to no one. To this response, ORUNMILA became angry and returned to heaven to live.

The very instance of ORUNMILA's leaving, the world was thrown into chaos and confusion, without his knowledge to guide it. The growth of life itself came to a stand still, as the following poem shows;

> Pregnant women could not deliver their babies.
> Barren women remained barren.
> Wombs no longer saw their menstruation.
> Semen dried up in men's testicles.
> Yams formed small but undeveloped tubers.
> Corn grew small but unriped ears.

So we can see, with ORUNMILA no longer around, the world was in even worst shape than just being upside down, it was on the road of being destroyed. People decided that ORUNMILA's sons should go to heaven and persuade him to return to the world.

The eight sons of ORUNMILA went to heaven where they met their father at the foot of "the much climbed palm tree with branches here and there and had sixteen huts like heads."

They tried, and tried to convince their father to return to the world, but he refused over and over again. Finally, being a father, he gave each son sixteen palm nuts, and instructions of the IFA Divination ritual, and said;

> When you reach home,
> If you want to have money,
> IFA is the one you should consult.
> When you reach home,
> If you want to have wives,
> IFA is the one you should consult.
> When you reach home,
> If you want to have children,
> IFA is the one you should consult.
> Any good thing you wish to have on earth,
> IFA is the one you should consult.

When the sons of ORUNMILA returned to the world, they started to use these sixteen palm nuts as instruments of divination ritual to find out the wishes of the Gods and Goddesses.

Thus, ORUNMILA replaced himself in the world with the IFA Divination ritual, and saved the world from destruction.

This is where IFA divination came from. It contains the knowledge of ORUNMILA, the Great Divination Priest of heaven.

The first poem ORUNMILA's sons taught the people, upon their return is as follows;

The day has its time.
The night has its time.
He who provides food for a child's mouth.
IFA divination was performed for the people,
Who was coming from heaven to earth.
If one has a problem,
One should take it to one's Ancestors.
One's dead father never fails to aid one.
One's dead mother never fails to aid one.
One's sacred divination palm nuts
Never fails to aid one.
One's ORI never fails to aid one.
One should honor and respect one's Ancestors.

This Ife story and poems are examples of the kind of negative effect Jealousy and Greed brought into the world, which includes negativity to the family structure itself. For it was Jealousy and Greed that drove Olowo to disrespect ORUMNILA. As to morality, the moral of the story and poems is, "Respect Ancestors."

Hospitality

The code of Hospitality is divided into two parts, one related to the responsibility of the host, and the other related to the guest.

Right away in the following IFA story, we can see that it is very old, for it is about an event that took place when the Gods and Goddesses were living among the people. The subject is about hospitality to one's guests, friends, as well as enemies. The IFA story is as follows.

"On an occasion when three strange men were to stay in his house; ORUNMILA did not even have one cowry shell (dollar) to spend. ORUNMILA called his wife, AABO, to take all of his belongings to the market to sell.

When AABO got to the market, ORUNMILA's iroke, which he bought for seven hundred cowries, was priced at one hundred and forty cowries. His horse tail ceremonial switch, which he bought for six hundred cowries, was priced at one hundred and twenty cowries. The ornament covered cloth of his Divination instruments, which he bought for sixteen hundred cowries, was priced at twenty one cowries. AABO wept.

Instead of crying aloud, she chanted IFA poems. She said that the materials were priced far less than they cost. ORUNMILA also answered her by chanting IFA poems, and instructed her to go and sell the materials. AABO then sold the materials at a loss, and took the money home to buy food. The three strange visitors, Death, Disease, and ESU ate, and they were satisfied, and ORUNMILA survived."

The moral of the story, is that hospitality has the power to protect one from evil. The value of which is shown in, that ORUNMILA made a sacrifice of his most valuable possessions to provide hospitality to his guest.

Now, even ORUNMILA, the God of Knowledge and Wisdom has to give hospitality at all costs. This means that this part of the moral code is a highly valued belief in the Yoruba religion.

On the other hand, there is a moral position related to the conduct of the one receiving the hospitality. The following poems tells what that is, and at the same time, shows some of ESU's police powers, and one of his tricks of enforcement when he receives his sacrifice. The IFA story goes as follows;

"Divination was done for ORUNMILA on a day, for one reason or another, he decided to steal Death's wife, the Fiendish One.

The Fiendish One was the only wife of Death, but ORUNMILA wanted to steal her just the same. ORUNMILA was asked to perform sacrifice for ESU, and he performed it.

After he had performed the prescribed sacrifice, he stole Death's wife. Death then took his club, and went to ORUNMILA's house.

He found ESU outside the house. ESU said, "I greet you Death, whose garment is always red with blood.

After they had exchanged greetings, ESU asked, "What is the matter?"

Death complained that ORUNMILA had taken away his wife. And vowed that he would kill ORUNMILA that day.

Then ESU asked Death to sit down. After he had sat down, ESU gave him food and drink.

After Death had eaten to his satisfaction, he stood up, took his club, and started to go.

ESU asked him again, "Where are you going?" Death said he was going to ORUNMILA's house. ESU asked, "Does one eat a man's food, and rise to kill him? Don't you know that the food you ate is ORUNMILA's food?"

When Death did not know what to do, he said, "Tell ORUNMILA to keep the woman."

Now we can see what the moral conduct should be of one that receives the hospitality, he must show positive appreciation in return, no matter what the cost. We can also see why ESU is sometimes called the Trickster God, he did trick Death into giving up his wife.

In this sense, hospitality promotes harmony, and it is harmony that molds society together.

Impatient

Also very high on the Yoruba's list of moral conduct, is that a person should not commit suicide. Self murder is destiny murder. This means that a person is rejecting OLODUMARE's gift, his or her ORI, as the following story will show.

"Once there was a man, Alukso, who had been having hard times all of his life. Every thing he tried to do, he was not successful. So instead of taking his problems to the IFA Priest, he gave up on life, and at the age of 39 committed suicide. After which he found himself standing at the Gate between Heaven and Earth.

On'ibode, the Sacred Gatekeeper, asked him why was he at the Gate before his time. Alukso complained that life was hard, and it was not fair. Plus, he could not see a reason for living.

On'ibode looked at him wondering why the man did not consult an IFA priest. Finally to teach the man a lesson; he locked him in a room and instructed him to keep listening.

Before long, there were foot steps outside, and Alukoso knew that those footsteps were the ones traveling to earth to be born that had arrived. He heard each of them recite what his or her destiny would be, and how it was sealed by On'ibode.

When they had all gone away, On'ibode sang;

Alukso,
Have you been listening?
This shows how one's destiny is ordered.

Thus Alukoso learned that, so far, the things that had happened to him on earth were according to his chosen destiny.

Next, On'ibode led him out and showed him an enclosure which contained many wives, and a room full of riches. All those, he was told, were to be his after the age of 40, according to his chosen destiny. However, he had forfeited every future by his impatience.

The IFA story concludes that at the sight of all that wealth, Alukoso burst into tears and pleaded so strongly, that OLODUMARE allowed him ten more years of life to enjoy his destiny."

On the other hand, there is a poem that states the case with another person and situation in another way;

"He who eats his corn meal without stew,

Complains of hard times.
What should he do that only has the
Wrapping leaves (plate) to scrape?
So declared ORUNMILA of Otewari,
Who decided to go into the bush and hang himself.
Otewari, do not hang yet.
Let us not run the world hastily.
Let us not grasp at the rope of wealth impatiently,
This should be treated with mature judgment.
Let us not treat in a fit of temper.
Whenever we arrive at a cool place,
Let us rest sufficiently well.
Let us give prolonged attention to the future.
And then let us give due
Regard to the consequence of things,
Dying and facing OLODUMARE after."

So we can see that, to the Yoruba, being impatient is a lack of Fortitude and caused the suicide, therefore, patience is high on their list of moral values.

Yoruba Articles of Faith
(Constitution of Highest Valued Beliefs)

Well Fellow Detectives, we have finally come to the end of our investigation of the structure of the Yoruba's religion. Now we can take a look at their highest valued religious beliefs.

For example, lets ask ourselves the question, what kind of people would record their religion and history, and everything else about themselves in poems and prose stories?

At the same time, establish a system, IFA Divination, to use the sum total of those poems and stories, not only as a means of teaching each generation their religion and history; but also use the knowledge of their history to solve personal and community problems. As well as give direction to their lives as a people? What is the foundation of the way they think about life? Answer, their Articles of Faith of their religion.

To begin with, we must deal with two questions, religion and faith. First, we must define what we mean by "religion." A religion is founded on "Articles of Faith." And Articles, in this case, means a group of ideas about the world, with special focus on the purpose of mankind. This, according to OLODUMARE, is their Chosen Destiny, better known as ORI.

In this sense, the Yoruba's "Articles", are the "constitution of highest valued beliefs," which is the power that molds them into who they are, the Yoruba as a people.

On the one hand, "Faith", means that a person believes "certain ideas of how the spiritual affairs of the world are managed, and thought to be absolutely true." When that person knows for a fact, that he or she does not know if what he or she believes is true or not." They have "Faith" that the ideas are true. However, they "know" that there is a "big benefit" in believing that they are true.

Now that we have some idea of the meaning of Articles of Faith, we can turn our attention to the structure of their spiritual constitution.

According to all of the IFA poems Grandpa has read, and there are hundreds of them, my conclusion concerning the major aspects of the Yoruba's Articles of Faith is as follows;

First Article: Have faith in the idea of a self-created Being, OLODUMARE, who is pure spirit, but is neither male nor female; known as the Great Artist.

Second Article: Have faith in the idea that OLODUMARE created male and female sexuality in the form of Gods and Goddesses, the Holy Family. Who, in turn, produced children, grandchildren, great grand children, and so on, to the number of 1600, known as the Holy Clan.

Third Article: Have faith in the idea that OLODUMARE next created the Universe; the Sun, Moon, Earth, and all of the stars.

Forth Article: Have faith in the idea that OLODUMARE'S powers were divided between the Gods and Goddesses, who became the Managers of the Affairs of the World.

Fifth Article: Have faith in the idea that people's physical body was created by the God ORISANLA, but ORI (their Chosen Destiny) is a gift from OLODUMARE.

Sixth Article: Have faith in the idea that they will be reincarnated within their family until their destiny is fulfilled, and ORI never dies, and will live in Ancestor land forever.

Seventh Article: Have faith in the idea of ritual sacrifice as a path of communication linking the Gods, Goddesses, Ancestors, and mankind together.

These are the major ideas that the Yoruba have faith in, or to say, they are the Yoruba's highest valued religious beliefs.

Now that we have an idea of how the Yoruba's religion is organized, we will next turn our investigative attention to the idea of putting their religion into practice.

Worship, Rituals, and Sacrifices

First we must get a good understanding of three Yoruba terms that we have mentioned but did not explain; Inner Head, Outer Head, and Inner Body. The Yoruba believe that the mind of man-kind is divided into three independent functioning parts.

ORI knows the purpose that a person was born with, a chosen destiny. ORI comes from OLODUMARE; and is known as a person's Inner Head.

Logic learns what that destiny is, and how to fulfill it in the world. Creative intelligence comes from ORISANLA; and is known as a person's Outer Head.

Fortitude sustains one throughout their existence. Fortitude comes from OLYA NAL; and is known as Inner Body. (For example, some people call, "having staying power," or "don't give up the good fight," etc, etc.)

This is what is meant when somebody answers the question, what is the Holy Trinity of the Yoruba religion? It would be answered, OLODUMARE, ORISANLA, AND OLYA NAL. As far as answering the question, what is the driving forces in a Yoruba person's life, the answer would be, Chosen Destiny, Creativity, and Fortitude.

Now when we mention the terms Worship, Rituals, and Sacrifice, we mean, a way of keeping harmony between these three. However, we are only going to define the terms at this point, we will look at how they work later.

ORI knows the purpose that a person was born with, their Chosen Destiny, and Logic learns what that Destiny is, and how to fulfill it in the world.

Logic is the function of the mind that creates intelligence. For example, the intelligence the Yoruba Ancient Wise Ones used to create Ifa priesthood as a storage place for the knowledge and wisdom of a people. On the other hand, logic is the most important tool history investors use to do their job; and is a subject that we will bring up a lot throughout our long study.

But for now, we will just say that logic is something a person is born with; it is the creativity given by ORISANLA. Logic builds up a body of knowledge that a person learns from experience in the world, from the day he or she is born, and gathered throughout childhood; and this body of knowledge, like ORI, becomes a guide in life.

At the age of puberty, logic and fortitude are supposed to combine into one functioning system to fulfill ORI (Chosen Destiny). This rarely happens, and leads to the possibility of "inner spiritual conflict." For example, ORI wants to go in one direction, and logic in another, which shows a lack of fortitude. This can happen on an individual, as well as a community level.

This is where the Ifa priest comes into the picture, to find out what ORI wants, and how much, if any, it is getting as far as its chosen destiny is concerned. To resolve this conflict is what the IFA Divination ritual, and one or another rituals in general are concerned. Now we will define the terms, worship, ritual, and sacrifice.

Worship is an attitude a person brings to rituals and sacrifices. The attitude of worship, if one is to be successful in conflict resolution, consists of a relationship of honor, love, and respect to the member, or members of the spiritual world in which one wants, or to whom one wants to communicate.

This brings up the question, what is a ritual? In this case, a ritual is a means of communion with the spiritual world, and one result of which is a spiritual conflict resolution process; for example, IFA ritual.

This means that a ritual is a specific act, or actions, that unify ORI with the logical part of a person's mind. At the same time, being as ORI is a part of the spiritual world of Gods, Goddesses, and Ancestors, a person is in the position to come into contact with, and communicate with these Spirits.

This is what the word ritual means, and is accomplished in a number of ways. For instance, praying, singing, dancing, and/or, chanting as the IFA Priests do. Or in the case of a community ritual, all of the above, in a great production like a play and concert combined.

The "act of a ritual", is in two parts, either a person is asking for something, and, or, the person is giving thanks for something already received. This brings us to the role of ritual sacrifice in the ritual.

If the person is receiving things from the spiritual world, it is only fair that he or she gives something in return, this something given in return is called a sacrifice.

The "act of sacrifice" is also in two parts, something is offered as a gift, and something is done with the gift in the ritual. First we will look at the something offered.

This something can be a number of things, but the most important thing about this gift, it must always be something the God, Goddess, or Ancestor personally likes. Just as important, the person gives up something he or she holds in high value. For example, a person gives something he or she would rather keep for themselves, in hopes of getting something else they want.

As we mentioned, each God, Goddess, and Ancestor must get a gift they like the most, and in most cases food is included. So since food is one of the most used sacrificed objects, we will use food in a long example of what happens to the sacrificed gift, as well as how a ritual works.

(Meanwhile, we must keep in mind, just like Marcus is studying to become a priest for ORUNMILA, each God and Goddess has a priest that worships at their shrine. A "shrine", is a place or thing that has been made Holy through the process of "consecration." We will define the words shrine and consecration in another place. At this point, we are concerned with sacrifices in particular, and ritual worship in general. Towards this end, we will return to Marcus and IFA Divination)

Divination and the Yoruba Artist

Marcus has now learned how to use the ritual tools, and how poems are used in IFA rituals. To get some insight into how IFA rituals work, and to demonstrate how the Yoruba use their history and Ancestors, we will move up in time when Marcus is 24 years of age.

About six months before he graduates a full IFA priest, he must commission an Artist, DionDi, to sculpture his tools which are to be presented to him as part of his graduation ceremony.

Recall what we said about the artist and the sculptured heads in our archaeology evidence. Now we will get a picture of how their approach is related to IFA Divination. With that definition of art in mind, we will analyze the Ifa ritual through the eyes of the artist and his works of art.

It is from insight like this, that hopefully will give us a picture of how the Yoruba religion, cultural and artistic beliefs relate to each other.

In this sense, a divination ritual itself is a work of art, designed to transform people into a spiritual state of being, and transports the spiritual world of Gods, Goddesses, and Ancestors of their beliefs into their mists.

A ritual, such as IFA, is one of many places where Yoruba culture is put on display, and shows the role it plays. At the same time, this ritual, with its creative spiritual expressions, should show us the full force of the power, uniqueness, and beauty of the Yoruba culture. Especially if we look at it through the eyes of the artist, and creativity, which will be our investigative approach.

Now, with this in mind, lets take a look at the symbolic meaning of the tools DionDi created for the soon to be priest, Marcus. Keep in mind that the tools are carved in the form of ritual art, like you might see in an African art store and museums all over the world.

First of all, there is a mask image of ORUNMILA, known as the God of IFA, who is the inspiration for the IFA ritual: He speaks through the IFA Priest, which means that he is the God that Marcus will worship. The mask is his shrine.

Second: There is a ritual bowl in which the sixteen sacred palm nuts are kept during the ritual ceremony. This bowl is sculptured in the form of a woman with a bowl on her head, a baby on her back, a vase, and pig at her side; showing Marcus' relationship with the Yoruba family.

Third: A small storage container to keep IFA Divination tools, which also may serve as a kind of altar in the ritual and, it is resting on the carved images of the heads of Marcus' Ancestors. On which the mask of ORUNMILA is placed during the ritual.

Fourth: A divining chain with the eight half nut shells, from which Priest Marcus reads the code of Odu, and symbolizes the way ORUNMILA's mind works, and is known as the gateway to Knowledge.

Fifth: Divining Tapers. One of these is used after Priest Marcus spreads the sacred yellow powder into the divining tray, tapping the tray to invoke the attention of ORUNMILA. The image on the tapers are that of the Yoruba Messenger God, ESU.

Sixth: The divining tray on which Priest Marcus spreads the sacred yellow powder, on which he marks the code of Odus. The art work around the edges of the tray tell the story of ORUNMILA giving the Ifa Divination system to mankind.

And seventh: Priest Marcus' walking stick; a shaft on which the main feature is an image of a bird on the tip. The bird symbolizes the Yoruba Earth Goddess OLYA NAL. A decorated shaft made of wood, which is always held carefully for, according to certain beliefs, it must never fall flat on the bare ground.

This means that Marcus and DionDi must spend a great deal of time in consultation during the time of the carving of the tools, because when taken together, these tools capture the spirit of Marcus as an Ifa priest, and at the same time, symbolically ties his spirit to those of ORUNMILA, ESU, OLYA NAL, Ancestors, and his Family; all through art.

This gives us an idea of how creativity and spirituality are bonded together in IFA ritual. Now let's take a close look at the nature of these all important poems and tools Marcus has spent so much time memorizing, by returning to a time just after Marcus' graduation, and his first client.

IFA Ritual
(Confronting one's Historical Cultural Self)

After graduating, Marcus returns to live at home. He is 24 years old and considered a man. Upon his return, he is the honored guest at a big celebration given by his family members, and every body in the community is invited. He is now known as Babalawo (Father of Knowledge).

He wears a blue robe and lots of beads. The main beads are called Ide (symbolizing Knowledge), which he ties to the wrists and neck. He is carrying a bag made of cloth which he hangs on his shoulder containing his sculptured ritual tools. He is also carrying a walking stick.

Most of the time a Yoruba usually seeks the services of an Ifa priest to learn about the values in their religious beliefs and history, (like we did in our investigative approach).

Other times, and just as important, he seeks the service of an Ifa priest when he or she is seeking answers, or information about questions he or she is having about positive or negative things happening in their life.

The following day, Priest Marcus gets such a case, his cousin Michael. Michael has a strong case of paranoia, and he doesn't know where it is coming from.

After pouring libation for ESU and ORUNMILA, and setting out his ritual tools, Priest Marcus begins the ritual by handing his tools to Michael.

While holding the divination tools in his hand, Michael whispers and states what is on his mind to a coin, and then throws the coin among the tools in his hand.

This is considered the same as whispering it to ORUNMILA, who will give his answers through Priest Marcus and the ritual tools. Meanwhile, Priest Marcus does not know what Michael whispered.

The next stage of the ritual begins when Priest Marcus takes the tools from Michael, and spreads the yellow powder in the divination tray. He then starts taking the sacred palm nuts in and out of his hands reading the Odu code making marks on the dust covered tray.

Or, if Priest Marcus chose to use the diving chain instead of the sacred palm nuts, he takes the chain in the middle, and throws it on the ground before him, reading the ritual code of the chapter that appears.

However, in either case, he then chants a poem about the character and meaning of that chapter, for example, the fourth major chapter, Odi Meji, which means negativity (evil) is close to Michael.

Naturally Michael will want to know more about this negativity. This is when the Ibo ritual tool comes into play and spells out the details which are done as follows.

The Ibo used in the ritual is based on two opposite possibilities of "yes or no" as answers. It is the belief of the Yoruba, that it is the ORI of Michael that makes the right choice when the Ibo is used. As Priest Marcus learns very early in his training, the Ibo consists of two cowry shells tied together, and a piece of animal bone.

Therefore, after finding out the character of the chapter's meaning, that negativity (evil) was close to Michael, Priest Marcus gives the set of Ibo to Michael and asks him to put to it questions requiring the answer yes or no. For example, is the negativity close to Michael in the form of another person? Which is whispered to the Ibo, and again, Priest Marcus is not allowed to hear.

Michael then drops the set of Ibo on the tools of divination while Priest Marcus picks it up immediately and touches the tools, and gives it back to Michael. After saying the cowries mean yes, and the bone means no, Michael then puts the cowries in one hand and the bone in the other, without Priest Marcus knowing which hand has the cowry, and which hand has the bone.

Priest Marcus takes up the divining chain again, and throws it on the ground twice. If the chapter obtained during the first throwing of the divining chain is senior to the chapter obtained during the second throwing, Priest Marcus asks Michael to show the piece of Ibo in his right hand. But if the chapter obtained during the first throwing of the divining chain is junior to the one obtained during the second throwing, he asks Michael to show the piece in his left hand.

If the piece of Ibo kept in the right hand turns out to be the cowries, it means that the answer to Michael's question is yes, which of course means that the negativity close to him is another person.

In this case, Michael uses the set of Ibo to ask other questions, for example, is the negativity close to me one person, or a group? This continues until he finds out where the negativity lies; in this case, a group.

Usually the process is followed until all of his questions are answered. Therefore, Priest Marcus may have to throw the divining chain many times when using the Ibo to find out a specific point.

When Michael is satisfied that all of his questions are answered, he tells Priest Marcus the actual problem for the first time.

Michael's problem is then discussed, and Priest Marcus helps further by chanting poems from the first chapter that came up, Odi Meji.

When Marcus chants a poem that fits the problem, Michael becomes interested and stops him. (This is the poem we analyzed when studying the structure of IFA poems).

Now we will turn our attention to the poem Michael chose. The poem and our analysis are as follows; and at the same time, we can get some insight into what Marcus learned about the role of sacrifices in poems.

Most of the time, a person's problem is solved by one Ifa priest, in one sitting. However, to get a better understanding of Ifa poems, we will present a long poem with three priest' on five occasions. Two of which made two complete divination rituals with no results, while the third found a solution.

The Tall One……..(First priest' nick-name).
The Heftyman…….(Second priest' nick-name).
Walk Slowly………(Third priest' nick-name).
IFA Divination was preformed for Oloofun…..(Name of the ancient person who came to the IFA priest).
When he would take the land of the King to farm upon……(The ancient person's problem).
He was asked to make sacrifice to the Ancestors of his household……(first priest' instructions).
But his sacrifice was not accepted…..(Results).
He was asked to make sacrifice to the Goddess of the Market…..(First priest' second instructions).
He made sacrifice to the Goddess of the Market……
….(Followed instructions).
But his sacrifice was not accepted. The Market Goddess refused his sacrifice…..(Results).
He was asked to make sacrifice to his ORI…(Second priest' first instructions).
He made sacrifice to his ORI repeatedly
Until his head became bald…(Followed instructions, no results).
He was asked to make sacrifice to OLYA NAL………. (Second priest' second instructions).
He made sacrifice to OLYA NAL….(No results)
He was asked to make sacrifice to the Father of Sacrifice of three cows, two goats, fifteen chickens, and 6,000 cowries. (Third priest' instructions)
He said that he knew that his father is the Ancestor of his household…..(Questioned third priest)
He said that he knew that one's mother is the Goddess of the Market.
He said that he knew ORI to be one's head,
And He knew OLYA NAL to be the Earth Goddess.
But he said that he did not know
What was called Father of Sacrifice,
The third priest told him that people's mouths,

People's mouths were referred to as the Father of Sacrifice.
What is it that we worship at Ife?
Their mouths.
I have given to those over there...(Followed the third priest' instructions).
I have given to those over here,
Their mouths.
Their mouths can no longer,
Their mouths cannot work against me.
I have given to those in my household,
I have given to passer-by.
Their mouths cannot,
Their mouths can no longer fight against me.
Fight against me (successful results).

Marcus helps further by telling Michael the story of the poem.

"Once long ago, a man was trying to get some land from the King on which to make a farm. His attempts were all unsuccessful, because the people in his community were all saying bad things about him to the King. He was the kind of person that was very unfriendly.

Thus he took his problem to two Ifa priests before he found the answer with a third priest.

He gave a big celebration at which was plenty of food, and he spent 6,000 cowries on drinks, and had a big band to provide music for dancing and singing". (This gives us some idea of the role of sacrifice. Everybody enjoyed themselves, and there was no problem getting land from the King.

The moral of the poem is, in order to be successful in life, you must be a friend to your community, otherwise the whole spiritual world of your religious beliefs cannot help you.

Then Marcus would explain to Michael that he picked the poem that made him feel his paranoia feelings; or to say, his ORI picked the poem. The poem means that his paranoia comes from the negative way the people in his community think about him. Plus, the reason people were having negative thoughts, is the disrespecting way Michael related to them.

Grandpa thinks that now would be a good time to look at the role of the sacrifice involved in the poem; and at the same time, see what purpose a sacrifice is to serve.

To every complete ritual, there is always a prescribed sacrifice, as we saw in the poem. Therefore, after the completion of the divination ritual, Marcus will tell Michael the sacrifice that goes with the solution of the problem; designed to restore harmony between Michael and his community.

We see that the main objective of the ritual is for the man to "cleanse himself of a problem," and this is what Michael must do.

Now if we recall, the third Ifa priest' instructions were three cows, two goats, fifteen chickens, and 6,000 cowries (African Bush money.

Michael then goes home to get the articles required, and he performs the sacrifice, the same as the Ancient man in the poem, and his paranoia goes away.

After selecting a suitable place, like a park, the ritual sacrifice would begin by inviting the Earth Goddess, Goddess of the Market, Ancestors, Ori, and all of the people in his community, Michael would cook the three cows, two goats, and fifteen chickens, along with all the things needed for a great meal, with the 6,000 cowries spent on palm wine and the hiring of a music group for a festival in the community.

After which, to begin the festival, the Earth Goddess, Goddess of the Market, ORI, Ancestors, and the people of the community are asked for forgiveness.

This is followed by everybody having a good time, singing, dancing, praying, and eating together; thus Michael would be cleansed of his paranoia.

Now let's take a close look at what was accomplished in the ritual process. Michael had a strong feeling of paranoia, and he did not know where it was coming from; which was a psychological or spiritual problem.

Ifa not only identified where the paranoia came from using Ifa ritual, but also gave a successful way to cure it, and prescribed a sacrifice; all by using the knowledge in IFA poems.

We only wanted to give a quick picture, not only to show the purpose Ifa Divination rituals serve, but also see the role of sacrifice in the ritual. As well as, show how the Yoruba's use their Ancestor's knowledge to find answers to the problems of the day. All the while staying in harmony with the spiritual world of their religious beliefs.

Since food is one of the most used sacrificed objects, we will use it as an example of what happens to the sacrifice, and at the same time, see a different kind of ritual.

In this example we will say, Tyree, his second client, goes to Priest Marcus with a problem. After the IFA ritual process, he finds out that the God ORISANLA (creativity) is the answer, and that he must sacrifice a chicken; this meant that he had to see that God's priest to make the sacrifice.

Tyree goes to the house of the Priest of ORISANLA, Orchester III, with a chicken, and tells Priest Orchester why he has come.

Both proceed to the Shrine. Which in this case consists of an open space; a cone shaped roof covering the alter of a circular mound of earth about four feet high with at least one earthen bowl on the top of the mound. To which a student priest brings the things that Orchester will need, and Tyree brings the chicken (gift).

On their arrival, the student priest places Orchester' instruments near the inner part of the shrine where only Priest Orchester may enter.

Then Priest Orchester opens the ritual by first calling on the Gods, Goddesses, and Ancestors. After this, a very short greeting, and Priest Orchester goes on to sound the praises of ORISANLA as follows:

> ORISANLA, God in Holy cloth!
> He who created man from clay.
> He who is able to answer a man
> Boldly and with impunity!
> Father ORISANLA!
> You give just when I am hungry!
> ORISANLA whom we owe our life!

Priest Orchester now states Tyree's problem, and prays that God grants the solution. At the end of this prayer, Tyree responds, "Yes! That is my problem! Priest Orchester then takes the chicken and waves it towards the shrine and back again three times saying,

> In the name of OLODUMARE
> In the name of ORISANLA
> In the name of OLYA NAL

Then Priest Orchester, holding the chicken by the wings, cuts of it's head off and sprinkles the dripping blood on the earthen dish half buried on the altar.

Next, a fire is made in the shrine area. Priest Orchester' helper and Tyree cook the chicken with yams, salt, and other seasonings.

When the cooking is over, Priest Orchester has to make another sacrificial offering. This time, it is done by throwing bits of each type of food towards the altar, and with a cup, he throws libation of cool clear water. (In most cases palm wine is used for libation, but recall, ORISANLA cannot drink palm wine).

Meanwhile, Priest Orchester keeps praising ORISANLA, and asking him to grant Tyree a solution.

Then, Priest Orchester and Tyree eat the remaining food. End of ritual..

This should give us an idea of what is meant by the ritual act of sacrifice. And at the same time, is an example of the "something done to the object being sacrificed," as well as an outline of how a ritual is performed.

However, more importantly, dealing with Michael and Tyree's problems are other examples of how the Yoruba use history to solve everyday problems. Thus is how the Yoruba use the creative they receive from worshipping Orisanla.

THE YORUBA'S
ANCIENT CITY OF THE GODS; IFE

The cultural center of the Yoruba tribe, with its 35,000,000 members is the city if Ife. As evidence for our investigation, we will use archaeological data, art, and religious and political oral history. Ife is a very ancient city in southwestern Nigeria, on today's map. It is about 80 miles from the Atlantic Ocean, and 150 miles from the Benin border. Ife was, and is, the spiritual center of all Yoruba's, and the place where their Kings originated.

There is probably enough evidence in oral traditional stories of migration, to show that all Bantu people, (so called Negro people), originated in the area of the Niger River's mouth, or southern Nigeria. .

Art symbolizes, and is inspired by the spirituality of the artist's innermost self, and this is what makes art religious. (Human beings are a work of art.) Therefore, when an artist is at his creative best, he is in harmony with his soul. To the Yoruba artist, this means being in harmony with his soul, his community, his King, and his God.

Creativity plays a strong role in an African's means of self-expression. For example, the African dance is creative competition, in the sense that each dancer is trying to, 'out do the others' in a creative manner. However, music, singing, and dancing, are not the only creative forms of African art by a long shot.

We will look at the Yoruba's sculptures in brass, stone, and terracotta. Terracotta is a term used for sculptures made in pottery, and its color depends on the condition in which it is fired or baked. Even so, all African art represents a reflection of religious ideas.

The force and power of a religion, when expressed, has an effect on people's lives in a very strong way. Now we are talking about three things in one, religion, history, and art. These things are in harmony in a way that cannot be separated, and one cannot change without the other two changing. For example, when European artist in the late nineteenth and early twentieth century began to appreciate the highly imaginative forms of African sculpture, they were greatly stimulated, and under its influence, set out upon a course of experiments in artistic form which completely revolutionized European art, liberating it from its nineteenth-and early centuries of Victorian morality. This set them on a path that would change their way of thinking about religion and history, because, a person has to change their way of thinking about religion and history in order to change their art.

However, they did not know the morality that went with the African art that they were copying. At least not until Dr. Martin Luther King, Alex Haley, and Malcolm X. told them what it means in religion and history in the 1960's, which was some 60 to 70 years later. We will examine European's religion art in the next section, 'the middle passage'. For now, we want to see where the art came from that the Europeans were reacting to.

Art gets to the heart of religion, because rituals are a work of art, in the same way that a stage play is a work of art. Art, as a creative force, plays a very strong role in a people's culture; the same kind of role that male and female sexuality plays in peoples lives. We could even say that, Art is the sexuality of a culture. Therefore, we can see the kind of impact that African art had on Europe.

The impact of African art started the European's school of impressionist, and others, and the appeal to the European artist was the freedom the African artist enjoyed in expressing his own personal ideas of the harmony of the world around him.

This was un-heard of in Europe. Nevertheless, Europe had another artist shock coming. It came as a tremendous surprise to the European art world when, in 1938, a group of bronzed sculptures of heads of life-size and of natural appearance were found during the digging of foundation trenches for a house in the middle of the city of Ife.

These sculptures were quite unlike the African art that they had in their mind's eye. Who could possibly have made these heads? What a remarkable achievement this was, to model heads to look like real people, but even more amazing, to have cast them in bronze! The people represented were Africans, so the heads were made in Africa, but how could Africans have made them? Africans are too dumb to do something of this nature!

Those who could see no beauty in the abstract mode of much of African sculpture, had no difficulty in appreciating the beauty of these heads. Their appeal is immediate, even to those who have had little or no experience in African sculpture.

In fact, these finds were not the first to be made in Ife. An incomplete face in terracotta of about half life-size had been brought to Europe before 1910, by which date, a plaster cast was already in the British Museum. We do not know who brought this piece out of Africa, but it is now in a private collection in America. It was probably taken from the Iwinrin Grove in Ife (Africans held church services in beautiful groves of trees) where a large number of terracotta sculptures used to be kept.

There is some evidence that there used to be many more pieces in this grove than there were in 1934 when they were brought into the Palace in Ife for safekeeping, and later transferred to the Ife Museum. No one paid much attention to this piece until the German anthropologist, Leo Frobenius, visited Ife in 1910. He collected a large number of ancient works of art, which he was forced to surrender, including a bronzed head with a crown which had been found in the middle of the nineteenth century in the Olokun Grove outside the town to the north, and had been kept there every since, being dug up for the annual festivals, and reburied afterwards.

However he took it back to Germany, seven fine terracotta heads, and a number of other important fragments. Frobenius made sweeping claims about his discoveries in articles in the German press, claiming that here in Ife, he had found traces of a Greek colony on the Atlantic coast of Africa. He thought that Olokun, the sea-God of the Yoruba, in whose Grove the head had been found, was the same God as the Greek's Poseidon.

Although anthropologist paid some attention to Frobenius, his discoveries appeared to have been largely ignored by the European art world. Yet, during the years that followed, a number of accounts of Ife were published in Talbot's four volume work 'The peoples of Southern Nigeria', which showed eight terracotta sculptures not previously known in Europe.

The art critics seemed not to have seen these books, so they were quite prepared when, late in 1938, thirteen bronzed heads were discovered at Wunmonije Grove, only a hundred yards from the back door of the palace. (Each Yoruba God had a special grove of his own.) Shortly afterwards, early in 1939, four more bronzed heads were found together with the upper part of a male figure wearing a beaded crown, an elaborate beaded neck-ring, armlets, and necklaces.

One of the heads were brought to Britain, where it was brought for the British Museum. Two others were brought by an American anthropologist, Professor W.R. Bascom, who was working in Ife at the time of the discoveries. He gave these two heads back to the Ife Museum when it was opened, so that now there is only one bronzed head known to be outside of Nigeria, namely, the one in the British Museum. The original 'Olokun' head, described by Frobenius, has disappeared. The head in the Ife Museum, which was supposed to be this one, has been found to be a copy made by a modern industrial casting technique, not by the traditional African method.

Apart from the bronzed head, the British Museum has a terracotta head, three fragments of terracotta sculpture, and a quartz stool. In addition to these, the terracotta face in private hands in America and the items brought back to Frobenius, are the only known pieces from Ife outside of Nigeria. The bulk of the art of Ife is in consequence still in the town where it was made. There is a great deal of which is now collected together in the Museum in the Palace, though much of it is still in use in shrines and groves in the town.

Scarcely a month ever passed without some new item turning up as new roads are cut, or foundations are dug for new buildings. It is amazing how often these new discoveries are unlike pieces already known, so that the range of creativity is unlimited.

Since 1943, we have had increasing evidence from Central Nigeria, of a group of people whose culture straddles the Later Stone Age and the Early Iron Age, the bearers of the 'Nok Culture', who themselves possessed a rich sculpture tradition which was discovered, and has been described by Bernard Fagg and his brother. It is the studies of William Fagg, the brother, since 1947, that have made sense of this great art centre.

From these studies, and from the study of more recent sculptures, especially in Nigeria, made principally by the same two brothers, Fagg on the Nok cultural art, and Frank Willett on Ife culture, we can get an idea of the relationship between the two cultures, and see that the Ife and the Nok culture are one and the same, and this will put the art of Ife into its historical setting.

In considering where the art of Ife originated, we do not need to look far, for there is in Central Nigeria, a culture of great antiquity about 150 miles north-east of Ife, and where the Niger and Benue Rivers meet, which had produced very rich remains in terracotta sculpture. Bernard Fagg interpreted these dates as indicating that the culture probably began some time well before the middle of the first 1,000 years A.D., and probably later. Moreover, Grandpa does agree with that. The idea was that, the time range had already been reached tentatively purely on geological grounds some years earlier.

In September of 1960, two terracotta figures of women sitting on round stools, or perhaps upturned mortars, were discovered at Taruga, which is south-east of Abuja. The heads of these figures were both missing, but small diggings conducted on the site in December of 1960 by Bernard Fagg, discovered the head of one of them. The site also produced evidence of iron-working and abundant charcoal, dated by radiocarbon to 280 B.C. + 120 years. This date is conveniently in the middle of the range of dates already established, and adds further weight to them. This site is not a riverbed deposit, but is evidently an occupation site where people worked, even if they did not actually live there.

It is hoped that further excavations on this site will extend our knowledge of the Nok culture, and the way of life of the people. The sites, which have produced Nok Terracotta sculptures, are spread across Central Nigeria in a wide band running diagonally across the country. There are many sites in this area. At least twenty are already known, apart from a large number grouped together close to Nok. They have produced sculptures showing considerable variation in style and treatment yet, all quite clearly in an African mode.

It is impossible to doubt that all the pieces are distinctly African, for they all show a very free use of the imagination in representing humanity, although the animals are not so impressionistic. Indeed, although the eyes of animals (like the elephant), are represented in much the same way as the eyes on the human heads. The animal sculptures achieve a much greater sense of realism than do the human figures.

The reasons for this are difficult to establish. If one were able to ask a Nok sculptor why he represented human beings in one way, and animals in another, he would no doubt give the same kind of answer as a modern African carver does; 'this is the way in which we so do it'. In modern Nigeria societies, like the Yoruba, we find the idea that every human being has a spiritual soul, which needs to be nourished to ensure the person's well being.

Witchcraft operates in many cases by attacking the spiritual soul. While we have no direct evidence about the Nok sculptor's ideas, it would seem not unlikely that they were afraid to some extent from making natural representations, because they felt that it might give them power over the individual recognizably represented. On the other hand, it was perhaps desirable to exercise power over the animals around them. It would be unwise to attempt to press this explanation very far, because we just do not know.

The principle means of sculptural expression in the whole of Africa is wood, and the forms of the sculptures at Nok are in many cases reminiscent of woodcarving. One fragment of a face shows the blocking out of the lips in a manner, which would be much more appropriate to wood carving, than it is to the way that soft moist clay is used.

Another way of looking at it is, many of the sculptural forms seem to derive from the round form of a log of wood. In woodcarving, the limits of the trunk of the tree set a boundary to the outside shape of the sculpture. The effect of transferring from wood sculpture, in which a tradition had evidently been well evolved, into the more pliable medium of Terracotta, was one of the freedoms of the artist. The artist was able to conceive his forms in soft terms, instead of in such rigid forms as wood had made him use.

The head from Katsina Ala, in contrast, is much more round in form. There are several heads of this general type, either a round or cone set at an angle on another cylinder, which is the neck. This is one of the characteristic forms of Nok sculpture. It is a basic structural form which is found in the later sculptures of Esie, and in the Nomoli figures of places as far away as Sierra Leone and the Kongo. (This is part of the evidence that we will use later to show that all Bantu people originally came from southern Nigeria.) The small head from Jemaa is again an intensely soft form. It is a little different from the larger head from Jemaa, which was one of the first examples of Nok sculpture to be published.

It is noticed in comparison that in all cases, the eyes are pierced, as are the ears, and usually the mouth as well. The eyes normally take the form of an inverted triangle, or a semicircle with eyebrows above, often arched to sweep over the lower edge of the eye, and that the eyes are a little larger than normal. This form of eye is not only very characteristic of Nok sculpture, but is also very closely similar to the eyes of modern Yoruba Gelede masks. Bernard Fagg has pointed out a great many parallels between the art of Nok, and the Arts of the present day Southern Nigeria.

The Nok people lived in a period between 2500 and 3000 years ago, which saw the introduction of iron working into West Africa. The digging has produced large quantities of stone axes, and evidence of iron working in the form of slag and nozzles for bellows, as well as a small number of iron artifacts, including two iron axes, which closely resemble stone axes in their form.

Three of the sculptures show figures carrying axes over their shoulders, but it is impossible to be sure, whether these are of stone, or of iron. Many of the stone axes from the digging are extremely small, and it is likely that these were intended for use as wood carving tools, while at the other end; some very large ones may have been used as hoes for cultivating the swampy river banks on which they lived.

The Nok people evidently used vegetable foods from the seed of the ATILI, (an oil bearing plant) as well as the shells of the oil palm, together with small stones with pits in them, which are thought to have been used in cracking open the nuts to extract the kernel, and stone hand mills for grinding these and probably other seeds. Stone arrowheads are also found, and with these, we can say that they were hunters, as well as collectors of wild seeds and nuts. The extent, to which they can be considered farmers, is difficult to determine; whether they were deliberately cultivating crops, or merely encouraging wild plants by weeding is hard to say.

One of the Terracotta figurines carries on his head what appears to be a bowl of eggs, while another seems to represent a domestic cow. However, no bones of any kind have been found in the digging to support the idea that they were in any way cattle raising people.

The sculptures are richly decked out with beads, and many stone beads have been found in the archaeological deposits, together with quartz cylinders, which are thought to be an ear, nose, and lip plugs. A grinding stone, too, has been found, which appears to have been used for making ornaments.

There is no sign at all of cloth on most of the figurines. Those from Taruga for example, wear beaded waistbands from which hangs a small apron. However, this is not clearly of cloth, and is more likely to be of beadwork, or possibly of bark cloth, or leather. One incomplete but originally large figurine from Kuchamfa, however, wears a wrapper which hides the feet and carries a groove parallel to the edge apparently representing a hem. The treatment of this detail is almost identical with a fragment of Terracotta from Ife, and is very similar to the hems represented on the bronze figures from Ita Yemoo. The other figurines wear ornaments on the pelvis, which are evidently composed of basketwork, while one has beadwork and a bell, which appears to be of iron.

A great deal of domestic pottery has been found with the figurines, most of it rather heavy and coarse, though well made. They seem to have been more or less globular vessels with slightly out-turned rims.

Some evidence of buildings survive, for pieces of burnt clay bearing the impression of wattle-work (thin, flexible twigs woven together) have been found frequently, together with more strong fired clay from furnaces, or bricks.

So many features of the Nok culture, particularly of its art, are found in later cultures else where in West Africa, and it is difficult not to believe that the Nok culture, as we know it, represents the sculptural tradition of all of West Africa at that time. While it is conceivable that there were other cultures not yet discovered in different areas producing work similar in style to that of the Nok culture.

In addition, Grandpa believes that the Nok culture is the Ancestors to the Yoruba people. That is why the art is similar, and, it is in this sense, that we shall discuss the influence of the Nok culture on Ife. When we do this, we must be kept in mind that the amount of archeological work that has been done in West Africa so far is very small, and it is quite likely that entirely unknown cultures will be found in the future. Also, keep in mind that the Nok culture is 2500 to 3000 years old, and our point is, that the Yoruba and Nok are one and the same.

Many of the elements we have described from Nok are also found at Ife. These two cultures are the only ones we know from the whole of Africa, which have attempted anything near life-size sculptures in Terracotta. The human figures in both culture's art wear lots of beads, anklets, and bracelets, but particularly heavy beaded collars. Body and limb fragments are often very similar; they are normally rather stylized and simplified at Ife, despite the intense natural like faces. William Fagg has gone so far as to say that, "If fragments of the limbs and bodies from Ife and Nok were to get mixed up, it would be very difficult on grounds of style alone to distinguish them apart."

The typical Nok eyes are very similar to those of Yoruba wood sculptures. The most vigorously treated type of nose at Nok, with widely flaring wings, appears again in some Ife heads, and at Yada, as the basic from of nose at Benin and in Yoruba sculptures.

Some of the Nok heads have forehead rings, a feature repeated at Ife. Rarely, the heads in both these cultures have the hair treated as a raised ring with a hole in the center at Nok, or an iron nail at Ife. The treatment of the lower leg of the knee line figure from Nok, is in the same spirit as the Ileesha pieces in which the leg is attached to the middle of the foot, while the left leg of the male of the Ita Yemoo pair show a comparable approach in making body structure fit the sculpture form. The globular base that supports the Nok piece is found again at Ife, and at Zuru. Nok figures wear heavy rolled beaded collars, while the Ife figures wear a variety of heavy collars.

A round, or conical head mounted on a neck is characteristic of the Nok style, and reappears at Esie. Further away, in the Nomoli, figures were found in Siera Leone, and in the areas west of Nigeria; for example, the Senufo of the Ivory Coast, and east of Ife and Nok, as far as Kenya, and south to the Gabembe on the lower Zaire River, and the Bajokwe of Angola, and even the Zulu of South Africa. Character Ife sculpture has come to light in a variety of ways. In many cases, ancient objects of art are used in the rituals in the shrines and temples of modern day Ife, 2006.

At the annual festival of Itapa in the Temple of Orishanla, there is an ancient terracotta head still used in worship. In addition, the Ogun Ladin shrine has not only the ancient stone mudfish, but a quartz cylinder with holes drilled in the end, and a pear shaped droplet of wrought iron weighing well over 100 pounds. This is a remarkable example of a blacksmith's skills, since it must have been built up from small fragments of wrought iron. Another shrine, Epinbodo, had until recently a pair of stone stools, both broken; one in granite is of the round column type, the second, in quartz, originally had four legs.

Antique ritual art from many of the groves, like the Iwinrin Grove, were brought into the King's palace for safe keeping as long ago as 1937. And this process of bringing them together has continued every since, being helped now by the existence of the Ife Museum which opened in 1953.

In the Holy Groves in the forest, these objects are not safe. More recently, the ancient stone carvings in the Ore Grove were brought into the museum for greater safety. Some of the shrines use more sculptures that are recent. For example, a small shrine for Obalufon in the center of the town of Ife, has a very modern stone carving.

Other art pieces have been found by digging for them. The digging in the Groves of Olokun Walode conducted by Bernard Fagg in 1953, and of Obameri by Oliver Myers in 1964, have revealed fragments of sculptures, none of them complete, but brought together in these shrines at some time in the eighteenth or nineteenth centuries. Frank Willetts's digging at Ita Yemoo, has produced evidence of different types of shrines.

The first, dug in 1959, contained the remains of seven terracotta sculptures, which appeared to have been complete, and in position at the time the site was abandoned. They had been weathered and eroded for some time before the building collapsed upon them. A second shrine on the same site dug in 1962, or 1963, had contained dismantled sculptures.

These were the remains of the two figures of about three-quarters life size, which appear to have already been broken when they were placed together in the shrine. Their positions were so jumbled, that they could hardly have arrived at such disorder if they had been originally complete, and had merely been smashed by the collapse of the building.

The other main source of discovery of Ife antique ritual art of course, is by casual finds. Since 1956, there has been an archaeologist resident more or less continuously in Ife, and the Museum was there three years before that.

Antique ritual art of Ife is not restricted to the town of Ife. A number of sites have been dug a few miles from Ife, Abiri and Agidi, but there are others. A terracotta ram's head was found at Oshogbo, thirty miles to the north, and a human head is still worshipped at Ikirun still further north. A terracotta hand, holding a staff, was found in Ijebu-Ode, seventy miles to the southwest, though this piece is not in the classical Ife style.

Stone sculptures at Erumu, Eshure, and Kuta, should be mentioned, while fragments of glass making crucibles have been found at Ede. One of the most characteristic features of Ife architecture was pavements made of broken potsherds, which have been found at

Benin, Owo, Ifaki, Ikerin, and Ede, and also in Dahomey at Letu, and Dassa Zoume, and in the Kabrais district of Togo.

The houses in which the ancient Ife's lived have collapsed, and are extremely difficult to recover in digging, because the unusual method of building in Ife consists of digging a number of irregular holes. Often, one inside area is designed to become a room. Water is poured into the loose earth in these 'borrow pits', and the earth troddens into a thick paste. This may then be used to build a course of mud wall about eighteen inches high, which is allowed to dry out for a day before the next is added.

More recently, the mud has been put into a rectangular mold, and then tipped out on the ground to dry in the sun. The most advanced technique of all are smaller molds that are used, and after drying, the bricks are fired in a kind of clamp. This technique of building does not require the use of foundation trenches. As a result, the walls themselves are almost impossible to find. Fortunately, the houses in Ife were paved inside with layers of potsherds laid on edge, often arranged in decorative patterns.

These patterns are sometimes revealed in present day roads and footpaths, and have proved to be extremely durable. Therefore, the archaeologist must dig down to the potsherds pavement, clean the area, and then there is the outline of the ancient houses. In some cases, these seem to have been pavements under the verandas around open courtyards. In others, they were the pavements of small courtyards, known as an impluvium.

Akodi is an open space in the roof to receive rain. This is the traditional method of building houses in Yorubaland, so that the opening in the roof is over the center of the room and allows light to enter, and of course, the rain as well. The rain is collected in a tank nowadays, and in large water pots in the olden days.

A near by pavement had an old grinding stone which was worn out completely so that there was a hole through the center of it set on edge beside the pavement to conduct the water through the mud, while protecting it from erosion. The pavements vary considerably in style. Sometimes they are simple straight rows of potsherds laid side by side, and in other instances, lines alternate with lines of white quartz pebbles. Occasionally, the rows of pottery are set in herringbone style, or the lines of potsherds intersect to form rectangular spaces, which are filled quartz pebbles.

From the plans of pavements like this, we are gradually learning something about the architecture of ancient Ife. The doors were of wood, hinged by means of an iron loop attached to the wall above, and passing around a tab on the door, while a similar tab at the bottom corner is turned in a cup shaped stone; two of which were found close to pavements at the St. David's digging.

The ancient bronze and terracotta sculptures of Ife show evidence of other crafts. The clothing worn by the figures are evidently of cloth with hems sewn around, while in some cases, embroidery is present. Both types of looms are currently used in Yoruba land. The broad loom on which women weave wide cloth, and the narrow loom used by men to make narrow strips which are sewn together to make wide pieces seemed to have been in use.

Most of the figures wear sashes that were probably woven on narrow looms. The figures are also decked out with beads, which can be interpreted both from the paint that has been applied to them, and from the shape in which they are modeled. Many of them appear to be red stone beads of a variety of shapes, while others are evidently intended to represent blue glass beads. Both kinds are found in the diggings.

In addition, there are a great variety of bracelets. Some are of smooth glass, metal, or ivory. While more elaborate ones are certainly of metal, with some having expanded trumpet ends. Others have opened work decoration, and many of them are sculptured to represent human and animal heads, as well as ideas of an abstract nature. Many of the figures wear caps and badges which appear to be made of small beads, although their embroidered caps are not closely done in the sculptures. Around their necks, these chiefs are wearing beads; two of them have long beads of blue grass know as Segi.

The manufactures of the glass beads in Ife appear to have been a major industry. All over the town, there are fragments found of crucibles used in the process of glass making. There were pots made of a white paste, usually thickly coated with glass, both inside and out. Some scores of fragments of these crucibles were found in the course of the digging at Ita Yemoo, while a complete one was used to store beads on the shrine with seven terracotta figures.

Music and dancing play an important role in African ritual life. We can safely say, these are two of the major African creative art forms, although they are very difficult to discuss, because there is no easy way of recording them in a book. However, there is some evidence in the archaeological material of musical instruments. Drums are represented on the elaborate ritual pots, while metal bars have been dug up, which resemble the Owo, which are struck in rhythm during modern festivals. Iron gongs have also been found.

Our subject is the Yoruba art form over a 2500 to 3000 year period of time, which allows us to see the continuity of the Yoruba's religion of creativity in their long history. Now we will turn our attention to the Yoruba's religion of creativity in the twenty-first century.

GELEDE;
Where Yoruba creativity and history come alive in the performance of a ritual

Well fellow Investigators, now we will move into looking at the Yoruba history, and beliefs in creativity from the point of view of a community ritual. There are a lot of authors that have researched and studied the ritual called Gelede from different points of view, and all of them have described in great detail what people were doing in preparation and performing the ritual.

H. Ulli Beier (1958), Frank Speed (1968), Peggy Harper (1970), Jacques Kerchache (1973), Jacques Bernolles (1973), Anthony Asiwaju (1975), Afolabi Olabimtan (1970), Gabriel Fayomi (1982), Benedict Ibitokun (1981), Emmanuel Babatunde (1988), Robert Farris Thompson'(1971), Henry John Drewal and Margaret Thompson Drewal (1983), and Babatunde Lawal (1996). The point being, is that all of them gave the same description of what people were doing in preparation and performing the ritual, which means that we can think of it as true, and is evidence we will use.

However, each one of the authors look at the same evidence from twelve different points of view, for example, ancient women ruled the Yoruba by making a film, the role of dance, art objects, the historical significance of Gelede, literary, linguistic, dramatic aspects, sociological, aesthetics of dance and costume, woman power, and social control. But Grandpa is going to look at the evidence from the point of view, that this ritual is no different than a Black Baptist Sunday ritual.

The evidence shows that the people come together, sing and dance, and a sermon is preached related to the spiritual health of their community, based on the code of conduct of the "Good Character" given to the Earth Goddess, OLYA NAL, by the Great Creator, OLODUMARE, before people were created. Just as the Christians come together, sing, dance, and a sermon is preached related to the spiritual health of their community based on the Ten Commandments and the teaching of Christ.

The only difference between the two is that when the Christians do it, it is to bring Christ's love into their mist; and when the Yoruba do it, it is to bring ORISANLA's creativity into their mist.

For a description of the ritual, we will begin our investigation with two books from the above mentioned authors. We will use the description found in,

Gelede: Art and Female Power Among the Yoruba (Traditional Arts of Africa) by Henry John Drewal and Margaret Thompson Drewal. Bloomington; Indiana University Press, c1983

And check the description against the book;

The Gelede Spectacle: Art, Gender, and social Harmony in African Culture. By Babatunde Lawal: Seattle: University of Washington Press c1996
The *author*, art historian *Babatunde Lawal*, is himself a Yoruba, and brings a participatory insider's view of the Gelede tradition, because he grew up seeing it performed.

(For more on Gelede, and art on the internet, Yahoo or Google the word Gelede, or the author's names.
And, or visit.
http://www.randafricanart.com/Yoruba_gelede_mask_birds.html   *for beautiful pictures of the dances and masks in color).*

I picked Henry John Drewal and Margaret Thompson Drewal's description, because it is from the point of view of women's spiritual power. And I think that my granddaughter Investigators will find it very interesting, being as you are now grown up young women with families of your own. I know you are interested in woman power in man-woman relationships, in your family, and in your community at large.

I am so impressed with these two descriptions, that when my money gets right, I am going to buy each one of my granddaughters a copy of both books. Not because I agree with both authors point of view, but because I think that if you think of art and womanhood on that level, you will get some insight into the major role that woman power plays in your personal life.

Meanwhile, Grandpa is going to focus on the same ritual evidence from the point of view of **Yoruba worship of creativity**, and how it has transcended time to the twenty-first century, some 2500 to 3000 years later.

We will examine a community-involved ritual, which will clearly show different art forms as they relate to a rituals creativity. This time, the sculptures will be in the form of masks carved in wood. Now, let's look at what people were doing in preparation and performing the ritual.

First, we will break down the Yoruba word, GELEDE, which means; GEL, 'to soothe, to pacify, to pet, or coddle'; ELE, refers to a woman's private parts, those that symbolize women's secrets, and their life-giving powers; DE, says, 'to soften with care or gentleness'. Together, these ideas give the meaning of the Gelede ritual, performed carefully, and I think, conceived and executed to put creativity to work in the community, to pay homage to women, so that the community may receive ORISANLA's CREATIVE POWER, in the same sense, as Christians seek Christ's LOVE POWER.

Gelede ritual consists of two kinds of performances. There is the nighttime Efe, which is the voicing of the Mother's love power, and the daytime dance, that makes love power visible in the form of a masquerade stage play that represents a highly visible and artistic expression of a Yoruba belief; that women, primarily elderly women, possess extraordinary love power from the Earth Goddess OLYA NAL who is the guardian of Motherhood, and the Gelede shrine.

A ritual that essentially belongs to the mothers, and lasts nine days and nine nights. Gelede provides an elaborate artistic and symbolic system of ideas with which to explore and evaluate the ideas and images of women in an African society, women's spiritual and social roles in Yoruba culture, and the man-women relationship. With the sanction of the Mother's, and OLYA NAL, Gelede has the power to 'bring together' the forces in the Yoruba spiritual world for the well-being of the community. A view that is reflected in praises acknowledging them as 'our mothers', 'the Goddesses of society' and, the 'owners of the world'.

With this power, the 'mothers' can be either beneficial or destructive. Through the Earth Goddess, they can bring health, wealth, and problems to people that interfere with the smooth running of the community, and fertility to the land and its people. The 'mothers' can also bring disaster.

Gelede ritual is a celebration, but, at the same time, this is a process through which the Goddess female ancestors, and the community mothers maintain social control. Gelede comments on male and female roles in society, which show that the male and female have equal power in the belief of the Yoruba religion, or to say, there is male and female power involved. Comments are made on traditional and modern fashion, creativity, and achievements. Community concerns are also shown, and brings the communities desires into actual existence through visual and musical art forms. It likewise criticizes antisocial individuals and deeds. The art forms constitute Gelede's comments on society, both individually, and as a community group which produces a beautiful performance that involves seeing as well as hearing, in addition to the other senses. But the bottom line is that Gelede is a church service like a Christian church service, only on a grander scale.

To understand the content of Gelede ritual, that is, the ideas it contains, is to understand a 'mothers' love creative capacity to shape the lives of her children. We also want to pay special attention to the sculptured wood masks that are worn in the performance, and what they communicate to the people; including the relationship of the

1970's sculptured art, and the Nok's ancient sculptured art, along with the nature of the sculptures relationship to spiritual ideas.

Gelede is presented in a festival manner, but most of all, its a community ritual to motherhood; and has a purpose, which is, to show respect, and to make sure that motherhood, or mothers love is involved in the communities affairs, both spiritually and physically. This is thought of by the Yoruba as, bringing 'female life force' (love) into the community.

Why is Gelede performed in the market place? Numerous stories involve the market place. Hunter's tales describe the way animals in the bush remove their skins, and transform themselves into human beings and go shopping on market days. Other stories tell of spirits in human form who frequent the market place, marry people, and bear their children, only to disappear one day, taking the children with them.

The inter-mingling of people and spirits in the market place during Gelede is suggested by an Egbado King, who contended that when Gelede is a success, spirits, known as 'strangers' visit the performance. They appear as people, and are identifiable by the fact that they are unknown to the community. When strangers are present, it is felt that the community has been successful, through performance, in communication with the spiritual world. As a Gelede elder explained, "We realize that our prayers have been answered, when strangers visit in the night. Young children, grownups, and old people come, and then disappear at day-break".

It is not by chance that the market is a major setting of social and economic activity involving primarily women. Trading is the most common profession among women in the Yoruba community. Indeed, women control the market. Its administrative head, the Iyalode, holds a position on the King's council of chiefs. Women are economically independent, and through trading, they can acquire greater wealth and higher status than their husbands can.

By bringing the ritual into the market, the Gelede society introduces it directly into the women's world, the place where their collective social power is consciously felt. The marketplace is thus a most appropriate setting for a ritual that seeks to gather all segments of the community in order to pay homage to the special power of women, and to use their influence.

Gelede mediates between the owners of society. Those who generate, manage, control, and punish it, and the community. Through praise and criticism, prayers and curses, Gelede ritual carries out the will of the mothers. The community is responsive in turn by lending its support. The art forms that make up the ritual thus become instruments of regulating society. Most important of all, Gelede confirms patience and indulgence, qualities thought to be possessed by women, as an ideal means of correcting problems, and maintaining peace.

The art of Gelede touches upon different concerns in many ways. The way that the different art forms work together, tell the community about the awesome power involved in 'Motherhood's Love', because love and power' are the nature of OLYA NAL, the Earth Goddess in the Yoruba religion, who is the Goddess of Nature; and as we know, Mother Nature is a very powerful Goddess indeed.

The enormous range of Gelede visual art, in mask form, can be said to evaluate everything that exists, women, men, ancestors, Gods, animals, plants, and objects, within the realities of the mothers, the 'owners of the world', in terms of their influence on the living, who are the 'children of the mothers'.

Things (mother's love) seen as contributing to the 'togetherness' of the Yoruba society are celebrated, while those detrimental to the community, are exposed, ridiculed, and made fun of in devastating creative images. Competing spiritual forces operating in the Yoruba spiritual world, whether religious or social, are carved in scenes of multiple human figures or animals in the super-structures of the masks. Similar imagery also serves and functions as 'visualized' proverbs, histories, or stories, passed down from generation to generation.

Thus, the heritage of the past is preserved, and new things are added in the sculptured masks. At the same time, all of these ideas are presented by the masqueraders to honor, respect, and please the mothers of the community. Having created appropriate images and performed the necessary rituals, the community felt secure in the belief that, as long as they continue to act according to traditional values, they will receive the benefits of the mother's power, channeled to positive ends. 'You cannot afford to make the mothers mad'. The Gelede creative art is in the form of dance, songs, words, and especially the talking drums and masks.

The Gelede Ritual

An Ese Ifa poem states:

Patience and good judgment was the ancient wisdom of the Egbe

Patience and good judgment was the ancient wisdom of the Ijesa

It was divined (Ifa) for Orunmila, who was going to the town of the owners of the birds (spiritually powerful women)

That he must put on an image (mask), head ties, and leg rattles

He obeyed, he put them on, he arrived in the town of the owners of the birds and he survived

He rejoiced in dancing and singing

'I have covenanted with Death, I will never die

Death, worrisome Death

I have covenanted with sickness, I will never die

Death worrisome Death'

This is said by the talking drums at the beginning of the Gelede ritual, as the masqueraders enter the arena to perform and retell the spiritual origin of Gelede masquerading. Ifa instructed Orunmila, the God governing Ifa Divination to exercise great caution in entering the domain of spiritually powerful women known as the 'owners of the birds', by putting on a mask, female head ties, and leg rattles; three main elements found in all Gelede costumes.

Orunmila did not confront these powerful women aggressively; rather, he sought to please them. As one elder comments, "It is the Great Mother who gave instructions, saying, anyone who worships her must have patience". For, the mothers from the left and from the right, and from the front and from the back are asked to descend and join the gathering; their reply comes from the trees in the form of bird cries.

Another elder, this time a priestess, says, "These masks are like the vital power (ase) that the ancients used in the past, which they called (eso), a thing done with carefulness. They must not perform it nakedly". With the proper dress and attitude, Orunmila journeyed safely into the midst of the 'owners of the birds', where he sings and dances. Gelede performances recreate this spiritual journey.

THE GELEDE RITUAL PERFORMANCE

As darkness approaches, the community completes its preparations for the sounds and sights of Efe Night. (the beginning of the ritual) Between 9 and 10 p.m., a large crowd gathers in the central market. Men, women, and children come bringing with them lamps, mats, chairs, and food. They arrange themselves in a large circle.

The performer's entryway into the circle, known as the 'mouth of authority', keeps the crowd's attention pointed in that direction. Families with titled elders, especially women and other important people, are given the best seats along the edge of the performance space. This large crowd of people, sometimes numbering 1,000 to 2,000, including Gelede shrine (church) members, relatives of local people who live in other towns, (each town has their own Gelede ritual, performance) and 'strangers'. (A term used for spirits as well as 'children of the world') From all parts of the town, neighboring villages, and from all age groups and lifestyles, the people assemble to the Efe (nighttime Gelede) ritual.

The drummers arrive first and set up for their ensemble within the arena just opposite the masquerader's entrance. The ensemble of four to six drums contain two large lead drums, approximately three to four feet high; the larger is called 'mother drum', the other, 'daughter drum'. The mother and daughter drum together, beat verbal messages by reproducing the rhythmic and tonal structure of the spoken Yoruba language. The smaller supporting drums, 'the male drums', are fixed at different pitches, and maintain a rapid complex poly-rhythm. Over this background rhythm, the mother drum and the daughter drum weave well known proverbs, and praise the Gods, Ancestors, and Elders while awaiting the arrival of the chorus of singers.

The singers are known collectively as, 'carriers of the news' and consists of male and female members of the shrine. Upon leaving the Gelede shrine, they proceed to the gathering, singing a song such as the following, which announces that all are in place and ready;

It is now time to start, it is time.
Bush fowl lives in the forest, it is time.
Teak is found in the grasslands, it is time.

The lavish display is prepared. It is evening, and it is time to start. The stage is now set for a series of masqueraders to appear. Men perform all of the masquerades, but the costuming and movement may represent either males or females. Efe night opens with a series of introductory masquerades known generically as, 'spirits of the earth'. The first is Ogbagba, who represents the divine mediator Esu/Elegba, the Trickster God. As mediator between men and the Gods, Esu/Elegba is honored first, and encouraged to 'open the way' for a successful ceremony. He appears twice, first as a 'young boy in a white cap and raffia skirt' as the people sing, 'Esu comes when light leaves', then, as a grownup wearing banana leaves and iron anklets, as the ritual members sing lines such as these;

Esu/Elegba carries leaves
On all the rubbish dumps, he has picked up the eko leaves
He comes carrying leaves.

Arabi Ajigbale follows Esu/Elegba. As the name implies, Arabi is, 'the-one-who-sweeps-every-morning', which literally means, he 'sweeps, and thus clears and cleanses the marketplace. His costume is of shredded palm leaves, and his clearing actions refer to Ogun, the God of iron, for both, he and Esu/Elegba serve to 'open the way' for all men's communications with the spiritual forces. At his appearance, people may sing;

Arabi, the-one-sweeps-every-morning
The cloth of another is good for sweeping

Fire is the focus of the next masquerade pair. The first, Agbena, or the fire carrier, appears with either a mass of blazing grasses, or pot of fire balanced on his head and a costume of white cloth. The performer moves quickly through the space, as sparks fly, forcing the crowd backwards as it sings;

The fire in the bush starts without warning

Farmers with fields near the bush, beware

These series of masquerades ritually re-enact the steps taken in establishing a shrine, a house or a settlement, actions of entry, clearing, and finally, burning off the remains; actions presided over by Esu and Ogun. As the God of iron, and the one who clears the way, Ogun in particular, is regarded as the major God of this process. Agbena, disappearing as quickly as he appeared, may be immediately followed by Apana, the 'fire extinguisher' who sings;

Owner of fire, kill your fire!

The hoopoe (a bird with a decurved bill) is coming

Put down your load,

Because one does not light fires

The performance enters a new phase now that the marketplace has been ritually prepared. All lights are extinguished as the impending ,'bird of the night', the most sacred of Efe and Gelede forms. The Great Ancestor Mother, IYANLA, appears either as a bearded woman, or as a bird called Eye oro, spirit bird, or Eye Oru, bird of the night. In the darkness, the Great Mother comes trailing a white cloth. While she performs, all lights must be extinguished. As she moves in a gentle slow dance matching her steps with the drum rhythms, the elders of the Gelede shrine flock around her. Her headdress, worn almost horizontally is fastened to a long white cloth that often trails on the ground. The sacred image gives expression to the awesome aspect of the mothers. These masks are of two distinct forms, yet the idea and function are the same, they represent the very essence of Gelede, and are the very 'foundation' of the society. They dramatize the spiritual side of womanhood in two of its aspects, a bearded woman, often called the Great Mother, and (Iyanla) and Spirit Bird. (Eye Oro)

The Great Mother's mask has two parts, the head, and a long flat board like extension below the chin. Together, the head and projection (between 15 and 36 inches in length) produce a massive headdress. The head is built to fit over the upper portion of the performer's head and forehead. The features are strong, massive, and clearly defined. Deep-set bulging eyes dominate the face, while heads are shaven, or simply indicating a hairline. A variety of hairstyles, or more dramatic, a prominent tuft of hair (osu) crowns the center of the head. The only superstructure is a snake encircling the head, or a bird perched on top. Aside from these few designs, surfaces are plain, somewhat rough, and usually white.

The board like projection from the chin of the Great Mother mask is identified as a beard. A beard defines an elder as having knowledge and wisdom. Nevertheless, in the feminine world, the beard takes on additional meanings, for by definition, a bearded woman possesses extraordinary spiritual power. Beards pictured in other Yoruba sculptures are much smaller and are sometimes darkened. The exaggeration and elongation of the Mother's beard emphasis her extraordinary nature, for the beard on a woman 'will not be like a man's own'. The additional element of whiteness emphasizes these qualities, for the Yoruba say, 'old age (wisdom) is shown by white hair, and maturity is shown by a beard'. The beard also symbolizes the 'transformation powers of the mothers', if we recall, birds are a common symbol of the mothers in a transformed state.

The Bird Mothers, like the bearded Mothers, are awesome in their bold simplicity. The whiteness of the cloth and mask dominate. The long, sharply pointed peak thrusts outward from the domed or crested head with its small eyes. Its blood-red tip highlights the beak's deadly quality; these sculpted images closely resemble descriptions of the mothers transformed into birds. For example, when 'elderly women wear plaited hair crowns on their head', or they praise names of the mothers, 'the one with two bodies', (abaara neji) or, 'the one with two faces'.(Oloju meji) The power of transformation referred to in these praises, originates in the ideas of the nature of women's life force, (ase) and their spiritual head.

The two mother masks symbolize two different sides of the Great Mother's spiritual head; First, it is said, 'nobody can love' as hard as a mother, and nobody can 'hate' as hard as a mother.

The procedures used in sheltering the Great Mother's image between performances, reveal the attitudes of the great feeling of love to this sacred form. She rests in the shrine of OLYA NAL, the Earth Goddess; The male religious leader says a greeting to the Great Mother, and carefully knocks three times before opening the door. In the center of a darkened room, raised on an alter is Iyanla. A spotless white cloth covers her completely, barely revealing the form. Only the leader and his assistant are permitted to approach the mask, because of the presence of powerful spiritual forces. A song offered at the Great Mother's appearance invites her to dance;

'Honored elder Apake come and dance with us

All birds come dance with us'

The Great Mother masquerader plunges his torso forward, and maintains a crouched position throughout the performance. His elbows and knees are bent and spread laterally to look like old age. Ankle rattles echo the Gelede drum rhythms, as the mother masquerade slowly advances to them, and retreats using small jumps that barely leave the ground. The Great Mother does not speak. A series of songs and drum rhythms accompany her, creating layers of messages. If the masquerade represents Spirit Bird, the chorus and crowd sing;

Spirit Bird is coming
Spirit Bird is coming
Ososobi o, Spirit Bird is coming
The one who brings the festival today
Tomorrow is the day when devotees of the Gods will worship
You are the one who brought us to this place
It is your influence that we are using
Ososobi o, Spirit Bird is coming

If, on the other hand, the masquerader appears as a bearded mother, the community offers the following song;

Iyanla come into the world, our mother
Kind one will not die like the evil one
Oaosomu come into the world
Our mother the kind on will not let you die like the evil one
Ososomu e e e
Honored ancestor apake e e e
Mother, Mother, child who brings peace to the world
Repair the world for us
Iyanla, child who brings peace to the world o e

As the song praises the Mother, the drums approximate the tonal patterns of Yoruba speech and simultaneously offer another message;

Mother, Mother, the one who killed her husband in order to take a title
Come and dance, the one who killed her husband in order to take a title, come and dance
Stand up, stand up, come and dance
One who killed her husband in order to take a title, come and dance
Honored ancestor Apake, come and dance
Come home immediately
One who killed her husband in order to take a title, come home immediately
One who has given birth to many children, come home immediately, come home now
I make sacrifice, I receive glory, the day is proper
I sacrificed, I sacrificed, I sacrificed
A woman will not describe what happened during travel
A woman will not tell what we have done

A woman cannot have Ajanon title in Oro
In this world, in this world, in this world
In darkness and completely surrounded, Iyanla circles the performance area and quickly returns to the shrine, where the mask, wrapped or draped with white cloth, serves as the shrine, and the focus of worship for the elders of the OLYA NAL shrine.

With the departure of Iyanla, the first singing mask arrives. It is known in some places as Tetede, (the one who comes in good time) in others as, Aiye Tutu. (Cool world) The role of this masquerader is to prepare the way for Oro Efe with chants that honor the mothers, the Gods, and the assembled elders, and then to call Oro Efe, ensuring that he may safely begin his night-long solo song sermon;

Amulohun, if I call you the first time, and you don't answer
You will become an anthill
If I call you a second time, and you don't answer
You will become a piece of wood
If I call you the third time, and you don't answer
You will become a savage beast
With the call of this introductory singing masquerader, two attendants of Oro Efe come into the area and kneel before the entryway, or 'mouth of authority'. They carry special medicines to protect Oro Efe throughout his performance. From the area in front of the entrance, the female ritual head of the Gelede shrine and her assistant, both dressed in white in honor of the 'Cool' Gods, and OLYA NAL, the Earth Goddess, called the Great Mother Goddess, strike the four-sphere bell. They ritually call Oro Efe to the world, and announce his coming, and insure that he is protected. Oro Efe is, 'the one who speaks for the Great Mother', or preacher of ritual, or to say, church service. That is a big responsibility.

Next, a flute player appears with a short burst of music praising Oro Efe, and calls him by name, then he silences the crowd. The slow insistence beat of Oro Efe's leg rattles announces his coming, as he appears in the 'mouth of authority'. He sways slowly, swinging horsetail whisks in each hand. With his first high piercing note, the flute ceases.

With everything ready, and ripples of expectation and excitement running through the crowd, the drums fall silent, and Oro Efe, accompanied by the flute, reply to the first singing masquerader;

When you called me the first time,
I had been doing a task for the Apa tree.
When you called me the second time,
I was providing service for the Iroko tree.
But when you called me the third time, I answered in a clear, resounding voice.

Now that you have finished calling me, go home.

The term Efe literally means, 'a play on words', and Ase means, 'the power of the word', and Oro means, 'King'. Therefore, Oro Efe means, 'King of the power of the words', or, a singing preacher, which has a humorous side of Ese night, and is apparent in numerous songs ridiculing, or mocking foolish, or antisocial behavior. Yet his very serious side will become evident as we examine the list of things that Ore Efe must do in his night-long performance. For, Oro Efe's words have the power of Ase. The power to make his meaning, with the communities backing, come to pass. An elderly Efe singer and priest of Ifa, 'the God of Wisdom' mention this force;

"The Ifa God is a prophet. If something bad were going to happen, and the Ife God sees it and tells us that, today, he wants us to celebrate Efe, it should be done. After doing it, the bad thing which was to happen would be sent away. What prevents the happening from coming to pass is what Ifa predicts is wind, and the Efe that we do is also wind." (voice, words)

A deep philosophical idea is involved in these words. Efe songs possess vital power, (Ase) which is activated in the pronouncing of the words of all Efe songs regardless of the subject matter. Efe is, in effect, the public equivalent of private prayer that occurs during sacrificial ceremonies, Ifa Divination, and in each individual striving to communicate with the Gods, Ancestors, and the Mothers. Stated another way, the voicing of prayer to bring something to pass, or to prevent something from happening is likened to, 'wind combating wind.'

Likewise, the manner in which Efe is presented, adds to its powers. Oro Efe as a male elder of the ritual, is chosen and controlled by the female ritual chief priestess, Iyalase. He is thus sanctioned both spiritually and socially; indeed Oro Efe is considered to be the 'servant' of the mothers. Because of this role, he is protected from any repercussions from the community, as a result of his words and deeds. This double sanction creates a special status for Oro Efe, which is shown in his song presentation and his costume.

The subjects of Efe songs have a wide range. Oro Efe, 'the king of the power of the word', begins respectfully honoring forces greater than himself. They include the Gods, the Ancestors, and the Mothers. He appeals to them to secure their benevolent intervention in the affairs of the community. These honoring prayers are followed by a change in attitude, intent, and direction, as Oro Efe turns to other matters. He first builds-himself-up as a means of protection in his temporary and vulnerable position as the verbalizer of the mother's desires and opinions. He must not falter or stumble. Then, he devotes the remainder of his song-sermon to community concerns, always mindful that the traditional attitudes and morals he presents, are those most desired by the Gods, Ancestors, and the Mothers.

He seeks to please them by teaching these ideas, and by ridiculing, condemning, and cursing all who contradict the wishes of the mothers. The community, well aware of the consequences of wrongful actions by any of its members, adds its combined force in 'call and respond', backing up Oro Efe. No transgression is left uncondemned, no contribution left unpraised, for the act of voicing community opinion carries with it sacral power.

While Oro Efe's opening words of honor are based upon very ancient prayers, his list of social commentary songs are composed only a short time before each performance to ensure that they will be up-to-date. All of the male shrine-church members who have performed Efe in the past compose the songs. As one of them explains;

"We will dream a situation, and in our minds, we will compose a song about the situation. We will meet in a private place, usually the Gelede shrine, about 10 of us, and sit down and think of songs. The songs sing about the situation presented."

Other elders, especially the women, may also offer suggestions for songs that 'follow up-to-date events', the happenings of the times.

The main body of Ife sermons may be divided into five major subject categories, with subdivisions, although some could be classified under more than one heading. We shall analyze each category briefly, on the basics of motivation and content, and then examine specific songs in each category and subdivision. The categories are;

1. Showing honor and respect to the spiritual powers

2. Prayer
    a. Self-affirmation
    b. Prayer
    c. Curse

3. Comments about community affairs
    a. Sexual behavior
       Sex roles
       Morality
    b. Politics
       External
       Internal
    c. Religion

   d. Seniority

4. History

5. Funeral commemoration

    Showing honor and respect to Oro Efe, he does so by means of his initial chant, or incantation, (Igede) which means, 'prayer of honor and respect'. It always occurs at the beginning of Oro Efe's performance, as a singing preacher, unlike the other songs before, do not go through a phase of choral repetition. Oro Efe directs his 'prayer of honor and respect' to those beings more powerful than himself, the Gods, Ancestors, and the Mothers, who could disrupt the performance or cause him harm. Performing an act of self-protection, he invokes and honors them with praises from oral literature and stories associated with these Holy Beings. Oro Efe thus compels them to support and protect him by voicing prayers that amuse, exalt, and flatter them.

    The following 'Prayer of honor and respect', as Oro Efe proclaims the commencement of his performance, and demands the silence of the large crowd. As the noise dies down, he begins the prayer. The order of invoking the God is based on their roles in the ritual. Therefore, like the order of appearance of the night masquerades, those who 'open the way', Ogun and Esu come first.

    Being a 'hot' God, Ogun has a strong, arrogant, aggressively masculine temperament, and the prayer imagery reflects these traits. Ogun is believed to have been the King of Ire, and one of his praise names recalls this event with 'Ogun Onire', (line 2) and tells of his bravery, violent temper, and thorough vengeance. (lines 3-7) His manliness and virility are praised in, (lines 8-10) when, with extreme audacity, he exposed himself in the presence of the King's mother, who by definition is a spiritually powerful woman. (line 11)

    Esu is honored next. All men wishing to communicate with the Gods, must present a portion of their offering to Esu, for he serves as messenger to the Gods. Oro Efe praises Esu's mischievous, unpredictable nature with acting images. Esu sheds tears of blood in mock sympathy with mourners, and then succeeds in frightening a defecating man by excreting intestines rather than feces. (lines 12-13) These verbal praises remind humans of the countless possibilities that can confront them when dealing with spiritual forces that are not bound by the rules of the living.

    Oro Efe then honors the Mothers. He calls upon them using their 'owners of birds' image, and talks of the sick and elderly bird that refuses to be warmed by the fire, or sun, (lines 16-17) for the obscurity of the cool night is her abode. He also refers to the belief that, the destructive mothers, in agreement with their favorite males, bury certain powerful substances in the earthen floor of their homes. The singer intones her praises descriptively, "my mother", and playing upon the sacred and awe inspiring words, set up the final honor and respect parts. (lines 18-20) He then recalls the female mysteries of the mothers and their controlling power over human creativity in referring to the vagina and pubic hair, (lines 23-24) private parts that symbolize the secrets that women will never reveal to men. The final lines mention the mother's spiritual eating of a victim trapped as a result of her whims.

Oro Efe thus secures the support and protection of Ogun, Esu, and the Mothers by the prayers that invoke their participation. For Ogun, these prayers flaunt the male ego, the strength, virility, and audacity symbolized by the lengthened penis, and invokes his overt, aggressive power, and his quick vengeance. Esu's power surfaces in his ability to 'mess things up'. Esu, the God at the crossroads, simultaneously offers many options, and 'opens the way', by forcing a direct channel of communication to the spiritual world, and giving Oro Efe access to a vast reservoir of creative power. Finally, invoking female power represented by the 'mothers', Oro Efe summons power that is secret, puzzling, and hidden, thus amazing spiritual support to assure that his words will take effect. It is presented this way;

1. Honor, honor, honor today, honor to the Gods
2. Honor to Ogun Onire, My husband
3. Ogun the brave one in firing, in firing
4. Ogun left (killed) his wife in the bathroom
5. Ogun killed the swordsmen
6. He destroyed them with one blow
7. Ogun, I asked you to chase them, not to lick their bones
8. Honor to the one whose penis stood up to father a child in the room
9. He makes his penis lengthen to father a child in the house of Ijana
10. We heard how the penis struck those in the market
11. Ogun, the one who saw the king's mother and did not cover his penis
12. Esu Laroye, the one who weeps with tears of blood
13. When on began to excrete feces, you frightened him by excreting intestines
14. Honor,oooooo (elongation of particle used in greeting to indicate respect) honor today, ooooo
15.Odulebe, (destructive mother) I, I honor you today
16. Old bird did not warm herself in the sun

18. Something secret was buried in the mother's house
19. A secret pact with a wizard
20. Honor, honor today, ooooo
21. Honor to my mother
22. Mother whose vagina causes fear to all
23. Mother whose pubic hair bundles up in knots
24. Mother who set a trap set a trap
25. Mother who had meat at home in lumps

His performance begins with honor and respect properly given to powerful forces, Oro Efe can now begin the list of songs that will be repeated by the chorus, picked up, and sung repeatedly by the crowd.

The actual presentation of an Efe song takes two distinct forms, the solo rendition, and the choral repetition. During the entire solo, Oro Efe sings with minimal accompaniment to a relatively silent crowd, thus, enhancing his presentation. He is set apart further by his distinctive costuming and physical acting. Everything is set up to make sure Oro Efe's words are distinct and understandable, if not, the chorus may sing a reproach to an inexperienced Oro Efe if his song and intent are not clear;

> Efe we would be grateful for an explanation
> You had better explain very well so that we understand
> Be direct, like the penis splitting the virgin's vagina
> Efe, we would be grateful for an explanation

The chorus must learn and respect the songs. Choral repetition completes the precise transmission of the Efe song text. At the same time, it adds the combined power of the united community voice. As one word for the chorus, Alagbe implies that these voices 'carry' the song to all parts of the crowd, thus, teaching it and encouraging full audience participation. After Oro Efe's solo, the chorus moves as a group through the performance area. They are supported by the rhythm of the drum ensemble; the chorus sings the text through completely, and repeats it as many times as necessary for the entire audience to learn the melody and the words. The chorus makes public, the sacred words, continuing to sing until the entire audience joins in the performance in a united and spiritual manner.

This full participation means acceptance of the support for the opinions expressed by Oro Efe. This united expression of public, has the power to strengthen the communication with the spiritual beings, the Gods, the Ancestors, the Mothers, as well as the practical power to compel antisocial individuals to 'mend their ways', or face public ridicule, ostracism, or banishment.

The weight of public opinion, voiced by Oro Efe and intensified by the communities consent, can, and does, have the power to affect the future of that community; it has the power of Ase.

Prayer; One of the first songs offered by Oro Efe, is a self-affirmation, or Ikase, which means, 'to step out slowly, with measured tread', which follows the, 'prayer of honor and respect'.

The following Ikase demonstrates self-affirmation. Oro Efe begins by challenging the audience to solve the riddles he will sing, (lines 1-4) and compares himself to the Awoko bird, which is well known among the Yoruba for its singing ability. (line 5) He shows his wisdom in knowing the proper moment to begin his voyage, (his performance) just as the boatman knows the safe time to sail. (lines 6-9) He then establishes his importance in relation to the audience by using 'pecking order' example.

First, he associates himself with a rich man in relation to a pawn, a debtor who offers himself as a bondsman to his creditor. Second, using sexual example, he is the pointed hook that pierces and subdues his wife, the fish. (line 11) Third, with political example, he becomes the 'King of Efe", for whom all must honor, just as the magnificent King of Ketu recognized political domination by the white man during the colonial times, when whites ruled Africa, and Agura Quarter bowed down before Ademola, the paramount king, or Alake of Abeokuta. (lines 12-14) Then, emphasizing his royalty, he demands respect from his audience. Oro Efe can now voice his opinions, his positions, and in his vital power; he sings,

1. Ayandokun, a riddle, a riddle, riddle, riddle
2. Okegbemi, a riddle, riddle, riddle, riddle
3. If I gave a riddle, who could solve it
4. I will take a song and fool you
5. The Awoko has come from a journey, the head of the singers has come
6. I, wise one, have come out, have come out, may my coming be good
7. When the river is in flood, the boatman sails
8. Aresa, I have come out, come out, may my coming be good
9. When the river is in flood, the boatman sails
10. A pawn never equals a man with money
11. A hook is a husband of a fish
12. The king of Ketu salutes the white man with 'sir'
13. Agura Quarter prostrates before King Ademola
14. I have become the King of Efe, all youths prostrate before me
15. A dog can never rival a leopard

In a shorter added piece, Oro Efe likens his dramatic performance to a blazing fire, (line 1) his power to that of a leopard, (line 5) and his voice to the sweetness of honey. (line 7)

1. Wood is burnt to a knot
2. People of Aiyetoro, I have really come
3. Wood is burnt to a knot
4. People of Aiyetoro, I have really come
5. If a dog spies a leopard, he will tell himself to be careful
6. If a dog spies a leopard, he will tell himself to be careful
7. Eeeeeee!!! Honey has come, throw away the bean cakes

Finally, before launching into songs on various topics, Oro Efe marshals his company of performers, drummers, and singers, as he boasts of his memory;

1. Drummers stand up! I am about to sing
2. Olojede don't waste any more time
3. Omele drummers it is in your hands
4. Iyalu drummers begin to form well
5. All who are to sing, don't be playful
6. Singers are you correct, we are correct
7. Tell Salawu that the singers should be correct
8. I, the one with endless wisdom, will recite the history including

Not only the exact day we came to settle this land, but who cooked and what they ate!

Next comes the prayer for blessings on the community as a whole. Oro Efe expresses the communities longing for good fortune and fulfillment in life, which includes health, wealth, peace, and long life. He appeals to the spiritual forces to hear and except these prayers, and the people add their agreement with raised voices.

In the following Efe song, Oro Efe asks the mothers to explain the sudden unexpected deaths that are occurring, and to end them. He reminds the mothers that he, (the community) has offered certain medicinal leaves to calm their anger, but that farming and hunting accidents continue to occur. (lines 1-4) The reference to hoe and knife accidents may mean deaths caused by Ogun, working on behalf of the destructive Mothers, who 'hide under all of the Gods', and whose vengeance is sometimes symbolized by knives. Then, in an appeal to Sango, God of lightning and thunder, who is most angered by untruthfulness, Oro Efe insists upon honesty. (lines 3-4) He points out that a thunderbolt would never strike a young Ose. The Ose refers to the Ose Sango, a double-celted wooden dance axe carried by worshippers of Sango, and placed in Sango shrines. The idea is that Sango would never destroy one of his own children. Oro Efe asks, have you, Oso and Aje, who are our ancestors, forgotten us? (lines 6-11) He pleads for the mother's forgiveness and their protection from sudden death, and calls for the support of the community. (lines 12-16)

Throughout this request, Oro Efe shows sensitivity towards superior and unpredictable power. He attempts to reason with, and calm the mothers in proclaiming sincerity in his concern. He pleads with them to hear his words. He even suggests that one of the Gelede shrine members may have 'offended', and, if so, the offender alone should be made to suffer the consequences. The tone is persuasive yet respectful, far different from the last song where he was self-assertive in tone. Oro Efe must exercise caution, and above all, patience in dealing with the powerful mothers,

1. Orifio leaves charmed you to forgive my misdeeds
2. Never have we suffered death from hoes, never from knives
3. Have I lied?
4. Never have we seen a thunderbolt strike a young Ose
5. Wizard in the house were you not the one who fathered me
6. Are you not our fathers?
7. Why do you not know us any longer?
8. Powerful mother in the house were you not the one who gave birth to us
9. Are you not our mothers?
10. Why do you not know us any longer?
11. It is prohibited for a dog to devour its child
12. Our mother Opake forgive us our misdeed
13. If a ritual member had offended, expose him
14. Join us in our offer of thanksgiving to Agobojo
15. Onidofoi was the one who saved us from death
16. Youths, elders, family members, and visitors, greet me for my dangerous journey

The third category of prayer is the Epe, or curse. Just as the prayers invoke the Gods for positive ends, so can a curse call upon those same forces for the destruction of an enemy. A curse has the same power as the other prayers with limitation that 'a curse reflects before it attacks'. In other words, an undeserved curse cannot take effect; and in fact, may return upon the curser. Nevertheless, if someone has offended society, Oro Efe will compose a song predicting his doom, and the song will come true. Keep in mind that Oro Efe symbolizes the community's spirit and how they feel and think about things.

The following curse was sung by an Oro Efe, whose house in Aiyetoro was burned, along with other houses in the community during the political problems in Yorubaland in December 1965, and January 1966. Lines 5 and 6 offers blame to those who think they can hide the terrible things they have done in the past. It recalls another Oro Efe song that says, character 'follows you wherever you go'. In lines 7-9, Oro Efe calls on Aibo and Idofoi Quarters of Aiyetoro to avenge him with a horrible death, that 'implies' destruction by the mothers, 'with eyes plucked out like shells'; (line9)

1. Fire spread swiftly on Alapa's house
2. People of Aiyetoro you are treacherous
3. Fire spread swiftly on Alapa's house
4. People of Aiyetoro you are treacherous
5. The wickedness you seek to forget will find you
6. The wickedness you seek to forget will find you
7. Aibo is the next to avenge me
8. Idofoi, come and avenge me
9. All who set fire to my house may you die with eyes plucked out like shells

In another curse, Oro Efe attacks those who have slandered the community unjustly. (line 1) Calling the mothers by their praise 'the one with knives Songa', (lines 3-4) he asks them to punish the offenders;

1. Those whom I did not offend are slandering me
2. Mother I leave it in your hands
3. My mother Songa bring trouble to him
4. Mother I leave it in your hands, The-One-With-Knives-Songa

Comments on the community affairs; The bulk of Oro Efe's performance, consists of commentary on events that have occurred in the community since the last Gelede festival. The singer-preacher looks into all aspects of community life that affect its continuity and stability, especially sexual behavior, politics, religion, and competition. On the topics, Oro Efe utilizes two methods of persuasion; positive reinforcement through praise and blessings, and negative reinforcement through ridicule, condemnation, and curse. The weight of such judgment is not Oro Efe's alone, for in one united voice, the entire community adds its collective social pressure and power.

Criticism of improper behavior, usually between the sexes, is popular in Efe night, and Oro Efe seems to derive as much enjoyment from such scandals as does his audience. Songs of this sort are usually in a mocking tone that highlights exaggeration, and the grotesqueness of the situation. In a direct reference to a sexual scandal within the community, Oro Efe criticizes the wrongdoer;

> Who owns the child, who owns the pregnancy?
> Pregnancy caused a fight in the house of Ajele
> Who owns the child, who owns the pregnancy?
> Pregnancy caused a fight in the house of Ajele
> You can't have one pregnancy by two persons

In the second song concerned with sexual behavior, Oro Efe expresses a clear-cut opinion about morality, and alludes to several traditional values that have been violated. The first and most serious crime is adultery, referred to in lines 3-4, when Oro Efe asks, 'Did Ogunsola marry his wife for you?' A second transgression compounds the crime, for it is committed by a rich and conceited man against his elder. In the traditional setting, wisdom is based on age determined status. But, with changes in the economic system, money has begun to play a determining role in prestige and power. In this case, money makes the junior feel superior to his elder, thus upsetting the social and moral laws of the ancestors. Oro Efe, as the symbol of order and justice, exposes the foolishness of a man who would 'pull on a snake's neck', and voices the Yoruba belief, "What goes around comes around";

1. The conceited man with all his money is teasing his elder
2. The conceited man with all his money is teasing his elder
3. Did Ogunsola marry his wife for you?
4. Did Ogunsola marry his wife for you?
5. Wicked person who pulls on the snake's neck
6. Wicked person who pulls on the snake's neck
7. If the viper bites you, should I be concerned?
8. Wicked person who pulls on the snake's neck

Men and women clearly defined sex roles in a community where, the husband has a number of wives. Although women have economic independence, they have less overt power in their domestic roles as co-wives, since they are strangers in their husbands homesteads. In such a situation it would be regarded as ridiculous for a man to 'cook, wash, and grind pepper', as it would be for the wife to 'threaten her husband with a cutlass', (an instrument that symbolizes masculinity and physical force.) Oro Efe as critic supreme, utilizes striking contradictory imagery to underscore the absurdity of the situation, and of the individuals involved. In line 5, he implies, the wife is 'something else'; since she causes trouble. The husband is called 'Sango', a male God noted for his strength, courage, and hot temper, in order to highlight his lack of these qualities. Biting sarcasm and repetition combine to create a direct statement on improper behavior;

1. For a husband to grind pepper and grate cassava
2. For a husband to grind pepper and grate cassava
3. For a husband to cook cassava meal and wash pots
4. For a husband to cook cassava meal and wash pots
5. The wife you married, Sango, is something else
6. She threatened her husband with a cutlass at the market
7. She threatened her husband with a cutlass at the market
8. I heard him shout to all around, 'help me'!
9. She threatened her husband with a cutlass at the market

Politics is another popular topic in Efe songs. Oro Efe concerns himself with both external and internal affairs. The external affairs include wars or disagreements with neighboring towns or areas, boundary disputes, colonial administration, and, after independence, political parties; while internal affairs usually involve chieftaincy controversies, headship claims, and land disputes. In these songs, Oro Efe utilizes positive and negative reinforcement, or merely serves as mediator of the dispute by emphasizing the community's desire for settlement.

In the following song, Oro Efe attempts to settle a dispute between Panku and IPO, two towns within the political domain of Ketu. He reminds the troublemakers that they are one, and should not disagree, (lines 3-7). In line 5, he calls for the return of balance with 'the right cannot do without the left'. Oro Efe rebukes the opposing parties in line 8, stating that there is no glory in disorder, 'dust' in a household, and in line 11, he asks Aka to reconcile both sides. Oro Efe stresses intelligence and reason to restore harmony and order between communities;

1. Panku must join together with Epe
2. They should not disagree
3. Do not be annoyed child of Ori, we are of the same blood
4. Do not be annoyed child of Ori, we are of the same blood
5. The right hand cannot do without the left
6. It is not good in front of the youth
7. Let us not hear of disunity
8. I have not seen glory of dust in the house
9. Broken wall must be rebuilt for biting tongue can belittle our town
10. Rebuild for disagreements can belittle the town

11. United to convince Aka in this matter
12. That Ketu may rise to success

A more contemporary commentary refers to the mid-1960s crisis in Nigeria that led to the downfall of the government. Oro Efe came down on those politicians whose carelessness, audacity, and disregard for the people led to their downfall at the hands of the mothers and praise those who have worked for their people;

This world is harsh for you politicians
Anyone who wants to live in this world must be very careful
Watch what you say, for the world is heavy
You politicians, the world requires caution
Those who were doing it whom we told were not doing it properly
The world' cut them away as bananas are cut from the stem
Those who were doing it whom we told were not doing it properly
The world' blew them away like shafts from wheat
Sardauna died, we saw Balewa no more
People of the world' killed Bello, Okotiebo packed up and left
Adegbenro with Odebiyi prepare to avenge
You did not allow a single child to suffer
Those who behave wickedly, the 'people of the world' will curse
It is a bad death that Akintola died

Oro Efe songs also deal with the expected behavior in the performance of religious obligations. The proper execution of fundamental religious rituals is necessary for continuity and stability in the community. Oro Efe condemns any changes from the accepted, traditional normal way of doing religious things. In the following song, Oro Efe cites a funeral at which certain adults showed great disrespect for the dead. The mourners had carried the coffin to the market, where they slaughtered a goat and shed its blood on the ground as they should. Afterwards, as one group was about to take the meat home to prepare and share it, a fight broke out regarding the rightful owner of the goat. Oro Efe, in condemning foolish and sacrilegious behavior that directly attacked the individuals. Directness and repetition reinforce harsh judgment of lack of character, which is equivalent to lack of wisdom, a regrettable situation for elders whose wisdom is expected to be above that of the general population;

Because of the deceased's goat, you began to fight in public

Because of the deceased's goat, you began to fight in public
Okanlawon came and claimed to own the goat
Okanlawon came and claimed to own the goat
You elders have no character
You elders have no character
Tell Disu that the goat he is collecting belongs to Egbedokun
You elders have no character

The last category of social commentary deals with 'Youth and Age'. This reflects various levels of wisdom, for it is age, not wealth, position, or book knowledge that brings wisdom. In the following song, obvious exaggeration (line 1) mocks the foolishness of youth, while pointed understatement completes the statement. (line 2) In an example, the one who was sent simply to collect the soup had the nerve to try to improve it, failing to consider that the specialist is more knowledgeable. (lines 3-4) These lines are a reminder to bigheaded youth, that men, like animals, acquire their own capabilities through experience, but they may be suitable for one thing and not for another. (line 5) This lesson is also embodied in the proverb, 'If a young man wants to behave like an elderly man, the date of his birth will not let him';

1. Ah, truly young children are very wise
2. However, I say they are not as wise as their elders
3. We called you to get the soup, but you went to add water to it
4. But you are not as wise as the one who cooked it
5. A goat is different from a horse; a white man is different from a Yoruba
6. You are not as wise as the one who did the cooking

Speaking of History, Efe songs not only comment of the present-day scenes, but also record and preserve the past by means of historical recitations. In the major Yoruba capitals, such as Oyo, Ketu, and Ili-Ife, there has always been a King's court lineage family responsible for the preservation of oral tradition and history. These accounts include ancient kings and major historical events, or conditions that characterized each kingship's government, and how it related to the people or event. Smaller towns and villages, however often, have no official court historians. The task is left to Oro Efe, who in song, not only preserves recent occurrences, but also recalls events, and King's personalities spanning many generations. Such historical Efe songs include significant political events as well as religious history. The following historical Efe song recalls the names of six Kings (oba) who have ruled a small town called Aiyetoro, Egbado, since it's founding early in this century 1902. Oro Efe does not simply recall them; he characterizes their time of rule, and fills the text with praise names;

> Seriki was the leader who enjoyed life like a king
> The turn of events overcame him
> Debeodero was next to enjoy life
> He fought well and died
> Peluola spent a short time before his death
> Then came Akinola, the hero who reigned at an old age
> It came to Asamu, the King who stepped with dignity
> Life came to you Omidokun, be tenacious

Another historical song credits a man named Edun, a name given to a twin, with the introduction of Gelede and its spread throughout thirteen towns in the Ketu kingdom;

> Edun of Ibadan was going on a trip
> When the evening came, the drumming of the ocean could be heard
> Father, where does one dance at this hour, asked the people?
> It is Edun who brought (imported from another Yoruba kingdom) Gelede
> It is Edun who brought it
> And we are proud of it
> The Gelede dance arrived at Iranjin, then from there to Igan-Gura
> It is Edun who brought it!
> We are proud of it
> The people of Ika went with two small goats as payment to ask for it
> The dance quietly made its appearance at Ofia
> The people of Omu having learned about it came to be initiated
> From there Gelede arrived at Odogbo
> The people of Iju quickly went to get permission to do it
> The children of Ibepere having learned of it came to be initiated
> Quietly the dance came to Awayi
> In the same way, it makes its appearance at Idie
> Those of Gbogburo ran to receive it
> Those of Issaba ran to be initiated
> Father, this is the history that was told to me and which I have kept in my memory
> It is not before me that Gelede began; it existed a long time ago
> Men and women, you must take it seriously

Those of you who are present, inform those who are absent
Men and women, be attentive
That was the work of Edun the Originator

Now for the Funeral Commemoration: Funeral commemoration songs are heard at the annual festivals and at special Gelede ceremonies in honor of a recently deceased member of the society, or a prominent citizen in the community. On such occasions, Oro Efe commemorates the deceased with songs of praise and honor. He recalls the person's stature, character, and role in life, and prays that his positive influence may still exert its power for the good of the community.

In the following commemoration, Oro Efe urges the chorus to sing more to honor the death of a great man, (lines 1-2) and lines 3 and 4 seem to be equaling the death of a prominent man with that of an elephant and buffalo, two impressive and powerful animals. The meaning of the 'pot' in lines 3-4, grandpa is not sure, but one possible explanation may be, 'no matter how powerful an animal may be, it eventually dies and becomes nothing more than meat cooked in a pot'.

Oro Efe tells the chorus to sing well, and to continue calling their deceased father home. He then asks other Oro Efe, and several sing at Efe in some Egbado towns to sing with a mournful voice. This probably means that the deceased, a Gelede shrine member and singer, died at a relatively young age. (lines 7-11) In line 11, the whisk symbolizes what traditionally belongs to a family, as in the Yoruba saying, 'the horse dying leaves the tail behind; the children survive the parent'. Thus, although the father had died, his presence continues a reflection of the Yoruba belief that the family lineage is eternal;

1. I am looking at you to see how you do the ceremony
2. You chorus have not sung enough
3. Elephant died in the farm and the pot ate it up
4. Buffalo died in the farm and the pot ate it up
5. You sung well during Bello's performance
6. All Oro Efe who are in the market
7. We must all use mournful voice in singing
8. We are calling upon you to come, come, father Adebayo, sleep no longer away from home
9. We are calling upon you to come, come, Akewe Bello, sleep no longer away from home
10. He could no longer rise up, could no longer sing
11. Father Labode, death caused the whisk to fall from the hand of the religious member

A ritual song, commemorating a departed mother, wishes her well in her journey home to the spiritual world. Oro Efe thanks the family of the deceased for its generosity during the funeral ritual, (line 4) and prays that the mother will watch over her family;

1. Grandmother sleep, mother went to the spiritual world undisturbed
2. I say the spiritual world is home. Grandmother greet them when you reach your home
3. Mother of Juli went to the spiritual world a good person
4. Greetings for spending money, greetings for looking after the house of the deceased
5. Mother will protect your home

Oro Efe directs his song to spiritual forces, especially to the mothers, as in the songs of social commentary concerned with anti-social behavior. Sanctioned by the mothers, the Efe ceremony becomes the epitome of united community voicing of power with choral repetition and audience involvement.

The entire community participates, young, old, male, female, Christian, Muslim, devotees of all the Yoruba Gods, and the mothers. So do those not of the world, but Ancestors, who also influence the lives of men either positively or negatively. The power of Efe however does not dwell in the act of voicing alone; indeed its power also comes from the masks and costumes that give Gelede its reputation as the ultimate ritual spectacle.

Finally, the closing masquerades: Just as introductory masqueraders bring the ritual into the world, other masqueraders mark the conclusion of Efe night. One closing masquerader is symbolized by a towering stilt dancer dressed in cloth of raffia, and a carved mask in the form of a hyena.

He holds long wooden staffs in both hands using them for balance and poking gestures that compliment his gaping teeth-filled jaws saying something like, 'I used to kill people' don't you see my teeth?' Then a mask representing Esu/Elegba arrives to conclude Efe night. His headdress is covered with magical gourds and a tuft of hair. Esu/Elegba 'chases Oro Efe from the Market', thus marking the end of the ceremony.

The performance continues throughout the night with only brief interludes, during which the drum offers a variety of praise poems, proverbs, jokes and riddles. As dawn approaches, and after Esu/Elegba's performance, the crowd of people collect their belongings and slowly go to their homes to rest, because Oro Efe's performance last the whole night, from 9 p.m. until sunrise. They will return in late afternoon for the next part of the Gelede ritual; the daytime dance of Gelede.

YORUBA RELIGION IN PRESPECTIVE

Linda:

"I can understand the Yoruba religion as related to their highest valued beliefs, but somewhere, didn't you mention something about an African Traditional Religion? I took this to mean that there is one religion for all of Africa."

Orchester Sr: "As to African Traditional Religion, as we use the term, does this mean that all of the Black people living south of Africa's Sahara Desert have one overall religion, based on the beliefs that the Spiritual World consists of a Great Creator, a Holy Family of Gods and Goddesses Who created and maintain mankind?

All Africans believe that the purpose of a religion is to provide people with what they want. In other words, the Heart and Soul of African Traditional Religions function is to make it possible for mankind to fulfill a Chosen Destiny, i.e. what they want.

However, different groups of Africans began to want different things from life, and they organized their religion accordingly.

So I can say, African Traditional Religion is a Parent Religion which has a lot of Children Religions; and each of the African nations are based on one of those Children Religions, as is the case with the Yoruba.

For example, we see that the Yoruba know that there are 1600 Gods and Goddesses in Heaven, yet they selected a combination that symbolized the things they wanted. Meaning, they want to choose the purpose they serve in life, and ORISANLA (creativity) and OLYA NAL (character) were the means they chose to accomplish that purpose.

In other words, African Traditional Religion allows each nation the freedom of choice in how they want to organize their religious beliefs, while still being true to the Parent Religion.

However, we should take special note that this means that each African nation has their own religion concept; nor, as we will see later, they do not have the same "Highest Valued Beliefs." This is because they have different chosen destinies. And this is why there are many religions in Africa, yet one African Traditional Religion.

In this respect, the Yoruba is the best of all African nations in Africa to use as an example of African Traditional Religion, in that they deal with more of the Gods and Goddess than any other African nation.

Elaine:

"But how does the Yoruba Culture fit into the picture of their Religion?"

Orchester Sr:

"We learned that OLYA NAL organized Yoruba Society into Kingdoms; Royal life style. While the Yoruba religious beliefs unified these Kingdoms into a nation of people with the same moral code. Which means that these Kingdoms were unified and had a national function.

This in turn means that the people in these Kingdoms, as a people, were doing more than just fulfilling their personal chosen destiny, they were also doing things as a nation, or to say, fulfilling a national destiny.

This is to say, the Yoruba nation has a collective ORI, and a collective chosen destiny. But what do we mean by Collective ORI and a Collective Chosen Destiny?

This means that the Yoruba Society has a national Spirit of its own, and this Spirit has a Destiny, which is expressed in the Yoruba Cultural Art forms. By that we mean, Cultural art is the image of the spirit of a culture.

Cultural Art transforms the spirit of culture into something a person can see, touch, hear, feel, smell or taste, or any combination of the six. Or to say, art displays the spiritual expression of culture in a way that can be experienced on a personal and social level, i.e. religious ceremonies and festivals.

For example, on a personal level, the physical expression of ORI is a creative act, and in that sense, life is a work of art of ORISANLA. ORI is spiritual, and life is the physical act of expressing the spirituality of ORI; i.e. a personal creative lifestyle. The same is the case with the Yoruba creative social lifestyle.

And what is a Creative lifestyle? This question returns us to the approach and attitude and the Yoruba Artist' we mentioned in an earlier chapter; for this is our clue to the approach and attitude of the Yoruba people in creating their culture.

We defined an Artist, as one whose creativity is shown by his or her talent in capturing spirits into physical forms.

We saw that the full force of the Yoruba religion on the people as a whole, is to give them the talent to capture the spirit of their beliefs. This put them into a position of controlling their physical life style; like an artist in a constant state of creating their culture.

Or we can say that the Yoruba captured the Spirit of their religion and express it in their culture. This means that the Yoruba have an Artistic Culture, and means that a culture comes into existence as the results of the creative way of living their religious beliefs. This also means, like ORISANLA, they are Artist that transformed them and their surroundings into a work of Art based on their religious beliefs. This is shown in the nature of the Yoruba's man-woman relationship and family.

For example, what turns a Yoruba woman on sexually is a man that is creative in his lifestyle; and what turns a Yoruba man on sexually is a woman that has great character.

These two values become the nature of the Yoruba family they produce. Their family sets the stage for their Society and culture; because Society is only a large number of families, each of which were started by a man-woman relationship. This shows the range of Yoruba Culture;"

On the other hand, the Yoruba believed in the existence of 1600 Gods and Goddesses, and an uncountable number of Ancestors, all of which are creatively expressed in their Society in the form of ritual ceremonies and festivals.

Each of these ceremonies and festivals are a huge production that calls for creative expression on many levels at the same time. For example, singing, dancing, music, and ritual tools like masks.

These ceremonies and festivals give you some idea of the vastness of the creativity in the Yoruba's culture. In this sense, the Yoruba produced more "Ritual Art" than any other people in Africa; and it is ritual art, ceremonies, and festivals that produce the experiences of Culture.

But we are getting ahead of ourselves. We will get to "Ritual Art and Cultural Symbolism" when we deal with our Ancestors the Akan in the third section of this book; and this will expand our understanding of African Traditional Culture as a whole.

Conclusion

Orchester Jr; "You are always talking about world views, what is the Yoruba's World View?"

Orchester Sr:
In the introduction we learned from shipping records that our Ancestors came from West and Western Central Africa. After further study we learned that this area consists of seven nations of people, the Yoruba, the Igbo, the Akan, the Aja, the Secree, the Wolof, and the Nzere Bantus; each with their own religious beliefs. Meaning that our Ancestors are divided into seven different religious groups.

We began this investigation looking for evidence about the highest valued beliefs of our ancient Ancestors. From this, we learned the highest valued beliefs of the spirituality of ourselves as Black Americans. We did this while working from the premise that, the soul of our spirituality came from our Ancestors. This also means that the constitution of our spirituality can be divided into seven parts.

Therefore, in our investigation of the Yoruba, while looking for their highest valued beliefs, we were looking for a part of the highest valued beliefs of Black America's spirituality.

On the other hand, we must keep in mind that another one of our stated goals was looking for the most influential nation in a given area of our Ancestral homeland, and what this influence consists of. In this case, Ifa Divination Ritual System. That is the very heart of the Yoruba Culture, their Ifa Divination System, as a way to make history useful to create Culture Growth.

Ifa influenced the culture of people throughout Nigeria, Benin, Togo, and to some extent, people in Ghana. And after the slave days, influenced Black people in North and South America; all of which is based on information from the Yoruba Ifa Divination poems and stories.

For one example, there are Yoruba Churches in Sierra Leone West Africa (especially Freetown), Europe, the USA, Brazil, and throughout the Caribbean Islands today, in 1998. Thus is the extent of the influence of the Yoruba's Spiritual Culture. With this in mind, let's recap the progress of our investigation up to this point.

First, we found that the Yoruba nation is over three thousands years old, and this showed us that the Yoruba religion is at least that old, and Grandpa thinks it is much older.

Finding the Yoruba Bible, which is Ifa Divination Rituals and poems followed this, which records Yoruba history and religious beliefs. And from that we learned about their spiritual world of the Great Creator, Gods and Goddesses, Ancestors, and ORI, and the role they play in an Individual's life.

This was followed by the religious Ifa story of the creation of the world, and some of the major events taking place at that time; especially the negative effects of jealousy and greed on the world.

We also saw how the world, and people were created, including how ORI chose a destiny, and came to earth to be born into a human being.

Finally, we constructed the Yoruba's Article's of Faith. We reached the conclusion that the purpose of the Yoruba's morals and character are designed for social living, and later, to turn the world right-side up, after jealousy and greed turned it upside-down.

Now if we follow this line-of-logic, we see that well over 3000 years ago, a group of Africans put together a combination of beliefs, their Articles of Faith, and became the mother and father of a new African Nation. Also over the years, guided by their chosen destiny, they developed a unique religious, social, and economic system for living life in a world ruled by Jealousy and Greed.

The application of their creative way of seeing things to the governing of their actions and reactions to life, was their way of dealing with, and seeing the world around them. Thus is the Yoruba's World View as Seen through their Religious Beliefs.

Now, Fellow Detectives, with all that we have found, let's see if you reach the same conclusion that Grandpa did, in answer to our major question. This is what history Detective work is all about.

The Yoruba religion, like all African religions, as we will see later, gives a person freedom to choose. You choose which nation to be born into. You choose which community to be born into. You choose your family, and you choose what you want to do in life. In other words, you choose a destiny.

Plus, you have all of the Gods, Goddesses, and the wisdom of your Ancestors to help you fulfill the destiny you chose. Therefore, if you are doing all of the choosing, there can be no excuses for "not doing what you told OLODUMARE you wanted to do in the first place."

However, if you don't stick to your choice, and don't do what you said you wanted to do, none of the Gods, Goddesses, or Ancestors can help you if you don't know what you want out of life.

Most important of all, your own ORI (Soul) is at its weakest point when it is not working to fulfill its destiny. And you are helpless and at the mercy of jealousy and greed.

On the other hand, this means, technically speaking, that when a person chooses his destiny, he or she is at the same time choosing a moral code of conduct.

For example, everything that you do that helps you to fulfill your destiny is a "good thing to do." In addition, everything that you do that hurts the fulfilling of your destiny is a "bad thing to do." Which Grandpa calls, "ORI's Moral Code."

This is where the Gods and Goddesses come into the picture. They symbolize the tools that you need to fulfill your destiny. For example, ORISANLA symbolizes "Truth," ORUNMILA symbolizes "Knowledge," OGUN symbolizes "Justice," ESU symbolizes "Reality," and SANGO symbolizes "Righteousness." OYA symbolizes "Determination." And OLYA NAL symbolizes "Fortitude." These are the values of the Yoruba's "Highest Valued Beliefs."

With these values as part of your ORI, there is no fear of not fulfilling your destiny. Thus is the nature of Yoruba religion.

The Game of Wari

Wari is a game played throughout West Africa. The game Wari will give us some insight into African Traditional Intelligence; in fact we can say that the game of Wari symbolizes this Traditional Intelligence.

This is very exciting part of our investigation. Jealousy and greed are the best pieces of evidence that we have found up to this point. We are in a position to see the details of the driving force of how Traditional Africans think. This is a Major Key in Understanding Why they did what they did; for example, how they organized their Religion, and Why.

Now as History Detectives, we have a means of understanding our subjects as a people; living their lives by the way they Think and Ritually Act to their Beliefs about The Spiritual World of Gods and Goddesses. This put us in the position to use the Logic-Line of their Intelligence to see what they see, and how they see it as related to what they think is the evil force that has taken over the world.

Now we must define what we mean by the game of Wari symbolizing African Traditional Intelligence. The way a mind is exercised determines how the mind develops. Wari, like most national and inter-national games, is governed by a set of logic rules, and based on an idea of putting two people in a situation where one can create a problem for his opponent.

Although Wari is played by the general public, men, and most women use it as entertainment. It is a game symbolizing the nature of conflict that took over society when jealousy and greed turned the world upside down.

On the other hand, intellectuals, like Kings, Queenmothers, Clan Chiefs, and War Chiefs, especially play it while developing certain skills in a method of out-thinking each other; based on the principals of observation and discovery of methods to defeat each other on a kingdom and clan level. In this regard, Wari is the ultimate in Traditional Conflict Resolution.

From this point of view, we can say that Wari type thinking symbolizes, and defines the nature of African Traditional Intelligence. However, this means that Wari symbolizes the approach and attitude that Africans can create Answers to Questions on any subject; for example, child education, man-woman relationships, etc, etc.

Now Grandpa has not taken the time to really learn this game of Wari, anyway, not to the extent of becoming real good at it; but as the name implies, it is related to warfare. Each player is a King with six Clans villages of four men, represented by four pebbles like small marbles, each in six holes on one side of a wooden board.

His opponent has the same number of men and villages. In the game, these Kings fight each other to see who can win and have more men in the end; and therefore can take the wealth of that Kingdom.

Now as Fellow Detectives, Grandpa thinks that you GrandKids should at least check it out to the extent that you understand the tactics involved. This will make you a better History Detective, because you can better understand the motivating forces behind the actions and reactions of other Ancestors we will study.

However to see how the game is played in detail, as Grandpa did, we will present it as it is written down by a European, G. T. Bennett which is located in a book, 'Religion and Art in Ashanti,' by another European, Capt. R. S. Rattray. Maybe one of my GrandKids will learn this game and teach Grandpa to be good at it.

Anyway, we will quote Mr. Bennett word for word, who Grandpa thinks does a very good job of explaining it. However, we will use two names of you GrandKids as players, "Tyree and Rory."

"The game of Wari is a game for two players using as apparatus, 48 pebbles, and a board hollowed out into two parallel rows of six cups. (A dozen shallow cups-pans and four dozen marbles make a convenient substitute).

Capital and low case letters are inserted for convenience of reference to each player in the description of the game that follows to be given.

The players, Tyree and Rory, sit facing each other with the board between them. The six cups 'ABCDEF' are on Tyree's' side of the board, and are here named in alphabetical order from his left to his right hand. Similarly the six cups 'abcdef' are on Rory's side of the board and are lettered from left to right as seen by him.

The large extra cup, 'Z', at Tyree's extreme right hand is for holding the pebble won by Tyree; and the extra cup 'z' at the opposite end is similarly used by Rory to hold the pebbles won by him.

When the board is set ready for play, each of the twelve cups ABCDEF and abcdef holds 4 pebbles each (the cups Z and z being empty).

This initial position may be denoted by the numerical scheme

```
Rory   f e d c b a
       4 4 4 4 4 4
   z          Z
Tyree  4 4 4 4 4 4
       A B C D E F
```

With a similar notation for any subsequent position, each number representing the contents of the cup which has the corresponding position. The players Tyree and Rory then play alternately and observe the following rules.

(Rule 1)

When Tyree plays, he empties any one of the six cups ABCDEF on his own side of the board, and deals them around the board cyclically until they are exhausted. In this cyclic sequence, the cup F is followed by cup a, and the cup f by cup A.

Thus if Tyree opens the game by emptying cup C, he places one of the four pebbles in each of the cups D, E, F, and a, in that order, and leaves the following position;

```
Rory   f e d c b a
         4 4 4 4 4 5
       z         Z
Tyree  4 4 0 5 5 5
       A B C D E F
```

When Rory plays, he empties any one of the cups a b c d e f, and deals around its contents according to the same cycle. Thus, if Rory plays from cup e in reply to Tyree's opening from C, he puts one pebble in each of the cups f A B C, and leaves the following position.

```
Rory   f e d c b a
         5 0 4 4 4 5
       z         Z
Tyree  5 5 1 5 5 5
       A B C D E F
```

The play that has led to this position may be recorded as Ce.

(Rule 2)

Tyree wins pebbles by his dealing when, and only when, the last pebble falls in one of Rory's cups a b c d e f and, there falling, makes 2 or 3 pebbles in that cup. He then captures the 2 or 3, whichever it is, and places them with his winnings in cup Z.

Similarly, Rory captures 2 or 3 pebbles from one of Tyree's cups A B C D E F, when the last pebble he deals, procures a 2 or 3 when it falls in the cup.

Thus, after play CeF, if Rory plays d, he captures 2 pebbles from cup C, and the position is;

```
Rory     f e d c b a
           6 2 0 5 5 6
      (2)z        Z (0)
Tyree    6 6 0 5 5 0
         A B C D E F
```

after play CeFd. The captured 2 are shown as placed in cup z.

(Rule 3)

Captures by Tyree may consist of any number up to 6, of 2's and 3's, provided only that they are in consecutive cups of Rory's, and that the last of the series of cups receive the last pebbles dropped. That is, when Tyree captures a 2 or 3 from one of Rory's cups, he captures also the contents of the next cup of Rory's to his (Tyree's) right. If that also has become a 2 or 3; and so on for as many 2's and 3's as are consecutive.

This if the position was

```
Rory   f e d c b a
```

```
            1 2 1 7 2 0
         z        Z
      Tyree   1 1 0 6
            A B C D E F
```

with Tyree to play, and if he plays cup F, he captures 2 from f, 3 from e, and 2 from d; (but not from b, because it is not in consecutive order).

The position becomes;

```
      Rory   f e d c b a
             0 0 0 8 3 1
         (2) z        Z (7)
      Tyree  1 1 1 1 0 0
             A B C D E F
```

Captures by Rory, similarly, are made from Tyree's cups only, and consists of 2's and 3's consecutive with the 2 or 3 captured from the last cup.

On the other hand, Rory's 7 in cup c was a threat to capture 8 pebbles, 2 2 2 2 from A B C D. However, Tyree's play of F, besides capturing 7 pebbles, has converted Rory's 7 at c, into an 8. And if Rory then played c after Tyree's played F, his last pebble would fall into an empty cup at E, and he would win nothing.

(Rule 4)

A heavily loaded cup, may in the course of play accumulate 12 or more pebbles, and the playing of this cup full will give a deal making more than one complete cycle of the board. For the cup emptied is always to be left empty. The cycle of cups which receive, by dealing, the contents of the cup emptied are therefore in effect the 11 cups remaining after the omission of the one emptied.

Thus if Tyree plays the cup F containing 15 pebbles in the position

```
      Rory   f e d c b a
             3 6 1 1 0 0
         z        Z
      Tyree  4 2 1 0 0 15
             A B C D E F
```

he drops the last pebble in cup D, making a 3 in that cup, and captures 3 3 2 2 from d c b a respectively.

(Rule 5)

An exception to Tyree's free choice of anyone of his own cups, from which to play its contents, occurs when Rory's cups are all empty. If Tyree is able to play from a cup which feeds pebbles into Rory's cups, he must do so; he may not play a cup which does not reach Rory's cups.

If, however, no move of Tyree's plays pebbles into Rory's cups, then Tyree captures the whole contents of his own cups.

Thus in position
Rory f e d c b a
      0 0 0 0 0 0
   z   Z
Tyree 0 1 3 2 0 6
      A B C D E F
Tyree, if it is his turn, must play F (the 6), for no other cup puts pebbles into Rory's cups.
In position
Rory f e d c b a
      0 0 0 0 0 0
   z   Z
Tyree 0 1 3 2 0 0
      A B C D E F
However, Tyree has no move which feeds Rory's cups, and so Tyree captures the whole contents (6 pebbles) of his own cups.

Of the case in which Tyree is unable to feed Rory's empty cups, he takes possession of the entire contents of his own cups. The most extreme occurs when, Tyree's cups hold 5-A 4-B 3-C 2-D 1-E, AND 0-F pebbles. Each of his cups fail to reach cup a, and Tyree secures all of the 15 pebbles.

Similarly for Rory, when Tyree's cups are emptied, Rory must, if possible, play so as to feed Tyree's cups; and if Rory cannot do so, he captures the whole contents of his own cups.

If Rory's cups are empty, and it is Rory's own turn to play, Rory's cups having just been cleared by Tyree, then, also, Tyree becomes owner of the total contents of his own cups.

Thus in position,
Rory f e d c b a
      0 0 0 0 2 1
   z   Z
Tyree 1 3 1 4 0 0
      A B C D E F
With Tyree to play; if Tyree plays D, the 4, he captures 5 pebbles, and leaves Rory with empty cups, and becomes owner of the remaining pebbles in his own cups. Similarly for Tyree, with empty cups after Rory had just played; the contents of Rory's cups become Rory's.

An exceptional fulfillment of the feeding rule occurs when feeding is done by emptying a heavily loaded cup, during the first circuits of the deal. And the enemy cups are totally emptied by captures made on the completion of the deal. The playing of 17 pebbles in F would be an instance of this.
(Rule 6)

When very few pebbles remain in play, it may happen that they circulate in a cyclic and periodic chase with no captures possible for either player. Each player then takes the pebbles which are circulating through his territory.

Thus with 1 in A, and 1 in a, and either to play, each player will take 1. Or with 1 in f, 1 in E, and 1 in F and Rory to play, Rory will take 1, and Tyree will take 2. In this last position, if it were Tyree's turn to play, Rory would, with correct play, win all 3 pebbles.

The Tactics of the Game

Some notes may be added on the more elementary tactics of the game. After very little experience of actual play, it will be found that the simple items of policy here described form but small parts of the complicated considerations that will dictate the best move. As the player's foresight increases, the intricacy of the play will continually develop, and he will find an unlimited field for move advanced analysis.

Threats of Capture: The ordinary threat of capture from a cup containing 1 or 2 pebbles, occurs when any one enemy cup contains a number of pebbles equal to the number of steps that separate the cups. Thus, the Cup B, when containing 1 or 2 pebbles, is threatened by 2 in f, 3 in e, 4 in d, 5 in c, 6 in b, or 7 in a.

In looking for a threat (or arranging to produce one) it is quicker (rather than checking the cups according to their range) to count backwards from the cup to be threatened. Noting when the tally agrees with the number of pebbles in the cup arrived at.

Counting backwards from cup B, the numerals 1 to 7 correspond to the cups A f e d c b a respectively. And any cup among a b c d e f, threaten B, when the numeral of his backwards count matches the number of pebbles in the cup.

In the exceptional case of a cup containing more than 11 pebbles, the method described applies after subtraction of 11.

The threats of a player's six cups are most effective when they are aimed at different enemy cups. Concentration on one is usually a waste of force.

Hence, it is generally a weakness to have cups whose contents have differences equal to their distance apart (the contents diminishing pari passu as the cycle proceeds forward). E.g. if Rory has 6, 4, and 3 in cups b, d, and e, respectively they all threaten cup B

Defense against Threats: The defense of a single pebble threatened by the opponent, may be effected either by moving it into the next cup (leaving the threatened cup empty,) or by playing so as to add one to the threatening cup (which increases its range beyond the cup threatened).

Thus in position,

Rory f e d c b a

```
          0 3 1 2 0 0
        z         Z
Tyree   0 0 1 3 3 5
        A B C D E F
```

Rory plays d, so that his cup e threatens to capture 2 from C, Tyree may play C, and so empty the cup threatened; or he may play F, so that cup e then overshoots C and reaches D.

The player may also leave the threat undefended, and prepare an immediate reprisal, the equivalent of the threat or exceeding it.

Thus, if Tyree plays D in the position just given, his cup E threatens to capture 3 from c at his next move, if Rory plays e. To counter Rory's play of d, there is thus for Tyree the choice of C, F, or D.

The defense of a 2 against threat of capture may be affected as for 1, by moving it on, (and so leaving the cup empty) or by playing a pebble into the threatening cup, or by preparing an adequate reprisal. Defense may also be effected by playing a pebble into the threatened cup and so converting the 2 into a safe 3.

Thus in position,

```
Rory    f e d c b a
          0 3 1 2 0 0
        z         Z
Tyree   2 0 2 3 3 5
        A B C D E F
```

Rory plays d so that e threatens C, Tyree may play C, which empties the threatened cup; Or F, which overloads the threatening cup e, or D which threatens a reprisal from E on c, or A, which makes C a safe 3.

Against attack from a cup with a load of more than 11, the cup threatened with capture contains 1 or 0, and the defense is more restricted. The 1 must not be moved on, (leaving the zero attacked and losing 2 pebbles) but increased by 1 to a safe 2. The overloading of the threatening cup and the preparation of a reprisal are only alternatives, as for an ordinary threat. For a threat against an empty cup, these last two are the only defense available.

Thus, for Tyree to play, with the position,

```
Rory    f e d c b a
          1 4 0 0 0 0
        z         Z
Tyree   1 1 1 0 0 0
        A B C D E F
```

His only move to save the immediate loss of pebbles is B, making a safe 2 in cup C; and if his pebbles were 1-A 1-B 0-C 0-D 0-E 0-F, loss would be inevitable, but could be restricted to 2, by playing A. If he played B, he would lose 8.

The extra loading, whether by himself or by Tyree, of any cup of Rory's which attacks cup F at once, causes it to have cup a as the point of fall. So that Rory's 'gun' fires into its own territory, and is harmless to Tyree.

Thus position,

```
Rory  f e d c b a
      6 1 7 2 0 3
      z       Z
Tyree  4 0 3 8 1 2
       A B C D E F
```

with Tyree to play, allows to move D to annul the attack of cup f on cup F. The same move simultaneously defends cup E from the attack of cup d.

In all these methods of countering a threat from one cup to another, care must be taken lest the annulling of the one threat should create fresh ones. It is of no avail to move forward a threatened 1 into the next cup, if that cup is 0 and already threatened. Nor to move on a 2, or convert it into a 3, if other cups fall under fresh threats in the process.

Nor is the overloading of a threatening cup of avail if it then attacks a 1 or 2 in the cup next beyond the threatened cup. Nor if other enemy cups are brought into attack, and fresh threats in any way arise.

An instance of a choice of evils for Tyree is shown by position,

```
Rory  f e d c b a
      5 4 0 5 0 0
      z       Z
Tyree  2 0 2 0 0 5
       A B C D E F
```

He is threatened by a loss of 3 at C, if Rory at his next move, plays e. If he evades this by emptying the threatened cup C, then Rory can play f, and win 4, 2 from D and 2 from E.

If Tyree overloads e by playing F, then Rory can win 3 at C by playing c. And if Tyree plays A, so as to convert C into a safe 3, Rory can win 2 at B, by playing c. Move A gives the smallest loss, and appears the best.

But it may be remarked as a caveat that the best move is not always the one giving the smallest immediate loss.

Slow-motion in End-Games: Rule (5), prescribing the feeding of the opposite set of empty cups, if possible, and the capture of all remaining pebbles by the player unable to do so, exercises a large influence on the end-game, when the pebbles left in play are few in number.

It becomes of importance to each player to have as many of the pebbles in his own cups, and as few in his opponent's as he can contrive.

By keeping his pebbles spread in many cups, rather than being concentrated in few, and by playing the 'smaller cups' in preference to the 'large', he retards the rate of passage of the pebbles through his territory, and may contrive to make the inflow greater that the outflow.

A unit cup causes an advance of 1 unit when played, a 2-cup causes an aggregate advance of 3 units, a 3-cup of 6 units, 4 of 10, etc.

As a simple case of this spreading and slow motion, the position,

```
Rory   f e d c b a
         0 0 0 0 0 0
       z       Z
Tyree  3 0 0 0 0 1
         A B C D E F
```

With Tyree to play, allows of his winning all four pebbles. The play is FaAbDcCdBeCf. Any other play fails to gain all four pebbles.

A Marching Group: When the board is only scantily filled, it is useful to notice that a set of consecutive cups, diminishing by unity, with a unit cup leading, and with empty cups ahead, is a configuration that may march unaltered. Thus, with 432100 in Tyree's cups ABCDEF, if he plays A, the new position is 004321. This process may continue round the corner Fa until the configuration is entirely in Rory's cups abcd.

An important and simple case of this bodily transfer occurs with two cups having 1 in front of 2 and empty cups ahead.

If the 3 pebbles are in Tyree's cups, and are played forward until the 2 and 1 are in E and F, then on playing E, the pebbles left are 2 in F, and 1 in a. If b is empty, Rory cannot play cup a without allowing Tyree to make a capture at b from F. This 2- and 1- method may on occasion be repeatedly used as a means of taking toll of pebbles that must necessarily be passed round the corner. Of the 3 that passed, 2 are captured.

Thus if Rory's cups are empty, and Tyree, in play, has in his cups 011121, he may win 4 of the 6 pebbles by playing EaFaDbCcBdCeDfEaF. The two pebbles remaining in B and a make a perpetually circulating chase, and are taken one by each player.

Heavily Loaded Cup: The destructive effect of a heavily loaded cup on a row of nearly empty cups on the opposite side of the board, may be sometimes increased by delaying its use until a few moves later that its first opportunity of action.

Thus for position,

```
Rory    f e d c b a
        0 0 0 0 0 1
   z        Z (10)
Tyree   0 0 3 2 1 11
        A B C D E F
```

And Tyree to play, the game may continue EaDbEcCdEeDfF, with a gain of 10 pebbles for Tyree at the last move.

If Rory had 2 or 3 pebbles in his cups, he might have contrived to maneuver so that the cup threatened by Tyree always safely contained 2 pebbles. Or at least that a 2 occurred in a cup close to Tyree's left of the cup threatened, thus preventing a wholesale sweep by Tyree from cup F.

Openings: If a treatise on the game came to be written, it would, in addition to a treatment of the middle-game and end-games, include also an examination of openings. They are very numerous. If Tyree starts, he has a choice of 6 cups to play from, and Rory then has also a 6-fold choice. The number of 2-move openings is therefore 36.

At his second move, Tyree may find that the cup he emptied has remained empty, in which case, he has a choice of 5 cups to play from; otherwise he has again a 6-fold choice. It will be found out that the 36 2-move openings, 26 leave an empty cup for Tyree, and 10 leave Tyree's cups all occupied.

The number of 3-move openings is thus, 190 (=5x26+6x10). Of these 190 3-move openings, 126 leave Rory with one cup empty, and 64 leaves all of Rory's cups occupied. The number of 4-move openings is thus 1,014 (=5x126+6x64). The earliest possible captures occur at the fourth move.

Among all of these openings, there seems not much to choose between those which begin by emptying cups from the player's left, (ABC and abc) and those which empty cups from the right (DEF and def).

The ABC openings disadvantageously leave a blank cup that the opponent may at once fill with a unit. The threat of a capture of 2 that ensues had to be countered.

The DEF openings, certainly, leave a blank which the opponent finds out of reach for a while; but the player himself, is soon forced to play units into his own blanks, and finds the enemy range increased meanwhile, and the temporary advantage seems more than nullified.

Analysis might reveal strong and weak openings that are not apparent superficially. But it will be found that the player with some experience gains his chief advantage over the novice rather in the handling of the middle and end-games, and in the use of heavily loaded cups.

Rules in brief: A concise summary of the rules, (intelligible only after the fuller statement) may be appended finally as useful for separate reference.

Four pebbles at the start in each of the 12 cups.

Each player in turn empties one of his own cups and deals its content round 'backwards', leaving his cup empty.

After the deal, he wins a final 2 or 3, or a final unbroken sequence of 2's and 3's from the enemy's side, if they occur.

If the player finds the enemy cups empty, he must play to feed if possible; if no move feeds, he gains all the pebbles left.

If the player finds his own cups empty, the enemy gains all the pebbles left.

A few final pebbles circulating endlessly are divided as they pass in transit across the two territories, each going to the player who is moving them."

Grandpa's conclusion, as mentioned, is that playing the Wari game symbolizes the Art of using African Traditional Intelligence as a Method of Thinking. In this sense, the game of Wari is major elements of a unique process of answering questions in creating and solving problems.

Therefore, in this sense, Wari demonstrates the "Logic" of how this process works. This means that it is a good symbol of African Traditional Logic, and this is the major key to our Investigation.

This is why Grandpa wants you to take a close look at the Wari game, because we will be using this logic a lot in the remaining adventures into the world of our Ancient Ancestors. This is why Wari is such a great piece of useable evidence.

And this brings us back to ORISANLA, and His problem of loving people too much for their own good, which led to jealousy and greed, turning the world upside down.

This left the world in a state whereas, people had to find a way to deal with the world as "it is," and still find a way to redeem their Soul, i.e., fulfill the Destiny they chose on an individual, family, and Kingdom level, in order to stay in the good graces of OLODUMARE. And this is what the Yoruba religion addresses, and where it fits into the picture of a world ruled by Jealousy and Greed.

This means that since Wari is played throughout Africa, all Africans have the same moral concept related to jealousy and greed. Wari was the solution to dealing with the world as "it is," and although they took different approaches, their religions are designed to take responsibility of fulfilling their Chosen Destiny under these circumstances.

Now you can see what a great position this puts us in as Detectives. We have a solid foundation to reach conclusions of not only how Traditional Africans see the World, under the control of Jealousy and Greed; but we can also see their approach and attitude in dealing with what they see, symbolized by the logic in the game of Wari. Those are the best tools a Detective can have to come to solid conclusions about our Ancient Ancestors, and their Highest Valued Beliefs.

ANCIENT IGBO GAME

Using the example of the things that Christians do and believe to bring love into their lives to save their souls through the father-son Gods of their Religion, Jesus Christ and Jehovah: The following are some of the things that the Ancient Igbo did and believed, in order to bring Social Equality and Personal Freedom into their lives to become a nation of families through the worship of the husband and wife God and Goddess of their religion, Igwe and Ala; Which is the game they played in life.

Igbo Holy Spiritual Family

CHINEKE: "The Greatest of the Great Chi." The same as the Yoruba's "The Great Creator."

IGWE: "The Great Father God." The same as the Yoruba's "ORISANLA." Also, administrator of mankind's affairs. "The Rain God"

ALA: "The Great Earth Goddess." Also known as "The Great Mother Goddess." The same as the Yoruba's "OLYA NAL." Makes the rules of moral conduct.

ANYANWU: "The Sun God."

AMADIOHA: "The Thunder and Lightning God. The same as the Yoruba's SANGO.

EKWENSU: "The Trickster God." The same as the Yoruba's ESU.

CHI: "The Soul of Mankind." The same as the Yoruba's "ORI."

IKENGA Statue: The symbol of manhood.

UMUNE leaves: Symbol of womanhood's wisdom of the womb.

DRINKING FROM ANCIENT WELLS
The Igbo, (Pronounced E-boo)
Well Fellow Detectives, in dealing with the Igbo, we will get a good chance to use our newfound understanding of African Traditional

Logic; because they are going to present us with a different kind of investigative challenge.

Igbo land covers about 15,000 square miles, and has one of the largest populations in Nigeria, which is bigger than the Yoruba. However, their land area is smaller than the Yoruba area.

This means that Igbo land is somewhat crowded, especially in the locations where the land is more fertile, but not to the point where each family did not have a farm.

Like the vast majority of Africans, farming is the foundation of Igbo economics, and plays a strong role in their social and spiritual life as well. In fact, the Igbo people live in farming villages surrounding a central market place, which is their second major economic factor. But we are getting ahead of ourselves.

The Igbo, like the Yoruba, have a long history in their present location. This is, according to what Grandpa could find from the archaeology work that was carried out in eastern and western Igbo land. The pottery found indicates a relationship to modern day Igbo pottery, and not Yoruba. We can assume that the same people lived in that area for the 4500 years, or at least as long as the Yoruba lived in their location. Which means that the Igbo and the Yoruba were ancient neighbors. This takes care of the "Ancient" in the title "Drinking from Ancient Wells of the Igbo."

Igbo Religion

To stay in tune with our investigative approach, we will begin our investigation with the spiritual side of Igbo life. On the other hand, we will look for the "Well", in the title, "Drinking from Ancient Wells of the Igbo.

The Igbo, unlike the Yoruba, did not have a body of knowledge in a ritual form, like a divination ritual. This means that Grandpa is going to take a different approach in our investigation than we took with the Yoruba.

With the Yoruba, our focus was on the highest values in their religion, and how they related to the individual's chosen destiny. Whereas with the Igbo, we will focus our attention on the highest values in their religion, as related to their family social values and economics; with a special focus on African Bush Intelligence (African logic).

This is because the Igbo's major focus is on their Ancestors. The Gods and Goddesses play a lesser role in their lifestyle, i.e., and social order.

On the other hand, our investigation is also made complicated by the absence of a lot of information about the Igbo's religious beliefs as far as their Gods and Goddesses are concerned.

Grandpa had to find bits and pieces here and there in over a hundred pieces of research material, until I could put this logic line together.

For example, they only had one religious story that covers the creation of the universe and mankind, although there are other stories dealing with other subjects; even this one story was hard to come by.

Anyway, this story will to serve as the "Well", and later, the "organization and function" of the Igbo people themselves. Their "sociality" has to be the "content" of the "Well" we will "Drink." We have to make the connections between sociality, and the people's lives, and this gives us some indication of the purpose we expect African Ancient Bush Intelligence to serve.

From what Grandpa could find from a lot of different sources, the Igbo believe, CHINEKE, the Greatest of the Great Being, created the universe and all therein, using parts of Him-her-Self. (This means that everything a person can see, touch, taste, smell, and hear is CHINEKE).

Another way of saying the same thing, the sum total of every thing in the universe, including the Gods and Goddesses, are the parts of one being, CHINEKE; like the parts of the human body, including the mind, is a part of one being, You.

This means that each of the CHINEKE's parts are inter-dependent on each other, but each, with a will and purpose of their own. On the other hand, we can say, the universe consists of the logical order of the parts of CHINEKE; for example like the heart, lungs, stomach etc, etc., of the human body. This is such an important concept in the Igbo's religious beliefs; that we should go into more detail.

From a sexual point of view, CHINEKE's mind is divided into a female side, and a male side, and each side is inter-dependent on the other, yet, each part has different functions.

The parts on one side are called Gods, and the other side are called Goddesses. However, both sides have the job of managing the affairs of the universe. The same way the left and right side of a person's mind manages their affairs.

This means that Heaven is the Mind of CHINEKE. Therefore, the activities of the Gods and Goddesses show how that Mind works. The relationship of the Gods and Goddesses to each other symbolizes the structure of the African Bush logic we mentioned.

For example, as a symbol of the unification of the mind, the Igbo believe that in the center of heaven is a Holy Marketplace. This is where the Gods and Goddesses conduct all social, ritual, and economic business of managing the affairs of the universe.

Symbolizing how the Gods and Goddesses relate to each other as a unit to form the logic of this Great Mind; the Holy Family harmony is a united state of mind. This shows that the Igbo believe that the universe is the body, and heaven is the mind of CHINEKE.

It is very interesting that the Igbo think of the center of heaven as a marketplace. We understand this to mean that there was a trade between the Gods and Goddesses in the name of harmony. Things were traded, and wealth was accumulated on all sides in the trade; spiritually speaking.

Whereas a marketplace is the creator of wealth through trade, which means that CHINEKE is the Great Creator of trade for the purpose of creating wealth.

On the other hand, this means that each Igbo believes that they are also a part of CHINEKE, and their purpose in life is the same as the Gods and Goddesses.

Meanwhile, although we used bits and pieces of information about the Igbo beliefs from a large number of sources, the evidence is still solid, and lays a foundation of the Igbo's world view.

We will use this world view as evidence in constructing the Igbo creation story, and later verify the story when we investigate the Igbo's social and economic lifestyle. Our purpose in doing things this way is to give a time line flow to our investigation.

Again, we must keep in mind that this is a story that Grandpa put together from things known as Igbo religious beliefs. For example, it is known that the Igbo believe that the God IGWE and Goddess ALA created mankind, and, the organization of Igbo society is based on how they believe heaven is organized. The story is as follows:

Creation Story

"For a long time things worked very well in heaven, however, all of the Gods and Goddesses lived in one place. Each was individualistic, and therefore very independent. This was the cause of a big problem; Jealousy and Greed came in the picture.

It seems that each God began to want all of the powers of the other Gods. The question was, who had more authority. The Gods became greedy. The same thing happened on the female side, the Goddesses became jealous of each other's powers, and things got worse and worse.

Finally, it got so bad that the affairs of the universe began to suffer, and became a threat to CHINEKE's existence, who was about to be destroyed by parts of HIS-HER own mind (A super schizophrenic case).

CHINEKE began thinking of how to solve the problem, and came up with a Master Plan in the form of Laws of Social Equality and Personal Freedom, based on Equal Value of each of the Gods and Goddesses Values.

Thereafter, to establish the family, a God and Goddess were to pair up and build their own place in heaven, surrounding a market place. And, the families' relationship was one of contract and trade, with the God EKWENSU, the Trickster, acting as an enforcer in the market place.

In other words, heaven was divided into equal parts. Each God and Goddess had a domain of their own that the Igbo call a Holy Homestead. And the Holy Marketplace is their symbol of social harmony.

Now we will focus on one of the pairs, the God EGWE and the Goddess ALA, whose domain consisted of the earth and sky.

Although they are like husband and wife, they do not live in the same house. IGWE lives in the sky, and ALA lives on the earth. To the Igbo, the earth and sky merge to form the Holy Homestead in which mankind was created.

ALA and IGWE created 8 people, 4 males and 4 females. In the process of creating mankind, IGWE and ALA used 4 kinds of materials which were sticks from the Ofo tree as bones and clay, and chalk for flesh. After they were formed and dried in the sun, ALA wrapped them in Umune leaves from the Umune tree for nurturing the five senses and sexuality. And as the creators, they had the responsibility of educating them as well, especially the 7 cycles-of-life, and the rituals related to the rites-of-passage that a person must past through in life;

(1) Sex-act and birth: (nine months)

(2) Babyhood: (Birth to about three years of age)

(3) Childhood: (Three years to the age of twelve)

(4) Adulthood: (developed between the ages of thirteen and twenty)

(5) Parenthood: (twenty to forty year age group)

(6) Grandparenthood: (Forty to sixty years)

And (7), Great grandparenthood and Ancestor- hood: (Sixty years to forever after death).

In addition, they were taught about the substance-of-life that a person must have to live. This was taught by the preparation for the up coming celebration-of-human life.

ALA and IGWE went out in their garden-of-life to get the things necessary for the ceremony. The 4 women went with ALA to her garden and gathered corn, melons, okra, pumpkins, beans, peas, greens, cassava, coco yams, red pepper, rice, bananas, plantain, peanuts, and palm oil. Meanwhile, IGWE, and the 4 men went to his garden to gather palm wine, kola nuts, alligator pepper, yams, and a wild goat.

ALA, being the Great Mother of nurturing, retired to her domain to prepare the food, including the 8 yams and goat meat given to her by IGWE.

While the food was being prepared and cooked, ALA taught the 4 women the mysteries of womanhood, wisdom of the womb, and the rituals related to the female 7 cycles of life; symbolized by Umune leaves.

Meanwhile, IGWE retired to his domain where the men were his guests, to whom he showed hospitality, as he taught them the rituals related to the male 7 cycles of life, and the mysteries of manhood symbolized by Ikenga, a statue of a man with ram horns on his head. The men were also taught about OFO.

Then the 8 people were brought together where they were taught that the contribution of the energy of life, in the creation of mankind, comes from IGWE. Meaning, IGWE is Head of the Holy Homestead, in the sense that he has the power to keep the homestead spiritually alive and functioning. This makes IGWE the Chief Administrator of mankind's Affairs.

On the other hand, ALA makes the rules of moral conduct; especially as related to the earth, called, the laws of the land. Thus is the authority of Umune. And IGWE enforces these laws, meaning he is also the judge, police, and priest, as well as a warrior-protector, thus is the Authority of OFO.

Just as important, as far as the men and women are concerned, each of them asked questions about what concerns them as individuals, and received individual answers. Thus, the 8 people not only learned about their roles as men and women, but also their roles as independent beings unto him or her self, even in their relationship with ALA and IGWE, their Creation Mother and Father.

When the food was prepared, ALA and IGWE invited the God AMADIOHA (the thunder and lightning God), ANYANWU (the sun God), EKWENSU (the Trickster God), and the Goddess of the Moon. All gathered in the Holy Market Place.

This was followed by the ceremony called, the celebration of life, which was performed in the Holy Market Place where there was a big festival of music, dancing, singing, talking, trading, and everybody having a good time.

After observing how the Gods and Goddesses related to each other as equals, and traded with each other, and all made a profit, the people learned the laws of social and economic relationships based on social equality and personal freedom.

Meanwhile, the 8 people Chose a Destiny to become a Wealthy Nation, based on Family Values and Trade; and to that effect, IGWE drew up the Contract as 7 Articles of Faith;

1. The Great Creator, CHINEKE, Created the Universe and all therein using Parts of HIM-HER-SELF; and is known as the God of Wealth.

2. The major members of the Holy Family, Those that concern people, consists of ALA, IGWE, ANYANWU, AMADIOHA, EKWENSU, and the Goddess of Mysteries (the Moon Goddess); Who CHINEKE bonded together with Laws of Social Equality and Personal Freedom.

3. CHINEKE, The Great Creator, created the Human Spirit who is given a personal Chosen Destiny; this Spirit-Destiny is called a Person's CHI (which means the same as the Yoruba's ORI).

4. The Earth Goddess and Rain God, ALA and IGWE, are Husband and Wife, and people are their Created children.

5. Ancestor Worship is the guide in building a nation.

6. Divine Manners of Kinship and Trade are the guide in life.

7. Negotiation, based on this Contract, is the Path-way to Spiritual and Economic Success; Wealth.

When the people, and the Gods and Goddesses put their seal of approval on this destiny, it became a Holy Contract between the spiritual world and a human being.

After the approval of this contract, the 8 people left the Holy Market place, and went out into the world, and multiplied into the Igbo nation. This chosen destiny later became the foundation of their religious beliefs and social lifestyle.

When the people reached the outside (of heaven), they took the names of the values of IGWE and ALA.

For example, the 4 women took the names Determination, Fortitude, Peace, and Unity, and the men took the names, Justice, Truth, Trust, and Righteousness. They got married, and formed the original 4 Igbo couples and families.

When IGWE and ALA created the original 8 people, they were pure in body and spirit. Even when they left the holy homestead and went out into the world, they had pure marriages, built pure homesteads, and raised pure families. Which grew into 4 pure clan towns, with a pure market place, and therefore created a pure society. (Here, pure means, copying the Holy Family).

People lived in perfect harmony, trade was perfect, and they were living in the paradise of the wealth of a perfect society. All of which was based on the 12 relationships that constituted a family (we will deal with constitution of family later).

Then, as the Yoruba say, jealousy and greed turned the perfect and pure society upside down, and destroyed the perfect family relationships.

Well GrandKids, let me tell you, when old jealousy and greed hit town, it was like a hurricane. Everything of value in society was being destroyed at a very rapid rate of speed. The town was falling apart. The original 8 people were not effected, they were too pure.

Because the original 8 people were the oldest Elders in society, all of the people held a meeting presided over by them. This is how the Igbo's first government came into reality, and here, the original eight people came up with a master plan.

Their plan called for each of the original 8 people to create a ritual to restore people to the purity of the 8 values of society. Since the original 8 people were taught by IGWE and ALA in the Holy Homestead, they knew something about the ritual process. This means, it was they who created all Igbo purification rituals for fighting jealousy and greed.

For example on the male side, Mr. Righteousness created the ritual to restore righteousness. Mr. Justice created the ritual to restore justice to society. Mr. Truth created the ritual to restore truth to society, a Mr. Trust created the ritual to restore trust to society.

On the female side, Miss Determination created the ritual to restore determination to society. Miss Peace created the ritual to restore peace to society. Miss Unity created the ritual to restore unity to society, Miss Fortitude created the ritual to restore fortitude to society.

After which, the original 8 people returned to live with IGWE and ALA in the Holy Homestead, and from there they became Messengers between the people of the world, and the spiritual world. So, Ancestor worship is the ritual relationship to one of these 8 values. (End of story)

Well Fellow Detectives, this completes Grandpa's little creation story on how the Igbo believe the universe and mankind was created, as far as Grandpa could put together from bits and pieces of information found here and there in a large number of books about the Igbo. But it is well known, that Africans build their religious beliefs and social lifestyle from their creation story.

Now we will turn our Detective type thinking to the conclusion Grandpa reached from other information found in researching the story.

In that case, the story means that the original 8 Igbo saw the relationship between IGWE and mankind, as one of ritual contract negotiable through petitions. On the other hand, IGWE is the source of ethic laws of spiritual politics and governmental conduct. In the Igbo beliefs, IGWE symbolizes Trust, Righteousness, Justice, and Truth; as related to Personal Freedom.

However, the Igbo have a totally different type of relationship with ALA, the Great Mother of mankind. ALA is the source of moral laws of social conduct related to Social Equality. She loves all of her children equally. She is thought of as the symbol of Peace, Determination, Fortitude, and Unity, related to Social Equality.

On the other hand, their relationships with the other Gods and Goddesses are of a different nature. They have what we will call a contractual agreement between equals, which the Igbo think of as hiring a God or Goddess.

They are hired as messengers and negotiators, and if a God or Goddess can be hired, they can be fired. No matter what his or her status is in the Holy Family, with the exception of IGWE, ALA, and EKWENSU.

The Igbo believe in ritual results. If they send a God or Goddess to CHINEKE, IGWE, or ALA with a message for something they want, and if they do not get it, they blame the messenger God or Goddess for being poor negotiators, and send him or her back to try again.

And if they still do not get positive results, they fire the messenger God or Goddess, take his or her shrine to the edge of their territory, cuss them out, and burn the shrine.

Then, they seek another messenger, and send him or her with the same message. In other words, any God or Goddess who can successfully negotiate with CHINEKE, is the God or Goddess of choice for ritual worship and sacrifices.

On the one hand, this means that the Igbo have two major forces in their religious beliefs, ALA (Social Equality), and IGWE (Personal Freedom); and everything else flows from those beliefs.

On the other hand, the other Gods and Goddesses, for the most part, have the role of lawyer-messenger. This also means that the Igbo, with two exceptions, never take no for an answer from anybody.

Like all Africans, the Igbo include a ritual relationship with their Ancestors in their religious beliefs. However, like with the Gods and Goddesses, Ancestors also are in a negotiated relationship. The important point is that, Ancestors are part of their religious beliefs.

Finally, there is another religious belief that we should give some attention, CHINEKE's relationship to mankind, which concerns CHINEKE's creation of spirits to be born on earth.

CHINEKE only creates human spirits once every three years, at which time a large group of spirits are created to be born at different times in the upcoming three years.

Then, there is an interesting twist in that time period, for example, let's say CHINEKE created all of the Igbo spirits to be born in a certain town in the following three years. After each spirit in the group approaches CHINEKE and chooses a personal destiny, then the group approaches CHINEKE and chooses a group destiny. This means that when those spirits are born, they have a double bond, one to their family, and the other to the group. Both bonds are very strong, the Igbo call the latter bond, an age-group.

Age groups are part of a generation, for instance, if we say a generation is 21 years, this means that generations can be broken down into 7 age groups who inter-act competitively and constitute the dynamics of that generation.

This belief plays a strong role in Igbo society where each generation is expected to bring some creative innovation to the society for the betterment of the whole, or face being publicly ridiculed. This innovation can be in any one of three areas, religion, political, and economical.

The point being, this is also the case in the spiritual world of their Ancestors, their generation, too, is divided into age groups.

This means, in Ancestor worship, each living age group has a direct ritual relationship, and is in competition with their Ancestral counterpart. For example, do more for society than their Ancestors did.

There is not only competition between age groups; there is also competition between the individuals within the age groups itself, as well as competition between generations. From that point of view, we can say that personal and group competitions are the dynamic forces that energize and give form to the Igbo family-society.

However, this brings up a number of interesting questions. What is the relationship between Igbo social practices of contracts and competition, and of their spiritual beliefs in social equality? And, how do personal and social ambitions and competitions work as a positive social force? In other words, what is the constitution of spiritual and social authority?

By authority, Grandpa means, the authority to manage the affairs of society in a manner that assures that each member is socially equal, and has the freedom to fulfill a personal destiny.

This means that the spiritual constitution of a village-town deals with a constitution of laws. Laws that cover the spiritual, social, and economic conduct of everybody in the village in the form of a social contract. A social contract made by their Ancient Ancestors (the original 8 people).

Now we come to another interesting question, how can a people have a constitution of laws that they must follow, and at the same time, have personal freedom to choose? This is where the Igbo's spiritual constitution of authority comes into the picture.

To bring the spiritual constitution of authority to light, means that we will be dealing with the two subjects we mentioned in our little creation story, OFO and UMUNE trees which are the physical symbols of IGWE and ALA's authority. This is in the sense that they created mankind, and therefore are the foundation of the Igbo religion, as well as the premise of Igbo world views.

In the process of creating mankind, ALA and IGWE use 4 kinds of materials, sticks from the OFO tree as bones, clay and chalk for flesh, and UMUNE leaves from the UMUNE tree to nurture the five senses and sexuality.

Thus is the nature of the sacredness of the IFO and UMUNE trees, as well as clay and chalk; and especially the sacredness of the Heaven (homestead) where the creation took place. All of which is the foundation and symbolism of the spiritual constitution of authority.

This means that the Igbo think of their family homestead, from a spiritual point of view, as sacred, and makes their family divine; and their homestead as a heaven-on-earth.

Another way of saying the same thing is that, each Igbo man and woman thinks not only of themselves as a King and Queen, and their homestead as their Kingdom, they also think of every other man and woman in the nation as Kings and Queens.

The Igbo build their homestead in the same pattern as the Holy Homestead of IGWE and ALA. They create (sexually speaking) children. Thus is how the Igbo think of a family homestead. It is a part of their religious beliefs as a place to create children.

Each man holds the position in his homestead, as IGWE holds in the Holy Homestead; and the women hold the position as ALA. And this is the spiritual basis of the society of the family homestead, and the village-town (We will explain the village-town later).

Like ALA and IGWE, in the Holy Homestead, nobody else has any social or spiritual authority in or over the family homestead or its members; the authority is shared only between the Father and Mothers (Same as all Africans, the Igbo believe in a man having more than one wife).

Materially speaking, the symbol of this male authority, OFO, is a tree that grows throughout Igbo land. The only thing unusual about it is that its limbs have joints, six to twelve inches apart, similar to human bone joints. It is one of these joints that is the physical symbol of OFO.

On the other hand, the UMUNE tree also grows throughout Igboland, which isn't unusual at all. It is the leaves that are the physical symbols of its spiritual authority. Clay and chalk are also plentiful everywhere. Anyway, this symbolism is important to the Igbo's idea of spiritual authority.

For example, as a spiritual symbol, OFO symbolizes the qualities of IGWE, Righteousness, Truth, Justice, Trust, and is the authority of Fatherhood. At the same time, OFO symbolizes a spiritual link between CHINEKE, IGWE, Ancestors, the living, and the unborn.

Furthermore, no serious ritual or ceremony is performed without the OFO symbol. Even political laws cannot be ratified and consecrated without OFO, and none is valid without it being used.

More to the point in our investigation, OFO is also the symbol that gives authority to the father to choose a destiny for the family homestead, which will become the chosen destiny of the clan village his family will produce.

This is also another area where competition between men in an age group takes place, based on success in fulfillment. The point we want to keep in mind is, there is a family destiny chosen on the authority of the father of the family.

We should also take special note of another very important male symbol in the male Igbo society. In the Holy Homestead, the energy-of-life came from IGWE. This energy-of-life is symbolized by a wooden statue of a man with ram horns on his head, called Ikenga, and is a ritual symbol of manhood as the energy-of-life in the family homestead.

We will next turn our attention to the female symbol of authority. UMUNE symbolizes the qualities of ALA, Peace, Unity, Fortitude, and Determination, all of the qualities that give authority to motherhood; qualities known as Wisdom of the Womb. From this wisdom, ALA makes the laws of the land, laws that deal with family-social relationships.

For example, all of the relationships between ALA, IGWE, and their Brother and Sister Gods and Goddesses are sacred, and have ritual symbolic value on the spiritual side of society. When we speak of family, we are speaking from this point of view.

There is the relationship between father and sons, father and daughters, mother and sons, mother and daughters, brother and sister, brother and brother, and sister and sister.

Being as Igbo think of their uncles and aunts as mothers and fathers, and their cousins as brothers and sisters, we do not have to count them as separate relationships.

Then there are the grandparent relationships, a Grandfather and grandsons, grandfathers and granddaughters, grandmothers and granddaughters, grandmothers and grandsons. We must not forget to include the man-woman relationship in the family structure; for a total of 12 special relationships in a living family.

On the other hand, the Igbo believe that in-law family relationship are just as important as their extended family, and they too, are thought of in terms of these 12 major family relationships.

For instance, there are mother-in-law and son-in-law, mother-in-law and daughter-in-law, father-in-law and son-in-law, father-in-law and daughter-in-law, etc., etc. For a total of 12 relationships, for a sum-total of 24 relationships in the constitution of an Igbo family.

Now, being as ALA is the Great Mother of mankind, she is not only concerned with the above 24 family relations symbolizing Social Equality, she is also concerned with the relationships between all of the families of the Igbo nation. This means that she loves everybody in the nation equally.

Therefore, when anything is done to hurt, physically and mentally, everybody in the nation is guilty of a crime. These laws cover everything from murder, to disrespecting elders; and governs everything social from birth to death; thus is the nature of the Wisdom of the Womb.

We do not mean to imply that OFO, IKENGA, and UMUNE are the only important ritual symbols. Only that they are the foundation of a group of symbolic objects that make up the symbolism of the Igbo ritual relationship with their social and religious beliefs.

In fact, everything involved, or related in any way with the creation of man kind has symbolic ritual value, and is considered sacred, including the clay, chalk, and food for the celebration of life, and especially the Holy Homestead itself.

We will take the laws of hospitality in the Holy homestead; enforced by IGWE. In every homestead in Igbo land, the husband and wives are very hospitable; enforced by the husband, and taken to an extreme.

For example, no matter what a guest does or says, he or she cannot be abused either verbally or physically while in their homestead. It is one of the oldest laws governing the homestead. It states that is the duty of a host to entertain and protect his guest at all cost.

This is even in the case of uninvited guest, for instance, someone running into a man's homestead to avoid the penalty of breaking some law. The husbands are supposed to keep and protect his uninvited guest until the pursuer is gone, no matter what the uninvited guest has done.

In addition, regardless of how strong or annoyed the husband is, an Igbo man is not expected to touch his offender if he runs into another man's homestead. If he does, and he is wounded or killed in the process, nobody will be held responsible.

Likewise, if the husbands chased a person into that person's homestead to fight him, and they are maimed or killed, nobody cares.

Now following our line of logic from IGWE and ALA to the Igbo family organization, Grandpa has to conclude that the 24 family relationships are based on Ancient Ancestor's beliefs about the Holy Family of CHINEKE. And this is what makes these 24 relations spiritual in nature, with a Holy foundation.

And like with the Yoruba, we will use our family name, only in this case, go back to your great great grandfathers and mothers; as the original 8 Igbo people.

For example, on your Grandma Victoria's side of your family, we will focus on Westly and Bertha Winfield, and William and Corena Franklin; which are your Grandma Victoria's great grandparents.

Whereas, on your Grandpa's side of your family, the Ancient Couples to whom we will focus our attention on are George and Kate Benjamin, and George and Serena Talton; Grandpa's great grandparents.

With these names in mind, we are going to say George and Kate Benjamin, as two of the 8 original Ancestors, moved into an area and layed claim to 24 square miles of land. They built a homestead, cleared enough land for a farm, and settled down to raise a family.

While George and Serena Talton, William and Corena Franklin, and Westly and Bertha Winfield also lay claim to 24 miles of land, built their homesteads, cleared land for farms, and settled down to raise families.

However, since Grandpa knows more details about the Benjamin history, we will follow them in a demonstration of how a Village-Town comes into existence. And also show the relationship between the Benjamins, Taltons, Winfields, and Franklins as we go along.

To begin with, it is the construction of the homestead itself we will focus our attention. The homestead is enclosed with a boundary wall from four to ten feet high, made of clay, with a narrow thatched roof along it's full length to protect it from the rain. The houses inside, also with thatched roofs, have clay walls. The floors are composed of beaten down clay raised about a foot or two above ground level. The walls and floors are polished by the women with clay water and look like polished marble.

As to the numbers at the entrance of the homestead, they are the locations of shrines. (1) Is a shrine to ANYANWU (Sun God), (2) Is a shrine to IGWE (Rain God), (3) Is a shrine to AMADIOHA (thunder-lightening God), and (4) Is a shrine to EKWENSU (Trickster God). (5) In the husbands house is George Benjamin's shrine room where his Ikenga, Chi, and shrine to the male Ancestors of his family are located. (6) The guestroom where visitors are shown hospitality. (7) Is George Benjamin's bedroom. The space between the husband and wife's house, (8) Is a shrine to ALA (Earth Goddess).

Now for the wives house: (9) Is where Kate's Chi shrine, and shrine to the female Ancestors of her family are located. (10) Is her kitchen and food storage area, and (11) Is her bedroom.

George and Kate's food crops, like in the Holy Homestead of ALA and IGWE, consists of corn, melon, okra, pumpkin, beans, peas, greens, cassava, cocoyams, yams, red pepper, rice, bananas, plantain, peanuts, and oil palm trees all raised on Kate's farm. Kola nut trees, alligator pepper, and palm wine trees are raised on George's farm.

They also hunt, fish, and raise domestic animals like sheep, goats, pigs, and chickens. This is some of their meat protein sources.

As far as their calendar is concerned, how they organize their time is called a lunar month of 28 days. It consists of 4 days per week, and 7 weeks per month, which governs market days as well as the days they work on the farm or perform certain rituals.

To get a better image of their symbolic ritual objects and shrines, and the front entrance of their homestead, check out the next two pages.

We can see all the shrines that all of the major Gods, Goddess, and Ancestors are present in, as well as the shrines to George and Kate, (their Chi shrines). This means that living in an Igbo homestead, is like living in a Church, and George and Kate are the Chief priest and priestess.

Along with their self-supplied food source, the homestead symbolizes an independent family unit, qualified to take care of all of its spiritual and economic needs; independence is the foundation of Personal Freedom.

However, to see how Igbo families and towns are organized, we will look at how their land is inherited. Being as, according to Igbo land laws, land is inherited through the male line; we will focus on the land belonging to George Benjamin and George Talton.

Over time, George and Kate Benjamin had five sons, Ben (oldest son), George, Jesse, Johnny, and Sonny, and three daughters, Julia Ann (Oldest daughter), Lizzia and Lizzie.

George and Serena Talton had 3 sons, Thomas (oldest son), Charley, and William; and 2 daughters, Sedona (Oldest daughter) and Lizzie.

Eventually the sons, the second generation of the families, got married and ended up with two wives each. They built houses near their father's homestead and settled down to raise their families.

The Igbo family organization is based on the father's side of the family, and legally the children belong to their father's family. The men stay in the village of their birth, and marry women from other villages. This means, an Igbo village is made up of an extended family of fathers, brothers, sons, and their wives and children. Their sisters and daughters, who, when they grow up and get married, will move to their husband's village.

Next we will look at how the kinship of family grows into a village-town; in other words, how a family grows into a clan, Igbo style.

When George Benjamin and George Talton grow old and die, according to Igbo land laws, their land is divided equally between their sons. Ben Benjamin and Thomas Talton, their oldest sons, inherit their homesteads, and their brothers build homesteads on their own land and clear their own farms on their father's land.

Ben Benjamin had two wives, Julia and Judy, and 6 sons, Anderson (oldest son), George, Ben Jr., and Elisha, Bo, and Willie; and 3 daughters, Mattie (oldest daughter), Carrie, and Erna Mae.

Thomas Talton had two wives, Georgia and Elnora; and 3 sons, Walter (oldest son), Norris, and George; and 4 daughters, Bertha (oldest daughter), Rena, Esophine, and Hester.

Ben Benjamin's son, Ben Jr., married Thomas Talton's oldest daughter Bertha and had 3 sons, Orchester (oldest son), Ben III, and Walter; and one daughter Clovis Rena (oldest daughter).

Orchester had 1 son, Orchester Jr. (oldest son), and 2 daughters, Linda (Oldest Daughter), and Elaine.

Orchester Jr. had 1 son, Orchester III (oldest son), and 3 daughters, Rachel (oldest daughter), Omni, and Nikki.

We have seen how the Igbo physically organize their family village-towns, based on kinship relations and independent family units; and kinship relations are social relations, and social relations are what make up a society.

This is the foundation of the Igbo Society, and this is what gave it its equality nature; the rights of each family to be independent, and their beliefs that every other family also has the right to be independent. Thus, everybody is equal, as far as family relationships with other families are concerned.

So we can say, social equality means individual family independence; for a family to be independent, the father and mothers must also be independent, and of course, independent parents produce independent children.

Now, to check Grandpa's little creation story and conclusions about related evidence, we have to take a detailed look at the organization of their society and how it functions; and there is lots of evidence on their lifestyle.

Since the Igbo believe that, they are the direct descendants, and follow in the footsteps, of the original 8 people created by IGWE and ALA at the beginning of time, we can think of the Igbo society as being created by these 8 Ancient Ancestors.

In fact, since the Igbo live where they always have lived, there is no evidence that they ever changed their lifestyle. We can use modern Igbo evidence; say about 1619 when Africans were first brought to America.

This is where we have more than enough research material to get us deep into the area of the wisdom of the original 8 Ancestors in building a society based on the contract with the spiritual world.

This brings the original 8 people into the picture to be investigated as the Most Ancient Ancestors, and creators of the Igbo Society from their experience in heaven with IGWE and ALA. This will serve as the foundation of the approach we will take in our investigation.

In any case, Grandpa thinks we have established their Ancestors and Igbo Society, as the "Well." We will next do some "Drinking" of the "Content" of the "Well," as used in this chapter title "Drinking from Ancient Wells," the Igbo.

Igbo Society

Well Fellow Detectives, Grandpa thinks that with all of the above information in mind, especially the spiritual symbolism, we should be about ready to take our investigation into how these ritual symbols were used in the every-day life of the Igbo.

Now Grandpa has reached the conclusion that the best way to investigate the Igbo society as a whole, and to see how it functions, we will focus on what they teach their children.

We will do this by following those children growing up and living their lives. Since we have put emphasis on the oldest sons and daughters, we will begin with the Igbo's society educational system as related to them. (We will explain their role later).

To set up a background, we will move up in time, say to the forth generation of George and Kate Benjamin, to the oldest son and daughter of Orchester Benjamin Jr., Orchester III and Rachel.

We will begin our investigation with the rituals related to Orchester III and Rachel before they were born. We will follow them through the rituals of their birth, childhood, adulthood, and old age;

including the rituals related to age-groups and generations associated with group and personal chosen destinies we mentioned in the section of Igbo religious beliefs; and ending up with the rituals of wealth.

In addition, we will put special emphasis on how the children are taught about economics (trade), independence, social equality, and personal freedom in Igbo society, through rituals and stories.

In the process, we will also be able to see how the Igbo applied their religious beliefs in their regular lives. To Grandpa, this is the most interesting part of our investigation, because, we will be dealing with lots of rituals.

For example, when Orchester III and Rachel's mother became pregnant, the children in the same generation became involved.

In both cases, when she is about five months pregnant, she goes to the market place carrying a calabash containing a coconut, a piece of meat, and sixteen cowries (ancient African money).

At the market the mother meets young boys and girls of near puberty age. (A pre-arranged group of future cousins 9 to 11 years old of the unborn baby) They take the coconut and meat, and cut them up and give them back to her. Then she gives them the sixteen cowries. (This symbolizes the mother's unborn child trading with his and her generation).

Upon her return to the homestead, she cooks the meat, and serves all of the children three years old and younger who are the unborn child's age group, meat and coconut.

So from a spiritual symbolic angle, before they are born, Orchester III and Rachel are inter-acting economically with their generation, the older boys and girls. At the same time, giving gifts to their age group, the children under three years of age.

Eight days after their births, Orchester III is circumcised, and Orchester III and Rachel are given their names. More important, their mother and father establish a CHI shrine (Soul shrine) to each, for their personal chosen destinies, and they make sacrifices before their shrines, on their behalf, throughout their childhood.

This is important, because it shows that Igbo children are made aware that they have a chosen destiny throughout their childhood, and they take over their CHI shrine when they reach puberty.

When Orchester III and Rachel are 28 days old (one Igbo month); Orchester Jr. provides a feast for all of the children in his extended family. Each child brings a pottery bowl which Orchester Jr. fills with soup, and each child is given a cooked yam.

The children take their soup and yam outside the homestead and eat their meal there, and when they have finished, they break their pottery dish in pieces by stomping on them. This symbolizes a communion meal between the Ancestors reborn within the children, as well as the Ancestors reborn within Orchester III and Rachel.

After the feast, all of the children go to a stream and bath, and on their return, they paint fancy patterns on their bodies with body paint. Then one of the boys (in the case of Orchester III), and one of the girls (in the case of Rachel), take some palm wine in their mouth and spit it over the fire in Orchester III and Rachel's mother's house. This he or she does until the fire is extinguished. The mother then sweeps out her house, while the boy or girl go and obtain fresh fire from a neighboring homestead.

After the rituals, the boy or girl, in the case of Rachel, rubs some chalk on Orchester III's forehead saying, "If your mother or father sends you on a message do not refuse to go. But, if an evil spirit sends you, say that you have no feet. Let not anything that your parents eat (do or say) cause harm to you."

Recall, CHINEKE only created human spirits in groups to be born over a three year period; and this group of spirits is what we call an age-group. In the process, each individual spirit chooses a personal destiny, and the group also chose a destiny which in turn bonds them together.

As we mentioned, an age-group is one-seventh of a generation, and generations also have a chosen destiny that play a role in society. Therefore, when Orchester III and Rachel are born, he and she are spiritually bonded to their family, age-group, and generation.

Thus is the meaning of those rituals, and these bonds are a dynamic force in their lives throughout their lifetime, and even after they die and become Ancestors. Thus is the nature of the major rituals of childhood.

Now we will look at childhood, and this means that we will focus on another side of the Igbo educational system, where children stories are the teaching tools.

So we will now direct our investigation to the kind, and meaning, of stories Orchester III and Rachel are taught throughout their childhood, up to, but not beyond the age of puberty.

The Igbo children stories are designed to teach children, and remind grown ups, not only the game of life, but also how the game is played; especially how to successful play the game.

As we mentioned, the Igbo see life as a market place of competition on three levels, between individuals, between age-groups, and between Ancestors, living, and unborn generations.

However, it all depends on how the individual plays the game of life, therefore, Igbo children stories focus on the individual person playing the game in society.

We can see, from this point of view, that their stories benefit children as well as the grownup storyteller; they are the assurance of the smooth flow of information across generations.

In traditional Igbo stories, like most Africans, sometimes the characters are animals, when in fact, they are not merely animals, but human creatures, living or dead in animal shapes. For example, in some stories, it is often said of a person that he is a leopard. In other words, that he is quick of action, or has other qualities of the leopard.

On the other hand, in Igbo, children's stories are always about animals, only the major character has the qualities they want to instill into the child.

In this regard, the major character is always a tortoise (turtle). The Igbo think that the tortoise has a good habit of acting with deliberation and discretion, while using sound judgment, and, by nature, he is a trickster. These are the qualities they want their children to have most of all. Therefore, the Tortoise is a symbol of EKWENSU the Trickster God; and as a symbol, in the stories, the Tortoise teaches the children how to get along in Igbo Society, and just as important, teach them independence (individualism).

From that point of view, the following story teaches children, Orchester III and Rachel, that success is the thing to be respected; one must follow one's Chi (Chosen Destiny), and how to use forces more powerful than one's self.

"One day, the Tortoise noticed that he was not getting the respect he thought he deserved. He had heard, that for one to get respect, he must follow his CHI, so he made a sacrifice to his CHI. Then the Tortoise challenged a buffalo to a tug-of-war.

The buffalo made fun of him, and said who will give you strength to pull against me? The Tortoise replied, Never mind, wait and see. So they appointed a day and drew up the rules for the contest, deciding particularly upon the signal for starting. Right away, the Tortoise went and challenged an elephant, and also made arrangements for a contest on the same terms.

When the appointed day arrived, the Tortoise fastened one end of the rope around the neck of the buffalo, and then acted as if he were to take the other end. But the rope was so long that, when stretched, one competitor was out of sight of the other.

The Tortoise called the elephant and tied the rope on his neck, and went into his act, like he did with the buffalo. At the agreed signal, the buffalo and elephant began to pull and strain, and the struggle became so furious that it ended in the death of both.

The Tortoise congratulated himself on the strategy, whereas he had obtained so much meat for so little trouble. He cut up the meat and sold it in the market place. He became very rich in cowries, and built a big homestead, and married wives and had children. After this, everybody sang praises to the Tortoise saying, He who follows his CHI is very smart indeed."

The above story shows that Igbo children stories are symbolic, and this one deals with the fact that one must use ones mind, regardless of outside physical powers much larger than one's self, to get respect. Respect for oneself, and from others is the cornerstone of independence.

Now we will next look at a very interesting story, because it deals with the inter-conflict between greed and manhood. Little girls can learn something from the story, but for the most part, it is a story for little boys.

In this story, the Ram represents the Tortoise's Ikenga Shrine (symbolizing his manhood), and shows what happens in life when a male works against his manhood. On one hand, its shows the loyalty of manhood; on the other hand, it also deals with the problems that come up when the Ancestors (and parents) are disobeyed; which is the major reason for the inter-conflict in the first place.

"The animals once disobeyed their Ancestors, and as a punishment, a great famine started throughout their Kingdom. There was scarcely anything to eat. Their hunger got so bad that the King of the animals organized a series of wrestling competitions.

This is not the ideal way to solve our problem I know, but it is about the most effective, he told the animals. Any competitor, who defeats his opponent, is free to kill him and eat him as food. If, however, the defeated wrestler offers a ransom, he will be released if the victor so wishes.

Most animals were pleased with this arrangement. The Ram and his friend the Tortoise, got ready the next day to go and try their luck. The Ram defeated all of his opponents and killed them. The Tortoise was always defeated, but not killed because of his friend's influence. The Ram always saved him by paying a ransom.

Look for a competitor smaller than you are, the Ram warned the Tortoise.

The next animal to wrestle with the Tortoise was a Bat. He carried the Bat up, and it seemed he would appear victorious, but the Bat was experienced and could not be thrown down. It was the Tortoise who was finally defeated. The Bat picked up a sickle to kill him, but the Ram quickly intervened. The Ram gave two of his games to the Bat for the release of his friend. The Tortoise was again spared.

A couple of hours later, the Tortoise saw a very weak little sickly Goat. He asked the little Goat to wrestle with him. The challenge was accepted. For the first time in his life, the Tortoise emerged the winner. The mother of the sickly Goat wanted to pay a ransom, but the

Tortoise was not ready to listen, not even to the pleading of his friend the Ram.

He quickly killed the Goat and cooked the meat. He gave one ear to the Ram. He waited for a little time, and then went to the Ram to demand his piece of meat back. This was immediately given to him. I am joking, eat your meat. Let's go to the lake and drink, the Tortoise said.

On arrival at the lake, the Tortoise made certain that his friend did swallow the meat. As they were going home, the Tortoise wanted back his piece of meat. The meat had already been swallowed.

I want my meat back. Nothing but the ear of the goat I gave to you. The surprised Ram gave him one of his games, but he refused to accept it. Finally the Ram gave all of his meat to Tortoise.

At home, the Ram thought of ways to teach the Tortoise a lesson he would never forget. Suddenly a thought came to him. He made a statue of his father with eso (a very sticky substance). He left the statue in front of his house.

Late in the evening, the Tortoise passed the Ram's house. And in spite of the Tortoise's smart mind, the Tortoise never failed to greet his elders. Not aware of his friend's trick, he approached the statue of the old man and offered his salutation. Good evening Sir, he said. There was no response whatsoever.

I say, good evening Sir, he repeated. Again there was no answer.

With all his might, the Tortoise gave the old man statue a slap. His hand was held by the eso. He used his left hand, and the same thing happened. Next he used his legs, which were also held fast.

He shouted in pain until the Ram ran out. You killed my father, the Ram shouted. Wife, Wife, he called, wife bring me a sharp knife. Please do not kill me, the Tortoise pleaded. He was released when he promised to give all of his property to the Ram.

Now that he had lost all of his property, the Tortoise planned his own trick. He fashioned a statue of his grandfather with pounded cassava. He carried the statue to his friend's house, and climbed a coconut tree to see what would happen.

But as soon as the Ram saw the statue, he knew what his friend had up his sleeve. He called on his wife; She prepared a soup immediately, and sent a messenger to go and ask all of the animals to come for a meal.

The statue of the Tortoise's grandfather was pounded into fu-fu, and the animals enjoyed the food. The disappointed Tortoise rushed out of his place of hiding up the coconut tree, and joined the festival."

The above story teaches the children, especially the boys, the nature of the relationship between a man and his manhood, and the role it has in his life.

The following story deals with other major symbols; Ofo, which is a symbol of fatherhood and male leadership, and also UMUNE, which is a symbol of motherhood and female leadership. It deals with these two symbols in the sense that it deals with self-discipline.

The lack of self-discipline leads to the person becoming destructive, in the sense of destroying the things they love the most, in this case, their children.

On the other hand, the story not only deals with the value of tricks, but also deals with the subject of repaying good with good, and not with evil. Not in respect to the effect it has on the other person, but how it breaks down a person's self-discipline.

"One day the Tortoise looked into his storehouse, and low and behold it was empty. Suffering from shortness of supplies, the Tortoise hired a Rabbit to dig a tunnel from his hole, to the market-place.

When the people were assembled with their things to sell, the Tortoise and the Rabbit, remaining hidden in the tunnel, began to sing, Ubwaw jisaw tijin tintiji tiji.

When the people heard the unfamiliar sounds, and could not see where they came from, they were frightened and ran away, believing that evil spirits had invaded the market.

The Tortoise and the Rabbit thereafter ran out of the tunnel and got enough goods left by the people to restock their storehouse. They continued to practice this trick when ever their storehouse got low.

Later on, the suspicions of the market people were aroused, and they accused the Tortoise of trickery. He strongly denied the charge, and declared his readiness to submit the case for trial. A day was fixed for swearing on the Gods.

Meanwhile, just before the trial day, the Tortoise made a contract with the birds called Asha; He put a large number of them into a pot and instructed them to utter cries in accordance with a code of signals.

The Tortoise concealed the pot under a weird looking awe-inspiring shrine that was in itself sufficient to put something on the minds of the people. And when the birds began to sing, it was too much for the assembled crowd, and they refused to proceed with the trial. Thus the Tortoise escaped by means of his skilful trickery.

Tortoise returned to his house carrying the pot containing the little birds with him. They served him loyally, but he returned evil for good. He placed the pot upon the fire, and when the birds cried for mercy, he mocked them.

Presently he removed the pot from the fire expecting to find all the birds ready for eating. As he lifted the cover, one bird flew out, the only survivor, and landed on the head of Tortoise's oldest son.

The Tortoise became so angry that he lost his self-control. He cried out to his son to stand quite still, seized a big knife and struck viciously, but the bird hopped to one side, and the blow fell upon the head of Tortoise's son, killing him on the spot.

This still did not quiet the Tortoise's anger; he turned and saw the bird perched on the back of his oldest daughter. Striking blindly in his fury, he was again deceived by the bird's quickness, and consequently, killed his daughter also.

The bird flew to the top of a tree, and watching his opportunity, landed swiftly on the back of Tortoise himself. The Tortoise who was by now was completely out of his mind, tried to think of how he might overthrow his little enemy. Finally, he decided to climb a tree, intending, when he reached the top, to throw himself down, and turning a somersault, to fall upon the bird on his back and crush him.

Once more, however, the bird was equal to the occasion, and as the Tortoise dropped from the tree, the bird slipped off his back and flew away. Tortoise fell heavily to the ground and was almost killed.

Thus the Tortoise, in the many months it took for his injuries to heal, learned the value of self-discipline (or to say, lose your cool and become a fool)."

In the above story, besides showing the value of tricks and self-discipline, it also shows the value of repaying good with good, and not evil. This is important for children to learn, because it plays a big role in Igbo society.

We can see that the Igbo also think that a person's attitude is very important in the game of life; from the point of view of, "what goes around comes around."

Finally in the following story, we will take a look at the games the Igbo play with each other's minds; which is their way of exercising their mental skills. In this story, the Tortoise is married to the daughter of EKWENSU, the Trickster God who in this story is called Agadi.

In addition, this is not only a story about a mind game between a son-in-law and father-in-law, but also how a person can let his pride become an obstacle to his growth in knowledge.

"One day the Tortoise wanted to find out if he was cleverer than his father-in-law. He called is wife and told her, See, I'm cleverer than your father. I wonder why people say your father is the father of tricksters. You're still a child, his wife told him. My father started his own tricks before any person was born. The Tortoise fell down from where he was sitting; he laughed, and laughed again at his wife's folly.

Now tell me, who were the victims of your father's tricks, since no person existed at the time he started his own tricks. You see why I say its useless discussing things with women. You've contradicted yourself. Anyway, I believe in action, not words.

In the evening, the Tortoise sent his son Nwambe to his father-in-law Agadi, to tell him to buy him good wine. He was expecting some very important visitors, he said. Nwambe went to Agadi and gave him the message according to the Tortoise's instructions; the wine should neither be locally produced nor imported.

Agadi knew the type of son-in-law he had. A few minutes later, he sent a messenger to him to say that the wine was ready with one condition attached, it was that any person other than a male or female should carry the wine.

This was above the Tortoise's intelligence. He could not find an answer. After waiting in vain for is son-in-law, Agadi sent another messenger to tell the Tortoise that anyone could carry the wine, provided such a person did not touch the gourd containing it. This condition was as difficult as, if not more difficult, than the first.

The Tortoise called his wife and told her what her father had said. The wife laughed and added; I told you that my father is an experienced trickster. I don't expect you to compete with him in any way. What you ought to do is to ask him to teach you some of his tricks.

The Tortoise would never admit any failure. He told his wife that he was simply finding out what sort of father-in-law he had."

Now when we look at these stories from an educational point of view as teaching tools, we can see that the Igbo child is taught how to function in society beginning at a very early age. For example, the story about the problem that developed between the Tortoise and Ram.

This is an instance of a man that has let greed overcome his manhood, Soulview, or, what is happening inside. A man is dependent on his Manhood Ikenga (Ram) in ways that can cause problems in his mind. The man is fighting his own power to act.

The story about the Tortoise and his father-in-law is very plain; this story teaches that one should learn from the Trickster God. On the other hand, the story about the Tortoise, the Elephant, and the Buffalo, is an example of a lesson in Worldview, or what is happening in the outside world of Spirits. And as we mentioned, how to deal with these Spirits in ways that are a benefit to oneself; by using what is learned from the Trickster God.

Whereas the story about the Tortoise, the Market People, the Rabbit, and the Birds, show a complete breakdown in a man's integrity. The birds symbolize the Authority of Ofo, Truth, Trust, Righteousness, and Justice; which the Tortoise disrespected by using them in a con game.

The results was the death of Tortoise's oldest son and oldest daughter, which is a direct attack on, and the destruction of, Fatherhood; (We will take a more detailed look at the role of the Oldest Son and Daughter in the Family, and Fatherhood later).

Igbo Tortoise children stories fascinated Grandpa. As teaching tools in their education system, they are like a study in psychology and philosophy on a child's level, of how the Igbo Society works. And how to use the workings of the mind to relate to one's self, as well as the outside world, and at the same time, teach the child how to use his inside forces to deal with outside forces.

This gives the child the confidence to trust his own mind, and therefore, become independent in the sense of not depending on someone else to do his or her thinking.

There are hundreds of Tortoise stories, as well as some that are centered around other animals, nevertheless, all of the stories follow the same pattern. As teaching tools, they focus and give spiritual support to independence of the individual person, as do Igbo religious beliefs. Thus is one of the teaching tools of the Igbo educational system, but there are also other methods.

For example, we should recall, 8 days after an Igbo Child is born, the mother or father, depending on whether it is a boy or girl, establishes a CHI Shrine (to his or her Chosen Destiny) on the child's behalf. And from that point, to the age of puberty, the child, with the help of parents, make sacrifices to it.

Therefore, a child grows through childhood knowing what he or she came into the world to do, and the Tortoise stories teach him or her how to be successful. This is still yet another learning experience of Orchester III and Rachel in the educational system.

Finally, there is another point about Orchester III and Rachel's childhood learning experiences that we should mention before we move on. Recall the rituals between the children and the new baby, before, and after he or she is born. Recall what we said about generations and age-groups. This is also reflected throughout childhood in the sense that the children take some of the responsibility of educating themselves; however, this needs some explanation.

Children learn by watching and imitating all of the grown-ups in their family in the form of play-acting; and the homestead playground is their stage. The playground is the world of the children, (the area we called children reality in Ben Sr. and Kate's homestead. Children are on their own a good deal of the time, from the age of three years until puberty. This area is governed by the children themselves, the oldest watching out for the younger, especially the oldest brother and sister.

So, from about the age of three, the Igbo child is thought of as sufficiently advanced to be left more or less to its own devices in the care of older children. In the sense, he or she begins to spend the day and evening on the playground with children of his age-group and generation. In some ways the playground is sacred. For it is believed that it is here that children, as age-groups, learn the skills necessary to fulfill their Group Chosen Destiny; and this is the area of the IGWE and ALA's Holy Homestead, the 8 original Ancestors that were created.

Thus is the case throughout the generations; and in this respect, we say that children of a generation raise themselves. Therefore, this too, is part of Orchester III and Rachel's childhood learning experiences.

We do not mean to imply that Igbo parents are not deeply involved with the children's practical education, this is shown by the stories they tell them. This brings us up to, and beyond their ages of puberty where they begin another type of education. It is as if they have finished grade school and are now ready for high school and college.

Puberty Rituals and Education

To understand what puberty means, we must recall that the Igbo believe that the World is owned by ALA, the Mother Goddess, and IGWE, the Father God. They are the Administrators of the World's Affairs. And this is the foundation of Igbo society. Women are the owners, and men are the political administrators.

In addition, we must understand that children are not a part of society. They belong to their father and mother, and are part of that family; and they do not take responsibility for their lives.

Therefore, the goal of childhood education is when a child reaches the age of puberty, 13, 14, or 15 years of age. He or she is ready to begin to take responsibility of their spiritual and social lives; become responsible adults.

This means that Orchester III and Rachel, after puberty, have the right to become involved with the ritual symbolism of Ofo and Umune. In that respect, they become their own chief priest and priestess; as well as something like Prince and Princess in relation to Society; they will become like Kings and Queens when they get married and begin raising a family.

In other words, for all practical purposes, at puberty, Orchester III and Rachel become young adults and have equal rights with all other adults up to the limits of their experiences. Or to say, Rachel becomes a co-owner of the society along with the other women, and Orchester III becomes one of its administrators with the other men.

Thus is the meaning of puberty, the spiritual transition from childhood to adulthood, which consists of rituals, followed by an education process that lasts from the age of 12 until they get married.

Marriage takes place for boys in their early twenties, and for girls in their late teens. Therefore, the puberty age education process can last anywhere from 6 to 12 years. Naturally this spiritual transition begins with puberty rituals; one for boys and one for girls.

This is also an educational process in the independent use of ritual symbols related to fatherhood and motherhood, Ofo (IGWE) and Umune (ALA); which according to Igbo beliefs are the Ultimate in Adulthood.

Puberty for Rachel began with her first menstruation period and ends nine months later. During which time through ritual transformation, she gains spiritual knowledge related to the wisdom of her womb. However, she still has a lot of practical things to learn before she takes her position in society as an Igbo woman. (Grandpa could not find any information on this ritual process).

On the morning after her ninth period, Rachel performs a ceremony before her CHI Shrine; called "greeting her destiny." Where she takes an Umune leaf, folds it, fills it with water, and empties it over the symbol, saying CHI, wash your hands and eat. After which, a female chicken is sacrificed, and some of its blood is allowed to fall on the Shrine.

Later, after prayers by the oldest woman in the Family, the same ceremony is performed before her mother's female Ancestor Shrine, representing all of her female Ancestors, especially her grand and great grandmothers.

Next, Rachel's mother cooks a female chicken seasoning it with Umune leaves for a sacrifice meal which Rachel shares. First with her age-group, as a sign of her age-groups destiny, then with the females of her family, young and old, as a sign of sisterhood. Rachel is now ready to begin learning all about being a woman, wife, mother, and her role in society.

On the other hand, Orchester III, when about 13 or 14 years of age, his father, Orchester Jr. convened all the males in his family.

Meanwhile, after a ritual at his CHI Shrine to "greet his destiny," Orchester III goes to the forest to find an Ofo tree to his liking, where he selects a joint of an Ofo branch. And along with the Ofo stick, he presents a male goat and male chicken to the senior male of the family; the ceremony is as follows:

As the senior male takes the Ofo stick, in ceremony fashion he says, "This Ofo, which we are about to confer on our son, is not an Ofo which will take the life of an innocent man. He has collected and presented to us all of the traditional materials, and we confer the Ofo with free will. He is not taking it by force.

Ofo, lend a ready ear to whatever truth he tells to you, but if he speaks lies, turn away from him. Ofo, avert all evil from this man and increase his family. Ofo, you are a witness that we, both young and old, are assembled here in this man's house for a good, and not an evil purpose."

The senior male kills the goat and chicken, and allows the blood to drip on the Ofo. The meat is then cooked, and a sacrificial meal follows. After the meal, Orchester III stands up and holds out his hands, palms upwards.

The senior male takes the Ofo. And the senior woman of the family places her hands on his as he says these words: "We are now giving to you this Ofo, an Ofo that confers life and children, and not an Ofo that takes away life."

The senior male and senior woman then both say simultaneously; "May IGWE stand with you." Thus Orchester III enters the position of Social Equality and Personal Freedom in society. But, this is not the only puberty ritual for boys, there is still the Ikenga ritual.

The Ikenga ritual consists only in Orchester III going to a divination priest. Then to a wood carver for an Ikenga statue of a man with ram horns. Orchester III then gets the biggest and fattest Ram that he can find. The priest, through divination, finds out which of Orchester III's successful male relatives is to be the presiding priest in the upcoming Ikenga ceremony.

On the appointed day, a meeting of all of the male members of Orchester III's age group gather, and the ram is held in readiness. The male member of his family who is to act the role of priest, plants a special tree and places the new Ikenga statue at its base with the following prayer,

"IGWE, I have come today to ask that You be-store your powers on this Ikenga. From You, I have derived energy for success, whether I went to the right or to the left, grant that things go equally well for Orchester III. May his homestead family grow big and strong, may he be successful in governing, may he grow rich."

After which the ram is killed, and a few drops of blood are allowed to fall on the Ikenga statue before it is cooked and a big sacrificial meal is prepared, of which only age-group members may eat. The ritual ends in a celebration dance in Orchester III's honor.

Thus Orchester III is entered into the world of manhood, and is unified with his age-group as a political force involving the age-group Chosen destiny. He is also in a position to Choose a Destiny of his future Family homestead when he gets married.

The two rituals, Ofo and Ikenga, are the point of departure to put Orchester III in the position to begin to learn to administer the affairs of his life and his village Society.

However, we should take special note. Although Ikenga symbolizes the power of manhood, Ofo is still the authority by which political power can be used. This means that political power is self-disciplined, just as Orchester III must be self-disciplined in administering the political affairs of his future homestead Society.

This completes our investigation into the symbolic spiritual side of Igbo puberty. Next we will turn our attention to the practical side of puberty age education. For instance, the things that Orchester III and Rachel must learn about the organization and government of Igbo Society. First, we will deal with the organization.

Social Organization

We saw that two of the Original 8 people, George and Kate Benjamin, had a family that grew into 5 Extended Family Villages; Ben's village, George Jr.'s village, Jessie's village, Johnny's village, and Sonny's village.

We must keep in mind that the 5 villages of the Family village group surrounded a common market place; this means that it is considered a village-town. Also that each village consisted of an extended family of fathers, brothers, and their wives and children; in Igbo land, a Clan consists of the offspring of George and Kate's 5 sons for 6 generations, following the male line.

We are going to say that there is an average of 20 homesteads per village; and in each homestead there is an average of 15 people, men, wives and children. 15 times 20 homesteads gives us an average of 300 people per village, and a total of 1500 people in the original Clan of George and Kate Benjamin.

Meanwhile, we must not forget the clans of George and Serena Talton, William and Corena Franklin, and Westly and Bertha Winfield. To keep round numbers, we will say that each of those clans population was 1500, for a total of 6,000 people in the original Igbo nation.

The population of the Clan, we will call the local society, combined with all of the other Clans, equals the Igbo General Society. However, George Benjamin's son, Ben Benjamin's village is the one that we will deal with in detail.

Political Authority

We should note that our investigation is directed at Government of Society This means that we will now focus our investigative attention on the spirituality and politics of Ofo and Ikenga, authority and power. And the constitution of the Family-homestead form of government.

There are three sets of laws that form the heart of government; Unchanging laws of the Gods and Goddesses (especially IGWE and ALA) and laws that change to deal with the changing times made by different Ancestors throughout history, and lastly, man made laws of the living.

Now if we mix these sets of laws with the authority and power of Ofo and Ikenga, and the nourishment of Umune, and modeled it on the Holy Homestead, we can see the constitution of laws of Government. From this, we should get some support for Grandpa's conclusion that social equality is a definition of personal freedom.

It is also important at this point, as far as government is concerned, to emphasize the role of the Oldest Son and Daughter in Family and Society affairs. As well as their cross generation co-ownership of family and society with their parent's generation, (recall the rituals the young children had with the mothers of Orchester III and Rachel before they were born and when they were babies).

Children are raised to be independent, and they are taught that their generation is also in some degree independent from their parent's generation.

This means that each generation is owned and governed by its Oldest Sons and Daughters. For according to Igbo traditional laws, the Oldest Son and Daughter, and their age-group, have as important of a role in government as their parents and grandparents generation, especially after they pass the age of puberty and get married. So, we can see that government covers and harmonizes three generations of society.

Remember, Ben is the oldest son of George and Kate, and Julia is their oldest daughter. As the Oldest Son, Ben would inherit the homestead when old man George died, and more important than that, he would also inherit old man George's Ofo ritual Shrine. The same would be true of Julia. As the oldest daughter, she would inherit Kate's Umune Shrine of the Female Ancestors.

Ben's oldest son Anderson, would inherit his Ofo Shrine and homestead, along with his Ofo Shrine; and Julia's oldest daughter Mattie, would inherit Kate's female Ancestor shrine. This is where the oldest sons and daughters get their authority.

In addition, the Ofo of each of the younger brothers would also follow their oldest son, and the Umune shrine of their wives would follow their oldest daughter. This brings us to the third son of Ben and Julie Benjamin, Ben Jr. and his wife Bertha.

Their oldest son, Orchester Benjamin, your Grandpa, would inherit Ben Jr's Ofo shrine, and their oldest daughter Clovis Rena, would inherit Bertha's Unume shrine.

Orchester Benjamin's oldest son Orchester Jr., would inherit Ben Jr.'s and Orchester Sr.'s Ofo shrines; and his oldest daughter, Linda, would inherit Bertha's Unume shrine.

This is where we find Orchester III and Rachel in possession of the future priest and priestess of Ben Jr. and Bertha's Ofo and Unume shrines. This gives them authority in Ben Jr's village, and Ben Sr's village town.

Meanwhile, we should also note, Ben had two wives, Julia and Judy. This had the effect on Ben's village being divided into two sections, Julia's section and Judy's section; and this too is a part of the organization of Ben Jr's Village.

This means that the men of the village are united on their father Ben's side, and divided on sides of their mothers, Julia and Judy. But in any case, for the purposes of our investigation, we now have Orchester III and Rachel as the Priest' Oldest Son and Priestess' Oldest Daughter of the village Family.

This is also the case with the other 4 villages in the group. For example, in George's village, his Ofo Shrine would follow a similar line of oldest sons and oldest daughters up to our time period, as would George's wives Umune Shrine of their female Ancestors follow a line of oldest daughters.

The same thing took place in Jessie, Johnny, and Sonny's village. However, George and Kate's Ofo and Umune Shrines in Ben's village means that his is the Senior Village in the Brother group.

Orchester III, being the Oldest Son of a line of oldest sons all the way back to Ben Jr., and Rachel being the oldest daughter of a line of oldest daughters all the way back to Bertha; puts them in the position of the highest officials in the male and female sides of Government of Ben Jr's village. As well as equals in the Government of the other four George Benjamin village-towns.

Recall the villages that make up the village town up to the 7th generation (6th cousins) are considered kinfolk, and the villagers cannot inter-marry. On the other hand, after the 7th generation they are not considered kinfolk, and the Clans break apart and begin the process all over again.

This means that we are dealing with a time period when the villages town is considered a full Clan, and Orchester III and Rachel are the Oldest Son and Daughter of this clan's leadership. Thus is the nature of political authority, now we will turn to the political Constitution side of government.

Political Constitution

Just because Orchester III is the Priest of Ben Jr.'s Ofo Shrine, does not mean that he is some kind of ruler over the village politically. He is only an officiate at Ancestors ceremonies. The Igbo have a line between the spiritual, and the political sides of their government; not that the two are really separated.

In fact, in the Igbo nation, every man is a King, and there can be no central ruler, although Orchester III is the Chief Priest to the male Ancestors as far as his villages is concerned.

This is where the Igbo's form of government gets interesting; for example, we will do a comparison between the Igbo's form of Government, and the Government of the United States. Both of which are supposed to function in a manner which provides social equality and personal freedom for the people.

In the United States, the people vote and elect a ruler who is supposed to govern in a manner that follows the will of the people; and this is the U.S.'s definition of political freedom. Although their goal is the same as the Igbo, they have a ruling central government who is balanced against State Ruling Governments.

On the other hand, in the Igbo nation, the central government is the spiritual world of IGWE, ALA, and the Ancestors balanced against individual Family and Clan government; which is the Igbo's definition of spiritual-political freedom.

Be that as it may, the point that concerns us is the fact that in the United States, the seats of government are located in the National capital building, and the State's capital building. In Igbo land, the seats of governments are located in the head of the Homestead and the Market place of the village town.

Thus is why Orchester III is not a ruler of the Family-village just because he has the Ofo Shrine of the Founding father, Ben Jr. In fact, this does not give him any direct political advantage, only spiritual respect; and he officiates at Government meetings. His Ofo shrine has an equal role along with the Ofo shrines of the other villages in the village town's political activities.

There is still another point we should make in our comparison between the Igbo and the U.S.A. Society, which is in the area of constitutional government; both are a government in a society where everything is negotiable between man and man. However, in the case of Igbo, things are also negotiable between man and the spiritual world, as well as between man and man. This means that most of all, both are Governments of Compromise.

However, both have constitution laws that must not be compromised. In the case of the United States, a constitution written by Thomas Jefferson; and in the case of the Igbo these are the laws of ALA, the Earth Goddess, called the Laws of the Land. This comparison will throw some light on the Constitution of Igbo Government.

Anyway, ALA is considered the Owner of Mankind whether living or dead. She is the Symbol of Human Morality, and therefore a principal of legal sanction.

The cases of murder, incest, adultery involving wives of fathers, brothers and sons, Stealing (especially certain ritual objects and food), arson, having sex on the Land (sex lying on the ground), kidnapping, poisoning, etc, etc.; these are all regarded as ALA constitutional laws, and each involves sanctions equal to the offense. Some call for drastic action.

For example, if members of one extended family kill a member of another extended family, the law calls for an eye for an eye. The killer, or a member of the killer's family, can be killed to balance things out. However, the major point being, these types of laws are thought of as moral laws, and therefore are not negotiable. Thus, ALA is related to Social laws of Family-Society relationships.

On the other hand, the laws of IGWE, the other Gods, Goddess, and Ancestors laws that people make to meet changing situations in a changing world, is of a negotiated contractual nature, related to Chosen Destiny. Thus, the Igbo Government is a balance between moral constitutional law and contractual ethical law.

The function of the Government is to tie all of those dynamics together, and maintain and promote harmony between them.

These are some of the things that Orchester III and Rachel learn about the government of society during their puberty years.

Next, we will turn our attention to a few of the many things that Orchester III and Rachel had to put into practice as related to the constitution and function of their Government.

Courts

Since we are now interested in Government in action, we need some situation on which it is to act.

Therefore, to handle this portion of our investigation, we are going to create some situations which call for some kind of Governing action; one involving social problems on a homestead, extended family village, and village town level.

However, we need to set up a cast of characters to perform on this action. We are going to move up in time when Orchester III is about 60 years of age, and has five wives, Sara being the Senior Wife, and about 20 children ranging from 12 to 40 years of age; his oldest son is named Steve, and his oldest daughter named Fay, and naturally there is his oldest sister Rachel.

Plus, there are his brothers. Uncles and cousins of Ben, Julie and Judy's village, who along with Orchester III, form the Elders of the village. Then there are the Oldest sons of the other villages. To make it easier to follow, we will say they are named for their founding fathers of their villages.

Therefore, we have George Jr., Jessie Jr., Johnny Jr., and Sonny Jr., who with Orchester III, form the Elders of the village town of George and Kate Benjamin's Clan. Thus we have the major players in Igbo Government.

Although we will include Rachel and the other Government members as we go along. We can find more answers to our questions about how the Government deals with Social Equality and Personal Freedom if we focus our attention and create our problematical social situation around Orchester III and his three Ofo Shrines.

Legal Situation
(Homestead)

Grandpa is going to have some fun in dealing with the Igbo Government. After reading and studying novels and Historical and Anthropological work, written by Igbo Authors among others, we are going to combine this information as evidence to present Orchester III in a personal way, in creating our legal situation. At the same time, remain true to our logic-line of their religious beliefs to present a picture of the Igbo government in action.

Orchester III, as Husband and Head of a Homestead Family, must deal with hundreds of factors. Maintaining peace and order between five independent minded wives, plus their relationship to him is just one example.

Then there are a large number of independent minded children to deal with. In addition, if we add to that, all of the economic needs of a growing family. While at the same time, he is the Priest between his family and the Gods, Goddesses, and especially Ancestors.

He must assure that each member of his family has social equality and personal freedom. He must be successful in dealing with these situations if his homestead family is to be successful, and his homestead being successful is the foundation of his fatherhood and manhood. Things can get very interesting.

So we can see why the Igbo are surrounded by shrines in and outside of their houses, and especially why they pray a lot, and we do mean a lot. In fact, we can learn a lot about the position of the Igbo Husbands by the nature of their morning prayer.

For this is the time and place where they get together to deal with the upcoming day's affairs of the homestead and his Village, and the Clan Village town. With this in mind, we will set up the scene by creating some problematic situations.

Orchester III is now a very successful 60-year-old man in every thing he does, his homestead family is the most smooth and successful in the whole of the village town. However, when we meet him, his mind is troubled.

He had just returned from a month long trading trip which took him a long way from home, and in his absence, a certain situation has developed that he learned about the evening before. So we meet Orchester III early the next morning as he wakes up.

Like all Igbo husbands, the first thing he does upon waking in the morning is to go into his shrine room. As we said, Igbo husbands pray a lot. The traditional morning prayer consists of giving thanks for the well being of the family through the night, and asking for blessing for the family in the upcoming day's activities. This ritual is performed before the Ofo shrine and general Ancestor Shrine.

On this morning however, although his ritual and prayer is typical, Orchester III has a lot of things he wanted to get off his mind. This in turn will give a good opportunity to see the contractual nature of his relationship with the spiritual world. This gives us an idea of what we mean by saying, Morning Prayer is a process by which a man gets himself together to deal with a serious situation.

At the same time, show the hiring and firing of a God, with the Gods and Goddesses serving as Witnesses. For in Orchester III's absence, jealousy and greed had turned life in his homestead upside down. Nothing was as he had left it; and he was angry with the God that was supposed to protect his homestead.

This morning's ritual consisted of Orchester III first retrieving the Shrine in front of the homestead belonging to the God who is the Protector of the Family.

Along with his Ofo shrines and a new God shrine, a kola nut, alligator pepper, and palm wine is placed before his oldest Ancestor Ofo shrine, the Ofo of Ben Jr. He then draws white chalk lines, also lines around his left eye, and offered the following prayer.

"Tradition that will never end,
Following the footsteps of our Parents,
Should do us no harm.

Regret shall meet the person rushing,
I say we shall go slowly to meet the day ahead.
Ofo that leads the innocent,
Stands for Truth, Justice, Trust,
And Righteousness,
This is the foundation of the Society
Of the living and the dead.
All allocations have been done,
I take my place.
But if anyone is jealous,
Let him go to his father's grave,
And if he knocks at the grave and his father answers,
Let him inquire how it was done in traditional times.
The wine taper should not talk
About funerals from the top of the palm tree,
Since he is near death where he is.
When I speak listen,
No one comes into the world an Elder,
You listen and keep.
A righteous man always receives welcome
When he comes back.
I am unacquainted with the movement of things,
How then can I wade into the fight!
CHINEKE, IGWE, ALA, ANYANWU, AMADIOHA,
EKWENSU, CHI, Ancestors
Eat kola nut and pepper.
All Spirits in our land,
Great and small Ancestors,
Good is for the Good
And evil for evil.
A child cries after his parents and no more.
No amount of anger can destroy a hill.
Good for nothing that allows
The outsider steals the values of the house,
Who eat sacrifices and do not respond,
With a blow you shall meet your end."

With these last words, Orchester III smashed the old shrine to the floor and placed his Ofo shrine near the new shrine. Thus the Old God-the-Protector-of-the-homestead is fired, and another God hired. The broken shrine is later taken to the edge of his property and thrown in the dump.

However, this does not end Orchester III's morning prayer, as we said, there were lots of things on his mind concerning attacks motivated by jealousy and greed, made by people inside and outside of the homestead. All of which were having a negative effect on the homestead from a number of directions.

These too, had to be dealt with spiritually in his morning prayer, as the following part of his prayer shows.

"My Ofo will raise my Ikenga,
And crown me with success likewise
IGWE and ALA, this is my witness.
My prayer is that none
Suffer what he or she has not caused.
I (Orchester III) did nothing to you (evil doer),
But you have gone after me,
You will only see disaster on your way.
May your front become your back,
And vice versa.
Whoever steals from his kin,
Whoever prevents his kin from prospering,
Whoever seduces the wife of another,
Whoever causes abortion in his neighbor's wife,
Whoever tampers with the crops of his neighbor,
Whoever takes the life of another,
Let them stand before
The righteousness, truth and justice of Ofo.

Our Ancestors have always stated,
In time of trouble like this,
That the eagle should perch,
While the hawk also perches,
If one should forbid the other,
Let its wing be blown off.
Amen."

The first prayer indicates the contractual nature of the relationships the Igbo have with Gods and Goddesses, with the exception of CHINEKE, ALA, and IGWE. On the other hand, we see that Orchester III has the freedom to hire and fire; again we have another link between equality and freedom.

But more important than that, it shows that the contract is based on success, and the high value success has in the Igbo beliefs. If the God was not successful in protecting the homestead, he broke the contract, and therefore he could be fired, and this frees Orchester III to hire another Protector God.

In the second prayer, we not only find out the things that happened in Orchester III's absence, we also get to the major laws the Government is to defend. We should take special note to the last two lines of the prayer, which according to the Ancestors, states the law of punishment, an eye for an eye or, that punishment should fit the crime equally between law and justice.

Nevertheless, the prayer as a whole tells us a lot about the nature of the approach and attitude of Orchester III's position as Head and Administrator of Affairs in the Homestead and Village. Upon finishing his morning prayer, Orchester III retires to meditate, until after breakfast, for he had a lot on his mind.

The reason these problematical events have such an effect on Orchester III is one of the things we want our investigation to highlight. It is Orchester III, as father, that Choose the Destiny for the Family homestead, and it is his responsibility to guide the Family in fulfilling that Destiny by administrating its affairs. Something has gone very wrong.

This has a negative effect. Not only the Destiny of the Family, but the Destinies of the Age-groups, Generations, Clans, and especially the Destiny Chosen by the 8 Ancient Ancestors (Wealth). For Orchester III knows that if the logic-line of Destiny Fulfillment is not repaired, the whole Society of the Clan will be destroyed.

This called for serious meditation; for the Morning Prayer only addressed the spiritual side of the situation. Although the Government has a spiritual constitution, its main function is to deal with social and economic issues. He knew that the problems still had to be dealt with on a legal, political, and social level by the Government.

This is what we mean when we say that Orchester III, as the oldest son, husband, head of a homestead, senior Elder of the village, and village group, must get, and keep himself together at all times.

This means, being as the problems he mentioned in prayer effect the well being, not only of the homestead, but also the well being of the Family village and Clan village group.

And being the Oldest Son of the Family village and Clan village group, according to Ancestor law of government, it is Orchester III who must convene a court of inquire and conclusion to look into the matter. Which is the operating system of political government, or to say, it is a cause for the government to assemble and act.

Although it is somewhat misleading to call the Igbo government a court, it is better to say that it works like a court of law. However, it also has legislative powers and can create laws, as well as enforce justice related to those laws along with traditional laws, while at the same time, being democratic by nature.

Therefore, although Orchester III is the most honored and respected man in the village and village group, he has no more political and legal power than anybody else, even the people who are the source of the problems.

Nevertheless, it is the working of a government based on Truth, Trust, Justice and Righteousness, that assures freedom and equality in Igbo society. So when Orchester III convenes court, the matter is really out of his hands, although he is part of Government.

To demonstrate government in action, we will select one of the serious crimes mentioned in Orchester III's prayer, Adultery. This case involves Ben's village members.

It seems that at a given festival, one of Orchester III's sons and the young wife of one of his Uncles of the same village got drunk and did or did not commit adultery. Nobody knows for sure.

If it is true, this was not only a crime against the Uncle and the village family, but also against Orchester III and his Family homestead. Not to mention, it is a crime against the Ancestors and ALA.

The case is also a good chance to demonstrate Rachel and the Oldest Daughter's role in government. As we mentioned, Adultery, especially when it happened between extended family members, is very serious indeed.

These type of situations caused feelings to run so high that the family village itself could be destroyed. Therefore, there is a special relationship and responsibilities between the Oldest Son and Daughter and their family. Likewise, there is a special relationship and responsibility between the Fathers, Brothers, and Sons, and their Sisters and Daughters.

Although Sisters and Daughters grow up and do not live in their village of birth, the village belongs to them in the same sense that the family unit belongs to the Oldest Son and Daughter. In fact, the sisters and daughters have some authority over the wives of their brothers of the village. Thus is Rachel's position in Ben's village government.

Even before Orchester III returned from his trading trip, there was a question that adultery had happened. The sisters and daughters, lead by Rachel, returned to their home village from the villages of their husbands to investigate the situation in detail. And it was Rachel that fills in the details to Orchester III.

To get back to the case, it is Orchester III's responsibility to assemble the government. So after breakfast, he sent his Oldest Son, Steve, with a message to all of the Head of Homesteads in the village, and all concerned, to assemble at a given time in front of his homestead.

At the appointed time and place, all of the Head of Homesteads called the Elders of the Village, and assembled and laid their Ofo shrine in a line between the shrines and doorway of the homestead. They stood to one side of the line of Ofo.

The defendants (the son and uncle's wife), their witness, and the prosecutor (the uncle) and his witness, along with the spectators standing behind them, stood on the other side of the line of Ofo. Rachel, and the Elder sisters and daughters of the village, stood near the shrines to the Gods.

Finally, behind the male Elders, stood Steve (Orchester III's oldest son) and his Age group of oldest sons of each homestead in the village, who are the policemen of the government, and maintain order during the proceedings.

Meanwhile, Orchester III has gathered a white rooster, kola nuts, alligator pepper, and palm wine, which he is to use in one of the two rituals to open the government for business.

He breaks the kola nuts into as many pieces as there are Ofo shrines on the ground, and kills the rooster. And according to seniority, he presents a bit of kola nut, pepper, some wine, and a few drops of blood from the sacrificed rooster to each of the Ofo, as he says the following prayer to each:

"Ancestors, come drink, eat kola nut, pepper and chicken.
We are told that your law has been broken.
And if a man or woman who did this and denies,
Do kill him/her off.
May his goats not increase;
And may he not be reincarnated,
Let him miss his way.
Our ancestors do hear.
Allow not a liar to escape,
Nor an evil doer,
To live in the land you gave to us.
Amen!"

When he finished, Rachel and the sisters and daughters presented the female Ancestor shrine pots. Those of Julia and Judy, and placed one on each end of the Ofo line.

Meanwhile, Rachel had gathered holy water, kola nuts, and a white hen. And before each Ancestress shrine, she proceeded to drop a few drops of holy water from a Umune leaf, a bit of kola nut, and some blood from the sacrificed hen into each pot, as she chanted the following prayer:

"We acknowledge that what one does in childhood,
Kill him in old age.
What the hen does during the dry season;
Kills it during the rainy season.
It is he who carried the fruit of Spirit
That looks behind.
The time a thing is cut.
Is not the time it dries up.
The opening underneath the she-goat
Is for young one to pass easily.
May the guilty repent,
Live and let live.
Help the willing to make peace,
This is reality within which we are,
Preserve men and preserve women.
Let human being please be human,
The person addressed,
Let him listen!
The one rushing always met regret,
But we wish to go gradually
To meet better days ahead.
Amen!"

After Rachel finished her prayer, the government is then open for business, and Orchester III begins the business of the day with a summation of the nature of the legal and spiritual problems involved.

"We have a grave situation before us today, it is grave if this deed has been done, and it is grave if someone is being falsely accused. Either way, the peace and order of the family's unity is damaged, or at the same time, the laws of ALA and our Ancestors have been broken.

Also, there is now tension between two generations of the extended family; the Son's and Uncle's generation. Did not the age groups of two generations choose a collective destiny before CHINEKE? Was not that destiny to move the community destiny forward? Does not a community's destiny depend on the generations working in harmony?

This still doesn't cover the whole situation. As if that is not bad enough, the Son is from Julie's section of the village family, and the Uncle is from Judy's section. Each section stands with its own and is angry with each other, our family is on the verge of attacking itself! Uncle! Son! What do you have to say for yourself?"

We won't get into the next stage of the trial, details of the debate between the Son, Wife, Uncle, and Witnesses; we will only point out the major elements of the government at work. The Son and Wife are the Defendants, the Elders of the village are the judges, and all of the other members of the village are the jury.

Rachel and the Daughters observe to see that Justice prevails for the village itself. The Wives of the village are also Observers to see that Justice prevails for the Wife on trial.

Anyway from the trial we presented, we can see why a charge of adultery is so serious, and at the same time, we can see how the extended Family court is constituted and governs itself.

We are going to say, the majority of the community finds the Son guilty. This brings the other elements of government into play.

For instance, the Son would again be put on trial, but this time, before the court of his Age-group. And the Daughters would then bring the guilty wife before their court, where she must stand trial by women.

The Wives of a village also have a court, and they would be Observers in the Daughter's court to see that justice is done.

If the wives agree with the verdict, they also would hold a Wives Court and put the wife on trial; however, if they do not agree with the verdict, all of the wives would go on strike by returning to their home villages, and not return until justice prevails.

On the other hand, if the Son and Wife are found innocent, the Uncle is automatically guilty of falsely accusing the Son and Wife of adultery, he would be put on trial by the Elders Court, and the punishment would be decided.

His punishment would be the same as the Son and wife would have gotten if they were found guilty. Injustice is a crime against IGWE, Who stands for Justice, Truth, Trust, and Righteousness; Although the crime itself came from a law of ALA.

Now we should take special note that there are four elements involved in Government, we will call mini-governments. The court of the Ofo Elders, the court of the Umune female Elders, the court of the Age-groups, and the court of the Wives of the village.

This means that everybody in the community has their own mini-government who can work on their own or, when working together, form the Government of the Society of the village. We can see by the constitution of the Government that it is in a good position to assure Social Equality and Personal Freedom in all of Society.

For example, let's look at the function of the Government from another angle. When we look closely at the whole situation, we see that everybody involved in the Government is kin to each other, by blood or marriage. This makes it a Family policing itself. For your family to convict you of a crime, the evidence has to be overwhelming.

However, the Ofo Elders of the village are the key to the success of the government. It makes no difference if the Son and Wife were found innocent or guilty; the Ofo Elders job is the same.

The rules of law and punishment come down from ALA, IGWE, and the Ancestors. However it is the Elders responsibility to repair the damage done to the family and family village by the trial itself, and no matter which way it goes, there would be hurt feelings, and hurt feelings are obstacles to harmony in Society, which must be maintained at all times.

This is where the Elders must use all of their knowledge about their Society. For all social crimes are based on one principle, somebody did not relate to another as equal. If the Son and Wife are found guilty, the bottom line is, they are guilty of not relating to the Uncle as equals. And the Society must have social equality to fulfill its destiny.

This is what is on the Elder's minds when they retire to consider the verdict. And, whatever they come up with, will heal and re-unite the Family along the lines of Destiny Fulfillment is the verdict they will hand down as a statement to the village at large.

Thus is the function of the Elders in the Government. The four mini-governments deal with punishment in their courts in most cases.

This gives us an idea of how government works in a homestead and family village. It doesn't matter if it is a criminal case, or a case of making new social laws, the same process and 4 mini-governments are involved. But what about the Governmental legal and social relations between the Family villages in a Clan village group?

If Steve, Orchester III's oldest Son is accused of a crime in another village in the group, things can get complicated.

In this case, Steve would be put on trial in the other village, but only if the Elders, including Orchester III, are present as observers.

If Orchester III does not think justice is done, he could call for a meeting between the Ofo Elders of his village, and the Ofo Elders of the other village. The Elders from the other three villages, as observers would oversee the negotiation between the two village governments until it is worked out.

If they can't come to some kind of settlement of the matter, there would be a fight between the two villages, and it gets settled that way. However, this type of fighting is not a full war, because ALA's biggest law concerning mankind's social relations is, thou shall not spill Igbo blood under any circumstances.

So even when fighting, there is not very much, if any killing done. Thus, are the relationships between Clan village groups, and how conflict is resolved in that situation. Thus is the constitution of a

Clan's Government. This leaves the question of how problems are solved between clan groups.

Each Clan group is thought of as equal to every other Clan group. In other words, each Clan group lives their lives the way that pleases them, and believes every other Clan group has the same rights. Thus is the spiritual bond that holds the nation together.

On the other hand, on the social side, the Clan village groups have in-law-family relationships with each other.

Recall, the men in one group cannot marry the women in their village group, they are blood kin. Therefore, the men's wives come from other Clan village groups, which makes the Clan village groups have in-law family relationship that also bonds the nation together.

This means that the constitution of the Igbo nation as a whole is made up of independent Clan village groups that have a spiritual relationship with each other that is also based on Social Equality and Personal Freedom.

This gives us some idea of how their Government handles conflicts within a homestead, village, and clan village town. Along with an idea of how the nation is bonded together. We will deal with how clan towns solve conflicts between each other in detail later.

Now we will turn our investigative attention to what Grandpa thinks is the more interesting aspect of the Igbo; their economic system.

Market Place, Trade, and Wealth

Grandpa can see that my Fellow Detectives are beginning to wonder, and rightly so, since the whole of the Igbo nation has a Chosen Destiny to be Wealthy. What does social equality and personal freedom have to do with the National Chosen Destiny? What are the connections?

You saw that the Original 8 Ancestors made it very clear to the Gods and Goddesses, that the Igbo people wanted to trade and make money; and their 7 Articles of Faith is a contract to that effect.

Well, that is an Investigator's job, making connections that lead to conclusions, and demonstrate that the conclusions are true. This is logic, and logic is what you are using when you are thinking.

So logic is the process of thinking, and this means that thinking is the logic line of Destiny fulfillment, i.e., African Traditional Intelligence. So with that in mind, let's see what we will have to do to make this connection between the Igbo destiny and Wealth.

We must be very careful. Sometimes finding the right question is as complicated as finding the right answer, for example, why do the Igbo want to make money?

The first answer we think of is to get rich. But the Igbo would think, to become wealthy. Then we automatically think that being rich and being wealthy are the same thing, and the Igbo think that they are different. The Igbo answer is that wealth is accumulated high values. For instance, money is a high value. There are also other high values like, family, land, food, friendship, respect, justice, etc, etc., all of which a man must have to be wealthy; however, it is money that gives power to wealth.

So the right question is; What is the connection between social equality and personal freedom, and making money and wealth? This is the question and answer we must demonstrate in our investigation.

On the other hand, if we take a close look at how the Igbo define a wealthy man, this throws a completely different light on why the Igbo want to make money. We can reach a conclusion, that making money is only part of a ritual to become Divine. Recall, CHINEKE is Wealthy. We will find that the Igbo's Chosen Destiny is for everybody in the whole nation that is working to be become wealthy; and becoming wealthy is becoming Divine, like CHINEKE.

This means that we will next have to show that the belief and practice of social equality and personal freedom are the approach and attitude that becomes a process of fulfilling their chosen destiny of making money and becoming wealthy.

To show why, relative to other nations like the Yoruba, in the Igbo area and maybe on all of West Africa, the Igbo are the best businessmen and women.

This is what trade is about, and where the market place fits into the picture. Money is made in the Market Place through Trade. The most interesting thing about that is, the Igbo play the trade game different from any body in West Africa.

For example, we will also have to show that, since the Igbo are not warriors by nature, and don't have an organized national army like the very warlike Yoruba, and, since jealousy and greed had turned the world upside down, and wars were a everyday affair all around them, they could not only grow rich, but also they could not capture new territory without warfare.

So, GrandKids, the right question always brings a family of interesting little questions along with it. We must make these small connections and answers, to form a logical line into a conclusion.

That is the answer to our big questions, what is the relationship between Social Equality, Personal Freedom, Making Money, and Wealth in Igbo Society? To make these connections is where our understanding of African Traditional Logic comes into the picture again.

To begin with, we need some solid information about the economic layout of the Igbo Nation as a back ground to the Igbo's thoughts and practices that go into their economic system.

Each Clan village group functions like a Town, or we should say, a Town-State, because of its independent government. Each Town has a Marketplace which is its Religious, Government, Social, and Business Center. This is where the tactics of War take place, not with an army of Warriors, but an army of Businessmen.

Economic Background

If we recall, the Igbo nation covers some 15,000 square miles, and in the time period we are most concerned with, from about 1500 to 1619, their population would have been around 2,000,000 people. The biggest social and political unit in the whole of the nation is the extended family village group, and the Clan Town. Just for an example, we will say that each Town population averages about 3,000 people.

If we divide the Town population of 3,000 into the total nation's population of 2,000,000, we come up with 666 Clan Towns throughout the nation. The point being is that there are 666 Market Places.

Finally, to fill out the picture, the Igbo, like most Africans, also have a calendar for measuring time; however, the Igbo have an 8-day week symbolizing the Original 8 Ancient Ancestors; four male days and four female days. However, we are only concerned with how the 8-day week regulates the marketplace.

The national marketplace is divided into a little over 83 market districts, and each district operates on an 8-day cycle. A district is 8 Clan Towns that are relatively close to each other.

For example, in each district, one market would be open for business on the first day of the week, another on the second day, still another on the third day. This would continue until each Town in the 8 Town market districts have a market day; then the cycle repeats itself.

Everybody in a district doesn't go to market every day, but everybody does go to a market at least 4 days, out of a 8 day week, in his or her own district, or some other districts.

So we can say that the Igbo spend half of his or her time with their farms and other work, and the other half is spent in the market. Nevertheless, everybody in a town goes to the market on their town's market day.

Now let us review what we have. There are 666 Town market places in the Igbo nation. This means that there are about 84 marketing districts, and on any given day of the week (given the 8-day cycle), there are 84 markets open and doing business.

This also means that the 84 districts, divided into the total population of 2,000,000 in the nation, have a population of near 24,000 people per district.

Finally, this means that there is a web of markets throughout the nation with money flowing within each marketing district, as well as flowing between districts every day of the week.

Economic Constitution

All markets are like a big flea-market in the United States, you can buy just about anything you need, food, clothes, tools, etc, etc. However, within a given 8 market district, each market will also specialize in one given product.

For example, a town near a river where there are many fish will specialize in dried-fish which is very popular. On the other hand, a Town where there are a number of blacksmiths will specialize in farming tools. Each of the Town Markets in the 8 market districts will have something the other doesn't have, and need. This is a free market economy, energized by capital investments.

This means that in order for this market system to work, there needs to be a means to raise capital to invest; like a banking system. This is taken care of by what the Igbo call the Money Pot between eight friends, based on an 8-week, or 8 day Cycle.

For example, these 8 friends meet on a regular basis, like once a week, and each one puts a given amount of money in a pot, let's say 1,000 cowries. This means that each week there is 8,000 cowries in the pot. Then, each week one friend, in his turn in a 8 week cycle, takes the 8,000 to invest in a trading trip.

Now, we will say that this friend doubled his money to 16,000 cowries. He has 8,000 cowries to pay his 1,000 cowries into the money pot for the next 8 weeks until it is his turn to take the money from the pot; and he has 8,000 cowries to save.

On the other hand, if a man does not want to invest when his turn comes around, he simply returns the 8,000 cowries over the next 8 weeks. The same is the case if the money pot is based on a 8 day cycle, which is popular with women, where the 8 week cycle is a favorite with men.

Now, a man or woman can be a part of as many money pots as he can afford, and can arrange for his turn to fall on the same week for each pot. For instance, if our same friend belongs to 10 such groups, and he collects 8,000 cowries from each, he will have 80,000 cowries to invest in a long range trading trip, even in non-Igbo territory. This means that the Money Pot between friends is the Igbo's Investment Bank.

Now if we look at the Igbo's marketing organization and banking system, and add to that CHINEKE's Law that relationships are based on the trading of values, and IGWE Law that the Path-way is Negotiation (see the 7th Article of Faith), we can see that the Igbo based his ability to make a profit through negotiation. This is where the Igbo's personal creativity comes into action, women and men.

This means that the Igbo have a Free-Market Economy where price is based on negotiation. Thus, this means that the Igbo's ultimate goal is to become a Master Artist in Negotiation, and deal with the Market Money Flow and Make a Profit.

We can say, from an economical point of view, the Igbo see the world as a market place, and trade, as the game of life. They believe that they are fully qualified to make the best deal, and make the most profit in any exchange. This makes the Igbo great traders and bargainers, and a unique kind of spiritual economic warrior.

There is no doubt what so ever in an Igbo's mind that he can beat anybody at their own game. Even when playing by the other person's rules, con the conman so to speak, or fight a person with their own beliefs, a man's man. And this is how the Igbo play the War Game.

For example, we will return to our old friend Orchester III, and the long distance trading trip where he visited a number of 8 market districts he took just before the trial.

First, he would collect his money from as many money pot groups as he belonged to. Then we will say that he lived in a Clan village group Town that specialized in blacksmith shops and farming tools. Orchester III negotiated a price with a blacksmith shop for a number of farming tools. He then goes on a trading trip with two or three of his sons.

First they take the farm tools to a Clan Town that specializes in farm food on their market day. Orchester III will sell the farm tools and his profit depends on his negotiation skills. We know that Orchester III is a Master Trader and his profit margin is high, for we said he was very successful. But, before he leaves that Town, he takes part of his profit and negotiates a low price for, say yams.

Next, Orchester III takes the yams to a Town that specializes in salt, which is always in high demand in Igbo land, where he again negotiates a high price for his potatoes, and a low price for some salt.

He continues this process through his, and or other market districts. When he returns home he has lots of money made from profits of his creative negotiation skills. Plus he brings back something to sell on his town's market day.

On the other hand, within local Town markets, there is a lot of money changing hands between local people, especially the local women, who are even better traders than the men. But any way we look at it, the Igbo make money through Trade and negotiating a profit in the Market place.

We should take special note of how negotiation works as a path-way to making money. Also notice how this approach fits in with the Igbo's religious beliefs. We can see that negotiation is the foundation of Igbo thoughts and actions in life. He depends on it to solve his problems, and depends on it for one of his biggest pleasures in life, negotiation for the sake of negotiation, the Igbo love debating about anything.

In this sense, negotiation is really one on one competition, where both sides can make a profit. For example in trading, the buyer makes a profit because he thinks he got a bargain, and the seller, because he made a return on his investment.

This gives us an idea of long distant trading in the national market place, and how it functions.

Now we will turn our investigative attention to the dynamics of a market place on market day, from the point of view of Orchester III and the local people of his town.

While the men are concerned mostly with long distance trading, women totally dominate the local trade in most goods. Even when local men have certain things to be sold in their market, they want their wives or sisters to do the selling.

So we can see that the dynamics of local market's money flow is in the hands of the women in the town. However, there are exceptions, especially where certain goods are concerned.

Market Day Dynamics

On the one hand, and other than on market day, the market place is used for community rituals to the Gods and Goddesses, and especially rituals to the combined Ancestors of the Clan, also, as the play ground for the older childhood children for the combined villages.

In other words, the marketplace is where all Clan spiritual and social activities take place; on other than market day, no trading takes place. And if we recall in the Igbo's creation story, we can see that the Market Place is a social and economic Sacred-Space.

On the other hand, a clan town's market day is a town festival, where old out-of-town friends meet and have a visit, and where new friendships are born. It is a news center, and a gossiping paradise. There is dancing, where younger boys and girls from different clan groups meet, and older boys and girls talk about getting married. Nevertheless, the major purpose of market day is making money.

As far as we are concerned, market day is where, and when the Town Government meets to take care of Town business, especially business with other towns, and see to it that trading runs smoothly in the Market place.

So we can say that market day is when the entire Town's Society is on display. This means that every market day, a town turns its market place into a big social festival event of making money.

In this, and all situations, we should remember that the Market Place itself belongs to the Women of the Town's Society, and it is the Men of Society that Manage the Affairs of Society.

So we will make our investigation through Orchester III and his role as a leading Elder of Society and a member of the Town's Government when it is managing the affairs of market day. And this will give us a picture of how the Game is played out in the Marketplace.

Economic Government

To deal with this subject, we should recall, Orchester III is the Senior Leading Elder in Ben Jr.'s village, and has Ben Sr.'s Ofo shrine. On the other hand, the Oldest Sons Senior Leading Elder of the other four villages that make up the Town have the Ofo shrines of George, Johnny, Sonny, and Jessie. So there are 5 Ofo senior Leading Elders that form the heart of the Town's economic government.

Then there are the leading Elders that are Family Heads in Ben Jr.'s village who, although they do not have quite as high a status as Orchester III, are equal in authority, and are senior Ofo Holders in their own right. In addition, they go to make up Ben Sr.'s village government. The other 4 village governments are formed on the same pattern, and means that the Town's government is those 5 village governments functioning as a single government.

For example, Orchester III and three of his Town's leading Elders meet with four of the leading Elders of each of the other 4 village governments.

Thus we have a 20-man government with 5 leading Ofo Elders as senior negotiators, and 15 leading Elders as Councilors. Together, they are going to manage the affairs of Market Day, along with their own Oldest Sons as police officers.

This is what we call a Representative Government. Even though the Town's leading Elders can make laws for the whole Society. Each Senior Elder must later bring the law before his village government, and the village people for approval; before any village will follow any law made by the Town government. But as far as market day peace and harmony is concerned, the Town Government has the power to punish any village member.

This is because the Town government is motivated by the fact that all of the Towns in the nation are in high competition over who has the most successful and peaceful market day. And by that standard, reach the conclusion to which Town has the most successful Society; so the whole Town Society's pride is involved with their market day success, peace and harmony.

As we mentioned in the trial, Igbo Society is made up of the Elder group, the Oldest Sons age group, Oldest Daughters age group, and the Village Wives group, and each group is really governing themselves as mini-governments. This means that the Town's government not only has Checks and Balances, but is actually in competition with itself.

For example, the Elders from one village are in competition with the Elders of the other villages, and this is the case with the Oldest Sons, Oldest Daughters, and Oldest Wives. Plus, all of the groups are in competition with their Ancestor counter groups.

Even the Town market is in competition with itself in making money. For instance, each village in the Town sets up their market goods near where their village road enters the Town's market place. And they too are in competition with each other in selling their goods.

All of this competition is focused on one purpose, what the Igbo call, "Lifting the Town toward wealth," which is their Chosen Destiny. This is the driving force in Town government as well as the Society as a whole, and the basis of their Town Pride. The Igbo believe in Progress.

The market place itself is like a big park with lots of trees to give shade from the hot sun. There are four special big trees, some distance from each other which are the Elder's Tree, the Oldest Son's Tree, the Oldest Daughters Tree, and the village Wives Tree, called the 4 Government Trees of the Market Place.

Note that the Government Trees surround a Shrine of the Trickster God, EKWENSU. The people under these 4 Trees symbolize the Igbo Clan Town Government, and EKWENSU Shrine symbolizes the Laws of Negotiation and Trade. And each village belonging to that Clan has a space surrounding the 4 Government trees where they do business.

We will now turn our investigative attention to the dynamics of a Market Place on Market Day, from the point of view of the local people of Orchester III's Clan Town. This will give us a picture of how "The Government and Money Game is Played."

Spirit of the Market Place

When we returned to Orchester III early on Marketing Day, the Town Government is on his mind. Today his morning ritual is focused on his Ofo, Ikenga, and Ancestor shrines, and his morning prayer is focused on Business.

"Ancestors managing the affairs of a market in our Society that is made up of independent minded unpredictable people can be an interesting job, where mis-understandings between buyers and sellers can lead to hard-feelings, and even fights.

Let's not mention all of the thieves, tricksters (conmen), and people that just love trouble more than they love themselves. They have been a problem since ancient times. I know that Ancestor Elders want peace and harmony among their children as much as the living Elders. So I know that you will give your help without asking, Amen!"

After his Morning Prayer and breakfast, but before he goes to the market place, Orchester III performs a special ritual before his Chi shrine. Followed by a ritual in his First Wife's kitchen. (However, these rituals are related to a big announcement he will make in the market place at the end of market day which we will deal with later).

About 9 a.m., Orchester III and his oldest grandson, the oldest son of Steve, we will call Lil Ben, along with three others above puberty age grandsons, carry their Ofo shrine (sticks), with lots of palm wine and kola nuts and leave for the Market Place. As would be the case with the 4 Senior Elders of the 4 other villages in the Clan Town.

The Grandsons of the Elders role is to carry their grandfather's things, help them in giving Hospitality, act as messengers, and especially, learn the art of Government. All were headed for the Elder's Government Tree.

They arrive well before the market opens for business at about noon. There is a lot of Town's business that needs to be taken care of before the market opens, and being as Orchester III is the holder of the most senior Ofo, he is the Official Host, and like all Africans, he believes in hospitality.

In fact, this is what IGWE showed the Most Ancient Original 8 Igbo Ancestors. So not only does hospitality have a ritual religious meaning, it is also good for business and part of their pride thing.

Once all of the Elders have gathered under the shade of their Tree and greeted each other, they settle down on their stools or mats and Orchester III begins the ritual of Host.

As the Host of the meeting, it is his privilege to perform the ritual of presenting Kola to his guest, the other Senior Elders. The kola nut meat inside is in four sections, and acts like a stimulant when chewed. This is a ritual performed in three operations, the presentation, the breaking, and the distribution of kola nuts, called Kola Hospitality.

Orchester III has his grandson, Lil Ben, select enough kola nuts so that each Elder has a section, which is then put into a bowl and passed around to the Senior Elders. They are divided into sections according to the seniority of their village in the village group. As one Elder receives the bowl, and before he passes it to the next, he tells a proverb, for examples,

"You do not scold a leopard." (You do not talk to a strong man carelessly, or you will be very sorry that you did).

"If an ear refuses to listen, it will be cut off along with the head." (If a person fails to listen and take in vital information, it endangers the person's life and security).

"When the eye starts crying, the nose also cries." (A problem for one member of a family is also grief for all of the other members of the family).

"Muddy water always becomes clear again, starting from the edges." (To solve a problem one must surround it).

"A person who eats with evil should use a long spoon." (Or the evil will consume you).

This continues until all of the Senior Elders blessed the Kola nuts, and then the bowl is passed back to Orchester III.

This is followed by a prayer by the eldest man present regardless of his Ofo status, or, if he is a Oldest Son, one of the men from one of the other villages. This ends the presentation ritual.

Next, Orchester III breaks the Kola nuts with a prayer calling on the Great Creator, the Gods and Goddesses, and the Ancestors to eat a Kola nut, asking for good health, wealth to nourish it, progress for all, and peace to the Town. Lil Ben then divides the meat of the nut into sections and returns them to the bowl. This is called the breaking ritual.

The distribution of the kola sections by Lil Ben also follows a ritual pattern. Orchester III gets the first share, which he eats to demonstrate that it is wholesome and free from poison. The senior leading Elders from the other villages that take their share, then each senior from Orchester III's village takes their share, all according to seniority. As each Elder eats his share, he dips it into a rich gravy of alligator pepper in a wooden bowl also carried by Lil Ben.

Once this part of the ritual is complete, the same process follows with a big bowl of palm-wine. Orchester III takes the first drink, and Lil Ben passes it according to seniority to all of the Elders, who take a drink. This is called the Distribution ritual, and ends the ritual of Hospitality.

The designed-purpose of the ritual is not only to create harmony between the Elders to enable them to function as a union, but also, to invoke the spirit of truth, justice, trust, and righteousness of Ofo to posses the meeting. The Town Government is now constituted, and opened for Clan Town business.

The Elders begin by talking over the affairs of the relationships between the five villages, and if there are any problems causing disharmony in the town, they will discuss a means of restoring unity.

Recall, it is the unity of the 5 villages that make a Clan village group into a Clan Town. Therefore, unity is important to the very existence of a Town Government, and its ability to advance the town toward being successful on all levels, the Igbo call "Lifting the Town."

However, the Elders are mostly in the role of a Supreme Court, reviewing the events since the last meeting. It is the village government that calls on the village governments to take corrective action on any of its members that may be causing problems.

If the village government fails to act, and the problems continue, the only course open to the Town Government is to kick the entire offending village out of the union.

Therefore, the social function of town government Elders in a case of village group relationships problems, is not so much to find out which village is right or wrong, but to restore harmony by the method of negotiating a compromise. Harmony is one of the qualities that Lifts a Town to Success.

Meanwhile, the Oldest Sons of the Elders, led by Steve and their age group, are meeting under the Oldest Son's government Tree. They too, are discussing the affairs of the Town. They are concerned with the market place and enforcing harmony from a physical point of view.

For example, reminding themselves that as the Oldest Sons, their responsibilities are to look out for thieves and con-men, and especially look for problems that could lead to a fight, and stop it before it takes place.

But just as important, the Oldest Sons are to show hospitality to all the guest traders and visitors, and generally see to it that everybody enjoys themselves and have a good time. This too, plays a role in lifting the Town to Success.

Whereas, under their Government Tree, hosted by Rachel, the Oldest Daughters are also concerned with the town's affairs, but they are concerned about the women's social conduct in the marketplace in general.

They are fully aware that women are the dominant force in market trade and money flow. But how the women of the town act socially, can make or break a market day success economically and socially. This is where the Daughters do their police work, as well as enhance hospitality. Positive Women's Social Conduct can really lift a town to Success.

While under the Government Tree of the Oldest Wives hosted by Orchester III's first wife, they too are concerned about the success of the Market Place on Market Day. For the most part, the wives are the saleswomen of the market, and are concerned with the harmony between selling and buying, which also lifts a town to Success.

Remember, the market place is a sacred space, and therefore, a place to put the Spirit of Town Society on display where it can shine in the brightness of its Success. From this angle, the four Governments are the Priest and Priestess of the Spirit of the Town's Society. Thus is the nature of what is taking place in the market place before it opens for business to outsiders.

We can see that the full Town Government is four dimensional, and the role of its operating parts, including Elders, Oldest Sons, Oldest Daughters, and the Oldest Wives. We can also see how the internal affairs of the Town's Society are cared for. Especially how they are focused on lifting the Spirit of the Town's Society.

We investigators have to be careful and stay on track. We are only interested in the economic side of the Town Government and how it manages the internal and external affairs in the Art of Making Money.

This is the exclusive job of the Elders, with the Senior Elders being the Spokesmen, and this means, now we will turn our full attention on the activities under the Elder Government's Tree, where the Elders are focused on the mechanics of making money and the 8-market districts.

Money is one of the path-ways to Wealth, and Wealth is the path-way to lifting the Town Society to its Chosen Destiny.

The Town Governments taking care of internal affairs begin about 9 a.m. Meanwhile, the market area begins to fill with people. Traders are setting up their trading space. Children begin to appear and play. Friends meet and have lunch, and lots of general socializing takes place.

More important, as far as the direction we will take our investigation is concerned, market day is when out of town government visits to take care of inter-town business. At about noon, the Elders settle down to the Money Business of the 8 market districts.

Economic Situation

The Elders, through their Clan Town Government, make the decisions on which Clan Towns they want in their marketing district through negotiating with other Clan Town Governments. If there is not the right combination, along with peaceful relations with the other Towns in the district, there will not be much money flowing into town on market day.

This is where the Igbo politics come into the picture; making and enforcing contracts with others that come to their market day. When people from out-of-town come to market, they bring out-of-town money with them, which is left in the pockets of the Town Market Traders. Who, for the most part are the Women of the Town.

So, as more and more people come into town, among them are a number of Elders, Oldest Sons, Oldest Daughters, and Oldest Wives from other Town Governments. And they head right for their counter-part's Government Tree, where they are shown hospitality, and the Politics begin.

Politics bring jealousy and greed into the picture. This is where negotiations are so very important, because when it comes to money matters, the Igbo people are very serious, and the eight Market Districts are a Big Money Matter.

To see the political side of Town Government, we must take a deeper look at the dynamics of the 8 marketing districts. Each town has seven trading partners, but the eight towns do not necessarily all trade with each other. For example, Orchester III's Town may have two trading partners that do not trade with each other.

Plus, trading partners have disagreements, and break their contract. This means that a Town's 8 market district is ever changing for one reason or another. But a District is always locked into the 8 day week cycle. The point being, when trading partners break up, the Town starts negotiating with another town that has the same marketing day as the one it broke with in order to continue its 8-market district.

However, like we mentioned, most of the time it is jealousy and greed that breaks up trading partners. So to understand Igbo politics even better, we will bring up a case of this sort before Orchester III and his Town Government.

We will set up the Situation like this, Orchester III's town has a trading partner, Moe Clan Town, and lots of Moe's Town people come to his town's market day. Plus, Moe's Town people are friendly and easy to get along with, and Orchester III's town has 6 other such trading partners in its district.

This means that Orchester III's town would have the largest and economic successful market in its district. A well balanced 8 market district is hard to come by, and this is the prime path-way for jealousy and greed to come into the picture.

There will be Towns that will want to take one or more of Orchester III's Town trading partners. One such Town we will call Eddie Clan Town, who is not in Orchester III's district, and has made a move to break up the relationship between Orchester III's Town and Moe's Town.

So the main players in the political game are Orchester III's Town, Moe's Town, and Eddie's Town, featuring Ontrack Orchester III, Slow Moe, and Slick Eddie, who are the senior leading Elder's in each of the three Town's Government.

Orchester III is what is called an up-right-man. He plays the political game just the way the Ancestors designed it to work. He stands on truth, justice, trust, and righteousness. And this is what has led his Town to being the most successful and respected town in the area in a group of 8 marketing Districts of 8 markets, called an Extended market District.

Slow Moe is a man you think of as slow, but sure. Always peaceful and friendly, and kind of gets things done in his own way. His economic understanding is just as sharp as Orchester III's, and his town is almost as rich.

Slick Eddie is a man you always have to keep an eye on. Although his Town does not have near the status as even Moe Town, he is ambitious and very tricky, and not above breaking the rules of man or God. He is trying to build what Orchester III already has, and he is very serious.

Although the Elders deal with the problem from an economic point of view, there are also social implications. For instance, when two towns are old and good trading partners, they also have a habit of marrying each others sisters and daughters.

Therefore, this also makes the problem a concern to the Oldest Son and Oldest Daughter in Government. For example, Rachel is married to Slow Moe, and Orchester III's first wife is Slow Moe's Sister; plus one of Orchester III's sons is married to a woman from Moe's town. On the other hand, there is also inter-marrying between Orchester III's town and Eddie's town.

So we can see that things get very interesting when these three men meet under the Elder's Tree. Ontrack Orchester III and Slow Moe are there to repair the harmony between their towns, and Slick Eddie is there to try to take advantage of a problem that he created in the first place. This problem is one of the worst things that could happen in Orchester III's 8 market trading districts.

Without Ontrack Orchester III and Slow Moe knowing anything about it, Slick Eddie had instigated a big problem for them through intrigue, witchcraft, and any other thing he could think of. It seems that a big fight broke out between a group of people from Orchester III's town while they were shopping in Moe town, and the Moe town people drove Orchester III's people from their marketplace.

Nobody has any idea of how the fight really got started except Slick Eddie, Mr. Jealousy and Greed himself. This is the major problem for the day for Orchester III and his town government.

Meanwhile, there are a number of Elders from other Town governments that have a stake in the outcome of the meeting between Orchester III and Moe.

So when all of the Elders are present, and hospitality has been shown to the out of town guest, the Elders get to the heart of the matter, and Orchester III presents the problem in short and sweet terms.

"It is a big disgrace for one town to drive people from their market place. It is a bigger disgrace for people to start a riot in their Host's market place. Who is the blame here? This is a direct violation of the laws of CHINEKE, IGWE, ALA, not to mention our Ancestors. Just as important, it is against the laws of making money, and therefore a sin against Wealth and Destiny!"

According to inter-town government operations, just being present allows any of the Elders, regardless of what town they are from, to enter the discussions of any problem Orchester III's government is dealing with, including Slick Eddie. And this opens the door for all kinds of political games to be played.

Slick Eddie wants to form an alliance with Slow Moe to blame Ontrack Orchester III, and in doing so, win Moe town as a trading partner. The reaction to this could cause Orchester III's trading district to fall apart.

Then, Slick Eddie has a chance of negotiating a winning combination of trading partners. His town can take Orchester III's Town place as the biggest and most successful market town.

Ontrack Orchester III and Slow Moe have more to lose than just the money flow between their towns, not only is their towns pride involved, this also hurts their economic future.

What upstanding town wants to do business with a town that causes big fights in market places? Slick Eddie has everything to win and nothing to lose if he is not found out. Either way if possible, Orchester III and Moe would like to negotiate a compromise to restore harmony, and they can only win what they already had.

This is a very explosive situation. The danger lies in Slow Moe knowing that his town did not start the fight, and Orchester III knowing that his people are innocent, so both are beginning to think the other is the blame.

On the other hand, if it becomes known that Slick Eddie is behind the whole thing. Orchester III and, or Moe could lay a heavy fine on Slick Eddie. If he doesn't pay, they can send the Oldest Sons to collect, and naturally there would be fighting. It is a matter of Business and Pride.

So the stakes are high all around. Every Senior Elder in the 8 market districts has an interest in the outcome, along with a number of other Elders looking for opportunities.

We won't go into all of the details of the negotiating discussions and compromises made. But we can say, as the Elders made decisions, messengers were sent to the Oldest Sons, Daughters, and Wives who were having the same discussions with the Oldest Sons, Daughters, and Wives of Moe's town. Our point was to show the dynamics forces at work in the Market Place.

But to give it a happy ending, we can say Slick Eddie was found out and his Town was given a big fine which was to be divided between Orchester III and Moe's Towns. Like we said, it's a matter of Business.

Anyway at the end of the day, with things back in harmony and market day a big success, Orchester III makes a big announcement; he is going to take a Title. This electrified everybody in the Marketplace, especially the people of his clan town. Thus ends Igbo Government activities on Market Day.

Well GrandKids we have used African Traditional Logic to Drink a lot of information from the Igbo's Ancient Well. This means that if we have followed a logical line from Igbo Religious Beliefs to their Government, we should have a good idea of the answers to the questions about Society we started with.

We investigated the Igbo Government to show the Spiritual, Social, and Economic role it plays as a way of getting a picture of Igbo Society. Finally, we only have to extend our logic line to the answer the question, why is Making Money such a serious a matter in Igbo Society?

That answer should complete our understanding of the Igbo's definitions of Social Equality and Personal Freedom as the foundation of their Society, and how all of this relates to their Chosen Destiny of Wealth.

This means that we must focus our investigation in the direction of what Orchester III meant by, "I am going to Take a Title," and, especially why everybody in his Clan Town was so excited?

This leads us to the Igbo Original 8 Ancestors and the role of Titles in Igbo Society, especially the Ozo and Umada Titles. This will tell us what the Igbo want to accomplish in Playing the Money Game.

Society's Rituals of Wealth

The Ozo and Umada Titles are called the Titles of Oldest Sons and Oldest Daughters, in the sense that they must have the Title before any of their brothers and sisters can take a Title. Now the questions become, what are Titles? How do they fit into Society?

When the 8 people left the Holy Homestead, each had one value from IGWE and ALA which became their last names. For example, the men's last names were Truth, Justice, Trust, and Righteousness, symbolized by the Ofo shrine. The women had Determination, Fortitude, Peace, and Unity as last names. (For instance, we had George Justice and Kate Unity in our examples of how the eight people started Families).

Anyway, the eight people married each other and began the Original 4 Families, and each pair had sons and daughters. Their children inter-married, and so on to the fourth generation.

By this time, each male had the four male name-values, and the females had the four female name-values. They were the first generation of Igbo Society carrying the 8 values as their Soul which became the Soul of their Society. For this reason, the numbers 4 and 8 are sacred in the Igbo society Ancestor rituals.

The Taking of Titles, as the Igbo call it, is a series of rituals by which any man or woman can lift themselves to a point of spiritual purity of the mentioned values. This allows them to become spiritually possessed by the spirits of the 8 ancient values of their Ancient Ancestor's Society.

Still another way to think about it is, taking titles is a pathway along the ranks of Society spiritual values; which leads them to becoming Divine, or a Living Saint. Anyway we think of it, taking titles is a spiritual transformation, or lifting of the living individual spirit in Society's 8 Values of Truth, Trust, Justice, Righteousness, Peace, Unity, Fortitude, and Determination to a Purified Spiritual State.

In this process, the Spirit of Orchester III and Rachel's Clan are also lifted up. Thus is why the people in Orchester III's Clan Town were so excited. So the question becomes, what does making money have to do with spiritual possession of Society Values? This is related to the Re-distribution of Money and Lifting Society.

Grandpa knows that my GrandKids are wondering how I came to those conclusions. Where is the evidence? Your wondering is good; for those are the kinds of questions History Investigators must always ask themselves, where is the evidence? However, Grandpa's conclusions are only a guideline for what we are looking for; we still have to demonstrate a logic line of information before we can give any possible reality to my conclusions.

We will accomplish this by looking for evidence from a spiritual point of view in Orchester III and Rachel, and the ritual of taking the Ozo and Umada Titles; with special attention being paid to the way

Orchester III and Rachel's money is being redistributed throughout their Clan Society, and that will teach us a lot about Igbo Society.

Now for a definition: Taking titles is to become an owner of something, for example, like receiving a title to show our ownership of a car. To the Igbo, taking the title means the same, only they are talking about taking the title to Society Values. For instance, in the ritual where he received his Ikenga shrine, he was taking the title to the spirit of manhood, and the manhood spirit became his private property, in the sense that through the ritual, he was transformed from boyhood to manhood.

However in the Ozo ritual, he is being transformed from a regular man into a Living Saint. The same is the case with Umada rituals and Rachel, at the end of which, she too will become a Living Saint.

In reality, Orchester III and Rachel would not perform their ritual at the same time, even though we will present them together to see the relationship between the two.

Society's Values are in 4 groups symbolizing, and, created by, the 4 Ancient Ancestor Families. They are Religious Values, Personal Values, Family-Society Values, and Economic Values.

A point we should note at this time is that, the Igbo's Society Spirit is the Marriage between Igbo Male Society Spirit and Female Society Spirit, symbolizing the marriage between the Original 4 Women and 4 Men.

Before we get into the Ozo and Umada ritual activities related to the Spirit of Society, lets take a close look at Orchester III and Rachel's life as related to these 4 groups of Male and Female Society Values.

Orchester III and the Ozo Title

(1) Orchester III is about 60 years old, and he is in harmony with the Gods, Goddesses, and Ancestors of the Igbo religious beliefs, and regularly worships at their shrines.

(2) He is in harmony with his CHI (spirit-destiny) and his Ikenga (manhood and energy of life). He has identified his Destiny and fulfilled it for the most part (with the exception of becoming a Living Saint, which he is about to do).

(3) He has five Wives, many Children, and even more Grandchildren. His Homestead is full of his Manhood Energy of Life, from which he always shows Hospitality to his Guest.

(4) He has a powerful relationship with his Oldest Wife, Oldest Son and Oldest Daughter.

(5) He has taken the titles of horse and cow killer. This means that he sacrificed a horse at his father's funeral, and a cow at the funeral of his mother. This is the ultimate in funerals given to Parents by their Children.

6) He has also paid for all of the arrangements for his Wives and for his Sons, which is a father's responsibility and funerals and wedding are very expensive. And just as important, he is on very good terms with his In-law Families (the families of his wives).

(7) During his adult life, he has become very rich. Just to use a number, we will say that he has accumulated 100,000 Cowries (dollars). This means he has mastered the art of Negotiation and Trade. And the fire of competition, on a personal, age-group, family, and clan level has grown into a raging forest fire. For example, we saw that he worked very hard to improve the economic situation of his Clan Town.

(8) Orchester III also has a reputation in his town and marketing district as an Upright Man whose business relationships are always based on Social Equality and Personal Freedom. He is Mr. Truth, Justice, Trust, Righteousness himself.

Plus, when Orchester III decided to take the Ozo Title, this meant, from an economical view, he has decided to invest all of his money, including all he can borrow in his local society (town). He is expecting to make a profit on his money.

This means making money out of society, to invest in society, to make even more money out of society values. Which is the highest of Society economic values, and the one that Orchester III now is seeking.

These four groups of values are the highest and most respected values in the Igbo Male Society, and is a part of Orchester III's Spirit-Soul. His soul also has some values that are not so valuable to Society, or himself.

The Ozo Title, as a Purification ritual, is a process of washing away all Jealousy and Greed, and leaves the 4 groups of values in sole possession of Orchester III's spiritual self.

Ozo is a series of 16 rituals, we call ritual steps that serve two purposes, clean Orchester III's Soul of any Evil, and redistribute his money in and outside of Orchester III's Clan Town, especially his Family Village. All of which are to transform (lift) him up from being a man, to the spiritual level of a living Saint of Society.

At the same time, and just as important, economically and spiritually lifting Society itself. The key to understanding what each of the 16 Ozo rituals mean, we must keep our eyes on ritual sacrifices and money flow. In this way, we can get a picture of the very heart and soul of Society, and the role Social Equality and Personal Freedom plays.

Thus, this not only shows that Wealth is the Values of Society, but also what purpose the Ozo Title ritual serves. Now with these 4 groups of Male Society Values in mind, lets follow Orchester III through the process of taking the Ozo Title, which should also give us some insight into why making money is so important in Igbo Society.

To set up the background, and just to keep an even number to deal with, we will say that there are already 50 Ozo Title men in Orchester III's town, more than any other clan town in his area. Divided between the 5 villages, 10 each. These 50 Ozo men form the organization that is to confer the Title.

Recall the spiritual rituals Orchester III performed before his CHI shrine, and the ritual performed in his First Wife's kitchen, before he left for the market place on market day. We will begin our investigation with those rituals, and continue through the other 15 ritual steps.

1st step: Although Orchester III made the decision before his CHI shrine after his morning prayer, he goes to perform a small ritual at the kitchen of his First Wife, and all of the wives and children are present.

Once he made the decision, before his CHI shrine after his morning prayer, this is the first place he makes a public announcement that he wants to become an Ozo man. For the Ozo Title concerns them as much as himself, and they too, receive some of the spiritual benefits, especially his First Wife, Oldest Son, and Oldest Daughter.

According to Igbo beliefs, Orchester III, his wives, children, and homestead are a spiritual unit, and after all, Orchester III is the spiritual energy that gives life to the homestead. Therefore, what he does to lift himself also lifts his homestead Family.

Together, his wives have more money that Orchester IIII. Remember, an Igbo man and wife are economically independent to each other. This means that the money she makes in trade, other than what she sells for him, belongs to her alone; and the Wives make a money donation.

This ritual takes place before the alters, (a special cook pot) of his wives CHI shrines with Umune leaves, and his shrines to Ikenga, CHI, and Ofo, Symbolizing the Unity of the Family in his decision; (Note in this case, money flows into Orchester III's pocket).

2nd step: Orchester III contacts all of the males of his extended family of Uncles, Brothers and Sons after they returned from Market Day. This is most of the male grownups in the Family village, and the oldest male Ofo holder presides over a ritual of announcement before their Ofo's and the shrine of Orchester III's mother and father.

Here, if there are any grievances in the extended family against Orchester III, they will be voiced and a proper settlement made. From them, he is seeking "Witnesses of his Uprightness" in his upcoming quest for the Ozo title, and they too make a money donation. (This is the only other time in the process where money flows into Orchester III's pockets).

3rd step: Now Orchester III begins seeking the approval of the Ozo men. He invites all of the Ozos of his Family village to a feast in his homestead. Recall that there are 10 of them for a ritual ceremony of planting four Iroke trees which are symbols of the wealth of the 4 groups of Society's values.

This is presided over by one of the Ozo members indicated by a Divination Priest. He plants the trees, he says a prayer ending with, "May you (Orchester III) and your wives and children live a good old age." A Sacrifice of palm-wine and cassava mixed with oil put beside the sapling, and the blood of a chicken is sprinkled over it.

Some of the blood is sprinkled on the Ofo of the members of Ozo who left their Ofo lying on the ground until they were paid 200 cowries each. The person chosen to plant the trees receives a special fee of 400 cowries. (Now we see the money is beginning to flow out of Orchester III's pocket into the pockets of others).

4th step: Later, on another day, he gives another feast. This time for all of the Ozo men of his Clan town, including his village which include about 50. To this group he gives a gift of 8 pots of cassava mixed with oil, cooked oil beans, 8 pots of palm-wine, 8 yams, 1 pot of oil, 16 kola nuts, and 4,800 cowries to be divided between them. This gives him the privilege of having a special Ozo stool made with his carved designs.

5th step: When the stool is complete, again the Town's members of Ozo are invited to a feast. This time they plant 8 Iroke trees in his homestead symbolizing the Original Ancestors. This time the prayer ended with "May Orchester III and his family live long, and may he be able to obtain all of the money necessary for his Title." The same gifts were given as before, including the 4,800 cowries to be divided between them.

(Note how the money is flowing into other people's pockets. Add to the fact that everything used in these rituals including all of the food for feast and sacrifices must be bought at the market. Nothing from Orchester III's homestead storehouse is used. Next, Orchester III deals with the Ancestors).

6th step: First, he gives a big feast and makes sacrifices at the alter at the shrine house of his father's Ancestors. This is presided over by the oldest living man in the family who ends his prayer with, "ALA,

IGWE, and Ancestors, come and eat. Bless Orchester III and cleanse his Soul of any spiritual miss-conduct."

Here, the same gifts are given to the oldest in the family, only this time they are doubled, and 9600 cowries are given to be divided between them.

7th step: He performs the same ritual at the Ancestor shrine house of his mother's family. With the same gifts, including the 9,600, cowries and everything is divided between them. Also, the same ritual is performed at the Ancestor shrine house of his father mother's family; with gifts and 9,600 cowries to be divided.

8th step: Orchester III makes an equally important sacrifice before the shrines of his in-laws, his wives family shrine. Where he provides foods and 9,600 cowries, for example, he has five wives, which means that it will cost him 48,000 cowries, 9,600 for each.

9th step: Next, Orchester III made a sacrifice at the Shrine of ALA, presided over by an ALA Priest. At sunset the same day, a small tunnel is dug in the ground by the Priest, and a rooster and a hen are sacrificed, and the blood and some feathers are put into the tunnel.

The Priest then takes the right arm of Orchester III, and pushes it into the Tunnel with the following words; "May Ozo Title prove to be a thing of value to you." And the same thing was done with his left arm. After which, Orchester III holds both arms to his chest. (This meant he was cleansing himself of any wrong doing against the ALA law of the land (Society).

10th step: Orchester III again giving sacrifices at the shrine house of his father's family Ancestors, and a feast and gifts of wine and food follows this, and as before, 9,600 cowries are divided between its members.

11th step: The same is performed at the shrine of his mother's family Ancestors, at a cost of a feast and 9,600 cowries.

12th step: Then as before, this is followed by a feast and the division of 9,600 cowries for sacrifices at his father mother's family Ancestor Shrine house.

13th step: This time around, Orchester III also makes sacrifice at the shrine house of his mother father's family Ancestors, and naturally, a feast and division of 9,600 cowries. (Now we enter the final three steps).

14th step: On a chosen evening, the Ozo men in Orchester III's village assemble in his homestead. After the Divination Priest makes a selection, this Ozo man builds a small platform of clay beside the wall of Orchester III's house in which he plants 4 camwood sticks. This becomes the symbol of Orchester III's Purified CHI, known as CHI Ozo.

After the completion of the symbol, the same Ofo man kills a goat and hen, then pours the blood over the camwood symbol. Then he sticks some of the hen's feathers in the blood, offers a prayer for Orchester III, followed by a ritual sacrifice meal, and the division of 4,800 cowries.

15th step: The next morning a mound of clay is built by the oldest Ozo man. With eight branches of the Iroke tree, and having waved them around Orchester III's head, he plants one of them in the mound of clay.

The remaining 7 are planted by other members of Ozo so as to form 2 lines, 4 each. Eight pieces of camwood sticks which have first been dipped in a special spiritual solution, were also passed around Orchester III's head and planted in the mound.

The Ozo man then kills a goat and rooster and sprinkles the blood over the symbols, with a prayer ending with, "May this title prove to be a cool thing (peace) and not a hot thing (trouble)."

A big feast is prepared for all, including women and children, and dancing and singing follow.

During the evening of the same day, the oldest Ozo man sits Orchester III down on a specially woven mat, and all of the Ozo members sit around him holding their Ofo. The oldest man then calls out, "May Orchester III live long to enjoy his title!" The other members shout "yea!", then they strike the ground with their Ofo.

Again the man calls, "May Orchester III derive wealth from his Title," and again they shout "Yea" and strike the ground with their Ofo. As the evening wore on, they fell asleep. It's customary for the members of Ozo to spend this night in Orchester III's homestead.

(The final step of the purification ritual, after which Orchester III will be so shinny clean and full of spiritual energy, he will almost glow in the dark, is related to the oldest of the Original 4 Male Ancestors, Mr. Righteousness; who created the Ozo Shrine, Nze, and the series of purification ritual steps leading to a state of a "Pure Upright Wealthy Man."

The Great Nze Shrine in Orchester III's town is a small hut located in a grove of trees near the marketplace where all of the ritual ceremonies are held in Secret. (We will deal with secret societies in detail elsewhere). The Shrine contains, as the Altars, the ritual objects are the treasure box and Ozo Staff of the foundering Father of the Town, Ben Sr., who was himself an Ozo man.

The Sacred Treasure Box is made of two identical blocks of kola wood about a foot and a half long. Each carved into the shape of a pyramid with the top point cut down about 6 inches. Each was dug out in the base, so that when the two blocks are fitted together at their base, there is a big sized space inside. This is where the Sacred Symbols of the Town's Values are kept.

Related to this Sacred Treasure Box is a ceremonial walking Ozo staff, a star apple tree stick about 4 feet long carved at both ends, and ringed with three iron rings that jingle when the staff is stamped on the ground, or when walking. This Staff serves the same purpose as a regular Ofo.

Parts of the remaining ritual steps are preformed in this grove in secret before this ancient treasure box and staff, plus a necklace and an ankle bracelet during the last step of purification rituals).

The16th and final step takes 8 days to complete. Just before sunrise the following morning, the oldest Ozo man raises Orchester III from his mat, and leads him outside the homestead and plants a branch of the Iroke tree. Orchester III sits down on his mat with his back against this branch where he is ceremonially washed (baptized) with holy water in which the leaves of Umune and four palm nuts have been soaked. When Orchester III rises after his baptism, he places his Ofo against his breast, while the old man chews some alligator peppers and kola nuts and blows the fragments over the Ofo.

After which, the man gives him a new name. Also Orchester III's Oldest Son and Oldest Daughter and another member of Ozo give him a new name. He now has 4 new names, and no longer answers to his old name. He is now known as Onye-Nze or Wealthy man, and congratulated by all with shouts and drum beats.

After this, all the Ozo men, with shouts and cheers, escort Orchester III in a procession through the village chanting, "Has money, has money!" As he walks, he is followed by a virgin girl who serves as his soul-bearer by carrying his CHI Shrine.

He is led to the grove of the Great Nze (Ozo) Ancestral shrine hut where he sacrifices 2 goats, and gives a big feast and a gift of 28,800 cowries to be divided between the Ozo members.

However, he can't go to his homestead, for he is to Pure of Spirit to enter it, nor can he have contact with the members of his family. He is now a Saint, and goes into seclusion for 8 days in the Shrine hut.

During these 8 days, Orchester III arranges to get the major symbols of his new position. This consists of a wooden divine bowl, a staff, a sacred treasure box, an elephant ivory horn, a necklace, and an ankle bracelet, which is given to the Nze Priest to hold. Then his head is shaved, with one little tuff of hair left on top.

On the night of the 7th day of seclusion, before the altar of Nze shrine house, he takes the Great Ozo Oath. Which ends with" I will, from this time on, speak with responsibility and avoid the pitfalls (jealousy and greed) of ordinary men. I will uphold this purified status in honor of our Ancestors."

Then he is taken in darkness to a special little room in the Nze shrine house. This is where the Nze Priest (the oldest Ozo man in town), anoints him with white chalk taken from the Sacred Treasure Box, therefore cleansing his body of any past mis-conduct. Now he is as pure as their most Ancient Original 8 Ancestors who are collectively called Nze.

An eagle feather is placed in the small tuff of hair on his shaven head. A male goat is sacrifice to Nze, and his new staff is sprinkled with its blood.

While holding the Great Ofo of Nze (staff), the Priest consecrates the achievement of Ozo Purification, and calling Orchester III by a name that symbolizes the money he spent, meaning "Wealth of the Child." He is now a full Living Saint of Nze. Or to say, a Living Saint of the Most Ancient 8 Ancestors.

On the morning of the 8th day of seclusion, Orchester III's Ozo friends go to prepare his wives to re-new a contact with him. Each wife must give these visitors ceremonial gifts of food and drink, and an unknown (by Grandpa) amount of cowries, and each takes a Title name glorifying herself spiritually.

In the afternoon during the public "Dance of Ozo," Orchester III and his wives are re-united is a special dance. He arranges for 2 cows to be killed, and provides fish for a general feast.

The Ozo men assemble and emerge in procession to the town marketplace. Circling around Orchester III and the virgin girl with his CHI shrine, they sing praises to him and his family. They address him by his Title name, and blow elephant ivory horns in his honor while he dances, chanting, "I have emerged!"

Thereafter, Orchester III performs a ceremony which expresses the magnitude of his accomplishment in re-distributing his money in Society. As a new Ozo man, he holds a mock market, during which he makes gifts of food to all of the members and their wives and children of the town. This costs him thousands and thousands of cowries. And this ceremony ends the 16 ritual steps of Ozo purification rituals.

For the next 28 days, an Igbo month, Orchester III spends all of his time performing the ceremonial ritual of "Washing hands of Ozo" in various homesteads in the villages of his town to which he has been invited. There, he spends the blessing of his new "Holiness."

When he enters a house, a virgin girl of that homestead hands him a calabash of water. Seated on a goatskin, he immerses his hands in the water and prays for the good health of all members of that family homestead.

After all other Ozo men present have also dipped their hands in the water, the calabash is returned to Orchester III. Again placing his hands in the water, he picks up the money the Host had placed in the bottom of the calabash, and keeps it as a sign of the privileges associated with his new state of purity.

The virgin girl then takes the calabash outside of the house and pours its water through the main doorway into the room, so that these blessings of purification will flow to the benefit of all the homestead members.

Thus is the ritual of blessing Society, and washing hands of Ozo which Orchester III performs for Society. This begins a long process of putting money back into Orchester III's pocket, which is a return on his money investment. Thus, Orchester III is a Living Saint doing good work for Society.

Rachel and the Umada Title

The Umada Female Title sometimes called by the symbol of its authority "The Pumpkin Seed Rattle," relates to "sisterhood of wives" in a clan town. Sisterhood is the foundation of the Oldest Wives who govern and protect women living away from home in their husband's village. Spiritually speaking, the Umada Title relates to Umune.

For some background, Rachel is 57 years old, a very successful trader, and the mother of many children.

This means that she is deeply involved as saleswoman in her married village and clan marketplace, where she has made lots of money on her own.

She has a reputation of being a highly respected wife and mother, and her homestead family is the ultimate in harmony between the wives and children. She is also an Elder in the Oldest Wife's social and economic Government in her husbands village.

Rachel is also a medicine woman who specializes in childhood illness, and she is well known and respected in this area. No matter day or night, when a child is sick, there is where you can find her.

However as the Oldest Daughter, she is in a different position than Orchester III as Oldest Son. Her loyalty is in two places.

She is spiritually, socially, and economically obligated to the home village family of her father where she was born and raised.

As important in her life, she is also spiritually, socially, and economically obligated to the Homestead and village family of her husband where she will spend all of her married life, and where she will raise her family. She is especially obligated to the living Wives, and dead Wives (Ancestors) of her husbands village, who will confer the Umada Title on her.

This means that in the ritual steps leading to her title, she will re-distribute her money and make ritual sacrifices in two clan towns, and before three groups; her family and ancestors, her husbands family and ancestors, and the wives group and ancestors.

We saw her role and authority as Oldest Daughter in her father's village family. Now we must set up her role and authority as Oldest Wife in her husbands family village.

She is the First Wife of her husband who is an Oldest Son of his village family and clan, Slow Moe. (It is a tradition for Oldest Sons and Daughters of different Clans to marry each other).

Rachel begins her series of ritual sacrifices and money flow like Orchester III with a prayer alone before her CHI shrine before breakfast.

After breakfast, she makes her intentions known before the CHI Shrines of her husband Slow Moe, and her children; where they make a large money contribution.

Next, she makes a public announcement at the shrine of the Ancestors of her Age group. Her age- group makes large money contribution also.

This ends the money flow into Rachel's pocket Then she visits her father village, and the money begins to flow out of her pocket. She is now ready to perform the series of Purification rituals of Umada.

In her father's village, she makes the announcement at a ritual sacrifice before the Ancestor shrine of her extended family village. She gives a gift of 8 bundles of Umune leaves, 8 pots of cassava in oil, 1 pot of oil, and 4,800 cowries.

This is followed by a ritual sacrifice before the Ancestor shrine of her Father's family, and a gift of food and 9,600 cowries.

And one is performed before the Ancestor shrine of her mother's family, and a gift of food and 9,600 cowries. Then she returns to her husband's village.

Here, she performs a ritual sacrifice before the Ancestor shrine of the Wives in her marriage village, with the Wives of the Oldest Wife Government, and the wives and mothers of her husband's village family. They are the ones that confer the Umada Title, and make a gift of food and 4,800 cowries.

Next she performs a ritual sacrifice before the Ancestors shrine of the females of her husband mother's family, and she makes a gift of food and 9,600 cowries; and before the Ancestor shrine of the females in her husband father's family, she makes a gift of food and 9,600 cowries.

After which she performs a small ritual before the shrine of the Wives for permission to have a Pumpkin Rattle carved as the symbol of her Authority with her designs, and she makes a gift of food and 4,800 cowries.

Rachel's final day of rituals will be very interesting. Grandpa has mentioned that the Igbo, and Africans in general, believe that a man should have more than one wife. In fact, African women do not really have much respect for a man that has only one wife. Grandpa also knows that you do not have any way to understand this way of thinking, being born and growing up in a country where one wife is the rule of law.

So the question becomes, what is the relationship, not only of the wives of one husband, but also the wives of the entire town? This is really what the Umada Title is all about. Wives and mothers, and their spiritual and social positions in their husband's village.

But most important, Rachel's final rituals of purification show the bond that she forms with her husband and children, and has to do with Family-in-laws relationships; which is just as powerful and important as regular family relationships in the Igbo Society.

For it is in her husband's village where she will carry out her mother and wife spiritual responsibilities governed by laws of ALA, the Great Wife and Mother Goddess.

However, a point we should keep in mind is that, the Umada Title is not related to the nature of the man-woman relationship. We will deal with that subject in another book. It is related to the Sisterhood of Wives and Mothers.

Rachel is to perform two rituals before two different shrines in different locations near her husband's town on the same day. The first ritual is performed before the shrine of the Foundering Mother and Wife of the town. Now we need a definition.

For an example of a Foundering Mother and Wife Shrine, we will use our family names. When Kate, George Benjamin's wife died, her oldest daughter, Julia Ann would have taken one of her cooking pots; the one used to cook Umune leaves, and is her CHI Shrine to a spot in the forest. This is where she would plant a special tree, and half-bury the pot at its base.

Kate's CHI pot becomes the spiritual shrine of the wives and mothers as long as the town exists. Thereafter, Kate is worshipped as the foundering mother and wife, who are called in prayers, "Lolo."

When your great grandmother Bertha married your great grandfather Ben Jr., this meant that your Grandma Bertha would perform a ritual before the shrine of Ben Jr. is grandmother Kate, and this would be the case with the founding Mother of Rachel's husband, Slow Moe's clan town.

The foundering mother shrine of Slow Moe's Village is located in a isolated place in the forest between the town and a fresh water stream. The shrine consists of a half-buried cooking pot at the base of a special tree, and the pot is filled with Chalk, Umune leaves, and other spiritual symbols, called "Medicine."

Rituals before the shrine of the Foundering Mother and Wife are performed once a year. Meanwhile, weeds and underbrush grow over the path leading to both shrine places, and part of both rituals are the cutting of a new path with long knives.

On ritual day, all of the men either leave town, or remain in their homesteads all day. The women take over the whole town. Now let's take a quick look at the ritual to the Foundering Mother, the Igbo call "Lolo."

On the appointed day, about 8 a.m., all of the wives and mothers are called to the marketplace by the oldest woman with her pumpkin rattle. After all of the women assemble, they begin cutting the pathway to Lolo's shrine. Once the shrine is reached, the women clear all bush in a wide circle around the tree and shrine, and cut the grass like it was mowed with a lawn mower.

We must keep in mind that all of the women in town are married to the Foundering Mother's great and great great etc, etc, grandsons. And the women approach the shrine and ritual with prayers from that point of view.

The ritual itself consists of the women dancing in a circle around the tree while singing songs of praise. Some women will be complaining that she is not being treated right by her husband, which is against the rules of the sisterhood of mothers and wives, and a thing that Foundering Mothers would frown upon.

Some women would be complimenting the Foundering Mothers for giving them such good sons for husbands. Most prayers consist of all of the things a daughter-in-law would talk about with her mother-in-law under the rules of a very strong bond related to Sisterhood of Mothers and Wives across generations.

Only on this occasion, Rachel's prayers would also be more of a ritual cleansing nature. For example, "Lolo (in-law Ancestor mothers), mother of our husbands, we come in peace, our thing and yours (sisterhood) is in peace (and harmony)."

Today I am going to take the Umada Title, and as all of the women of your town are witness, I have devoted myself to being a good mother and wife and my homestead is in peace. I have stood strong with my sisters in all things, and there is not a woman here that has a bad thing to say about me. Thus is the nature of Rachel's prayers to Lolo as she continues to name things that she has done to up-lift the sisterhood of the wives and mothers of the town.

The women cutting a path from the shrine to the fresh water stream follow these prayers, where they symbolically wash (baptize) away all ill feelings one may have for another.

After which, the women return to the marketplace to refresh themselves with food and drink, and get ready for the afternoon ritual ceremony.

Meanwhile, the women dress in their finest clothes, and paint their bodies in beautiful colored female symbols, for Umada is a festival occasion.

About mid-afternoon, the women begin cutting the path to the Umada shrines of the Original 4 Wives and Mothers, which every Clan Town has.

Another point we must add is although this is a festival occasion, the women also have a militant protective attitude, and their singing and dancing have a warrior approach. This shows the feeling they have about their sisterhood; called, the Women's "Dance of the Long Knives."

The four shrines symbolize Motherhood, Wifehood, womanhood, and selfhood, and these are the spiritual values the women praise and protect in their songs and dance.

Their feelings run so high, that the men leave town for the day for fear that one may do or say something that the women may think of as an insult, and they will be attacked.

Only one priest may remain to perform a sacrifice, and he then will immediately leave town. Now we will take a detailed look at the Umada (sisterhood) ritual.

The shrine itself is a group of 4 trees with two pots at their base. One of the pots are filled with water to wash one hands, and the other, half-buried in the ground, contains Umune leaves, white chalk, and other spiritual properties used to cure spiritual and physical illnesses.

After the cutting of the actual path, some of the oldest women approach the shrine, and kneel near the trees, and began clearing away leaves and grass. They are very careful that nothing is rooted up, only cut or brushed away.

All the while, singing that it is the Ancient Wives and Mothers who uphold and give them power to do anything, and it is because of them that the women are proud. And anyone who has bad feelings against them or takes any actions against them, let the Ancient Wives and Mothers kill them.

When this is finished, the Priest comes up carrying a female chicken. He is to perform the actual sacrifice, this being a Priest' work, (in Igbo land, women do not perform blood sacrifices because they make a personal blood sacrifice once a month).

He stands in front of the shrine and swings the chicken around the heads of the assembled women, and bumped it on each of their heads in turn.

As he does so, he calls on the 4 Ancient Wives and Mothers to bless the women with long life and lots of children.

He then pulls some feathers out of the chicken's neck and cuts its throat, letting the blood drip on the half-buried spiritual medicine pots of the shrine. After which the Priest leaves town.

An old Priestess now approaches the shrine. Using her hand, she stirs up the Medicine in one pot. She then approaches Rachel who is standing in front of that pot, and smears medicine with her hand over her eyes, and makes designs on her face.

Next, she stirs the medicine in the second pot, and smears it on Rachel's chest, followed by smearing her back from another pot, and finally her legs from the last pot, as a symbol of receiving the values of the Ancient Mothers and Wives.

The entire assembly of women then start dancing near the shrine, making a circle of dancers with Rachel in the center of the shrine trees, while singing protective and praise songs of sisterhood.

There is great excitement and banishing of knives in this dance, as the Old Priestess presents Rachel with her Pumpkin Rattle of Authority. Rachel is now a Saint in the Sisterhood of Wives and Mothers.

Finally, Rachel blesses the women by rubbing medicine in their hands, and this ends the ritual of Rachel's Sainthood. This gives us some insight into the nature of Igbo women's Sisterhood.

The women parade back to the Market, where Rachel promotes having a ceremony for all of the children under the age of puberty. This is a festival occasion with food, singing, dancing, and the children are the guests of honor.

Her ritual steps now begin to follow the same pattern as Orchester III, at the end of which she will have re-distributed as much, or more in Society as Orchester III, and becomes a Living Saint of Society.

That night, when all of the men return, Rachel is paraded through her husbands village with a young boy as a Soul Bearer, and she dances with her husband, sons and daughters in the marketplace, and sing "I have emerged."

And she too, spends the next 28 days going around the Clan Towns blessing the wives and mothers in their Kitchens. Because according to Igbo beliefs, kitchens are a Sacred Place symbolizing the values of Nurturing, which is what mothers and wives are all about. Thus, ends a rough out-line of the series of rituals that transform Rachel into a Living Saint doing good work for Society.

The question arises about Igbo beliefs in one man having more than one wife? This is a good time to raise this question, because it relates to sisterhood. So the question is really about sisterhood and the bonds that allow 4 or 5 women to be married to one husband.

To Igbo women, Sisterhood is on a much higher level than jealousy of a man. The bond of sisterhood is very spiritual and powerful, based on ALA, the Great Mother and Great Wife. A man is only a means of becoming a mother; their ultimate goal is to produce society.

On the other hand, the rituals of sisterhood also showed that Igbo women are ready to protect each other; and this is the case throughout Africa.

For an example of the depth of this bond, in 1929 the Igbo sisterhood of women from many towns organized themselves into an army. And with no men allowed, declared war on, and went into battle with the English army over an issue of an insult to the Igbo women; which is known in Igbo history as the Great Women's War.

This gives us some insight into the meaning in the ritual of dancing around Rachel, banishing their long knives while singing protective and praising songs.

Which not only bonds her into sisterhood of living wives and mothers of the town, but also with the values of the ancestor wives and mothers; the values of the Original 4 Wives and Mothers of the Igbo nation. This is what the Umada Title is all about.

Just as important, as far as our question is concerned, this sisterhood is not only the bond that makes up Igbo Female Society, but also the bond that holds 4 or 5 wives to one husband.

Market Place, Trade, and Wealth Conclusion

Well GrandKids, we have finally reached the point, after looking at the Ozo and Umada rituals as evidence, where we can reach a conclusion about the Ozo and Umada Titles.

They are a series of ritual steps that transform Orchester III and Rachel's spirit Soul into a state of Sainthood, i.e., wealth. This is designed in such a way, that the rituals lift Society as well; thus is the beauty of African Bush Intelligence, i.e., African Logic.

This conclusion was followed by the question, why do the Igbo use all of their creativity in making money in trade, and what does it have to do with this spiritual transformation? And this led us to follow the money flow in, Taking Titles.

We approached the answer to this question from the point of view that, taking titles is a spiritual and economic investment in Society values, with money made out of Society's Marketplace.

If we take note that Orchester III and Rachel, in order to take their titles, made economic and spiritual sacrifices to all members of their families, including in-law families; as far as we are concerned the question becomes, what does Ozo and Umada Titles mean as to the nature of Igbo Society.

We mentioned that Orchester III's and Rachel's money was divided between different groups, and this brings up the question of sharing. We can go so far as to say, sharing is one of the major factors that promote harmony in Igbo society. For example, there is a law on how this money is to be sub-divided down the line until every body in the group has a share.

One such law is that, for instance, the division of 4,800 cowries between the 50 members Ozo group in Orchester III's town is base on seniority. The man that has the oldest Ofo staff gets a little larger share than the next man in line of seniority, and this works down to the last man on the seniority list who gets less than all of them.

On the other hand, this process also works for the wives and daughters. For instance, the wife of the senior Ofo holder, Orchester III's wife and oldest daughter, will get a larger share when money is divided in groups to which they belong. So we can see that in this way, Orchester III economically lifts his wives and daughters, and his sainthood make their share even larger.

Next, we should take special note that the Ozo and Umada Titles are the major series of rituals and money flow that transforms an Igbo into a Saint of Society.

There is also a group of lesser titles where there is less ritual and money involved. For example, the titles of 'Horse and Cow Killer at the funeral of one's father and mother we mentioned. And there are others, all of which allows a person to lift himself and family to some level of Sainthood, which also makes them Wealthy to some degree. However, there is another advantage to taking titles.

We will take the example of Orchester III. For investing all of his money into Society, as an Ozo man and member of the family, he will share in the cowries of all of those that take the Ozo Title for the rest of his life.

Let's also say, he took the Title when he is 50 years old, and he lives to the age of 70. He will have collected cowries from his money investment for 20 years, which is also the case with Rachel.

Now when we take into consideration of the large number of cowries it costs to take the Ozo and Umada Title, and the length of time they collect interest; Orchester III and Rachel could make a profit of 10 times on their investment, 10 times 100,000 cowries equals 1,000,000 cowries.

Of course these are not real numbers; but they make the point that, returns on investments are very high; but what about his spiritual investments?

Now let's think of how you would you feel about somebody that has given you and all of your family a big spiritual lift, like Orchester III's 28 days of blessings the community. And at the same time, has put lots of money in the pockets and food in stomachs of you and your whole extended family.

According to the Igbo, that man or woman deserves the highest of respect and honor, and, receive money for the rest of their life. So Orchester and Rachel receive Respect, Honor, and Social Security in return for their spiritual and economic investment. Thus is the role money plays in Taking Title's to the Wealth of Society.

The point is, we can say that every member of Igbo Society is in one stage or another of becoming Wealthy in the highest values of Society, which is the Destiny Chosen by their Original 8 Ancestors. And it is these titles and money flow that create the constitution and dynamics of Igbo society.

IGBO IN PRESPECTIVE

Orchester Jr.

This leaves us with two questions. One, it seems to me that the same amount of money is changing hands in Igbo Society, how does the total amount of money in the Igbo nation grow? And two, how did they capture new territory, especially since we said that the Igbo don't have a national army of warriors.

Orchester Sr.

It is true that the Igbo were not organized around a central government, and did not trade on a national level, and this made the growth of Igbo national money supply slow.

They do not have an organization of warriors, but they did have an unorganized army of traders. In this way, as individual Traders in foreign territory, especially the small nation to their south, and the Yoruba to their west, they were bringing new money into the nation.

This provided economic growth, at least, more than enough to keep up with the growth rate of the Igbo's national population; which gave the Igbo economy a slow but sure Growth rate.

This not only provided a slow but sure growth in their national money supply, but also provided a method for the growth of Igbo territory as we will see later.

But the most important point about Igbo economy, is that their money supply was continuously re-distributed throughout Society through the large number of Titles to be taken, which gave their economy a dynamic cycle in its money flow.

All of which provided a solid spiritual and economic social security system, to give a lift to the spiritual health and economic welfare of Society.

However, on the one hand, from another point of view, the answer to both questions are the same, EKWENSU, the Igbo name for their Trickster God, and this means that we should answer the questions in some detail.

While in the Yoruba's religious beliefs, they used their Trickster God, ESU, in the role as Messenger between mankind and the Gods and Goddesses, and Enforcer of the Rules of Ritual Conduct.

On the other hand, in Igbo Religious Beliefs, their Trickster God has the role of being the Source of Creativity in the Art of Making Money, Negotiation, and Enforce the Laws of the Money Flow of Trade. Recall, in the Igbo creation story, CHINEKE appointed EKWENSU as Chief Enforcer of the Laws of Trade in the Holy Market Place, and this means that He is the God of Money Flow. This also means that the Igbo use EKWENSU, as Trickster, to successfully Make Money (Negotiation) inside and outside of their nation, and at the same time, expand Igbo territory.

For an example of how this expansion takes place without the support of an army of warriors, I am going to quote an Igbo Writer, Mr. Mazi Elechukwu Nnadibuagha Njaka, in a study entitled Igbo Political Culture. I think he can do a better job of explaining the process than I can, especially since he has the experience of being born and raised in the Igbo Society. We quote out of context.

"One of the main attributes of the Igbo is the ability to negotiate a bargain. This is manifest in their markets, in their religion, among themselves, and among Family villages and Clan Towns.

In fact, every facet of Igbo life is full of negotiations. Daily negotiation is carried on in Igbo within the membership of the family, with the umunna (Clan Town), or with the rest of the world. They take place anywhere--at work, at the market, at political meetings, and at all social gatherings.

This continuous process of negotiation in itself presupposes change. The Igbo negotiates even with spirits (Gods, Goddesses, and +), and this quality of negotiation stimulates him to undertake adventures. Each adventure gives him vigor and self-confidence, which encourages his assumption that, come what may, he will attain at least part of his goal (in making money). Any failure is attributed to a (bad) CHI (Destiny)--a scapegoat in this instance--but it does not deter him from making further attempts.

The (Igbo) proverb, "Tomorrow is pregnant, nobody knows to what it will give birth," explains why the average Igbo is constantly ready to negotiate with both men and spirits. Nothing prevents him from trying to advance upward in life except the refusal of his Chi (its not part of his Destiny). Quick wit and cunning (EKWENSU) in negotiation is necessary for advancement, as suggested by the following parable.

Once upon a time, a traveler was stopped by a group of spirits who would not let him pass unless he danced for them. At the same time, he was warned that if he danced he would die.

The traveler looked up and down, then turned to the spirits, and asked if they were ready to witness his performance. When they replied in the affirmative, the traveler told them that he would dance, and demonstrated a few steps.

But suddenly, he announced that he was not prepared to dance after all, and walked a short distance. Then he changed his mind again, and begin to dance, then once more decided to walk.

Thus he deliberately refused to make up his mind whether he would dance or walk until he had passed the spirits and left them busy wondering whether he had danced or walked!"

This gives a look at the kind of influence EKWENSU had on the Igbo. Now for a look at the kind of laws He Enforced. Again we quote Mr. Njaka out of context.

"Consequently, the Igbo city-state (Clan Town) continued a more or less peaceful coexistence buttressed by self-regulation and reciprocity. Several Ibo proverbs expressed this goal in external relations, for example: A traveler should have no enemy; A person who kills a guest does not demonstrate power or strength.

The implications stress the Igbo philosophy, which is based on accommodation, restraint, honor, mutual reciprocity, and self-regulation among individuals and among states (Clan Towns). As a result, all possible measures were taken to protect travelers.

If such a crime did occur on the market day, the criminal had to be apprehended and handed over to the victim's town-state (Clan Town).

Thus a traveler could move freely and safely among the various city-states if he took care to move within each on its market day.

On his journey, he could carry money, cloth, tobacco, bracelets, or other commodities, secure in the knowledge that he and his possessions were safe; as long as he traveled on market days, or with an escort for the short distances in a state where the market was over."

Now we get to what Mr. Njaka has to say about how the above relates to economic expansion into foreign territory.

"Their methods of expansion were essentially peaceful and can be identified as penetration, attraction of relatives, absorption, and assimilation.

An experience I (Mr. Njaka) had when I was a district officer at Degema (an Igbo Town) illustrates these processes of expansion.

In 1957 an elderly Kalabari man (non-Igbo people and territory) came to the district office at Degema (town) to complain about a younger Igbo man who, many years earlier, had arrived in a village near Bakana (A town in foreign territory).'

There he had worked hard until he was able to purchase some land where he built a hut. As he prospered, that hut became a magnificent house containing his wife and children. He acquired more land until he owned more that forty-five acres.

Gradually he bought in more families from Igbo country, had the entire area surveyed and registered with the Ministry of Land at Enugwu (another town in foreign territory), and established himself as ruler of his domain.

The complainant was not disputing the younger (Igbo) man's right to his property, or even his being a chief in accordance with the Kalabari tradition.

Instead, he (the old Kalabari man) complained that this Igbo immigrant had learned to speak the Kalabari language. But, when the old man went to borrow some money from him, the new chief required that he speak in Igbo before the chief would listen to his request.

The old man had therefore walked out in anger without obtaining the loan. When he came to the divisional office however, he made his complaint in Igbo.

This story demonstrates some of the methods of Igbo expansion. One Igbo had penetrated, and begun to attract people from Igbo country. Before doing this, he had assimilated himself in his new environment by learning the language and culture.

As soon as he had firmly established himself--all legally--he embarked on the final method of absorption, which the old man resented. But it was too late--he had already been absorbed enough that he made his complaint in the Igbo language."

Mr. Njaka not only gives the role of EKWENSU, and the economic trade laws He Enforced, but also His role in economic expansion into foreign territory without the use of an army of warriors.

We must come to the conclusion that the Igbo, with their great understanding of the nature of "money flow" in the "Market Place" means that they can dominate the money flow anywhere.

While all of what Mr. Njaka says is true, from the evidence I have seen, my bottom-line conclusions of the real reason the Igbo were so successful at the art of making money, and expanding into foreign territory is as follows:

The Igbo, with his great understanding of the nature of the Money Flow in the Market Place, means that he can dominate any market in which he does business. This is shown in how he turns the money flow to himself; and the Yoruba man was borrowing Yoruba money from an Igbo.

But in any case, the above is how they bring more money into their nation, while at the same time, expand their territory on individual levels without the use of an army of warriors.

Out of all the African nations we will investigate, the Igbo are the only ones that do not have, or need, an army of warriors to survive.

Igbo, Grandpa's Conclusion

Recall the Igbo saying, "Everything one can see, feel, think, touch, taste, is IGWE." To sum-up Igbo's religious beliefs, we will take a look at their World view and their Soul view. By looking at the logic in the harmony in the relationship the physical world surrounding mankind, and the spiritual world that exists within mankind's Soul.

However, in reality, the Igbo do not see any space between their inside soul view and their outside world view. One cannot exist without the other. It is a matter of looking at the same thing from inside or outside. Both are the foundation of their religious beliefs; "everything is IGWE, and IGWE is everything."

The Igbo worldview, is that the World is a Market Place filled with unpredictable situations. They see these situations as opportunities to take advantage of. In fact, the Igbo see the world as a constant state of change.

This means that the Igbo's approach and attitude towards life is to be maneuverable and ready for change at all times. For example, recall the Spirit of their Market Place.

This calls for each individual to be self-disciplined and fully qualified, and relying on the principle of negotiation under shared authority in a democratic Society. To be able to take advantage of every opportunity to the fullest, means that the Igbo are Traders by Religious Conviction.

This approach and attitude translated into thoughts and actions related to their religious beliefs, which allows the Igbo to succeed in himself, his family, his society, as well as in hostile foreign territory.

It is in seeing and thinking about the world from this point of view, that allows the Igbo to live and expand in areas where they are surrounded by warlike nations like the Yoruba and others in their area.

This is where the Igbo had a big influence on Black Americans. We too, live and expand our Society totally surrounded by a warlike nation in the U.S.A; and we don't have an army. The only difference between Black Americans and the Igbo is that, the Igbo do it economically, and we do it spiritually; but the process is the same.

Being as this subject is a very big issue in now-day Black-American concerns, this is a very educational investigative adventure. After all, Black-Americans have been fighting to obtain social equality and personal freedom for the last 381 years (1619-2000).

From this point of view, the Igbo are a clear symbol of the roots of Black-American's powerful beliefs, especially concerning social equality; which shows a direct spiritual relationship between the Igbo and Black-American Society.

However, the whole subject of relationships between Igbo and Black-Americans is only a part of an overall goal of finding the relationship between Black-Americans and Africans period. I only mentioned it here and there to remind ourselves of our major goal; and suggest we have a similar world view. We will deal with this relationship, along with other African nations in more detail in another book: Now to return to Igbo World View.

To better understand how the Igbo see the world, Grandpa will demonstrate what we mean in the form of the nature of the relationships between Igbo Soul and World View of life; according to their Religious Beliefs. Grandpa wanted to shows that CHINEKE, IGWE, and ALA are the Holy Trinity, or center of the Igbo religious beliefs. They are the foundation or beginning point of Igbo thinking about the world, and where they fit into the picture.

This means that the Igbo's religious beliefs are really a logic-line of their World View. Their Society is the results of "living this logic."

This also means that the ideals that are found in their Soul View, are also found in the Family and Clan social and economical area of their Society; as we have shown.

For example, the Igbo really think of their Society as a place where every man is a King, and every woman a Queen; and their homestead is their Kingdom. However, this does not have any thing to do with "Royalty," this is a "Pure Democratic Society" based on "Kinship Relationships."

In our investigation we saw lots of strong evidence which demonstrated these Democratic Relationships of Kinship at work in Igbo Society. Which also demonstrated Igbo World Views in the reality of their Society; where its designed-purpose (goal) is to Lift Society's

Chosen Destiny to be a Wealthy National Society ever closer to Fulfillment.

At the same time, this means that we must, according to the logic of Igbo World View, come to the conclusion that in the framework of a Democratic Family-Society; IGWE, ALA, and CHINEKE symbolizes the Igbo's highest valued beliefs, we call SOCIAL EQUALITY, PERSONAL FREEDOM, and WEALTH.

Plus, this is the Second Aspect of Black America's Holy Trinity of our Spiritual Constitution.

ANCIENT AKAN GAME

Using the examples of the things that Christians do and believe to bring *love* into their lives to save their souls through the father-son Gods of their Religion, Jesus Christ and Jehovah; the following are some of the things that the Ancient Akan did and believed, in order to bring *Ideas* into their lives to become a nation of *Philosophers* through the worship of the father-mother Gods and Goddesses of their religion, *Odomankoma, Nyankopon, and Asase Yaa Afua*: Which is the game they played in life.

DRINKING FROM ANCIENT WELLS
(Akan and the Ashanti Kingdom)

Well Fellow Detectives, now we will get a detailed look at the impact of Jealousy and Greed on the Kings, Queenmothers, Clan Chiefs, Chief Priests, and War Chiefs; and see how they affect a Kingdom.

This should be very interesting because in the process, we can also look for the connection between the Akan, the Igbo, and the Yoruba's relationship to African Traditional Intelligence. With this in mind, let's begin our investigation of the Akan.

Since the Ashanti Kingdom is part of the Akan speaking people, (The Akan Nation) we should begin our study of archaeology and religious beliefs of the Akan as a whole. But first we should define the difference between a kingdom and a nation as we use the terms.

A kingdom consists of an alliance of a group of Seven Clans who elect a King to be their leader. On the other hand, the Akan Speaking nation consists of a large group of Kingdoms that speak the same language, have the same religious beliefs, form of government, and the same Most Ancient Ancestors.

In this sense, the people speaking the Akan language are a nation which is located in an area that covers the southern half of Ghana, western Togo, and eastern Ivory Coast.

We should note that the Ashanti Kingdom is located in the lower central area of the country of Ghana, which puts them just about in the center of the Akan Nation. And it is in the Ashanti general area that we will begin our archaeology investigation.

For our archaeology evidence, we will turn to a Ghanaian archaeologist, James Anquandah from the University of Ghana; and who is himself an Akan. His book, "Ghana Past" contains the results of his radiocarbon dating figures, and his findings are what we will use as our reference point. We quote:

"Sometime between 2000 and 1000 B.C. farming began in areas which are today inhabited by Akan speakers. Ruins of stones used in village communities that probably kept livestock, and perhaps cultivated crops, are known in the Borng and Ashanti regions.

There was a matrilineal (Many) development of proto-Akan (original Akan). Social units are in a number of areas such as the northern Borng savanna grassland, the Adensi forest land, Etsi coast land, and Assin. That these social groups were probably the descendants of stone age farmers who spread out to inhabit the forest land between the River Comoe and the River Volta about 500 BC.

The corroborative evidence of archaeology, oral traditions, linguistics, and ethnic patterns of this region, suggests that it is somewhere in this area that the Akan language and the political and social institutions associated with the Akan must have commenced their revolution. They are diffused (spread out) between the Comoe river in eastern Ivory Coast, and the Volta river in western Ghana, and on into Togo.

The indications are that the Akan cradle (where they originated), if there was one, is likely to have straddled the geographical area between Borng, Adensi, an Assin (areas), especially since the Borng dialect is known to exhibit some of the most archaic (ancient) traits on the Akan language.

In a traditional libation prayer in Adensi preceding the narration and documentation of tradition of origin, the local Elders and Chieftains declared; "The first of the Akan states (Kingdoms) is Adensi; Adensi stands at the head of the entire Akan Nation."

According to Adensi cosmogony (story of creation), Adensi was the traditional 'Garden of Eden' of the Akan."

Our conclusion is that, from Mr. Anquandah's data, people were living in the Akan area for 3,000 to 4,000 years; between 2,000 and 1,000 B.C.

About 2500 years ago (500 B.C.), a group of people in the center of the Akan area put together a combination of beliefs that were the roots of a religious culture that grew into the present day Akan Nation.

This means that the Yoruba-Nok, Igbo, and Akan, from an archaeological and historical point of view, had put together a combination of religious beliefs about the same time, at least 2500 years ago, and as much as 4,000 years ago.

This tells us one of two things; either there was a Spiritual Revolution taking place throughout Africa during those time periods, or as Grandpa believes from other sources, that Africans belief systems are much older than the evidence shows. Its a matter of the Investigator's research methods and translation of evidence.

However, as far as our investigative goals are concerned, this doesn't matter. What matters is that African belief systems are older than Christianity, and as old or older than the Jewish Bible history. And this is what we will use as a reference to begin our time line in investigating the history of African and Afro-American traditional religious beliefs.

But anyway, getting back to our point, this also means that the Akan are very ancient, which takes care of the word "Ancient" in the title of this chapter, "Drinking from Ancient Wells of the Akan."

As usual, we will start our investigation by looking for the Akan Bible; or to say, look for the "Well" in the title "Drinking from Ancient Wells of the Akan."

In the case of the Akan "Well", we don't have to look far, only at the *Talking Drummers*.

The Talking Drummer

First, we should define what Grandpa means by "Drum talk." The Akan language is tonal like all African languages, with meanings often dependent on rising or falling inflections (change of pitch or tone in speaking); like singing.

This means that any musical instrument can easily translate their language. This also means that any musician can use his instrument to hold a conversation with people. The drum is king of African musical instruments, and is used to do most of the talking. The talking drummers form an institution unto themselves, much like a college presided over by old Master Drummers. Who, like Professors, teach the younger generations of students from a large body of knowledge in the form drum poems, proverbs, and stories; and this is what the Talking Drummers talk *about.*

In this sense, the Akan and Yoruba deal with their history in the same way. Like the Ifa Priest in Yoruba-land, the Akan Drummers are trained from early childhood, and in 10 to 15 years, if he has the talent, determination, and a very good memory, he will get his degree, so to speak.

He must memorize the history and all of the poems, proverbs, and stories that contain the ideas of the spiritual world and wisdom of life. Moreover, over a long period, the student's mind slowly becomes a storehouse of the Akan's traditional knowledge.

However, the student drummer is not trained to be a priest like the Ifa Priest, even though they serve more or less the same purpose, as far as Grandpa can see. Akan Drummers are trained more like a Philosopher of Knowledge.

The point being, we have found the Akan "Well." And now that we have, to our satisfaction, established the "Ancient", and the "Well," next we will investigate the "contents" of the "Well," or to say, deal with the "Drinking" in the title "Drinking from Ancient Wells of the Akan."

Religion, Philosophy, and Chosen Destiny

In looking into the Akan's well, as far as Grandpa can see, they took a philosophical approach to life. This means that we will take a philosophical, as well as a spiritual approach to our investigation.

This also means that we will be dealing with the relationship between 'philosophical terms; like ideas, logic, and reality,' and, 'religious terms; like God, soul, and spirit.'

Being as we are already familiar with religious terms from dealing with the Yoruba and the Igbo, we will begin from a philosophical point of view, that *Ideas are where reality comes from*; for an example, we will deal with the question, how did a car become a reality?

First there was an idea of an engine, and somebody built it. Then there was an idea of a transmission, and that was built. This was followed by an idea of a differential (rear end), and that too was built; this is followed by ideas of fenders, hood, seats, doors, top and trunk. To build those ideas, is to bring them into reality.

Logic organized these ideas and realities into the idea and reality of a car. This is what we mean that ideas are where reality comes from!

Now to take our example still further; the three major things that make a car a car is (1) engine, (2) transmission, and (3) rear end. Without them, there can be no such thing as a car. They are the foundation of the car's existence, and everything else is built around them; so we can say those three things are the soul (trinity) of the car.

The point is, ideas have souls, which come first, and, through the results of logic, reality follows. The same is the case with a Kingdom's Chosen Destiny; it is a big idea which is the logical results of a number of other ideas.

This brings up the question, where do ideas come from. Our answer is, they come from beliefs, and in the case of the Akan, from religious beliefs. In this respect, ideas and beliefs are the same thing, or to say, beliefs are ideas about things.

This question comes close to Grandpa's personal belief-ideas. The closest thing that Grandpa has to a religious belief, is the belief in the power of historical ideas.

Grandpa believes that in the past, African-American men and women have had good ideas that are still having a positive effect on Black people as a whole.

Grandpa also has an undying belief that Black people will produce the men and women who will 'come up' with a 'good idea' of how to deal with any Black problem that may come in the future.

For example, in Grandpa's life time, Dr. Martin L. King and Malcolm X came up with ideas that, when brought into reality, moved Afro-Americans forward. Their ideas are still working for Black's benefit; although both are now dead, their ideas live on.

The point being, their ideas not only have life, but also have spiritual power, or to say, ideas, if powerful enough, are a spiritual force that can bring itself into reality. In addition, their ideas can also maintain themselves for hundreds and even thousands of years.

Grandpa goes a step further, and believes that, old Black ideas, and new Black ideas are related to each other as a mother is to her child.

Better still, the relationship between old and new ideas are similar to the extended family member's relationship to each other, including the Ancestors.

Now, if we hold the position that a big idea consists of little ideas, or to say, the logical organization of little realities result in a big reality, we can come up with a historical Idea of reality that is a driving force in a Kingdom's Chosen Destiny, or Soul.

It is important to take note that the above short introduction into Grandpa's philosophy of life, is not just a 'side-trip', as will soon be shown.

The world of ideas are the only way Grandpa has of explaining the inner workings of the Akan Religious beliefs, and especially how a Kingdom's chosen Destiny comes into reality.

Thus is the nature of our philosophical approach to investigating the Akan's Highest Valued-Beliefs, and the process they believe of how the world became a reality.

ODOMANKOMA, the Great Creator.

Well Fellow Detectives, as investigators, we must really put on our thinking caps. For, 'Drinking' from the Akan's "Well", we will find that the Akan have a thinking mans religion.

The Akan's name for their Great Creator is ODOMANKOMA. This means that, OLODUMARE of the Yoruba, CHINEKE of the Igbo, and ODOMANKOMA of the Akan have the same meaning, The Great Creator of the World and everything therein.

So now with the Akan's ODOMANKOMA, and Akan religious beliefs being the subject of our investigation, we will begin by asking the question, what is the process the Akan believe ODOMANKOMA created the world?

Our first piece of evidence comes from an Akan Scholar, Dr. J.B Danquah, who wrote a book, "The Akan Doctrine of God."

We are dependent on this writer in two ways. First, his collection of drum poetry and proverbs, but more importantly, his translation of key

Akan words into English, although we did crosscheck with other sources. It is from his translation of religious terms, that we will begin our look for the Akan religious beliefs; beginning with the Great Creator.

Mr. Danquah writes that ODOMANKOMA is "....also called BOREBORE, which is translated, Hewer, Carver, Originator, the Architect, and Inventor....; and there is the title, BO-NNA-MMERE-ESON, translated 'Who created the Seven Eras; a third title is, Onye DOMANKOMA ba, which translates 'ODOMANKOMA is an Eternal Spirit, Who has no beginning or end, always was, and always will be."

This gives us a pretty good idea of how the Akan think of what ODOMANKOMA does, and is; a Super Great Spirit Who is a Great Architect, and creates by bringing ideas into reality.

Mr. Danquah defines ODOMANKOMA as "The Great Architect, Who alone created the World." And we defined OLODUMARE of the Yoruba as, "The Great Artist", and CHINEKE of the Igbos "Is the World."

To Grandpa, these terms mean the same thing; a Super Great Being, Who causes the world to come into existence. This means that all African Nations believe in the Same Great Creator. However, they do not believe in the same process by which the Great Creator created the world.

On the other hand, to get more insight into Akan religious beliefs, we must see how Mr. Danquah reached his conclusions of what those words mean; his definitions. First of all, we can see that he is saying that, in Akan language, names are not just words, but are Ideas about something; and we quote how he deals with the three titles he mentioned above.

"......BORE-BORE is really the artistic action of ODOMANKOMA. BO means 'to create;' BORE, to scoop or dig, is a duplicative of BO, the particle-RE, being the Akan's grammatical manner of expressing a continuous or repetitive action. For example, 'oko' means 'he goes,' but o-re-ko means, 'he is going' or, 'he keeps going,' progressively.

Now in BORE-BORE, we have as many as two BOs and two – Res, which means that ODOMANKOMA means, (the one who) continuously and progressively excavates and creates. Who invents or hews out, as it were, carving out the idea of creation into reality. ODOMANKOMA is BORE-BORE, The Super Great Creative Genius of the Universe. ODOMANKOMA represents Creative Intelligence."

ODOMANKOMA's title BO-NNA-MMERE-NSON Who created the Seven Eras; the phrase is made up of the following; BO (to create), NNA (day), MMERE (time), and NSON (seven); which means, Who Created the Idea of Seven Days to measure time.

This refers to the seven day week; of which each day was, and still is, ruled by a planet, the Sun, the Moon, Mars, Mercury, Jupiter,

Venus, and Saturn. Each of which symbolizes a Guardian God or Goddess and their character and personality.

These are Guardian Gods and Goddesses of the days, and each person born receives his character and personality from the Guardian Spirit of his or her birthday. (Importantly, as far as our interest is concerned, this means that ODOMANKOMA created seven Gods and Goddesses, and a purpose for each gives character and personality to mankind).

"The third title of ODOMANKOMA is 'oney ODOMANKOMA ba,' which means, ODOMANKOMA is dependable, who has always been on the scene, and always will be. The meaning also goes further than that to mean, 'Who will always be ODOMANKOMA the Almighty Creator and the source of the human soul and destiny."

Mr. Danquah goes on to write. "These three titles mean that the Akan think of ODOMANKOMA as having three major qualities, (1) an artistic quality, (2) the qualities of the seven Gods and Goddesses of the days, and (3) the quality self-existence (self created).

Add these three qualities together, and we have what is called a 'Godhead' or, 'pure idea' or, 'a pure Spirit,' HONHOM (Soul) as it is called by the Akan. For HONHOM is not a 'thing' at all, it is 'the spirit of the thing.'

The Greek have a name for it, they call it 'idea,' The Akan calls it 'adee;' but all are referring to the idea of the Universe; and means that ODOMANKOMA first created the 'idea' of the universe, and then, 'made the idea into reality." And this is the process we mentioned that the Akan are most concerned with.

Of the religious terms Mr. Danquah defined, HONHOM concerns us most at the moment. For it is a good example of what we meant by our example of how a car comes into reality. HONHOM is the logical organization of ODOMANKOMA's qualities.

In our example of the car, these three major qualities are the engine, transmission, and the rear end, which is the car's soul. In this respect, the three qualities of ODOMANKOMA is the Soul of the Universe.

According to Mr. Danquah's definition, this gives us some insight into the 'process' by which the Akan believe the Great Creator Created the Universe.

The second term he used that concerns us is 'Adee.' Now we are going to get into Mr. Danquah's translations of Drum Poems. He next defines the word O-BOO-ADEE as meaning 'O (ODOMANKOMA), BOO (created), and ADEE (the idea.)'

He had already defined the word BOREBORE to mean, 'The creative Activity of ODOMANKOMA, or, the Act of Bringing the Idea of the Universe into Reality.' With this in mind, let us investigate his translation of the drum poem he uses as the foundation of his conclusions.

Mr. Danquah presents the poem in the Akan language, then, translates it into English; Grandpa thought it would be a good idea to present both forms.

"ODOMANKOMA
BOO ADEE
BORE
BOO ADEE
O boo deeben?
O boo Esen
O boo Kawukwabrafo
Di Tire."

(His translation)
"ODOMANKOMA
He Created the Idea
ODOMANKOMA created what?
ODOMANKOMA created Court Crier
ODOMANKOMA created Poet-Drummer
ODOMANKOMA created touch and die:
The big Executioner:
As Principals."

Next, Mr. Danquah defines the key words in the second half of the poem, and then interprets the poem as his conclusions, by asking himself three questions. Now, what is a court crier? What is a Drummer-poet? And what is touch and die, executioner?

"The court crier is the King's spokesman; his duty as such is to keep order in the assemblies. From time to time he utters the words; 'tie! tie! Meaning listen! Or, 'berew! komm! komm! Meaning Quietly! Orderly! Orderly! The quintessence (purest form) of his function (job) is therefore that of 'Keeping Order."

"Order (logic), it is said, is Heaven's first law, and when the Esen's (Spokesman's) name is mentioned first in the list of things ODOMANKOMA created. It is obviously an attempt by the Akan to symbolize the spokesman the primordial (original) Orderliness of (the) Creation (idea) itself."

Mr. Danquah goes on; "Next the drummer or poet-drummer of the talking drums. The drummer is not, as in other orchestras, merely the 'big noise' man.

The talking drummer, called Kyerema, is a poet and historian. His mind is a storehouse of the people's traditional knowledge. He could not play a single bar on the talking drum unless he knew what the "talking" was about, playing the appropriate poem on the appropriate occasion, or for the appropriate person.

The poet drummer is from childhood trained in poetry, stories, and proverbs of the people. And there is not knowledge of nature, or of man which is beyond his comprehension as the language of the talking drums testify.

He is therefore the Akan's symbol of knowledge, ODOMANKOMA's second creation." (This is why Grandpa says that the Akan drummer is a philosopher).

"Then there is the Executioner. He clearly symbolizes Death, and was created by ODOMANKOMA; third in the order."

Mr. Danquah goes on to not only re-translate, but also to interpret the meaning of the poem as follows;

"ODOMANKOMA
He created the Idea
Hewer-out Creator,
He created the Universe.
What did he create?
He created Order,
He created Knowledge,
He created (Life and) Death,
As it quintessence (as the purest form of the idea")

Well Fellow Detectives, Grandpa believes that we now have reached a point from which to begin our investigation into Akan religious beliefs; Drum poems.

We think that Mr. Danquah's evidence well established the Akan beliefs, concerning the creative ideas of ODOMANKOMA, by showing the logical organization of the ideas of Order, Knowledge, and life-death. (Which means that Ideas have life, purpose, and death), or HONHOM, is the process by which the world came into reality; or to say, a group of ideas are the ultimate source of reality, and ODOMANKOMA is the ultimate source of ideas.

Now we will turn to another drum poem to see the connection between the Akan people and ODOMANKOMA.

"The stream crosses the path,
The path crosses the stream,
Which of them is the elder?
Did we not cut a path?
To meet the stream.
The stream had its origin,
Long, long ago.
The stream has its origin
in ODOMANKOMA."

To interpret this poem, we have to ask ourselves two questions, what is the "stream?" In addition, what is the meaning of "did we not cut a path to meet the stream?" We think that the 'stream is the process by which ODOMANKOMA create an idea of the Universe, and brought it into reality.'

To the second question, we think it means that the Akan "learn the process by which ODOMANKOMA created the Universe," learning is the path.

The main point being, the Akan as a people, believe that they must come up with their own ideas and bring them into reality as a way to live their lives; in other words, be like ODOMANKOMA. This concludes the meaning of ODOMANKOMA's title BORE-BORE.

Now we turn to Mr. Danquah's translation of ODOMANKOMA's title 'BO-NNA-MMERE-NSON, Who Created the Seven Eras;' Seven Gods and Goddesses of the seven days of the week. But we need to take our investigation further to really learn the functions of the Seven Eras. For this answer, and a number of other answers, we will look at four drum proverbs;

"ODOMANKOMA created Death before Prophecy." (Which we interpret to mean that ODOMANKOMA created Death after a plan to bring the idea of the Universe into reality).

"ODOMANKOMA created Death, and was killed by Death." (Grandpa thinks the meaning of this proverb will become clear later).

"ODOMANKOMA, having died, left the affairs of the Universe in the hands of the Seven Eras". (Whom we found to be Seven Gods and Goddesses)

It was none but ODOMANKOMA Who made Death eat poison." (This means that ODOMANKOMA defeated Death with a ritual process called death and resurrection).

We will deal with the third proverb first, which to Grandpa, means that ODOMANKOMA created the Seven Eras, Gods and Goddesses, before the Universe was made into reality, and their functions seem like with the Gods and Goddesses of the Yoruba and the Igbo, to be that of *Managers of the Affairs of the World.*

After all, they were present when the whole process of the world's reality took place, which means that they are well qualified to do their jobs. However, we can see that they work different from the Gods and Goddesses of the Yoruba and the Igbo.

On the other hand, as far as the four proverbs are concerned, the theme of death is related to the first poem, "ODOMANKOMA created touch and die, the big Executioner." Then we are very interested in the last proverb, "it was none but ODOMANKOMA Who made Death eat poison."

Which we, like Mr. Danquah, take to mean that ODOMANKOMA defeated Death, or escaped Death, or what we like even better, ODOMANKOMA died, and was resurrected, which would mean that ODOMANKOMA created Death and Resurrection; a subject that we will get deep into, especially in investigating Akan Kingship.

But at this point, we want to investigate the role of the Seven Eras still further.

Mr. Danquah gives the names of the Seven Eras, the ancient Gods and Goddesses, as 'AWO' symbolized by the planet Moon and day Monday. 'ABENA' symbolized by the planet Mars and the day Tuesday. 'AKU' symbolized by the planet Mercury and the day Wednesday. 'ABERAW' symbolized by the planet Jupiter and the day Thursday. 'AFI' symbolized by the planet Venus and the day Friday. 'AMEN' symbolized by the planet Saturn and the day Saturday. Finally, 'AWUSI' symbolized by the planet Sun and the day Sunday. These are the most ancient Gods and Goddesses in Akan Religious Beliefs.

At this point, we will deal with two more questions, first, how the Seven Gods and Goddesses manage the affairs of the world, and how they are organized. Second, how mankind came into reality? However, to begin looking for those answers, we must introduce another God, NYANKOPON, and another Goddess, ASASE YAA AFUA.

This means that we need Mr. Danquah to translate the God's name; and, we will translate the name of the Goddess.

"........The Akan have a particular name for the God of Religion (The God that Created Mankind), who is called 'He of Saturday, NYANKOPON KWAAME. Any male child born on Saturday is called Kwame. Saturday is recognized by the person born on that day as particularly appropriate for (personal) Soul (Kra) worshipping, or washing. Those born on other days of the week observe the equivalent ceremonies of their souls as the Saturday-born do for Saturdays.

The God of Religion is therefore called 'He of Saturday,' either because He is supposed to have been born on Saturday, or that Saturday is the appropriate day for His worship. On every fortieth Saturday, called Dapaa or Dappada, Open or Free Day, special ceremonies are preformed in respect of Saturday's God. There are nine Dapaa days in the Akan Calendar." (We will deal with the Akan calendar in more detail later).

We will consider here the significance of the name NYANKOPON. Apart from recognizing that NYANKOPON is 'He of Saturday', NYANKOPON is most obviously derived from 'The only Great Shining One,' or, 'He Who alone is of the Greatest Brightness.' NYANKOPON is the Greater God (as far as religious worship is concerned)."

This seems to indicate that NYANKOPON is also symbolized as the planet SUN (Sunday) as well as SATURN (Saturday).

Now that we have defined and translated His name, next we want to find out the position NYANKOPON holds in Akan religious beliefs; so naturally we turn to the Drummer-Poet.

"(Spirit of) Asiame Toku Asare,
Twiaduampon Who made God.
The Long Table has settle authority,
Asiame NYANKOPON,
The ODOMANKOMA Drummer says;
If He went elsewhere,
Behold, He has risen up,
The Rooster crows at dawn,
The Rooster crows with intent,
Early, early, early,
We are telling you,
And you will understand."

We are going to attempt to interpret this poem ourselves from translations we have made. For example, it is known that the word Twiaduampon is another name for NYANKOPON.

Therefore, we interpret the second line of the poem "Twiaduampon Who made God," to mean that NYANKOPON is made Chief Administrator of the Affairs of the world.

The third line, 'The Long Table has settle authority,' we take that to mean that the decision was made by the 'Seven Original Gods and Goddesses,' AWO, ABENA, AKU, ABERAW, AFI, AMEN, and AWUSI.

The fourth line, Asiame NYANKOPON, is hailing NYANKOPON as Chief Administrator. And the fifth line, and the second half of the poem, identifies NYANKOPON as the rising Sun. Note Mr. Danquah's translation of the name as 'The only Great Shining One' or, 'He who alone is of the Greatest Brightness.'

Now, we can see where His authority comes from, The Seven Eras; and the position He holds, Chief Administrator of the Affairs of the World. Recall the proverb, 'ODOMANKOMA having died, left the affairs of the Universe in the hands of Counselors,' this means that the Counselors elected NYANKOPON to do the job.

Next let's see, according to a Drum poem Morning Prayer, what purpose NYANKOPON serves the Akan people as God of Religion.

"The Universe is wide, wide, wide;
The Earth is wide, wide, wide.
The one was lifted up,
The other set down,
In ancient times, long, long ago
NYANKOPON

We serve you.
When NYANKOPON teaches you something,
You profit by it.
If we wish white we get it,
If we wish red we get it,
Twiaduampon,
God, Good morning
God of Saturday,
Good morning"

To expand on the relationship between NYANKOPON and the Akan, we will look at seven proverbs that mention this relationship; the Drum poet says,

1. "If all men suffer NYANKOPON together, the individual does not suffer."

2. "I face upwards and can't see NYANKOPON, but what of you sprawling downwards."

3. "To save fraud, NYANKOPON gave each person a name."

4. "Let living men empty your goblet of wine, NYANKOPON would refill it."

5. "Unless you die of NYANKOPON, let living men kill you, and you will not perish."

6. "If you will tell NYANKOPON, tell the wind."

7. "If you would serve NYANKOPON, be thorough, attaching no conditions."

So the question becomes, where did NYANKOPON come from? He is not one of the original Seven Eras Whom ODOMANKOMA created? Mr. Danquah sidestepped this question when he said, "either He is supposed to have been born on Saturday, or that Saturday is the appropriate day for His worship."

Mr. Danquah also mentions a Goddess of religion or, the Goddess of worship, NYANKOPON's female counterpart, ASASE YAA AFUA, however he did not translate Her name, or where She came from. Therefore, we must do some translating ourselves.

ASASE YAA AFUA; it is well known that in the Akan language, the word asase, sometimes spelled asaase, means 'the earth.' It is also true in Akan language, Yaa is a female name meaning 'She of Thursday', whose planet is Jupiter. And Afua, also a female name is 'She of Friday,' and is related to Friday, whose planet is Venus.

So the translation is 'Earth, She of Thursday and Friday.' So, we can say that the Akan Goddess of worship is 'ASASE YAA AFUA, She of ABERAW-Jupiter and AFI-Venus.' In any case, it is well known that ASASE YAA AFUA is the Great Earth Goddess or Great Mother Goddess.

However, we have the same question about Her as we have about NYANKOPON. Where did She come from? She also is not one of the original Seven Eras.

To answer that question, we must take into consideration that All Africans believe that the Gods and Goddesses are organized into a Holy Family; and all Africans organize their families in the same pattern as the Holy Family. Since the Akan family pattern is known, we will take a quick look at the Akan family organization to get some insight into the organization of the Holy Family.

The Akan have a unique family organization, as far as the Afro-American family is concerned. Their children physically, and legally belong to their mother's family. The mother's family, and the mother and her brother, the children's maternal uncle, have responsibility for the child's welfare. Therefore, when an Akan child is asked, 'who do you belong to, the answer would be, 'I am of' the name of his mother and, or, uncle. (We will explain this further when we get into the organization of the Akan Royal Family and Kingship).

Meanwhile, it is also well known that in Akan religious beliefs, as we will see later, AWO, the Moon Goddess, is the Mother of NYANKOPON. It is from these two known facts that we will construct the organization of the Holy Family.

How NYANKOPON and ASASE YAA AFUA
fit into the picture

Recall, ODOMANKOMA created the idea of the Seven Eras, and brought them into reality. This means that ODOMANKOMA created male and female sexuality, symbolized by the Gods and Goddesses, which are in themselves a means of reproduction.

Grandpa believes that the seven Gods and Goddesses had Children Gods and Goddesses, like the Gods and Goddesses of the Yoruba. This is where NYANKOPON and ASASE YAA AFUA came into the picture.

This means that AWO is NYANKOPON's Mother. Add to that, the identifying NYANKOPON as 'He of Saturday, means that the ancient God, AMEN is his Maternal Uncle.

Which again means that AWO and AMEN are Brother and Sister; this being the case, who is His Father? Now if we recall, NYANKOPON is symbolized by the Sun, the ancient God AWUSI, and we think is His Father.

On the other hand, when we come to ASASE YAA AFUA, She of ABERAW and AFI, who, we conclude is Her Mother and Uncle; and they are Brother and Sister, which leaves the question, who is Her Father?

The most important point about NYANKOPON and ASASE YAA AFUA, is that they are the ones that created human beings; (More on this later).

They also had God and Goddess Children; known as Abusua, who is the Goddess of female Clans, and Ntoro, Who is the God of male Clans. We will define Abusua's role later.

For now, we will look at these Ntoro Clan Gods, who are symbolized by bodies of water, for example, rivers and lakes. We will begin with their names; while keeping in mind, that in the Akan language, the word for God is Bosom.

God Symbol	Messenger		Day of Worship
Bosom-MURU Muru River	Python		Tuesday
Bosom-TANO Tano River	Elephant		Saturday
Bosom-PRA Pra River	Leopard		Wednesday
Bosom-TWE Twe Lake	Kwakuo	Monkey	Sunday

There are 12 Ntoro Clan Gods in all. The Akan do not ask each other which God they worship. They ask which Ntoro do you wash; in other words, what God's water do you use to purify yourself (Baptize yourself.)

According to Akan beliefs, when people first came into reality they did not know anything about sex and childbirth, as the story goes.

"Very long ago, NYANKOPON sent a Python, who made its home in the river Muru. At that time, these men and women did not bear children. They had no desire, and conception and birth was not known.

One day the Python asked them, the people, if they had no offspring, and on being told they had not, He said he would cause the women to conceive.

He made the couples stand face to face, and then He plunged into the river, and rising up, sprayed water upon their bellies with the words "kus," and then ordered them to return home and lie together.

The women conceived and brought forth the first children in the world, who took Bosom MURU as their Clan God, each male passing on this God to his children.' This means that Clan Gods are what is known as male fertility Gods."

We will deal with the first two Gods, MURU and TANO, when dealing with King's Clan God, and the God of the Kingdom. Thus is the organization of the Akan spiritual world of Gods and Goddesses, and their position in Akan Religious Beliefs.

Take into consideration that ODOMANKOMA's title, 'Who Created the Seven Eras,' and Mr. Danquah's statement, that 'this refers to the seven days of the week. Each day is ruled by a planet, Sun, Moon, Mars, Mercury, Jupiter, Venus and Saturn, each of which symbolize a Guardian God or Goddess, and their Character and personality.

Each person receives their character and personality from the God or Goddess of their birthday, and that the Akan's Soul and Chosen Destiny comes from NYANKOPON.

Now, let's take another look at the poem and the statement, "did we not cut a path to meet the stream?" Our interpretations were that this meant that the Akan came up with an 'idea' of how to 'learn, and use ODOMANKOMA's process of bringing ideas into reality. And thus is how the Akan deal with the fact that Jealousy and Greed had turned the World Upside Down.

This puts Grandpa in a position to come to a conclusion about the Akan's Articles of Faith; or to say, the major Aspects of Akan religious beliefs.

If we break down the information we have gathered up to this point, as far as Grandpa can see, it will support the following conclusions as to what are the Akan's religious articles of Faith.

(1) Believes that ODOMANKOMA got an idea of a Universe, and through inventing, shaping and forming, brought that idea into reality through the process of logical organization; The Spirituality of The Logic in the Thought process; Thinking.

(2) Believes that ODOMANKOMA had an idea of NTORO (male) and ABUSUA (female) Sexuality, and brought those ideas into reality in the form of the 'Seven Eras,' or Seven Gods and Goddesses.

(3) Believes that the Seven Ancient Gods and Goddesses are the Managers of the Affairs of the Universe, Who Elected NYANKOPON to be Chief Administrator of the Heaven and Earth.

(4) Believes that NYANKOPON had an idea of Human Beings, and ASASE YAA AFUA brought that idea into reality.

(5) Believes that people have the responsibility of creating their own ideas, and bring them into reality; in this way, people take responsibility for themselves.

(6) Believes in Chosen Destiny.

(7) Believes in their Ancestors.

To Grandpa, this means that the Akan have an astrology-numerology organized religion, regulated by numbers and the stars. To demonstrate what this means, and how the Akan religion works, we will turn to another interesting aspect of Akan religion, their Ancient Calendar.

Ancient Religious Calendar and Kingship

For this information we will turn to an English anthropologist, Ms. Eva L.R. Myerowitz, who collected more information on the Akan's Ancient Calendar than anybody else that Grandpa could find.

The Spokesmen for the King, and the head custodian of the royal cemetery, is in charge of the calendar. He counts with nine bundles of forty sticks; each bundle contains a stick, which is of a different color, representing the first day of a 40-day month.

The Calendar consists of nine forty-day months, plus the months are broken down into weeks of seven days each; the names of the days of the week, and their meaning are as follows,

(1) Sunday (Sun), 'under the Sun.'
(2) Monday (Moon), 'calm, peace.'
(3) Tuesday (Mars), 'emotional, quick tempered.'
(4) Wednesday (Mercury), 'fame, heroic.'
(5) Thursday (Jupiter), 'strength, powerful.'
(6) Friday (Venus), 'growth.'
(7) Saturday (Saturn), 'the most ancient God.'

The seven weekdays are also given another name each (a prefix), the prefix and meaning;

(1) Mono, 'fresh or new.'
(2) Fo, 'fertile, generous.'
(3) Nwona, ' shielded, protected.'
(4) Nkyi, 'destructive, anger.'
(5) Kuru, 'exalted, sacred.'
(6) Kwa, 'free, open.'

As there are only six prefixes for seven days, the last day of the week is given the prefix of the first, and therefore the prefix falls back a day with each week. The new year always starts on a Mono-Wednesday, new years day, and the first month of the year is as follows, as an example of how the prefix falls back a day, as the weeks pass within a 40 day month;

1. Mono-Wednesday, 'fresh or new Wednesday.'
2. Fo-Thursday, 'fertile Thursday.'
3. Nwona-Friday, 'protected Friday.'
 4. Nkyi-Saturday, 'destructive Saturday.'
5. Kuru-Sunday, 'exalted or sacred Sunday.'
6. Kwa-Monday, 'free or open Monday.'
7. Mono-Tuesday, 'fresh or new Tuesday.'
8. Fo-Wednesday, 'fresh or new Wednesday'
9. Nwona-Thursday, 'protected Thursday.'

10. Nkyi-Friday, 'destructive Friday.'
11. Kuru-Saturday, 'exalted or sacred Saturday.'
12. Kwa-Sunday, 'free or open Sunday.'
13. Mono-Monday, 'fresh or new Monday.'
14. Fo-Tuesday, 'fertile Tuesday.'
15. Nwona-Wednesday, 'protected Wednesday.'
16. Nkyi-Thursday, 'destructive Thursday.'
17. Kuru-Friday, 'exalted or sacred Friday.'
18. Kwa-Saturday, 'free or open Saturday.'
19. Mono-Sunday, 'fresh or new Sunday.'
20. Fo-Monday, 'fertile Monday.'
21. Nwona-Tuesday, 'protected Tuesday.'
22. Nkyi-Wednesday, 'destructive Wednesday.'
23. Kuru-Thursday, 'exalted or sacred Thursday.'
24. Kwa-Friday, 'free or open Friday.'
25. Mono-Saturday, 'fresh or new Saturday.'
26. Fo-Sunday, 'fertile Sunday.'
27. Nwona-Monday, 'protected Monday.'
28. Nkyi-Tuesday, 'destructive Tuesday.'
29. Kuru-Wednesday, 'exalted or sacred Wednesday.'
30. Kwa-Thursday, 'free or open Thursday.'
31. Mono-Friday, 'fresh or new Friday.'
32. Fo-Saturday, 'fertile Saturday.'
33. Nwona-Sunday, 'protected Sunday.'
34. Nkyi-Monday, 'destructive Monday.'
35. Kuru-Tuesday, 'exalted or sacred Tuesday.'
36. Kwa-Wednesday, 'free or open Wednesday.'
37. Mono-Thursday, 'fresh or new Thursday.'
38. Fo-Friday, 'fertile Friday.'
39. Nwona-Saturday, 'protected Saturday.'
40. Nkyi-Sunday, 'destructive Sunday.'

Nkyi-Sunday is followed by Kuru-Monday and Kwa Tuesday, and the forty third day is again Mono-Wednesday, which restarts the cycle.

Thus, is one example of how the prefix falls back a day as the weeks pass within a 40 day month; however, Grandpa will give another example of how the calendar is formatted on paper as follows to show the same thing. I will show the last month of the old year as the example.

NINTH (LAST) MONTH OF THE YEAR

1 Fo-Monday Fertile	2 Nwona-Tuesday Shielded	3 Nkyi-Wednesday Destructive	4 Kuru-Thursday Exalted	5 Kwa-Friday Free	6 Mono-Saturday Fresh	7 Fo-Sunday Fertile
8 Nwona-Monday Shielded	9 Nkyi-Tuesday Destructive	10 Kuru-Wednesday Exalted	11 Kwa-Thursday Free	12 Mono-Friday Fresh	13 Fo-Saturday Fertile	14 Nwona-Sunday Shielded
15 Nkyi-Monday (Destructive)	16 Kuru-Tuesday (Exalted	17 Kwa-Wednesday (Free)	18 Mono-Thursday (Fresh	19 Fo-Friday (Fertile	20 Nwona-Saturday (Shielded)	21 Nkyi-Sunday (Destructive)
22 Kuru-Monday (Exalted	23 Kwa-Tuesday (Free	L-Adae Mono-Wednesday (Fresh	25 Fo-Thursday (Fertile)	26 Nwona-Friday (Shielded)	27 Nkyi-Saturday (Destructive	28 Kuru-Sunday (Exalted
29 Kwa-Monday (Free	30 Mono-Tuesday (Fresh	31 Fo-Wednesday (Fertile)	32 Nwona-Thursday (Shielded	33 Nkyi-Friday (Destructive)	34 Kuru-Saturday (Exalted	35 Kwa-Sunday (Free
36 Mono-Monday (Fresh)	37 Fo-Tuesday (Fertile)	38 Nwona-Wednesday (Shielded	39 Nkyi-Thursday (Destructive	40 Kuru Friday (Exalted	41 Kwa-Saturday Free	B-Adae Mono Sunday Fresh
43 Fo-Monday Fertile	44 Nwona-Tuesday Shielded	45 Nkyi-Wednesday Destructive				

We should note that a year contains 365 days, and the Akan have 9 months with 40 days each, 9X40=360. To the 360 days, the last of which is a Kuru-Friday, should be added Kwa-Saturday, Mono-Sunday, Fo-Monday, Nwona-Tuesday, and Nkyi-Wednesday to make the full 365 days. That means that the last month of the year really has 45 days instead of 40 days. (See the above calendar).

To start the New Year again on a Mono-Wednesday, the Kuru-Monday, which falls on the 342nd day of the year, is changed to Fo-Monday. This results in the 365th day falling on a Mono-Wednesday; which is celebrated as the first New Year's Day, and Fo-Thursday is the second New Years day. But the calendar starts on the Mono-Wednesday, and seems from this angle, the year has only 364 days or 52 weeks.

Thus a day is lost, and to bring New Year's Day back to the first day of Fall, three days were added every third year; like a leap year in America. The Calendar fixes New Years Day at the Autumnal Equox, which is on the 21st, 22nd, or 23rd of September.

However, Grandpa drew a calendar of the first two months not only to show the new years beginning on a Mono Wednesday, but also to show two ritual holy days, Big and Little Adae, on the first day of the new year and the ninth day.

FIRST MONTH OF THE YEAR						
L-Adae Mono-Wedsday (Fresh)	2 Fo-Thursday (Fertile)	3 Nwona-Friday (Shielded)	4 Nkyi-Saturday (Destructive)	5 Kuru-Sunday (Exalted)	6 Kwa-Monday (Free)	7 Mono-Tuesday (Fresh)
8 Fo-Wednesday (Fertile)	9 Nwona-Thursday (Shielded)	10 Nkyi-Friday (Destructive)	11 Kuru-Saturday (Exalted)	12 Kwa-Sunday (Free)	13 Mono-Monday (Fresh)	14 Fo-Tuesday (Fertile) Ku
15 Nwona-Wednesday (Shielded)	16 Nkyi-Thursday (Destructive)	17 Kuru-Friday (Exalted)	18 Kwa-Saturday (Free)	B-Adae Mono-Sunday (Fresh)	20 Fo-Monday (Fertile)	21 Nwona-Tuesday (Shielded)

22 Nkyi- Wednes day (Destru ctive)	23 Kuru- Thursd ay (Exalte d)	24 Kwa- Friday (Free)	25 Mono- Saturda y (Fresh)	26 Fo- Sunday (Fertile)	27 Nwona- Monday (Shielde d)	28 Nkyi- Tuesda y (Destru ctive)
29 Kuru- Wednes day (Exalte d)	30 Kwa- Thursd ay (Free)	31 Mono- Friday (Fresh)	32 Fo- Saturda y (Fertile)	33 Nwona- Sunday (Shielde d)	34 Nkyi- Monday (Destru ctive)	35 Kuru- Tuesda y (Exalte d}
36 Kwa- Wednes day (Free)	37 Mono- Thursd ay (Fresh)	38 Fo- Friday (Fertile)	39 Nwona- Saturda y (Shielde d)	40 Nkyi- Sunday (Destru ctive)		

SECOND MONTH OF THE YEAR						
1 Kuru- Saturda y Exalted	2 Kwa- Sunday (Free)	3 Mono- Monday (Fresh	4 Fo- Tuesday (Fertile)	5 Nwona- Wednes day (Shielde d)	6 Nkyi- Thursda y (Destruc tive)	7 Kuru- Friday (Exalt ed)
8 Kwa- Saturda y (Free)	B-Adae Mono- Sunday (Fresh)	10 Fo- Monday (Fertile)	11 Nwona- Tuesday (Shielde d)	12 Nkyi- Wednes day (Destruc tive)	13 Kuru- Thursda iy (Exalted)	14 Kwa- Friday (Free)
15 Mono- Saturda y (Fresh)	16 Fo- Sunday (Fertile)	17 Nwona Monday Shielded	18 Nkyi- Tuesday (Destruc tive)	19 Kuru- Wednes day (Exalted)	20 Kwa- Thursda y (Free)	21 Mono- Friday (Fresh)
22 Fo- Saturda y (Fertile)	23 Nwona- Sunday (Shielde d	24 Nkyi- Monday (Destruc tive)	25 Kuru- Tuesday (Exalted)	26 Kwa- Wedmes day (Free)	27 Mono- Thursda y (Fresh	28 Fo- Friday (Fertil e)

29 Nwona-Saturday (Shielded)	30 Nkyi-Sunday (Destructive)	31 Kuru-Monday (Exalted)	32 Kwa-Tuesda (Free)	'L-Adae' Mono-Wednesday (Fresh)	34 Fo-Thurday (Fertile)	35 Nwona-Fridaiy (Shielded)
36 Nkyi-Saturday (Destructive	37 Kuru Sunday Exalted	38 Kwa Monday Free	39 Mono Tuesday Fresh	40 Fo Wednesday Fertile		

As to the religious nature of the Calendar, it serves two purposes, one, it shows the days of worship of Ancestors (called adae). This takes place every sixth Sunday and Wednesday. In addition, it gives the daily moods of the Gods and Goddesses.

As you can see, there are two Adae (ritual holidays) per 42 day period. The big Sunday Adae, where the focus is on the Royal Ancestors, and the little Wednesday Adae, where the major focus is on all of the non-royal Ancestors of the Kingdom.

The Sunday Adae involves the King and Queenmother directly, and the Clan Chiefs and Family-heads in-directly. On the other hand, the Wednesday Adae involves the Clan Chiefs and Family-heads directly, and the King and Queenmother in-directly.

Since there are two Adae rituals, one preformed on a Mono-Sunday, and the other, a Mono-Wednesday, means that they are evenly spread throughout the year; each Sunday Adae is 42 days apart, and the same is true of Wednesday Adae, and the months contain only 40 days that causes the rituals to come at different times of the month.

However, Ms. Eva L.R. Myerowitz says. For example, in the first month, Mono-Sunday falls on the 16th, and the next Mono-Sunday is 42 days later, on the 18th of the second month, and a like time also elapses between each Mono-Wednesday.

Note, in the second month, the ritual holidays fall on the ninth and thirty-third day of the month. I don't know if Ms. Eva L.R. Myerowitz made a mistake in her math, or a mistake was made in Grandpa's calculation when I was drawing the calendar: I have the first month Mono-Sunday on the 19th in the first month, and in the second month, on the 9th <u>if the first day of the first month of the year always falls of a Mono-Wednesday</u> like she said; (See first and second month calendar above). But I was never good at math, and like I said, the point is that there were *two ritual holidays per forty day month. We will get deeper into Adae rituals and Royal Ancestors later.*

The period between one Mono-Sunday and the following Mono-Wednesday is 24 days, and between the Mono-Wednesday and the next Mono-Sunday is 18 days; and this pattern continues throughout the year.

On the other hand, the days are the symbol of a God or Goddess, and the prefix and suffix symbolizes their personalities and moods. We see that their personalities stay the same; however, they are continually having mood changes. Then we can see that the designed purpose of the calendar is to let the Akan know in advance, for ritual purposes, what mood a given God or Goddess will have on a given day throughout the year.

This allows the Akan to understand and use their Ancient Gods and Goddesses to their best benefit. For example, if a person was sick and needed strength, he would ritually approach the Goddess of Strength in Her generous mood, Fo-Thursday, and She will be generous with Her Strength.

On the one hand, if a person were going to war, one would approach Her on Nkyi-Thursday when She would give Her destructive strength. So we can now see one of the many roles that the religious calendar serves.

This gives us some indication of the two major purposes the Ancient Calendar serves; the relationship between the Most Ancient Akan Gods and Goddesses, and the Akan, as well as the relationship between the Akan and their Ancestors. Moreover, it also serves a purpose for the individual Akan; as the following example will show.

Birthdays and days of the week

There is a specific name for each person according to the day of the week he or she is born. For example, any male Akan born on Saturday is called Kwaame (he of Saturday),and for a female it is Ama (she of Saturday; This means that Saturday is that person's "soul worshipping day" or "soul washing" day. Those born on other days of the week do the same thing on their birthday. In America, one celebrates their birthday once a year, whereas the Akan celebrate theirs every week.

However, the Akan take their birthdays to another level, because the celebrating is related to the God of that Day, symbolized by one of the stars in the universe. For instance, their birthday name is the name they use in rituals relationship with the Gods and Goddesses.

Day of birth		Birth day name		Honor	Child of	
English	Akan	Male	Female	God	Akan	Star
Sunday	**Kwasida**	**Kwasi**	**Akosu a**	**Awusi**	**The Sun**	**Sun**
Monday	**Dwowda**	**Kwadw**	**Adwoa**	**Awo**	**Peace**	**Moon**

		o				
Tuesday	**Benada**	**Kwabena**	**Abena**	**Abena**	**War**	**Mars**
Wednesday	**Wukuda**	**Kwaku**	**Akkua**	**Aku**	**Fame**	**Mercury**
Thursday	**Yaoda**	**Yao,Yaw**	**Yaa**	**Aberaw**	**Strength**	**Jupiter**
Friday	**Frida**	**Kofi**	**Afuaf**	**Afi**	**Growth**	**Venus**
Saturday	**Memenda**	**Kwaame**	**Ama**	**Amen**	**Ancient**	**Saturn**

Along with each person's birth day name, he or she also has a personality name, which is also the personality of the God who is the Guardian Spirit of that day of the week. This name is used only on the "talking" drums or horns, and at religious ceremonies: The personality names is as follows;

Kawasi (He of Sunday) is known as Bodua, "Tail of the Beast."

Kwadwo (He of Monday) is known as Okoto, "warm hearted."

Kwabena (He of Tuesday) is known as Ogyam, "the compassionate."

Kwaku (He of Wednesday) is known as Ntoni, "the Hero."

Yao (He of Thursday) is known as Prekp, "love to fight."

Kofi (He of Friday) is known as Okyin, "Wonderer."

Kwaame(He of Saturday) is known as Atoapoma, "Always sexual."

As we saw; the record of time for religious purposes is thought of by periods of forty days, every fortieth day there is a festival called "great Adae" festival; twenty days later, there is a festival called "little Adae." The great Adae festival is always celebrated on the sixth Sunday of the forty day period, and that of the little Adae on the third Wednesday of that same forty day period; although some Akan kingdoms celebrate little Adae on the Wednesday following the Sunday of the great Adae. But I don't think that makes any difference to the purpose of the Adae.

The days of the week are divided into three masculine, and four feminine days; Wednesday, Saturday, and Sunday are masculine days; Monday, Tuesday, Thursday, and Friday are feminine days. To put it another way, three Gods and four Goddesses each have a day of the week in which they rule. These seven days symbolize these seven Ancient Gods and Goddesses are the creator and ruler of the universe, and they are also the Guardian Spirit of the people born on their day of the week.

The numbers, three for males, and four for females, along with seven for the ancient Gods and Goddesses, we will come into contact with later in different forms through-out our study of the Akan's religious life style, along with the forty day period. Twelve is also a male number. On the other hand, the Moon calendar is Female, and the Religious calendar is Male

We must keep in mind that our purpose in investigating the Akan religious beliefs is to lay a foundation to focus on how their religious beliefs in Ideas is related to their Kingship, Kingdom, and Chosen Destiny. Better still we should say, laid a foundation, which leads to the process by which a Kingdom and its Chosen Destiny comes into reality from an idea.

To make this connection, we must understand the thing that makes a Family Divine. According to Akan beliefs, the thing that makes them Divine is that they are ritually related to NYANKOPON and AWO, the King and Queenmother of Heaven.

This being the case, by investigating the ritual symbolism of the Akan Royal Family and Divine Kingship, will not only tell us how their spiritual world is organized, but also answer our major questions about Kingdom Chosen Destiny.

There is one other point that we should draw to our attention before we leave the subject of the Akan religion organization. That is, the Akan area was in the middle of one of the biggest gold fields in the world.

Gold was so plentiful until people could just find gold nuggets on top of the ground washed up by the rain, and it rained a lot. There was also silver in supply, though not as plentiful as gold; made silver more precious than gold.

The point is, gold and silver play a major role in Akan religious beliefs, and especially in the Royal Lifestyle of the King and Queenmother.

Gold symbolizes the Sun, and, the Sun symbolizes NYANKOPON, and as a Divine person, the King is thought of as the Divine Son of NYANKOPON. And being as NYANKOPON is also thought of as 'The King of the World', gold is a symbol of the King's relationship with NYANKOPON.

The same is the case with the Queenmother and silver, which symbolizes the Moon, AWO, the Queenmother of the World; and the Queenmother is thought of as the 'Daughter of AWO,' and silver symbolizes that relationship.

The Akan Nation

To begin our investigation, we must first investigate the dynamics of the social organization of the Akan nation as a whole, to use as a background to see how the Ashanti fit into the picture.

Recall how we defined the difference between a Nation and a Kingdom. The Akan Nation consists of all of the people living in the Akan area; the southern half of Ghana, parts of Togo and Cote D'Ivore on a map of West Africa who speak the same language and have the same religious beliefs.

However, the people and the area are divided into independent groups of Seven Clans who elect a King to form a kingdom, like States in America; only the kingdoms are not tied together by a federal government. The Ashanti is one of those Akan Kingdoms.

But before we deal with the Ashanti Kingdom, we must give a picture of the general dynamics involved in the state of affairs throughout the Akan Nation to fill in our background; and this brings up the subject of economics.

All over Africa, in our time period, we noticed that Africans are fighting each other. The same was true in ancient times; but it is the motives of these wars that interest us.

Like the Yoruba said, jealousy and greed turned the world upside-down, and this was no less true in the Akan Nation. Each Akan Kingdom wanted to dominate ever other Akan Kingdom physically and economically.

The way this operated was, once a Kingdom dominated another with its army in war, the losing Kingdom had to pay the dominant Kingdom tribute, like a tax which could be very high.

This caused the losing Kingdom to have to come up with more money, which they did by dominating a lesser Kingdom and forcing them to help with their taxes. This means that directly or indirectly, all of the valuables were flowing to the major dominant Kingdoms, which became even more rich and powerful.

But this also meant that every Kingdom was trying to get themselves in a position to knock-off the Kingdom to which they had to pay taxes. So being a dominate Kingdom was not easy. In fact, they were always fighting with some Kingdom or others who got out of line.

As to their other motives for fighting, trade goods were flowing from two directions into the Akan Nation, from the north and from the south.

Recall, the Akan Nation was sitting on one of the biggest gold fields in the world, and the world wanted that gold, thus the flow of trade goods.

European trade goods from England, France, Spain, Germany, Italy, Dutch, Portugal, and Belgium, were arriving by ship on the southern Coast in large numbers.

Northern African trade goods, from Morocco, Algeria, Tunisia, Libya, and Egypt, were coming over land in camel caravans across the Sahara Desert.

The dominant Kingdom also wanted to control all of that trade. Which would mean that all of those trade goods flowed to the dominant kingdom. Thus is the economic dynamics of the Akan Nation.

Thus was the situation when the Ashanti came into reality as a Kingdom. They became one of those Kingdoms fighting to dominate. However, they chose a destiny to dominate not only all of the Kingdoms in the Akan Nation, but also those in the surrounding Nations as well.

How they organized themselves spiritually, socially, and economically to reach this goal is the subject of our investigation.

To begin with, we must define the spiritual and social difference between a Clan Chief and a King. A King and Queenmother worship at the shrines of NYANKOPON, and His Mother, AWO. A Clan Chief and Chief mother worship at the shrine of NYANKOPON and His Wife, ASASE YAA AFUA. Other than this difference, the rituals related to Kingship and Chieftainship are the same, and their government is organized on the same pattern, spiritually speaking.

On the other hand, socially speaking, a Clan is a large extended Family on the mother's side of the family. Recall, according to Akan tradition, the children belong to their mother's family. This means that they belong to their mother's clan, and inherit titles and things. Or to say, everybody that is blood kin to your mother is your clan; and they are organized into a clan government, headed by a Clan Chief.

These Clans can be quite large. For our purpose, we will use the number of 10,000; anyway, they elect a older male member, who is qualified to be the leader of the clan. This leader is called a Clan Chief, who is head of that clan government. The point is that a clan is a family affair. Now we will turn our focus on spiritual authority of Kingship.

This is where the Akan religion fits into the picture. Seven Clan Chiefs, symbolizing the Seven Ancient Gods and Goddesses, can elect a member of a Royal Family to manage the affairs of the combined Clan Chiefs, and indirectly, their extended families, as King. Thus you have a Kingdom with a population of 70,000.

Just as the ancient Gods and Goddesses elected NYANKOPON to be the Manager of the Affairs of the World, a King is elected to manage the affairs of a small world, a Kingdom. And these seven Clan Chiefs are the King's Counselors, just as the Ancient Gods and Goddesses are the Counselors to NYANKOPON.

When a Royal family member is elected King, his mother, sister, or niece (on his mother's side) is automatically elected Queenmother. And when a Clan Chief is elected, his mother becomes Chief mother, which means that when NYANKOPON became King of Heaven and the world, His Mother, AWO, became the Queenmother of Heaven and the World.

And one of the many authorities a Queenmother has is over the King's wives. This means that AWO has authority over ASASE YAA AFUA, the Wife of NYANKOPON; and ASASE YAA AFUA is the mother of mankind.

Now we have reached a point where we can deal with our major subject, the Ashanti Kingship, and Chosen Destiny.

The Ashanti People

The question becomes, according to Akan tradition, where and how does the Ashanti Royal Family come into the picture, beings as all of the people came from ASASE YAA AFUA? For that answer, we will begin our investigation of the Ashanti in the Adensi area of the nation.

The Adensi location has been producing generations of Kingdoms for thousands of years. As we mentioned, this is where Mr. Anquandah did the Akan archaeology work. In addition, Adensi was one of the later generations of Kingdoms that formed in that location.

They began forming about 1000 A.D., and grew into one of the biggest and most powerful Kingdoms of that time, but began to fall a part by the late 1500's.

The Ashanti is made up of seven sub-clans that decided to leave the Adensi area about 1600, and those seven clans grew into the Ashanti Kingdom beginning about 1620.

It is the dynamics of the spiritual, physical, and economic history of the Ashanti that we will next turn our investigative attention, to answer our questions about their Royal Family and Kingship, and NYANKOPON and ASASE YAA AFUA, and the Ashanti ideas of the process of the creation of mankind.

For evidence, we will quote what an old Ashanti Queenmother said on the subject of the creation of mankind and the Royal Family.

"Very long ago upon a certain Nkyi-Monday night (see calendar), a worm bored its way into the ground, and out came seven men, five woman, a leopard, and a dog. The names of these men and woman I cannot repeat, save only on a Nkyli-Monday or Tuesday. (The names follows).

Males	Females
Adu Ogyinae	Takyuwa Brobe
Opoku Tenten	Aberewa Noko
Adu Kwao	Aberewa Samanate
Adu Kwao	Aberewa Musu
Kusi Aduoku	Abrade Kwa
Ankora Dame	
Odehye Adjews Sabene	

All of these people with the exception of Adu Ogyinae, were bewildered by the new and strange sights that they saw around them (on earth), and their eyes roved wildly about in fear.

Adu Ogyinae laid his hands upon them one by one, and soothed them. By Wednesday they had begun to build huts, but while so engaged, a tree fell upon Adu Ogyinae and killed him. That is the real origin of the great oath of Ashanti, the wukuda oath; (for example, "I swear by the name of Adu Ogyinae)."

The dog went away and brought back fire in his mouth, food was laid upon the fire, and the dog was fed this, and as it grew fat (from eating cooked food), men came to eat cooked food.

The first of our Ancestors settled at (the village of) Nampansa, where the soil is very red. The men and women who came from the ground were of the Aduana Clan, The Oyoko, and the Royal Clan that was later to sit upon the stool of Kumasi (produced the King to rule the Ashanti). Also up from the ground at (the village of) Santemanso, (the site) of one of the archeology sites in Adensi.

ODOMANKOMA, on His journey about the Earth making things, met people already settled here, (and) took one of our Ancestors with Him as His Spokesmen. We had His staff up to the reign of (the Ashanti King) Kakari when it was lost.

The eight pots (Ancestor Shrine) in the forest are for the men and women of our Clan who came up from the ground at that spot (a grove of trees that serve the purpose of an Ancestor shrine in Santemanso).

The King of Ashanti always sent a cow (for sacrifice at the Ancestor ceremony held at Santemanso), but they were never allowed to go there in person."

The first thing we want to deal with is the symbolism of the old Ashanti Queenmother's statement, "...a worm bored its way into the ground, and out came seven men and several women, a leopard, and dog.

Grandpa's conclusion is that this means that NYANKOPON, who is called the Great Father God, had sexual relations with ASASE YAA AFUA, who is called the Great Mother Goddess, and mankind was born.

Or to say, the statement symbolizes that in one way or another, the Ashanti believe NYANKOPON and ASASE YAA AFUA created mankind.

On the other hand, to use Ashanti terms, when people first came into reality, they already had a leader, Adu Ogyinae, and at least one Royal woman that produced Royal Clans. This Royal person had to be a woman, according to Akan Traditional Family; Royalty follows the women's side of the family.

This also means that, being as Royal means Divine, half man or woman and half God or Goddess, is in one way or another related to AWO, the Queenmother of Heaven and the World. However, there is not much evidence to make that point.

But the old Ashanti Queen mother's comments did show that the Ashanti King had a ritual relationship with the ancient Ancestor shrine. In any case, we are more interested in Her statements about the Oyoko and Aduana Royal Clans.

If we recall, in Akan traditional beliefs, a Kingdom is a Confederation of Seven Clans who choose a King from one of these Royal Families to lead them. The purpose of the Kingdom, with the combined population of the Clans, is to put together a big army, and become rich and powerful.

So when a Kingdom is defeated, there is really no reason for the Clans to support it. The Confederation falls apart, and the Kingdom does not exist any more, and each clan is left on their own for survival.

This has a negative effect on the Clans and their Chief, not only do they not have any money coming in, but they also still have to pay taxes to the dominant kingdom that defeated them, and still care for their clan people economically. This means that from an economical point of view, the Clans have a very serious problem.

For example, when the Adensi Kingdom was defeated by the Denkyira Kingdom, some of the Clans remained in the same area, while others decided to move to another territory to try to improve their situation. The Oyoko, Aduana, and five common people clans, decided to move to another territory.

Now, throughout the Akan Nation, all land is occupied and owned by some other Clan or Kingdom. On the other hand, Clans are powerful in their own right. For instance, a Clan can have a population of over 10,000, which means that a Clan Chief can have an army of over 2,000 warriors.

This means that when the Oyoko and company made a decision to move to another territory, it automatically included a decision about warfare, and the approach and attitude to take land and people.

So we now have a situation where Clans are fighting Clans for land, and economic advantages, and they still must pay taxes to the Kingdom that dominates in the area.

When a Clan defeated another Clan, one of three things happens. Either the defeated Clan joined the winning Clan, and stay in the territory and pay taxes to the winning Clan; or they in turn move to another territory and attack a weaker Clan. But in most cases, the loser will join the winner. In this respect, a Clan can move, and grow in population at the same time if they are strong enough.

Between 1600 and 1620, Adensi Clans made their move from Santemanso, in Adensi, some 50 or so miles north along the northern trade route, with hopes that in that way they could improve their economic position. The area they had in mind was owned and occupied by the Domaa, Tafo, Amakom, Atwima and the Kwabiri people who were large Clans.

How this worked out, the Adensi Clans sent a few members of their Clan to the areas they wanted, and asked permission of the Clan Chief of the area for a little land, and built a small village. This was easily accomplished, because nobody saw them as a threat, plus they paid taxes.

In this way, seven small clan villages were founded in new territory by the Clans from Adensi; the villages were, Kumasi, Asumegya, Juaben, Bekwai, Nsuta, Kokofu, and Mampon. Over the 20-year period, the Clan members were continuously coming from Adensi, and the new villages soon grew into large towns; this is when the fighting began.

The Clans from Adensi wanted to control the land and the people they found in the new territory. This was especially the case with the Royal Oyoko Clan who began with the village of Kumasi. The northern trade routes lead to one point at that time. The dominate Kingdom at the time was Denkyira.

The ambitions of the Oyoko Clan, when they moved to their new village, found that all trade routes met up at their village Kumasi. Which put them in position to control all trade leading to the dominate Kingdom if they became big and powerful enough to defeat Denkyira.

They were in a good position to accomplish this if they could dominate the surrounding land and people in the new territory. Thus we have the motivation for warfare.

On the other hand, all of the new villages' locations are on the two major northern trade routes; which shows that all of the Adensi Clans had the same ambition as Oyoko Clan. Even though at that point in time, they were independent Clans, and fighting their own war with the people in their area.

Now we must keep in mind that all of the land in the Akan nation was owned and occupied by some Clan or Kingdom. For example, the Domaa, Tafo, Kkofu, Amakom the Kwabiri people owned the land on which the Adensi Clans moved; and they, along with the Adensi Clans, were paying taxes to the Denkyira Kingdom.

Also note that the Adensi Clans did not have to move very far from Santemanso, and could travel from their home Village to the new village in a day or so. It was only about 50 or 60 miles.

In the framework of the economic situation that developed when the Adensi Kingdom fell apart, and the decision by some Clans to begin new villages in a new territory, we will next deal with these villages over the years, 1620-1700, to see how they grew into the Ashanti Kingdom.

Although warfare played a big role in the process of development, we are more interested in the Kingdoms spiritual side; with questions like, how does a clan village become big and powerful? How did the Spirit of the Ashanti Kingdom come into reality? What are the rituals related to Kingship? What is the major community ritual of the Ashanti? Who is the God of the Kingdom, and His role? And just as important, what role does the concept of War play in the fulfilling of a Kingdom's Chosen Destiny? We will begin our investigation to answer those questions by first focusing our attention on the history of the new village of Kumasi, the Royal Oyoko Clan, and the origin of the Ashanti Kingdom.

Kingdom's Chosen Destiny

According to the Ashanti, as told by members of the Royal Family, the origin of the village of Kumasi, the Capital Town of Ashanti, is as follows:

"In a thick forest called Kwaman, some 50 miles north of Santemanso, a hunter from the Kingdom of Dagom opened a small market under a okumaninasi tree on the north-south trade route, in order to sell meat of the animals he hunted to traders.

Soon other hunters and farmers from the northern countries gathered around him to supply food and shelter to long distant traders. The small village at this time was called Okumanyinasi, after the tree. The people from all over began to build villages near-by and the area grew rich on trade.

About 1600, the first large group of people from the south in Santemanso, an Aduana royal sub-clan, settled side by side with Okumaninasi, and founded the village Asafo under their Clan Chief 'Otuinfi Bi;' who became Clan Chief of both villages over time, and the two villages began to inter-marry.

Otuinfi Bi was followed by his younger brother, 'Kwabia Amenfi as Clan Chief.

Meanwhile, a 'Clan Chief, Oti Akenten,' of a 'Oyoko royal sub-clan' moved from Santemanso to Okumaninasi-Asafo with a large number of his Royal Clan. Moreover, in one way or another, 'Oti Akenten became the Clan Chief of the combined village which he re-named Kumasi.

This is how the royal Oyoko Clan gained leadership over Kumasi from the Aduana royal clan; though both were royal families from Adensi, and related to each other.

Anyway, Oti Akenten, (as far as Grandpa could fine) is the one who established the future Ashanti attitude and approach to conquer people in, and close around Kumasi in order to provide themselves with land and people, and take control of the trade route.

Oti Akenten became Clan Chief of Kumasi around 1630, and died about 1660. He was followed as Clan Chief by 'Obiri Yeboa,' his nephew (sister's son). Obiri Yeboa took up where Oti Akenten left off fighting for control of land and trade.

This was not easy; for instance, there were the Tofo people, who were then an old and prosperous trading town. Their wealth had already attracted other settlers like the Domaa, Amakom, Kwabiri and Atwima; all of which had villages within a few miles radius of Kumasi.

During these times, the struggle for power in the Kumasi area between the old settlers and the new arrivals was a do or die situation. Especially with the Domaa; for the Domaa and the Oyoko of Kumasi were evenly matched, and that war, off and on, lasted for years.

Meanwhile, Obiri Yeboa was also fighting the Tafo, Amakom, Kwabiri and Atwima. Finally in the late 1690's, Obiri Yeboa was killed in one of the wars with the Domaa. He was followed as Clan Chief by his nephew, 'Osai Tutu,' the man who later founded and became the 'first King of the Ashanti Kingdom.' He was out of the country at the time Obiri was killed.

Osai Tutu

To bring Osai Tutu into the picture, we must go back about 25 years before Obiri Yeboa was killed. Obiri became Clan Chief in 1660, but from the first he had a problem, he had no one to inherit his position.

As we mentioned, Clan Chiefs are followed in office by his brother on his mother's side, or nephew on his sister's side.

However, Obiri Yeboa had no brothers and only one sister, 'Manu Kotosii,' who was old and well pass child-bearing age, and had no children; though she had been married three times.

This was a problem because the Oyoko Royal Clan would lose its leadership role to the Aduana Royal Clan; therefore, Obiri Yeboa sent his sister to a famous Shrine, of 'the God OTUTU' to solve the problem.

This was a 'Shrine, and God known for miracles.' After sacrifices and other rituals were preformed, the High Priest of OTUTU had Manu Kotosii lay on a board on her back naked, and poured Holy Water over her body.

After she returned home she became pregnant with a son, and thereafter daughters. The son she named Tutu in honor of the God OTUTU who caused the miracle to happen, for she was an old woman; and this is how Osai Tutu came into the picture and got his name.

Obiri Yeboa took personal charge of the raising and educating of Tutu from the time he was old enough to walk and talk, 5 or 6 years old, until he became a young man. This was his responsibility being the brother of Osai Tutu's mother as we mentioned.

The Oyoko of Kumasi-town was continuously at war with the Domaa, Tafo, and others, and Obiri Yeboa was Clan Chief and therefore War Chief as well.

This means that Obiri took Tutu every were he went, even on the battle field, as well as Clan business meetings; Osai Tutu grew-up knowing the meaning of warfare as well as the art of leadership.

When Tutu became a young man, Obiri Yeboa sent him to work in the palace of the King of Denkyira. He wanted Tutu to learn how a dominate Kingdom operated, plus the Denkyira King always liked to check-out future Clan Chiefs of Clans that were paying him taxes.

Right away in Denkyira Osai Tutu got into big trouble. He got the King's sister and a few of his wives pregnant, and had to flee for his life. On the other hand, this action shows just how bold Tutu was, for those charges carried the death penalty, and he knew it.

Tutu escaped to the semi-dominate Kingdom of Akuapem whose King was a friend of Obiri Yeboa. This is why Tutu was not in the Kumasi when Obiri got killed. This is also why Adu Gyemfi had to act as Regent until he could safely come home. After all, the Denkyira King was just waiting for Tutu to come home so he could punish him.

Meanwhile, the Akuapem King took a special liking to Tutu, and not only gave him safety, but also taught him the art of using and keeping power in a dominate Kingdom.

At the same time, being as Akuapem is near the sea coast and European trade centers, Tutu could study the Kingdoms blocking the trade route north to Kumasi-town; As well as the Europeans, and how to deal with them.

It was during this time period that he developed a burning ambition to rule the entire Akan nation. He got the idea of a plan to bring his ambition into reality; a 'Master Plan.'

As important, while in Akuapem, Tutu met a 'Master Priest, Anokye,' who was chained to a log (African jail) for some offense, to which Tutu used his influence with the King to get all charges dropped.

After which Tutu told Priest Anokye of his 'master plan', and right away 'Priest Anokye' came up with a 'master plan for the Spirit of a kingdom;' Osai Tutu and Priest Anokye became very close friends.

Meanwhile, Osai Tutu and the King of Akuapem became lasting friends; after all, the famous Shrine of the God OTUTU was located in Akuapem. And it was the same King that gave Obiri Yeboa permission to send Manu Kotosii, Yeboa's sister, to receive the miracle of pregnancy, which resulted in Tutu being born.

After two or three years in the Kingdom of Akuapem, and one year after Yeboa was killed, it was safe for Osai Tutu to return to Kumasi and become Clan Chief of the Royal Oyoko Clan.

The King of Akuapem gave him a troop of three hundred men to assure a safe journey, led by a War Captain with whom Tutu had also became close friends.

Amankwa Tia

When Tutu told the War Captain of his master plan, and seeing that Tutu needed a special army to carry out the plan, he came up with a master plan of his own. His plan consisted of how to organize an army, and inspire it to greatness; this mans name was 'Amankwa Tia.'

However, before a kingdom can become dominate, it must have physical power. A Master Warrior, or War Chief, and a powerful army; and this is where Amankwa Tia's Master Plan (Amankwa ideas) came into the picture.

When he was appointed to take Osai Tutu to Kumasi, he could put his plan into action; his plan was in the organization of his army, as follows;

```
Scouts
L          Advance Guard                       R
e                                              i
f          War Captain                         g
t                                              h
w          Main Army                           t
i          War Chief Amankwa Tia               W
n                                              i
g          Drummer-Osai Tutu-Priest Anokye     n
Rear Guard                                      g
```

The job of the scouts was to locate the enemy, determine their number, and report back to the War Captain of the advance guard.

The advance guard would attack the enemy from the front, right wing on the enemy's right side, and the left wing on their left side. This forces the enemy to close ranks in a neat little package, where the main army could finish them off.

Naturally, the rear guard is to protect the army's rear. On the other hand, while traveling, the advance guard, right and left wing, and the rear guard have the main army of, Osai tutu, Priest Anokye, and Amankwa Tia surrounded, to defend against a surprise attack.

The point is that the army is commanded from the center, which means that the War Chief pushed, rather than lead his army into battle. It must be noted at this time, when ever a Kingdom or Clan goes to war, the King or Clan Chief goes with the army.

This is what we mean that Amankwa Tie came up with an idea of how to organize his army. And this is how Amankwa Tia succeeded in traveling in hostile territory to bring Osai tutu and Priest Anokye to Kumasi. In the course of which he proved himself to be a Master Warrior, being out numbered in most of the battles he had.

Priest Anokye

On the other hand, before a Kingdom can come into reality, it must have a soul, i.e., spiritual unity. This is where Priest Anokye came into the picture.

Anokye was born in a place called Akrokyere in Adensi. His mother was of the Asenie clan, and his father of the Bosommuru Clan God. Both were holy people. His father a priest, and his mother a priestess.

Anokye's elder brother was Yamoa, who also became a priest, but was killed along with Obiri Yeboa in the Domaa war; but Anokye did not grow up around his brother, who was much older and had a different mother.

Tutu's father was also of the Bosommuru Clan God, but not in the same family line as Anokye's father; they were like third or forth cousins.

In any case, it is said that Anokye was born with strong spiritual powers; in Ashanti words, "he was born holding two lumps of spiritual magic made of balls, and a cow's tail in his hands."

Throughout his youth, Anokye was called a "Prophet" and could predict the future, "curse or bless at will. "People said, "He got the Power!" But being inexperienced, this got him into a special kind of trouble in his early adulthood.

For example, once, as a young teenager, Anokye and his mother were in the kingdom of Denkyira attending a big community ritual.

When he went into a trance, he predicted that a woman with discolored hands would bring evil to the Kingdom; and his mother had discolored hands, before he came out of the trance, the King had Anokye's mother killed. Even though she was not the woman he was talking about in the trance.

This is what we meant when we said that Anokye's 'special powers' got him in special kinds of trouble. It made him an orphan, and it changed his life. Being in a strange land, knowing no one, Anokye was on his own, and really raised himself from that point on.

So at the age of 12 or 13, he began to travel all over the Akan nation studying under master priests at times, serving different Gods, practicing all kinds of rituals, and generally educating himself in spirituality; and as always getting into trouble. Thus is how he came to be chained to a log in Akuapem when Osai Tutu found him.

However in the process of the many spiritual experiences, Anokye became well educated in spiritual matters, and a gifted Priest and Prophet.

His only problem was that he did not have a purpose; Osai Tutu's Master Plan was the perfect thing for him to pull himself together. This opened the way for him to become the Super Master Priest-Prophet-Miracle worker he became.

However, we must define what we mean by the terms 'Priest-Prophet-Miracle worker.'

A Priest is a Man that understands the workings of the Spiritual World. A Prophet is a man that can look at a situation and see what it will lead to in the future. A Miracle worker is a man that can create a situation that will lead to a future of his own design. All of these have to do with rituals.

So to understand Anokye, we must remember first of all that he is an Akan, and Akan's believe that everything or situation has a spirit. That ritual allows a person establish a relationship, and sometimes control the spirit of that thing, or situation.

Therefore, to deal with a thing, or situation, one must deal with its spirit, and the only way to deal with spirits is through rituals.

But as a Miracle worker, Anokye was not following traditional rituals. He could create a ritual to fit the spirit of any situation, and a situation to fit any spirit. This knowledge allowed him to be able to know what was going to happen in the future, because he could make it happen, as we will see. This is the meaning of Priest-Prophet-Miracle worker.

Therefore to create a thing, like a powerful Kingdom, one must also create a powerful spirit, or cause a powerful spirit to possess it, like a God, and, or, Goddess.

So When Osai Tutu became Clan Chief of the Oyoko clan, and declared war on the Domaa for killing his uncle, Priest Anokye was well prepared to take care of the spiritual side of Tutu's war plans, step by step.

Ashanti Kingdom

Now, let us define what we mean by Osai Tutu coming up with a 'Master Plan.' We mean that upon learning the nature of the art of King Leadership, from the King of Akuapem, and looking at the nature of the economical situation on the Coast, he came up with an idea of how he could control all the Akan trade activities.

He could become the King of Kings in the Akan nation, or to say, the Royal Family he was a part of, could rule the whole of the Akan nation; Osai was a very ambitious young man with lots of courage.

The question becomes, how is the Master Plan (Osai Tutu idea's) to be brought into reality? To transform Osai Tutu's Master Plan into a reality, he needed a Kingdom which took this idea to dominate all of the kingdoms in the Akan nation, as its Chosen Destiny. This is where Priest Anokye's Master Plan (Priest Anokye's ideas) came into the picture.

Anyway, immediately after his arrival in Kumasi-town, and becoming Clan Chief, Osai Tutu made Priest Anokye High Priest of the Oyoko Royal Clan, and Amankwa Tia War Chief of its army.

With all of this in mind, we will next direct our attention to how these three 'master plans' were transformed from a group of seven Adensi Clans and their Clan Chiefs, into a rich and powerful Kingdom; with special emphasis on the role of the Priest Anokye in that transformation process.

Now, according to the Old Ashanti who are the direct descendants of Anokye, we will take a look at what they had to say about the long line of events, and spiritual activities, that brought the Spirit of the Ashanti Kingdom into reality; Which was the spirit of Osai Tutu's Master plan as the Destiny of the new Kingdom.

Meanwhile, the first step Osai Tutu made in this direction as Clan Chief, was to declare war on the Domaa.

However, the Domaa were tough, and had defeated the Oyoko before, and killed Obiri Yeboa. For the most part, the Domaa and Oyoko were evenly matched.

Neither could defeat the other in any final way. What Tutu needed was something to swing the balance of power to the Oyoko side; this was Priest Anokye's job.

The first thing Priest Anokye did, after Tutu declared war, was to call a meeting of the Clan Chiefs of the new Adensi villages of Bekwai, Nsuta, Kokofu, Juaben, Mampon, Asumegya, and of course Tutu of Kumasi, and use the occasion to discuss their unification to fight the Domaa.

When they agreed, the unification was sealed by a ceremony of everybody present drinking palm wine mixed with secret spiritual properties. This left the question, who was to be the leader of this new loose confederation of Clans?

To settle this question, a test was made to find out who this leader should be. One of Priest Anokye's assistants planted a cutting of the tree called Kumnini in the seven Adensi villages. Those of the other villages died, and the one at Kumasi lived.

This was taken as a sign that the Clan Chief of Kumasi, Osai Tutu, should be the leader. Next, Priest Anokye buried gold, silver, brass, copper, lead, and iron bars at a special spot; as a sacrifice to Mother Earth, ASASE YAA AFUA, to make the union strong.

Priest Anokye then buried a python under the raised earthen platform upon which Osai Tutu, as clan Chief, sat on great occasions; the python is the Messenger of Tutu's father Clan God, BOSOMMURU.

Take special note, before we get ahead of ourselves, that the Gods and Goddesses we are now referring, unless already explained, are the Sons and Daughters of NYANKOPON and ASASE YAA AFUA; this is the case with the God BOSOMMURU. These were the ritual steps of establishing Osai Tutu as leader of the confederation.

Following this, Priest Anokye instructed Amankwa Tia to go and stand at a special place in the forest, where he told him he would meat a leopard. He ordered Amankwa Tia to lead the leopard by its left paw and bring it to him.

Amankwa Tia did as he was told, met a leopard, and led it to Anokye by the left paw. Osai Tutu then cut off its head, and its skin was made into a hat for Amankwa Tia; and he was given the title of War Chief of all the warriors of the seven Clan Chief's villages. The leopard's head was buried in a special mound of dirt, around which all of the war councils were to be held. The remaining parts of the leopard were given a human type burial with all of the funeral rituals.

Grandpa thinks we should stop at this point and review this ritual act of Priest Anokye. For example, let us just think what it will take for a man to be able to confront a wild leopard, and lead him by his left paw! Why the left paw? Why did they make a hat from his skin and give it to Amankwa Tia? Why use the leopard's head as an alter for war counsel meetings? And, why give the leopard a human type funeral?

This brings up the subject of the Leopard that came up from the ground with Human Beings that the Old Queenmother mentioned. We know the purpose that the Dog serves. He gave mankind the art of the use of fire. But what purpose did the Leopard serve? The leopard, whose title is BOHEMO, is related to the Ancient War God of Tuesday, ABENA, whose War title is SANTEMAN; the leopard is His Son, or to say, the leopard symbolizes the Spirit of the Akan War God.

This is why the Old Queenmother could only recite the names on the Original Ancestors on a Monday or Tuesday. Monday being the Day of the week when the Ancestors came up from the ground. And Tuesday is the day of the Leopard's Father. So Monday or Tuesday were the proper days to speak the names.

Now back to the ritual sacrifice which transformed Amankwa Tia into the War Chief of the 7 Clans.

Priest Ankoye stood on one side of the mound of dirt, where the leopard's head was buried. He took a cup of wine in his right hand, leaned over the mound, and spoke as follows, while a sheep was held across the shoulders of Amankwa Tia who stood beside him as he spoke;

"SANTEMAN KOBINA, here is wine. By your kindness today is Tuesday. That is the day on which you eat (is sacrificed too). I hold this sheep and wine and give to you; let no one tie a knot in his head (plot) that the swords come into play (start a war between the seven Clans). Permit no bad thing whatever to come upon this people of SANTEMAN. Your son is Amankwa Tia who has brought a sheep and wine for You. Let him have life, do not let his ears become closed, do not let his eyes become covered over."

Priest Anokye then pressed a small pointed knife into the sheep's throat, saying as he did so, the following words as the blood dripped on the mound;

"SANTEMAN KOBINA, receive this sheep and eat; life to the Royal Clan mother, life to the Royal Clan Chief, life to the Chief of Warriors. May Chief Osai Tutu never have to say 'what shall I do?' May the Clan Mother Manu Kotosii never have to say 'what must I do?' And May Amankwa Tia never have to say 'how must I fight?'"

Next Priest Anokye, with the wine cup in his left hand, poured some on the mound, saying,

"Bohemo the leopard, who springs to the left, we are giving your father something to eat, and you who shake the foliage around the Ashanti territory, here is yours."

Grandpa's conclusion is that Priest Anokye was ritually establishing Amankwa Tia as war Chief before the Akan War God, as well as before the six Clan Chiefs. This made him the leader of the combined armies of the seven Clans, symbolized by the leopard skin hat.

In making the leopard's head, an altar at war counsel symbolizes that the approach and attitude of the army was to be that of a leopard; note the organization of the army. And giving the leopard a human burial symbolizes instituting the leopard's spirit with those of the seven Clan Chiefs.

This interpretation of the rituals Priest Anokye performed, not only tell us what he was accomplishing, but also give us some insight in the Akan symbolic way of thinking. On the other hand, this should give us some indication of the role leopards play in Ashanti's religious beliefs.

However, we will deal with ritual symbolism in more detail when we get deep into the nature of Kingship. As for now, we will remain with Priest Anokye and his ritual activities related to the Osai Tutu war with the Domaa.

Priest Anokye then ordered Osai Tutu to make swords and hand them out to his War Captains, with a special one for Amankwa Tia as

War Chief. He created an oath they should take; this is how the taking of an oath before war was instituted. Priest Anokye himself took one of the swords and, standing before Osai Tutu, swore;

"I speak the name of the father of Osai Tutu (his spiritual father, the God Otutu), the great forbidden oath that, if I do not go to this war on which you have sent me forth. Or, if I go and show my back to the enemy, and if I run away, then I violate the great forbidden oath.

If it is a choice between dishonor and death, death is my choice. If I go forward, I die, if I flee, I die of the oath; better to go forward and die in the mouth of battle." Amankwa Tia, war captains, and the warriors of the seven Clans took a similar oath.

Next Priest Anokye asked Osai Tutu for one of his cousins, and was given Saben, a son of his uncle Obiri Yeboa. Anokye gave Saben a shield, and he was told that so long as the front of the shield was present towards the enemy, they would retreat.

Saben was also informed that the spiritual rule of the shield was that he should never drink palm wine while holding the shield. Then Osai Tutu attacked the Domaa.

The fighting lasted several days, and the warriors had nothing to eat. One day, Saben saw a woman carrying a pot of palm wine. He forgot all about the spiritual rule of his shield, and drank, and turned the face of his shield away from the enemy, who rallied and turned upon the unified forces of Oyoko warriors, who retreated.

Priest Anokye was accused of being a fake, but was able to show how Saben had violated the spiritual rule. All of the swords that had been made were now cast, by Anokye's orders, into a stream; new swords were forged by the blacksmith, and the oaths were again taken.

Saben was warned that he would be killed in the fighting. This was the origin of an old Ashanti saying, "What ever happens, Saben will die." The Oyoko were this time victorious; but it took two wars to do it.

At this time the Tafo people were very powerful; they had not taken any part in the Domaa wars, but their Ntabera talking horns and Fontomfrom talking drums could be heard in Kumasi, talking about how powerful they were.

Osai Tutu demanded that these instruments should be handed over, and when the Taros refused, he attacked and defeated them, capturing and killing their Clan Chief.

This is how Fontomfrom drums and Ntabera horns first came to Kumasi as part of their ceremonies. Chief Tutu and his War Chief, Amankwa Tia's warriors were on a roll. And it was not long before the Kwabiri, Atwima, and Amakom were defeated, and the whole area was under the control of the Seven Clans from Adensi; almost.

Then came the third war with the Domaa, who now had a new Chief, Domaa Kusi, who rebelled against Osai Tutu, and was again defeated; but he was not killed as was the case with other defeated Chiefs.

He was sent to Mampon, where Priest Anokye had a temple built, to be a priest to NYANKOPON. The reason for this was that Domaa Kusi had two sisters, and Priest Anokye married both, by which he had a son by each. This was the first step of making the Ashanti Kingdom a reality.

Most importantly, when Domaa was defeated the third time, Priest Anokye captured the Spirit of their God, 'TANO,' and put it in a brass pan (which is used as Shrines by the Akan) and brought Him back to Kumasi, and appointed a Priest as His custodian; thus the Confederation of 'Seven Clans had a God of Unity.'

This brings up a big question, how does a Priest capture a God? This is very interesting because we will look at the ritual of making a Shrine, which is to be the home of a God. For this answer, we will quote from what an Ashanti priest had to say on the matter.

"To begin the process, Priest Anokye allowed himself to be spiritually possessed by the God TANO on the banks of the Tano River. TANO then instructed him to prepare a brass pan, and collect water, leaves, and *spiritual medicine* of a specific kind. Then Priest Anokye danced for three days to the accompaniment of drums and songs, with short intervals for rest.

Quite suddenly, he plunged into the river and emerged holding something he had brought up. He folded this thing to his breast, and water was at once sprinkled upon it to cool it, when it will be thrust into the brass pan and quickly covered up.

The *spiritual medicine* is then pounded and placed in the brass pan, along with the original object already inside (what the man brought up from the river bottom), while the following prayer is repeated;

'Supreme Being (NYANKOPON), upon whom men lean and do not fall, Earth Goddess (ASASE YAA AFUA), Leopard, and all beasts and plants of the forest. Today is a sacred Friday; and You, TANO, we are installing, we are setting You (here), that we may have long life.

Do not let us get death; do not let us become impotent; life to the head of these Clans; life to the young men; life to those who bear children (women), and life to the children of these Clans.

O tree, we call Odum Abena, we are all calling upon you that you may come, one and all, just now, that we may place within this Shrine the thoughts that are in our heads.

When we call upon You TANO in the darkness, when we call upon You in the sunlight, and say, do such a thing for us, You will do so.

And the laws that we are decreeing for You, this new God of ours, are these if in our time, or in our Children's, and our grandchildren's time, a King should arise from somewhere, and come to us.

And say he is going to war when he tells you, and You well know that should he go to the fight he will not gain the victor, You must tell us so. And should You know that he will go and conquer, then also state that truth.

Yet again, if a man is ill in the night, or in the daytime, and we raise You aloft and place You upon the head, and we inquire of You saying, is so and so about to die? Let the cause of the misfortune that You tell him has come upon him be the real cause of the evil and not lies.

Today, we all in this town, all our Elders, and all our children, have consulted together and agreed without dissent among us. We have all united and with one accord decided to establish Your Shrine, You, TANO, upon this a Sacred Friday.

We have taken a sheep, and a chicken, we have taken wine, we are about to give them to You (as sacrifice) that You may reside in this town and preserve its life. From this day, and so on to any future day, you must not fly and leave us.

From this day, to any future day, You, O TANO's fire, in anything that you tell us, do not let it be a lie. Do not put water in Your Mouth and speak to us. Today you become a God of the Clan Chiefs (Osai Tutu and the other six), today You have become a God for our spirit Ancestors.

Perhaps upon some tomorrow one of the Clan Chiefs may come and say, 'my child so and so is sick,' and ask You to go with him, or may be he will send a messenger here for You; in such a case You may go and we will not think that You are fleeing from us.

And these words are a voice from the mouth of us all."

Now to Grandpa, from what the old Ashanti priest said, this not only shows how a shrine comes into reality, but also the prayer shows us the nature of the relationship the Ashanti established with the God of that Shrine. Although they showed honor and respect, they are the ones that laid out the rules of the relationship. By making rules, they place themselves in the position as future judges of the God's conduct.

And we should notice the straightforward logical approach; there was nothing emotional about the prayer, and the calling of other spiritual forces as witnesses, which gave the ritual a legal touch.

This is what Grandpa means by the statement that the Akan Religious Beliefs are a thinking man's religion, and what they are seeking from the God is information and positive energy. This is especially shown in their statement, "We may place in this Shrine the thoughts that are in our heads."

This ritual is called, "The consecration of a Shrine, or, the bringing of the Spirit of God into the Shrine, or, the making of the brass pan and its spiritual ingredients into a Holy Altar of a God."

The Shrine is consecrated with prayer, and the sacrifice of the sheep, chicken and palm wine. With some of the blood of the sheep and chicken, along with some palm wine being place in, and mixed with the other ingredients in the Shrine, the ritual is completed, and the God is captured. This follows a joyous celebration of drumming, singing and dancing.

Our major point is that, in capturing a God, Priest Anokye invoked the God TANO to take possession of him, and he consecrated a shrine as the God's new home, and moved his to Tutu's clan village. This is how TANO became the God of the Seven Clans from Adensi; He is their God of Unity, or to say, their beliefs in TANO unified them into one people. Now to return to the wars with Domaa.

The three wars with the Domaa pointed to a problem, why did Osai Tutu allow the Domaa to regroup to fight the second and third wars?

For example, when the Amakom were defeated, Osai Tutu appointed his favorite, Edu Panin, to be Chief of Amakom, and gave his sister to him in marriage. The off spring of this marriage was Opoku Ware, whom Osai Tutu named to be his successor, being his sister's son, who became the second King of Ashanti; but we are getting ahead of ourselves.

The three wars not only pointed to a problem in defeating, but especially, keeping an enemy defeated. At the same time, it shows how a Clan enlarged its population. This is what Osai Tutu's sister and Priest Anokye marrying into the enemy's leading families' deals with.

There are one of four things that happen when a Clan is defeated; either marrying into the ruling family as we saw; or, defeating a clan and appointing, from their ruling family, who is to be their Clan Chief. Naturally, this is one that agrees with the winning Clan's plan.

Another one is defeating a Clan, and forcing their Clan Chief to 'Drink the Gods,' make a great oath to serve Osai Tutu, or to say, accept Osai Tutu's Master Plan. Finally, in the defeat of a Clan, capture their God, and the people will follow. As finally was done with the Domaa.

This was the second step in the formation of the Seven Clans into a Kingdom. So now we can turn our attention to the very interesting events that led up to the final stage in bringing the Ashanti Kingdom into reality.

The Denkyira Kingdom, being the dominate Kingdom in the area, had been watching the war activities of the Oyoko Clan, and saw them as a upcoming threat.

To deal with this situation in their area, Denkyira sent a big brass bowl to the Oyoko group, with the demand that it be filled with gold dust, also that the favorite wives of the Seven Chiefs be sent to the King.

We must remember that all of this time, the Seven Clans from Adensi, as well as the Clans they were fighting, were paying taxes to Denkyira.

This was Denkyira's attempt to bring the Oyoko into line, by either making them accept an insult, or by war; for they had to protect their reputation as the dominate Kingdom in the region.

However, Denkyira did not take into consideration the powers of Priest Anokye. We now come to the final step of how the Spirit of a Kingdom comes into reality.

When the Officials from Denkyira arrived with these demands, Priest Anokye caused Osai Tutu to summon all of the Clan Chiefs who had taken part in the Domaa wars to come to Kumasi.

Meanwhile, he gathered some secret spiritual properties, which he mixed with palm wine. A great meeting was held; Osai Tutu sat on the raised mound of earth beneath which the python was buried.

The messengers from Denkyira stood before them and renewed their demands, which was answered by a shout in union "We shall not pay!"

The Chiefs became so angry that one of the Clan Chiefs of Juaben picked up a sword and struck the Denkyira Chief Messenger, wounding him and cutting off one of his ears.

The Messengers were sent back to Denkyira empty-handed. This meant that it now was insult for insult. It was a big insult to wound a King's Messenger, for it is the same as wounding the King himself. In this way, the Oyokos had declared war on a dominate Kingdom.

All of the Chiefs now asked Priest Anokye what they should do next; he said they should prepare for war, and meantime not make any other wars.

In fact, warfare is how the Ashanti got their name. The King of Denkyira said *"it is only because of war these people have come together."* So Osai Tutu named the new confederation of Seven *Clans* *"The because of war people,"* in the Akan language, *"The-esa-nti-fo,* which means the *Ashanti people," or "the warrior people;"* thus is how the Ashanti people got their name.

Meanwhile Priest Anokye went to Denkyira where he turned into a red-skinned girl, and sat in the market selling fish.

The Denkyira King's servants saw her, and reported to the King that they had seen a beautiful girl in the market selling fish.

The fish Anokye was selling was mixed with secret spiritual properties, so that the heart of anyone who ate them would become like that of a weak woman.

The King was fascinated with this girl as his woman, and while he was asleep, Anokye (symbolically) took the Kings heart, and then escaped and returned to Kumasi.

Now he was ready to perform his masterpiece of a ritual, the bringing of the Spirit of the Ashanti Kingdom into reality; and at the same time, make Osai Tutu the first King of that Kingdom, and his mother, Manu Kotosii, its first Queenmother.

To the people of the Seven Clan villages, Anokye announced that on a certain Friday, the day of worship of their new God TANO, a special ceremony was to take place in Kumasi; to be attended by everybody in the confederation, men, women, and children.

When this Friday came, it was a beautiful clear day. A multitude of people had gathered around a giant Wawa tree in the center of Kumasi. The air was charged with a serious kind of excitement and expectation.

The Clan Chiefs and Chief mothers were sitting on their Clan Stools of Authority. They were dressed in their most impressive clothes near Osai Tutu, who, on his Stool, was sitting under the tree itself placed on the mound where the python was buried.

Everybody knew that something special was going to happen, but what? Not a word was spoken; even the children were quiet and serious. The only sound to be heard was the small drums that were beating out a strange new rhythm just above the sound of the leaves blowing in the breeze. All eyes were on the man of the hour, Priest Anokye.

Finally Priest Anokye moved into the clearing facing the Chiefs and Chief mothers, and began to dance. Soon he was possessed by the God TANO, who he had captured from the Domaa; then Anokye began to speak.

"We are all alike, we have the same traditions, now we the same Master Plan; let us unite. Lets us then ask this God to send us a symbol of our unity to seal our victory with a pact that will last beyond the time when our children who are not yet born are wise and white-haired men and women. If there is a desire among you for all of us to join together, let this new God of our people now speak!"

At this point the sky burst with a flash of lightning, and a clap of thunder. A thick cloud of white dust appeared in the branches of the Wawa tree; and then, slowly, there descends from the cloud a wooden Stool trimmed in gold, and decorated with mysterious carvings.

Inch by inch it floated down, until finally it came to rest gently on the knees of Osai Tutu; this symbolized the Spirit of the Kingdom called the Golden Stool.

From Osai Tutu, Priest Anokye received twelve strands of hair from his head, six from each ear, and six from each nostril, six from his mustache, six from his beard, and twelve public hairs, and clippings from each of his fingers and toe nails. This symbolized the Osai Tutu Master Plan as the Kingdom's Chosen Destiny.

From each of the Chiefs and Chief mothers, he takes clippings of fingernails and a lock of head hair; symbolizing unity, fortitude, drive, and determination of the people.

Then he takes a cup and half-fills it with water from the Tano River; symbolizing the God TANO. This was followed by taking the heart he stole from the King of Denkyira, and burning it to ashes; symbolizing the enemies of the people.

All of the hair, finger and toe nails, along with the ashes of the heart, he placed in the cup of Tano river water. He crushed them and mixed them into a thick paste; then, moving in front of Osai Tutu, with the Golden Stool still on his knees, Priest Anokye ritually spread the paste onto the Golden Stool with the following words;

"This is our symbol, Our God has blessed our hope and desires for unity. But this Stool, which He has sent us is not just a Clan Stool such as those upon which you now sit; it is a special Holy Stool. Now, at this moment, our Golden Stool contains the Soul and Spirit of each one of the Clan Chiefs and the Clan mothers gathered here.

Each one of you are tied to the Golden Stool, and it is tied to each of you. In it, rests the entire Soul and Spirit of all of our people, all of our Ancestors, of our God, and now, of our new Kingdom. It will be forever the outward and visible sign of the fortitude, drive and determination which now binds us into a Kingdom. It is the symbol of our Kingdom, the Ashanti Kingdom!"

Thus the Ashanti Kingdom was brought into reality, along with a Master Plan as its Chosen Destiny.

Then the Ancestor Stools, symbolizing the Soul and Spirit of the Clan, being brought from the Clan Stool house of each of the seven villages, was placed in a circle around Osai Tutu and the Golden Stool.

At which time, an albino (man) was placed on the Golden Stool, and Priest Anokye struck him upon the head, and he disappeared into the Stool; this gave the Golden Stool life.

Then Anokye hung seven bells on the Stool, three of gold, one of silver, one of copper, iron, and brass. This was followed by taking small pieces of gold, silver, copper, iron, and brass, and distributing them to all of the Chiefs and Chief mothers; thus sealing the Unity of the Kingdom. And at the same time, sharing with the Clan Chiefs and Clan Mothers some of the spiritual authority which lay in the Golden Stool. However, it was understood that Osai Tutu was to be the King of this new Kingdom called Ashanti, with the rituals of Kingship to follow later.

This was the third and final step, the transformation of Seven Adensi Clans into the Ashanti Kingdom with a Chosen Destiny. This took place in 1700.

The new Ashanti Kingdom went on to defeat Denkyira, naturally with additional help from Priest Anokye.

This was in 1701, and for the next two hundred years, 1701 to 1901, they dominated all of the Kingdoms and Clans, at one time or another, throughout Ghana, and parts of Togo and the Ivory Coast. This was Osai Tutu's Master Plan from the beginning, to become a Super Dominate Kingdom spiritually and economically.

However, as we mentioned, we are more interested in the spiritual side of the Ashanti Kingdom more than what they accomplished in physical warfare.

Meanwhile, this is not the end of Priest Anokye's activities. He founded a village which became the village where Priests came for training in Priesthood called Agona Akuapem, about three years after bringing the Spirit of the Ashanti Kingdom into reality. There, he spent his time making rules, regulations, and ceremonies to keep the Kingdom spiritually operating smoothly. For example, the 'National Odwira Ceremony' which we will look at later.

Finally in 1713, Priest Anokye informed Osai Tutu that he was about to set out on a quest to find a spiritual medicine to defeat death itself. He asked Osai Tutu to call his nephew, Kwame Siaw, and of the Priest Elders of his village, Agona Akyempim, to come to Kumasi.

When they did so, Priest Anokye informed them that his nephew, Kwame Siaw, was to be the new Chief Priest of Ashanti, and that he would be absent seven years and seventy-seven days and nights. And during all of that time, no one must weep, or mourn for him, although he appeared to be dead.

He returned to his village and gave orders that he was not to be disturbed for seven years and seventy-seven days and nights. He entered his house, and there he "died."

The village was placed in charge of his Seven Priest Counselors, who were the Chief Priest of the Seven Clans. This meant that the Ashanti Kingdom had a Chief Priest, and each Clan also had a Chief Priest under Priest Anokye.

For seven years and seventy days, seven days short of his orders, the last day of 1719, his nephew declared that his uncle Anokye was really dead, and that people should weep, and that guns should be fired.

The door of Anokye's house was open; it was empty. On that very day, a man walking on a road outside of the village met a man who asked him what was happening in the village, as people were weeping.

He replied that they were holding the funeral custom for Priest Anokye.

The man then said that he was Priest Anokye. He had obtained the medicine to defeat death, and was returning with it. But as his kinsfolk had disobeyed his orders, he would go away for ever, and the Ashanti would never find the medicine against death.

Nobody ever saw Priest Anokye again, but it is believed that he is still alive this very day, for he had found the medicine to defeat death." Osai Tutu was killed in war the seventh day of the year 1720.

However, we are not interested in the warfare side of the new Ashanti Kingdom. Our major focus is on the spiritual side of the kingdom. For example, we will look at the nature of the God Priest Anokye stole from the Domaas, TANO the Great War God: The role of the Royal Ancestor and the spiritual side of Ideas: And the nature of Kingship.

As to the God TANO, when a God inspires a Unity and Destiny of a Kingdom, means that it is not only gives power to a Kingdom to come into reality, but also the power to fulfill its chosen Destiny.

This power is called *'Fortitude, Drive and Determination,'* which to Grandpa's thinking, is the meaning of 'spiritual power itself, the power to live and succeed.'

This tells us what the Ashanti were seeking from their new God as a Kingdom. We can see that it was not a master plan they were seeking, because Tutu thought it up himself before he knew anything about the God TANO.

Therefore the only thing they needed from a God was spiritual unity of purpose, power to fulfill the plan they chose themselves; the getting of this power is the purpose Priest Anokye's rituals served.

But Who is this God that sent a Golden Stool of Authority from Heaven as a symbol of the Unity between these Clans? This is TANO, the God Anokye captured from the Domaa; Who became the God of the Ashanti Kingdom, and the God of worship of the people in the Kingdom.

The Ashanti call TANO the Great, the God they are dependent on to provide the spiritual power of fortitude, drive and determination to bring the Ashanti Kingdom's Chosen Destiny into reality; from start to finish. TANO is the "God of Unity of Purpose.

Thus is the major thing Priest Anokye accomplished with his supernatural powers.

We mentioned that the Akan religious beliefs were based on the Idea that people do their own thinking, and create their own ideas.

However, to get some insight into how a Kingdom becomes a spiritual and physical reality from the three groups of ideas, master plans, of Osai Tutu, Priest Anokye, and Amankwa Tia, we should return to Mr. Danquah's final interpretation of the Drum poem;

> "The stream crosses the path,
> The path crosses the stream;
> Which of them is the elder?
> Did we not cut a path to go and meet the stream?
> The stream had its origin long long ago.
> The stream had its origin in the Creator.

> He created the thing,
> Pure pure TANO
> He created the idea
> What did He Create?
> He create Order (Osai Tutu),
> He created knowledge (Priest Anokye),
> He created Death (Amankwa Tia),
> As the purest form of the idea of a Kingdom"

So what is the relationship between these three men and order, knowledge, and death, have to do with a Kingdom coming into reality?

Osai tutu=order vision of a destiny; destiny brings ordered life, and gives directions to a Kingdom.

Priest Anokye=knowledge; A kingdom is a living being, and according to African Traditions Beliefs, all living things have a spirit and, a Kingdom is a living thing; so knowledge means spiritual knowledge of the Spirit of a Kingdom.

Amankwa Tia=death. A War Chiefs purpose is to kill. Death is one of the most powerful forces in the world. Only ODOMANKOMA (and the Gods and Goddesses) could defeat death, therefore, death means power; this is what a War Chief gives to a Kingdom, power.

This means that the God TANO used the master plans (ideas) of Osai Tutu, Priest Anokye, and Amankwa Tia to create a Kingdom. This is called, in African Traditional Kingship, the holy trinity of the spiritual and physical reality of a Kingdom.

However, we can see that it was Priest Anokye that 'cut the path to meet the stream' of what the God had to offer, a Kingdom. This is another thing Priest Anokye accomplished. Now we will turn our attention to the constitution of the Kingdom.

If we recall, Anokye came from a Clan of priest. Not only was his father, mother, uncles and aunts Priest and Priestesses, his older brother was the priest to Tutu's uncle, Obiri Yeboa. As far as the direction we are taking our investigation, this brings up the question of Clan Spirit and its Destiny; and in Anokye's case, his Clan's destiny.

In one sense, we can say Anokye not only helped bring the Ashanti Kingdom and Destiny into reality, he also was fulfilling his, and his Clans chosen destiny. For his family's destiny was to be the chief priest to the King of Ashanti.

For example, when Anokye retired, he sent his nephew on his mother's side to Tutu as Chief Priest of the Kingdom. And his nephew when he retired, sent his nephew, and so on through the generations for the life of the Kingdom. Thus was the destiny of his Clan, to serve as Chief Priest to the Ashanti King, as well as priest of the Clan Chiefs.

Just as Osai Tutu's Royal Family was destined to serve the Kingdom as King. Osai Tutu was followed in office by his nephew on his mother's side, and his nephew would be followed in office by his brother or nephew, and so on.

But this is the nature of all Akan institutions in a Kingdom, the Clan is the one that supports and keeps them alive over the generations. This was the case of every position in the Kingdom, from the King to the average man; this means that a Kingdom is one big family of Mother Clans; with the exception of War Chief, who had to prove himself in battle.

On the other hand, a Mother Clan is a family of families, and their Clan Chief is chosen from one of those families. This continues throughout the life of the Clan; for example as we saw with the Oyoko Clan. Obiri Yeboa was followed as Clan Chief by his nephew, Osai Tutu.

However, this does not mean that, for example, Osai Tutu's fathers side of the family-clan does not play a role in Kingship and Clanship, as we will see later.

Being as every generation is following in the footsteps of their Elders, what role does their Ancestors play in a Kingdom?

The value of the Ancestors is summed up not only to the person following in their footsteps, but also in the purpose of what is called, Ancestor worship, and what purpose the rituals to Ancestors serve? The means of staying in harmony with the Kingdom's Chosen Destiny, which is the driving force of everybody in the Kingdom.

So since the Akan believe that spirits of people never die, the spirit of the Ancestors was around, and the people naturally called on them for help in finishing what the Ancestors had begun in the first place. So we can see the reasoning behind the rituals of what is generally called 'Ancestor Worship.'

Worshipping Ancestors is the same thing as worshiping the idea of their collective Destiny; or to say, keeping the Spirit of the Destiny alive and functioning in the direction of its fulfillment. Therefore, the interest of the 'Ancestors and their living relatives, were tied together and kept alive by the Destiny of the Kingdom.'

This means that the Ancestors play a strong role in Kingship. In this sense, for instance, if Osai Tutu chose the Kingdom's Destiny, and a Kingdom lasts for hundred of years, naturally Tutu is not going to be alive long enough to lead the Kingdom to fulfill its Destiny.

This is the job of the Kings and Queenmothers that follow him and his Queenmother. Each King and Queenmother, through the generations, bring the Kingdom a step further along the pathway to its Destiny.

Therefore, there are ritual links of communication from Osai Tutu in 1701, through the generations of Kings, to the King of today; all of which is working to the same end, fulfilling the Destiny of Tutu's Master Plan.

Therefore, the Ancestors play a very strong spiritual role in a King and Queenmothers actions as Leaders of the Kingdom, they are the link between the Kingdom and its royal Ancestors.

Finally, this brings us to the subject of Kingship rituals related to the relationship between the King and the people of the Kingdom, and the relationship between the King and the Spirit of the Kingdom; and the King's relationship with the Ancestors of the Kingdom. All of which is based on the following proverb,

"I exist because we exist, we exist because I exist."

'I' means the King and Queenmother, and 'we' means the people in the Kingdom. Which indicates that a Kingdom is a solid inter-working and inter-related group, tied together through Kingship; there is a 'Oneness' about it.

Everybody identifies with the Kingdom, and the Kingdom identifies with everybody. The Kingdom's destiny controls everybody's actions and re-actions, as a group, and as individuals, on a spiritual and physical level.

Thus is the constitution of the Ashanti Kingdom, the Kingship institution is the thing that keeps everything in this relationship running smoothly.

The King's Palace

Although we will not deal with the subject in any detail, we must keep in mind that a Kingship is also a Government that deals with trade business, and law and order in the Kingdom.

The King spends the vast majority of his time in his household, the King's palace. The only leaves it once when he is first elected to let the people see him as King, or when he goes to war. His palace is the center of Kingship Authority, physically as well as ritually; this means that the Palace is a kind of Shrine Government.

So we will begin our investigation of Kingship by first taking a look at the physical lay-out of the Palace itself, which is really a small walled city containing hundreds of people, as a background to the King's spiritual and physical functions.

(1) The main entrance; the door way is made wide enough for the Kings umbrellas, when open, to pass through.

(2) An oblong courtyard where the King sits and presides over important cases, and holds big receptions.

(3) An open room containing, in this case, the King's special Mpintini drums; (Open rooms have three walls, a floor and roof, but no front wall ,and usually opens into a courtyard).

(4) Open room containing the King's special Kete drums.

(5) Open room occupied by the Drummers.

(6) Open room, in which the King sits after special ceremonies, or on other important occasions, and serves out wine.

(7) A small courtyard where lesser disputes among the Palace Officials are heard by the King in his capacity of house-father.

(8) An open room used as a kitchen for the cooks.

(9) A closed four-walled room in which the bathroom attendants sleep.

(10) An open room where the King sits, oils, and dresses himself after his bath.

(11) The Bathroom, containing a bath, a white Stool, and two elephant tusks; on the tusks the king will place his bare feet to avoid contact with the ground.

(12) An open room for the King's young subject, and the person in charge of them.

(13) A courtyard, known as the approach to the Chapel of Stools, where the Stool of the Royal Ancestors is kept.

(14) A sleeping room for the Chief of the Royal Chapel of Stools.

(15) An open room where the Chief of the Royal Chapel of Stools eat.

(16) A pen for sheep and goats to be used for sacrifices at the Royal Chapel of Stools.

(17) An open room facing the inner courtyard where the King sits at ceremonies.

(18) A closed four walled room containing the blacken stool of the Chief of the Royal Chapel of Stools and his other belongings.

(19) Courtyard of the Royal Chapel of Stool.

(20) An open room; here sits the Messengers and Minstrels at ceremonies.

(21) A courtyard in front of the Royal Chapel of Stools.

(22) Stool house of the King's ancestral blackened Stools.

(23) Five closed sleeping rooms used by attendants of the Royal Chapel of Stools.

(24) Room of where the skeleton of dead Kings are kept, called the Spirits of Kings.

(25) An open room containing the ritual objects of the Odwira Ceremony, (which we will see later).

(26) An open room where the King sits at ceremonies in connection with Ancestors.

(27) A courtyard where all the lesser ordinary court cases are heard.

(28) A narrow raised ledge.

(29) An open room where the King sits when cases are being tried before him.

(30) An open room where the War Chief sits during the hearing of court cases.

(31) An open room where the King's Chief Spokesman sits.

(32) An open space where small boys attending the King's wives play.

(33) An open room where the King eats.

(34) A courtyard where any subjects of the King or any stranger might come and receive hospitality at the King's expense.

(35) A four walled room, facing away from the courtyard, containing boxes of the King's clothes.

(36) A big sleeping place.

(37) An open room containing eating utensils.

(38) The King's sleeping room.

(39) An open room where the King's wives come to visit him.

(40) A yard behind the sleeping quarters.

(41) An open room where the King eats when he wants to be alone.

(42) An open room where the King's wives comes to sit and visit among themselves.

(43) A four walled room containing the King's storage room.

(44) A four walled room containing a chair and table.

(45) A four walled room sometimes used as a sleeping room for overnight guest.

(46) A four walled room used as a storeroom for food items.

(47) A yard leading to the lavatory; also where household rations are issued, and sheep are killed.

(48) The King's lavatory.

(49) Ritual house of the King's Clan God, BOSOMMURU.

(50) An open room where the King's umbrellas are kept.

(51) A courtyard in which the King and his Counselors sit to discuss matters in private, before they are finally made public.

(52) An open room where Goldsmiths sit and work for the King.

(53) An open room which serves as a kind of miscellaneous storage room.

(54) A four walled room containing a bed. Here the King sits and rests in the evenings, and receives any complaints from his wives.

(55) Another miscellaneous storage room.

(56) A four walled room used as a storage area for ritual objects.

(57) The entrance to the area where the King's wives live.

(58) A Street running all around the back of the Palace, facing the houses of the King's wives

(59) The King's wives houses.

(60) An exit, leading to the Kitchen garbage dump.

(61) An exit, leading to the place where water is drawn.

(62) A four walled room for the Spirit of the dead wives of the King.

(65) Farms of the King's wives.

We can see, the Palace is really a self-contained town in itself, and sometimes can be over a square mile, and have a population of hundreds of people. On the other hand, we can also see that a 'King's Palace is a big Male Royal Shrine to the Idea that became the Kingdom's Chosen Destiny.'

This is the lay out of a King's Palace, but the Queenmother also has a Palace of the same design and size. The only difference is the sex of the population to some extent. For example, in the Queenmother's Palace, there is a large group of houses fill with young Princess' of the Royal Clan, the King's sisters, whose sons can also become King.

Their is the Queenmother's nieces on her mother side, and the daughters of high ranking Clan Chiefs, all of which are there to study under the Queenmother. The 'Queenmother's Palace is also a big Female Royal Shrine to the Idea that became the Kingdom's Chosen Destiny.'

Our conclusions is that a Palace is a living Shrine in which a ritual is continuously in operation, and it is from this point of view that we will take a look at the spirituality of the Palace as a Shrine.

Kingship spiritual position

Well Fellow Detectives, now we are getting to the subject that really fascinates Grandpa, the Spiritual Constitution of the King and Queenmother as Divine Beings of the Kingdom; what we call, *'The Royalty of the King and Queenmother.'* So our question now become, what is the spiritual laws and constitution of Kingship according to Akan religious beliefs?

The King is a spiritual power among other spiritual powers. For instance, the Gods, Goddesses, and Ancestors, which means that he has a number of ritual rules to follow which make up the spiritual constitution and laws of Kingship.

For example, there are some things that a King must and must not do, like, his feet must never touch the Earth, and the Sun must never shine on his head. Meaning he must wear sandals, and travel under a very large umbrella. If his feet touch the earth, he is in the Earth Goddesses, ASASE YAA AFUA's, and domain; and if he is in the Sunlight, he is in the Sun God, NYANKOPON's domain.

The King has a spiritual domain of his own, the spirituality of the Kingdom; in this sense that the King is Divine. A God in the domain of the Spirit of the Kingdom, and his palace is his shrine.

At the same time, the King's job is to maintain a harmonious relationship between his spiritual power, and those of a number of Gods, a Goddess, and Ancestors. For example, the God of his father's Clan, BOSOMMURR, the God TANO, the God NYANKOPON, the Goddess AWO, and the Royal Ancestors. This means that a King must live his life in such a way as to maintain this harmony, which means that he lives in a continuous state of ritual symbolism, in which he is a Divine Symbol.

This is the case of the Queenmother. Also She is a Goddess in the domain, and in the Spirit of the Kingdom. Her job is to maintain a harmonious relationship between her spiritual power, and those of a number of Goddesses and Gods: For instance, the Queenmother of Heaven AWO, Earth Goddess ASASE YAA AFUA, the God NYANKOPON, the God TANO, the Goddess of her mother's Clan OYOKO, and the Ancestress of the Royal Family.

This means that the Queenmother owns the Kingdom. Just as the Moon Goddess owns the universe, the Earth Goddess owns the Earth, Clan mother owns the Clan, and Mother owns the family.

On the other hand, this means that the King manages the affairs of the Kingdom. Just as NYANKOPON manages the affairs of the world, the Clan Chief manages the affairs of the clan, and the Uncle manages the affairs of the family.

This is what we mean by the *Royalty* of the King and Queenmother; and this is what the nature of Kingship is all about.

We have concluded that a Palace is a Big Shrine, the King and Queenmother are the God and Goddess, and Kingship is a continuous Ritual inside the Shrine; and by continuous, we mean 24 hours a day for 365 days of the year.

We will make the point that while on the one hand, the King is the Chief Administrator of the Spiritual Affairs, and he is also the Chief Administrator of the social and economic Affairs as well; with the aid of his Queenmother. This means that the Palace is a Shrine and a Government. The King is a Divine and Political Leader; and these two positions must always be in harmony with each other.

On the other hand, this leaves us with the question of who maintains the harmony in the affairs of the Palace and Kingship rituals?

Up to this point, we have focused on the King's mother side of his family and his sister's sons. This brings up the question, what role does the King's father and sons play in Kingship?

Now according to Akan beliefs, the King's father is the Priest of the male Clan God, BOSOMMURU. On the other hand, and what interests us the most is, his sons consists of the ones he fathered, and serve his male clan God BOSOMMURU. Plus the ones he inherits from the last King; all of which are called the King's sons even if some of them are older than the King.

All of these sons are Gyase Chiefs. More to the point, Chiefs and sub-Chiefs of the Gyase people. But what role does the Gyase people serve?

They are concerned with the well being of the King and his household, being as 99% of the King's life is spent in the Palace, means that they are a part of, and are concerned with the King's Royal lifestyle.

In other words, the Gyase Chiefs are the Palace Officials of the functionaries who maintain the smooth operation of the King's Royal lifestyle, physically and spiritually. Thus is the role of the King's sons.

The following is a list of the major Gyase people who are under the Gyase Chiefs and sub-Chiefs:

Title	Functions
Akyeame	King's Spokesmen
Akonuasoafo	King's Stool-carriers
Asokwafo	King's Drummers, horn-blowers
Akyiniyekyimfo	King's Umbrella-carriers
Barimfo	Caretakers of the Royal Mausoleum
Agwareyefo	King's bathroom attendants
Akragwafo	King's Soul-bearers and washers
Aboprafo	King's Elephant-tail switchers
Papafoafo	King's Fan-bearers
Sodofo	King's Cooks
Asoamfo	King's Hammock-carriers
Akokwafo	King's Floor polishers
Sana hene Afotuosanfo	King's treasurers and sub-treasurers
Nseniefo	King's Heralds
Afonasoafo	King's Sword-bearers
Atumtufuo	King's Gun-bearers
Akyemfo	King's Shield-bearers
Kwadwumfo	King's Minstrels
Abrafo	King's Executioners

Being as working for the King is a highly honored and respected position with great benefits, Clan Chiefs from far and wide send their sons and nephews to become Gyase people of the King to learn leadership. Recall, Osai Tutu's Uncle sent him to work in the Palace of the Denkyira King.

We must keep in mind that the King is the Symbol of the Kingdom and its Chosen Destiny. Keeping the Kingdom and Chosen Destiny spiritually pure, clean, and protected is the job of the Gyase people. For instance, a Gyase Chief is Chief of the King's bodyguards as well as an essential player in the King's ritual ceremonies.

This means that the Gyase people, and especially Gyase Chiefs, are more than just common servants of the King, and are deeply involved in the rituals of the King's Royal Lifestyle; so, we can see that the King's sons play a big role in Ashanti Kingship.

While we gave some indication of the role of the sons in the King's family, his Gyase Chiefs and sub-chiefs, we have not mentioned the King's daughters and their spiritual and physical position.

In many ways, the King's daughters have the most interesting position in the symbolism of Kingship. They, especially the King's oldest daughter, is thought of as the wives of the King's Clan God, BOSOMMURU, in the sense that they are the Chief Priestesses of His Shrine. On the other hand, they symbolize the King's wealth and spiritual authority.

The King's daughters, in the King's ceremonial procession, display the symbols of the King's wealth and spiritual authority in the form of all gold symbols, including his symbol of spiritual authority, the Elephant tail, over their left shoulder. A King is thought of as spiritually poor if he does not have any daughters.

We mentioned the King's Elephant tail-bearers, and his daughters carrying elephant tails, without stating the symbolic meaning of the tail.

There is an Akan proverb that says, "God has the head of authority, and the King has the tail." The elephant is the animal symbol of BOSOMMURU.

This means that the King's Male Clan symbol of authority is the elephant tail, and the elephant head is the symbol of the God of his Clan, and the God of the Kingdom, TANO.

To the Ashanti, the Elephant also symbolizes the Fortitude, Drive and Determination of the Spirit of the Kingdom's Chosen Destiny; big and powerful. The King's and Queenmother's stool, on ceremonial occasions, rests on elephant skins. This brings us to the Queenmother.

As we mentioned, the Queenmother also lives in a Palace which is as big, or bigger than the Palace of the King. Her household is located close to the apartments of the Royal wives, and the King's wives, which are under the Queenmother's supervision.

The Queenmother has Gyase people; however, whereas the King's Gyase people are all male, those of the Queenmother are all female, her daughters and nieces, and hold pretty much the same titles and functions, for example to name a few:

Title	Function
Okraa	Soul-bearers
Akrafo-ba-panyin	Chieftess of soul-bearers

Abrafo-ba-panin..................Master of ceremonies
Akyeamehemaa.................Chieftess of Spokeswomen
Gyasehemaa......................Chieftess of functionaries
Sodohemaa........................Chieftess of cooks

Then there are Adowahemmaa, who are in charge of the Adowa drumming and dancing. Patomfo, who dress the Queenmother and groom her everyday. Adwarefo are the maid servants who help her to bath. Nkuruwafo, who are responsible for her drinking water, palm wine, and are cup-bearers and wine-bearers at ceremonial occasion. Mmagyefo are the nurses of the Royal children.

In addition there are also her stool-bearers and cushion-bearers (a soft cushion is always placed on the Silver Stool on which she sits), and, Sandal-bearers (for a Queenmother's feet, like the King's, must never touch the Earth). Fan-bearers; and the list go on.

Before we get too far ahead of ourselves, Grandpa should mention all that we have said about how the organization Kingship fits the pattern of Akan Traditional Kingship System. This is at least 2500 years old, according to the archaeology done by Mr. James Anquandah.

This means that all Akan Kingdoms follow the same pattern; the thing that made the Ashanti Kingdom unique among Akan Kingdoms, and was the innovations in the pattern made by Priest Anokye.

For example, one such innovation is when the Golden Stool came from the cloud and settled on Osai Tutu's knees in front of all of the people of the Seven Clans. And Osai Tutu was spiritually transformed from a Clan Chief to a Divine King of a Kingdom. Now we can begin to get some idea of what made Priest Anokye so Great.

This meant that Priest Anokye not only ritually created a King, but the spirituality of a Kingdom as well.

This also means that Osai Tutu had the vision of a Kingdom's destiny, and Priest Anokye brought that vision into spiritual reality in the minds of the seven Clan Chiefs and their followers. This was one hell of a spiritual transformation for all concerned.

Being as all of what Priest Anokye ritually created is spiritual by nature. For the Kingdom to function, the Spirit of the Kingdom must be brought into physical reality on a cultural level; this brings us to the subject of Ritual Symbolism and the Artist.

Therefore, we will next turn our investigative attention to the ritual symbolism, or to say, the inter-working of the spirituality of Kingdom; especially the role of gold, silver, and the Gyase people played in Kingship.

Kingship Ritual Symbolism

This brings us to the Akan Artist, especially the Goldsmith and Silversmith. For they, like the Yoruba's artistic creation, are the ones to capture the different spiritual aspects of Kingship, especially in Gold and Silver, but also metals, such as brass and copper, and wood as well.

As we mentioned, gold and silver symbolize NYANKOPON (Sun) and AWO (Moon). Therefore the Akan Artist used this belief in the design of gold and silver Ritual Art to show the King and Queenmother's Spiritual relationship to NYANKOPON and AWO, the King and Queenmother of the World.

So when we put the Gyase people and the work of the Artist together around the King, we have the Kingship Spirit symbolized in physical form.

This means that the Gyase people must give living physical expression to each of the Kingdom's spiritual aspects; which is our definition of Ritual Symbolism in the spiritual world in which the King lives.

And this is where the Gyase people and Artist fit into the spiritual symbolism of Kingship. Although we will focus on the King, and gold, we must always keep in mind that the Queenmother has all of the symbolism a King has, expressed in silver, as well as some in gold. This together gives the full picture of the spirituality of Kingship and Queenmothership.

We mentioned that the Akan nation was located on one of the biggest gold fields in the world, and that gold symbolizes the Spirit of NYANKOPON. The King is thought of spiritually as His Divine Son. So gold plays a big role in Kingship symbolism, especially if we keep in mind that NYANKOPON is the origination of the Spirit and Chosen Destiny of the World, Kra (Soul).

In this respect, gold represents the Spirit and Chosen Destiny of the Kingdom as well, which is also what the King represents. So we can begin to get an idea of the symbolic role gold plays, it symbolizes the Unity between the King and the Kingdom's Soul and NYANKOPON.

Just like the American President needs one kind of "Administration" to help him govern physically, and the Catholic Pope needs another kind of "Administration" to help him govern spiritually. Being as the Akan Kings have both titles, President and Pope; he needs a special kind of Administration to help his govern. Every body in his Administration must reflect the Unity of the Kingdom, and NYANKOPON, with gold symbols at all official and, or, ceremonial occasions.

Of the above type official gathering, a European writer in 1818 had the following to say about the amount of gold he saw on display; of course he did not know the symbolic meaning of what he observed. But we are only interested in what he had to say about gold, and other things that have a ritual meaning.

"A delay of some minutes while we (some Europeans) severally approached to receive the King's hand, afforded us a thorough view of him. He wore a fillet of aggry beads round his temples, a necklace of gold cockspur shells strung by their largest ends, and over his right shoulder a red silk cord, suspending three sapphires cased in gold.

His bracelets were the richest mixtures of beads and gold, and his fingers covered with rings; his cloth was of dark green silk; a pointed diadem (crown) was elegantly painted in white on his forehead; also a pattern resembling an paulette (a ornamental badge) on each shoulder, and an ornament like a full blown rose, one leaf rising above another until it covered his whole breast (Soul-disk).

His knee bands were of aggry beads, and his ankle strings of gold ornaments of the most delicate workmanship, small drums, sankos, stools, swords, guns, and birds, clustered together; is saddle, of a soft white leather, were embossed across the instep band with small gold and silver cases of sapphires; he was seated in a low chair (stool), richly ornamented with gold. He wore a pair of gold castanets (clappers) on his finger and thumb which he clapped to enforce silence.

The belts of the guards behind his chair, were cased in gold, and covered with small jaw bones of the same metal (gold); elephant tails, waving like a small cloud before him, were spangled with gold, and large plumes of feathers were flourished amid them.

The royal stool, entirely cased in gold, was displayed under a splendid umbrella, with drums, sankos, horns, and various musical instruments cased in gold, about the thickness of cartridge paper.

Large circles of gold hung by scarlet cloth from the swords of state, the sheaths as well as the handles were also cased in gold; hatchets of the same (gold) were intermixed with them; the breasts of the Ocrahs(?), and various attendants were adorned with large stars, stools, crescent and gossamer wings of solid gold.

The King's four linguists (Spokesmen) were encircled by a splendor inferior to none, and their peculiar insignia, gold canes (shafts), were elevated in all directions, tied in bundles like faces.

The keeper of the treasury added to his own magnificence by the ostentatious display of his service; the blow pan, boxes, scales and weights, were of solid gold."

Whereas the European writer thought that the Ashanti King and the Gyase people were just trying to 'show-off,' we can see that the symbolism of gold is representing the spirituality of Kingship. As well as the harmony of the unity of the Spirit of the Kingdom; thus is what we mean, that the King lives in the world of spiritual symbolism, and gold is the symbol of that harmony.

And being as the Europeans were there concerning trade and other economic issues, we can say that what the writer saw was the symbolism of the Royal Government.

We have now seen the role of gold in the Kingship of the kingdom, which reflects the male side of the Kingdom: And being as, according to Akan traditional beliefs, everything has a male and female spirit, we will next turn our attention to the female side of the Spirit of the Kingdom; the symbolism of Queenmothership.

From a spiritual point of view, the King is the Chief Administrator of the Affairs of the Kingdom's Destiny, and the Queenmother is the Owner of the Kingdom itself, and all of the people therein. Her symbols reflect her as the Mother of the King and of the Kingdom, as well as her relationship to the female side of the Akan religious beliefs, which is her spiritual position in the kingdom, and its Chosen Destiny. This is shown in the symbols on her Stool of Authority, the Ashanti Queenmother's Silver Stool.

The Stool, as well as its Chair is trimmed in silver, and has a Soul Disk design in the center of the seat of the Stool, and on the backrest of its Chair.

But unlike with the King, her soul disk symbolizes harmony in the relationship between the Queenmother of Heaven, the Queenmother of the Kingdom, and the Kingdom's reality; and the silver soul disk is the design of the full moon.

Plus, as Owner of the Kingdom, the soul disk on her Stool symbolizes her approval and support of the Chosen Destiny of her Kingdom; And through her, the approval and support of the Moon Goddess, Earth Goddess, and the Ancestress of the Royal Family.

The display of symbolism of the Queenmother is on a grander scale than that of the King; for example, we will quote a Writer in those times; ".......the Queenmother is regarded as one of the greatest persons of the Kingdom. She has her own court and is surrounded by the greatest luxury imaginable. She has precious jewelry, rich cloths, silver vessels---everything the King possesses (in this respect) she has in abundance."

What this Writer thought of as precious jewelry is really ritual Art symbolizing her spiritual position.

Although the Queenmother uses all silver for her ceremonial occasions to symbolize the physical reality of the Kingdom, she and the other women of the Royal Clan, the Princesses, also wore gold jewelry as did the Royal Wives; to symbolically show their relationship with the King, and the Spirit Destiny of the Kingdom. Although they wore gold, they also had identical pieces in silver, but gold or silver, the design pattern symbolizes the Moon Goddess's spiritual powers. Her Soul-disk is decorated with swirls and curls in the design patterns of female symbolism.

This design symbolizes the power, mysterious by nature, of female spirituality and sexuality, which according to Akan beliefs is the nature of AWO, ASASE YAA AFUA, Royal Ancestress, Queenmother of the Kingdom, Clan mothers, on down to the Family mothers, and ends up in puberty aged young girls.

Now we will get into the relationship between the Unity of the Queenmother's female spiritual powers of authority, symbolized by silver, and the Unity of the King's male spiritual power of authority, symbolized by gold. Recall that gold symbolizes NYANKOPON, and silver is of His Mother, AWO.

The symbolism showing this relationship, is also shown in the designs of gold and silver beads used to make up necklaces, and arm and leg bracelets. Also, this is shown in the Royal male and female smoking pipes; one of the pipes is cast in pure gold, and the other in pure silver. And again, there are the Royal smoking pipes, one is of silver, and the other is of gold.

So when we add the symbols on the beads, to the symbol of the necklace, this shows the unity and harmony of the male and female spiritual forces that go to make up the Spirit of the Kingdom, which in turn, becomes the powers of the Kingdom to fulfill its Chosen Destiny. Which if we recall, came from an idea of Osai Tutu, the Ashanti first King.

These is some of the ritual symbolism related to the Kingdom. But most important of all, as Owner, and Mother of the King, and Kingdom, the Queenmother is thought of as "giving birth to the Kingdom, and the women are thought of as her daughters.

This is shown in certain special ritual ceremonies related to Queen motherhood, which is expressed only in silver. This is when, on a full moon night, the Queenmother is carried through the crowd dressed in silver cloth and jewelry; with a bowl of silver dust from which she throws clouds over the women as a symbol of the blessing of the Moon Goddess.

We saw that the Queenmother's daughter, who is the King's sister, whose son is eligible to become King, is her Gyase Chiefs.

This gives us some idea of the organization of the symbolism of Divine Kingship and Queenmothership, to sum-up; we will look at the ritual that transforms a Prince into a King.

To show this, we will return to the history of the Ashanti, say to the time of their second King, Opoku Ware, Osai Tutu's nephew: Whom he raised to follow in his footsteps, and see the ritual that transformed him into the Ashanti second King.

Osai Tutu was what is called a Philosophy-king. All that he dealt with was ideas, and although he went to the battlefield to give moral support and spiritual force to his warriors, he was not involved in the war strategies. Nor was he thought of as leading his warriors into battle. The actual execution of the over all war was in the hands of his War Chief, Amankwa Tia.

Our point being, Tutu was King for nearly to twenty years, from about 1701 to 1720, when the Akyem Kingdom temporarily defeated his army. Tutu was supposedly killed, but his body was never recovered. But in any case, the Ashanti had to install a new King, Opoku Ware, who was even more ambitious than Tutu. Opoku Ware became the Greatest Warrior-King that the Ashanti ever had; who really built the Ashanti Empire.

Opoku Ware was his nephew, and was raised and taught the art of Kingship by Tutu himself. And chosen by him to be the next King, the process by which Opoku Ware was installed as King still involved a number of different groups.

For example, like the Queenmother and her Counselors. The Seven Clan Chiefs and their Counselors, Tutu's Gyase people, plus the general public, must give their approval before anyone is made King; and this same group can kick him out later if he messed up.

Now we must remember how this Kingdom and its Chosen Destiny comes into reality; through the activities of Osai Tutu, Priest Anokye, and Amankwa Tia.

Then through symbolism, we saw the Spirit side of the Kingdom symbolized by Ritual Art. At the same time, we saw that the Spirit of the Kingdom came from the God TANO, and Osai Tutu created the idea of the Destiny of that Spirit. Both of which became the Soul of the Kingdom, which symbolically rest in the Gold Stool.

This means that for a man to become king, he must become possessed by the Spirit and Destiny symbolized by the Gold Stool.

So, the approval of those groups of people, and being possessed by, and, or, coming into harmony with all of the Spirits, is what makes up the Kingdom. Including the Spirit of the King before him, Osai Tutu, is the ritual process by which Opoku Ware became the second King of Ashanti.

After an Ashanti King dies, or is kicked out of office for some reason or another, the first group to act is Osai Tutu's Gyase people.

They take possession and become the armed guards of the Golden Stool, or to say, guard the Spirit of the Kingdom in its time of no leadership.

With the Spirit of the Kingdom protected, the next group to act is the Queenmother and the Royal Clan. This is the group that makes the decision on which male members are to be presented to the people as the candidate for King.

Although a recommendation was already made by Osai Tutu that Opoku Ware become the next King before he died. It is only a recommendation, the process of choosing must be made by different groups of people, and the Royal Ancestors consulted, to see if Opoku Ware is qualified for the job.

The Queenmother then formally presents Opoku, her grandson, to the Tutu Counselors, and the Seven Clan Chiefs, who in turn must consult their Clan members before they can give their approval.

But a King still cannot be installed without the Golden Stool. Which is in the possession of Tutu's Gyase people, (his family on his father's side), who consults the Gods and Ancestors (including recent-dead Tutu), who must give their approval.

The disapproval of either group means that the Queenmother must choose another member of the Royal Clan, a brother or nephew of Tutu, and repeat the process all over again. At this point, we should take special note of the democracy and balance of power in a Kingdom.

Each step of the process includes ritual sacrifices. But the rituals involved in the installation of a King, and the ritual with the Golden Stool are the ones that that interest us the most. Or to say, the one that causes the Spirit of the Kingdom to possess him which in turn transforms him into a King.

This transformation is symbolized in a small ritual involving the Seven Clan Chiefs, Queenmother, Gyase Chief, and the War Chief. In this ritual, Opoku Ware makes a pretense of sitting on, but not touching, the Golden Stool three times; after which, he is considered possessed by the Spirit of the Kingdom, which symbolically rest within the Stool.

From that point on, Opoku Ware is a Divine King of the Ashanti, and their Chief Administrator of Affairs. And especially from our point of view, he became a living symbol of the Spirit, and Destiny of the Ashanti people; the Destiny that came from Osai Tutu's vision of the Ashanti's Greatness.

This ritual shows us how the Kingdom's Destiny passed from one generation of Kings to the next. And at the same time, shows the process of the installation of a Queenmother, and how the ownership of the Kingdom is passed from one generation to the next generation Queenmother. Because when Opoku Ware became King, his mother, Osai Tutu's sister automatically became Queenmother.

Organization of the Royal Family

Grandpa believes that we have reached a point where we will change to using our names in the Royal Family.

In this way, Grandpa thinks it will be easier to understand the Akan family system. "The children of a family legally and physically belong to their mother's side of their family, and spiritually belong to their father's side of the family."

As Grandpa uses the terms, children belong to their mother's family, it is not to become confused with the terms, 'matriarch and patriarch' which means that it is a male or female dominated family structure.

Anyway, this is not how Africans define these terms, the child not only belongs to his or her mother and father, but equally to the extended families of their mother and father.

The major point being, a child's family has two sides, and each side takes certain responsibilities, and the children inherited certain social positions from both sides. Africans do not think in terms of a male or female dominated family, only the mother's side and the father's side.

However, we are more interested in which side the child inherits his social status. For example, we saw with the Igbo that Rachel and Orchester III inherit their social positions of Oldest Daughter and Oldest Son from their father's side of their family.

But with the Akan, and especially the Ashanti, it is the other way around. The King and Queenmother inherit their social position from their mother's side of the family.

Because the Akan believe that children inherit their blood from their mothers, in this case Royal Blood, called, a 'Royal Blood line' through generations of 'Prince' and Princesses;' they are the only ones that can become King and Queenmother.

And, it is from this point of view, that we will super-impose the names of four generations of the female side of your family; Meaning, using your Grandma Victoria's family names onto the Royal Family, Kingship, and Queenmothership of the Ashanti.

Your Great Great Grandma Corina Fulton, would be the foundering Queenmother of a sub-clan of the Royal Oyoko Clan. One sister and one brother, Sadonia and Remus; and she had four daughters; your Great Grandma Rushie, and Great Aunts, Rosita, Dolly and Gladys, and five sons, Earnest, John, Henry, Willie, and Earl, who would be Prince' and Princesses.

Your Great Grandma Rushie had two daughters, your Grandma Victoria, and Grand Aunt Earline, and three sons, your Great uncles William, Kirk, and Ricky Dee, who would be Prince' and Princesses.

Your Grandma Victoria had two daughters, your aunt Linda and Elaine, and two sons, your Uncle Orchester Jr. and Uncle Larry who would be Prince' and Princesses.

Your Aunt Linda and Elaine, each had one daughter, Tiffany and Maya, and one son each, Marcus and Michael, who would be Prince' and Princesses.

The point being is that all of the Children, Grandchildren, Great Grandchildren, and Great Great Grandchildren of Great Great Grandma Corina and Sadonia, would be prince' and Princesses. In addition, in each generation, one of the Prince' and Princesses would become King and Queenmother, following the line of Grandma Corina's daughters; after an election based on their qualification to be leaders.

However, if any of Corina's daughters did not have any sons, the line of Kings and Queenmothers would follow the line of Great Great Grandma Sadonia. This was the case with Osai Tutu's mother before she visited the Shrine of the God OTUTU. We are going to say that the qualified ones, were one of the prince' and princesses of your Great Great Grand Mother Corina.

On the other hand, your Grandpa Orchester Sr. (me) also has a role and place in the picture. Recall when Osai Tutu (Uncle Kirk) became Clan Chief of the Oyoko Royal Clan, and defeated a number of Clans in the area, the Domaa, Tafo, Kwabiri, Atwima, and the 'Amakom' is where Grandpa comes into the picture.

When the Amakom was defeated, Osai Tutu (Uncle Kirk) appointed his favorite of the Amakom leaders, one Edu Panin (Orchester Sr.), to be Clan Chief of the Amakom, and gave his sister (Grandma Victoria) to him in marriage.

The offspring of this marriage was Opoku Ware (Orchester Jr.), whom Osai Tutu (Uncle Kirk) named to be his successor, being his nephew, as the second King of Ashanti.

This means that Grandpa is the Clan Chief, and Chief Priest of the Kings male clan whose God is BOSOMMURU; which will be shown through the ritual symbolism in the upcoming Odwira Ceremonies.

However, to return to the organization of our family names superposed on the Oyoko Royal Family; this would mean that Obiri Yeboa (Great Great Uncle John's) mother, would be Great Great Grandma Corina Fulton, followed by Osai Tutu's (Grand Uncle Kirk's) mother, we will call Great Grandma Rushie, followed by Opoku Ware's (Orchester Jr's.) mother we will call Grandma Victoria.

In this sense, the major characters would be, in your grandma Victoria's royal family; Queenmother Victoria, King Orchester Jr., Princesses Linda, Elaine, Tiffany, and Maya.

Then all of your Grandaunt Earline's sons and daughters would also be prince' and Princesses, and King and Queenmother if anything happens to Grandma Victoria's family.

And your granduncle William, Kirk, and Ricky Dee are considered older wise Prince', called, "Keepers of the Tradition."

On the other hand, DionDi, Tyree, and Orchester III would be Chief of King Orchester Jr's Gyase people, Chiefs of his bodyguard, and Priest to Grandpa Clan God BOSOMMURU.

While Rachel, Omni, and Nikki would be Priestess to the Clan God ,BOSOMMURU, and the owners and symbols of King Orchester Jr's Wealth.

Now to round out our understanding of how the Ashanti Royal Family is organized, there is one other point we want to keep in mind.

Although we will not mention this in the ritual symbolism, everything that King Orchester Jr. does in carrying out his kingship duties, is observed by Marcus and Michael, for they are in line to become the next King. Another point that we should keep in mind is that we can see that it is King Orchester Jr., his sons and daughters, and father, that is really the governing forces of the Kingdom spiritually and economically.

Take note that it is the Gyase people that have control of the Golden Stool when a King dies. While Queenmother Victoria is concerned with, along with the 7 Clan Mothers and Clan Chiefs, the election of a New King; meaning that Gyase people (father's side of the family) maintain the spiritual symbolic power of the Kingdom.

However, to fill out our picture of the spirituality of the Ashanti Kingdom and its Chosen Destiny, we must next focus our attention on the two major community rituals related to Kingship.

One for the Royal Ancestors, called 'Adae;' where the King and Queenmother are in the role of Priest and Priestess.

And the other, for the well being of the Spirit of the Kingdom, called 'Odwira;' where the King and Queenmother are in the role of God and Goddess in the spiritual world of the Kingdom's Spirituality.

We will now return to Ashanti history, and King Orchester Jr. (Opoku Ware), their second King. And focus our investigative attention on how He, and Queenmother Victoria (Osai Tutu's Sister), performed these two rituals; beginning with the Adae ritual for the Royal Ancestors.

Sunday and Wednesday
Adae Community Rituals

As we mentioned (see calendar), there are two Adaes per 42 day period. There is the big Sunday Adae, where the focus is on the Royal Ancestors, and the little Wednesday Adae where the major focus is on all of the non-royal Ancestors of the Kingdom.

The Sunday Adae involves the King and Queenmother directly, and the Clan Chiefs and Family-heads in-directly. On the other hand, the Wednesday Adae involves the Clan Chiefs and Family-heads directly, and the King and Queenmother in-directly.

This shows the major differences between the two, and at the same time, shows the relationship between the two. With that in mind, we will now look at a Sunday Adae.

All preparations are made the day before Adae, a Free-Saturday, which means a day of no ritual activities. Fire wood, food, palm wine, a sheep to sacrifice, King Orchester Jr's white stool, and cooking pots are washed with holy water (from the Tano river).

Because work of no kind is allowed on the day of the ritual, with the exception of King Orchester Jr's and Queenmother Victoria's cooks, who must cook the sacred food for the Ancestors.

Adae is a one-day ritual which takes place in the Chapel of the Stools, called a Mausoleum; that is, in the room where the Ancestral Stools are kept.

Remember that the Ashanti believe that a person's favorite stool in life becomes the shrine of his or her spirit when they die; Sunday Adae is concerned with the Stool-shrine of the Royal Ancestors, especially the Ancestral Kings and Queenmothers. (We will quote an observer :)

"About nine o'clock on the morning of Mono-Sunday the musicians, drummers and horn blowers, and other Gyase people and the general public assemble at the Chapel of Stools.

In front of where the King sits between the Chapel of Stools is where the Heralds and Minstrels sit (number 20).

Soon thereafter, King Orchester Jr., led by his Chief Stool-bearer, and Orchester III, DionDi, Tyree and other Gyase Chiefs, make their way to the door and enter the Chapel of Stools. They are the only ones to enter the room itself.

On the east wall of the room (chapel of Stools), opposite the door, is a long low platform, raised about three feet off the ground. Upon which rest three blacken stools covered with a cloth, which belongs to now dead King Kirk (Osai Tutu), Royal Clan Chief John (Obiri Yeboa) and Royal Clan Chief Remus (Oti Akenten), which are the founding fathers of the Ashanti Kingdom.

All, including King Orchester Jr. are dressed in their oldest cloths and no jewelry. On entering, King Orchester Jr. bared his left shoulder and slipped his sandals from his feet, stand on them, as signs of respect shown to Ancestors as being superior to himself; he speaks to the Stools as follows,

"Ancestor Grandfathers, good morning," and sits on his white Stool.

His Chief stool-bearer (Chief of the Royal Chapel of Stools, who is Orchester Jr's Uncle Walter on his father's side), then comes forward and removes the covering, exposing the three blacken stools laying on their sides with the seats facing the worshippers.

A small pot of holy water is then brought into the room and poured into a jar, and Gyase Chief Walter pours some on the ground with these words, "Grandfather (Ancestors) receive this water and wash your hands."

Following this, the Chief-cook brings sacred food, mash yams or plantains. From this, the Chief stool-bearer takes a spoonful, and hands it to King Orchester Jr. who slips his sandals and bares his shoulder, approaches and places the food on the oldest Ancestor Stool with these words,

"Grandfather Remus, today is Sunday Adae, come and receive your food and eat; help this kingdom prosper; and permit the bearer of children to bear children; and may all the people who are in this Kingdom get riches."

This was repeated with the Stools of John and Kirk, after which the rest of the sacred food was thrown on the ground, for the Ancestors of the Gyase people of those leaders, as King Orchester Jr. returned to his stool.

Next, a live sheep is brought in, carried slung across the shoulders and neck of one of the cooks, and presented to the Stools with the same prayer by King Orchester Jr., as with the other sacred food, "Ancestor Grandfathers today is Sunday Adae, etc, etc."

After which, while the sheep is held tightly by the cooks, King Orchester Jr. makes a little stab in its neck and allowed a little blood to fall on the floor.

And with a wooden bowl held under the wound, as the sheep was taken outside where its throat was cut and the blood caught in the bowl. Then in preparation for a sacrifice meal, the sheep is cut into small sections.

Meanwhile, the bowl of blood is carried back into the Chapel of Stools, and the Chief stool-bearer smears the blood on the seat and edges of each Stool.

The covering of fat on the lower intestines of the sheep were next brought in, and placed on the center support of each Stool. The blood, intestine and lungs symbolize AWO, ASASE YAA AFUA, and the breath of life from NYANKOPON. All of this was done in a hush silence.

At the same time as this was going on, the meat-cutters are outside cutting and threading choice pieces of meat on small skewers, three pieces each, which are sent to the Chief stool-bearer's wife to be cooked.

When cooked, they are brought back and laid on a wooden dish, and taken into the Chapel of Stools. A golden bell is then rung to announce that the Ancestor Spirits are about to eat.

A skewer of roasted meat is place on each Stool by the Chief Cook. With King Orchester Jr. saying to each one, "Ancestor Remus, here is meat, receive and eat; Ancestor John, here is meat, receive and eat; Ancestor Kirk, here is meat, receive and eat."

After the offering of cooked and un-cook meat had been arranged on the Stools, a jug of palm wine is produced; and the Chief stool-bearer pours a few drops on each Stool with these words;

"Grandfather Remus, your wine, life to the people of Ashanti; for one who would wish evil on this kingdom, let misfortune fall upon his own neck. Grandfather John, your wine, by your kindness let this Kingdom have life. Grandfather Kirk, your wine, does not permit any bad matter to come to this Kingdom.

The remainder of the palm wine is passed around to all as a kind of sacrament, along with a skewer of roasted meat, symbolizing harmony between the Royal Ancestor Leaders, King Orchester Jr., and the people of the Kingdom.

In this respect, King Orchester Jr. is the Priest standing between the Royal Ancestors and the people. This ends the ritual sacrifice for the Royal Ancestors in the Chapel of Stools."

Recall, King Orchester Jr. was dressed in his oldest and plainest clothes. He now retires to dress for the Festival of Royal Ancestors," to entertain them so to speak. Or to say, he had communion with the Ancestors, and the next thing was to party and talk business in their presence and seek their advice.

But we must not forget that Ancestors of Queenmother Victoria are also Royal Leaders. In addition, Sunday Adae was also performed for them in the Queenmother's Palace at the same time, and same way, as Adae was performed in the King's Palace.

To show what we mean, we will quote an old Ashanti Queenmother (Queenmother Victoria) about her role as Priestess of the Royal Ancestor Queenmother Adae:

"My stool-bearers (who are women, and her Gyase people) prepare eto (mash yams or plantains) and fish from the lake (Bosomtwe): BOSOMTWE is the Clan God of her father) and perhaps otwe (antelope) meat. My head stool-bearer pours a little water upon the ground that the Spirits may wash their hands. I then take a spoon and place the eto upon each stool.

There are three Queenmother's blackened stools in my stool house (Chapel of Stools). Not every Queenmother who dies has a stool blackened for her; for should a Queenmother have a great number of such stools in her charge, and should war come, and she should have to fly (run away), they would be a great encumbrance and she might not be able to save them all.

As I place the eto (sacrificial food) upon the stools, I address my Ancestors, saying: "Give me health and strength, and give health also to the King, and to the people of Ashanti, and to the women of the Kingdom, and to strangers in the towns. May the women bear children and the men gain riches. Any one who wishes evil to the Kingdom may that evil fall upon him."

Of the eto that remains, my stool-bearers will place some upon any rock near the Tano River. (When asked the reason for this, she said); "Any stone or rock may after dark become the abode of a Spirit." (Meaning the offering was made for the God TANO).

The meat is then placed upon the stools and wine is poured over them. I then sit down and wait for King Orchester Jr. to finish his Adae.

The King may not go home until I have visited him even should I delay for a long time. He will send for me, begging me to come quickly. When I go to him he gives me wine, and I first pour a little upon the ground as the Talking Drummer is speaking to the Spirits, (first is NYANKOPON):

"The earth is wide, wide, wide,
The one was lifted up,
The other was set down,
In ancient times, long, long ago
Supreme NYANKOPON, upon whom men lean and fall not,
We serve you.
When NYANKOPON shows you something
May you profit by it.
If we wish white we get it,
If we wish red we get it.
Him upon whom we lean and do not fall,
God, Good morning
You whom we serve upon a Saturday,
Good morning.
    Then the Drummer speaks to TANO,
The fowl has crowed in the morning,
The fowl has awakened and crowed, Very early,
They are addressing me and I shall understand.
Next the Drummer calls the god of the Kingdom, TANO,
The stream crosses the path,
The path crosses the stream;
Which of them is the elder?
Did we not cut a path to go and meet this stream?
The stream has its origin long, long ago,
The stream had its origin in the Creator.
He created things (Kingdom and Golden Stool),
Pure, pure TANO;
Come here, TANO;
He devours rams (as sacrifices)
Health to King Orchester,
Health to Queenmother Victoria,
Health to the Kingdom,
Let no bad thing come upon this Kingdom.
TANO, the great One, the powerful One
Whom we serve upon a Monday"

"No woman who has her menses may enter my stool house. If I were 'ill,' my head stool-bearer would officiate for me. I do not eat any of the offering placed upon the stools myself; the children of the stool-bearers may do so. If any man or woman be impotent or barren, the remains of the offerings will enable them to beget or bear children."

We should take note, the part of Adae that takes place in the Chapel of Stools, only the Royal Ancestors who were Leaders, and Queenmothers, were at the center of the ritual sacrifices. Not only were there no other Ancestors involved, no Gods or Goddesses were called upon either: Until the Queenmother Victoria entered the Palace of King Orchester Jr., when the Drummer began inviting all of the Spirits to the Festival of the Ancestors. As we saw, beginning with NYANKOPON and TANO while King Orchester Jr. goes to change clothes.

While he is gone, the Drummers continue, and now speak to ODOMANKOMA's Holy Drummer, the Royal Elephant, and the Royal Ancestors, as follows.

"Oh, Holy Drummer,
I am scarcely awake and have risen up.
I, the Ashanti porcupine King's drummer,
I am scarcely awake,
I have made myself to rise up,
I am about to sound the drum,
If you have gone elsewhere
And I call you, come;
The fowl has crowed in the morning,
The fowl has awakened and crowed,
Very early, They are addressing me and I shall understand."

This is followed by calling on the Spirit of the Elephant who symbolizes the Fortitude, Drive and Determination of the Kingdom.

"There are swamps, swamps, swamps, Which can swallow up the elephant.
A river may lie small in the valley
Between great hills
But it flows on for ever and ever.
If You (Spirit of the Elephant) have gone elsewhere
And I call upon You, come. The fowl has crowed in the morning,
Very early,
They are addressing me and I shall understand."

Next the Drummer calls upon the Royal Ancestors who were the subject of the sacrifice in the chapel of Stools:
I lay down, but I did not feel sleepy,

I lay down but my eyes did not close,
For three watches of the night
I think about my friends who have left me.
And are asleep (dead).
Remus, John, Kirk, (Oti Akenten, Obiri Yeboa, Osai Tutu,)
The old Birds whose bones have grown strong
Fowl, good morning, good morning
The fowl has crowed in the morning,
The fowl has awakened and crowed,
Very early,
They are addressing me and I shall understand.

Finally, the Drummer calls upon King Orchester Jr. to return for the second part of Adae ritual, the Festival of Ancestors. Which consists of giving honor and respect to the King as Priest between the Royal ancestors and the people; the Drummer begins by giving information about the progress of the King dressing for the occasion,

"He is coming, he is coming
Little by little, slowly, slowly
Be careful not to stumble,
Little by little, slowly, slowly
You will come and sit down,
King, you will come and sit down.
The Great man has sat down (to dress).
The King has sat down,
He who destroys towns has sat down,
He who never forgives (enemies),
He has taken a stool and sat down.

This goes on throughout the time the King changes cloths and ends when he is fully dressed and about to appear; when the Drummer says,

"The King is going to rise,
The destroyer of towns is about to rise.
Rise!
Rise!
Rise!
Little by little!
Carefully! Carefully!
Take care you do not stumble.
King, lead us forward."

With these last few lines, King Orchester Jr. dressed in a beautiful cloth, and a velvet headpiece inlaid with gold. His fingers, arms, neck, legs, and ankles are so loaded down with massive rings, necklaces and bracelets, that he could hardly move.

But slowly, carefully, and little by little, he steps into the courtyard number 7 and is met by his Gyase people carrying ostrich feathers, gold swords with handles bound with leopard hide, and a gold leaf.

His Daughters carry elephant tails, and are so decked out in gold until they had to be carried.

Spokesmen with gold shaft, sandals-bearers carrying spare gold in-laid sandals. Umbrella-bearers carrying the immense silk and velvet gold topped umbrellas. Under which slowly, carefully, and little by little, lest he should stumble, King Orchester Jr. is escorted to his place (number 6) and seats himself on his White Stool.

The Drummers have been following his progress all the way.

"The King has sat down,
The destroyer of towns has sat himself down,
The great man has sat down
He has taken a stool and sat down."

King Orchester Jr. sits surrounded by his Gyase people with a space, one step back and to his left, reserved for Queenmother Victoria's visit. He is now ready for the second, short, stage of Adae; where the King is honored and respected, by the Clan Chiefs, as the Priest between the Royal Ancestors and the people.

Meanwhile, King Orchester Jr's Gyase Chiefs, shield-bearers, horn blowers, drummers, sword-bearers and men of the King's bodyguard, form a double lined ally that extends from the gate of the Palace (number 1) to where the King sits (number 6) through which the Clan Chiefs, who have been waiting outside, one by one march to pay homage and greet the King as follows:

Slipping their sandals from their feet and bearing the left shoulder, they bowed from the waist, saying, 'Grandfather, good morning,' and retired, making way for another, with the King acknowledging their salutations by the slightest possible inclination of his head.

After the Clan Chiefs had all greeted the King, everyone seated himself upon his stool in the place appointed to him according to his rank, and surrounded by their own Clan Gyase people.

At this point, the courtyard (number 2) is packed with people, the Gyase people of the Clan Chiefs, as well as the general public.

The King's wine-bearers now pass palm wine to all present, including the King, and some is poured on the ground for the Gods, Goddesses, and Royal ancestors as sacrament.

This communion is climaxed by the Clan Chief of the Royal Clan (who would be your Aunt Earline's Son) coming before the King, slipping his sandals and bearing his left shoulder, and saying 'Grandfather, I thank you.' After which everybody sits and waits for Queenmother Victoria's visit, and nobody can leave before her appearance, including the King.

Queenmother Victoria's arrival is led by her stool-bearers with her Silver Stool and cushion; which is placed on the same elephant skin as the King, to the left and slightly behind him.

She is decked out in some gold, but mostly silver jewelry more so than the King. As she progresses from the gate (number 1) down the ally of the King's Gyase people, the talking Drummer follows her progress as was the case of the King.

"She is coming, she is coming,
Little by little, slowly, slowly,
Be careful not to stumble,
Little by little, slowly, slowly.
You will come and sit down,
Queen, you will come and sit down.
The Great Mother,
Nurturer of all, come and sit down
Owner of the Kingdom,
Come and sit down."

And finally, upon reaching the King and pouring libation, and sat down, the Drummer continued with:

"She has sat down,
The Great Mother has sat down.
The Queen has sat down,
The Owner of the Kingdoms sit down."

This ends this stage of Adae. King Orchester Jr. now retires to his sleeping quarters (number 38), to refresh himself in preparation for the third stage of Adae; the Royal Wives' Adae.

The Royal Wives' Adae ritual takes place in (number 39). Where the Royal wives led by Chief Wife Norma, one by one, like the Clan Chiefs, greet the King. After which, they dance with the Queenmother's (female) Drummers accompanying them on drums.

Finally, they are presented with palm wine, which they drank as the Senior Wife Norma pours libation for the Royal Ancestor Wives (symbolizing sisterhood). At the same time, the female minstrels call out the name of the wives of Oti Akenten, Obiri Yeboa and Osai Tutu; which ends the third stage of Sunday Adae.

Late in the afternoon, people begin to gather in front of the King's and Queenmother's Palace Celebration of the Royal Ancestors. This is really a festival which last throughout the night, with drumming, dancing, and singing for the Royal Ancestor's great deeds. This is the fourth, and final stage of Sunday Adae.

We mentioned that there were two Adae's per 42-day months, Sunday and Wednesday; we will now look at the Wednesday Adae.

The major difference between the Sunday and Wednesday Adae is that Sunday ritually revolves around the King and Royal Ancestors, whereas in the Wednesday Adae, the ritual activities revolve around the Clan Chiefs and Family-Heads. Which is related to their Ancestor Clan Chiefs and Family-Heads; as well as between Clan mothers and Family mothers, and their Ancestor Clan mothers and Family mothers: and Clan mothers, and Family Heads and Family mothers are the Priest and Priestess of Wednesday Adae; the King and Queenmother are not directly involved.

The other difference is the location of the ritual, which takes place in the Seven Clan Towns, and each families homestead. Other than these differences, Wednesday Adae follows the same pattern, in detail, as Sunday Adae, including the use of Gyase people.

Thus ends our look at the Sunday and Wednesday ritual ceremonies called Adae. Now we will focus on what Adae means in relation to the Kingdom's chosen Destiny.

First off, we should take special note that the Gods and Goddesses were not called upon in their prayers. Although the Ashanti think of their Ancestors as a powerful spiritual force, their prayers do not have a begging quality. In fact, other than a general blessing, they do not ask them for help to solve any of the Kingdom's problems.

Therefore, the Ashanti do not pray from the point of view of "Oh God or Ancestor help us to do this or that," they think it is their responsibility to work it out for them selves. Or to say, come up with their own ideas for a solution.

They think that NYANKOPON gave them a strong Spirit, and it is a insult to God not to use it. This is why Grandpa calls the Akan, and especially the Ashanti religious beliefs, a thinking-man's Religion.

But the major point we wanted to bring to light by going into the details of Sunday Adae, is how the Kingdom's Chosen Destiny, chosen by King Osai Tutu, moved into the next generation of King Orchester Jr.; and how he spiritually maintained that connection by renewing it every 42 days.

This means that King Orchester Jr. is the next step in the long march of the Kingdom's Destiny toward fulfillment; followed in office by Marcus or Michael, who will be followed by Desmond or Dominick.

The purpose of Sunday Adae is to maintain the spiritual continuity of that Destiny across generations. In other words, the purpose Sunday Adae serves, is to unite the King and Queenmother and the Royal Ancestor Leaders into a common cause.

Remember, a Kingdom's Chosen Destiny is different from, for instance, an Individual's Chosen Destiny, (Yoruba) which is fulfilled in one lifetime, and a family Chosen Destiny, (Ibos) which is fulfilled in three generations.

A Kingdom's Chosen Destiny, (Akan) unfolds over many generations and hundreds of years; therefore it is very important to maintain continuity for the survival of its Destiny.

On the other hand, Wednesday Adae symbolizes the continuity of people supporting the Kingdom's Chosen Destiny from one generation to the next.

This is a ritual communion between the Ancestor Clan Chiefs, and Family-Heads as supporters of Oti Akenten, Obiri Yeboa and Osai Tutu. And the Clan Chiefs and Family Heads that are the supporters of King Orchester Jr.

In this respect, Wednesday Adae is as much about the Kingdom's Destiny as the Sunday Adae. Both draw the King, the people, and all of the Ancestors into one functioning unit. This becomes the Spirit of the Kingdom, whose purpose is to bring an idea into reality, or to say, fulfill a Destiny symbolized by the Golden Stool.

On the other hand, we must not forget the point about the nature of Ashanti prayers, especially the part about taking responsibility. The question becomes, what gives the Ashanti the self-confidence to take on the job of creating an idea, and bringing it into reality as a destiny?

For this means that it is up to the King, Queenmother, Clan Chiefs, Clan mother, Family head, and Family mother to deal with all situations that come up; for example, maintaining the continuity of one idea across generations.

However, that is not the end of the responsibility. We mentioned that there were two major community rituals, Adae, which we have investigated in some detail, and now we will turn our attention to the second, "Odwira."

Odwira background

Up to this point, every thing we have investigated in the Akan Kingship and Queenship spiritual symbolism, including Sunday and

Wednesday Adae, is part of the Akan Traditional Kingship rituals, and is performed by every Kingdom in the Akan Nation.

But now, we get into ritual symbolism that is only performed by the Ashanti Kingdom; created by Priest Anokye especially related to the Ashanti Chosen Destiny.

We must now recall that 3 years after the Ashanti defeated the Denkyira, Priest Anokye retired to a small village. And while there, we mentioned, without going into any detail, that Priest Anokye created a community ritual called 'Odwira,' for the health and welfare of the spiritual side of the Kingdom. 'Odwira means, in Akan language, cleansing and purification.'

The Akan think of a Kingdom as a living Spirit, and if we recall, in Yoruba Traditional Beliefs, a person must spiritually cleanse, purify, and energize his spirit and destiny, ORI, as a means of spiritual health and destiny fulfillment.

According to African Traditional Religion, this is the case with any living spirit, and therefore is the case with the Living Spirit of a Kingdom. This means that it is the responsibility of the Ashanti themselves, to clean, purify, and energize the Kingdom's Spirit, and this is where the Ashanti's great ritual creator, Chief Priest Anokye's Odwira's ritual comes into the picture.

We should also keep in mind that in the beginning, we came to the conclusion that Akan Traditional Beliefs had three parts, spirituality, astrology and numerology, which go to make up, what we call a thinking man's religion.

We also looked at the Akan religious calendar, which symbolizes the organization of these three parts into a functioning religion.

Priest Anokye not only showed his spiritual genius in bringing the Spirit of the Ashanti Kingdom into reality, as symbolized by the Golden Stool, but he also was a Creative Artist, in that he had to create a place for that Spirit in Ashanti general Religious Beliefs.

This meant that Priest Anokye had to create a new ritual. He had to design it to ritually fit into, and be in harmony with the Calendar organization of the Akan basic beliefs about the activities of the Original Gods and Goddesses; who have an influence on every thing in the Universe, including the Spirit of the Ashanti Kingdom.

This also means that, depending on its nature, Anokye's Odwira ritual ceremonies must be performed when the desired Day God or Goddess is in a certain state of mind. But each God and Goddess changes their state of mind six times in a six week period, or to say, six times in one Akan month.

Which means that Priest Anokye fits Odwira into the mood swings of the Day Gods and Goddesses; however, the major point being, that Priest Anokye created the Odwira rituals.

Now to get to the subject at hand, and deal with the question, if a Spirit must be cleaned and purified before it can function at its best, how do the Ashanti cleansed and purify the Spirit of the Kingdom?

The answer is that Odwira Ceremony is performed at the end of the Year to rid the Kingdom of all evil, and at the same time, renew its energy.

By this we mean, clean and purify the God TANO and the Ancestors, King and Queenmother, Clan Chiefs and Clan mothers, Family-Heads and Family mothers, as well as the general population. And we can see that this is one hell of a job, however, it is the designed purpose of the Odwira ritual ceremony to deal with this job.

For example, Adae deals with the continuity of the Kingdom's Chosen Destiny, and Odwira deals with the Kingdom's Spirit and the 'evils' that have accumulated over the year, to make ready for the new year.

First we must define what is meant by 'evil' in Ashanti beliefs; that is, *evil means any thing that becomes an obstacle to the Kingdom's destiny fulfillment*, as we will see.

Odwira, a Community Ritual

To begin our investigation, we must return to the Calendar. Take note that the Odwira begins around harvest time, and ends the first days of Fall, September 21st, 22nd, or 23rd; called Fall Equinox, the beginning of the Akan new year. Odwira is performed in a period between a Sunday Adae and a Wednesday Adae which is New Year's Day; (See Calendar).

Odwira itself is a group of 8 independent rituals, some lasting only one day and others lasting up to nine days. This group of rituals are called Odwira.

This means that each of the 8 rituals involve one or more of the Seven Day Gods or Goddesses, and His or Her attitude-mood on the day or days the ritual is performed.

For example, the first day of Odwira ritual activity falls on a Generous-Monday, following a Sunday Adae; which is the Day of the Goddess AWO, NYANKOPON's Mother, when She is in a Generous Mood. This means that the Ashanti are beginning Odwira with Her permission and support. This is the meaning, and reason that certain rituals are performed on certain Days.

Moreover, at the same time, we can get a better idea of how the Akan Calendar serves as the Path Way and regulator of their ritual activities.

So with that in mind, let's return to the time of King Orchester Jr., and take a detailed look at how the Odwira ritual unfolds.

On the morning of Generous-Monday, in the last month of the year, King Orchester Jr. and his Gyase Chiefs DionDi, Tyree, and Orchester III, with Marcus and Michael as observers, make a ritual visit to the Chapel of Stools. This is where gold dust (Ancestor money) is kept, to borrow some money to buy things for the up-coming Odwira rituals, like palm wine, food, etc, etc.

There, showing honor and respect by slipping his sandals and bearing his shoulders, and sacrificing a sheep and feeding the Royal 'Ancestors, King Orchester Jr. makes the following prayer.

"The edge (end) of the year has come around, we are about to celebrate the rituals of Odwira. Don't permit any evil at all to come upon us, and let the New Year meet us peacefully."

Thereafter, King Orchester Jr. takes a certain amount of gold dust out of a special brass container kept in the Chapel of Stools, which ended the ritual.

This ritual, the borrowing of money from the Royal Ancestors, symbolizes their support as well as a kind of announcement to the Royal Ancestors that the Ashanti are taking care of things as they should. We call it borrowing, because it will be replaced.

In the afternoon, the business side of the up-coming ritual continues between King Orchester Jr. and his Gyase Chiefs, especially his Royal Treasurer and Book-keeper (Tyree).

A meeting is held in the courtyard to work out the cost of the major rituals. The ones that take place in King Orchester Jr's town of Kumasi, parts of which take place in his Palace. We must keep in mind that the role of a King is that of a Businessman, as well as Divine Being and warrior.

After taking into consideration the money borrowed from the Royal Ancestors, King Orchester Jr. sends Messengers to all Clan Chiefs and sub-Chiefs the day they are to be in Kumasi. And how much money they are to contribute to Odwira's expense.

The Clan Chiefs and Family-Heads follow the same pattern as King Orchester Jr., for they too, on a smaller scale in their town, have a Chapel of Stools of their Ancestors from which they ritually borrow money.

But the borrowing from Ancestors is more ritual and symbolic, and does not by a long shot add up to the actual amount of the huge amount of money to pay the full expense of Odwira; nor is it ever meant to.

Each person, including King Orchester Jr. and Clan Chiefs, makes large contributions out of their pockets. From this point of view, the Ancestors are temporary paying their share as Co- Authors and Actors in the cleansing and purification of the Kingdom.

Thus, we can see that the first day of Odwira's activities are concerned with planning and economics. And all levels of Leadership are involved, from King Orchester Jr., down to the Family-Heads, and include the Queenmother, down to the Mother of the Homestead. This means that Odwira is supported directly by the general public, and means that every body in the Kingdom is involved. And thus is the first day of ritual activities of Odwira.

As we mentioned, the first day was a Generous-Monday (21st) that meant the next day was a Protected-Tuesday (22nd).

From that Protected-Tuesday (22nd) to the next Sacred-Wednesday (30th), nine days later, are spent by everybody physically washing everything in the Kingdom with holy water, and repairing everything that needed to be brought up to standard.

For an example, we will take what was happening in King Orchester Jr's Palace as the nature of what was happening throughout the Kingdom. Houses were repaired; the Kingdom's regalia, chairs, stools, drums, and umbrellas were cleaned and overhauled.

Cooking and other household utensils, wearing apparels, jewelry, tools, weapons, and just about everything used in everyday life is cleaned and blessed.

And as we said, this was taking place in every town, village, and homestead in the Kingdom. Thus is the designed-purpose of the 9 day cleansing ritual, which ends on a Sacred-Wednesday, the 30th.

We will continue with our point, in our investigation, that King Orchester Jr. and the Queenmother Victoria's ritual activities, on one level or the other,are taking place throughout the Kingdom by all male and female Leaders.

The next day, the 31st, a Free-Thursday, is spent in a ritual designed to *clean up the relationship between the people and the Ancestors.*

Free-Thursday is begun by King Orchester Jr., and naturally his Gyase officials, making a visit to the door of the Chief Stool-bearer of the Golden Stool (DionDi). Where King Orchester Jr. pours palm wine on the ground as a libation for the Ancestors with these words, "Spirits of the Dead, receive this wine, let no bad thing come. We are about to celebrate Odwira ceremony;" where he is joined by the Chief stool-bearer carrying the Golden Stool upon the nape of his neck.

This is an impressive sight, with King Orchester Jr. under his great umbrella, surrounded by his officials. And the Golden Stool under its even greater umbrella, called the "Covering of the Kingdom" also surrounded by an equal amount of attendants including drummers and ministers.

From there they made their way to the Chapel of Stools, stopping now and then to play music and sing songs (like their National Anthem) to the Golden Stool. Recall that the Ashanti believe the Golden Stool contains the living Spirit of the Kingdom.

Upon reaching the Chapel of Stools, King Orchester Jr. pours libation and sacrifices a sheep with the same prayer, 'Spirit of the Dead, receive this wine and sheep, we are about to celebrate Odwira.'

The group next moved to the Chapel of Spirit, where the skeletons of Royal Leaders are kept (another Mausoleum). Here, King Orchester Jr., slipping his sandals and baring his left shoulder, faced the skeletons of Oti Akenten (Remus), Obiri Yeboa (John), (but not to Osai Tutu (Kirk) because his body was never found). And to each, poured libation and announced that he was about to begin the Odwira ceremony.

This was followed by King Orchester Jr. and the Golden Stool leaving the Palace, and going in turn to where the houses (still kept up) of the (dead) fathers of Remus, John, and Kirk, and finally to his fathers (Orchester Sr.) house; and at each, pouring libation and announcing Odwira's ceremony.

This is followed by the group going to the Queenmother's Palace to pour libation and sacrifice a sheep at the Chapel of Stools of Queenmother, again announcing Odwira.

Finally, and by this time it is late afternoon, King Orchester Jr. and the Golden Stool visit the major crossroad in Kumasi (the shrine of the Trickster God, ANANSI the Spider). And there, libation was poured and a sheep sacrificed for Priest Anokye, the creator of the group of rituals that make up Odwira.

Our conclusion is that, these activities on Free-Thursday are designed to cleanse and purify the relationship between the Royal Ancestors, including the now Royal Priest Anokye, and the Kingdom, by inviting them to the upcoming ceremony. This ends the cleansing rituals on Free-Thursday, the 31st.

The next day, Fresh-Friday the 32nd, the Seven Clan Chiefs of the seven Clan towns, who are the Counselors of King Orchester Jr. arrived in Kumasi. They are under their Clan umbrellas and surrounded by Clan Gyase people, and displaying Clan symbolism and wealth. Therefore, the day is spent in their settling in. Although their arrival is ritual in nature, no ritual activities take place on Fresh-Friday, the 32nd.

The activities on Generous-Saturday, the 33rd, involve the Kingdom's Royal Government, and the assembling of that Government Body to cleanse and purify itself; which means an assemble of all of the high ranking Officials in the Kingdom.

Although King Orchester Jr., and his Council of Seven Clan Chiefs are the center policy decision makers in Government Administration; the Gyase people, especially their Chiefs, for example Chief Spokesman (Orchester III), are also high ranking government officials, and key players in the functioning of Government.

Therefore Gyase people are as much a part of the physical body of government as they are in spiritual symbolism; as is Queenmother Victoria's Royal Family.

First, we will show how the Ashanti assemble as a government body, followed by how they clean and purify the Spirit of Government.

The Government Body is assembled (in one of the courtyards in the King's Palace) facing west with an entrance through the Palace's main gate.

King Orchester Jr. and Queenmother Victoria sit on their Royal Stools. Behind of which are the Gyase people from the King's father's side of his family, like chief stool-bearers, Chief Executioner, etc, DionDi and Orchester III and others are the drummers and horn blowers.

Facing the King on his left, and facing the King on his right, are the Seven Clan Chiefs. Behind the Clan chiefs, sits their Sub-Chiefs. The Chief Treasurer (Tyree) holds a big pot of gold dust, and the Chief of all the Gyase Chiefs and people, along with Grandpa Orchester Sr.

A line of Sword-bearers, and a line of 'court Officials; the King's twelve Spokesmen, and is the War chief and his second in command.

To the King's far right, are high ranking Army Leaders. Along with Chief Priest to NYANKOPON, Chief Priest to TANO, Chief Priest to BOSOMMURU, Orchester Sr. Chief of the chapel of Stools, and Chief of the Chapel of Spirits (skeletons).

Thus is the assembled Body of Government from where the business of the Kingdom is administered. In this case, the cleansing of the Government itself; the goal is to begin the New Year with all parts of Government clean and pure.

To clean the Kingdom's Government means to put all of the Governments business dealings left over at the end of the year in its proper relationship with itself, as well as deal with the health and welfare of the Kingdom as a whole. Now we will take a look at how they do this.

To begin, the Royal Treasurer pays all of the Government's debts, and at the same time, collected all debts owed to the Government; no matter how large or small.

Next, all old laws that are weak or not working are made stronger or gotten rid of, and new laws made, based on what is thought of as being good for the Kingdom as a whole.

The relationship with other Kingdoms is analyzed, and decisions are made about trade, war, and peace in the upcoming year.

Economics are discussed, for example foreign trades as well as the economic health of the Kingdom itself, and problems, if any, are taken care of with new policies.

Any lingering court cases, felonies, and misdemeanors are disposed. Government Official's conduct are looked into, including the

King, and if any wrong-doing is found, a warning is given, if this is the second time, he or she is replaced.

As we mentioned, a Kingdom is a confederation of Seven Clan Chiefs. This means the Government came into reality by them pledging an allegiance to the King.

Therefore, it is very important that the relationships between the Clan Chiefs, and their relation to the King, be clean and pure in order for the Government to function. Therefore, so those allegiances are renewed in the cleansing process at this time.

Finally, and most important, the relationship of the Government to the women and children are examined in detail; represented by Queenmother Victoria, who is sitting to the left side of the King Orchester Jr. as these proceedings take place. She has veto power over all matters that concern the women of the Kingdom.

If the women and children are having problems legally and, or, economically, solutions must be found that meet the Queenmother's approval. This gives us an idea of the kind of activities that takes place on Generous-Saturday, the 33rd.

The next day, a Protected-Sunday, the 34th, the Government's cleansing operations continue, but in a different direction. On this day, King Orchester Jr. deals with the un-desirables of the Kingdom's society, or to say, capital punishment.

He also deals with the fact that the Ashanti believe that Ancestors have spiritual power. This also means, the Ancestors of people defeated by the Ashanti also have spiritual power, for example, the Ancestors of the Denkyira Kingdom have to be dealt with.

The following rituals can also give us some insight into the answer to the question, why are certain rituals performed on certain days?

This is a Protected-Sunday, and the rituals performed on this day are designed to protect the Kingdom's Spirit and society from possible evil effects of the undesirables of his own Kingdom, and the Ancestors of other Kingdoms. So lets look at this kind of cleansing ritual, beginning with the undesirables.

Un-desirables are Ashanti citizens that have committed capital crimes, like murder, rape, and other crimes that carry the death penalty. They are kept in a special village until the end of the year.

When they are sent to the Ancestors to deal with, in the form of a mass execution carried out in front of the Chapel of Spirits in the Palace on the morning of Protected-Sunday, the ritual activity is as follows.

King Orchester Jr. and his Gyase Chiefs, especially his Chief Executioner, the Talking Drummer, and of course the prisoners, gather in front of the Chapel of Spirits. The prisoners are put into three equal groups; for example if there are six prisoners, they are put into three groups of two each.

The Talking Drummer positions himself near the door of the Chapel enough to see what is taking place inside.

King Orchester Jr. enters, slipping his sandals and baring his left shoulder, standing in front of the skeleton of his Great Uncle Remus. As he poured libation, the Drummer sends the message to the Executioner, who cut off the heads of the first group of prisoners with these words, "Off with you to the spiritual world to serve Remus."

The same process took place as the King poured libation for Great Uncle John and Uncle Kirk. Therefore, the Kingdom was cleansed of that evil element in the society. This ends the ritual execution of the Kingdom's capital criminals.

In the afternoon, King Orchester Jr. begins the dealing with the Ancestors of the enemies of the Ashanti, first, by having the sculls of the Kings and War Chief, who were captured and killed in the various wars. These sculls are bought from the Chapel of Spirits and placed on the ground before King Orchester Jr. as he sits with the Seven Clan Chiefs.

As each scull is placed before him, he places his feet on it with the following words; "Uncle Remus of my Ancestor killed you, Uncle John of my Ancestor slew you, Uncle Kirk of my Ancestors gave me your scull;" as the case of which scull his foot was on at the time.

This was followed by King Orchester Jr., Gyase Officials, and the general public, making a trip to the edge of town to the bush-forest. And from there they make a sacrifice of new-year yams in a disrespectful way and threaten the enemy Ancestors.

King Orchester Jr's Spokesman, and Orchester III go to the edge of the forest and shout, "Hay You! Hay You! Hay You!"

From the forest comes a voice symbolizing the enemy Ancestors with, "Yes! Yes! Yes!"

And the Spokesman says, "The edge of the Years have met, we have come to celebrate the Odwira. Come and receive this food and eat. Any one of you who does not wish to serve the King of Ashanti, let our hand slay him as we slew you and your kinfolk."

A number of yams are thrown into the forest and the congregation turned their backs, and walk back to town without looking back; which ends the ritual.

Finally, the last ritual of the day consists of dedicating Odwira to King Kirk, the first King of Ashanti.

The groups of eight rituals that make up Odwira are symbolized by a pair of horns of the bongo antelope, the sacred animal of Odwira, and the shrine of Odwira. Anyway, it is upon this shrine that the dedication ritual is performed by King Orchester Jr.

For this ritual, King Orchester Jr. is dressed in plain cloths and wears no jewelry. He only has designs painted on his forehead and arms with a red dye made from the roots of a special tree that has protective spiritual powers. The red dye symbolizes protective spiritual powers.

Upon the Odwira Shrine being set before him, King Orchester Jr. draws protective designs on it with the same red dye, and with these words;

"Odwira of King Kirk, accept this wine and drink, anyone who does not wish to serve you, (the Kingdom's Chosen Destiny) let me get him, and let me kill him, and let me display his scull under my feet on Odwira."

After which, he painted protective designs on the forehead of the Seven Clan Chiefs. This ends the ritual activities on Protective-Sunday, the 34th.

The next day, Destructive-Monday the 35th, again shows us how the ritual activity relates to the mood of the Day God or Goddess.

But most important, Monday rituals lead us to the subject and meaning of 'Death and Resurrection Rituals, that ask the question, what is the deep meaning of 'Baptism', which is the heart and soul of any 'purification ritual, including Christianity.'

We should also at this point take note; in this case, the Death and Resurrection ritual really covers two days, Destructive-Monday and Sacred Tuesday. In this respect, the rituals on Monday are related to 'symbolic death' of King Orchester Jr. and his male Clan God BOSOMMURU. And the rituals on Tuesday are related to their symbolic resurrection (coming back to life, somewhat like the death and resurrection of Christ in Christianity).

We will begin with the two rituals on Destructive-Monday. And take note that this is the Day of the Queenmother of Heaven, and that Odwira was started on Her Day when She was in a Generous mood, and now She is in a Destructive mood.

Now, the death of a God or King is a serious matter, even if it is only symbolic. Therefore, when King Orchester Jr., Gyase Chiefs, Clan Chiefs, and the public gather early in the morning in front of the Palace, they are wearing protective red dye; which protects them when dealing with the symbolic death of the King's male Clan God, BOSOMMURU.

An ox, the sacred animal of BOSOMMURU, symbolizing His strength, and should not be harmed in any way, is disrespectfully dragged before King Orchester Jr.

Who rises up and takes the Great Gold Sword, the Shrine of BOSOMMURU, and strikes the Ox three times, repeating with each blow, "This is Yours! This is yours! This is yours!"

The striking of a God's sacred animal with His own Shrine is the ultimate in disrespect, and symbolically kills the God. This ends the Kings part of the ritual.

The morning ritual is very short, after which the Clan chiefs and Family-Head return to their own towns and villages. Where each of these Leader's male Clan Gods are symbolically killed in the same ritual manner as used by the King.

Therefore, the symbolic death of these Clan Gods are really the death of male spiritual leadership, which is based on the idea that *'disrespect kills spiritual powers.'*

Now we come to the second ritual of the day, held in the afternoon. For the second ritual of the day is held all over the Kingdom, including in each homestead; where the King, Clan Chiefs and Family-Heads are symbolically killed with disrespect.

However, the ritual serves two purposes, besides the symbolic killing of the Leadership (King, Clan Chiefs, and Family-Head). at the same time, it has a cleansing effect, the relieving of the penned-up frustration the people feel about how their leaders are doing, using negative words, without being charged.

For example, we will look at the kinds of things being said to King Orchester Jr. in Kumasi as an example of what is being said to Leaders throughout the Kingdom.

In late afternoon, King Orchester Jr. Chief Spokesman, and Orchester III go throughout the town making the following announcement:

"King Orchester Jr. says that I am to tell you that upon this Odwira festival which has come around, you are to celebrate it by abusing him.

And during this time, if anyone of you have a cause to quarrel with anyone else, or if your friend should seduce your wife, or someone should insult you and you do not keep your temper, but lodge a complaint, then you are bound by the oath (of the God and Goddess) of Wednesday, and of Thursday, which makes you liable to a penalty."

So in the afternoon, King Orchester Jr. is carried in a hammock, dressed in his finest, including gold jewelry, throughout the town, stopping here and there and listening to people singing abusive songs, for example as follows;

God, TANO, Says if we have anything to say,
Let us speak it,
For by so doing
We are removing misfortune from the Kingdom.
Your head is very large,
We are taking the victory from out your hands
O King Orchester Jr., you are a fool.
We are taking the victory from out your hands.

O King Orchester Jr., you are impotent
We are taking the victory from out your hands.
Do you people know the child who is head of this town?
The child who is head of this town
Is called 'the helpful one.'
When he buys palm wine
He helps himself to the pot as well.
Did I buy and give you to eat
That when they are leading me away
(Captured by enemies)
You should laugh at me?
These times have changed Orchester Jr.,
O Orchester Jr., these times have changed.
They know nothing about wars,
The Ashanti leaders know nothing about wars.
Had they known about wars
We would control all trade in the Akan Nation.
And be much more rich and prosperous.
We know that a Brong man eats rats (is a coward),
But we never knew that one of royal blood eats rats.
But to-day we have seen our King,
Orchester Jr. eating rats.
We are the Creator's stars.
When we say something it is important.
To-day all is well and we may say so, say so, say so.
At other times, we may not say so, say so, say so.

Every time King Orchester Jr. hears one of these songs and, or, an abusive speech, some of his kingship symbols and jewelry are taken off and returned to the Palace. And finally, the rich cloths he is wearing are removed, under which, he is wearing the poorest of cloths, even his Gyase Chiefs returns to the Palace and leaves him alone; symbolizing the ritual death of the King.

On the other hand, the Kingdom-wide abusiveness serves another very important purpose, of which we will quote an Ashanti Chief Priest explanation,

"You know that every one has a Spirit that may get hurt or knocked about or become sick, and so make the body ill.

Very often, although there may be other causes, like witchcraft, ill health is caused by the evil and the hate that another has in his head against you. Again, you too may have hatred in your head against another, because of something that person has done to you, and that, too, caused your Spirit to fret and become sick.

Our forbears knew this to be the case, and so they ordained a time, once every year, when every man and woman should have freedom to speak out just what was in their head. To tell their neighbors just what they thought of them, and of their actions, and not only their neighbors, but also the King or Clan Chief, or Queenmother.

When a man has spoken freely thus, he will feel his Spirit cool and quieted, and the Spirit of the other person against whom he has now openly spoken will be quieted also. The King of Ashanti may have killed your children in a unjust war or as an unjust criminal, and you hate him.

This made him ill, and you ill too; when you are allowed to say before his face what you think, you both benefit."

So we can see that the Destructive-Monday afternoon ritual is a process by which every Spirit in the Kingdom is cleansed and purified. As well as the Spirit of the Kingdom itself; one brings about the other. Thus ends the symbolic death of a God and King, as well as the death of all evil intentions on Destructive-Monday the 35th.

On the morning of the next day, Sacred-Tuesday the 36th is in the same spot and at the same time that the ox was sacrificed on Monday. King Orchester Jr., Gyase Chiefs, and the public gather this time at the Shrine of BOSOMMURU. The Great Gold Sword resting on its own Stool, is placed before the King.

A sheep is brought to King Orchester Jr., held over the Golden Sword Shrine, its throat was pricked, and the blood was allowed to fall on the Shrine.

Roots and leaves of certain plants are also squeezed into the bowl with water from the sacred river, Muru, in which white clay had been mixed. With this, the Shrine is also sprinkled. The following words are spoken by King Orchester Jr.,

"O BOSOMMURU the edges of the years have met. You were sharp, but I took that thing which you abhor (death) and touched you with it yesterday. But, today I sprinkle You with water in order that Your powers may rise up again.

When I and my equal (King of another Kingdom), some War Chief, or other, meet, cut off his head and give it to me; and along with the water, with which I sprinkle You, here is a sheep." This ends the morning ritual, BOSOMMURU is now alive; thus is the resurrection of the God.

In the afternoon, beginning in the same spot and time as on Monday, King Orchester Jr. is again carried in a hammock throughout the town. Only this time, he begins dressed poor and ragged with no gold jewelry, and people sing songs of praise, like,

Orchester Jr. is a Great King
Ashanti is honored

King Orchester Jr. will lead us to health and wealth
Ashanti is honored
Father Orchester Jr. is not a pet of one person alone
Ashanti is honored
Etc, etc, etc.

With each song, part of Orchester Jr's Kingship is returned to him in the form of the King's symbolic jewelry and fine clothes. Thus is the resurrection ritual of the King, keeping in mind that the same thing is happening throughout the Kingdom with Clan Chiefs and Heads of Homesteads. And this ends the ritual activities on Sacred-Tuesday, the 36th.

There is not an Odwira ritual activity on Free-Wednesday, the 37th, or Fresh-Thursday, the 38th; the next ritual day is Generous-Friday, the 39th, which needs some explaining.

The combined rituals of Destructive-Monday and Sacred-Tuesday give an insight into what is called a 'death and resurrection' ritual, and the purpose it serves; but it is incomplete. TANO and Kingdom Spirit are not yet 're-energized.' This brings up the question of baptism.

To fully understand Baptism, as a Death and Resurrection ritual, we should remember certain things about Akan beliefs. For example, life-giving water called "Ntoro' is what brought people into reality, which came from NYANKOPON, Who has Sons, One of which is TANO, symbolized by the Tano River.

Therefore, water from that river has cleansing (in the sense of killing evil) as well as life-giving (brought human life into reality) powers.

Baptism simply means that all evil has been washed away, and you have the experience of being as spiritually pure as you were the day you were born. But more important, have the spiritual energy you had the day you were born. This is why being baptized is called by Afro-American Christians, 'being born again.'

In other words, a person's spirit can be so burdened with evil, that it takes all of their spiritual energy just to deal with it. This leaves them in a very poor position to fulfill their Chosen Destiny; Baptisms remove the evil, which leaves them in a position to use all of their spiritual energy to fulfill their Chosen Destiny.

The same is the case with the Spirit of their God, TANO, and Kingdom's Spirit, they too must be Baptized to re-new their spiritual energy (powers) to fulfill their Chosen Destiny. Thus is the nature of the ritual activity on Generous-Friday the 39th.

For an account of this ritual activity, we will quote an Ashanti Priest who was involved in the Community Baptisms of the Kingdom rituals;

"The King and his court (Gyase people), dressed in their best, and preceded by the golden Stool and the Royal Ancestral blacken stools, Odwira shrine, BOSOMMURU shrine, the shrines of the Gods, together with all the paraphernalia of the household (Palace), stools, chairs, drums, horns, etc., were marched to the river (Tano).

Here, the War-chair called fwedom (drive back the enemy) was set up, and upon this was placed the Golden Stool. The numerous blacken stools, and the shrines of the Royal Ancestral Spirits, were held in front of the bearers, each by its respective stool-bearer.

The King held in his hand a branch of the plant called BOSOMMURU Adwira; this he dipped into a large brass basin that had been filled with the sacred water (from the Tano River). And with it, sprinkled the Golden Stool (symbolizing the Spirit of the Kingdom), repeating as he did so the following words;

> Friday, Stool of Kings, I sprinkle water upon You,
> May your power return sharp and fierce.
> Grant that when I and another meet (in battle),
> Grant it be as when I met Denkyira (King);
> You let me cut off his head.
> As when I met Domaa (Clan Chief);
> You let me cut off his head.
> The edge of the years have met,
> I pray upon You for life.
> May the Kingdom prosper;
> May the women bare children.
> May the hunters kill meat
> We, who dig for gold, let us get gold to dig,
> And grant that I get some for the upkeep of my Kingship.

Then, the Odwira, BOSOMMURU, blacken Ancestral stool, Shrines of the Gods, and the assembled people were likewise sprinkled, and similar prayers offered up, asking for prosperity for the Kingdom, freedom from sickness, plentiful crops, and many children.

Then, every one returned home; sheep were sacrificed to the Spirits of the Dead Kings, and wine and new yams were (it is harvest season) offered to them, with these words;

> "The edges of the years have met,
> I take sheep and new yams
> And give that you may eat.
> Life to me
> Life to this my Ashanti people
> Women who cultivate the farms,
> When they do so,

Grant the food comes forth in abundance.
Do not allow any illness to come."
Fresh yams were also placed on the shrines of various Gods, on the Odwira, and on BOSOMMURU, and the shrines of all the Gods and Goddesses, burial-places of the Royal Family, and all Ancestor shrines, with the following prayer;

"NANKOPON, upon whom men lean and do not fall,
Goddess of Earth, ASASE YAA AFUA,
Creature that rules the Underworld,
Leopard that possesses the forest,
Tano River,
By Your kindness it is time to harvest Your gifts;
Here are first-fruit yams,
Here is wine,
Eat and drink to the harvest."

Only after the Gods, Goddesses, Ancestors, and other non-human spiritual powers have partaken of the new crops of yams, might the King, Clan Chiefs, and the general public eat them.

The rest of the day, and throughout the night, is spent in a festival of songs, dancing, drumming, and general merry-making in celebration of the Kingdom meeting the new year purified, energized, and inspired." Thus ends the final ritual day of Odwira, and ends Odwira period, as told by an old Ashanti Priest.

Recall, we mentioned that Odwira is performed in the harvest season; yams and sweet potatoes, are the staple food of the Ashanti and are very important in their diet. But yams are also the staple food in the spiritual world of Gods, Goddesses and Ancestors, Who is to receive, in ritual sacrifice, the first-fruits of harvest, which is an honor bestowed on the spiritual world Who are the spiritual powers of the Kingdom. In this sense, giving the first-fruits of harvest are purifying the relationship between the people and their spiritual world.

Next, we will summarize the 8 rituals of Odwira. Now we can begin to see what Odwira is all about, and what is meant by cleansing and purifying the Spirit of the Kingdom; and we saw that Baptism, death and resurrection, is the process by which cleansing and purifying takes place.

Therefore, we can say, Odwira means cleansing and purifying as a means of renewing and re-energizing life. In other words, to make stronger. In our case, the Spirit of the Kingdom, and lets not forget its Chosen Destiny.

Spirit and Chosen Destiny equals one thing, Soul; therefore it is better for our understanding if we think of Odwira as cleansing and purifying the Kingdom's Soul, which is the collective Souls of the Ashanti people, with the help of the Gods, Goddesses, and Ancestors; this is made clear in the rituals themselves.

Odwira gives us some indication what we mean by maintaining the health and welfare of the Kingdom's Spirit and Destiny. On the other hand, and just as important, we saw the flowing of this Spirit and Destiny across generations in the Adae rituals.

This brings us back to Priest Anokye, the creator of Odwira group of rituals; all Akan Kingdoms performed Adae rituals that are as old as the Akan people. However, the Ashanti Kingdom was the only one to have an Odwira Ritual, which gave the Ashanti the edge. Their Kingdom's Spirit was in better health than the other Kingdoms; unhealthy Kingdom Spirits are the cause of a Kingdom becoming weak, and at the mercy of other Kingdoms. To prevent this is why Priest Anokye created Odwira.

To the Ashanti, their destiny was to become the riches and most powerful Kingdom in all of the Akan Nation, This is shown in the nature of the prayers of Odwira.

This means that Odwira, in cleansing and purifying the Spirit, is really a key protective measure to assure the preservation and fulfillment of its Chosen Destiny. The thing that made Odwira so successful was that Priest Anokye brought the whole of Akan Religious Beliefs to purify and energize the Chosen Destiny. This shows the spiritual genius of Priest Anokye, and shows him to be the "Christ" or Source of Spiritual Power of the Ashanti.

Kingdom's Power and Warfare

If we recall, in Odwira, the Kingdom's Shrine, and the Golden Stool was placed on a War Chair. Which means that the Ashanti had a Spirit of War symbolizing the leopard, and this was His Chair.

And if we also recall that Amankwa Tia, the Ashanti Great War Chief, created, inspired, and Organization of the Army, and this Chair symbolizes these three qualities. This means that the Chair really symbolizes the Spirit of Amankwa Tia; and his spirit is the Spirit of Physical Power of the Kingdom's Army.

This Power Spirit also must pass from one War Chiefs generation to the next. However, unlike with the King and Chief Priest, War chief ship does not follow a family line. A man must, like Amankwa Tia, prove himself in battle before he can be elected War Chief.

This election by the King, Queenmother and the Seven Clan Chiefs take place in a small ritual before the War Chair, and the new War Chief must pretend to sit on the chair three times; where it is believed that the Spirit of the leopard (Amankwa Tia) possesses the new War Chief. Thus is how the War Spirit flows across generations.

However, for the most part, we have only shown the spiritual side of the Ashanti Kingdom's Chosen Destiny. Next we want to see how a Destiny unfolds into reality over time; as we will show, a destiny needs Physical Power to grow into reality.

Now, if we remember, the Ashanti Chosen Destiny was to become the richest and most powerful Kingdom in all of the Akan Nation. Foreign trade goods were flowing from two directions into the Akan Nation, from the north and south.

But we found that every Kingdom wanted to economically dominate every other Kingdom, and more important than that, each Kingdom wanted to control the foreign trade goods coming into the Akan Nation; this meant the control of the trade routes.

This also meant that each Kingdom was trying to get themselves into a position to knock-off those Kingdoms which were standing between them and the source of the trade; and for the most part, all of the Akan Kingdom's were not only organized the same, but their armies and war skills were evenly matched. So all of the Akan Kingdoms were in the position whereas they could not make any mistakes or show any weakness just to survive, much less grow rich and powerful.

Therefore, we can see that Amankwa Tia's idea of organization and inspiring his army gave them an edge, and played as big of a role in the Kingdom's Chosen Destiny coming into reality as Osai Tutu and Priest Anokye's ideas.

ANCIENT AJA GAME

Using the examples of the things that Christians do and believe to bring *love* into their lives to save their souls through the father-son Gods of their Religion, Jesus Christ and Jehovah; the following are some of the things that the Ancient Aja did and believed, in order to worship the *Friendship between the mind and five senses* to become a nation of *psychologist (I call voodoo magic)* through the worship of the father-mother-baby Gods and Goddesses of their religion, *Mawu-Lisa and Legba*: which is the game they played in life.

DRINKING FROM ANCIENT WELLS
(The Fon (Dahomey) Kingdom of the Aja nation)

Well Cool Grandkids, after a long intermission, we should be ready for another African adventure. If we recall, we are to deal with your Parent's questions concerning the so-called Trickster God (so named by the Europeans), Voodoo (named witchcraft by the Europeans), African funerals, the spiritual world of Ancestors, and how Africans define History. From this point of view, Grandpa thinks this just may be the most interesting adventure we have taken up to this point.

Although we have mentioned those subjects before, here we will go into much more detail about how they function; as related to African Traditional Religion. On the other hand, the Aja are our direct-line Ancestors, and we want to find their Highest Valued Belief.

Although the Aja's are as ancient as the Yoruba, Igbo, and the Akan, they always had a serious problem.

Like the Igbo, they were a nation of people who had to find a unique way of fighting to survive, or, they would be crushed out of existence between the jaws of those powerful Akan Kingdoms and the equal powerful Kingdoms of the Yoruba.

What made them different was that they were just the opposite in their approach; where the Igbo did not believe in warfare, the Aja took warfare to an extreme.

As we saw, when an Akan Kingdom dominated another Akan Kingdom, there was not any pressure to change their way of life, they only had to pay taxes. And the same is true if one Yoruba Kingdom dominated another Yoruba kingdom.

However, if the Akan or the Yoruba kingdom dominates an Aja Kingdom, the Aja Kingdom had to not only pay taxes, but were also under pressure to understand the people who were doing the dominating to be able to fight them.

In this sense, the Aja were spiritually and physically influenced by the Akan and the Yoruba. However, the Aja did, and still do, have their own language and religious structure.

For example, to show the kind of influence the Yoruba had on them, we find that the Aja have the same divination system, they call FA, as the Yoruba's IFA. They are organized around "Priest of Knowledge", and a "God of Wisdom" like the Yoruba Ifa system.

However, Grandpa doesn't want to give the impression that the Yoruba dominated their religion, or that the Aja are just a combination of Yoruba and Akan. They are a people in their own right, with their own history, social organization, religious beliefs, and their own world view; which is totally different from the Yoruba, Igbo, and Akan.

The point being, the Aja have a "Bible" of poems and stories, organized like the Yoruba's Bible, which they call "Facts of History and Religion." This makes our job of investigator much easier, as far as "getting to the evidence" is concerned; like with the Yoruba Ifa poems and stories, and Akan drum poems and stories.

From this we will learn all we need to know about the nature of the Ancient Aja as a people; especially their Highest Valued Beliefs. Plus, answer your parent's questions about "Trickster God," "Voodoo", funerals, and more insight into the spiritual world of Ancestors, and why they are worshipped.

Anyway, the Aja are as ancient as the Akan, Igbo, and Yoruba, and they too are part of what happened when Jealousy and Greed turned the world upside down. Therefore, their conflict with the Akan and the Yoruba are from ancient times, and so is the organization of their religious beliefs.

Now that we have taken care of the "Ancient" and "Well," we can deal with the "Drinking" in the title "Drinking from Ancient Wells of the Aja." We can turn to some of the "Contents of the Well" of what we will be "Drinking;" stories in the Aja "Bible," beginning with the history of the Fons.

They will be the focus of our investigative attention; because they are the most influential Aja Kingdom in the time period we are concerned with.

History of the Fons

The information we are looking for, the history of the Fons coming into reality, is buried deep in the Fon's history stories, which means that we need to get a deeper understanding of the stories themselves.

Especially how to translate the symbolic language of the stories, by comparing them to information we have from other sources, mostly from historians who are themselves Fons, and some Europeans.

To accomplish this, Grandpa will present all of the information that he can find. And follow this with three history stories of the Fons about the same events; the coming into reality of the Fon's Royal Family, and their Kingdom's Chosen Destiny.

In this way, Grandpa believes we will better understand the Fon's way of recording their history in their Bible stories. Thus is our investigative approach. First we will deal with information from other sources:

The people that became the Fons, came from Aja-Tado, which was a very ancient Kingdom, founded sometimes well before the year 1200. And whose Kingship was patterned after the Akan, that the King's nephew becomes the next King, when the old king dies; which shows the influence of the Akan on the Aja.

Anyway, sometime between the years 1550 and 1575, a War Chief from the Oyo Yoruba Kingdom; where the title of War-Chief is "The Black Panther," came to the Kingdom of Aja-Tado to live.

He was kicked out of the Yoruba Kingdom because he was too war-like and strong willed, and therefore, uncontrollable. For he had his own vision of how a Kingdom should be ruled; in this way he had Chosen a Destiny for a Kingdom before he founded one.

Meanwhile, in Aja-Tado, this War-Chief, called the Black Panther, had a sexual affair with one of the King's wives. This resulted in the birth of three sons: "Ajaxuto, Te Ajbanli, and Agasu," who grew up to be great warriors like their father.

When the old King of Aja-Tado died, somewhere around the years 1595 and 1600, the Black Panther tried to make his oldest son, Ajaxuto, the next King, following the pattern of his chosen destiny for a Kingdom: A belief that a Kingdom and Kingship should be based on warfare.

However, the Aja-Tado people refused, and made the old King's nephew the next King, according to their traditional laws of Kingship they got from the Akan.

Ajaxuto had the backing of his mother's Clan, and a couple thousand Aja people. And with the Black Panther's blessing, naturally he decided to try to become king by force of arms, and a Civil War broke out in the Kingdom; and the Black Panther was killed.

Although Ajaxuto succeeded in killing the new King, he was still defeated in battle by the majority of the people, and chased out of the Kingdom. In fact, he was chased from Aja-Tado to a nearby place called Allada, a small Kingdom of other Aja people.

It was not long before Ajaxuto, his brothers, and mother's Clan defeated the original people in Allada. Ajaxuto set himself up as King, and became the founder of a new Kingship, with his Father's family as the Royal Family; hint, the three brothers.

This meant that Ajaxuto had founded a new Kingdom and a new Royal Clan; founded on the Destiny chosen by his father, the Black Panther.

The clan was called Kpodjito (the Black Panther people), wives of the King were called Kposi (Wives of the Black Panther), their children were called Kpovi (Children of the Black Panther), and the King was called Dada Kpojito (King of the Black Panther).

Recall, the War-Chief from Yoruba land was called 'the Black Panther, and the father of the three sons of which Ajaxto is the oldest, and this is why they became known as the Royal Black Panther Clan.

The now, King Ajaxuto of Allada, and his royal brothers, had their father's War-Chief nature and his vision of how a Kingdom was to be ruled, and what purpose it should serve. This became the Chosen Destiny of the new Kingdom and Kingship.

And, naturally, coming from a War-Chief's vision of Kingship, based totally on Warriorship, they had a Warfare approach and attitude as a way of life. This means, not only the royal family, but all of the people thought of themselves as warriors, male and female. Thus is the nature of the Destiny he chose for the Kingdom.

But the most important point is that it was Ajaxuto, with the aid of his brothers, that formed the Kingdom in the image of their father's vision. This meant that they had to make new social, economic, and to some extent, religious laws to govern the people. Things worked well with Ajaxuto as King until about 1620.

The two younger Brothers were too ambitious to be satisfied for too long; all of them wanted to be King, but there can only be one King per Kingdom, what were the two youngest brothers to do?

Being brothers of a War-chief father, and after a little fighting between themselves and their followers, they decided to divide the people of the Kingdom between them.

Ajaxuto remained King of Allada; Te Agbanli moved southeast to a place he named Porto Novo, and Agasu moved north to a place he named Abomey. Both set up Kingdoms in their area. And later became known as the three kingdoms of the Fons; the Black Panther people. Agasu and the area of Abomey is the major subject of our investigation.

This completes the history of the Fons, and the major events that led to their Kingdoms becoming a reality, from all of the sources Grandpa could find in his research of history written by African and European historians.

This was presented first for a reason. In this way, we can better interpret the spiritual symbolism of the stories and poems from the Aja's "Bible" as source material dealing with the same events.

In this regard, we will present three "Bible Stories" about the "force migration" and foundering of the Fon Kingdoms. Now we will turn to the first Fon "Biblical History Story."

"In the very beginning of time, when animals and human beings lived together in a place called Ajatado. In this region, there were two women, the wives of the same man, who were always quarreling and gossiping.

When one of them got pregnant, the other said, "it is an animal who has made you pregnant." When the woman gave birth to a son, Ajaxuto, and the gossip was all over the Kingdom that this child had been fathered by Kpo, the Black Panther, and the women quarreled until they fought. Ajaxuto, as he grew older, was angered by this gossip, and leaving Aja-(Tado), he went to Allada.

The people of Aja-(Tado) pursued Ajaxuto, and a war began which was fought from Ajadji to Allada. The pursuing forces were more numerous than those of Ajaxuto, who when he saw this to be the case, stationed a friend at a strategic place, and instructed him to send a warning when the pursuers were sighted.

But this friend went to the people who were making war against Ajaxuto, and plotted with them to bring Ajaxuto into the power of his enemy. Ajaxuto however, knew what his so-called friend had done and killed him.

Now, the name of the friend was Kozoe, and from that time on Ajaxuto took a new name, saying, "I am now to be called Ajanu Kozoexuto (a man of Aja Tado who killed Kozoe).

As Ajaxuto warred against his enemies, one of those who aided him was named Tedo, and another Agasu. Agasu hunted for the other two, and kept them supplied with food. Today all three are worshipped as (Ancestor) Gods who came to Allada, the home of the Aladaxonu Kings, but it was Agasu who first arrived there, for as the hunter, it was he who found the road to this place.

When the three reached Allada, Tedo said, "I am tired. I want to rest." So he took a side road and sat down to rest, and it is here where the Temple of Tedo is found today.

Ajaxuto went deeper into the bush; the people of Aja-(Tado) continued to follow him. But, Ajaxuto had Vudu-logic, (some people call witchcraft, which we will define later) and he carried a lance.

He put his cloth on the ground and said, "Let a river spring up, so that I may be separated from my enemies," and a river appeared. He took his lance and said, "I am going to throw you, and where you fall, there let me come and live without being molested by my enemies."

As he said this, he threw his lance and told the people who were with him to find where the lance, had fallen. But he warned them saying, "when you see the lance, do not touch it."

When the people told Ajaxuto they had found his lance, he went with them and said, "Good, it is here that I shall stay." The place where he settled is called to this day Ajaxu town, "the house of Ajaxuto," and it is here that people go when they perform ceremonies for Ajaxuto.

When Ajaxuto settled there, he took wives who bore him children. These children were called Kpodjito, the people born of the Black Panther and his wives were called Kposi.

They began to conquer their neighbors, and they became Kings, so that when anyone saw a King's wife, they called her, "wife of the Black Panther." Also, when one of their children were seen, he was called kpovi, a "child of the Black Panther."

Everyone feared the descendants of Ajaxuto, and feared to touch anything that belonged to them. If a person saw a descendant of Ajaxuto, he called out, "Dada Kpokito--O King, descendant of the Black Panther." All were afraid to meet the Black Panther's wives, since it meant the death of one who did so.

Agasu was the child of the tohwiyo (Saint) Ajaxuto, and while the Royal Family was united in Allada, they worshipped Ajaxuto as the founder of their family.

However, as time went on, new differences arose among "the children of the Black Panther," and some of the family made their way north to a place called Abomey, where they extended territorial sway over a progressively greater area, until finally they came to rule over all of Dahomey.

These people took Agasu and left Ajaxuto in Allada, and it is for this reason that Agasu is the principal tohwiyo (Ancestor Saint) of the Royal Family in Abomey." End of story.

The above story verifies the information found in the works of African and European historians, concerning the founding of the Fon Kingdoms.

At the same time, it also introduces two subjects we will deal with later; ancestor worship and friendships. In this regard, the following story should be just as informative.

"Once, in the early days, a male Black Panther emerged from a river, and for a period of time, layed with one of the wives of the King of Aja-(Tado). The King, who alone shared this secret, revealed it to his principal wife, herself childless.

By spreading the news, this wife brought about opposition to the secession of these Black Panther children to the throne of Aja-(Tado).

The three brothers that had been born to the now "wife of the Black Panther," killing their enemies, fled from their pursuing country men to Allada: Where they established themselves in time as ruler over the Aizonu people (the original Aja people of Allada).

The three brothers however, could not live harmoniously together, and the restless blood of their animal parent and, lusting for war, brought about their separation after serious quarreling.

The Hunter, Agasu, left with his followers to penetrate northwards. Ajaxuto remained at Allada, while Te Agbanli, the third brother, went southward with his descendants, eventually to rule over the Aja people in what is now known as Porto Novo.

The supernatural Black Panther Father showed greatest favor to Agasu, however, since with the passing of the centuries, it was his descendants (the Fons of Abomey) who came to rule ancient Dahomey, Porto Novo, Allada, and many lesser Aja Kingdoms.

Now where as the Father of Ajaxuto, Agasu, and Te Agbanli was a warrior, and true to his species, a lover of shading human blood, their mother was a peace-loving woman who had enjoined peaceful ways upon them.

Being sons of their father, they observed their mother's prescription of warfare by a subterfuge. For, having conquered an enemy Kingdom southwest of Allada, they commanded the people who lived there to live forever at peace, and in this, to act as their spy." End of story.

Finally, we come to our third history story, and still another angle to the major events of the foundering of the Fon Kingdoms. Or to say, a story with information not included in the other stories.

"Ajaxuto, Agasu, and Te Agbanli were brothers, all born of the same mother. They conspired against the successor who had been named by their father, the King of Aja-(Tado), before his death, and after some bloodshed, found it necessary to flee the country for safety.

As sons of a Great War Chief, they experienced no difficulty in gaining sway over the people of Allada and the adjacent Kingdoms. There they remained rulers until their ambitions, once more active, caused a break, since the younger brother had no taste for remaining in Allada, while the oldest of the three enjoyed the Kingship.

Therefore, Agasu went to the north and Te Agbanli to the southeast, the first to what is now Porto Novo. Their leaving Aja-(Tado) had "something to do" with determining whether succession should go through the mother's family or through that of the father, a question that, in the olden days, used to give much trouble.

However, with the formation of the great Royal Family, and as a result of the escapades of these brothers, it was ordained that the line must descend on the side of the Father.' End of story.

The above story gives us the added information. The problem between the brothers was related to the question, should the King be chosen from his father or mothers side of the Royal family?

Moreover, this shows how the Fons used symbolism, for example, animals to make their point about the nature of things in their physical and spiritual world.

Thus is what Grandpa means about using symbols to demonstrate, what the Aja call, the "facts of history and religion" in their stories as evidence to reach a conclusion about their spiritual beliefs.

This will put us in the position to better understand the symbolism in their stories of their religious beliefs; for these stories provided a direction for our investigation to take; Voodoo Logic (witchcraft), and later on Ancestor Saint. (Ancestor worship)

First, we will deal with the word Vudu. The Afro-American words 'Voodoo or Hoodoo' comes from the Aja word Vudu or Vodun; meaning any God or Goddess.

But as far as Afro-Americans are concerned, Voodoo (witchcraft) means using the power of ritual as a defensive or offensive weapon against another person; which the Fons do.

On the other hand, when Afro-Americans use the term voodoo, we also mean, the Fon's relationship with the Trickster God, LEGBA. But in reality, we are talking about the Fon's religion and a way of life, in this study we call, Vudu-logic or Vuduism.

We do not mean to imply that the Fons were only depending on Vudu-logic as their only weapon, for they were some of the best physical warriors in West Africa. In fact, the Fons of Aboney defeated the Ashanti in the only battle they had, and they were continuously winning and losing wars to the Oyo Yoruba.

The Fon warriors were divided into male and female armies, with the female warriors being the best of all. For example, when you hear of the fighting Amazon warriors in West Africa, in most cases, the Fon female warriors are who they are talking about. In any case, they fit the Amazon category; a lean mean fighting machine. But we are leaving our major subject.

Our question becomes, how did the Fons organize their Aja beliefs of Gods and Goddesses around a chosen destiny to be a warrior people; to fight the Akan and Yoruba and remain a people unto themselves?

Now if you Recall, Grandpa concluded that an Afro-centric Worldview had four (4) Dimensions in African thoughts about how to deal with the reality of the World.

In that context, Grandpa's conclusion is that the Aja Religion is one (1) of those Dimensions. Therefore, Grandpa's questions will give our investigation its direction, along with looking for their highest valued beliefs.

This also means that this time we will get a chance to see African Traditional Religion from still another angle. For as we said, there are hundreds of nations in Africa, and each one has a different spiritual approach to fulfilling their chosen destiny; meaning that there is a large number of spiritual path-ways in African Traditional Religion.

This also shows that there is a large number of different things the religion can do, or to say, a large number of ways it can be used. And voodoo-logic is one of those uses, the position the Aja took.

In addition, there is only one of the major African Gods that has the "Power of Voodoo-logic," as we will find out in the following stories. That would be the Trickster God, whom the Fons, Haitians, and Afro-Americans call LEGBA, the God of the Crossroads; the Yoruba call ESU, the Akan call ANANSI, and the Igbo call EKWENSU, which is also related to the crossroads. However, most Africans who have become Christians think of the Trickster God as the Devil.

But, once LEGBA is understood correctly, as you will see, we can get away from the "The Trickster God as the Devil." The image European missionaries made famous throughout Africa as part of a colonial attack on African Traditional religion; and restore HIS real function, that of "Best Friend to mankind."

We are getting ahead of ourselves; we must begin with bible stories to see just where LEGBA really fits into the spiritual world of the Aja.

Aja Creation Story,
The Gods and Goddesses

Well Fellow Detectives, we can see that the Yoruba's influence was in the area of Divination ritual, and the Akan's influence in the area of the organization of Kingship.

However, as mentioned, when it came to the organization of the Aja's religious beliefs, we will find that they are not influence by anybody in all of Africa.

For this reason, Grandpa knows that the following stories of the Gods and Goddesses will seem strange to you compared to the Gods and Goddesses of the Yoruba, the Igbo and the Akan. This is because the Aja have strange Gods and Goddesses and a strange religion, as we will soon see.

Grandpa thinks you will begin to see what I mean after we see some of the symbolism in their stories about the Gods and Goddesses;

beginning with the one about how the Aja believe the spiritual world came into reality.

Meanwhile, we should keep in mind, that the Aja word for Gods and Goddesses in *"Vudu,"* pronounced *"Voodoo;"* and we quote.

"MAWU-LISA, The Great Creator, is one Being with two faces. The first face is that of a Goddess, MAWU, whose eyes are the Moon. The other face is a God, LISA, whose eyes are the Sun. MAWU is Calm and Cool like the Moon, and LISA, is hot and ruthless like the Sun.

Since MAWU-LISA is one Being who is both God and Goddess, MAWU became pregnant. The first to be born were a pair of twins, a God child called DA ZODJI, and a Goddess child called NYOHWE ANANU.

The second birth was SOGBO, who had the form of his parent, God and Goddess in one.

The third birth was also of twins, a God, AGBE, and a Goddess, NAETE. The fourth to be born was AGE, a God.

The fifth, GU, also a God: GU is all body. He has no head, instead of a head, a great sword is coming out of His neck. His trunk is of stone.

The sixth birth was not a spiritual Being, but DJO, Air, atmosphere; Air is needed to create the breath of life.

The seventh to be born was LEGBA; MAWU said LEGBA was to be Her spoiled Child God, because He was the youngest.

One day the Goddess face of MAWU-LISA assembled all the children in order to divide the kingdom of the Universe. To the first twins, DA ZODJI and NYOHWE ANANU, She gave all the riches, and told them to go and inhabit the earth. She said the earth was for them.

MAWU said to SOGBO, He was to remain in Heaven, because He was both God and Goddess like His Parent. She told AGBE and NAETE to go and inhabit the sea and command the waters. To AGE, She gave command of all the animals and birds, and She told him to live in the bush (forest) as a Hunter.

To GU, MAWU said He was Her strength, and that was why He was not given a head like the others. GU is a Blacksmith God who makes weapons for War, and tools to build, thanks to him, the earth would not always remain wild bush. GU taught men about warfare and building houses and farms.

MAWU told DJO (air) to live in space between the earth and sky. To him was being entrusted the life-span of man. Thanks to Him also, His Brothers and Sisters would be invisible, for He would clothe them. That is why another name for *Vodun (Gods and Goddesses) is DJO, the Invisible Ones.*

When MAWU said this to the children, she gave the SAGBATA TWINS (DA ZODJI and NYOHWE ANANU) the language which was to be used on earth, and took away their memory of the language of

Heaven. She gave to SOGBO the language He would speak, and took from Him the memory of the Parent language. The same was done for AGBE and NAETE, for AGE, and for GU, but to DJO was given the language of man.

Now she said to LEGBA, "You are my youngest Child, and as you are spoiled, and have never known punishment, I cannot turn You over to Your Brothers. I will keep you with me always. Your work shall be to visit all of the Kingdoms ruled over by Your Brothers, and sisters and to give me an account of what happens." So LEGBA knows all the languages known to His Brothers and Sisters, and He knows the language MAWU speaks, also, LEGBA is MAWU's Spokesman. If one of the Brothers or Sisters wishes to speak, He must give the message to LEGBA, for none knows any longer how to address Himself to MAWU-LISA. That is why LEGBA is everywhere.

You will find LEGBA even before the houses of the Vudu (Gods and Goddesses), because all Beings, humans and Gods, must address themselves to Him before they can approach the Great Creator, MAWU-LISA. (End of story).

This gives some indication of what Grandpa meant by the Aja having strange Gods and Goddesses, as related to our usual way of thinking about the image of Gods and Goddesses. And at the same time, tells us how the Aja believe the Gods and Goddesses, and their functions and domains, came into reality.

The following story tells how the Aja believed the Earth was formed into its present shape, and introduces a mysterious Supernatural Being who is not a Son or Daughter of MAWU-LISA; which gives another strange twist to the Aja spiritual beliefs.

"At the beginning of the world, before MAWU had borne children, and before SOGBO existed, AIDO and HWEDO (God and Goddess twins), the Serpents, had been created by whoever created the world. Unlike other Vudu who revealed themselves to clans that They might be worshipped by men, AIDO-HWEDO is the God of no family group (mankind), and is the Child of none of the other Gods.

When LISA began forming the world as it exists today, He was carried everywhere in the mouth of AIDO-HWEDO, the Serpent, Who was His servant, symbolized by a pair of python snakes used in rituals related to LISA.

Wherever They spent their nights, mountains appeared out of the excrement of AIDO-HWEDO. Now, when the task of making the earth was done, LISA saw that He had put on it too great a weight for it to carry; for there were too many mountains, too many trees, too many large animals.

Something had to be done to keep the earth from falling into the sea. And so, AIDO, the male serpent, was asked to coil himself, tail in mouth, and lie below the earth like a carrying pad that men and women used to support pots and baskets which they carry on their heads.

But because AIDO does not like heat, the Creator gave Him the sea to live in. For food AIDO ate the bars of iron that the Creator commanded the red monkeys who live in the sea, to forge for Him.

From time to time, His position becomes uncomfortable, causing Him to move slightly. When this happens, there is an earthquake. Some day, when the monkeys have no more iron to give him, hunger will compel Him to eat His own tail.

And the earth, overburdened at the beginning, but now bearing a much heavier load of people and houses, will slip into the sea. That is when the world will come to an end. The female Serpent, HWEDO, did not like water, and lived in Heaven, and visited earth as a rainbow." End of story.

Being as LISA could not go anywhere without MAWU, means that the Aja believe that LISA created life, including mankind, at the same time as the world was created, and the Gods and Goddesses were created later.

Well GrandKids, as Investigators, we are confronted with a big question, who or what created MAWU-LISA and AIDO-HWEDO? And nowhere in Grandpa's research material has there been an answer found to this question.

The only conclusion could be that the Aja's don't believe in a Super Great Creator of the Universe, or they think that this Super Great Creator is too far removed to make a difference in their religious beliefs.

In any case, although most Africans acknowledged a Super Great Creator, nowhere is there a shrine of worship directly related to "HIM-HER-IT."

This means that the Aja simply took the concept a step further; they don't mention a Super Great Creator at all. Although this is an interesting question for Aja theologians, it is not really related to the Aja's Highest Valued Beliefs.

Meanwhile, we see the major forces in Aja religious beliefs, next we will look at how the Universe is Governed, and who is the Chief Administrator of the Affairs of the Universe in the following story.

Keep in mind that the first-born twins, SA ZODJI (God) and NYOHWE ANANU (Goddess), together are called SAGBATA. And SOGBO, the second born is the One God with a male and female face. However, the following story deals only with the Brothers, and their Sisters side is not mentioned. Now for the story:

"SAGBATA and SOGBO are Brothers. We are told that the Great LISA did not work any more after He created the world, but delegated His Sons, SAGBATA and SOGBO, to rule the world for Him. The two quarreled over who was to be the Chief Administrator of the World Affairs, and SAGBATA, the elder, who is calm and peaceful like MAWU, decided to leave Heaven and go down to earth. He took with him, since He was the eldest, all of His heritage, things that belonged to MAWU. The younger Brother, who was the more ruthless and hot like LISA, remained in Heaven and took the name of fire and lightning, SOGBO.

Before SAGBATA was leaving for the Earth, Their Father said to them, He would not justify the claim of either, in a quarrel over who is to be the Chief Administrator of the world. They must be together like a closed calabash and the world must exist inside them.

He said that since SAGBATA was the elder, He should be the lower part, and that SOGBO should be the upper. Their Mother told both of them to go and live in the world. SOGBO refused. He would not leave His Father.

When SAGBATA descended, He could not get back on high. He, therefore, descended lower and lower. SOGBO won all the of confidence of His father, and the Gods who surrounded Him. Then one day, SOGBO caused the rains to stop.

Now in the world below, SAGBATA had Himself chosen as King, and the people came to Him and said, "Since You came among us and we made you King, there is no longer any rain. We are dying of hunger." He said, "Yes, it is so, but in a few days you will have rain."

A year went by and no rain. Two years went by and no rain. For three years, still no rain. Now, two men came from Heaven. Those men fell down in a country called Fe, (this means they came down in Yoruba land, Ife).

They preached. They preached. They preached the writing of Fa (the Ifa Divination Ritual of the Yoruba). They traveled everywhere.

It is said that at that time, the world had no more than a thousand people.

Now, people came to tell SAGBATA that two men came from Heaven and preached something called Fa. He said that they should come. When they came, they spoke to SAGBATA the language spoken in Heaven, and SAGBATA knew at once that they told the truth. He asked them why there was no rain.

They said they did not know. Their errand was to preach Fa. What they did know, was that His Brother SOGBO was angry.

SAGBATA asked, "Why is He angry?"

They said that they did not know, but with Fa (divination ritual), which was the writing of SAGBATA's Mother-Father (MAWU-LISA), they would know at once. They took the divining seeds, and throwing them asked, why the rain did not fall in this country? The first combination of Fa that fell was called (chapter) Oyeku Gbuloso (like the Odu in the Yoruba system).

At once they told SAGBATA that there was a dispute between two brothers, who both wanted the same thing, and that the elder should submit to the younger to bring about reconciliation.

SAGBATA said that now Heaven was too far away, and that He no longer had the power to climb up. He said that before going down to earth, His Mother had given Him the right to take with Him all the riches.

These, He put in His sack. He said that it was He Himself Who had refused to take along water, because He could not take it in his sack.

But arriving on earth, the water which He had left behind had become very necessary. The two men said that water was now under the control of His Brother (SOGBO). SAGBATA asked these men what was to be done to have the rainfall.

The two men then said to Him, if He wished to make the sacrifice, He must give a portion of all the riches on earth and confide this to the bird Wututu, the great friend of SOGBO. They said, "When Wututu goes up there to talk to SOGBO, SOGBO will never refuse her."

SAGBATA heard. He gathered up a portion of all of His riches, and He had Wututu called, He said to Wututu, "Go tell SOGBO that now I, SAGBATA, surrender the Universe. I shall let Him have the country, and the homesteads, and the houses. He may take the sons and the father; the children and the mother. He, SOGBO, is to dwell up high and guard those below."

Once She was up high in the air, Wututu, in a voice which SOGBO knew at once, began to sing. "The earth, SAGBATA, charged me with a commission for you. Do you hear, SOGBO?" Wututu sang, "He said that He leaves you the Universe. He leaves you the country. You are to have the homesteads, and all the houses. He lets you have the sons and the father; the children and the mother."

When She said this, SOGBO recognized the voice of Wututu from on high. He sent a bolt of lightning. As the lightning flashed, He saw it was Wututu. SOGBO said to let her come.

When Wututu came up, SOGBO said, "Go and say to my elder Brother SAGBATA that though He is the elder who inherited all the wealth of our Mother, He was foolish to leave behind the two things that are the power of the Universe. With these two things, I, the younger, can control all the wealth of SAGBATA." Those two things are Water and Fire.

He told Wututu to return, and before even reaching earth, She would see what followed. Wututu flew away toward the earth. When She reached half way between heaven and earth, a great rain began to fall.

Wututu arrived. SAGBATA was very happy. And He commanded that Wututu was never to be killed. Should someone kill her by accident, a great ceremony is to be given. This ceremony consists of removing the head-pad, because it was she who had carried on her head the message from SAGBATA to SOGBO.

That day the Brothers were reconciled, and that is why each year Thunder visits the Earth. On that day SOGBO gave Himself the new name,

Fallen on the grass, the grass puts forth shoots;
Fallen on mankind, mankind becomes fertile,
The sprinkling dew gives glory to SOGBO." (End of story).

This story tells us how SOGBO became the Chief Administrator of the Affairs of the Universe.

We will next look at two stories which tells how the Aja, as a people, came into reality, as well as how Religious worship was established in Temples, and take a look at the Aja's Holy Trinity. The first story deals with MAWU-LISA.

"Tradition tells that in very ancient times, a man and a woman descended from Heaven to the district of Some in Aja (a place we will deal with later), and this was the first family founded on the earth.

They came bearing a long wand, wearing blouses that were much longer than those ordinarily worn today, and carrying a calabash.

It not only rained that day they came from heaven, but it continued to rain for seventeen days thereafter.

During this entire time they uttered no word, except to cry out the name of the Being Who had sent them, calling, "LISA! MAWU! LISA! MAWU!"

On the seventh day of rain, another man and woman descended from heaven, and these wore the white beads which are known even today as Lisadje, 'beads of LISA.'

These began to teach the worship of MAWU-LISA, and raised a Temple in their honor; and the Temple they established still exists in Aja today.

When the day came on which they were to offer sacrifices to MAWU-LISA, it rained once more, and with the rain still more Beings came from Heaven to aid them. But as soon as the ceremony was over, they went back to Heaven, leaving the others behind.

After this ceremony was out, three or four times, the second pair also returned to Heaven, leaving their beads behind them. Before they departed however, they left a daughter on earth, with the original couple who had completed the establishment of the Temples, one for MAWU-LISA, one for GU, and a third for AGE.

For MAWU, they killed a ram, for LISA a white goat and white chicken, to GU was sacrificed a white cock, to AGE a dog. And since that time, the sacrificial animals have been the same, for it is they who taught the doctrine of MAWU-LISA to mankind.

Later the woman gave birth to two children, the first a son, and the second a daughter. With each child came a small wand held in the hand and, as the child grew, this wand grew.

The children carried their wands with them everywhere, and they were never lost. Seven years after the birth of their children, the parents returned to Heaven whence they had come, and now each of the children in turn explained the teaching of the Temple to which they belong.

Since their teachings were good, the worship of the Gods and Goddesses of Heaven spread everywhere in the land of Aja.

When the original couple descended from Heaven, they were accompanied by a Chameleon who went everywhere with them as a dog goes about his master.

The Chameleon, who always walked before them, was sent by LISA to protect them. Because it was realized that when they taught the doctrine of MAWU-LISA, there would always be those who would refuse to receive their teaching, and who would conspire against them.

But with the Chameleon in front, an enemy who's intent was to attack, and was about to strike them from behind, they would see their assailants reflected in the smooth skin of the Chameleon, and be on guard.

For the body of the Chameleon, like that of LISA, is as smooth as a mirror. This is why the Chameleon is the animal sacred to the God LISA." End of story.

This story shows how people came from Heaven, in the beginning of time, and set up a Temple for MAWU-LISA and rituals for some of the Gods of Heaven.

We should also take notice; the couple that had two children born with a wand in their hands were the founders of the Royal Family, from which the King is chosen.

A Temple was not established for SAGBATA and SORBO. There is another story that shows that SAGBATA, (the twins DA ZODJI and NYOHWE ANANU), also sent people into the world.

And he too, set up a Temple and rituals, for Himself and His Sons and daughters, the Gods and Goddesses of the Earth, as well as a Temple for SORBO. SAGBATA story is as follows:

"One day in early times, during a heavy rain, a great cloud of smoke suddenly arose from the earth. In those times, the region of Abomey, in Aja land, was a great forest, and had no inhabitants.

The cloud of smoke issued was from the very center of this forest. When the smoke cleared, a man, followed by a woman, were visible. Each of them carried a sack at their side containing okra seeds.

On the next day there was another heavy rain, and again smoke arose; this time, sixty-six people appeared; thirty-six women and thirty men.

These people began to cut the forest and clear the earth so that it might nourish human beings. They cultivated the land and planted the okra seeds they brought with them.

The first man to appear was called Afblo, and he mated with the woman that accompanied him, and the people who followed them also mated and had children, and their descendants peopled Dahomey (the Kingdom of Dahomey).

Afblo and his wife eventually died, he in the morning, and she the same afternoon. The others were left to morn the loss of the two who, they said, had founded their people.

The bodies of these founders, then the body of a ram, which was sacrificed to their spirits, were added. And with this ram, they were buried in the hole in the earth from whence they had issued. (Indicating that they came from the God SAGBATA).

When the Founders of the people were buried, and the hole in the earth from which they had come was filled in, these people had no Gods to worship.

Some time later, a man called Cheyi was digging a well. When he reached a depth of twelve or fourteen meters, he found that he had uncovered a great road, along which many people were passing.

He started along this road, but soon he met a woman, who asked him why he had come. He replied that he was digging a well and had happened on this roadway. He was told that the place where he had dug was sacred to the Earth, and that he must be brought before the ruler of this place.

Cheyi was thereupon taken to a Temple. Although he saw no one, he could hear a voice which announced to him that he was now in the house of SAGBATA. It was SAGBATA Himself who had caused him to choose the spot he had selected for his well, so that he might come to this country, learn how to worship the Earth Gods, and take this knowledge back to his own people.

Cheyi was thereupon ordered to return to his home to close the hole and build a Temple for SAGBATA over it. Another place not far from this was designated, and here, he was informed, he must raise Temples for SORBO, the Gods of Heaven.

Finally, he received instructions to tell all of his people to worship these two Gods. He was also told that SORBO eats the male goat (as sacrifice), and SAGBATA the ram, and was taught the Doctrine of these two Gods.

When Cheyi emerged from the earth, he closed the hole that he had made as he was instructed. He built the two Temples, and brought before him all of the people of the village to inform them of what he had seen and heard.

The instructions given to him when the first ceremony was held, was that the first ram and goat sacrificed to SORBO and SAGBATA was accepted; a heavy rain fell, thunder was heard, and in an instant, the animals disappeared. The goat for SAGBATA also disappeared, for when it was put in the Temple; the earth opened and swallowed it.

Yet, though Cheyi was told which animals to sacrifice, he had not been instructed in the details of ritual worship of the Gods to whom he had erected Temples.

It is for this reason that, after a time, a man named Agamu appeared out of the opening in the earth. And spent sixteen days with Cheyi teaching him how to establish the Gods in their temples, and how to sprinkle their altars with the blood of the animals sacrificed to them.

Thus it was Cheyi who began the Temple of the Great God SAGBATA and the Great God SORBO, and it was he who appointed the first high-priest for each, SOGBO and SAGBATA. But one day, when he had grown old, the earth opened and he disappeared." End of story.

The major point of the two stories is that SAGBATA, as well as SOGBO, have established Temples on Earth. This made the Aja have three major Temples: One for MAWU-LISA, one for the God King of Heaven, SORBO, and one for the God King of the Earth, SAGBATA. This means that the Aja's have three centers of religious worship. Or to say, three Gods of religion.

Just as important, the two stories show that the Royal Family comes from Heaven. Also, the last story gives us a hint of where the Spiritual World of the Ancestors is located, in the Earth with SAGBATA (The God DA ZODJI, and Goddess NYOHWE ANANUA).

Thus, we not only have a good idea of how the Aja religion is organized, and the major players, but also how the Aja came into reality as a people.

We can see that people came from two sources, MAWU-LISA and SAGBATA, however, as was the agreement between SAGBATA and SORBO, He also had a Temple built for SORBO, and divided his people between Them. Thus is how the doctrine of their religion was established on Earth.

The two stories are very important, as far as insight into the Aja's Spiritual World is concerned, for they show the Holy Trinity of their religious beliefs. This means that the Aja's have three Gods and Goddesses, as pairs, in their Holy Trinity: MAWU-LISA, SAGBATA, and SORBO, symbolized by the three Temples.

Instead of having their Holy Trinity as an abstract spiritual concept, one in which most people know nothing about, the Aja established a Temple for each aspect of their Holy Trinity and worship them directly.

For example, the Yoruba, Igbo, and Akan only worship two aspects of their Holy Trinity, "the Great Father God, and Great Mother Goddess of Mankind," and don't have anything directly to do with the Great Creator of the Universe.

And with the Christian's Holy Trinity, of "Father, Son, and the Holy Ghost;" the Son, Jesus Christ, is the only aspect that is worshipped directly in their Church.

Now let's turn our investigative attention on the Doctrine taught in these Temples.

Doctrine of the Holy Trinity

This brings us to the subject of the Aja's beliefs related to the nature of the Soul of Mankind. They believe that MAWU created the Human Spirit; but it is LISA that created the Human Mind, and before whom permission for Human Spirit to Choose a personal Destiny is granted.

At this point of development, one of the Ancestors of the Clan to which the Human Spirit choose as its Earthly Family appears with some Sacred Clay of the Clan from which to form the body for the Human Spirit.

At the same time, this Ancestor becomes a part of the now completed Human Soul; that consists of a Spirit, Mind-Destiny, and an Ancestor as its Guardian, even before the Spirit is born.

The Clan Ancestor symbolizes the Clan's Community Chosen Destiny of which the Spirit-about-to-be-born is to become a functioning part. This means that a person is born with a history of their Clan Chosen Destiny.

Therefore, the Human Soul has three functioning components, a part of MAWU, a part of LISA, and, a part of an Ancestor, we will call the 'Holy Trinity of the Human Soul.'

The Aja's word for Soul as a whole, and its parts, is 'SE;' for example, Se-Spirit, Se-Mind-Destiny, and Se-Ancestral History; which goes to make up the "Big SE of their Soul." Therefore the definition of SE, is the same as the Akan's KRA, the Yoruba's ORI, and the Igbo's CHI.

Now let us turn to the subject of the function of these parts-of-the-Souls. For example, the role that the little Se plays in a trial before MAWU-LISA, where an account must be given after the death of a person. Related to how the Human Spirit did on its mission of fulfilling its Chosen Destiny; and the consequences if found guilty.

When the Se-Spirit is on trial, after a long life on earth, the Se-Ancestor acts the part of the Lawyer for the Defense, and the Se-Mind-Chosen Destiny is the Prosecuting Attorney. MAWU-LISA as the Judge, and the Gods and Goddesses the Jury.

Se-Mind-Chosen Destiny (Prosecutor) opens the case by making a statement of what the Se-Spirit did or did not do in life, which is checked by MAWU who keeps a written record of all Destinies.

If the record shows that Se-Spirit fulfilled his destiny, Se-Ancestor (Defense Lawyer) praises Se-Spirit before MAWU-LISA. However, if Se-Spirit did not fulfill its Destiny, Se-Ancestor reviews the case step by step, and makes a long plea of unforeseen circumstances before the Jury of the Gods and Goddesses, who make recommendations to MAWU-LISA. If found guilty, MAWU-LISA always commits Se-Spirit to Reincarnation.

The Aja, like all Traditional Africans, do not believe in a place like 'Hell' where one is punished forever. They believe that the Human Se-Spirit, once found guilty, must return to Earth, up to sixteen times, until the Chosen Destiny is fulfilled. Where they would still be re-born into their same Clan-family, in their own Great Grandchildren's Generation each time.

It is not known what would happen after the sixteenth time, and the Se-Spirit still fails, anyway Grandpa could not find such a case. Therefore, we must assume that before the sixteenth time, all of the Aja's would have completed their Destinies.

The point being, the Aja believes that the three parts of the Human Soul are a force in themselves, all working together as a 'Big SE; which can be reincarnated as much as Sixteen times; and must go to a Court of Judgment in the Spiritual world; this is the nature of the Human Soul. This is the Doctrine taught in the Temple of MAWU-LISA.

Now we will investigate the Doctrine taught in the Temple of SAGBATA.

Now the image of the Aja's Gods and Goddesses may seem strange to you, two faces on one body, and things like that. But this tells many things philosophically, for example, this means that the Aja's see things like love and hate as two aspects of the same thing. More important, this tells us the close relationship between the male and female principle as far as "getting things done" in the world.

Therefore, in the Aja's Society, men and women form close bonds in their relationships and families, and in their Society; especially as far as SAGBATA is concerned.

SAGBATA, as the twins SA ZODJI-NYOHWE, really symbolize the Mother Goddess and Father God of Nature, the Yoruba, Igbo, and Akan, call Mother Nature or, the Earth Goddess.

In this regard, SAGBATA is not only concerned with social relationships, but, just as important, SAGBATA is concerned with the growth and development life.

Therefore, the focus of SAGBATA's Temple teaching is on the 'Seven Cycles of Life;' which are as follows:

1. Pregnancy and birth (nine months).
2. Babyhood (birth to about three years of age).
3. Childhood (three years old to the age of twelve).
4. Manhood and womanhood (begins with puberty to about age twenty).
5. Fatherhood and motherhood (from about age twenty to about forty.
6. Grand father and grandmotherhood (from forty to sixty).
7. Ancestorhood (sixty to forever after death).

And this Principle-of-Seven applies not only on a individual level, but also includes the life of a family and Society; in which the individual is involved. This is the Doctrine taught in the Temple of SAGBATA.

Finally, we can turn our attention to the Doctrine of the Temple of SORBO. Here, we are dealing with the Government of society, family, and the individual; related to a "Doctrine of Truth, Justice, Righteousness, and Leadership" on each of those levels.

While the moral laws of conduct in Aja Society come from SAGBATA, the ethics of the Government of Society come from SORBO. This is what LISA meant when he said that the world is in a calabash and SAGBATA was the bottom, and SORBO was the top; in their dispute over which was to be the Chief Administrator of the World.

Nevertheless, we will get more insight into the Doctrine of SORBO when we deal with Kingship and Government. But this gives some indication of the Doctrine taught in the Temple of SORBO.

Voodoo-magic and Voodooism

The Aja use the Yoruba's Divination system as a model of a "place" as a storage for their Knowledge and Wisdom (facts of religion and history), and use their IFA organized ritual process to reach chapters containing poems and stories in their "Bible;" but this is not the case on the spiritual side. For example, LEGBA is the "God of Wisdom" in the Aja's divination ritual called FA.

There is a big difference between the nature of LEGBA, and the Yoruba's "God of Wisdom, ORUNMILA;" LEGBA became Chief of all the Gods and Goddesses. And life can be very interesting when living life by the wisdom and knowledge of LEGBA, in a world of Voodooism.

Recall, with the Akan, we use ritual symbolism in dealing with the spirituality of a Kingdom and Kingship. With the Aja, we will deal with the spiritual symbolism of LEGBA and Voodooism; to try to get some insight into Voodoo-logic.

Some people call it "witchcraft," some call it "magic" and some others call it "miracles;" the point is, there is a ritual process that makes a miracle happen. And the "logic" of the ritual process is what the Aja call Vudu-logic.

Now keep in mind that the Aja's word Vudu means God or Goddess. Therefore, the word Vudu-logic means the logic that Gods and Goddesses use to perform miracles. When we look at the symbolism of the stories, it shows some of the ways this miracle logic works.

This is especially the case if you think of what LEGBA is doing in the following stories is a voodoo ritual process. Now Grandpa doesn't like the sound of "Vudu logic or Vudu-miracles; "Voodoo-Magic" sounds much better.

Therefore, we will begin with how LEGBA became Chief of the Gods and Goddesses, by following the stories that refer to LEGBA, the very powerful Spoiled Brat of MAWU-LISA. And follow him as He carries out His assignment as Chief of the Gods and Goddesses, Messenger and Chief Policeman of the Universe, using Voodoo-magic.

And just as important, as far as our investigation is concerned, we are very interested in LEGBA as the Giver of Voodoo-magic to mankind. In this sense, LEGBA, with his many names, is the most interesting and powerful God in all of Africa.

Now lets turn our investigative attention on stories in the Aja Bible related to "LEGBA," as the "God of the wisdom and knowledge of Aja Divination system, FA." This means that in the following stories, LEGBA's activities are really a ritual of voodoo-magic in progress.

Therefore, the stories are about how to perform Voodoo-magic. This means that when the Divination Priest performs his ritual for someone, it is said that he is teaching them how to use the Voodoo-magic of LEGBA to deal with their problems.

LEGBA and Voodooism

Well Fellow Detectives, the organization of the Aja's Spiritual World, the nature of the Soul, the Doctrine of the Gods and Goddesses, and the Aja's Divination system is only a background.

We have now reached the point where we can deal with the major subject of our investigation, LEGBA, and His impact throughout the lives of the Fon Kingdom.

From this we can better understand the highest valued beliefs of the Aja, as well as get a better understanding of Voodoo-Hoodoo (witchcraft).

This means that we must take a careful and detailed look at the nature of LEGBA.

Grandpa knows that these stories will seem strange to you, especially with your young imagination. But we must remember that the symbolism in Voodooism is strange, because the Aja's religious purpose is unique; but once we get into them, they will make sense. So lets look at some LEGBA stories, and see if Grandpa is right:

"Long ago, LEGBA was the younger of the Gods. One day LISA said to the Gods, He would show them something. He would show Them Who would be Their Chief. LISA gave them a gong, a bell, a drum, and a flute, and said, whoever took all the instruments, and played the four together, and also danced to them would be their Chief.

SOGBO said, "I am very strong. I can do all." He tried and failed. GU came. He said He had much strength. He had fire. He made many things. He would do it. He tried, and He, too, failed.

Now, LISA called all of the Gods together and asked LEGBA to try. LEGBA tried and did all. He struck the drum; He played the gong; He rang the bell; He blew into the flute, and at the same time made all the movements of a beautiful dance. LISA said to the other Gods that LEGBA was the first among them. Now LEGBA said He would sing, and He sang,

"If the house is peaceful

If the field is fertile,

I will be very happy."

(More important of all, this part of the story tells the nature of Voodoo-magic. One must be able to do five things at the same time. Meanwhile, this also tells us a lot about LEGBA's relationship to the Gods and Goddesses. He is Chief and the Master of Voodoo-magic. And at the same time, we see what makes Him happy, and why Grandpa calls him the God of Friendship. More on this later, now let's return to the story).

"Now LEGBA had knowledge, and He began to use Voodoo-magic. He was the first. He made a serpent. Then He put the serpent down on the road to the market, and He commanded the serpent to bite the sellers and the buyers. Once the serpent bit them, LEGBA came and said to them, 'give me something, and I will cure you.' If they gave Him something, He went away to buy food, and drinking water. Then He ate all and drank all.

One day someone asked LEGBA, 'What is that' pointing to the serpent, 'that which bites people?'

LEGBA answered him, 'it is voodoo-magic.' LEGBA said to this man, 'bring Me two chickens, eighty cowries, and some straw. I will make one for you.' So LEGBA began to make voodoo-magic for this man.

LEGBA led this man down the road to the market, and He told him all that had to be done to make this voodoo-magic. When LEGBA said to throw the liana, the liana became a serpent and began to bite people. Then, LEGBA gave him the medicine to cure these people. This man was called Eja, and it was LEGBA Who gave voodoo-magic to him.

Now voodoo-magic spread everywhere. LEGBA began to give him other voodoo-magic so that if someone needed voodoo-magic he came to Eja, and Eja called LEGBA to his house. They made the voodoo-magic inside the house, and then carried them outside to give to those who came for them.

MAWU was angry. She called LEGBA and said to LEGBA, 'Now if someone does not see You, You will not do this again.' (She made Him invisible).

Now, LEGBA is forever a Vodun (a God, and cannot also be a man). Eja is a man, so he continued to make voodoo-magic. Eja became Chief of voodoo. When someone wished to make voodoo, he came to him and brought all that was needed. Eja took the place of LEGBA. So Eja went everywhere and asked who wanted to make voodoo-magic? Then He gave them voodoo and disappeared.

He gave voodoo-magic to everyone. He also gave voodoo to those who do evil (thus is the nature of witchcraft). He gave voodoo to pregnant women that the child should not come. Then when the woman was having a difficult time they called Eja, and they had to give him many things before he was satisfied. Then only would he give medicine that the child might come.

The Kings of many lands came to Eja to ask for voodoo-magic. If Eja met a child he would drop medicine on its body, and the body of the child became a ball.

Eja now said, 'I am going to see the world. Now there is enough voodoo-magic.' One day he brought cotton thread and silk, and all in one night he rolled the cotton into a ball. He did this from six o'clock in the evening until six o'clock the next morning. He left it. During the day he took the silken thread and he rolled it until night. He measured both, and he discovered that they were both the same length.

One day he climbed an ant-hill, and he threw the cotton and silken threads toward Heaven. LISA caught both threads. Then holding on to these two threads, Eja reached Heaven. LISA said to him, "What are you looking for here?"

Eja said to LISA, "my knowledge is great. I now seek to measure my knowledge with LISA."

LISA said, "show me what your knowledge is."

Eja cut down a tree. He began to make a human figure. He made the head very well, the face, the hair, and the arms. But the statuette could not talk. It did not breathe. It could not move.

LISA said to him," your knowledge is not enough. Wait, I'll show you."

On the same day, LISA took a grain of corn and traced a row and sowed it. The grain sprouted, and the same day they ate the ripe corn. They removed the corn from the cob, put it in the mill, brought the flour home, and prepared the dish that Eja ate.

LISA left Eja, and Eja went back to earth. But LISA sent Death to follow him. LISA said to Death, "men are evil. If someone does evil, (use voodoo-magic to do evil) it is necessary to kill him."

Eja tried voodoo-magic, and attacked Death. In those days, wood would not burn, for there was no fire. It was impossible to cook. So LISA said to Death and Eja, "if you, Eja, attack Death then whoever will prepare his food will find that food raw again." So, Eja let Death go, in order that, among men, one could put food to cook, and it would cook quickly, and people could eat. LISA said to Eja, "if someone is ill, you are to take good care of him. But if I like, I will send Death to kill him."

Eja mastered LEGBA's knowledge, and he became a practitioner of voodoo. Eja and Death are the two friends of the world." End of story.

We can see that the major point in the first part of the story is that LEGBA became chief of the Gods because He could do five things at the same time.

At this point we will say, the knowledge to do five things at one time is what we call Voodoo-magic, on the other hand, LISA could do thousands of things at the same time, as Eja found out. But in any case, this is how LEGBA became Chief Police of the Universe; and gives us some insight into His nature.

The next part of the story deals with how LEGBA gave the knowledge of voodoo-magic to the Aja people, through Eja; symbolically, Eja means the Aja people.

Also, we see LEGBA using voodoo-magic for His hustle. In the beginning the Gods did not have people making sacrifices to them and they were hungry. Thus is why LEGBA had to hustle to survive, until people started paying Him, and we see another part of His nature.

The third part of the story deals with the impact of Voodoo-magic on the Aja people, and how some misused it. They were beginning to think that they were more powerful than MAWU-LISA; as shown by Eja's challenge. Thus, we can see the power of voodoo-magic, and how dangerous it is.

But most important of all, in the final part of the story; we see LISA, the Great Creator, telling Eja (the Aja people) that it is o.k. to use voodoo-magic to help someone that is ill. Therefore, the Aja people have permission from the Great Creator to use voodoo-magic.

We have not clearly defined voodoo-magic at this point, and we have a long way to go before we can do that. Still, we can see the most important point about the story shows clearly that according to Aja religious beliefs, LEGBA is the Aja's God of wisdom and knowledge.

Or to say, He is the One that gave His type of Knowledge to mankind; and mankind uses this knowledge to live their lives. In the same sense that Christ gave his type of knowledge to mankind; and mankind uses this knowledge to live their lives.

Recall the story where LISA had the Gods attempt to do five things at once. He gave Them a gong, a bell, a drum, and a flute, and said, "Whoever took all the instruments and played the four together and danced to them, would be Chief of the Gods"; and LEGBA was able to accomplish this.

As we will see, the gong, bell, drum, flute, and dancing were symbolism related to the job of "Chief of the Gods and Goddesses." We can interpret this to mean,

LEGBA IS THE GOD OF LAW AND ORDER
LEGBA IS THE GOD OF KNOWLEDGE
LEGBA IS THE GOD OF SEXUALITY
LEGBA IS THE GOD OF FRIENDSHIP
LEGBA IS THE GOD OF DESTINY

And the "way he carries out His job" is "Voodoo-magic" as we define the terms. For example, next we will look at the nature of LEGBA's job as Messenger and Chief Policeman of the World of mankind, and how he performs his duties in the following story.

"In ancient times, LISA sent a Messenger (LEGBA) to earth daily to travel from sunrise to sunset. He did this all the time every year. One day, while on His errands, He reached Aja land and it was already night. He could go no more, and so He went into a house. There was a man who was also on the road. As night fell, he, too, went into this house. They gave them a place in the same house, the two strangers together.

LISA's Messenger asked the other, "Where are you going?"

He said, "I am going where the sun sets."

Good, LISA's Messenger said, "It is life that gives a companion. I myself am going to the same place."

The following morning, at first cockcrow, in a house beside theirs, was a sick child sleeping, and the parents were crying.

LISA's Messenger went to ask them, "Why haven't you slept all night?"

They said, "We have a child here who is very sick."

Now, LISA's Messenger had a sack in which He carried some powder. He gave some of the powder to a man to give to the sick child.

And He went back quickly to the man who was sleeping in his house and said, "Wake up! Wake up! We are leaving."

They took but a few steps away from the house, when all at once the people in the house began to shout, Where is the stranger? Where is the stranger?' The child was dead.

So they went away (LEGBA and His companion). They went until they came to Savalou (another village). There in Savalou they spent the night. They took shelter in a house beside the road. At first cockcrow, LISA's Messenger took some flint and made a fire. And this fire He put to the straw of the house where He had slept. He said, now, to the other man, "Wake up! Wake up! We are going." After they left, the house took fire. The people asked, 'Where are the strangers? Where are the strangers?' But they were gone.

They ran away and continued their journey. As LISA's Messenger did that, his companion, who was a human being, was astonished. He did not know that the other was a Vudu (God). So they reached Badahwedji where the sun sets. That is, they were almost there.

Now, there was a river that separated Badahwedji from where the two travelers were. In order to cross the river, one must put down a raft and pass on it. There was an old man from Badahwedji who was in the habit of coming to the river bank for leaves. He gathered them and went back. Now he was crossing the river for the second time. So LISA's Messenger came behind him and pushed him, so that he fell into the water.

When He did this, the man who came with LISA's Messenger ran away. LISA's Messenger saw him run and He called him back. "Come, come here," He said, "That's not where you are going. You are going to this place. Here it is."

The other said, "What I saw on the road here is too much. I am running away from it."

LISA's Messenger said, "Now, I'm not a man. I know you are astonished at all I did. But I'm not a human being. In the house where I killed the child, if that child had not died, its mother and father would have died when it took its first step. It is LISA who sent me to destroy that child.' He said, 'In that house this mother and father have borne many children, and this one child could not be allowed to spoil their lives."

He said, "The family where I burned the house has rich relatives among them. But they buried all their money and their children are poor. So I burned the house, so that when they break the walls to make them new and begin to dig the foundation, they will find the money."

He said, "I had the man fall into the river, because the King of Badahwedji is dead. To replace this king, a younger man should be named. If that old man were alive, a young man could not be named. That is why Lisa sent me to throw him into the water. The people still think the old man will be their King. But if that man became King, there would be no more goats, no more cattle, no more children in that Kingdom. SAGBATA would come to their Kingdom and kill them, because MAWU had ordained that one could not be King. With a young King, they will have goats, pigs and children also."

Then, He said, "I look into the hearts of men, and LISA sends me to look at things. You must not be astonished. Year after year, if I do not change into a man, I changed into a headache and kill men. I change into serpents and burn houses. And when, in the course of life, you see such things, you will know that is MAWU-LISA Who sends them." End of story.

It is clear from this story that LISA is concerned about the Destiny and it's fulfillment, on an individual, family, and Kingdom level. And as Messenger and Chief Policeman, we can see why LEGBA'S job is so complicated, and why he must know how to do so many things at the same time. The nature of LEGBA's job is to keep all Destinies operating in harmony.

On the other hand, LEGBA is the God of Friendship, as the following story shows.

The long tuft of hair on LEGBA's head is the sign of the Friendship of LEGBA and GU (the God of iron, war and hunting), who were especially close to each other. The following story shows how this Great Friendship came to be.

"During the time that the Gods and Goddesses were living on earth, when the Gods visited the house of GU they enjoyed meat, wine, and entertainment. LEGBA told GU that on the day of His death He would know who His real friends were. He thought that those who came to eat the food of GU were not His true friends.

One day GU decided to find out who His real friends were and test them. So He told His Sons to tell them that when they came to His house that He was dead, and they got a white cloth to cover him like a corpse. Then He told His Sons to yell in a loud voice that GU was dead.

As soon as the Gods heard this cry, they started to rush to the house of GU, and began to quarrel about which piece of property went to whom. But on that day, LEGBA was shaving His head. As He was finishing the sides and back with only a tuft on top left to shave, He heard the voices on the Sons of GU crying that Their Father had passed away.

LEGBA said; 'What a sudden death! Come to My Friend! He left His hair unfinished and ran, tears streaming down His face, to the house of GU. GU opened His eyes and looked at LEGBA and said, 'You are My real friend. You will be My Friend for ever more. I have seen you arrive with your hair unfinished. Henceforth, this tuft of hair will remain on your head as the sign of Friendship which is Genuine." (And the tuft came to mean friendship, and this is why most Aja artists, in creating an image of LEGBA, put a long tuft of hair on His head). End of story.

This means that LEGBA became the Best Friend of the Gods, Goddesses, and the Aja people. In this sense, if "CHRIST is the God of Love they Neighbor," "LEGBA is the God of Friendship with thy Neighbor." The question becomes, how did this Great Friendship originate and manifest itself to the Aja people? The answer is, He gave them the knowledge of the value of friendship.

The following two stories concern LEGBA and the divination system of Fa, which will show, He is the Continuous Source of Knowledge and Wisdom. We must take note of this, and it might be an advantage to go back and review the Yoruba's Divination System.

Anyway, Aja's word 'Gbadu' in Fa Divination means the same as the Yoruba's word 'Odu' means in Ifa Divination; 'chapters in a body of knowledge,' in story form, used in Divination rituals to tell the future of chosen destinies. With this in mind, lets look at the ritual symbolism related to the Aja's Divination system as related to LEGBA in the following two stories.

"GBADU, born of Her Parent (MAWU-LISA) as the child following the Twins AGBE and NATETE (the God and Goddess of the Sea) is like Her Parent, both male and female. She has however, sixteen eyes.

Her Parent instructed her to live on top of a palm-tree in Heaven in order to observe everything that transpired in the Kingdoms of the Sea, the Earth, and the Sky. But She was not told at this time the duties She was to perform. Thus GBADU always lived atop Her tree.

At night she slept Her eyes closed. And since She cannot open them herself, LEGBA has been charged by His Parent to climb the palm-tree every morning to open the eyes of His Sister.

When LEGBA climbs the palm-tree, He first asks of GBADU which eyes She wishes to have opened, whether those of the back or front, to the left, or right. GBADU however, is too wary to speak her reply fearing to be over heard, and so She makes Her wishes known to LEGBA through the kernels of Her palm-tree.

If She places one kernel in his hand it signifies that she wishes Him to Open two of Her eyes, and if She gives Him two kernels, one of Her eyes are to be opened. When LEGBA sees this, He Himself looks about to see what is happening in the Sea, On Earth, and in the Sky, and transmits this information to GBADU.

After a time, GBADU began to bear children. The first child was Minona, a daughter, and the second was also a daughter. The others, all sons, were named Aovi, Abi, Duwo, Kiti, Agbanukwe, and Zose.

One day GBADU confided to LEGBA that She was troubled because She has yet not been told what Her kingdom was to be. Since LEGBA alone could understand MAWU, He promised His sister that He would teach Her the speech of their parent.

Later, MAWU left with GBADU the key to the door that opened the future. It is said that the future is a house (where the chosen destinies are kept) which has sixteen doors corresponding to the number of GBADU's eyes, and that the name of the palm-tree on which GBADU stays is Fa.

As GBADU received the key, MAWU said to Her that since LEGBA is The Great Overseer of the World, GBADU must be the intermediary between the three kingdoms of the Universe; the earth, the sea, and the sky.

She said further that when men wished to know their future (chosen destiny) or to know what decisions to make, they should take palm-kernels and play with them as a ritual, and this would open the eyes of GBADU which correspond to the number of kernels that remained and the order in which they fell.

The kernels opened an eye which also corresponded to a door in the house of the future (house of the chosen destinies). A man who had the proper knowledge, (a divination priest), had but to look in order to see the (chosen) destiny of the one for whom he was divining.

Sometime after this, LEGBA informed MAWU that there was a great war on earth, a great war in the sea, and a great war in the sky. And that were it not for GBADU, all these three kingdoms would shortly be destroyed, since man did not know how to behave. The water of the sea did not know its place, and the rain did not know how to fall.

The reason for this LEGBA explained, was because those who had been given these kingdoms did not understand the language of their parent, and therefore, could only blunder.

When MAWU asked LEGBA what had best be done to correct this, LEGBA recommended that GBADU be sent to earth. But MAWU said " No, let GBADU remain here, but let an understanding of my language be given to some men on earth. In that way men will know the future (their chosen destiny), and will know how to guide their lives."

MAWU thereupon instructed LEGBA to send three men to earth on this mission. And LEGBA, choosing three sons of GBADU, dispatched them to teach the alphabet of MAWU to men. Also to tell them which alphabet was contained behind each door of the house of the future.

Thus Duwo, Kiti, and Zose came to earth to teach Fa. They brought palm-kernels with them showing men how to use them, and instructing each concerning the 'SEKPOLI (Chosen Destiny). Saying that *SEKPOLI is a soul which MAWU had given to all,* but which cannot be discerned until GBADU has been made to reveal it.

And they said further that it is always necessary to know the number of eyes GBADU has opened before calling this Soul. So that if a man knows the number of lines that Fa has traced for him, he will know his SEKPOLI.

Finally they taught that no altars are necessary for the SEKPOLI, because the human body itself is its altar. When the three had finished their teaching, they went back to Heaven.

MAWU thereafter sent all the Children of GBADU to earth where they were led by LEGBA. When they came, Zose took the name of Faluwono (meaning the processor of the secrets of the Fa ritual) which GBADU had given to Him.

Minona became the Goddess of women; and abides in the house of women where she spins cotton on her spindle.

Duwo resides in the house of Fa (Fa ritual itself), while Kiti stays with Duwo to help Zose do his work, since the task of Zose is to manipulate the palm-kernels.

Zose has only one foot, and in the beginning when He traced the lines by which He divined, people did not believe Him. His brother, Aovi (problems) was thereupon charged with the task of making people more respectful toward the Fa ritual. That is why if today one disobeys Fa, tomorrow Zose will tell His brother Aovi to punish the delinquent one.

A small clay figure of LEGBA was made and placed in a little house to one side of the Fa house. Abi was told to play for Minona the role which Aovi plays for Fa; Aabi becoming the ashes of the fire, and the one who makes women respect Minona.

Therefore, when a woman who had incurred the ill-will of Minona cooks, the fire burns her and her house. Little by little people began to understand the new ritual, and since Aovi is very severe, Fa ritual came to be respected, and the ritual of Fa has spread everywhere in Aja land.

Meanwhile in Heaven, LEGBA continued to have relations with GBADU, and when He came to earth He also lay with Minona. This went on for a long time, until one day He came to earth with GBADU to visit Fa.

As was Their habit, they shared the sleeping-mat (African mattress) together. Late that night He arose steely, and disguised Himself, and went to Minona. GBADU awoke however, and discovered that LEGBA had deceived Her with Her own Daughter.

A violent quarrel ensued between GBADU and LEGBA. Both returned to Heaven in anger to bring the case before MAWU. LEGBA denied that He had relations with a Mother and Daughter, but His Parent ordered Him to undress.

As He stood naked, MAWU saw how His penis was erect and said, "You have lied to me, as you have deceived Your Sister. And since You have done this, I ordain that Your penis shall always be erect and that You may never be appeased (never be sexually satisfied)."

To show His indifference to this punishment, LEGBA began at once to play (sexually) with GBADU before their Parent. When reproached, He merely pointed out that since His penis was always to remain erect, MAWU had decreed such conduct for Him. That is why, when LEGBA dances, He tries to take any woman who is at hand. (He dances the dance of sexual intercourse)" End of story.

First we should understand that GBADU is not a Goddess, but a divination system, even though the Aja relate and talk about the system as if it was Holy, which it is, being created by MAWU-LISA. This means that in the story, the sexual relations between LEGBA and GBADU symbolizes the close relationship between LEGBA and Fa Divination ritual; and some indication that it is a source of LEGBA's knowledge given to the Aja people.

On the other hand, the story gives us a very good idea according to Aja religious beliefs of how the spiritual side of their Fa Divination ritual came into reality. And at the same time, shows LEGBA's role in bringing the Fa ritual to earth. And if we look through the symbolism, we can see that it is organized and functions in the same way as the Yoruba's Ifa ritual.

Plus, the story gives another side of LEGBA; He is a God Who is always in a state of sexual readiness, but never sexually satisfied, which symbolizes that He is in a continuous relationship with Aja's divination system.

Now as to the second story, we will only quote in parts. It deals with how MAWU-LISA gave LEGBA the job of being the 'Guardian God of the Aja people, to be their Friend, and to assist them in the fulfilling of their Chosen Destinies.

"As time went on, though they (the Aja people) remembered that Fa is the will of the Gods, they forgot the importance of LEGBA. Thus it happened that sometime later, three other men came to earth at a place called Gisi.

The first was named Adjaka, the second Oku, and the third Ogbena. They came to tell the people that they should not forget that MAWU had said it is important that they worship LEGBA.

They reminded men that LEGBA is the Son and the Assistant of MAWU Herself. And that if people on earth are in need of anything, they must first of all address themselves to LEGBA who has all power to do what He chooses on earth.

To spread their message, the three emissaries of the Gods selected a man named Alaundje whom they instructed in the way of manipulating Fa ritual. When a man wishes to know his destiny, he must enter the forest and take the kernels himself and throw them and trace eight lines on the earth. These eight lines are the design of the (Chosen) destiny of this man.

He was told further how this same man must then gather the earth on which he has traced the lines of his destiny; put it into a small cloth, mix it with what is necessary and (sacred ingredients) after which this would constitute his personal destiny to which he must thereafter address himself. (This is to say, this small bag of sand is the man's alter to his soul).

Alaundje was further told that after a man has thus obtained his destiny, he must give the lines to one who can read them so that the knowledge of how to do this might be spread among mankind.

The Messengers from Heaven taught Alaundje the explanation of each line and, at the same time, the meaning of the lines of the hand which correspond to the traceries of his SEKPOKI (destiny).

This makes it known that it is by the writing on the hand of man, that MAWU makes known Her own writing. As well as the fact that this is why, when Fa is written, it is written like the lines on the palm of the hand. (So we can see that the Aja added the art of palm reading to their divination system, unlike the Yoruba).

Continuing, they taught him how necessary it is that LEGBA have a shrine outside each homestead facing the entrance to the dwelling-place, because in Heaven, He is always so with MAWU.

And because the writing that controls human destiny is in the house of MAWU, it is necessary that LEGBA, Who is always before the door of this house, be placed before the doors of the houses of men.

They said that before a man may eat, LEGBA must eat; (a sacrifice given to LEGBA) that when a person goes away from his home he must tell LEGBA, that he may be led by a good road. That when one is troubled, the trouble should be confided to LEGBA that He may bring aid. In short, when a man wishes to do anything at all in life, LEGBA must first be informed.

They told how, until a man had entered the forest to trace the eight lines of his destiny, he must never erect a great LEGBA (shrine) in front of his house, since where the writing of MAWU, Fa, is absent, LEGBA may not be present.

Therefore they explained how, when a boy approaches manhood he is to be given his partial Fa, his destiny as a young man. But that until he has passed from childhood and is a man, it is not permitted for him to have a great LEGBA in front of his house.

Finally, they prophesied to Alaundje how, after their departure, men and animals that were unlike ordinary beings would appear on earth for the purpose of creating families. Also how these beings would give to man, the Gods they would in the future worship.

The messengers, in parting declared that the people should know that all of the rivers empty into the Sea. Even though men were called to worship many different Gods, they must recognize that it is MAWU and LEGBA Who has given them their Gods. And that if they desire their Gods to be powerful, they must make a LEGBA (shrines) for all Vudu (Gods) and for all Ancestors." End of story.

We must take special note of the last paragraph of this story, They must make LEGBA shrines for all Vudu and all Ancestors. We will deal with the role Ancestors play in Aja religious beliefs later.

Meanwhile, this story gives us a good idea of the purpose Fa Divination ritual is to serve; it is the keeper of chosen destinies given by MAWU, and the voice of the knowledge of LEGBA of voodoo-magic. As well as more insight into the position LEGBA holds.

We can begin to see more of why we say that LEGBA not only was made the Guardian God, in addition to His other jobs. But also we see that He moved into the position that He really did not answer to any God, or have to follow any rules other than those He made Himself. This made Him the most powerful of all the Gods and Goddesses, this also made Him Chief of the Holy Trinity of the Aja's religious beliefs.

Of course the Aja worshipped the other Gods and Goddesses in Their Temples, and these Gods and Goddesses had their priest and community rituals. But LEGBA became their personal God, like their Best Friend; that is to say, LEGBA, the Trickster God is the 'Christ' of the Aja.

This made the Aja unique among African nations. All Africans believe in the Trickster God, no matter what combination of African Traditional Religious beliefs they happen to hold, or what ever name they happen to call Him. But they, for the most part, use the Trickster God only as a Messenger God to carry their prayers and sacrifices to the other Gods and Goddesses, and never ask Him for personal advice.

However, the Aja made the very nature of the Trickster God Their major focus. One Who gives them personal advice and voodoo-magic as a means of finding, and fulfilling their chosen destiny.

There is no Temple Shrines made for LEGBA, nor is there any community rituals held in his name; he is a personal God. Whereas all of the other Gods and Goddesses have their group of worshippers, Priest and Priestess, and day of worship. Every man and woman in the nation of Aja had a personal LEGBA shrine in front of their houses. And they relate to him through the Fa Divination Ritual, and face to face at the Crossroads on a group and, or, a personal level.

This means that LEGBA is the only God or Goddess, including MAWU-LISA Who people depend on, all the time, day or night. Thus is the role of LEGBA in the Aja's religious beliefs we call Voodooism.

Voodoo-magic and the Mind of Mankind

Now we come to a long story dealing with what we have called 'voodoo-magic and how it works on the mind; and how LEGBA became known as the Trickster God.

We will now get deeper into Aja symbolism. The following one long and two short stories are dealing with the Soul-mind of the Aja, and the role LEGBA plays in how it works. Especially as related to how voodoo-magic works.

On the other hand, in the following long story, and King Metonofi, nobody seems to have a definition for the name Metonofi as we will see later. However, Grandpa's conclusion is that the King symbolizes SAGBATA, the twin God and Goddess of the Temple of Family and Social relationships; meaning the Aja's Moral Code of Social Conduct. The long story is as follows:

"Agbanukwe (Chosen Destiny) and Kpoli (Personal Spirit) (chosen destiny and personal spirit equals the mind of a person) had three Children (three forces in their soul). The first, a daughter named

Minona, the second and third, who were sons, were called Aovi and Legba. Each had been married, but each had killed their mate.

When Minona killed her husband, she ripped open his stomach and intestines with a knife. Aovi killed his wife by cutting off her head, and Legba did away with his mate by hitting her a fatal blow on the head with a stick.

The three formed a little funeral band and, one day when a great man in a far away country died; they went to help at his funeral.

When they arrived at the place of mourning they played their drums and sang the funeral songs so well that all who were present were pleased, and they were rewarded with many cowries (money).

Fa (the name of the Fon's divination ritual), who was the master of Legba was also present at the funeral. The two always worked together, since it was necessary that Legba be at his side before Fa could speak.

Now, there was a King named Metonofi (King of the World) Who had given his eldest daughter in marriage to the King of Aja (King of Mankind).

But the King of Aja was impotent and unable to have sex with her. This had caused him so much shame that he gave the girl away to his eldest son.

This son of the King of Aja had come to the funeral to find Fa and tell him all that had passed between his father and the daughter of King Metonofi. And that his father had given him the girl as a wife.

When he recounted this, he asked Fa for a powder that would assure him potency when he has sex with the girl, for he wished to remove his father's shame from his family. Fa told him to go home, and that in three days he would send him a good powder.

But Legba, who kept the sack which contained the medicines of Fa said," Your sack is here. I can take the boy behind the house and give him the powder now."

Now Fa had two powders, a white one that gave potency and a red one that rendered men impotent. He told Legba to give the son of the King of Aja some of the white powder, but Legba gave him the red powder.

With the burial over, Legba, his brother, and sister started for home. They came to the cross-roads (which symbolized the spiritual home of LEGBA) where they sat down to divide what they had received.

They divided the cowries into three equal piles, but one remained over. No matter how hard they tried to make an equal division of the cowries, one always remained.

Minona said that since she was the oldest, she would take it. Aovi disagreed with her saying that since he was the second it should go to him. While Legba claiming that since the others had already had much to eat before he was born, it should belong to him.

After a long discussion in which they could not come to an agreement, a woman who gathered wood to sell in the market place was seen coming along the road with a bottle on her head.

They called to her and asked her to divide the cowries equally. She tried again and again, but one was always over. Finally she asked, 'Which of you is the eldest?" Minona replied, "It is I."

The woman then said that in her country when three divided something and there was one over it went to the eldest, and thereupon awarded the extra cowries to Minona.

At that, Aovi cut off the woman's head, while Legba gave her a blow with his club, and they threw her body into the bush. But Legba went where the body had fallen, and had sex with it.

When he returned, they resumed their dispute until another woman who was on her way to the well to get water came down the road.

They called to her and asked her if she would divide their cowries. She tried many times, but one cowry was always left over. Finally she asked,' who is the second eldest of you?' Aovi replied, "I."

In my country when three divide something and one is over, the eldest doesn't take, nor the youngest, but the middle one; and she gave the extra cowry to Aovi.

At once Legba struck her with his stick, and Minona ripped out her intestines and her stomach. And when they had thrown her body into the bush, Legba went where the body lay and had sex with the dead woman.

After a time, a third woman was seen on the road coming from the market, and they invited her to distribute the cowries. She tried as the other two had tried, but always one cowry remained. So she asked," 'Who is the youngest?" Legba said, "I am."

Whereupon she gave the extra cowry to Legba saying, "in my society when three divide something and there is one over, we give it to the youngest, for the elder ones have eaten before he was born."

At this, Minona rip open her intestines, and Aovi cut off her head. But Legba took her body into the bush and had sex with it.

By now Legba had enough of this, so he told the others that he was going into the bush to look for something, and he carried with him the sack of his master, Fa.

In the sack he found a figurine which turned into a dog. He whispered to the dog to walk past the three as they were attempting to divide the gifts they had received at the funeral, telling him what to do. He returned to them.

As soon as he came back, a dog was seen coming down the road, and they invited him to divide the cowries. He tried and tried, but always there was one over. So with his paws he scratched a small hole and said, "in my society, when three divide something and one is left over, it is for the Ancestors." And he buried the extra cowry in the hole.

All three were content, and they praised the dog. Minona said, "You will lead all the women I command; you will be their guardian." Aovi said, "You will lead all the Spirits I command; you will always be before them." And Legba said, "You will lead all men, and will never let them lose their way."

So they blessed the dog again, and he went on his way. But Legba went into the bush, and when the dog came to him he was once more changed back into a figurine.

When they returned home, the son of the King of Aja, to whom Legba had given the red powder was there with Fa. He said that he, too had become impotent.

Now in those days as today, all came to Fa before doing anything. When King Metonofi made known that the man who succeeded in having sexual intercourse with his daughter would be given half of his kingdom, all the men of the Kingdom came to consult Fa.

To all of them Legba gave the red powder, so that all the men of the kingdom became impotent. When they complained to the King that Legba had rendered them impotent, King Metonofi sent for him to punish him, but Legba escaped to the house of Ayo, his mother-in-law.

Now Legba's father-in-law was away, and Legba had to sleep in the same room with his mother-in-law. So that night he had sex with her, and in the morning returned to his village.

He was seized at once and brought before the King, who summoned all the men of the kingdom to come and make their complaints.

The men of the families of the three women who had been killed by Legba, Aovi, and Minona at the cross-roads, also accused Him to their deaths before the King. Legba's father-in-law also made a complaint that Legba had sexual intercourse with his wife. While all the men of the Kingdom accused Legba before the King of having given them the red powder which caused them to become impotent.

The first count, upon which he was tried, was the death of the three women. The King asked Legba if he had killed the women, but Legba said "No, it was Aovi," adding that, He himself had intervened and had tried to divide the cowries in order to save their lives.

The others however denied the guilt of Aovi, and said that a dog had settled the dispute. Legba now told how he had changed the figurine into a dog, and to prove his words, he took the figurine out and before the eyes of all, changed it into a dog.

Now all saw that Legba had spoken the truth, and King Metonofi ordered that thenceforth Legba should be guardian of men, of women, and of all the Gods. Minona was ordered to remain in the houses of women whom she commanded; Aovi was instructed to remain with the Gods; but Legba was told that he might live wherever he chose. So Legba came into the houses (of people).

The hearing on the second complaint took place after two days. Legba was asked, "Did you have sex with your mother-in-law?" This Legba admitted, but explained that he had done this because the woman slept in the place where his wife usually laid.

King Metonofi said that since he had named Legba guardian of all, he could not withdraw his law. But that in as much as Legba always created scandal, he should not live inside a house, but that his place must be outside and before the entrance to houses.

Two days later, the third complaint was brought before the King for judgment; this being the accusation that Legba had given the men of the kingdom the powder that made them impotent.

But when he was asked did you give the men the good powder? Legba said, "Yes." In order to verify the truth of his answer, he was told to bring the powder he had given the men so that all might see.

While he was gone Legba mixed the blood of a pigeon with the good powder making it red, and to the red powder he added water in which (white) caolin had been mixed, thus making it white.

When he returned with the two powders, King Metonofi asked the men, "What was the color of the powder given to you?" All cried, "The red, the red!"

So the King ordered Legba himself to take some of the red powder, and commanded all to return in two days, when it would be demonstrated whether Legba himself had been rendered impotent.

When all had reassembled, they found that King Metonofi had caused a little house to be built, and in it he had placed his daughter, the wife of the King of Aja.

The men were told to enter, each in turn to see if they could have sex with his daughter Konkoni. But none of them could accomplish sexual intercourse. There were some who said that it was not good to be tested with so many people about waiting expectantly.

But Legba said to the King that these men were fools; that as for him, he would have sex with his daughter in public if they wished it. King Metonofi told him to enter the house, and added that if he accomplished intercourse with his daughter he would reward him well.

Now Legba had brought his drums, and there, he caused to be played as he entered, and he was successful and she was a virgin. The blood was all over the entire house.

This done, he emerged from the house still naked with his penis erect approaching one bystander, now another, and went through the gestures of sex while the drums continued to play.

King Metonofi was pleased with what had happened. He gave his daughter to Legba as a wife, and ordered that from this day Legba's drum should be played everywhere in remembrance of his daughter.

He also decreed that Legba might sleep with any woman he chose without any distinction, and that since Legba was wise, he named him intermediary between this world and the next. And that is why Legba dances everywhere in the manner of a man having sex.

Legba gave the daughter of King Metonofi to his master Fa, and Fa invited all the men of the country to his house to celebrate the marriage. When all were there, Legba gave them drink which contained the good powder so that all became potent once again. On that occasion, Legba took the name 'Aflakete, Trickster God,' and gave the girl the name Adje, Cowries, since it was for cowries he had killed the women.

It is because of these happenings that Legba is now found everywhere. To go to a Vudu (God or Goddess), one must pass Legba; to consult Fa, one must pass by Legba, and every man and woman must have a Legba shrine as a guardian. And that is also why the dog is respected as the animal of Legba." End of long story.

First of all we should note that LEGBA gave Himself the Name of the Trickster. We must recall that in every African nation the Trickster God is the God of rituals and is a Messenger God; for example, we saw this clearly with the Yoruba.

Thus is the nature of the old Afro-American term, voodoo-magic, and the new Afro-American term, 'Making a Trick' out of somebody, and the Aja use the term, 'Trickeration,' however, the three terms mean the same thing.

Therefore, in that light, if we look at this long story about LEGBA's activities, we can see that His goal is to have a positive or negative effect on the minds of the people He was dealing with.

We also see that He is a Master of the Mind Game, which is our definition of Voodooism. This means that the nature of the African mind, especially the Aja's mind, is what Afro-Americans call 'Messing with somebody's Mind' with Voodoo-magic.

To better understand what we mean by 'Trickeration,' and 'Making a Trick out of somebody,' we will take an example of a man that owes three important and dangerous men money which he does not have to pay them. What is he to do?

He goes to the Fa Priest who uses the Fa ritual to find an answer which is told as a story of the use of voodoo-magic: First short story.

"Fa owed money to a serpent, a Leopard, and a hunter. The serpent was a poisonous one. Each of the three lived in a different village, and not knowing one another, had no means of finding out that Fa owed money to all of them. When the serpent came to ask for the repayment of his loan, Fa said, "Come tomorrow." When the Leopard came, he was told to return the next day, and so was the hunter. As soon as the three left, Fa washed the head of KPELI (baptized his Soul).

Then he divined, and the Du (chapter, like the Yoruba) was Gudamedji, which says that for a matter involving debt, the debtor must first find a raffia sack and put small stones on the type called gbadakeo inside it. Then close the sack. In those days, cowries were used for money, and these cowries were carried about in these raffia sacks, (gbadakeo stones look just like real cowries). The Du said that Fa should then put the sack against a wall of the house, and give a chicken to LEGBA, (sacrifice a chicken to LEGBA).

Fa did as he was ordered. The next morning, the Leopard was the first to come. Fa said, "I have your money here, but my son is away and will not be back for a short while. If you wait, he will help you carry away the money." The Leopard agreed and climbed a tree behind the house of Fa to wait for the son of Fa. In a few moments the serpent came. Fa showed him the sack (of fake money) and said, "Here is your money, but if you wait a short while, my son, who will soon return will help you carry it home." The serpent likewise agreed and went into the bush behind Fa's house to wait. Soon afterwards the hunter came, and Fa showed him the same sack saying, "My son has gone to the village with a friend, but he will be here in a moment and will help you carry this money away." And having said this, he asked the hunter to wait in the back of his house.

The three creditors had never seen each other before. Now when the hunter went behind Fa's house, he saw the leopard crouched in the tree. At once he aimed his gun, and shot and killed him. He had taken no more that three steps toward his prey, however, he was bitten by the serpent. As he felt the sting of the serpent, he threw his knife which cut off the serpent's head. That moment, the poison from the snake took effect, and the hunter died. Thus Fa rid himself of his creditors. He then gave another chicken to LEGBA (as a sacrifice)." End of first short story.

So we can see the kind of advice LEGBA gives to people through Fa divination system; when asked for help.

After reciting this story to his client, the Divination Priest instructs him to find a raffia sack, small stones, the skin of a leopard and of a serpent, a small piece of wood from which a toy gun is to be made, and two chickens.

These are given to the Priest who makes a sacrifice for the man with the problem. He takes up each object and touches his forehead with it before using it for shaping the sacrifice.

When it is finished, the client is told to carry it to a known sacred bush and to leave it there. The two chickens he had brought are killed as a sacrifice for LEGBA. This done, his destiny will permit him to find the means of side-stepping the demands of his creditors by using this approach, which we call voodoo-magic. But the question remains, what is the thing that makes it work between people?

Another way of looking at it is voodoo-logic comes from a deep understanding of how the mind works, and the dynamics of the mind's reality.

And from people's own personal experiences, they know that their mind plays tricks on itself. Therefore, the mind is open to trick-activities. Now if a person is fully qualified, like a Fa Priest, he can invoke the mind to start playing tricks on itself, or, use the tricks that the mind plays on itself to totally control the mind's thoughts and actions.

For example, the ritual symbolism of the serpent, the leopard, and the hunter is a clear case of a voodoo-magic divination Priest using the three dynamic forces in the mind to destroy itself. He demonstrated the spiritual ritual process involved in getting it done.

Therefore, we can say that the dynamics of voodoo-magic is the focus on how the mind works, and its function was changing the process of the mind's reality. This is why LEGBA does such strange things; messing with the mind's reality; and in the case of witchcraft, making the mind attack itself. Thus is the nature of voodoo magic.

Now Grandpa is fully aware that in your young lives in America, you have heard it said that voodoo-magic is evil, when you think of it as just Witchcraft.

Voodooism is a religion. Like any other religion in Africa, it can be used for good or evil. When used for evil is what is called Witchcraft. Nevertheless we saw in one of the stories, that MAWU gave mankind permission to use voodoo-magic for the good it can do.

However, with all of the jealousy and greed in the world, people have a big fear of anything that can change how their mind functions. This makes voodoo-logic a dangerous weapon, not only for what it can do, but also what people fear it can do.

Voodooism is much more than a super spiritual weapon. It is a religion with high family and community morals and ethics; values about how to live life.

For example, we can see that the major focus of LEGBA , and therefore the people, is on the Mind and Sex; but his sex does not seem to have a direction. This is where SAGBATA comes into the picture. He gives sex a purpose, producing a Family and Society.

This means that His Doctrine of the seven cycles of life is the role of sex as far as the man-woman relationship, family, and Society are concerned. Thus is the nature of SAGBATA Knowledge, which is a code of moral laws covering sex, man-woman relationships, family relations, and society's social conduct. On the other side is the Knowledge of SORBO, Whose Knowledge covers the Ethics of Power in Society, Governing these aspects of Society; which is the nature of His knowledge. Then there is LEGBA doing his voodoo-magic in the mist of everything; it is LEGBA's job to maintain harmony in the world.

This gives us some idea of what is meant by MAWU-LISA, SAGBATA, and SORBO being the Power-source of the Fon's Society. Their Knowledge is not the same thing, nor do they compete with one another. And if we focus on these kinds of differences, Grandpa thinks it will highlight and give us a clearer picture of not only the Fon's Society, but also the nature of their religious beliefs.

This means that the Fons really have four major lines of knowledge as the foundation of their Society, which aid them in the fulfillment of their Chosen Destiny. One line through LEGBA, and the others through MAWU-LISA, SOGBO, and SAGBATA temples. Thus is the function and purpose of Aja's Religion.

Now to put all of this into some kind of perspective, if we recall, the Akan cut their religious path-way with their Calendar; they themselves did all of the work.

On the other hand, LEGBA cut a religious path-way by becoming the thing that makes up the Aja's Articles of Faith, ordained by the Great Creator MAWU-LISA. LEGBA was seeking the Aja, they were not seeking Him. But once LEGBA had the backing of MAWU-LISA, the King of the Universe, SOGBO, and the King of the Earth, SAGBATA, the people naturally followed Him. His path-way was complete.

This was the final step. LEGBA then became the Key God, the major path-way, and played the central role in their religious lives.

Of course the Aja worshipped the Gods and Goddesses of the Holy Trinity, MAWU-LISA, SORBO and SAGBATA, Who had their Temple, Priest, and Community Rituals. However, every man and woman in the Aja nation has a LEGBA shrine in front of their house, and related to Him through the Fa Divination ritual, and meet Him face to face at the Crossroads.

In this respect, LEGBA became the Manager of the Affairs of their Mind, and in this way control their Lives. That is to say, LEGBA, the Trickster God, became the 'Christ' of the Aja.

This made the Aja unique among African Nations. All Africans believe in the Trickster God. No matter what combination of African Traditional Religious beliefs they happen to hold, or what ever name they happen to call Him. All Africans believe in voodoo-magic.

But they, for the most part, use the Trickster God only as a Messenger to carry their prayers and sacrifices to the other Gods and Goddesses, and never ask Him for personal advice; only the Witches do in other African Societies.

Nevertheless, Grandpa must say that the Trickster God is real cool just as a Messenger, as is the case with the Akan, the Yoruba, and the Igbo. But when we take a close look at the way LEGBA's Mind works, He is one Unique God. And in the case of the Aja, even His Family is Unique, especially his Mother-Father, MAWU-LISA; strange even for African Traditional Religion, which has the widest application of any religion in the world.

Or, maybe it just seems strange. If we focus our attention on how the Aja's religious beliefs function as the Guiding-light in their Society, it won't seem strange at all. We will begin with their education system, as taught from the Doctrine of the Temple of SAGBATA

SAGBATA TEMPLE TEACHING
Fon's Childhood Education System

The focus of SAGBATA's Temple teaching is on the development through 'Seven Cycles of Life;' which is as follows:

1. Pregnancy and birth (nine months).
2. Babyhood (birth to about three years of age).
3. Childhood (three years old to the age of twelve).
4. Manhood and womanhood (begins with puberty to about age twenty).
5. Fatherhood and motherhood (from about age twenty to about forty.
6. Grand father and grandmother hood (from age forty to sixty).
7. Ancestorhood (age sixty to forever after death).

And this Principle-of-Seven applies not only on an individual level, but also includes the life of a family in which the individual is involved. This is the Doctrine taught in the Temple of SAGBATA.

For example, the teaching begins with the childhood education system.

Now when we mention education systems in Society, we mean that there are Teachers. Of course, there are Priest', Priestesses, Hunters, Warriors, and economic Teachers in Fon Society But the 'Greatest Teachers' of all are the ' Fon Mothers,' especially throughout Babyhood and Childhood when the most important things are taught about the 'Traditions of Society.' And their method of teaching is with songs and stories.

Even at the stage of babyhood the Fon mother's method are song-stories, in these, the whole history and traditions of the family and clan are contained. And, by hearing these song-stories daily, it is easy for the baby to assimilate this early teaching without any strain.

At the time when the baby begins to learn how to speak, according to Fon's beliefs, babyhood ends. When a baby begins to talk and childhood begins. Care is taken by the mother to teach the child the correct manner of speech, and to acquaint him or her with all of the important names in the family, past and present.

These are also given in song-stories to amuse the child, who is never told that he or she is being taught. But in any case, the child is left free to listen to these songs when they like.

If the mother notices that they don't like certain songs, she at once introduces others with different phrases and melody containing the same teaching.

Therefore, when the child is able to speak well, they can answer many questions which are asked naturally to test how much they have learned, For example, questions like, what are the names of your father's family? What are the names of the family of your mother?

These questions go back for a couple of generations of Ancestors, and young children are able to answer freely without any effort or strain on their part.

These questions are never asked seriously, they are always taken in the form of amusement or conversationally. In this way, the history and traditions of the child's family becomes a stimulating influence in their life, and from a fitting background to the rhythm of the family and community.

These song-stories do more than just give knowledge; they also foster a special feeling of belonging. By the time the children are old enough to talk and understand, they already have a feeling of belonging to a family. This not only extends to all of their living relatives, but also those in the land of the Ancestors; especially the Ancestor that is their Guardian. In fact, the children learn to talk from these song-stories about their extended family.

So we can say that these song-stories are the methods the Mothers used to build this feeling in the children that they belong, and are of high value to this world of their extended family. This is what babyhood is all about. This feeling of belonging, love if you will, pulls the baby into the reality of the world of family and community of other children, and also make up this new generation. So we can see that their history and Ancestors are the first thing taught to children, beginning in their Babyhood.

On the other hand, there are another group of stories the Mothers sang at the same time, called 'Yo stories,' which were their way of teaching their children about LEGBA.

As we mentioned, LEGBA is not only the cornerstone of Aja religion, but also is at the very foundation of how the Fon's mind works as far as voodoo-magic is concerned.

This method of teaching beginning at birth is so effective, that by the time the child is five or six, they have a large number of stories in their subconscious mind. So that as soon as they can talk real well, they can tell these stories in the form of games that teach the children about the nature of LEGBA as the God of Voodoo-magic. Also, the morals and ethics of MAWU-LISA, SAGBATA and SOGBO. This takes place in Story Games.

Story games take place in late evening at the house of an older Woman of the homestead, more than likely their grandma or an old Aunt. The children of this age group of 4 or 5 to about 12 or 13 years of age gather to tell stories.

The game begins by the old woman asking a riddle like the following, 'Hole within a hole, hair all around, pleasure comes from inside?' (The answer is a flute being played by a bearded man).

We can see by the riddle that the Fons teach their children about sex at a very early age. For example, in order to understand the riddle, one needs an understanding of sex.

Anyway, if the selected child cannot answer, he or she must tell a certain number of stories, and this continues until all of the children have had to tell at least four to five stories.

All stories are supervised by an old Woman, who not only sees to it that they don't make any mistakes, but also tells the children new stories that they have never heard before.

For the most part, the children tell stories that were put into their sub-conscious mind by their mothers while growing through babyhood. Keep in mind that the children learn to talk by reciting stories, especially "YO stories.

As far as the focus of our investigation is concerned, highest spiritual values, we are more interested in the YO stories. But who, or what is "YO?"

YO, is a hard character to define from the stories. Some say that he is a super natural animal. While others think of him as a super natural child. Nor is it clear if YO adventures take place in Heaven or on Earth. To Grandpa's thinking, but without much evidence, YO is the Son of LEGBA, and serves the same role in childhood as LEGBA serves in Adulthood. He teaches the children the art of using voodoo-magic.

But in any case, LEGBA and YO are just alike, both use Voodoo-magic, Tricksters, and make their own rules, with one exception. Whereas LEGBA has an uncontrollable desire for sex like men, YO has an uncontrollable desire for food like a child; and too, Grandpa believes that YO stories represent a time when the Gods, Goddesses, and people lived together.

But as to the purpose of YO stories, there is no doubt that as educational tools, the stories teach the children about the nature of the logic of LEGBA and voodoo-magic in a form that they can understand. A good example of this is shown in the following very long YO story as told to children by the Old women.

"When people first came into the world, Dada Segbo (SOGBO, God King of the Universe) had no wife. He called all the people together and took out a cowry, (money, worth for example, a penny), and told His people to take that cowry and find a wife for Him.

The people said, 'What does the King mean? Can one get a wife with only one cowry? It is impossible everybody said. No, we cannot do it. A man can never find a wife for one cowry.'

Now, YO said that he could get a girl for one cowry. Dada Segbo said, 'Alright.' He gave him the cowry.

YO sent to buy flint and bamboo tender (Fon's matches). Then he went and found dry straw. With these, he set the straw on fire. The grasshoppers began to jump. YO had a sack beside him, and he collected the grasshoppers inside the sack.

So now he went on his way with this sack of grasshoppers until he came to the house of an old woman. Now, this woman was drying beans in front of her house, but the chickens came and ate them.

YO said, 'haven't you corn to give your chickens?' Now, this was the time of famine. There was nothing to eat. YO said, 'All right, I have grasshoppers here. If I throw these to your chickens, they will let you beans along.'

The woman said, 'yes.' So he gave the grasshoppers to the chickens, and when the chickens finished eating them, he took the beans.

The old woman cried out, but, YO, why are you taking away my beans?'

He said, 'didn't you tell me to throw my grasshoppers to your chickens?'

(YO sang)

The grasshoppers came from the straw;
The money for the straw came from Dada Segbo.
So YO went on. Now he came to a river where fishermen were fishing. He saw that the people from the village of Tofi were trying to fish, but that the fish had nothing to eat. So he said, 'If you like, I will throw my beans in the river. The fish will come to eat, and you will have a good catch.'

The people said, 'true, true,' and they told him to throw in the beans. So the fishermen caught many, many fish.

YO picked out the largest fish for himself. The fishermen cried out after him, 'YO, why are you taking away our fish?'

YO said, 'did you forget that you took my beans?
The beans came from the old woman,
The old woman took my grasshoppers;
The grasshoppers came from the straw;
The money for the straw came from Dada Segbo.
I do nothing without getting my reward.'

YO continued on his way. He came to a place where blacksmiths were working. There were many hoes on the ground. When he saw the blacksmiths, they were tired.

YO said, 'why are you tired blacksmiths?' Have you had nothing to eat? You cannot even lift your hammers. If you like, I will leave you my fish so you can eat.'

The blacksmiths said, 'true, true.'

They took the fish and ate. When they had finished eating the fish, YO took the hoes and knives and filled up his sack with them. The blacksmiths cried out, 'Where are you going YO? Where are you going with our hoes and knives?'

But YO said to the blacksmiths, 'didn't you know, before you took my fish,'
The fish came from the fishermen,
The fishermen took my beans;
The beans came from an old woman,
The old woman took my grasshoppers;
The grasshoppers came from the straw,
The straw came from the money I got from Dada Segbo.

Then YO came to a field where men were working. Now, these men had neither knives nor hoes. They worked with their hands. YO asked them, 'don't you want knives and hoes to work with?'

The men said, 'yes.' He gave them the tools, and when the men had the knives and hoes they worked fast.

YO stood and watched them. Now the men had with them a dish of beans and cassava flour called abla. YO went and gathered it all up.

They cried out, 'YO, YO, what are you doing with our food?'

YO said, 'don't you know?
The hoes and knives came from the blacksmiths,
The blacksmiths took my fish;
The fish came from the river,
The fishermen took my beans;
The beans came from an old woman,
The old woman took my grasshoppers;
The grasshoppers came from the straw,
The straw took by a cowry;
The cowry came from Dada Segbo.
I do nothing without getting my reward.'

So again he went on his way. He walked for a long time until he came to a house beside the road. In this house, there was a dead girl. All the people were wailing. They had nothing to eat.

YO went inside and said, 'I see you have nothing to eat. I have abla (beans and cassava) with me. Divide it among you and drink water with it. Then you will be refreshed, and you will find a way to bury your dead.'

So they made YO sit down next to the dead. YO was a stranger. At night, while the others were digging the grave, he took the body.

The people ran after him and cried, 'YO, YO, why are you taking the body?'

Yo answered, 'don't you know?
Abla came from the farmers,
The farmers took my hoes and knives;
The hoes and knives came from the blacksmiths,
The blacksmiths ate my fish;
The fish came from the river,
The fishermen took my beans;
The beans came from an old woman,
The old woman took my grasshoppers;
The grasshoppers came from the straw;
The straw came from one cowry;
And the cowry came from Dada Segbo.'

So he left with the dead body. That day, YO traveled from early morning till night. He went to see the King of the country and said to him that Dada Segbo had told him to go and look for a wife for him. As he had found her, he wanted a place to spend the night with this girl who belonged to Dada Segbo.

Now, he put the dead body in the house which they gave him, and went inside with it. At cockcrow, (sunrise) he left the body there and went away. At six o'clock, he came back to the house and began to wail.

'The people here killed Dada Segbo's wife! They killed her, Dada Segbo's wife! What shall I do? What am I going to tell Dada Segbo?'

The Head of the family now called together all the people. The people said, 'YO is lying. This woman was dead when she came here. No one saw her. No one went near her. YO is deceiving us.'

YO said, 'I dare not take this dead body to Dada Segbo. I must have another girl as fine looking as she.'

So all of the old people came together and talked this over. They said, 'We cannot anger Dada Segbo. YO says he brought this woman here alive. Now she is dead. She died in our country. We must find another woman.' And since the King of that country had a fine young daughter, they said that he must give that one to YO for Dada Segbo.

YO began to wail again. 'what shall I do? What shall I tell Dada Segbo?'

But they gave him the girl, and he went on his way. They came to a village called Bodenu-Mawu-Bode. From there YO sent a message to Dada Segbo that with one cowry he found a wife for Him.

The girl began to sing,
'Hungry come from afar,
Hunger has followed the road here;
The intestines come from afar
The intestines have followed the road here.'

Now Dada Segbo had many, many dishes cooked. He sent many men to meet YO on the way. So the girl and YO had much food.

When the food came, the girl said, 'swallow it fast.' And when the girl said this, the food disappeared. YO was amazed.

So the girl and YO arrived at a place called Todogba. YO sent another message to Dada Segbo asking for more food. Dada Segbo sent him much food, more than before. There were six hundred and forty calabashes of food. There was water. There were bowls of palm wine.

When the girl saw the food coming, she began to sing the same song again. And when the men and women came near with all the food, the girl called out, 'swallow fast,' The food vanished.

YO said to Dada Segbo's people, 'This woman amazes me. She never eats with her hand. But, when she says 'swallow fast!' the food disappears.' He sent a message to Dada Segbo saying he wanted forty guns and powder, and eight hundred calabashes of food.

When the girl saw this new food approaching, she began to sing the same song. The people went back to tell Dada Segbo that the girl was too much for them. The moment she saw food come, she had but to say, 'swallow fast!' and everything vanished.

But YO sent still another message to Dada Segbo that he wanted food. This time he asked for three thousand calabashes. This food came. Now, the girl did the same thing, and when she made the food disappear, she began to eat the men. The moment she saw a man approaching, she called out 'Swallow fast!' and the man was not seen.

A man hurried to tell Dada Segbo that the girl was too evil. She had finished the three thousand calabashes, and now was doing away with the men. Dada Segbo called all his counselors. They said, 'It is terrible to have a beautiful woman like this who eats people. It is very strange.'

They brought the girl to Dada Segbo. All the people of the country gathered before the King's door to see her. But the moment this girl fixed a man with her eyes and said, 'swallow fast!' the man disappeared.

Dada Segbo asked his Chief Advisor, 'What shall we do now? Here is a girl who eats much, and is not satisfied unless she eats men too. What shall we do?'

The Chief Advisor said, 'This woman knows only to kill. Let us kill her. YO has no family, so he is no man to send to find a wife.'

In olden times, one needed only to have a cowry to marry, but with that one cowry, a man often got a woman who was a Witch. That is why today, in order to marry, a man must have much money." End of story.

If we followed the story carefully, especially YO's actions, we saw that each one of his actions are related to the others. And each step formed a line that led him to his goal of finding a beautiful wife for the King.

Take special note that at each step of the way, YO used a trick to lead him to the next step. And most importantly, we saw that YO, like LEGBA, did nothing without being paid.

This made the story a logical line of voodoo-logic in a very simple form in which children can easily understand how it works.

It also teaches the children the kind of problems that can arise in this way of thinking. So we can see, in the story-game, the idea is to make the children think, and this story tells them how to think; using the 'Art of Voodoo-magic.

Which in turn will give them a foundation from which to understand Legba; and through LEGBA, Fa Divination, and the other Gods and Goddesses as well when they grow up into adulthood.

In this way, the riddles, and especially the YO stories teach the children about the spiritual approach and attitude of their Families, which is also the approach and attitude of their Ancestors.

At the same time, it gives them some insight into Voodooism. This begins when they are about five or six years of age, and lasts until they reach puberty, or throughout their childhood.

Thus is the form of education that lays the foundation of the children's spiritual growth in voodoo magic.

But from an educational point of view, we should take special note that this education takes place while the children are playing a game and having fun. Also, YO stories are designed to be funny to the Fon's sense of humor.

On the other hand, this story teaches a traditional rule of the Ancestors about things held in high value in the community. 'Don't be cheap, for you get what you pay for' and, 'No matter how slick a person is, there is always some one strong enough to blow your mind;' as the Witch did to YO.

But all children's stories are not about YO and his activities; there are other such stories that teach things like 'Friendship;' which is also related to LEGBA, as in the following story.

"There was a Hunter who hunted. This man was also a good farmer. So his best friend came and asked him to work in his field. He named the day. The Divination Priest came and asked him to come to work in his field. He named the same day. And his father-in-law came and asked him to come to his field. And he too, named the same day as the others. (Meaning the man was committed to work for three different people on the same day).

The day arrived. He (the Hunter) took his gun. He hunted for a long time. As last, he shot at an animal. But he did not even go to see whether he did or did not kill it. He left at once for his father-in-law's field.

He went to his father-in-law and he said, "my Divination Priest told me to come today to work on his farm, and my best friend too. Now, when I knew this, I went hunting to kill an antelope for you, my father-in-law. But when I shot, I killed a man."

The father-in-law said, "I don't want to listen. I don't want to hear anything about it. You went and killed a man belonging to the

King, and now you come to hide here? I don't want to know anything about it."

Very well, He went to his Divination Priest. 'You commanded me to work your field today. My father-in-law also asked me, and so did my best friend. I wanted to kill an antelope for you, but when I shot, I killed a man.'

The Priest said, "Ah, you and I have nothing to do with each other. You gave me your money, and I give you your destiny. You went and killed a man belonging to the King, and now you come here to hide? Go. You cannot hide in my house."

So he went away. He went to his friend. He said, "My friend, your day came. But my father-in-law also asked me to work his farm today, and my Divination Priest, too, named the same day. I wanted to kill an antelope for you, so that you might cook it for the people who came to work your field. But I shot a man." Very well". His friend said, "What? Did you tell anyone you killed a man?" He said, "No, I told no one."

So the friend said, "All right." He (the friend) took his hoe. He said, "Let us go and bury him." So they went to the forest. His friend did not even ask him the place where he had killed the man. He began to dig the grave. When he finished digging the grave, he said, "All right. I have finished the grave. Let us go where the man is."

The hunter said, "No, I don't want to go there. The place where I killed the man is over there."

So the friend went there. When he arrived, he hunted through the forest, and he separated the branches of the low bush until he came on a dead antelope.

The hunter said, "In the life that MAWU gave me, I wanted to know whom, among those three, one could follow until death, friend, Diviner, or father-in-law. Very well, He said, "I told this to my father-in-law. I told this to my Diviner. When I went to my father-in-law, he would not even let me tell him what happened. He said that he did not want to hear anything about it. I must get away at once, the same thing with my Diviner."

In life, when deciding among Diviner, father-in-law, and friend, one should always rely on the friend and leave the others to one side. It is the Friend Who is the First." End of story.

This story shows still another way the children are taught about LEGBA. By them teaching them His qualities, they will grow up to hold friendship as one of their highest valued beliefs. This is also the case with the YO stories, which are designed to teach the children voodoo-logic as one of their highest valued beliefs.

On the other hand, there are stories that teach the morals and ethics of their Ancestors, and why they should be respected. For example, in the following story, we will see how these values can solve problems of life. In the story, we must keep in mind that the word "Tohosus" is the name of the 'Spirit of the ancestors' of one's 'Extended Family.'

There was a girl whose mother died, and whose father gave her to his second wife to look after. One day the girl broke a water jar that belonged to this woman. Now, there was a stream some twenty-five miles from where they lived. The girl was sent to fetch water from that stream and she knew she would be eaten by the wild animals. For this was the stream where wild animals ate nothing but human beings.

This woman (the girls step-mother) had a son who was almost a man. She forced the orphan (girl) to go for the water. She thought, 'when the girl goes, she will not come back. She will be eaten by the animals, and all the possessions of the father will go to my own son.'

The girl went on her way until she came upon two stones fighting. The stream from which she was to get water was called Azili. The girl asked of the stones, 'which is the road to the Azili?' The stones said to her, 'one does not go there for water. It is forbidden. You cannot go there.'

The girl begged them, and she said, 'My mother is dead. My step mother mistreats me. I broke her water jar, and she sent me to get water from the Azili.'

The stones asked her, 'did you see anything just now?'

The girl said, 'no, I saw nothing.'

They said, 'all right, come between us, and we will keep you from falling.' She placed her feet between the two stones, and they immediately began to roll against them. They crushed the girl's feet until blood ran. The stones asked, 'do you see anything? Are you hurt?'

The girl said, 'no, I see nothing. I am not hurt.'

So the two stones showed her the road and she continued on her way. Then she met an old woman who took off her head, and began to pick louses out of it. The girl greeted the old woman.

The old woman asked her, 'where do you come from?'

The girl said, 'my stepmother sent me to get water from the Azili.'

The old woman asked her, 'child you see anything?' The girl said, 'No.'

The old woman said, 'go. There is your road.'

She walked on until she came to a crossroad. At this crossroad sat a woman whose body was covered with running sores. The girl asked her the way to the Azili.

The woman said to her, 'come and clean my wounds with your tongue. When you have done this, I will show you the way.' She did this and the old woman showed her the road.

She went on her way until she came upon two buffalos who were attacking each other. They said to the girl to come between them and they would not attack her. The girl came between them, and then the buffalos showed her the way. They said, 'here is the stream. The 'Tohosu' are there,' (as we mentioned, Tohosu is Ancestor. However, when some of them died, they became guards of the river Azili, between the land of the living and the dead).

The girl came to the banks of the stream and saw the Tohosu. One of them was bathing. He said to the girl, 'dry my back.' Now the back of the Tohosu was covered with knives, broken bottles, thorns and the claws of wildcats. The girl began to dry his back with her hand. When she did this, her hands were badly cut. The Tohosu asked her, 'is there anything the matter with you?'

The girl said, 'nothing.'

He gave her some water to wash her hands and when she washed them, her wounds disappeared. The Tohosu said to her, 'you are not leaving today. You are to sleep here.' At the house, he gave her a grain of corn and told her to grind it. This one grain gave much meal. He had her cook it, and everybody at the house ate some of it.

Then she went to sleep. They put her with the animals, and at night the goats urinated on the girl. The next day the Tohosu asked her, 'what happened to you during the night?'

The girl said, 'I slept. I know nothing.'

The Tohosu said to her to go to the stream, and he said, 'now there are little gourds there (very small pumpkin type fruit), and among those little gourds, the ones that say 'gather me' you must not gather.

But from among those that are silent, take seven. Then go and get water from the river.' They told her, 'when you are on your way, if you come onto something that obstructs your path, break a little gourd; and after three miles break the second.'

She walked on until she came to a closed road. She broke a little gourd, and at once the road opened. She broke the second and she saw many people appear. These at once began to cultivate fields.

She broke the third, and more people appeared who began to put up houses. She broke the fourth, and many women came, and animals. She broke the fifth and she saw large animals, like cattle and horses. When she broke the sixth, she came into possession of much money and gold.

With the seventh, she saw appear many storied houses everywhere, and hammocks and everything needed for a King. The water is no longer on her head. The jar was taken away by another. She is carried away by two hammock-bearers. Forty men accompanied her to her stepmother, to bring the water for which she was sent.

The stepmother greeted the girl, and was greatly amazed to see her arrive in this manner, accompanied by so many men. She gave her water to drink and spoke to her nicely. The girl refused the water. She (the stepmother) said, 'why are you angry with me, my girl?'

The girl said, 'no, I do not live here any longer. I have my house. I live now on the road to Azili.'

The stepmother said, 'all right.'

After having given the water to the stepmother, the girl went back to her own house. When the girl went away, the stepmother was very angry and she began to beat her own child. She said to him, 'here, now an orphan became rich. You, too, must go for this water so that you, too, may become rich.'

The boy did not want to go. To force him she went and brought some water, and placed it in front of him, so that he would be sure to break the jar and spill the water when he got up. He was asleep, and he did not know that the water was there.

He rose and as he did so, the jar broke and the water was spilled. The next day the mother was very angry. She said, 'you must go for the water today. If you do not go, I will give you nothing to eat. You will go hungry till you go.'

The boy went. On the road he came on two stones fighting together, just as had happened to the girl. All that the girl came across on the road, the boy too encountered.

The two stones asked, 'what do you see?'

As the boy was not discreet, he told them, 'I saw two stones fighting together.' Now, he said what should not have been spoken. 'ah, I never saw that before. But it's terrible all the same for two stones to be fighting.'

He continued on his way. He went along and saw an old woman take off her head, and busy herself picking louses off it.

The old woman asked him, 'where do you come from?'

As the boy was tired, not having eaten all day, he said, 'I am on my way to look for water, the water from the Azili.'

The old woman asked him, 'did you see something?'

The boy said, 'I am not blind. I saw an old head put down, and lice searched in it.' Now, he should not have said that.

The old woman said to him, 'so you are like that. All right.' She showed him the road.

He next came on two buffalos fighting. The two said, 'place yourself between us.'

The boy asked, 'but what for? I am not strong enough to fight against two buffalos

They said to him, 'alright, go ahead. Here is your road.'

The boy said, 'I must pass on. I did not ask you the way. I know my way.'

He went on and met a girl who had the plague. The boy asked her about the road to the Azili. The girl called to him to come and clean her wounds first, but the boy said, 'what do you take me for? I am not a fool. I am a stranger, and you ask me to clean your wounds!'

The girl said to him, 'all right, go on your way. Here is your road. You will see the chief of the Azili.' The boy reached the stream. There was the Tohosu bathing. The Tohosu asked him, 'what do you see?'

The boy said, 'it is terrible. You have knives, needles, broken glass, and thorns in your back. And now you ask me to dry your back, so that I should cut my hands. I did not come here to cut my hands.'

The Tohosu said, 'all right. You will see what you are looking for.' He showed him the road to the house. He said, 'all right, you will leave tomorrow morning.'

The boy said in anger, 'if you do not want to give the water, let me go back. Why should I stay here overnight?' He gave him a grain of corn. The boy said, 'what am I to do with one grain of corn?'

The Tohosu said, 'you are to pound it.'

The boy said, 'at my house, one gives this to chickens.'

The Tohosu said to him, 'all right.'

At night, he put him in a room with the goats. The boy protested, 'do you want me to sleep here? The goats shit everywhere. Where am I going to lie down?' The boy went to sleep.

During the night he began to cry out that the goats were urinating on him. He said to the Tohosu, 'it seems that you never gave birth to a child.'

The Tohosu said, 'why do you say this?'

The boy said, 'because you told me to sleep with the goats, and you yourself took a clean place. I could not sleep. And I believe that you slept well.'

The Tohosu said to him, 'you are a bad boy. You are good for nothing. You will see the reward of a bad boy before you leave. Misfortune always has friends.'

The next morning, he was sent to see the little gourds. Now, one should never gather the little gourds that ask to be gathered. One should take those that are silent.

Now, the Tohosu asked him to take seven of those that spoke. The boy went to take them. The Tohosu also told him to go and get the water.

After three miles, he broke a little gourd. When he broke it, the road closed and the boy could not pass. He wandered about in the forest like a blind man and did not know where to go. The boy began to cry and cry.

He broke the second little gourd. The road opened a little. He was on the road. After four miles he broke the third one. When he broke that, he found himself facing a river. At the stream he broke the fourth, and when he broke this he found his road. He went on again. He broke the fifth, the road closed again.

And many animals appeared, Panthers, Lions, and Elephants. Observing the situation was a hunter in a tree. The panther asked the boy to tell him what he had been about. The hunter was watching them. The boy was sized by the animals, before he could even break the seventh gourd.

And that is why one should not mistreat and annoy orphans. Now the hunter who saw the animals devour the boy, went home to the boy's mother and told her his fate." End of story.

This story shows that regardless of being in a bad situation, if one follows the morals and ethics of society, things will work out for the best.

However, just as important, the story has symbolic value, What is meant by getting water from the river, Azili, that stands between the land of the living and the Ancestors? This is a subject we will deal with much later, but we should keep it in mind.

Anyway, there are hundreds of YO and other children's stories, and the children are taught them throughout their childhood years. And as we mentioned before, all the stories have messages of morals and ethics of personal and social conduct.

But the point we wanted to make is, if we add the values told in the stories, to the knowledge gained from the children's imitation and observation of grown-ups, then we can begin to see that their childhood education is a foundation from which to become good Fon-men and Fon-women in Society.

This brings us to the next cycle of life, the Puberty years or sexual development years (we call teenage years).

Fon Puberty education system

Now that we have seen the Friendship and Voodoo-magic teachings about LEGBA, we will next investigate the God of Sexuality side of His Nature: With special focus on the Fon's sexual code and the man-woman relationship; and how all of this fit into their education system.

According to Fon's beliefs, children sexual development, both physically and mentally, begin at about the age of 10 or 11 years of age, some early and some later.

This is about the time they begin having sexual fantasy-dreams. The boys start becoming like LEGBA, always ready for sex, even at this early age it is a major subject in their thinking. About the same age, the girls begin growing breast, having menstrual periods, along with their sex fantasy.

As the Fons say, when this begins to happen, childhood is over, and sexuality takes control. It is the time when the children's sex education should begin, especially the girls.

To the Fons, sex education is more than just teaching the children about the act of sexual intercourse, it concerns the nature of Male sexuality and manhood, and female sexuality and womanhood, and at the same time, the relationship between the two; for example, the man-woman relationship.

The Fons also believe that Manhood and Womanhood covers a much bigger area than just the sexuality of the man-woman relationship: For instance, fatherhood and motherhood, and the bringing into reality, and educating, the next generation. All of which is in the spiritual domain of SAGBATA, as the God of Family.

Grandpa knows that all of this sounds complicated, but it gives us some idea of the dimensions of the Fon's beliefs concerning manhood and womanhood, and at the same time, helps us to understand their sex development and education that takes place in the children's puberty years, or teenage years, from about 12 to 20 years of age.

Although our major interest in on the spiritual side of the children education, in order to show the imitation and observation side, we must get a picture of the physical organization of the Fon's family-society.

The Fon's family is organized the same as the Igbo, towns containing the father' extended family, and the wives live in the town of their husbands. While the family unit, a man and his wives, consist of a walled homestead containing the husband's house and a house for each of his wives, who are farmers and warriors.

Throughout childhood the boys and girls live in the house of their mothers, although the boys go to work the farm with their fathers, and the girls with their mothers.

For the most part, the boys and girls play together without the Parent's close supervision. But at about the age of 10 or 11 this comes to an end, like we said, sexuality takes control of the children's minds, and the parents have to deal with it.

First off, at about this age, the boys must work together to build themselves a house inside the homestead, following the examples of their fathers, and move out of their mother's house.

Although each will continue to eat their meals at the house of their mother, they will spend their early puberty years in the house they built for themselves without supervision, or help from their older brothers, fathers or uncles.

And no matter how the house looks, they take pride in it, and the older people praise them, which gives the boys a certain amount of independence.

Still following the example of the grown up males, the boys also pick one of themselves to be the head of their house, their family-head so to speak, like a play-chief.

They are expected to govern themselves, with the older males correcting them if they are seen to be getting too far out of line. This is the boys first step into manhood.

Physical manhood, according to Fon's beliefs, consists in part, in knowing how to do four things very well, make a farm, build a house, be a good warrior, and contribute to the self-help system of their extend family.

By helping their fathers in the fields throughout their childhood, means that by the time they are this age, they pretty much have a good idea of how to make a farm.

And by building a house by group effort, they learn two things, they learn how to build a house, and they learn the value of self-help by working as a unit.

During their early puberty years, the boys also form little hunting parties, again like the grown up males, and hunt small animals like rabbits and edible birds, and have their mothers cook them.

Plus, the boys have their games of wrestling, running and jumping, sparing with sticks and shields, lifting weights, sling and stones (we call a sling-shot); and then they have homestead war-games.

The boys in one homestead have a mock fight with the boys of another homestead, under the supervision of the older males who give pointers here and there about Warriorship. And the best performers in these war activities are marked out for future war leadership.

All of this type training is in the form of fun and games, in the spare time, between still helping their fathers in the field. However, in the evening, as the sun is going down, the boy games change, and become boys looking for girls from a sexual point of view.

Thus is the nature of the transformation from childhood to early manhood, and we should take special note that the boys are not taught directly about sex.

Meanwhile, the girls are moving along the same kind of lines in making the transformation from childhood to womanhood.

For example, the girls in their childhood learn the art of cooking, washing, how to care for the house and babies, and go with their mothers to work on the farm. They learn the codes of morals and ethics taught by the Ancestors, and of course, contribute to the extended family self-help system. They too, must have the Heart of a Warrior; all of which lays the foundation of womanhood.

But there are two more steps in learning before a girl can become a woman as defined by Fon women. A woman must also know business (the art of trade), and just as important, know the art of sexuality in the man-woman relationship.

Thus is what Fon girls must learn in their puberty years, how to become economically independent, and detailed knowledge of the sexuality of womanhood. They must learn the "Wisdom of the Womb.

When Fon girls breasts first begin to develop, but before they have their first menstruation period, they stop helping their mother with house and farm work. Some remain in their mother's house, while others live with their grandmothers on their father's side. They are divided into groups of 10 to 15, from a number of homesteads, under the guidance of an economic and sex Teacher.

This Teacher is usually one of their younger Aunts or older cousins of the homestead, about 20 to 25 years old, who have a successful marriage (man-woman relationship), and have had at least one baby.

The 10 to 15 girls are to be under this Teacher's control throughout their puberty years until they marry. Note that the Teacher is about 10 to 12 years older than the girls, and are not their mothers. This makes communication between Teacher and student easier because of the closeness of their age. So, unlike with the boys, the Fon girls actually go to a regular school for at least 4 or 5 years, and are under their Teacher supervision even longer.

From an economic point of view, the Fon woman, like women all over Africa, play a big role in the general market place, and always have the opportunity to become economically independent.

The money made from her personal farm, and things sold in the market are her own, and not part of 'family money.' This economic independence is a big part of their beliefs about womanhood.

Even when a girl is in childhood and went to the market with her mother, she was given small articles to sell, like chewing sticks (African toothbrush), small cakes, etc, etc.. And the little money she made was her own to do with as she wished, even at the tender age of 5 or 6. Her mother would give her pointers about money-management.

And as she enters her puberty years, under a Teacher, making money and management continues as part of her schooling.

With supplies provided by the Parents, like salt, soap, chewing sticks, cornmeal, and flour; the Teacher makes sweets, cakes, and other little food snacks. Each girl fills her little calabash with some of these articles and goes about selling in the village or, on marked days, to the market.

If for example a girl does not do well selling one kind of article, the next day she is given another. This goes on until she finds something she is good at selling.

Now that we see how serious Fon women are about their economic independence, as far as their husbands are concerned, this should give us some insight into their independent state of mind.

Which brings up the questions, what effect does female independence have on sex education, as well as in the man-woman relationship? But more importantly, what do we mean by 'independent?

By independence, we mean that in the community as a whole, women are of equal value to men, or, we could say it the other way around, men are of equal value as related to women. Unlike in other places in the world where women are thought of by men and women as being inferior to men.

Therefore, this means that women maintain their values as women, and men maintain their values as men. And as far as the man-woman relationship is concerned, women maintain their half, and men their half, and both maintain the harmony between the two. Each knows the value of their values from the point of view of manhood and womanhood.

However, in this area of relationship of dependency, the question becomes, what is the nature of the "love" or "romantic" side of the man-woman relationship? We will answer this question in the following two long stories.

The first story is about a girl, 'Ahwala,' who had finished her education in sex, misused her new found knowledge, and the results that followed.

On the other hand, the story will show how a young girl 'gets herself a man;' it also shows it is the responsibility of the man to maintain control of the situation.

Although the story deals with the Priesthood, and a Priest trainee named 'Hundjo, it shows the power and dept of the love provided by a woman in the man-woman relationship.

At the same time, the story is interesting in the sense that it also shows the morals and ethics of conduct concerning female and male sexuality, as well as those in the man-woman relationship; and it has a happy ending.

However, the theme of the story concerns the Spirit King of Kings of all Aja land, Metonofi, and making rules favoring the man-woman relationship among young Priest and, or, Priestess: Now for the story.

"Ahwala and Hundjo"

"Long go, if a child was 'called to be a Priest' by a God, he went at the age of twenty to live with the Priest of that God's Temple for eight years. After eight years they gave him a wife. Formerly a man was married at twenty-eight. Both men and women entered these Temples for eight years. In those days, no one saw them. The Priest provided food for them.

There was a woman and a young girl, who sold cooked food and cakes. Now, no one might enter where the young man was, (especially women) for he was with the Gods. But the woman, while walking, saw the man. The woman said, 'you are a fine fellow, I like you.' And the young woman entered where the young man was and she said, 'I never saw you before. Yet the moment I saw you, I wanted to have sex with you.'

The man said, 'the Priest forbade me to touch a woman.'

The girl went away. Turning her back, she threw off her cloths, and she remained in beads along. Now she went back into the Temple to tempt the man. The girl said, 'today we will have intercourse, whether you wish it, or you do not wish it.'

The boy begged her to leave. 'Here they do not do such things.'

The girl said, 'you are not a man. A real man, seeing a young girl naked, would take off his clothes and would be naked with the girl.' She sang a song tempting him.

The boy now approached the girl. They had sexual intercourse. When this was over, the boy died.

The Vudu Priest, (Priest of the God of the Temple where the boy was in training), came and gave orders that the girl should be bound.

The girl said, 'do not trouble to bind me. I am here.' When she said this, she did not rise. She remained there seated. She sat beside the dead body (of the boy) keeping off the flies.

The Vudu came to the head of another male worshipper (the God of the Temple possessed one of the Priests). He said, 'If you wish the boy to come back to life, bring three bundles of firewood, and three jars of palm oil.'

They brought the things He (the God) asked for. They dug a hole before the door leading to the Temple of the Vudu. There they put in three bundles of firewood, and they poured three jars of oil on top of that, and they lit it. This made a great fire.

The dead boy was called 'Hundjo.' They went to take his body and put it in the fire. Now all the people of the village and all the worshippers of the Vudu were gathered there.

They said to them, 'those among you, who have courage to enter the fire with Hundjo, will come out from the fire with Hundjo.' Not a man was willing to go into the fire. Not a woman among these.

Hundjo's mother rose and said, 'if it is true that my son will come back to life, I will go into the fire. He is the only son I have.' She went close to the fire, but as she smelled the fire she said, 'no, I cannot enter. If I do not die, I will bear another son.'

His (the dead boy's) brother rose and he went to the fire. He said, 'I am going to take my brother.' He approached the fire, but he, too, lost heart. 'If I am not dead, I will have another brother.' (This is not a contradiction with men having more than one wife; a woman can have one son that has brothers on his father's side).

His best friend came. 'I am going to find my friend.' He approached the fire. But he lost heart. He went back. 'If I am not dead, I will have another friend better than this one.'

Now, there was no one else willing to go into the fire. The girl Ahwala, who caused his death now rose. She took out of her sack two pipes, a small calabash, two sticks for cleaning teeth, tobacco, and matches.

Now, if the fire subsided, they added oil; they added wood.

The girl put her calabash on her head, her pipe in her mouth, the other pipe, tobacco, and matches in the hand. They poured too much oil on the fire that it was a great flame. She began to walk round and round the fire. She said, 'Now, if I did not enter the fire, I would be ashamed. 'Then she sang a song,

> If I do not go into the fire
> I will not be able to live with my soul.

After having sung her song, she threw herself on the fire. In a few minutes, the two came out of the fire alive: (The boy and girl).

All the people in the village began to beat the drum to dance.

King Metonofi ordered all the people of the village to assemble. When the people came, King Metonofi said to them, 'If a child comes into the world and is named by the Vudu, he must not be kept secluded for eight years. From this day on, the ceremony of the Vudu initiation must be concluded in three years.'

When he said this, the man and woman was there. They now took the girl and gave her to Hundjo to marry.

Long ago, a child named by the Vudu was held for eight years without seeing the sun or playing with women. As Hundjo disobeyed, that changed it. Now they keep them for three years instead of eight. The disobedience came from Hundjo.

King Metonofi (SAGBATA) was born before Destiny. Destiny does his bidding. He is Mystery. We say that about all things that exist, and that we do not see, King Metonofi, Vudu, Yo, are Mystery." End of story.

Next we will deal with a story that has the same theme as above, only this time it is a boy that breaks the rules and deal with the death over his lover.

At the same time, it highlights the kind of problems that can come about in a situation where a girl is matched with the wrong man, and cheats on her husband.

The following story concerns itself with a Son that got involved with one of his Fathers younger wives, and even though it shows a great bond between a man and woman, it ends in a soap opera type tragedy.

"Now King Metonofi had a very, very beautiful wife, if they searched far and wide, they could not have found a woman to match her beauty. So King Metonofi shut his wife up in his palace, saying that no man but himself should see her.

Now, his eldest son, who was called Degeno, climbed the wall (around the palace) and had sex with the woman. One day King Metonofi surprised his own son with his wife. He was so angry that he denounced his son and killed his wife. They threw the body of the dead woman outside.

The story says that in ancient times when a person died, the vultures came from the sky to eat the body. For the vulture is the bird of Death. Now that night Degeno armed himself with two good sticks, and sat down beside the dead body of his loved one.

When Death sent the vultures to eat the dead woman, he threatened them with the sticks. So the vultures returned to tell Death that there was a man beside the dead body who kept them from eating it.

Death said it was not true. Death now sent the great vulture called Akun. But when Akun arrived and was no higher than a house top from the body, Degeno threw a large piece of wood at it, and wounded its wing. The vulture returned to Death and said it was not possible to eat the dead body.

Now, Death called his first servant, Headache, and he ordered Migraine to measure his eyebrows. It is said that Death's eyebrows reached to the earth.

He next called Diarrhea, and he called Measles, Influenza, and Yellow Fever, and said, 'go bring my hammock.' They brought the hammock, and Death himself went to the dead body; as He sang,

Death is going to appear,
Agbla is going to appear.

When he came within a height of several feet, Degeno called out, 'stop. If you do not stop at once all the little children will know him who is called Death,' (meaning he would kill Death). He took his stick and threw it at Death.

Death came softly towards Degeno, and he asked him why he did this. Degeno told him his story, and he said he would rather die beside the body of the woman he loved, than to let her be eaten by the vultures.

Death said to him that he had decided to revive this woman, but that sooner or later this very woman would cause Degeno's death. Degeno accepted Death's proposal, and Death brought her back to life. She became beautiful as before.

Now, Death gave Degeno two horse tails, one black and one white. He said if a war came to Degeno, he should take the black tail and wave it before the attackers, and all would instantly die. If he waved the white, he would revive them. Then Death gave him seven small calabashes, and Death said to him to go off into the bush and break these calabashes when he desired.

Degeno went to the bush and broke all seven calabashes. Instantly, he beheld a great palace with many people about, herds, and riches of all kinds. There was a house where he was to stay, and it had two stories (the house of a King). He lived there for several months.

One day his wife asked him permission to go to the market in Aja land. Degeno agreed. The woman left for the Aja market. That day the King of Aja went to market. When he saw the woman, he said he would give two thousand women to have one like her. He said she pleased him very much. And the King said all that could be said to win the woman. Now, the woman could not resist the King, and she did not return to Degeno.

When Degeno did not see her, he did not eat for three days.

But the woman said to the King of 'Aja that if he started a war against Degeno, one day Degeno would be captured. Before going to market, the woman had taken the two tails belonging to Degeno to amuse herself on the way.

Now Ajahosu (King of Aja) sent at once a war against Degeno. Degeno looked for his two horse tails to make the warriors die, but he could not find them. So he was killed by the King of Aja.

His wife, the one the King of Aja kept, ordered that Degeno's head be cut off and brought to her. Now, as the woman saw that the King of Aja was a great King, and rich, she spoke ill of Degeno to please him. She ordered that the head of Degeno be placed at the foot of a tree in the middle of the palace.

Every morning the children of Ajahosu showed the two tails to the head of Degeno and said, 'Degeno, here are the two tails.'

Then the woman sang to the head of Degeno,
See if Degeno still breathes.
Does he see?
Does he hear?
No, I do not believe it."

And she sang,

"Gather up for me his fat,
With which to light my lamp;
Give me his bones,
To use as firewood

She said it to please the King of Aja. He found it strange. When he heard it, he was displeased. He too began to sing,

Women are strange;
Do you remember the watch Degeno kept
Over your dead body?
Do you recall how he watched in those days?

Death from on high sent two strong vultures to take the head of Degeno. The birds came when the children were showing the two horses tails to Degeno's head. One bird struck with its wings the small child, and took the two tails. The second took the head, and they flew away.

They brought all this to Death. Death revived Degeno and gave him the two horse tails, and the birds were commanded to bring him down to earth. Degeno arrived with a great army, and sent a war to bring back as slaves the King of Aja and his wife.

Now, when they came, Degeno had these two brought before his court. The King of Aja said before Degeno's court that it was the woman who had wooed him, and the woman said it was the King of Aja who had wooed her. Degeno then gave great gifts to the King of Aja, and said that he could return to his kingdom, He had done no wrong. He said, 'I, Degeno, would do the same for a woman as beautiful as she.'

Now, he (Degeno) went to his house. He dug a hole and he covered it with a mat. On top of this he put down his pipe. Now, he told his women that when he sent for his pipe, it should not be one of them who is to bring it to him, but the woman whom the King of Aja had taken away.

Now, when the moment arrived, he asked for his pipe, and the wife that the King of Aja took from him, and hurried to bring it. At once, she fell into the hole. Now Degeno began to throw stones at her. Then he threw cloths, and cowries, as he sang,

> All that we have said,
> I shall never forget;
> We have talked of the pieces of cloth,
> here they are.

He threw them into the hole. He did the same with the beads and oil, and corn. Everything that must be given the dead, he gave. Now, when he had done this, he closed the hole (buried his wife).

Then He made a figure of a woman out of earth, there on the grave, and he made a roof over it, and he called it HWELI. This is the Vudu (Goddess of morals) of the woman of a household. She watches over women.

Where there is a HWELLI shrine in a house, She will keep the women who lives there from committing acts like these. And it is forbidden to this day to take an oath of HWELI." End of story.

The above stories give us an idea of the great depth of the spiritual bond that the Fons believe should be the foundation of the man-woman relationship. It also gives us some indication of the rules of conduct to maintain the commitment to this spiritual bond.

At the same time, it shows what is to define what this spiritual bond means; two people, a man and woman, making sacrifices to each other, even to the death. Thus is what the older teenagers are taught about the approach and attitude towards 'spiritual harmony' (love) in the man-woman relationship.

Marriage and family

Grandpa thinks that we will find the subjects of marriage, and married life a very interesting affair in all of Africa, and the Fons are no exception.

For unlike in America, they believe in, and practice what is called "polygamy marriage," where a man has two or more wives at the same time.

Although African women have a very strong sense of "sisterhood" as we saw with the Igbo; just imagine the cross current of positive and negative feelings involved with one husband and five or six wives living in one homestead.

An understanding of this situation will not only give us a deeper insight into the man-woman relationship, but also into the family unit itself. For example, the relationship between children that have the same father and different mothers, and grandfathers and grandmothers on their mother's side of the family.

We will get into this subject in detail in the section of the book that deals with the Secree, another Ancestor nation in West Africa; but we are getting ahead of ourselves again.

Plus, there is the issue, if one man has so many wives, it seems that there will be lots of men that can't have a wife at all; which has a different effect on the man-woman relationship.

For instance, women are in such high demand, a woman can always get another man, while it is very hard for a man to get a woman in any case. All of which gives a woman a lot of power in the relationship.

Then there is the big role that the woman's family plays in the marriage, and married life. For not only do they, in some cases, decide who the woman is to marry, but also a woman can be divorced from her husband by her family, whether she wants to leave or not.

This does not mean that women do not marry whom they choose, it is only an example of the kind of power a woman's family has if they want to use it.

The real consequences of this family control, is that the family must get paid in all kind of ways. As we mentioned, women are of high value in African society, and the family does not give up their daughters without some kind of compensation.

On the other hand, we will look at courtship and the marriage ceremony as an educational process that teaches the young men and women about the nature of the relationship between families. And the role of the man and woman to be married play in these in-law families. All of which sets the pattern of the man-woman relationship, and the married life that follows.

That is to say, after marriage, this man-woman relationship spiritually bonds their children to themselves, to their parents, and the families of their Grandparents, and becomes a big Extended Family, and marriage is the first step in the process. All of which relates to the Doctrine taught in the Temple of SAGBATA.

Therefore, we can see why the Fons are so serious about sex and the man-woman relationship; it is the foundation of their Society. And this is the area which concerns the Ancestors more than anything else, marriage and family life.

In this sense, the Ancestors are the enforcers of SAGBATA's moral code of conduct, which is the source of 'Ancestor's morals and ethics of family and social values.

Well Fellow Detectives, Grandpa has finally found a place to begin using some of our family names again; and bring your Great Grandpa Ben and Great Grandma Bertha into the picture, and follow them from marriage and the rest of SAGBATA's Seven Cycles of life. At their Funeral, we will also get more insight into Ancestor Worship; to answer your parents questions on the subject.

We will use the first names of your great grandfather and grandmother; from the time they got married to their deaths, funerals, burials, and finally, follow them into the spiritual world of Ancestors.

This should be fun and interesting all in one. Grandpa knows that you have wondered what the Ancestors do, and how they "live." Well we are going to find out; but we first must get Ben and Bertha married and on the long road to their funerals.

We are going to say that Ben and Bertha grew up in neighboring villages, and had many opportunities to get to know each other real well in their puberty years.

And we will say that they had a teenage crush on each other. So a few months after Ben's circumcision ceremony, they decided to get married.

This brings us to the interesting subject of the time-consuming traditions, and mandatory symbolic gifts, which give birth to the engagement and marriage of Ben and Bertha.

The first obligation Ben must perform, is one of showing respect. He makes a casual visit to Bertha's father (Thomas Talton), the head of her family, to seek permission to begin courting her.

Tradition calls for her father to say no!, and force Ben to tell him of his intentions; naturally Ben's response is that he wants to get married, to which Bertha's father again says no! This time to force Ben to show his mental abilities by convincing him that he can be a good husband. This conversation can go on for hours, even days, with Bertha's father saying no at every turn, and not giving the reasons why.

Bertha's father continues to say no until Ben is sharp enough to see what it will take to convince him. At which time he pleads that Bertha's father consult his Divination Priest and ask LEGBA if the marriage will be a good one.

If her father himself is convinced, he agrees. Some time later, after consulting his Diviner, and LEGBA's answer is positive, Bertha's father sends a message to Ben, "take good care of your mother-in-law." as a way of saying he gives his permission for the marriage.

Next, Ben makes an official visit to Bertha's father; this time he is accompanied by his mother, oldest sister, an Uncle and Grandfather, and brings with him a sack of corn, some palm-wine, tobacco, matches, and some money.

When Bertha's father receives these symbolic gifts, he divides them as follows. The tobacco and matches are distributed among the Elders of Bertha's family; the wine is poured as libation to Bertha's Ancestors; the sack of corn is given to Bertha's mother; and the money, her father keeps for himself.

These gifts symbolize an agreement between the two families of Ben and Bertha to their getting married. Ben is now officially engaged to Bertha, and now must begin to perform the traditional obligation he owes to her family as part of the courtship.

These traditional obligations are in three parts, those to Bertha's father, mother, and at the funeral of close members of her family. The obligation to her father consists of, for example, if his fields need clearing, or the ground turned, Ben would get some of his friends, and get the job done. Or, for instance, her mother's house needs a new road, likewise, Ben and his friends get the job done.

But by far, the biggest obligation of all, are those own to the funeral of one of her parents or grandparents. Even after marriage, as a son-in-law, Ben's funeral obligations are continued, (We will deal with this subject later, when Ben and Bertha get old, die, and have their own funerals).

Meanwhile, when the family of Bertha is satisfied that all obligations are fulfilled, which could take a year or more, Ben calls his Diviner and consults LEGBA on the day for the wedding ceremony.

After which, the Chief of Bertha's Clan (your great great grandfather George Talton), orders the marriage ceremony to be performed; which covers three or four days.

First day: Ben brings Bertha's Clan Chief, not her father, seven hundred and twenty cowries; one large man cloth; one woman cloth; a sack of salt; and a castrated goat ten to twelve years old that stands about two feet high.

Her Clan Chief sacrifices the goat to Bertha's Ancestors, to inform them that their daughter is to be married.

The salt is given to the household, as a symbolic act to preserve and give flavor to the future relationship between their families.

The cowries are thrown into the house where Bertha's Ancestor shrine is kept so they may be of use to the Ancestors "for the purchase of goods in the market of the dead."

The large man's cloth goes to Bertha's father. It is said that this cloth serves to replace the one on which Bertha's parents lay the night when her father caused her mother to conceive Bertha, who is herself about to be married.

The small woman's cloth is given to Bertha's mother, and is said to replace the one she used when she carried Bertha as a baby on her back; when this ceremony is over, Ben returns to his homestead.

This ritual ceremony is very important, especially the sacrifice of cowries to her Ancestors. This sacrifice stays in the Ancestor shrine house of Bertha for two days, and then the same sacrifice is transported to the Ancestor shrine house in Ben's homestead where it remains another two days. And this is what makes a marriage "legal."

Second day: Ben takes a special basket, used to carry cloths. In which he puts as many women's cloths as he can afford, and some small cloths, women's beads, head ties, and almond perfume. And that night, Ben's Clan Chief (your great great grandfather George Benjamin) sends two men and two women of Ben's family to carry this basket to Bertha's father.

When they arrive they say, "The head of our clan sends us with this basket to tell you that he is hungry.

At his homestead he has corn and yams, but there is no one to prepare them for him. He asks that you send him a woman." Bertha is called, but does not come, for tradition demands that she acts as though she was bashful and reluctant to leave her mother.

While they wait, the four visitors are given food, and when they have finished, someone enters to tell them that their woman (Bertha) is lost. And that they must give a traditional gift so the searchers may be sent to search for her. The traditional amount of cowries is given, and in a few minutes, they are told that the lost one had been found.

Third day: Ben arrives at Bertha's family homestead, and all the Elders of her family assemble; he displays all of the gifts he is giving to his new bride; and puts them in a pile before them.

In another pile besides his, Bertha's family displays the belongings of Bertha, the things she bought with money she made in the market, to show that she is a good trader. As well as things given by her Father and other members of her family, things she needs to set up her future home.

At this time, one of the oldest women of Bertha's family (her great grandmother) stands between the two piles of goods, and addresses Bertha as follows,

"My girl, you are going to be married. You will bear sons who in time to come will watch over the family of your husband, and the clan of his father.

You will bear daughters who will leave you to marry into other clans, and they will spread among those to whom they go the name of the clan to which you belong.

We hope to see born of you a child who, one day, will increase the clan in which you are leaving. May the spiritual bonds of your relationship last forever, and may you never be ill while you are with him.

May you be well cared for, and may you carry the children of your grandchildren in your arms. In the name of our Ancestors, I bless you." With these words, she pours libation for the Ancestors.

After which the Divination Priest is called, and a sacrifice of a rooster, palm oil and cornmeal are made to LEGBA, His favorite meal, and the destiny of Ben and Bertha's relationship is revealed.

At this point, Ben and Bertha are half-married, and leave for Ben's homestead, escorted by the young women of Bertha's family, where the remainder of the marriage tradition is to continue.

Upon their arrival, Bertha is given a symbolic bowl of beans, and spends the rest of the day and night with Ben's mother, and sleeps in her house.

Forth day: Bertha's young married friends arrive, and the young women of her family, in a kind of house warming party. They help her set up her new house, (for Fon men and their wives do not live in the same house); which takes up most of the day.

That night Bertha spends the night in the house of Ben, and Bertha's and Ben's mothers spend the night outside their door. In what is called a 'marriage watch,' As Ben and Bertha have intercourse for the first time.

Fifth day: Upon waking in the morning, Ben sends the mat on which he and Bertha had sexual intercourse to her father to show the blood spots to show that she was a virgin.

Later in the day, a festival celebration ceremony is held to which all the friends and neighbors of Ben and his family are invited. At which time Ben gives Bertha her married name, a pet name like "honey" or some other way he thinks of her, which is the name every one is to call her thereafter, himself included.

Music is played and Ben does a solo dance of his choosing, while Bertha wipes the sweat from his face with a small handkerchief which she carries for that purpose. After he performs, everybody joins in, and the festivities and feasting continuing the entire day. Ben and Bertha are now married, almost.

The most important point we should note is that it is Bertha's and Ben's Ancestors that make the marriage legal, and it is the two families that actually perform the marriage ceremony itself.

Even to their mothers making a "marriage watch" on their "wedding night," this means that marriage is totally a family affair. However, and another important point to note, the final stage of marriage is when Ben and Bertha's first child is born.

When Ben became a man just before he was circumcised, he built a house of his own in his Father's homestead. And when he got engaged to Bertha, he and his friends not only built a house for her near his own, but also cleared a piece of land for her personal garden. And it is in this setting that they settle down to married life.

Now to keep things moving along, we will say that Ben and Bertha's marriage did not have any problems, and in a year or two they had their first baby; me, Grandpa.

Being successful both economically and relationship-wise, having a family started, they set-up a situation whereas the traditions of the Ancestors demand that Ben gets another wife.

The Ancestors demand that his first wife, Bertha, who caring for her husband, and his position in the community, should help him get his second wife. In addition, the first and second wives should work together to get his third one, and so on.

Men that have many wives are held in high esteem by Ancestors, and the community as a whole, and so are his wives.

For this reason, it is Bertha that approaches another woman that she likes, and who likes her and her husband, to join the little family.

We mentioned the strong bond of sisterhood when dealing with the Igbo; however, this bond among Fon women is much stronger.

The Fons very nature is to be warriors, including the women. They had an all woman army, as well as a male army, and, that the women's army was better warriors than the men's army was.

This means that the women had to have a very strong sense of sisterhood to promote the kind of unity needed to make an army strong. Thus is the sisterhood bond in war and marriage.

In the mean time, Ben, along with his brothers, work his father's farm and share in his father's profits, and are other wise under his father's authority. In this respect, this period can be considered to be part of Ben's education in the art of managing the affairs of a growing family.

And if Ben is the oldest son, this continues until his father's death, at which time Ben will become the head of his father's homestead and all of the families living there. In any case, the sons and fathers are tied together economically until the sons reach the stage of full fatherhood.

For an example of fatherhood, when Ben's oldest child reaches the age of puberty, which makes Ben 32 or 33 years old, the Divination Priest is called. And through LEGBA, his personal family Destiny is revealed.

Or to say, he chooses the destiny of his personal family of five wives and all of his children by them; thus marks the stage which finalizes his 'sixth cycle of life,' fatherhood.

At the same time, Bertha's womanhood is finalized, and she enters the stage of motherhood; only there is no ceremony marking the occasion; but in any case, it changes their standing in the community.

After reaching this stage, Ben and Bertha, and his other wives when their oldest child reaches the age of puberty, is considered to be mature responsible members of society. Now they can not only sit on family councils, but also can take part in the management of the village government.

Since Ben is not the oldest son, he is not in line to inherit his father's homestead; therefore, he establishes a homestead of his own, for he is now qualified to be a Family Head.

In any case, Ben now takes full control of his economical affairs; he stops working for his father and make a farm of his own. If he has chosen to follow a trade, like blacksmithing, hunting, weaver, etc, etc., he now establishes himself in that profession. He can also hold high positions in the army.

But most important of all, he can now have his own shrine to LEGBA, and one for his Ancestors. This means that Ben, at this stage, takes over the control of his personal spiritual affairs from his father.

On the other hand, Bertha returns to her family homestead to worship at the shrines of her Ancestors on special occasions; just like the Igbo.

At this point, as far as their future is concerned, there is no limit to what Ben and his wives, as a family unit, can accomplish in the Fon society if they are ambitious and have themselves together.

After saying all of that, we will now turn our attention to the dynamic forces operating within Ben's polygamy family; consisting of five wives, and his and their many children, all of whom are living in the same walled homestead.

The success of any marriage and family depends on the harmony between its members, and this harmony depends on Ben and Bertha, especially in their choices of the second, third, forth, and fifth wives.

Do they love, respect, believe in, and are willing to contribute to the direction Ben, as Family Head and leader is taking his family? Do they believe in the Destiny Ben chose for his family?

And just as important, do they believe Ben has the ability to bring that Destiny into Reality? If this is the case, family-harmony is not too difficult. Also in this kind of marriage, there is a "Chief Wife," Bertha, who has the power to maintain harmony.

But most important as far as family-harmony is concerned, does Ben himself have the ability to deal with that many women at the same time?

For example, although Bertha is his Head-wife, and Head of the female side of the homestead, he must have a tight spiritual bond between himself and his wives. Especially as far as sex and his affection for all their children, and how much money he gives each to run their household is concerned.

Keep in mind; it is Ben's responsibility to care for the welfare of his wives and children. All the money his wives make on their own belongs to them to do with as they please.

Although if they are successful in the market, they will give Ben's money as gifts to show their affection; in some ways Aja women treat their men like Pimps. We will now take up the issue of their sex situation.

After Ben's second marriage, this wife spends eight nights with Ben, as a kind of honeymoon, after which she and Bertha take turns, and, this is the way it works with each new wife as she enters the family.

For example, this means that Bertha spends the first night. The second wife spends the second night. Third wife spends the third night, forth wife spends the forth night, and the fifth wife spends the fifth night; and the cycle begins again with Bertha.

When Bertha's turn comes, like all other wives, she cleans Ben's house and cooks his dinner, then spends that night. But, she never has dinner with Ben. He the man of the house and, if other male friends or brothers are not sharing his meal, he eats along.

On the other hand, Bertha has her meals with her children, as do the other wives. This works fine as long as Ben has an attitude that each wife is of equal value to him, and therefore shows equal amounts of love for each of them. But what about the wives relationship to each other that allows them to share one husband, for this is also very important to the harmony of the family.

To some extent this depends on Bertha, as Head-wife, and shows why she has a say in who the other wives are to be, and naturally she chooses women she can dominate to some extent.

Or, in any case, the wife who can dominate, or, we should say lead, becomes the Head wife, all of this comes under the rules of the Ancestors, as for example, in the case of sex.

On the other hand, the wives relationship is one of companionship of sisterhood based on spiritual bonds to the same husband, and especially their care and support for all of his children. For example if one wife dies, the other wives take full responsibility for the dead wife's children with the aid of the dead wife's mother and sisters; according to the rules of the Ancestors.

However, for the most part, harmony between wives is maintained by the wives as a group, for instance, if one wife gets out of line, the group works together to pull her back in line.

This leaves the relationships of the children, with their parents as well as with each other; having different mothers and the same father.

We must keep in mind, unlike with the Akan where the children belong to their mother's family and clan, the Fons are more like the Igbo, where the children belong to the father's family.

And just as important, it is their father's Ancestors that provide the clay from which they are made; recall what the Doctrine of MAWU-LISA'S Temple is. Also, we must remember that children are the ultimate goal of both sides of their family.

Another point to be made is that, all of the children in a polygamy family unit have the same grand parents on their father's side, but this is not the case on their mother's side.

For instance, the children of one wife shares the same maternal grandparents, and being as there are five wives, the children are divided between five sets of grandparents on their mother's side.

After saying that, being as the children belong to their father's family and Ancestors, they, especially their father's mother and his sister take special interest in their welfare. They are the ones that make all of the children feel like full sisters and brothers in one family unit.

On the other hand, like children all over the world, their mother is the center of their life. This is not only the case in their childhood when she is their teacher and trainer, but also after they have grown up. She is still the center of their honor and respect. This is especially the case with her parents and Ancestors, who, not having the responsibilities of their physical welfare spoils them rotten.

In this respect, the children's feelings of the security and being spiritually bonded are one of belonging to one big family that has two paths to what they need physically as well as feeling special.

Meanwhile, their Father's homestead is where they spend the majority of their time. The children's social center is their grandparents on their father's side.

The boys hang around and sometimes live with their paternal grandfather, and the girls center is their paternal grandmother.

For the Ancestors say, a person's grand children are their true children. Children are the 'star of the show' in the homestead throughout their childhood, and most of their puberty years as well.

This feeling is enforced even further in the children's many visits to their particular mother parent's homestead. For it is said that all of her Ancestors rejoice on that occasion, for their mother visits her Ancestors ceremonies on a regular basis.

This means that the children are the heart, and connection link between two extended families, all of which is concerned about their welfare; thus is the position of the children in a successful polygamy family unit.

Nevertheless, we should note that the above only deals with the ideal polygamy family. With human nature being what it is, we know that any man-woman relationship, and those between families, are going to have problems of all sorts.

For instance, there is always one family member, on one side or the other, that has a "bad understanding." Which brings disharmony, no matter how hard everybody works to keep things running smooth and calm, and this leads to divorce on many occasions.

Since we took a look at the marriage ceremony, and the role the woman's family and Ancestors played, we should take a quick look at how a divorce takes place, and the role of her family and Ancestors from that point of view.

Like we mentioned, a woman always belongs to her family, and is under their protection, married or not; therefore, her family gave her in marriage and can take her away from marriage; with just cause according to the Ancestors.

Divorce is really a simple affair. Her father or her clan Chief (Grandfather or Great Grandfather) sends for her to come home whether she or her husband wants her to leave or not, she cannot refuse. And if the husband refuses to let her go, it could cause a little war between the two extended families, and maybe even grow to a big war between their clans.

A woman's father, or Clan Chief can divorce her from her husband, only according to Ancestor rules, if her husband beats and otherwise abuses his wife, and if the husband does not properly fulfill his funeral obligation to his wife's parents and grand parents.

This also occurs when a brother or cousin of the husband commits adultery with the wife of his wife's father, brother or uncle. Also, if the husband does not come in person to the annual ceremonies of the Ancestors of his wife's clan, or, if a problem develops between the husband and her father, or between any member of the husband's wife family.

The above not only shows the reasons for divorce, but also how involved the woman's family is in the process.

However, before a divorce can become final, the wife's family must return all of the gifts given to them by the husband. Especially the gifts of cowries and goats sacrificed at the shrine of her Ancestors during the wedding ceremony. Only then is she free to marry someone else, but the children remain with the father unless they are very young.

Because of the way the marriage ceremony is performed, the husband, nor his family can begin divorce proceedings no matter what his wife does.

His only recourse is to deliberately break one of the above mentioned Ancestor rules. And thereby force the wife's family to take divorce actions; if they don't he must keep her as his wife.

For the husband, his family and Ancestors are in a different position than the wife's family and Ancestors; their relationship to the children is more direct. Recall, it is the husband's Ancestors that provide the sacred clay MAWU used to create the children in the first place, therefore they cannot reject a daughter-in-law that gives them birth. So according to the husband's Ancestors rules, he cannot begin divorce proceeding against his wife. On the other hand, the Wife's Ancestors provided the sacred clay for her existence, and she belongs to them, and they make the rules on how she is to be treated in the man-woman relationship; and these rules govern divorce.

Now we can begin to get a little more insight into the nature of the man-relationship and the family it produces. It does more than just bring the next generation into reality, it is also a bond between extended families, of which the children are a living example.

Therefore in this process, with each family becoming connected to a number of other families through in-laws, all of the families in the Kingdom are connected to each other.

Thus is what is involved in Ben and Bertha's state of Parenthood. But they still have another stage in the cycle of life to pass through, Grandparenthood, which puts them on the pathway to becoming Elders of the community as a whole; the Old Wise Ones.

SOGBO TEMPLE TEACHING
Eldership and Social organization

As we saw, fatherhood and motherhood (parenthood) deals with the dynamic functions of the family unit and married life. On the other hand, grandparenthood (elder hood) deals with the dynamic functions of the community's social life in which the family unit exists.

Or to say, grandparents are the enforcers of the social laws of conduct of the community as a whole.

It is out of the grandparent group that the Village Chief is chosen, as well as the Chief's council of Elders, who have the final say on how the affairs of the community are managed, i.e., village government.

This stage of life begins when Ben and Bertha's oldest grandchild reaches the age of puberty, and they are about fifty years of age.

We will say, upon reaching this state, Ben could become a chief; and as far as our investigative direction is concerned, Ben is made chief of one of the community's "major Friend-group organizations."

To put Ben and Bertha in that position, Grandpa thinks, will give us a bigger picture in which to place the "grandparent's stage of life."

And at the same time, show us one of the major ties that bond the community together along non-family lines; for example the 'Dokpwe organization.' So in our case, Ben is destined to become a "Dokpwe Chief."

Now we move into the Doctrine taught in the Temple of SORBO. To set this up, we need some background before we define what a Dokpwe Chief is.

We will say that Ben's father is a Dokpwe Chief, and he inherits the position upon his father's death; for in Aja Kingship, the line of Chief ship passes from father to son.

The Dokpwe Chief is an official position in the Kingdom's government; this means that the installation ceremony is performed before the King. At which time his duties are spelled out to him and he is given 'Authority'. And the King gets his Authority from SORBO's Doctrine of Leadership.

After saying that, sometime before his death, Ben's father, as Dokpwe Chief, sent the name of the son he chooses to inherit his chiefship to the King or one of the Chiefs in the Royal Family.

So when his father dies, after the funeral, Ben sends his name and his father's stool of authority to the royal palace, to let them know that in a few days he will come to be made chief. And when he arrives a day is appointed for the ceremony before the King.

Now a point of interest to us, and we should keep in mind, in this ceremony, the King symbolizes Code of Ethics of SORBO the God of Work and War.

On the day of the ceremony, the King gives his Chief Spokesman a large cloth and tells him to call Ben. Upon his arrival before the Chief Spokesman, the cloth is placed over Ben's back, and he is given a necklace of red beads, his father's stool, and his father's staff of office. The Chief Spokesman then gives him a hand full of sand, and asks for his name.

'My name is Ben."

The Chief Spokesman, speaking for the King who is present at the ceremony, replies, 'From this day, you will no longer be called Ben.

You will be called Dokpwega (Dokpwe Chief). And you will command all of the young men of your village.

"However, before allowing you to take leave, let me call to your mind the ancient prescriptions of the King: The definition of Dokpwe's position and authority.

"The Dokpwe is an ancient institution. It existed before there were Kings. In the olden times there were no chiefs and the Dokpwega was in command of the village.

"The male members of the village formed the Dokpwe as today, and the cultivation of the ground was done communally. Later, with the coming of Chiefs and Kings, disputes arose as to their respective authority.

"Once Metonofi (the God King of the Earth, SORBO) was King, he was no longer able to occupy himself with such matters as seeing that men and women obtained proper burial, so he put these matters in the hands of his Chief Spokesman.

"Again there was trouble, for the Chief Spokesman was not above being bribed and, in addition, used his power to humiliate his own enemies.

"One day King Metonofi saw a column of traveler-ants enter an ant-hill, and the Ants came out with the dead bodies of their victims which they brought before a large ant, one of their officers. As he watched them, the thought came to him that the 'Dokpwega' was the man to whose job it is of whom the work of 'burying the dead.'

"The King has said that in (the kingdom of) Dahomey, a Chief must see to it that everyone holds firm where his hand rest. He has said that Dahomey is AIDO HWEDO, and the Chief is the ironworker.

"If you go home and fall asleep, and DA had cut and eaten the bar of iron which is in your custody and given to your care, you will become a lizard with a black tail.(Meaning that Ben will be put to death if he neglects his duties),

"But if you care for the iron, you will be a red tailed lizard: (if he is a good Chief, he will have a long and prosperous life).

"Dahomey is great, and must come before all else. It is because of this that the King has said, a Chief must not do as the tailor who breaks his needle and tries to sew his cloth with his finger along, for this is stupid.

"The King has said that Dahomey is a vast land, and that everyone must confine his work to the place where he lives. For this reason, it is forbidden for any of the young men who cultivate the earth to stop work in the fields while the grass remains uncut.

"The King has said that a country must be loved by its people. And that is why he has forbidden his people to migrate from one part of the country to another; since a wanderer can never have a deep love for his land.

"The King has said that Dahomey is an enemy of the entire world, and that his Chiefs must use as much force in killing an ant as they would to kill an elephant, for the small things bring on the large ones.

"The King has said that Dahomeans are a warrior people, and that, in consequence, it must never come to pass that a true Dahomean admits before an enemy that he is defeated.

"The King has said that the Chiefs represent his authority in Dahomey. Therefore, he commands you never to denounce a Dahomean before an enemy, who provokes your country, because he does not wish another dog to bark louder than his own.

"The King has said that in the region of Dahomey which you will command, there are men who are big-headed, who, though they are rivers, have the will to imitate the ocean. Such small holes must be stopped up, and you must see to it that at Abomey along the sun may shine.

"The King has said that those in position like yours, who represent his authority, often do evil things. He forbids the strong to take the possessions of the weak. This is the way of the hawk that snatches away chicks without asking permission of the owner of the chicken yard.

"The King has said that the Chiefs are like the bellows that help the iron-worker make the fire even redder. So that if any of you keep for himself the air that is necessary for the fire of Dahomey, he will be used as coal to make the iron hot.

"In closing, the King orders you to allow even the poorest man to come to him, and the stranger who has no protectors in the capital, so that he may help them. And here is the rule of Dahomey; put dust on your head and rise to vow to the King your devotion, and give us your surname." Thus is the Doctrine of SORBO's Temple.

Ben now, throwing the sand given to him over his head in accepting these duties given by the Chief Spokesman speaking for the King. He responds in a 'call and response' inter-action with the crowd and high officials witnessing the ceremony which is taking place facing the King, as follows,

       Ben: "With the help of Agasu" (first King of Abomey).
       Crowd: "He will aid you."
       Ben: "With the help of the ancient Kings."
       Crowd: "They will aid you."
       Ben: "With the help of the present King."
       Crowd: "He will help you."

Ben now turns and faces his family, and they interact in the same manner,

Ben: "With the aid of my father."
Family: "He will aid you."
Ben: "With the aid of all the Dokpwe Chiefs
Who have once lived."
King, crowd, and family: "They will aid you."
Ben: "Today is my naming day."
Crowd: "Yes ! Yes!"

Again, Ben faces the King, and makes the following statement, "I shall work! At night I shall not sleep, during the day I shall not rest, because rest is not a thing of the day and sleep not a thing of the night.

The commands the Chief Spokesman as given me I shall not forget, but shall keep them for my pillow. When the King commands anything of the War Chief, I will see to it that he has all the young men in Dahomey instantly respond.

When he goes hunting, he kills much game; when he makes war, he takes many prisoners. I praise the King! From this day forth, I shall call myself Dokpwega (what ever his new name will be)."

Without another word, Ben marches three times around the palace shouting praises of the King, which ends the ceremony; Ben is now a Dokpwe Chief, and returns to his home village.

This ceremony shows clearly the Code of Ethics of SOGBO, the God of War and Work, symbolized by the instruction given by the King's Spokesman; in this respect, the Dokpwe Chief is a High Priest of SOGBO.

On the other hand, this ceremony is what the grandparent stage is about, authority, status and power in the community; this is what the Dokpwe Chief symbolizes in one area of community control.

The Dokpwe chief is chief of organized male labor; for instance, a War Chief organizes men to fight, a Dokpwe chief organizes men to work; which means a Dokpwe Chief and a War Chief have the same amount of authority.

Although Ben was installed in office by the King and owes certain obligations to him, he is concerned with the affairs of his home village, and answers to his village Chief. However, he is not involved in any way with politics, nor is a War Chief. The Kingdom's government consists of the King and his Councilors, District Chiefs and their Councilors, and the village Chiefs and their Councilors.

As he stated in the ceremony, he is concerned with nothing but work. Any job that uses more than four workers in his village comes under his authority, all the way from building a house to having a funeral. The Dokpwe Chief organizes how the job is to be done and the men to do it.

In the ceremony, this is what Ben meant by the statement, "I shall work! At night I shall not sleep, during the day I shall not rest..." As we can see, this is one hell of a commitment to work, just as strong as a War Chief is to fighting.

Also note his statement, "When the King commands things of the War Chief (declare war), I will see to it that he has all the young men."

This means that the War Chief commands men in war time, and the Dokpwe Chief commands them in peace time; which leaves the conclusion, in Fon land, all the men are organized under a commanding Chief all the time.

Thus gives us some idea of the position a Dokpwe Chief holds, and symbolizes the position of the Grandparent position in a tightly organized society; as well as how much power the King has in Society; given by SORBO.

Now we come to how the Dokpwe organization leadership is organized, which will also give some indication of how the Fon's Society is organized around the idea of 'Friend-group.'

Upon Ben's arrival back to his home village, he appoints, with the advice and consent of the Village Chief, three Dokpwe officials to aid him in fulfilling his duties: Chief assistant who is to be the general supervisor of work projects. Next comes the official who made the arrangements and sees to it that the men show up at the work site. And finally, there is his spokesman who speaks for the Dokpwe Chief at funerals.

This shows that Ben and the Village Chief are in partnership in dealing with the welfare of the community; as he is with the King in dealing with the welfare of the Kingdom.

Now we come to the nature and purpose of the Dokpwe organization itself. The word Dokpwe means 'workingmen.' And the organization is designed to give unlimited support to help each man in his obligations to his family and community.

This is based, not on family-ties, as is the case with most of Africans, but on the brotherhood of all men; for all men belong to the Dokpwe's organization no matter what family they belong to.

A man joins the Dokpwe when he becomes an adult, about the age of 20, and really remains a member until he is too old to work; this is also the case in the army. The point is that the army and the workforce are organized the same way, and really form one complete male society.

This means that Ben, as Chief, has status, power, authority, and receives respect and obedience; his word is not questioned. No man would without serious cause, refuse the call of the Dokpwe Chief to work on whatever task is at hand.

If a man fails to respond to a Dokpwe Chief, his wives would leave him, and he would be ostracized by the whole community. And his family punished also, none of his relatives could obtain burial; when forced to see the error of his ways and seek forgiveness, he must humble himself before the Dokpwe Chief whose word he had ignored, and pay a heavy fine.

Even if a man is not called to work, and he passes where the Chief is doing a job, he must stop and ask permission to go on his way; otherwise, he must stop and help with the work until it is finished. Thus is the power the Dokpwe Chief has.

But on the other hand, Ben has strict rules on how he can use his power; note in his installation ceremony, it was made very clear that if he abuses his position, the King will have him killed.

Now lets look at how the Dokpwe organization functions, and at the same time, see the approach and attitude of the men actually doing the work; toward each other, and between them and the man having the work done.

We will take a case of a man that is about to marry a new wife. If we recall, there are a number of big jobs the man must get done in preparation.

He must do some fieldwork for his future father-in-law, and maybe put a new roof on his future mother-in-law's house.

On the other hand, he also must build a house and clear a farm for his future wife, as well as work on his or his father's farm. Plus, there are a large number of men in the same position at any one given time. This means that there is a lot of hard man-work in the Fon's community; to get this work done is the job of the Dokpwe Chief.

Now let's look at the organization in action. In our case, the man wants a field cleared for a farm to belong to his wife-to-be. Once the decision about size and location has been made, he approaches his Dokpwe Chief, Ben, with some wine and a small number of cowries for a sacrifice of the Ancient Dokpwe Ancestors; and he tells Ben what he needs.

Dokpwe Chief Ben decides how many men will be needed and appoints a day, for instance, "I will have 50 men at that location four days from now, and the man returns to his homestead; that is all there is to it.

Then Ben instructs his Assistants of the job to be done and how many men to call, and they take care of the details of making the arrangements.

The number of men he calls is always twice as many as would be actually needed for a special reason, to make the work easier and faster on all concerned.

Early on the appointed day, all the men arrive at the work site in a festival mood; carrying drums, rattles, gongs, flutes, and singing work-songs.

The reasons for the festival attitude is that the men think of the job as a great honor bestowed on them by the man having the work done by letting them help his move forward in life.

It is such an honor, that the men who are not called by Dokpwe Chief Ben, hear about what is going on, and volunteer to join in on the work-festival. By the time the job begins, Ben has at least three times the men he actually needs, and this is as planned. The work progresses as follows.

A number of men are put to the task of cutting, taking away, and burning all of the small bush on the farm-to-be. Another group breaks up the land with hoes, followed by a third group making up the rows.

One reason for the presence of the extra men is to entertain the men working with work songs and music to add rhythm to their work.

Another reason is that no man works for long periods. Well before he gets tired, one of the men doing the entertaining takes his place, and he entertains for a while. Therefore, with three times the number of men needed, we can see that nobody really works hard, and the farm is made in one day or less no matter the size.

The point is, the man whose future wife the farm is to belong, owes these workers nothing, his only obligation is to help the Dokpwe Chief, when called, in the same way.

However, if he is a man of means, he will have a feast for the men upon their finishing the job, but if he is poor, the men bring food and have a feast for him.

As we mentioned, the approach and attitude of the Dokpwe is that of it being a great honor bestowed on them to help another of their, or a neighboring village to make progress in life.

In our example, the man can afford to have a much bigger farm. And after he is married and it is harvesting time, women part of farm work, she too, has a woman organization to help her to do her work.

In this way, a man and his wives can maintain a much bigger farm than if they had to do the work along. In this way too, a man can fulfill his obligation to his family and community, as well as grow rich in the process.

The Fons, being so tightly organized, were always on friendly terms, and help each other. This also made them very good warriors in their male and female armies.

Although they had affection for each other, they did not like anybody that was not a Fon; this is the meaning, in the installation ceremony, of the Chief Spokesman's statement, speaking for the King, said;

"The King has said that Dahomey is an enemy of the entire world. And that his Chiefs must use as much force in killing an ant as they would to kill an elephant, for the small things bring on the large ones."

"The King has said that Dahomeans are a warrior people, and that, in consequence, it must never come to pass that a true Dahomean admits before an enemy that he is defeated."

Now if we add the King's statements about the war-like nature of the Kingdom to its nature of Dokpwe work force, we come to the conclusion, that the approach and attitude of the Kingdom itself is one big self-contained-war-work machine.

As we saw, their Dokpwe work group is designed to enrich the community and the individual. On the other hand, even their army of warriors, males and females, enrich the Kingdom in the sense that they too add to the wealth of the Kingdom by taking goods from other Kingdoms.

Thus is the nature of the foundation of the Fon's Society, Family, Work, War, based on the teaching in SOGBO and SAGBATA temples.

On the other hand, our example of Ben as Dokpwe Chief, deals with the nature of Grandparent's position in Society; they are the leaders of the families and community. All of this is based on the Fon's beliefs that 'wisdom and knowledge come with age,' and the grandparents have the age, and this is also the reason the Ancestors are held in such high esteem.

Thus is the role of the grandparent stage in the cycles of life, and is what Ben and Bertha were involved with throughout their old age, with their pass-time being their grandchildren. Now we will focus on the final cycle of life.

MAWU-LISA TEMPLE TEACHING
LEGBA, Friendships, Funerals, and Ancestors

Now if we define Dokpwe work group as a group of friends helping each other with their obligation, then there are hundreds of traditional non-family self-help organizations that bond the Fons into a

Society, and every Fon belongs to a number of them, males and females.

There are also large numbers of Friend-group organizations that extend well beyond the village community. There are groups of people from different villages that also form Friend-groups organizations.

In fact, the whole population of the Kingdom is inter-related through non-family Friend-group organizations of this kind. And in this way, the whole Kingdom grows in wealth and well being.

Only unlike the Dokpwe, these are not organized like the army, or have anything to do with the King. They are related to the nature of LEGBA, who, if we recall, is the God of Friendship.

Nevertheless, the organization of Friend-groups are focused on the Individual and the Community Chosen Destines, and are supported by MAWU-LISA and LEGBA as their spokesman. Because in this approach, everybody helps the individual fulfill his Destiny, and the individual helps everybody fulfill the village and Kingdom's Destiny as well.

But along with the Fon's approach and attitude of Friend-groups between non-family members, they also believe that each man and woman should have a personal *Best Friend* to help with personal affairs.

To serve this purpose, LEGBA established the institution of *'Best Friend* that goes much deeper than economics, war, and social welfare.

For example, the Best Friend has a major role in all parts of a man or woman's life. A best friend is closer than a brother is. This is the Friend that one shares the problems and joys of life.

This is also the case between women, who they trust with their deepest wishes and goals. Thus is the Doctrine from the teaching of MAWU-LISA, as taught by LEGBA through the Divination system, Fa.

This brings us to Ben and Bertha's final stage in life that deals with death, funerals, and especially their conversion to Sainthood and Ancestor Worship; the Catholic Church term for Deified Ancestors. Meanwhile, we will get more insight into the Fon's concept of *Best Friend and Friend Groups*.

Or to put it another way, we saw the other transformation rituals between one stage of life to another, for instance, all of the changes between babyhood and grandparenthood. Which leaves the question, what is the transformation from grandparenthood to that of Ancestorhood?

This process begins with one of the most interesting rituals of all, the Fon's Traditional Beliefs, the Funeral and Burial, and ends in the *Land of the Dead Ancestors*.

So we must not forget, in the installment ceremony, Ben also was instructed that "The Dokpwe Chief was the man to whom the work of burying the dead should be entrusted, a tradition that was handed down from the King's Ancestors."

This means that the Dokpwe Chief is involved in the process of the transformation from the world of the living, to the world of the dead. As well as making the Ancestors into, what the Catholic Church calls, Saints to be worshipped with Prayer. This also means, the Dokpwe Chief is also a Funeral Director.

To keep with our Friend-groups theme, we will define, and investigate, funerals and burials as a number of Friend-groups working together; this means that there is a friendship between Friend-groups.

Because no where in all of Fon land are Friend-groups more evident than when a family is confronted with the death of one of its members. The family brings a person into the world, and the family sends the same person out of the world; meaning that funerals, like births, are a Family and Friends Affair.

To go forward, we are going to say that Ben lived a long life and died of old age, and he died before Bertha. Also we are not interested in his position as Dokpwe Chief, only as a common man to get an idea of the funerals of how every man and woman in Fon's Kingdom are performed.

However, as a starting point, there are a few things we should keep in mind as we proceed with our investigation of Burials.

(1) Although Ben is Dokpwe Chief, and his oldest son Orchester Sr. is to inherit his position, his son could not be the Dokpwe Chief to handle his funeral; a Dokpwe Chief cannot officiate at his own father's funeral.

(2) A funeral is a very, very expensive thing to perform, and consumes a tremendous amount of the family's wealth, symbolized by cloths, cowries, sacrificed animals, all of which are considered a sacrifice made to the dead person.

This is an obligation sanctioned by the Gods of Society and Ancestors; in other words, giving a family member a cheap funeral shows that that member isn't held in high esteem by the family.

And this is an insult to the Ancestors and MAWU-LISA who gave that person to the family in the first place. On the other hand, the sacrifices of wealth demonstrate the great spiritual bond between a family, and its member that just died.

When we use the terms, the family who has the responsibilities and obligations, we mean Ben's wives and children, his brothers and sisters and their children; we must include also his Clan Chief, and especially his Clan Mother who also has responsibilities and obligations.

(3) We should remember that each member of Ben's family belongs to different Friend-groups. For example, if Ben has 20 children, each would belong to his or her group, and have their own Best Friend.

This means that there would be at least 20 different Friend-groups to not only participate in, but also help with the cost of his funeral. But the people that play the lead roles in Ben's funeral are,

The Dokpwe Chief, who is the Funeral Director,
The Clan Chief, who is the oldest man in the Clan,
The Clan Mother, who is the oldest woman in the Clan,
His Head Wife,
His oldest Son,
His oldest Daughter,
His oldest living Brother,
His Best Friend,
And his Divination Priest

(4) We must not forget that Fon funerals are in three parts; the burial is three days after death, the funeral is eight days later, and the ritual of Sainthood is within the next ten years.

(5) Recall in the Igbo, where one could become a living Saint. Our conclusion is that the designed purpose of all African funerals is a ritual process of transformation into Sainthood; to use a Catholic's term.

Where as the terms used by the Fons, "so and so is an Ancestor." Meaning he or she is automatically worshipped as a Saint based on whether or not that person had a proper funeral given by his family, especially his children.

And also we will now use Ben's children's names, for example, your grand Aunt Clovis, and grand Uncles Walter and Ben Jr., and of course, (me) your Grandpa, and we will include your Great Grand Uncle Willie. Now let's get on with the burial.

Burial

Let's say Ben lays sick with some old age ailment, and takes a turn for the worst, and the doctor says that there is nothing more that can be done.

At this point he is surrounded by his wife Bertha, his older children, Orchester Sr. Clovis, Ben Jr., and Walter. Including his brother Willie, and sisters Carrie and Ernie Mae, his Clan Mother, and Best Friend, who comfort and care for him until the end.

Even when death is expected, it is still a tremendous emotional shock to the family when it takes place. To deal with this first shock is the function of his Best Friend.

Ben's Best Friend's function is to comfort the family. He pulls them together emotionally, and leads them in beginning the traditional activities that must begin upon the death of one of its members.

When the family is calmed down somewhat, the Best Friend, Bertha, and Orchester Jr., take charge of preparing Ben's body. After washing, all hair is shaved from the body, and the fingers and toenails are cut, all of which are wrapped in a small cloth and place beside the body.

Meanwhile, the Best Friend produces a medium size cloth which he wraps around the loin of the body of Ben in a manner like a diaper on a baby; and sings a song like the following:

"This day I bring you the cloth I promised you;
This is the day of misfortune,
The day we spoke of together;
You knew that when war came to you,
I would not fail to bring you aid;
That is why I have come."

Next Ben's body is rolled in a special large cloth that covers him somewhat like a mummy, and placed on a mat just inside the doorway of his house. A lamp is placed beside the body, and a bottle of palm wine at his head and another at his feet. At which time, his Clan Mother and Bertha take charge of the "Death Watch."

At this point on, with the exception of one wife, no cooking is allowed in the homestead. It is the obligation of Ben's son-in-law, Clovis' husband to send as much food as it takes to feed the family throughout the burial, as well as the funeral.

At the same time, this marks the beginning of a period traditionally called "Crying Time." This is when all of the family members, young and old, gather in front of the house to pay respect to the dead.

They relieve themselves of some of the burden of pain by drumming, singing, crying, shouting, or whatever way they, as individuals, feel like expressing their grief.

That night, Ben's children, Orchester Sr., Clovis, Ben Jr., and Walter sleep on the bare ground around Ben's house as a sign of respect.

The next morning, Ben's oldest living brother, Willie, calls a family meeting to arrange for the burial. And a message is sent to the son-in-law telling them how much money is expected from each; and also to the Gravedigger and to the Dokpwe Chief.

Later, Orchester Sr., Ben and Walter, led by Grand Uncle Willie, pay a visit to the Clan Chief. Who, after calling his Divination Priest and consulting LEGBA, gives the date of the burial and funeral; for instance, the burial is to be in two days, and the funeral eight days later.

Meanwhile Ben's body remains just inside the doorway, and the Clan Mother and Bertha continue their deathwatch. While the wife that cooked Ben's last meal before he died continues to cook for him, and brings the food to the Clan Mother who places bits of food near the body for a while, and then Bertha eats them.

The rest of the food is divided equally among his grandchildren, Orchester Jr, Linda, and Elaine. Next, Ben's favorite pipe and tobacco are brought, and is smoked by the Clan Mother and Bertha.

Also from this point on, three Dokpwe members sit facing the doorway, and take turns playing the funeral drum 24 hours a day.

On the second night the Gravedigger arrives, and is given a rooster, a calabash of fresh water and another of palm wine, and four hundred and fifty cowries. This is to make a sacrifice to the SAGBATA TWINS, DA ZODJI AND NYOHWE ANANU, the God and Goddess of the earth, for permission to dig the grave. The Fon's grave are dug under the house.

A hole is dug beside the house to the desired depth, and the actual grave is a tunnel that goes beneath the house. At burial the hole is filled, and this leaves the body in its little cave.

Now the Dokpwe Chief orders six Dokpwe members to line up, three on each side, facing each other with hands interlocked; the body is place on their outstretched arms, and they sing,

"O children support this body,
By its head and feet take it up.
When a man dies, his own children
Support his head.
He who lies dead is our kin,
Come, then, and support his head."

While they sing, Ben's children, in order of age with the oldest leading, come and individually pay their respect. After which the Dokpwe, holding the body sing another song, this time;

"A little hunchback came upon
A man with small-pox on the road, and said;
My small-pox will be cured
But your hump never will be broken.
Drummer, make ready your drum stick."

As the drum plays, the Dokpwe begin dancing with the body. They are relieved by Ben's brothers until all of the brothers have "danced the body," at which time they are relieved by the six Dokpwe members; about that time, the Clan Mother sing and dances,

"Bat, oh, Bat,
Return to your perch."

This is the signal for the body to be taken to, and turned over to the gravediggers who are waiting in the bottom of the grave with Orchester Sr.

With the utmost care, they lay Ben's body, with his head pointed south towards the Sea, in the position that Orchester Sr. saw his father resting in life; Thus Ben is "Laid to Rest."

Wood is place about half way down the grave-hole, and dirt is thrown on top of this scaffolding; meaning the grave is to be re-entered eight days later for the funeral.

When the grave is closed, the Clan Chief orders Ben's wives and children, according to tradition, to come every morning from this day until the funeral, to get sand from the grave to throw on themselves. This ends the burial ceremony.

Funeral

On the appointed day, eight days after the burial, before the night of the funeral, an area is cleared outside of the gate of Ben's homestead, where two temporary houses made of mats and poles are built.

They build the houses so that they face each other with a courtyard between them called "Sacred Space of the Dead." This is where the funeral will be performed.

One of the temporary houses is for the family and their friends, and the other for the officiating Dokpwe Chief, visiting Dokpwe Chiefs, and their officials and helpers.

About 8 or 9 o'clock in the evening, around dusk dark, Ben's Family, Friends and neighbors gather inside his homestead in some what of a festival mood.

This does not mean that the people are not sad that Ben died, they know, according to their beliefs; he is going on a journey to where their, and his, Ancestors are waiting to welcome him to their domain.

And they, especially his family, are now ready to send him on his way, and not only see to it that he has everything needed for the trip, but also every thing he needs after his arrival. This is what the funeral is all about.

Although this is a festival occasion, like a going away party, it is a happy-sad affair. They are sad to see Ben go, but they are happy he is going to their Ancestors. He came from the Ancestors in the first place, now he is returning.

Throughout the funeral ceremony Ben is symbolized by a burial cloth robe meant to look like a person is inside, placed in the doorway of his house, in front of which Family, Friends and Neighbors are gathered for pre-funeral activities.

Pre-funeral activities, a form of entertainment, consist of songs and drumming, performed by Ben's sons and daughters and their family unit.

For example, Orchester Sr., his wives and children, along with their drummers, form a little band and sing a song expressing this happy-sad mood we mentioned, like singing the 'blues.'

This continues until all of the sons and their family unit have performed. This is followed by the oldest daughter, Clovis, her husband, and children doing the same until all of the daughters and their family unit have performed.

This is a Family, Friends, and Neighbor's affair. The Dokpwe Chief remains outside of the homestead in his special house. Thus is the nature of the pre-funeral festivities.

It is now about 11 or 12 mid-night, at which time the Dokpwe Chief, who is waiting outside in his temporary house to take over, and for the actual funeral to begin.

The Dokpwe Chief sends his spokesman inside of the homestead with a message like the following,

"Silence! Silence! Be quite! The Dokpwe Chief who commands, bids me to come and say that the people of the homestead shall come to the Sacred Space of the Dead; that all outsiders (friends and neighbors) shall come to the Sacred Space. The Dokpwe Chief bids me say that he is there waiting for them."

After which the family leads their friends and neighbors to their temporary house outside of the homestead, facing the Sacred Space, across from which is the Dokpwe Chief and his group;

Spokesman: "Let the family come kneel before the Dokpwe Chief."

Family kneeling; "Let the Spokesman salute the Dokpwe Chief for us."

Spokesman: "The family greets the Dokpwe Chief."

Dokpwe Chief: "The Ancients, salute you."

After this, the family returns to their place. This is followed by Orchester Sr., producing a large cloth, five hundred cowries, and a calabash of palm wine to the Dokpwe Chief; which is received by his

Spokesman, who strikes the earth with the cloth with the following words,

"Attention! Silence! To him who is no longer living (Ben), King Hwegbadja (an ancient King of the Fons) has rented a piece of earth. Today we give the King a large burial cloth of twenty strips (very large). It is he who has decreed that men should cover the body of the dead; that the feet of the dead might not be seen; that the hands of the dead might not be seen.

Heed you! Heed you! To him who is no longer living Hwegbadja gives drinks that must be drank when a man is dead.

To him who is no longer living, Hwegbadja gives this money. Here it is. The King has said that he brings it to pay for food bought on the road traveled by the dead."

When the Spokesman finished his speech, the cloth, wine and money are place in the center of the Sacred Space. Then the Dokpwe Chief asks the family to kneel and repeat after him,

"All that the King does is good. The King goes to hunt, the hunt is successful. The King goes to war, the war ends in victory. I, the Dokpwe Chief, praise the King. When wood is brought it gives fire. The King has lived in this house; and even those who are not yet born to our grief stricken must praise the King."

This is called 'Opening the Funeral.' After the family returns to their place, the Spokesman comes and stands in the center of the Sacred Space; and the gift giving begins. Orchester Sr., gives the Spokesman a large cloth, who strikes the earth while saying'

"Heed you! Heed you! To him who is here no longer comes his oldest son. He gives a burial cloth of fifteen strips and says it is for covering the dead."

Meanwhile, the Spokesman places the cloth in the center of the Sacred Space. Orchester Sr. also gives a clay pipe and tobacco, a pot to hold water, soap, a sponge, a cloth worn like pants, cloth worn like a shirt, and a cap, which he piles in the center of the Sacred Space; all of which is symbolic of the things Ben will need in the land of Ancestors.

All of Ben sons, Ben III and Walter, according to age, who gave the exact same things, follow Orchester Sr.

The sons followed by the daughters, beginning with the oldest, Clovis also gives the same thing as the sons; with the exception that she also gives a special cloth (to carry the dead across the rivers of death), and forty cowries to pay his passage.

Next, Ben's Best Friend approaches the Spokesman with the same type gifts as the sons, as the Spokesman says,

"Heed you! Heed you! The Best Friend of him who is here no longer placed the loin-cloth about the body of his friend, and said My Friend, this cloth becomes you well. He came not to the Sacred Space without tears. Now he offers a cloth of fifteen strips to cover his friend."

With the offering of the Best Friend concluded, the remaining friends and neighbors, one by one, come with their gifts.

On behalf of the family, Orchester Sr. again approaches the Spokesman, this time with three pieces of cloth. One is for all the dead males of the family, one is for all of the dead females, while the third is for all of the women of other families who died after marrying into this family.

In giving these, Orchester Sr., asks his father (Ben), upon reaching Ancestor land, to present them to those men and women and wives of the family who have died over the years. This is to let them know that the living family has not forgotten them.

At this time the Clan Mother, who had maintained the death watch, approaches the center of the Sacred Space accompanied by the Grave-digger.

She takes up the cloth of Hwegbadja, and the first gift of Orchester Sr., and wraps it about herself. The Grave-digger takes two cowries, and as the Clan mother goes toward the house where the symbolic body of Ben lay, he holds each between his thumb and first two fingers, striking one against the other in a rhythmic sound.

When the Clan Mother enters the house where the symbolic body lays, She kneels for a while, and then returns to the Sacred Space where she turns her back to the Dokpwe Chief who throws cowries into the Sacred Space. Next, she turns her back to the family who does the same. This done, she drops the cloth she is wearing and returns to the house where the symbolic body is laying.

Ben's Best Friend now chooses a man to represent him, who takes up the cloths the Clan Mother dropped and wraps it around himself, picks up another, and wraps it around his head, and gets one of Ben's pipes. This man proceeds toward the house where the symbolic body lies, accompanied by all the members of the Dokpwe, singing funeral songs to the rhythm of rattles and gongs. The one representing the Best Friend sings;

> "My friend is dead.
> Would that my friend were still in life,
> Would that something might be found
> To bring my friend back to life"

When they arrive at the symbolic body, all kneel and sing;

"Behold what death has done.
What death has done to a family
Friend and friend are united,
The death of one leaves the other in grief.
The song itself cried out, and it says
Behold what death has done!
What death has done to a friend"

After which all rise and return to the Sacred Space singing;

"I went to drink with my friend
And I did not find him.
O death! you kill without a trial
One day I will see him again,
Yes, one day I will see him again
For I, too, am going toward death."

When the representative of Ben's Best Friend arrives at the Sacred Space, he repeats the ceremony of the Clan Mother, turning his back first to the Dokpwe Chief and then to the family, while they throw money at him.

When this is concluded, the Dokpwe Chief orders all the cloths in the Sacred Space folded real neat, and all the other gifts piled in a neat pile to the accompaniment of the following song,

"Truly death spoils all things!
Death, you spoil the good things.
Clap your hands
That the house may be sweet,
For death spoils all things.
A great thing has all at once become small.
Were it not that war had changed all things,
Do you think this ceremony would be so small?
A man must bring forth children,
If his death is to be a fine one
Yes, a man must not fail to bring forth children,
If his death is to be a fine one
For a man must be buried with many cloths,
Since it is not a thing for a child"

Once the gifts in the Sacred Space have been gathered together, the Dokpwe Chief orders these to be taken to the gravesite. Meanwhile, six Dokpwe members are given the symbolic body of Ben, who are 'dancing the dead'.

Only this time the body is danced out of the homestead and on into the village. To the house of his Best Friend, into the houses of relatives, and especially, to the major cross-road, the meeting place of LEGBA; this is called the "last visit."

Finally the Dokpwe Chief orders the symbolic body to be carried back to the house, where he sings;

"Come hold him by the head,
Children come hold him by the feet,
Let the kin of the dead come and hold him by his head,
One of our kingsmen is dead."

As he sings, Ben's oldest living brother, your Grand Uncle Willie, holds the symbolic body by the head and feet. As Bertha, Orchester Sr., Clovis, Ben Jr., and Walter come to face the dead, again giving gifts, especially cowries. For they want Ben to be a man of wealth in Ancestor land.

When this is concluded, the Dokpwe Chief orders the symbolic body to be taken around to the outside of the house to where the gravesite is located.

The Grave-diggers have re-opened the hole which leads to the tunnel grave where the real body of Ben lays, beside him all of the gifts are piled, as the Grave-digger sings to Orchester Sr.,

"Today you look upon your father for the last time,
See him there!
The makers of salt have thrown their salt into the water,
This salt you will not see again."

The symbolic body and rolled up mats are handed down the hole to the Gravedigger, who un-roles the mats and places them beneath the real body.

Next, all the gifts are given to the Gravedigger who places them in the tunnel grave with the body.

When this is finished, the Gravedigger, along with his helpers, fill in the hole with dirt which they stamp down with their feet as the final, "Act of Closing the Grave."

After this, the Dokpwe Chief leads the family back to the Sacred Space to listen to the song of the Ancient King, Agongolo; he begins by saying, "Agonogolo said that after every funeral this song is to be sung. Kneel, therefore, and listen to the voice of the King."

"If I had money
I should buy drinks to drink

One of three thousand cowries
Son of Ben, drink
Let all of you hear.
To have a pleasant thought,
Yes, yes, yes.
To have a pleasant thought,
He who has money
And hoards all for the future
Of him I do not think well.
In the coffers of the houses of the dead are many drinks.
Had he for whom this was bought drunk of it?
No, no, no
Sellers of drinks, give me drinks to drink
For today my head is turning.
I see it; there is no pleasure for the dead.
I say; what you eat in this world,
The pleasure of it goes with you.
I say; the wives you had,
The pleasure you had of them goes with you.
I say; the meat you ate,
The pleasure of it goes with you.
I say; the drinks you drank,
The pleasure goes with you.
I say; the pipe you smoked,
The pleasure goes with you.
Ben, my song praises you;
The wife of the unsuccessful hunter,
Does not blow into an animal horn
In life friendship has worth,
Come, lets us sing of joy and pain.
Let us drink to friendship begun in childhood.
Is it a friend with whom
One shares drink in a small calabash?
Has the seller of drink drunk of it?
Give me drinks while I am yet alive,
O, Ben, while in life, say
Friendship has worth.
Come; let us sing of joy and pain."

This song of understanding and consolation of the ancient King ends the funeral. It is now early morning, and the funeral has lasted all night.

The Dokpwe Chief, Family, Friends and neighbors now retire to rest for the rest of the day. For although the funeral itself is over, there are still two related ceremonies still to be performed: The first one later that same evening, and the second, three months later.

Early in the evening the Dokpwe Chief returns, and the Family, Friends, and neighbors again gather in the homestead. This time for a "Going away party" type ceremony for Ben. This is a time to have fun and entertain the dead. There is drumming, dancing, singing, drinking, playing games, and telling jokes and funny stories, all for the enjoyment of Ben's Spirit. This continues into the late night, and concludes with the Dokpwe Chief and Clan Mother leading everybody to Ben's grave.

At the gravesite, a sacrifice is made of two baby chicks, one hen, and one rooster, eighty-two cowries, one calabash of water, and one of palm wine, and two pots are placed on the grave. Meanwhile, as the Clan Mother sings,

> "An old woman weeps
> Amidst the leaves;
> A white-haired woman
> Weeps amidst the leaves of the forest
> And she says, the birds in the bush,
> The life of these birds is to be envied.
> How it is that man born into life
> Has no more generations?
> An old woman was burned in the bush.
> Oh singer, son of a singer, do not hide.
> The Great Sun lights the whole universe
> And I, myself, do not hide."

After which the Dokpwe Chief sings and performs, while the Family provides him with the things necessary to actually perform things said in the song on the actually grave itself; as follows.

> "To begin a pot
> Is it the same as to finish it?
> To die and leave life is not good.
> Death chooses badly;
> He who killed you must have an avenger.
> Give water for him to drink
> A drinker of water is dead.
> Give wine for him to drink
> For a drinker who drinks is dead
> Give tobacco,
> That someone may smoke it for him,
> For a smoker of tobacco is dead.

> Give a woman,
> that someone may lye with her,
> For a lover of women is dead.
> Give a spear,
> For a warrior is dead."

After the Dokpwe Chief's performance, he actually does each of these things on Ben's grave. This is considered a ceremony to send Ben on his three-month journey to Ancestor land. While symbolically, they give him the things that gave him pleasure in life.

With this ceremony completed, the Clan Mother authorizes Orchester Sr. Clovis, Ben Jr. and Walter, in the name of the Clan Chief to bath with soap, to shave their heads, and put on clean clothes to purify them from the death they have been involved with.

Meanwhile, Ben is on a journey that takes him across rivers and mountains, as well as an appearance before MAWU's Court before he finally reaches his Ancestors three months after his funeral.

During this time, Ben's family, sons, daughters, brothers, sisters, aunts, uncles, and daughter-in-laws wear the mourning color, indigo blue; the women wear a blue scarf around their waist, and the men on any part of their body they choose.

Three months later, the second ceremony is performed, called "the welcoming of Ben by his Ancestors." This ceremony assumes that Ben has arrived in the land of Ancestors.

On the night before the second ceremony, Ben's Clan Mother escorts Orchester Sr. and Clovis, your grand aunt Carrie, and Uncle Willie to the nearest cross-road to meet face to face with LEGBA.

Ben's Clan Mother is covered with a large cloth, and carries a small pot, some palm wine, a white cloth, and a baby chicken. Whistling the whistle that summons the Spirit of the Dead, she calls the spirit-Ancestors of the family to come to the following ceremony.

These include the spirit of the ancient men of the family whose names now forgotten, and the spirit of the ancient women of the family whose names are unknown. And also those killed by lightning, those killed by small-pox, those who died away from home without a funeral, and finally, the spirits of the Best Friends of the family through the generations.

All of these spirits enter the pot, symbolized by the chick, and are carried back to the homestead under the care of the Clan Mother.

The Dokpwe Chief arrives just before-daylight of the same night; and with his own hands removes the mourning cloths from the family members as a sign of the end of the mourning period. Which is his last act as Funeral Director, and he returns to his home.

When daylight comes, seven small huts, about two feet high, are built in a circle facing the pot and chick carried to the cross-road the night before. A large one for Ben, six slightly smaller ones for the six classes of spirits called by the Clan Mother; a large jar is turned upside down in the one for Ben. Now it is time to begin the second ritual ceremony we mentioned.

Also a great quantity of food, goats, chickens, wine, vegetables, corn flour, spices, and what ever else is needed for a great feast.

Orchester Sr. begins the ceremony by sacrificing a goat over the hut of Ben, allowing some of the blood to fall inside. Next Ben's Best Friend does the same; for each Ancestor hut a goat is sacrificed, and as each animal is killed, the Ancestors are asked to welcome Ben into the Family's Ancestor Clan.

After which all of the food is cooked and small bits are given to the Ancestors as the Family, Friends and Neighbors eat the remainder.

This is a happy affair, more like a family reunion between the living and the dead, all in celebration of Ben being established in Ancestorland. Thus is what the three-month-after-the-funeral-ceremony is all about.

Spiritual Journey of the Dead

Now that Ben is firmly established in the place of his Ancestors, Grandpa thinks it will be very interesting to see just what this three month journey consists of. Therefore, we will next take a look at the Fon's idea of what Ancestor land is like, and Ben's experiences on its way to this strange place. For this we will quote a story about a Fon who died and made that journey, but being as he was kidnapped and taken there, he was returned to life; his account is as follows.

"One day, as this man, whose name was Bokofio, lay sick on his mat, he heard a whistling in his ear, and soon found himself in a large clearing where two men came forward, one carrying a long rope, the other whip in hand. The first one said,' walk in front of us, we are going to leave this place.' and tied the rope about his neck. Holding the other end of it, he pulled poor Bokofio as he would a dog. The other walked behind him and lashed in to make him walk faster. As the three made their way up the path, they were climbing a high mountain. They did not stop when they reached the top, but descended to the other side until they came to a river.

They did not stop at the river, however, but continued on their way, walking on the water as though it were land. Although they met with some difficulty in getting up the bank of the river because it was slippery, they at last found themselves in a land of great banana farms.

After some time, as the three walked rapidly, they came upon a clearing and some low thatched houses in front of which were bamboo leaves. It held no shrines, apparently, as Bokofio did not even an 'aiza' (will explain later). He was also unable to see whether or not this village had any people, though he did notice smoke coming from one of the houses. Those who had him in charge passed quickly through the village; and when he tried to cry out, one of his captors put a hand over his mouth.

A little later they again came upon open country. Here there was nothing but earth; no trees, no water, no grass, just bare earth. Some distance ahead, Bokofio saw men seated one after another in a long row, and the road which they were following led to these seated figures. Arriving at the place where the row of stools began, his captors turned abruptly and went along a by-way which led to the slope of a second great mountain.

While making his decent down the other side of this mountain, Bokofio saw another river before him. Again, however, they walked on the water as though it were land. On the other side, they were met by two great, threatening dogs who barred their way, but the two who had Bokofio in charge cried out a 'strong name,' the power of which caused the animals to step aside.

Now a third mountain even steeper than the other two confronted them, a mountain whose summit receded from them as they climbed it, and the path grew steeper and steeper. At each step, guards, who asked his name, but refused to tell him their own, met Bokofio. All of this time his two captors continually urged him to go faster and faster.

When at last they reached the top, they came to an enclosure, watched over by a guard who was seated at a door constructed of plaited banana leaves. The guard told them to wait, and as they waited, Bokofio heard the soft sound of many voices, and knew there were a great number of people about. He was not allowed, however, to look within the enclosure.

Presently a guard came through the door, accompanied by a man dressed in raffia-cloth, who held a stone in one hand. On the stone were no marks that Bokofio could see, but the man who held it appeared to be reading something from it. After a time, a second man came out of the enclosure and this one held many banana leaves in his hand, which he examined like a note book, each leaf acting as a page. This second man whispered to the first, who then answered in a language which Bokofio could not understand. The second one, however, spoke the Fon language of Abomey itself, and asked Bokofio why he came. Poor Bokofio said that these two men brought him by force.

The man who spoke Fon then turned to the captors, and demanded to know who had sent them to bring this captive. When they made no answer, the man who spoke Fon called 'Adjoto!' The man in the raffia-cloth took up a stone and hurled it at the two who had brought Bokofio and they ran away, leaving Bokofio free.

The man who had first come from the enclosure looked at his stone again, and after scrutinizing it carefully, he ordered Bokofio to raise his head. As Bokofio raised it, this man spurted water at him from his mouth, and the stream covered Bokofio's face. At this time the guard took a great club and drove him away. Bokofio ran so fast that he had no idea how he ever surmounted all of the obstacles he had to pass as he retraced his way home.

At last, he found himself at home on his mat. Now it so happened that his son had been far away when his "death" had occurred and his body had been kept in his hut for three days, awaiting the first ceremony of burial. Therefore, when he revived, while he knew he lay on his mat, he could not see, and he felt his mouth tied. He began to toss about, and as he removed the bandage that covered his eyes, those watching him (Clan Mother and Wife) ran away.

When they returned with help, they found him sitting upright. The first words they heard Bokofio speak were a request for water. Then those who had courage undid his bonds and gave him water. He wanted no food, but laid down again and at once fell into a deep sleep. When he awoke, he was well, and hungry." End of story.

This is an interesting story, for it gives us a good idea of how the Fons view the spirit world of the Ancestors; we can begin to see the type problems Ben encountered between not only the grave and the river-of-death, but also the ones in the spirituals world itself. And at the same time, we can see some of the super-natural powers possessed by the Ancestors. All total, the story gives us some indication of the nature of the burial, and especially the funeral rituals, and the purposes they serve. However, the story also gives us other insights into other things Ben is confronted with on his three-month-journey; however, being as Ben was not kidnapped, he had to pay his way around the obstacles confronted on the "Road of Death. This is what the money and things given by his eldest Daughter were for, if you recall the funeral.

It is not hard to come to a conclusion about the first spiritual village Ben would have come to, where there were no people, only smoke coming from one of the houses. This is where Ben would stay while waiting for his trial before the Great Creator, MAWU-LISA, concerning his Chosen Destiny. However, it is hard to come to a conclusion about the two men at the enclosure. One was reading from a rock, and the other, from banana leaves. But it is known that the one who could speak the Fon language is the Chief of Ben's Ancestor Clan to which he will belong in Ancestor land. As to the man dressed in raffia cloth reading a stone, Grandpa will say, without any evidence, that He was LEGBA checking Bokofio's Chosen Destiny.

However, Ben is not entitled to his full place in the Ancestor community until still another ritual is performed by his living relatives, which transforms him into a Saint to be worshipped by the living members of his extended family; and is the final Cycle of Life. Now we come to your Aunt Elaine's questions.

Sainthood and Ancestor Worship

Now to deal with Aunt Elaine's question, what is the nature of Ancestor Worship and history? We must first define what is meant, according to Fon's beliefs, by the terms Ancestor, Ancestor Worship, and History, as a guideline in our investigation.

Ancestor Worship is misleading terms, we should think of Ancestor ritual as more to the point. The three terms have a close relationship with each other. For example, the Fons believe that Ancestors form a line through time. A living time-line that ends in their existence in reality; beginning with themselves, and reaching back in time to their Great, hundreds of times great grandparents, grand uncles and aunts, and their families. Thus is who the Ancestors are.

The Fons also believe that, on this living time-line, what their fore-parents thought, felt, and did in their experience in life, gave them a special kind of wisdom and knowledge that came from life itself. This wisdom and knowledge are what is called history.

Therefore, Ancestor rituals (worship) serve the same designed-purpose as the Fa Divination ritual serves with LEGBA's knowledge and wisdom. The Ancestors are made into Saints, and Ancestor rituals are designed to seek Ancestor knowledge in a problem-solving manner, and on a daily basis: The same as LEGBA. Thus is the meaning of Ancestor Worship.

To begin our investigation in the area of Saints and their place in Fons spiritual beliefs, we need a little background to set it up. First of all, what we call Sainthood is institutionalized into the family traditions. It is a thing that must be done for all Ancestors of an extended family. Sainthood ritual ceremonies are performed on a ten year cycle for every member of the family that died in that ten year time period. For example, in the ten years since Ben died, some of his wives, brothers and their wives, plus some of their children and grandchildren, would have also died for various reasons. They and Ben would be made Saints at the same ritual ceremony.

Meanwhile, those Ancestors that died in that time period have a low status in the Ancestor community, it is the responsibility of Ben's living family to secure a high status position for the family of the dead; especially Ben's children.

Upon Ben's death, Orchester Sr., inherits his homestead, and his position as Head of the extended family, and lives in the house under which Ben's body is buried; and he, and the family council, according to traditions, must perform the ritual of Sainthood for Ben and the other dead family members. This also means that he, Orchester Sr., is going to establish a shrine-house in the homestead where these Ancestors are to be worshipped. So this brings us to ten years after Ben's death, and the time for him to go through his final cycle of existence, his transformation to Sainthood.

A Sainthood ritual and a Funeral serve the same purpose. Both deal with the living. Moving the dead from one state to another; for example in the case with Ben, the funeral rituals had to do with his journey from the land of the living to that of the land of Ancestors. On the other hand, the Sainthood ritual deals with Ben's journey from Ancestor land to a Shrine among the living. Even the physical lay-out of a Saint and Funeral rituals are the same, in the sense that both are performed in a Sacred Space faced by two full sized houses; a large one for the family, and a medium sized one for the Dokpwe Chief and his group.

Once Ben's family decided it is time to perform the Saint ritual for their recent Ancestors, Orchester Sr., now the Family Head, approached the Dokpwe Chief about the Family's intentions, and they in turn, consulted Divination and LEGBA about the date and location. Unlike a Funeral, Saint ritual is performed deep in the forest, and not in front of the homestead.

Meanwhile, as the Dokpwe Chief and the Dokpwes clear the Sacred Space and build the two temporary houses, Ben's family gathers a large number of goats, pigeons, hens, roosters, baby chicks, ducks, small pots, lamps, money, cloth, and especially mats; this is another occasion where each family member's Best Friend and Friend-groups make a major contribution.

In the early evening on the appointed day, Ben's family, men, women, and children move into the largest of the houses in the forest, and the Dokpwe Chief and his officials move into the other. They are to stay for the next few days with food being provided by the son-in-laws of the family.

Orchester Sr. presents the Dokpwe with one cowry for each of the family members who have died in the last ten years, including one for Ben, along with a number of pots, lamps and mats. In the center of the Sacred Space, the Dokpwe Chief folds ten mats into little houses in which a cowry is placed, representing the ten recent Ancestors to be canonized to use a Catholic Church term; plus one is folded for the spirits of the Friends of the Ancestors in which a number of cowries are placed. This phase of preparation lasts until about mid-night at which time the Dokpwe Chief leads the older members of the family to a place where seven roads meet, (cross-roads always mean a meeting with LEGBA), carrying eleven pots, eleven baby chicks, corn meal, palm oil, and lamps.

The Dokpwe Chief has his long staff of office, and when they arrive, he draws a circle in the sand in the center of the cross-roads. In this circle, the sacred leaves, the chicks, and pots are placed there. The Dokpwe chief remains inside, and everybody else outside this circle.

The Dokpwe Chief, who wears a sacred cloth, takes a small pot and a little chick, and puts some of the mixture of cornmeal and palm oil into the pot. Stepping on a special ritual charm which he has placed on the ground in front of him, he leans toward Orchester Sr., and asks in a whisper, "who was the first of your family to die in the last ten years?" As the answer is given, Ben and the Dokpwe Chief whistle the name sixteen times, as he holds a small pot in one hand and a baby chick in the other. On the sixteenth time however, he throws the chick inside the pot in which cornmeal and palm oil have already been placed, closing it immediately with his hand. The chick symbolizes the soul of Ben, and the palm oil and cornmeal is its sacrifice. Orchester Sr. stands nearby holding many cloths, and when the Dokpwe Chief has covered the opening of the pot containing the chick with his hand, he presents it, covered, to Orchester Sr., who wraps it at once with a cloth.

This ritual at the cross-roads continues in this manner until the symbolic souls of the ten Ancestors are captured in the ten pots, which is passed to the oldest man of the family, the Clan Chief, while the Clan Mother and oldest women sing songs of the dead. Finally, the Dokpwe chief is given three pots representing an invitation to the souls of the Best Friends, in Ancestor land, of the dead family members to also become Saints; over these pots, forty-one chicks are sacrificed. The cross-road part of the ritual ends with the Dokpwe Chief leading the family, with the pots, back to the Sacred Space in the forest.

Upon their return, there is a ceremony performed whereas in each small mat house, along with the cowry already there, are placed the proper pot containing the soul called at the cross-road; also a lamp to burn day and night are placed in front of each mat house. By the time this ceremony is concluded, it is early morning of the following day; at this point the Family and Dokpwes retire to rest and get some sleep until late evening when the ritual is to resume.

Meanwhile, we should keep in mind that the Ancestors and their Best Friends were only symbolically captured in the pots at the cross-roads, or the pots were consecrated to become Shrines of the Ancestors and their friends; while their Spirits remained in the land of the dead.

The next stage of the ritual is concerned with the journey of the Ancestors from the world of the dead, to the world of the living where they are to become embodied in an Ancestor Shrine House, in the pots. In this respect, the ritual is just the opposite of the function of a funeral, one is to send the dead away, and the other is to bring them back.

Early in the evening of the second night, Orchester Sr. and the Dokpwe Chief send for a Master Drummer Chief. Those that drum at funerals, and whose drum-voice can communicate with the land of the dead, and he can find out what is taking place in the land of the dead. His function is to let the Family know when the Ancestors have gotten in their spiritual boat to cross the river of death that lies between the living and the dead. When this takes place, there is still a ritual that must be performed to power the boat across the river; which is the subject of the ritual on the second night. The children of each Ancestor must sacrifice a ram, two chickens, a pigeon and a duck for their Father, and a female goat and two chickens for their Mother, and begins with the Best Friend of each Ancestor sacrificing a male goat; this is what gives power to the boat.

This part of the ritual begins with songs as the Dokpwe Chief and Chief Drummer lead the Best Friend of Ben to the mat house and pot symbolizing Ben's soul; the Best Friend, if he is still alive, or a representative is carrying a male goat. Upon reaching the center of the Sacred Space, the Best Friend cuts the throat of the goat and allows some of the blood to fall on the mat house; with the following words,

"My friend, during your lifetime we told each other all. We promised each other that when one of us should die, the other would come to cover his body with a large cloth. That, I have already done. We also promised each other that when one of us should be on the other side of the river (of death), the other would supply him with the horns of a male goat to serve him as a bridge for reaching the other side. Here I bring you the goat. Come, visit us."

When this ceremony of the Best Friend is complete, Orchester Sr. does the same with a male sheep, two chickens, a pigeon and a duck; followed by Clovis, Ben Jr. and Walter. After the ceremonies for the fathers and male Ancestors who have died, those of the mother and female Ancestors are carried out in the same fashion, beginning with their Best Friend. This takes up the whole of the second night, and the ritual ends with the Clan Chief making a sacrifice of a male sheep for the souls of all the men of the whole Clan who have died, and a female goat for all the women, and eleven chickens for the Ancient Clan Ancestors.

The third and final night is festival in nature, consisting of dancing and singing with lots of music. To begin, the Dokpwe Chief goes to the center of the Sacred Space near the mat houses, where he draws seven circles in the sand; called "circles of gifts." This is the signal for the Family and Friends to place their gifts of money, cloths, palm wine, tobacco, matches, pipes, and beads in the circles as the Dokpwe Chief sing,

> "Your fathers and your kinsmen
> Shall never wear torn cloths because of the
> Neglect of their children who remain in life;
> And when fine cloths are worn,
> Your Ancestors shall appear in the finest of cloths.
> Give all you can to honor the memory of your dead,
> For when later you come upon them in their home
> They will tell you they have received all you gave.
> And you alone can make their boats go."

After which everybody dances and has a good time. This is in celebration of the Ancestors setting out in their boats on the river of death, beginning their journey back to the land of the living. This festival celebration lasts until mid-night. At which time, the Friends and neighbors return to their homes, and the Family to their temporary house. But the ritual is still not complete. There are still things that the Dokpwe Chief and the Clan Chief must do while the Family sleeps the remainder of the night.

This part of the ritual is performed in a place in the forest held sacred by Ben's Clan, in which the Clan Ancestors reside, not just the ancestors of Ben's extended family; recall, a Clan consists of a large number of extended families who have the same Ancient Founding Ancestors on the male side.

At this Clan Sacred Space, the Dokpwe Chief is given two yards of cloth, a chick, palm wine, and forty-one cowries for each of the ten Ancestors on the journey, plus seven castrated goats, seven roosters, seven female goats, seven hens, the ten pots from the mat houses, and all of the drums used in the ritual. The Dokpwe Chief now digs a large hole into which he places all the small pots which represent the dead men of the group; then he sacrifices the seven castrated goats and the roosters in the hole, and covers it up with dirt. For the souls of the women, he digs another large hole in which their pots are placed and the seven female goats and seven hens are sacrificed, and the hole is filled. Finally, he digs a third large hole in which all the drums used in the ceremony are placed and covered up with dirt. Then the Dokpwe Chief says a prayer to the Ancient Founding Clan Chief to welcome his new children, who have just come to earth.

By the end of this ceremony it is now morning, and the Dokpwe Chief and Clan Chief return to the temporary house where the Family sleeps; the Family is gathered together and the Dokpwe chief makes the official announcement that the Ancestors are in their boats and are crossing the river of death. He asks the Family when they want to meet the Ancestors at the riverside. Their answer is, in three months. Recall, according to Fon's beliefs, it takes three months to travel between the land of the living and the dead.

In conclusion, the Dokpwe Chief fashions three small ritual objects, one is to serve as a shrine for the male Ancestors, one for the female Ancestors, and one for the children who have died in childhood for one reason or another: which is presented to the Mother of the Family, namely the oldest woman in the Family. Then he instructs Orchester Sr. to build two full size houses in his homestead. One for the future shrine house for the worship of the Family Ancestors, and the other, to worship the Most Ancient of Ancient Ancestors of the Kingdom. Thus ends the first half of making Saints of the Ancestors.

Once the date is fixed for the upcoming second half of the ritual, the Family returns to their homesteads and regular life for the next three months. The Dokpwe Chief and Dokpwes also return to their regular life and homes, for this not only ends this part of the ritual, but it also ends the Dokpwe Chief's involvement in the ritual period. In the second half, the Clan Chief, who is also Chief Priest of the Clan Ancestor's Shrine will be the official in charge.

Meanwhile, the Family, under Orchester Sr., builds two houses in his homestead inherited from Ben which is to become the Temple of the Ancestors. One as a place of worship for the ten Ancestors on the river, and the other, for the worship of the most Ancient Ancestors who are collectively called DAMBADA HWEDO. Also, in preparation, the Family has to gather together gold, silver and brass ritual objects, many calabashes, two hundred and forty-one chickens, sixteen goats, two white cloths, red and white clay powder, two special drums, and added to that, two wide-mouth pots and a mat for each of the Ancestors on the river. Plus, the same number of everything for the Ancient Ancestors. With these things on hand, when the appointed day arrives, three months later, Orchester Sr. sends for the Clan Chief.

The Clan Chief arrives with two assistants and leads the Family to a river held sacred by the Fons, which symbolizes the river of death where the ritual is to begin. They took the pots and goats with them, and when they arrived at riverside, they sacrificed two goats and seven chickens; after which the family, with the exception of Orchester Sr. moves back a ways.

As the Family sang sacred songs, the Clan Chief walks into the river until he is up to his waist in the water. He carries one pot in his right hand, and one of his left, and asks the name of the first person of the Family who has died in the last ten years. When the name is spoken, the Clan Chief says a prayer, stoops, quickly fills one pot and covers it with the other. This is done for each of the male and female Ancestors, and one by one are lined up on the bank wrapped in its own mat. When he is finished with this part of the ritual, he calls the Family once more to the place where the pots are, and they sacrifice two more goats. The spirit of the Ancestors are now in the pots.

Now the Family is told to return to their homestead and wait in front of the newly constructed Ancestor shrine house; leaving the pots, mats, the two assistants and Clan Chief at the riverside. While the Family waits, the Clan chief and his assistants performed a sacred ritual, after which they too return to the homestead, empty handed.

On their arrival, the Clan Chief tells the waiting Family that their Ancestors are now present. When he says this, he is asked, 'where are the pots we took to the river?' The Clan Chief answers, 'they have already been brought home.' At which time the Family looks in the shrine house, and behold the pots and their mats are inside. The question remains, and the great mystery is, how did the pots get from the riverside to the Shrine house? Grandpa thinks it had something to do with the secret ritual of the Clan Chief performed after the Family left for their homestead, but be that as it may, the Ancestors are now Saints, in their own Shrine house, to be worshipped. And naturally there is a big celebration.

Although the Ancestors that were on the river were established in their Temple and considered Saints, we must keep in mind that Orchester Sr. built two Temples. This means that the ritual is still not over. The Clan Chief must establish the Most Ancient Ancestors in their Temple. These Ancestors are in two groups. One representing the Ancient, or First Ancestors, and the other, are Ancestors that were slaves in the Americas, or, others that were lost to the Kingdom, and did not have a proper funeral. Being as the names of both groups are long forgotten, or were never known, they are collectively called DAMBADA HWEDO. In Fon land, these Ancestors live in certain trees and mountains. Therefore, the second ritual is performed in the forest instead of at the riverside, but otherwise, follows the same pattern with the pots which mysteriously appear in the DAMBADA HWEDO Temple in the homestead.

Our major point is to show that the living family uses a ritual to transform their Ancestors into Divine Beings with supernatural powers. This ritual establishes them as semi-Gods and Goddesses to be worshipped; and though they use a different ritual, this is the same process the Catholic Church uses to make Saints in which they worship. At the same time, this lets the living family know what is going to happen to them when they die and become Sainted Ancestors. They too, are destined to become semi-Gods and Goddesses if they have children and friends. Thus is the belief that is the foundation of Ancestor Worship, and how it fits in with the Fon's religious beliefs.

Conclusion

Well GrandKids, we began this adventure with questions your Parents had about the Trickster God and Ancestor Worship, nevertheless, we should not forget that our ultimate goal, investigating the Fons, the influence they had on the Aja nation, and most important, find the Aja's High-valued Beliefs.

In "Questions of Black Salvation; Black History and African Soul;" Grandpa continually referred to the religious beliefs of our African Ancestor Nations as Pyramids. This needs some explanation if we are to understand how the Aja African nation fits into this idea. When we speak of pyramids, we are talking about the "form of the structure of the spirituality of a religion;" while focusing on the "God Head", or "Spiritual Energy Source" which is the "Usefulness" of a people's Highest Valued Religious Beliefs.

Mankind all over the world got the idea that they needed a solid physical form to be the symbol of their "God Head Spiritual Energy Source," as a physical symbol of this "Great Power."

A pyramid is made up of five geometric plans, four equilateral triangles, and a rectangle whose side's equal one side of the triangles. As far as the spiritual symbolism is concerned, this brings us back to the Holy Trinity every people have as the foundation, or, God Head of their religion.

A Holy Trinity is a spiritual principle of a triad of ideas, Gods and Goddesses in our case, working toward the same end; producing spiritual power. But as we saw in the first book, the Holy Trinity works on four levels, the God level, the nation-community level, the family level, and the individual level. So we have four triangles in a religion. By making an enclosure with these triangles to contain this idea, is what is called a spiritual pyramid.

However in doing so, the Base-foundation of the pyramid forms a rectangle square with equal sides, which symbolizes the four dimensions of the Holy Trinity, and completes the enclosure.

In this sense, a pyramid symbolizes a "Form that contains the Sacred Space for a Religion to Exist." And when thinking about pyramids in this way, we can see that all religions form a pyramid. But this is not the case with the Aja.

And this is what makes the Aja unique in all of Africa, they only focus on the "base" of the pyramid, and their religion has, instead of a "Holy Trinity," they have a "Holy Rectangle."

For example, the Igbo has "CHINEKE, IGWE, and ALA" as their "Holy Trinity," draw an equal line between the three and you have an "equilateral triangle form" for their "religion;" and the same is the case with the Akan and the Yoruba.

On the other hand, the Aja has "MAWU-LISA, SAGBATA, SORBO, and LEGBA," draw a equal line between them and you have a "rectangle square form", to symbolize their religion. So we can see that LEGBA changed the dimensions of Aja Religion when He became Chief of the Gods and Goddesses; and this is what makes Aja's religion so unique, Thus is the nature of LEGBA, The Trickster God.

The appearances of some of the Aja's Gods and Goddesses are strange looking, with two faces and so on. For the area of Africa we are concerned with, West and Western Central Africa; this is not the case in the rest of the world. For example, the Roman God, JUNUS, who has two faces; and the India Goddess has lots of arms and hands. So in this regard, the appearance of the Aja's Gods and Goddesses are not so strange looking as far as the rest of the world is concerned. However, Grandpa could not find any religion in the world that had a God like LEGBA as Chief of their Gods and Goddesses; especially as related to Voodoo-magic and Voodooism, the part of their religion that interest us most.

To begin with, we must make sure that we have our terms well defined, especially Voodoo-magic and Voodooism which related to two things, Gods and Intelligence.

The Aja's term "Vudu," pronounced "Voodoo," means Gods and, or, Goddesses, in this case LEGBA. And Logic means the Intelligence used to perform what is called miracles, and magic as the words are used in the English language, which means that we define "Voodoo-Logic to mean the 'Intelligence of LEGBA;'" and "Intelligence" as the "dynamics" of the Mind. So this makes "LEGBA the God of the Working of the Mind."

This being the case, we think that the evidence we presented demonstrated beyond a doubt that the Aja used this LEGBA Intelligence, not only to live their lives, organize their religious beliefs, their family and society, and everything else in their life, but more important, to "organize Their Minds;" which is the definition of

'Voodooism.' Therefore, we must conclude that one of the Aja's Highest-valued beliefs is in their LEGBA- Mind.

On the other hand, when we see the organization of the Fon's Society, and the things that mold and give its morals and direction, we must take into consideration the role MAWU-LISA and Destiny played; SAGBATA, their God of the morals and ethics of Family and Society played; and, SORBO, their God of Warfare and Work played; we see that they play as strong of a role as LEGBA's Intelligence does in the make up of their Society. This is especially true when we recall the role of Best Friend, Friend-groups, and warfare and work play in the Seven Cycles of Life of their Family and Society.

This means, we must come to the conclusion that a "quadrilateral" of the "Aja's Highest-Valued Beliefs" are in MAWU-LISA's -Destiny; SAGBATA's-Family-Society; SORBO's-War-Work; and LEGBA's-Mind.

Parent's Questions

Orchester Jr.: "In understanding the Aja's overall religious beliefs, there seems to be a few questions. There seems to be no doubt that LEGBA is concerned with how the mind works, being a Trickster God. There is also no doubt that being as the Aja follow LEGBA's way of thinking, Voodoo-magic, they are also deeply concerned with how the mind works. My question is, what does the strangeness of the appearances of the Holy Family as a group, have to do with how the mind works?"

Orchester Sr.: "Like with all Africans, here, we are dealing with symbolism. The Gods and Goddesses form seven parts that work together to form what we call the mind; they are the mind's reality. Or to say, using our example of the car, if three ideas form the power train of the car, its holy trinity, then those seven parts form the car as a whole; and each part has a function. Only the Aja think in terms of 'domains, they would say that the mind contains seven domains. In this respect, the holy Family is an image of the mind.

The strangeness of the appearances of some of the Gods and Goddesses, for example MAWU-LISA as having two faces, one male and one female, only indicates that this Being has two qualities, and this is no different from when the Yoruba's say, "God the Creator first created male and female."

On the other hand, this strangeness is related to the unique functions the Gods and Goddesses are to serve in the operation of the mind. For an example, we will return to the story where MAWU-LISA gave the Gods and Goddesses their Domains. However, in reinterpreting the story, even though I do not believe in any of the prevailing psychological theories, nevertheless, we will use psychological terms as an example; recall the story goes this way,

"One day MAWU-LISA (Ego) assembled all of the Children (Gods and Goddesses) in order to divide the Kingdom (of the Mind). (1) To the first Twins, SAGBATA, She gave all the riches and told them to go and inhabit the earth. She said the earth was for them. ((We interpret this to mean that MAWU gave them the domain of consciousness).

(2) "MAWU said to SOGBO He was to remain in the sky, because He is both man and woman like His Parents." (This seems to indicate SOGBO is to occupy to domain of Thinking).

(3) "She told AGBE and NAETE to go and inhabit the Sea, and command the waters." (This seems to indicate the domain of the Un-consciousness).

4) "To AGE, she gave command of all the animals and birds, and She told Him to live in the bush (forest) as a Hunter." (I think this is related to the part of the mind concerned with economics, curiosity, and learning).

(5) "To GU, MAWU said, He was Her Strength, and that was why He was not given a Head like the others. Thanks to Him, the Earth would not always remain wild bush. It was He who would teach men to live happy." (Being as happiness is an emotion, I will say He is to occupy the domain of the Emotions and Artistic Talents).

(6) "MAWU told DJO (air) to live in space between Earth and Sky. To Him was being entrusted the life-span of man." (This means the domain of the mind that is concerned with time and space).

(7) "She said to LEGBA. Your work shall be to visit all the Kingdoms (of the mind) ruled over by your brothers, and give me an account of what happened." (For LEGBA to carry out his job, he had to have the ability to see, hear, smell, taste, and feel; which is the domain of the Five Senses of the mind).

If MAWU-LISA symbolizes the Mind's Ego, and LEGBA symbolizes the 5 Senses, and being as the 5 Senses are the Source of Experiences, and Experiences are the Foundation of Knowledge, and Knowledge is the Energy of the Mind; This means that 5 Senses are Chief of the Mind. We can see why LEGBA is Chief of the Gods and Goddesses. Without Him, the Ego Mind cannot Function. This is why MAWU-LISA and LEGBA have such a close relationship.

Now if we interpret the story in this manner, we have to come to the conclusion, based on the Aja's focus on the mind as a way to deal with life, the Holy Family of their religious beliefs symbolizes a Super Holy Mind that Manages the Affairs of the Universe."

Still using our example that the Aja think of their Gods and Goddesses as symbols of the parts, and functions as a Super Holy Mind, this means that LEGBA is the Manager of the Affairs of this Holy Mind, and the minds of the Aja people. Therefore, we can clearly see that His job is to maintain Harmony between the parts of the mind. Meaning that each part of the mind answers to a Chief, and LEGBA, Who Promotes this Harmony through Tricksteration; or to say LEGBA Tricks the Gods and Goddesses to function in Harmony, and in this respect Harmony promotes Energy or Power.

Linda: "With all of the things LEGBA is involved with, and I can see that He is a very complicated God, how does this fit into the Man-woman relationship?"

Orchester Sr.: We defined 'Voodoo-logic' as meaning the 'Logic of LEGBA,' or the 'Intelligence of LEGBA' in the relationship between the Aja people themselves, and this is the logic which creates the kind of harmony which is the bond in the man-woman relationship which produces the Family and the next generation; and in this respect creates Society.

Now we have been defining this Harmony as the same as the English word Love, although the terms have somewhat different meanings as far as I am concerned; especially as to the man-woman relationship. The feeling that develops between a man and woman, in African terms, is "Harmony of Spirits: with a "Special Purse." It is from this point of view that we a get a better picture of the nature of LEGBA.

Marriage to the Fons and Africans in general, is based on one known fact, no matter what mankind thinks of religion and destinies, there is one purpose he and she knows without a doubt they must fulfill, they must raise a family! This means that the family is a kind of generator that powers life across generations. In this, mankind does not have a choice according to African beliefs.

In this respect, the man-woman relationship is under the powerful pressure of responsibility, it is reacting to the most powerful force in the world, and in mankind's nature, 'Life Force.' We mentioned the symbolism related to the Holy Family, now we must mention the symbolism of MAWU-LISA, Life Force. And if the power of life Force created the world and all that it contains, we would have to say that it is the most powerful of the powerful. And, the Man-woman relationships have to deal with this power directly.

From this point of view, the man-woman relationship is the process of a family's reality, or to say, the Man-woman relationship brings the family into reality in the same manner as MAWU-LISA brought the world into reality; sexuality.

This means that the harmony in the man-woman relationship is the key relationship of all, if the harmony in this relationship ceases to exist, humanity would end, there would be no people to give humanity any reality; for the man and woman create the family, and the family is humanity.

And this power is generated by the harmony of the Spirits of a man and woman. For example, take the power of MAWU-LISA Who is Male and Female in one Being, thus is the nature of the man-woman relationship.

As to the nature of LEGBA, it is hard to say, the Aja respect, honor, and obey all of the other Gods and Goddesses, especially MAWU-LISA, SAGBATA, and SOGBO Who have Their Own Temples.

Elaine: "I think the approach of using an education system to show the relationships between the seven cycles of life, living life, and especially as related to Ancestor Worship was educational in itself; plus, it showed how living life is related to the Aja's religious beliefs. The connection I think is missing is the relationship between Ancestor Worship and History you mentioned? Is Ancestor Worship the same as reading a history book?

Orchester Sr.: "First let's look at how the Ancestors are organized across generations that cover the dead, living, and unborn. For it is not hard to see that the Ancestors themselves went through the seven cycles of life in the past, including Sainthood. They themselves lived in the past, involved with the living family in the present, and they are involved with a person before he is born; this means, that Ancestors are deeply involved in the past, present, and the future.

But what is the past, present, and future? We came to the conclusion that we are talking about a time-line through human existence. However, History is also defined as a time-line through human existence. History tells of the major events of the past, and the Ancestors tell of the major experiences of the past.

This brings up the question, what is the relationship between events of history and the experiences of the Ancestors of those events as they were happening in that time period? For example, if there was a war in the past, which is the event, then, the Ancestors fighting that war are the experience; this is the kind of relationship we think exists between Ancestors and History.

The events of history are what the Ancestors did, the reason they did what they did, how they did it, and especially what they learned from what they did, covers their experiences of the event. So we can see that History and Ancestors are inter-dependent, history cannot exist without the Ancestor experience, nor Ancestors exist without history's time line. In this respect, the designed-purpose of Ancestor worship is a ritual by which a family and, or, family member can profit by the experience of the Ancestors in the form of their wisdom and knowledge from their experiences.

Therefore, we can define history as an account of a people's experiences while living by a group of high valued-beliefs about what is the purpose of life. These high valued beliefs are what is passed on a time-line from generation to generation by a chain of what we call Ancestors; and this is what we call a Soul. This is why history-of-Ancestors is not only very important as a means of knowledge and wisdom about life, but also is the only way I can think of as a means of Knowing Yourself.

On the other hand, there is also a physical stream flowing down the time-line. For example, each generation comes from the womb of their parent generation; which is shown in how they physically look. But there is also a spiritual stream that shows how a person acts and think, especially about religious beliefs. So from the Aja traditional point of view, the living family is only one time period in a long river of time and experiences that is forever moving between the past and the future.

In this process, the living family can use their Ancestor's experiences, add it to their own experiences of living to form a growing body of experiences to pass on to the future generation, which moves them forward in their family-society's Chosen Destiny.

Now to deal with the second part of Elaine's question, is Ancestor worship and studying history books the same thing? My conclusion is that there are many streams that make up the river of human existence through time. History books only deal with one of those streams, the stream of events. On the other hand, Ancestor Worship is involved in all of the streams, including the stream of events.

Therefore, I think history books and Ancestor rituals deals with the same subject matter, and have the same kind of effect on the one thinking about the past. However, I think Ancestor rituals goes much deeper than history books. Here we are dealing with the experiences of their experiences; where as reading a book we are dependent of our imagination of their experiences.

ANCIENT SECREE GAME

Using the examples of the things that Christians do and believe to bring love into their lives to save their souls through the father-son Gods of their Religion, Jesus Christ and Jehovah; the following are some of the things that the Ancient Secree did and believed, in order to bring wisdom and knowledge into their lives, to become a nation governed by the laws of the jungle through the worship of a husband and wife God and Goddess of their religion, Ngewo and Ndoi. Which is the game they played in life.

DRINKING FROM ANCIENT WELLS
(The Mende in the land of Secret Societies)

This should be a very interesting investigation. Grandpa thinks that the people in the land of Secret Societies, as we will call them for now, are going to present us with our biggest challenge as investigators. Unlike with the Yoruba, the Igbo, the Akan, and the Aja, each of whom we investigated as a nation of people; this is not the case with this investigation.

To lay the foundation to meet this challenge, we will begin by noting their physical location, and give them a group name. In this way, we can keep in mind who we are investigating. Since they are not a nation, or have a group name, this means that we must focus our investigative attention on what these different Clans have in common.

The People in the land of Secret Societies are a large group of small Clans; who don't necessarily speak the same language nor have the same most Ancient Ancestors.

They are located on a strip of land about 200 miles wide, and 800 miles long between the Atlantic Ocean and the Fouta Jallon mountain range. Which is an area covering the south western part of the Ivory Coast, all of Liberia and Sierra Leone, and parts of Guinea.

For the most part, this land is covered by rain forest, which among other things, is ideal for rice farming, their staple food. Therefore, they have "rice farming in common."

While socially, they have in common, like the Igbo, living in independent village-group towns, and Village Government is the Highest Authority; they do not have a Kingship System. So we can call them the "Independent Minded Rice Farmers."

This brings up the questions, where did these Rice Farmers come from? And, how long have they lived in this area?

Grandpa thinks that every kingdom has its Outlaw Families. The Land of Secret Societies became a dumping ground for such families, from the Akan Kingdom on the east, Wolof Kingdom on the west, and the Mali Kingdom to the north. These Kingdoms archaeology evidence goes back some 4000 years.

Anyway, these outlaw families took control from the original people that lived in the area in ancient times. This would mean, "Outlaw Families" from a number of places founded the Clans in "The land of Secret Societies" over the centuries.

This leaves the question, what are secret societies?

The people living in this 200 by 800 mile area organized their society into a number of smaller independent societies. Each of which have ritual activities that are held in secret from the rest of society.

And it is the sum-total of these ritual activities of those smaller societies, that give form to the spirituality of their Society as a whole.

On the other hand, secret societies are schools where knowledge is stored and designed to teach and train people for their role in society. It is the training and teaching that is held in secrecy.

To get an idea of how a secret society functions, we only have to recall the Igbo, and Orchester III's purification ceremonies to become a Living Saint in Society. And note, only secret parts of all the ritual ceremonies were held in the forest hut when no outsiders were present but a Priest.

Now if all of Orchester III's ritual ceremonies were held deep in the forest, and no outsiders were allowed to see what was going on, these ceremonies would be secret society ritual activities as we use the term.

Thus is where all of these Clans secret societies take place, in the forest. If anybody that starts nosing around, they are punished, even family members.

So we can see that Secret Societies are spiritual centers for ritual activities. This is most important, as far as we are concerned; secret societies, as a spiritual belief is what all of the Clans living in this area have in common.

Grandpa thinks we should name this very large group of Clans by the most powerful spiritual bond holding them together, their belief in the power of Secrets. So we will call them the "Secree," meaning "Outlaw Rice Farmers Who Believe in Secrecy as the foundation for their spiritual beliefs;" which is why we named this area the "Land of Secret Societies.

All societies in the world have secret societies. For example, the masons in America. This is the case throughout Africa. The thing that makes the Secree unique, as we will see later, is that they are the only people Grandpa could find whose whole life is governed by secret societies.

Now that we have established "Secree" as the "investigative name" of this large group of Clans, and the area as the "Land of Secret

Societies," and where they came from, we must now decide on an investigative approach and attitude.

The question becomes, what do we mean by Outlaws? From the research Grandpa did on the subject, "African Outlaw" means the same thing as we use the term "Pimp Gangster."

As far as our attitude is concerned, the language will show that we use "Street talk." This is the attitude we will take throughout the investigation. As to our approach, like always, we will look deep into their secret societies, the "Well" in the title "Drinking from Ancient Wells," and look for the "Spirituality of their Outlawness."

This means that we will turn our investigative attention to the Mendes, one of the most influential Clans in the area. And we will see how they came to be in the land of secret societies, and how their Society was spiritually related to secret societies. And this should give us some indication of the life of all of the People in the Land of Secret Societies; and in this way, find their Highest Valued Beliefs, as our Ancestors.

The Mendes, a Background

Whereas we don't know where all of the Clans came from over the centuries, we do know that one such Clan in the Land of Secret Societies came from the Great Kingdom of Mali; the Mendes, about 700 years ago. So we will turn our investigative attention on the Mali Kingdom, and see why the Mendes moved to the Land of Secret Societies.

The Mali Kingdom was founded when a large gold field was discovered in the Upper Niger area between the Niger and Sankarani. There lived a number of large Clans. Ten of these Clans used this gold to build the Mali Kingdom.

Like the Ashanti, they built their Kingship around a Royal Clan from which they chose a King, the Keita Clan. The Kingdom is made up of a number of large powerful Clans whose Chiefs are the Counselors to the King.

Throughout this area, for hundred of miles, were a number of outlying Clans, some large and some not so large, who spoke the same language. This meant that the King was able to, and did, raise an army of warriors who numbered in the thousands.

And even if any of the outlying Clans didn't want to become a part of the new Kingdom, it didn't take long for the warriors to whip them into line, and get their men to join their army.

Nonetheless, most Clans welcomed the idea of living under a rich Kingship, and the Kingdom grew very fast population wise, mostly in the north. However, the Capital city, Niahi, and the Kingdom's

Government rested in the hands of about 10 Clans between the two rivers we mentioned. The Great Kingdom of Mali, over time, dominated half of West Africa at one time or another from AD 1230 to 1650. This included the northern half of Guinea, the country of Mali, Senegal, Upper Volta, and parts of Mauritania. But they never dominated the Land of Secret Societies.

Mali, is the name given to one of the largest nations of Manding speaking people, Mandinka (Europeans call Mandingoes), and is used when referring only to the people of the Mali Kingdom.

On the other hand, going back in time, it was the different nations of Manding speaking people that founded all of the Great Kingdoms of the Sudan (Grassland of West Africa). For instance, the Great Ancient Kingdom of Ghana, A.D. 300-900; Soso (Songhay?), A.D. 900-1230, and so on.

All of these ancient Kingdoms grew rich and powerful through the Sahara desert trade with Morocco, Algeria, Libya, and Egypt. We will investigate the Mandinka Mending speaking people, and others, in another Chapter, meanwhile back to the new Mali Kingdom.

The gold field was discovered in the area between the rivers, and the Mali Kingdom came into existence. Like always, when dealing with a large Kingdom, the outlying Clans had to pay taxes, and at least one is going to be a rebel, and this is where the Mendes appeared.

The evidence indicates that, before the foundering of the Mali Kingdom, the Mandinka speaking people lived like the Igbo, in independent Extended Family-Towns. However, unlike the Igbo, their town had a Town chief, a War Chief and his Counselors, who were their highest government authority.

The Mendes refused to join the Mali Kingdom, and this made them outlaws as far as the Kingdom's government is concerned. They were overpowered and driven out of the Kingdom.

At this point we will make up names for the leadership of the Mendes to understand how they were organized, and to show why they were successful; and at the same time, set up a dialogue between them to show their spiritual motivation.

We are going to say that Old Man Mende, a Town Chief, had a large family of seven wives. Unlike the Igbo men who were focused on the Oldest Son of their first wife, Old Man Mende was focused on the Oldest Sons from each of his seven wives.

When these sons grew up, the oldest of the oldest sons became leader of old man Mende's village, and the others founded 6 villages on Old Man Mende's land. These seven villages called Mende Town, founded a few generations before the year A.D. 1230, when the Mali Kingdom was founded, and located some 50 miles south of the Mali capital, Niani.

By the year A.D. 1250, the Kingdom of Mali was strong enough to begin making the outline Clans pay taxes. And Mende Town had grown to a population of over 1500 men, women, and children; 100 of which were top level male warriors between the ages of 18 and 40.

Old Man Mende died the year the Kingdom was founded. On his dying bed, he made his 7 oldest Sons promise that the Mende small Clan would never give up their independence by paying taxes or serving the Kingdom; or anybody else, man or God.

He told them, The world is a jungle, survive by any means necessary, but survive you will. I leave this Clan in your hands. The (Mali) Kingdom is expanding to the north, but the day will come when they will expand to the south, into the homeland of our father, grandfathers, and great grandfathers; you won't be able to stop them.

"When that day comes, you must be prepared to go on a long journey, and don't stop until you find a new home where my Clan can live independently."

Then Old Man Mende spent seven days and nights teaching his Sons how to organize and govern themselves to make this journey. In the ritual process, He chose a destiny for his Clan to be a traveling Society of Outlaws; with a Purpose, find a new home. The point we are leading to, is that sometime between 1230 about 1250 Old Man Mende could clearly see that they could not win in a fight with the Mali Kingdom, and came up with a master plan.

He knew full well, not only that to travel means to fight one's way, but also that every inch of land in West Africa is owned by somebody who is not going to give any of it up without a fight.

So the wise old Clan Chief, Old Man Mende, decided to convert his Clan into a Society of Outlaws, physically and spiritually, seeking a home where they could live that lifestyle. Now we will introduce Old Man Mende's 7 oldest sons.

Bighead Mende, age 50, was chosen to be Leader because of his knowledge of traditional law and philosophy. He was a visionary; his job was to administrate the affairs of the Clan, and lead them to the promise land so to speak.

Priest Mende, the youngest of the seven Sons, was chosen because of his close spiritual relationship with the Ancestors; his job is to take care of the spiritual needs of the Outlaw Society. As the symbol of his authority, he was given three pots of three different sizes, so that they could into the biggest one; the shrines of the Clans Ancestors.

Killer Mende, 35 years of age, chosen to be War Chief because he not only knew how to organize an army of warriors, but he also was a master of planning offensive and defensive military maneuvers. Plus, because of his battle field fighting skills, he had killed three times more enemy warriors than any other man in the Clan. His job was to keep the warriors well trained, and be the driving physical force in the Outlaw Society.

Doc Mende, the medicine man, age 45, was chosen because of his knowledge of how to treat illness from the different plants in the forest. His job was to take care of the health of the Outlaw Society.

Ironhead Mende, the Blacksmith, age 40, was chosen because of his knowledge about creating and maintaining weapons. His job was to keep the warriors well armed, and to make farm tools if the need arises.

Stick Mende, age 39, was chosen because of his knowledge about house building, and building towns. His job was chief scout and make plans of attacks on towns and villages.

Money Mende, the long distance Trader, age 40, was chosen because of his many travels and knowledge of dealing with strange people. His job was to be the War Chief's negotiator with towns and villages.

The point we wanted to make is, these seven, a Leader, and 6 Councilors, are the model of the Mende Governing Body of an Outlaw Society; and the warriors enforce the rules inside the Clan.

This gives us a good idea of how a Mende Outlaw Government is organized, also the kind of knowledge needed in its leadership, and the kind of warriors needed to carry out its plans of action.

This means that the government are warriors by nature, and Outlaws by lifestyle; its purpose is for physical protectors, and economic providers of the Outlaw Clan by any means necessary. Now let's re-visit the mission this traveling government is to accomplish.

Lockjaw, as War Leader, was to lead an army of 500 warriors and a large number of women, children, and old people some 800 to a 1000 miles.

And they are to travel through territories of nations protected by governments and warriors who don't like strange warriors passing through their land; much less give them any land on which to live.

Anyway, the evidence shows that the Mendes traveled east, on the northern side of the Fouta Jallon Mountain range until they reached the Highlands in the Northern Ivory Coast where they came into conflict with the powerful Akan Kingdoms.

So they turned south, where they came into contact with the Land of Secret Societies in the south western part of the Ivory Coast. And they knew they had found the kind of place they could live the lifestyle that Old Man Mende had chosen for them. A place filled with people just like them, Outlaws, and there were no Kings. But they didn't have any land.

They fought their way south until they came to the Ocean, and they could not take any land, so they turned west and fought their way along the coast until they reached their present home in Sierra Leone.

The only things that Lockjaw and company carried with them was knowledge in leadership i.e., government, and lots of weapons and warriors who knew how to use them. We can just imagine the problems they had to solve.

However, as far as our interest is concerned, it is enough to say that the evidence shows that this Mende Clan arrived in their present location in Sierra Leone around the year 1250, some 25 years or so later. And they arrived with their government intact, and took some land from the Temne and Bullom nations and built a town, and grew into the Mende nation of this present day.

Well Fellow Detectives, since we see how the Mendes came to be in Sierra Leone, we are now going to move up in time to about 1260. The 25th Anniversary when Old Man Mende sent his oldest sons on a mission to establish a new home.

Now lets look in on Old Bighead, Priest, Killer, Doc, Ironhead, Sticks, and Money Mende, who although are very old men, are still War Chiefs and Elders of New Mende Town. We want to see what they are doing spiritual wise. They are celebrating before a special three-pot Shrine to their Ancestors, including the ones that died on the journey.

This is a private celebration which is taking place the night before the Great Anniversary day. It is held in a special room in Bighead's house, with these seven old men present with their memories of the long ago mission to find and build a home.

When we arrive, the Ancestors have been greeted with a sacrifice meal of one rooster, one hen, seven yams, and seven portions of rice that has been cooked. The old men are telling their Ancestors about the success of the 25 year mission. Let listen in on what they are saying;

Bighead: "Greetings Fathers! Welcome to Outlaw Paradise! We are coming to the end of our life's journey. Our sons soon will become the leadership of Your New Town. We are seeking your approval as to the progress we have made in fulfilling the Mission you gave to us, and we are going to give to our sons.

Our journey was in two parts, leaving Mandinka land, and entering Riceland, the Land of Secret Societies. I left Old Town with 500 warriors, and before I reached the Land of Secret Societies, I had over 800 of the finest warriors you could imagine. Some I took in raids, and others just wanted the adventure and a share of the rewards.

We did lose some warriors in the many battles on the journey; however, we killed or captured many more than we lost. Our journey took 20 years. However, our biggest battle of all came when we took land from the Temne and Bullom people; this fight took 3 very bloody years.

Now for 5 years I have protected, and provided Your New Town with all of its protection and economic needs from the outside world. Every year I have made successful raids on other towns to increase the wealth of your people. Although in the beginning, Your Town was also raided, but never successfully.

And every year Your Town has grown in size, not only have our women produced many grand and great grand children for you, we have also captured many whole families, given them land, and they are also part of Your Town population, which is some 5,000 people. We have not shamed you with failure!"

Killer: "We have 800 of the best warriors in all of the Land of Secret Societies and, we are feared and respected far and wide. Our reputation, as well trained warriors, is such that we only have to appear at the gates of a town, and they surrender. We have not shamed you with failure!"

Doc: "This land is rich in plant and animal life, and very good for farms, especially for growing rice; and as you can see, we have become Rice Farmers. We have our full measure of chickens, cows, and goats. Also, there are many fish in the rivers and streams. This is a hunter's paradise. There are herds of elephants, hippopotamus, bush cows (small Buffalo), deer, and more small edible animals than I can count. There are many kinds of wild fruits and vegetables to be found. We have not shamed you with failure!"

Ironhead: "Our warriors are well armed with the best swords, spears, and arrows in the Land of Secret Societies, and too, our farmers have the best farm tools; and our arts and crafts are producing more than we need. We have not shamed you with failure!"

Stick: "We have stockades in Your Town. It is surrounded by three war fences. The inner fence (wall) being made of a double-roe of logs 14 feet tall, and planted 4 feet deep. The middle fence is 8 feet from the inner, and built the same. The outer fence is 15 feet from the middle one; however, this one has spaces between the logs for defensive reasons. To make surprise attacks difficult still more, all paths leading to the Town are left overgrown and narrow as possible. This means that enemy warriors can only approach in single file; and only a single road leads into town, and it is easily blocked. Also the actual gate into town is so narrow that only one man can enter at once.

And finally, the houses in town are deliberately built close to each other in irregular patterns, so that the paths between them form a maze. That makes it very difficult for enemy warriors to find their way about, if they are lucky enough to get this far. We have not shamed you with failure!"

Priest: "Although Your Town functions by the traditional laws of old town, the ones you taught us in our youth, the Land of Secret Societies is a strange place. We now have some new institutions called Secret Societies. Even so, we have not shamed you with failure!"

Money: "Your Town is very rich, and has good trading relations with a number of big towns, plus the raids bring in lots of money; Your people are wealthy. We have not shamed you with failure!"

Bighead: "Honor! Honor! Honor! given to our Ancestors, honor given to their mission. This is Your Town; we are only its servants. We also seek your approval, and invite You to attend tomorrow's celebration by all of your people."

Eavesdropping can be a good way to gather evidence; we have not only seen how a Traveling Government accomplishes its mission, but also how it established its goal.

This gives us a good idea of the approach and attitude of the Secree in general. Especially when we take into account the defense around their town. We can see that they were living in the middle of a war-zone, which is something else all of the nations in the Land of Secret Societies have in common.

At this point, Grandpa should define how we are using the term OUTLAW. We mean a family, or a person, that makes their own laws of social conduct, and refuses to live within the laws of the wider society of which they are a part of.

In this sense, the Mendes are outlaws because they refuse to live according to the laws of the then new Mali Kingdom society's laws of a King.

However, with this definition in mind, once the Mendes moved into the Land of Secret Societies, they cannot be defined as outlaws outside of the Kingdom of Mali. Although, we can also see that the Mendes have an Outlaw Philosophy of life, "take what they wanted out life."

Now if every Clan that came into the Land of Secret Societies grew into a small nation had this approach and attitude, that would mean that all of the nations in the Land of Secret Societies are Outlaws as related to some Kingdom or other.

Therefore, we must come to the conclusion that the Secree Society, or to say, the Society in the Land of Secret Societies, is outlaw by nature. But the evidence also shows that the Mendes and Secree, were not only Outlaws from a physical point of view, but just as important, they also had Outlaw Religious Beliefs as well.

Secree Outlaw Religious Beliefs

As far as the Religious Beliefs of the Secree are concerned, they have a lot in common with the Aja, where the differences were only a matter of degrees, for instance, Ancestor Worship. Where as the Aja only took Ancestor worship to a higher level, the Secree took it to its final conclusion; its highest level.

In other words, the Secree's entire religious involvement is focused on their Ancestors. They do not get too involved with other aspects of African Traditional Religion. Whereas the Aja have one spiritual foot in the spirituality of their religious beliefs, LEGBA, and the other spiritual foot in their spiritual beliefs about their Ancestors; The Secree have both their spiritual feet planted firmly in their spiritual beliefs about their Ancestors, period.

Recall the Aja and the Igbo's social organization, where the village society consisted of Fathers, Brothers, Sons and their families, this means that a town society is one big family; a family bonded together by a combination of spiritual-(emotional) relationships.

This also means that the spirituality of the extended family and the spirituality of society are the same thing. This equals the spiritual relationships, Ancestor to Ancestor, the Living to Living, and the key, Ancestors to the Living. This three-way relationship is the Holy Trinity of the Secree's outlaw Society.

To demonstrate what we mean by Outlaw Religious Beliefs, based entirely on Ancestor Worship, we will take a look at the Mende's, and the Secree's beliefs about the role of the Gods and Goddesses.

<h2 style="text-align:center">Secree Religion
(Gods, Goddesses, and Creation)</h2>

As we mentioned, the Mendes are not focused on their religious beliefs as far as ritual worship of Gods and Goddesses are concerned, and the Secree are no exception. So there is very little evidence to work with concerning Gods and Goddesses, in fact, we only have two stories to work with.

In this situation, we Detectives have to do a lot of interpreting, to see the kinds of conclusions we can reach about their spiritual world. Mende's word for Great Creator is "NGEWO." The two stories are as follows, and we will interpret as we go along.

"NGEWO, before He was called NGEWO, was once a very Big Spirit who lived in a cave (Universe?). He was so powerful that all He said would be done, really took place (He created with Words).

One day He said, I have all of this Power, why don't I use it? I have lived alone for a long time with no one to talk to, and no one to play with. Then, He went to the entrance of the cave and said, 'I want all kinds of animals to live with me in this cave.'

So the animals came in pairs. Then He shut the door. After a while, He called them all together and gave them the laws of the cave. He said, 'I will give you anything you want, food (knowledge?),' and everything else, but you must not touch My Own food (special knowledge?).'

Then the Spirit looked round about and said, "This cave is too small," so He turned Himself around and the cave became very, very big (heaven?). The animals were now very happy because they had plenty of room to find food (learn). All they had to do was eat (think).

The Spirit too was happy; He had neighbors to talk to and to play with. The Spirit was so big that all the animals could not move even one of His legs. But the Spirit was very strict about the due observance of His Law.

One day one of the animals came to greet the Spirit. As it approached, it smelled some sweet smelling food. He saw some food (special knowledge called Hale) and took some and ate it. Immediately, it found itself in front of the Spirit.

The Spirit said, "What brought you here, you have violated My Law." The Spirit then threw the animal out of the cave and said, 'You! From now on, your name is cow.' Later, another animal ate the food, and again the Spirit threw it out of the cave, saying, 'You! From now on, your name is monkey.' At last, all of the animals were thrown out of the cave.

Some of the animals the Spirit called mankind. That is how animals got their names. All the animals and men are still wandering around in the world looking for this 'sweet-smelling food' (knowledge about life). The Spirit is now called NGEWO. He has now gone up far above men (in the sky), where He is sitting, watching to see who will eat His food (use His knowledge to live life). Man and animals are now removed from NGEWO.' (End of story)

(Second story)

"Long ago NGEWO made the earth and all things and finished by making a man and a woman. These two people did not know NGEWO's name; they only refereed to Him as 'MAADA-LE' (He is Grandfather).

One day NGEWO addressed them saying, 'Everything you asked me for, if you want it, you shall have it.' When they wanted anything or needed food (knowledge about things) they went to Him saying, MAADA, give us this; or give us that'.

When they began to come to Him very often, He said to Himself, 'if I stay near these people, they will wear me with their requests. I will make another living place for myself far above them.' The People went to sleep, and when they woke the next morning, they looked about, but could not see Him. They lifted up their heads and saw Him (as the sky). From this we say, NGEWO is Great (The Great God, or God the Creator).

From the place where He stayed, He made two living things, one for the man, and one for the woman, which He named Fowl. When He handed them over He said, 'Whenever one of you does wrong to his companion, you must call me, and when I come you must give me back my fowl' (sacrifice a fowl to Him). This has now become a signal for a curse. Whenever a person who does wrong hears these words uttered, he will apologize at once, instead of allowing NGEWO to come down for the fowl to kill it.

One day, NGEWO came down to them and said 'Farewell'. He then exhorted them, saying, 'See, I have made an agreement with you concerning your dealing with one another; therefore do not have a bad heart (bad feelings) towards one another.' They replied, 'Yes.' Then He went to His own place. From that time they called Him LEVE (Up High)." (End of story).

Grandpa just loves this part of Detective work, interpreting African creation stories, for we now must reach a conclusion from the () marked points in the two stories of creation. While keeping in mind that we are seeking the religious beliefs that the Mendes have in common with the other nations in the "Land of Secret Societies."

And in this way, come to a conclusion as to what are the religious beliefs of the nations as a group, the SECREES. We are going to accomplish this, as we mentioned, from interpreting the points in the two stories, and rewrite the points in one story of our own conclusion. Our made-up story is as follows;

NGEWO lived in a Cave of Paradise which had a door way, and this Cave was the only thing that existed in space. One day NGEWO became lonely and decided to use the Power of His Secret Knowledge in the form of Words to create the World and All Therein, including life in the form of Animals.

NGEWO was very happy, and gave the Animals the Laws of Social Conduct; the law of the jungle. This was followed by NGEWO giving the Animals a big gift; He allowed them to Choose their own Destinies by giving them everything they personally wanted. And NGEWO and the Animals lived in Perfect Harmony.

After a few generations, NGEWO saw that of all the Animals, Mankind was the only one misusing the Knowledge of Hale; while some were using it to help people, medicine men, priest, etc., others, like witches, etc., were using it to hurt people. In fact, jealousy and greed had grown into a big powerful two headed Spirit, people called EVIL.

NGEWO's Heart went out to mankind, and this is why Ancestor land is located in NGEWO's Heart instead of in Mother Earth, the Earth Goddess, and NDOI, Who are NGEWO's Wife.

Out of His deep concern for Mankind, NGEWO created a male and female weapon, Poro and Sande, and gave them to men and women; along with a Contract of Social Conduct as a sign of Forgiveness for what they had done in the Cave. (End of made up story).

Thus is the creation story of the SECREES, based on our conclusion from the () marked points of the above two Mende creation stories; but this does not end our story. We are now going to extend our story to cover another point about the relationship between NGEWO and Mankind; Ritual Worship of Ancestors. Which is to serve as a background for our next Mende story, our extended made up story is as follows:

Still seeing Mankind, after receiving the weapons, Poro and Sande lose fight after fight with the EVIL of Jealousy and Greed. NGEWO was at the point of condemning Mankind as a Lost Cause; this is when the Original Ancestors from the Cave-days came up with a Master Plan.

The Original Ancestors would take full Responsibility for the Redemption of Mankind, if NGEWO would teach Mankind the art of Ritual Worship (ritual communication), and Ancestors be allowed to Visit earth and become a Part of Mankind's Society.

NGEWO thought, "If I take into consideration that when People died they must climb a Mountain and cross a River, I can use mountains and rivers as a communication door through which Mankind can tell something to the last Ancestor to die. He tells it to the next, and so on, until it reaches the Original Ancestors, and they can negotiate with Me.

This means that all I will have to do is deal with the Original Ancestors, and we got along just fine in the Cave-days. After all, all of the Gods and Goddesses take responsibility for their social conduct, so why not give the Ancestors and Living Mankind the same responsibility, and allow them too, to become Gods and Goddesses in respect to responsibility."

So NGEWO agreed and this became a Contract between NGEWO and the Original Ancestors. Meaning, it is the ORIGINAL ANCESTORS that are the REDEEMER of MANKIND.

As we said, the extended part of our story was to be a kind of background to the up-coming Mende's story about how mankind learned ritual worship of Ancestors; the Mende story is as follows:

"In the beginning there was no form of praying at all. NGEWO sat and thought of all the people He had made, and how there was no way of making them follow His wishes. All the people did was to come to Him with their petty complaints.

Then NGEWO made a big mountain near the town where the people lived. He gave the mountain power to talk to people. NGEWO said, 'If the people get used to hearing the voice of the mountain (the Original Ancestors), and if they keep the laws set out by the mountain, in the future, they will keep My Laws.' Then NGEWO gave people the power to dream.

It happened one night that one of the old men in the town had a dream. The Mountain came to him in the dream as an Old Man (Ancestor) who said to the Dreamer, 'You are my friend, do you hear?' "Yes!'

The Old Man of the mountain continued; 'When you awake from this sleep, you must tell the Elders of this town that all the people must give me food to eat (make sacrifices).' The Dreamer agreed.

Then the Dreamer said to the Old Man, 'Where do you come from?' The Old Man replied, 'I have come from the mountain that you were looking at.'

The Dreamer turned to look at the mountain, but could not see it. He said to the Old Man, 'The Mountain is gone.' 'Yes' said the Old Man, 'I am the mountain!

Then, when he said good-bye, the Old Man went away saying, 'Do not forget what I said.' As soon as the old man had gone out of sight, the mountain appeared again.

When the Dreamer awoke from his sleep, he went at once to the Elders and recounted his dream. The Chief Elder then called his people together, and the Dreamer repeated his story.

They agreed to give the mountain food as requested, and asked the Dreamer to go to the mountain and say that its request had been granted.

He was also told to ask the mountain to help them catch the animals required for preparing the food. They, the people, for their part, would supply the rice and sauce in four day's time.

After a while, the Dreamer went towards the mountain. As he went, he picked up twenty stones. On reaching a certain spot, he cleared the bush and said, 'O Grandfather, you in this mountain, you were the one who came to me in my dream last night and said you had chosen me to be your friend (priest).

And that my people and I should give you food to eat. I have told them the dream, and they have agreed to grant your request.

But they say that I must ask you to help them to catch some animals, which we would cook for you. That is what I have come to tell you. I have brought these stones; please arrange them in such a manner as to indicate to me how many animals you want.' Then the Dreamer went back to the town.

The next morning he returned to the mountain and found the stones arranged as follows; ten were facing the man, nine facing the mountain, and one was placed in the center. This meant that in the hunt, nine animals would escape. The hunters would kill ten, but one must be saved alive for the mountain. This one was to be killed by the dreamer on the day of the ceremonies.

The dreamer explained this arrangement to the people, and they consented to abide by it. Then, they all went hunting. They killed ten animals, but the eleventh was kept alive, as the mountain had wanted of them. That same evening, the dreamer-priest again went to the mountain. He then addressed the following words to the mountain;

'Big Mountain, Big Mountain,
I have come to tell you here,
I have come to tell you that
The big pot (sacrifice) you asked for
We are coming with it tomorrow.
Therefore however high the sun may
 Rise tomorrow (how late)
Do not go anywhere until I arrive.
If it looks quiet, I have not yet arrived.'

To each of those statements the mountain responded, 'Woo-woo!" with a rising shrill tone.

Then the Dreamer-Priest went back to the town. That night, the people gathered rice, palm oil and salt from the women, and a public proclamation was made that on the next day everybody should go to the mountain. They set out the following morning, they set out together. When they reached a certain place, they stopped, and the Dream-Priest called out to the mountain;

'Big Mountain! Big Mountain!
The big pot (sacrifice) I mentioned yesterday,
I have brought it.
I said, do not go away until we come,
No matter how high the sun may be.
Now we have come.
The rice that we have brought
Is not enough for everybody
Therefore, please tell us
Who should eat it,
The men or the women?

The mountain responded, 'Whoo-whoo!' to each of the statements except the final question, to which the mountain replied, 'The men.'

When the men heard this, they drove all of the women away back to their homes. Then they brought the live animal to the Dreamer, who killed it by cutting its throat upon a rock.

They (the men) then cooked the meat with the rice and red palm oil. When the food was ready, they gave it to the Dreamer. He laid a banana leaf on the ground and set some of the meat and rice and palm oil on it. He also poured out some palm-wine on the ground and said to the mountain, 'Wash your hands, and eat rice, drink water.'

Then he took a kola-nut and split it in two. He held the halves in the hollow of both hands cupped together and addressed the mountain saying, "If this rice we have given you has really reached you, and you are pleased with it then show us a sign."

He then tossed the halves of the kola-nut into the air; and, when they fell on the ground, the white insides were facing upwards. This action was repeated four times with the same results. This sign made them feel glad as it indicated that the Ancestors) had accepted the food. Then the dreamer-Priest began to pray:

'O Big Mountain,
We did not put you to shame,
Do not put us to shame.
We have all come here today;
If there is any one sick amongst us,
Make him well.
As for our children,
Let not witches or any other evil people attack
them.
Here are our Elders and their wives,
Let no evil attack them.
Let no one bring war upon us.
But if war does come,
Let our town not be destroyed by it.
Let none of us be lost in war.
Let our women not die in childbirth.'

Then at that point, all the people spontaneously responded, 'NGEWO let it be so!' That spot near the mountain became a yearly praying place for the men, but not for the women.

Then, one day a woman had a dream, and was visited by an Old Woman, and in this way NGEWO provided for the women a praying place as He had done for the men." (End of story).

Thus was how ritual worship of Ancestors came to mankind, and the same process took place when a male and female praying place was established at the riverside.

Only in this case, visitors in the man and woman dreams were an Old man and woman who had a long chain for a body. The chain symbolizes the many linked generations of Ancestors. However in both cases, the ritual process was the same.

Now we will turn our attention to a Mende story that tells how the 'tree' became a praying place for family worship of Ancestors. The story is as follows:

"Long ago, this Tree did a very interesting thing. It changed itself into an Old Man and went to a certain person in a dream. This man's (the Dreamer) name was Sengbe. The Tree said to Sengbe, 'We will make a compact of friendship; if you give me food (sacrifices) I will make your town prosper.' Sengbe agreed.

The next morning Sengbe told the people in the town what had happened in his dream. They also agreed to take food to the tree, and they continued to do so regularly.

When the tree saw that the people were looking after it so well, it said to Sengbe, 'I will come to you yonder when I go walking.' Sengbe said, 'all right, but how can you walk in the town without the ordinary people seeing you?' The Tree then said, 'You will see a white cat, which will be me.'

One day, after they had taken food to the Tree, Sengbe said, 'Let us go back to the town now.' As they went back they saw a big white cat. It stayed in the town walking about until the evening, and then it disappeared. From then on, the Tree always used to appear and disappear in the form of a cat. In due course, when Sengbe died, the people turned the Tree into a Family praying place." (End of story)

Thus is how Ritual Worship of Ancestors came to Mankind; and a Mountain, River, and Tree became praying places.

However, the two points to keep in mind is that we do not mean to imply that the SECREES do not have a Personal Soul with a Chosen Destiny. Only that we are not looking in that direction. Our major subject is the Secret Societies and their role in the spirituality of Society itself.

Nor do we mean to imply that the people that make up the Land of Secret Societies are not fully aware of the other Gods and Goddesses of the African Traditional Holy Family. Only that they don't have a direct relationship with them, that's the Responsibility of their Ancient Ancestors.

In fact, the only time that NGEWO and NDOI, the Great Father God and Mother Goddess' name is used, is when someone Swears an Oath. Other than that Oath, the whole of the Secree's ritual activities, as far as worshiping is concerned, is focused on their Ancestors; which is why none of the Gods and Goddesses have Praying Places, only their Ancestors.

And this is why we say that the Secree took Ancestor Worship to its highest level. Their Ancestors are their Great Redeemer. This means that Ancestors are the Gods and Goddesses of the Society as far as ritual worship is concerned; (in the same sense that Christ is the Great Redeemer God of Christian Society.)

Well Fellow Detectives, it has been a long and complicated effort dealing with multi-nations who don't have one religion in common, nor speak the same language. The only thing they have in common is a belief in Ancestor Worship, and we will show later, Secret Societies. But Grandpa believes that we have finally gathered enough information to come to a conclusion about the Articles of Faith of these nations as a group.

Secree Religion (Secree's Articles of Faith)

(1) NGEWO, the God of Knowledge, and His Wife, NDOI, the Goddess of Understanding, Created the World of Life using Words of Knowledge and Wisdom.

(2) NGEWO gave all life (including plants) Laws of Social Conduct.

(3) Mankind broke NGEWO's Laws by Stealing His Knowledge of the Nature of Things, and now NGEWO's Knowledge is divided throughout Life forms; each Form of Life has Knowledge about different things.

(4) Life is Outlaws by Nature; because they Choose to Live outside of the Laws of NGEWO; especially Mankind.

(5) NGEWO created Ancestor Worship to Redeem Mankind.

(6) NGEWO has a Social Contract with Mankind; Mankind Worships NGEWO AND NDOI through the ritual of worshipping Knowledge and Understanding.

(7) Mankinds Chosen Destiny is to Find, Collect, and Store the Knowledge the Other Life forms (animals and plants) Stole, and add it to his own Stolen Knowledge. SECREES believe that Knowledge and Wisdom can cure any Problem, and this is why they call it medicine.

These Articles of Faith are our conclusion indicating the religious beliefs that all of the people in the Land of Secret Societies have in common. Being of different nations, no matter what other beliefs they may have that are different from each other; gives the 'Secree' a 'Spiritual Unity.'

Grandpa is fully aware that this is a big (logical) jump from two Mende creation stories, and two stories about Ancestor Worship. And also come up with that particular combination of beliefs for all of the nations living in the Land of Secret Societies.

But let's analyze these Articles from the known evidence we will demonstrate. It is very clear that the SECREES have an uncontrollable desire for Knowledge and Wisdom.

After all, people do not defy a God unless they think what they are stealing is of high value, like Creative Knowledge from a Creative Knowledge God, NGEWO, and, Creative wisdom from a Creative Understanding Goddess, NDOI. With knowledge and Wisdom comes Understanding automatically. Also, there can be no doubt that the SECREES are Outlaws by Nature and Choice, and created their society from that point of view.

But to get some insight into what this means, we must answer the question, exactly what kind of Lifestyle Mankind was living, that caused NGEWO to become so frustrated with them? He could only deal with them from a distance; and then, only in-directly through their original Ancestors.

This is an easy question to answer. All of the evidence, and there is lots of it, shows clearly that the Mendes never made any attempt what so ever to live under the Moral laws of NGEWO's Social Contract.

Their approach and attitude in life is to only concern themselves with the laws of the morals of the Society they created themselves. They were not only social outlaws within a Kingdom; they were also spiritual outlaws in the spiritual world of African Traditional Religious Beliefs.

Grandpa's conclusion is that, the Secree's lifestyle of outlaws is what Afro-Americans call, 'a Street Lifestyle Society.' For example, there is also evidence that shows clearly that the Mendes 'took what they wanted' by 'any means necessary'.

However, this is not the direction we are going to take our investigation; we have come to conclusions about history and religious beliefs. Now we must back up those conclusions with evidence, and come to a conclusion about the 'Well' in the Title 'Drinking from Ancient Wells,' and more important, the 'Content of that Well.'

After looking at the evidence, Grandpa came to the conclusion that, 'Secret Society' is the content of the "Well," which we will see is the Dynamic force in their Society. Thus is the direction we will next focus our investigation, Secret Societies.

Secree Religion
(Society and Secret Societies)

Now we can turn our full investigative attention on the Mende Society, and our major subject, Secret Societies. Where the focus is on how the Mende Society is governed, and their Outlaw Lifestyle; and see if the evidence proves Grandpa's conclusion that 'Secret Societies' are the 'Content' of their 'Well.'

But first we must define two words, Society and Secret Societies, and the relation between the two. When the Mendes use the term Society, they mean the Society of their own Clan Town, and don't include the Society of other Clans living in the area.

However, if the other Clans have the same highest Society values, we can think in terms of the 'Society of Secree;" although we will continue to investigate the Mendes as our example.

Next, we must define just what we mean by secret societies. The SECREES, and this includes the Mendes, believe that their society is composed of a number of smaller independent societies, each of which has ritual activities that are held in secret from the rest of society.

And it is the sum-total of these ritual activities of those smaller societies, that give form to the spirituality of their Society. On the other hand, secret societies are schools where knowledge is stored, designed to teach and train people for their role in society as a whole. It is the training and teaching that is held in secrecy.

To get an idea of how a secret society functions, we only have to recall the Igbo, and Orchester III's purification ceremonies to become a Living Saint in the Igbo Society. And the only secret part, the ritual ceremonies were held in the forest hut when no outsiders were present but a Priest.

Now if all of Orchester III's ritual ceremonies were held deep in the forest, and no outsider was allowed to see what was going on. These ceremonies would be secret society ritual activities as we use the term.

Now, we must mention that in the Mendes Society, they have two governments that work in harmony with each other, yet function independently. One government deals with war and outside economic issues, and the other deals with social and spiritual issues.

We have looked, in some details, at their war-economic government, and we have also looked at their Outlaw Religious Beliefs for good measure. Now we come to the good part, their social-spiritual government; and this is where secret societies fit into the lifestyle of Outlaw's Society.

The Mendes call Secret Society Government, Bush Schools, because they teach and train in the bush (forest); and secret societies because the schools are part of society that functions in secret; as all Outlaws do.

While the Mendes have a number of Bush Schools, there are 6 such Schools that directly govern their Society; they are as follows:

Poro School: Deals with the education of young boys starting at puberty age. The art of Manhood is taught, and trains them for their role in Society. As well as, enforces all rules and regulations of male social conduct throughout their lifetime.

Sande School: Is concerned with the education of young girls of puberty age. The art of womanhood is taught, and trains them in the role they are to play in Society. As well as enforce all rules and regulations of female social conduct throughout their lifetime.

Humui School: Teaches sexual conduct; and makes all of the moral rules of where, when, and with whom one can have sexual relations within Society. As well as deal with physical sexual diseases.

Njayei School: Is concerned with the mental health of Society. For example, insanity, or any other mental problems, big or small.

Kpa School: Is concerned with the medical problems of Society. For instance, the well being of the body in general; from problems with eyes, teeth, stomach, to setting broken bones etc, etc.

Then there is the Wunde School: Which is concerned with warriors and Outlaw activities, and is related to War-Economic Government, which doesn't interest us at this point.

These 5 Schools, and some schools that have sub-divisions, not only govern with the social side of Society, they also perform rituals related to Spirituality of Society. Each school has a Chief Priest, a Chief Medicine Man, a Chief Teacher, and at least 6 Elders as Councilors.

Plus each school, as a government, has the authority to enforce the rules they teach throughout Society. It is these 5 government Schools, working in harmony with each other, that govern the Social, Spiritual, Medical, and Spiritual Attitude of Mende Society.

Collectively, they handle general education; in the sense of social and vocational training, indoctrination of spiritual attitudes, regulating sexual conduct, and supervising political and economical affairs.

They also operate social services, ranging from medical treatment, to forms of entertainment and recreation. The major point being, is that all of the Clans in the Land of Secret Societies have the same 5 Bush Schools and Bush Spirit, including the same ritual approach to them; no matter what their beliefs are.

This leaves the question, what are the spiritual beliefs that the Mendes call "Bush Spirits." If we recall, in the first Creation Story, as NGEWO threw the animals out of the Sacred Cave, He gave each a name.

Grandpa's conclusion is that these names symbolized the nature of the knowledge they stole; cows stole knowledge of the nature of cows, monkeys stole knowledge of the nature of monkeys, and mankind stole knowledge of the nature of mankind. The point is that all of them stole, and are in possession of Knowledge.

Also, the Mendes, like all Africans, believe that knowledge has a spirit and certain powers. This means, being as all the animals, including mankind, live in the Bush (forest), the Spirit of the Knowledge they stole also lives in the Bush. This is why the Spirits of the schools are called Bush Spirits.

Now think of the five schools we mentioned, as meaning that the Mende Society is divided into 5 spiritual parts; each school specializes in the knowledge covering its part. Thus we have Bush Spirit-Knowledge as the Gods and Goddesses of Society. This means that the Mendes have a ritual relationship with Knowledge. Or to say, their Society worships the Spirits of Knowledge.

Whereas the Poro and Sande schools deal with knowledge of the nature of manhood and womanhood, there are other schools, for example Kpa School, for the benefit of Society, collects, teaches, and worships knowledge that the other animals and plants stole.

This brings up another interesting point. If the Mendes believe in the Spirit of Stolen Knowledge, and, they believe that NGEWO is the God of Knowledge or the Super Spirit of Knowledge; then indirectly, when they worship knowledge, they are also worshipping NGEWO and NDOI. This is especially the case with Poro and Sande Spirits.

On the other hand, the Mendes call Poro and Sande Schools, the Mother and Father of all bush schools, because of the role they play in sustaining Society.

They believe that children do not have a role in, or are a part of Society. Children must be born into Society as men and Women. This birth is one of the major functions of Poro and Sande Puberty Rituals; following the idea that Society grows in the same way as a Family, through birth.

This makes Poro and Sande, the Father and Mother that gives birth to men and women for the growth and strength of Society.

Therefore, if we take a detailed look at Poro School, and a close look at the Sande School, we can get a picture of the foundation of the social and spiritual activities of the Mende Society as a whole. As well as more insight into the nature of puberty rituals; which not only answers your Parent's questions, but also our question about the highest values of the Secree as our direct-line Ancestors.

Well Fellow Detectives, like Grandpa said, this is going to be an interesting investigation, because the subject is so unique to Afro-

Americans usual way of thinking; an Outlaw Society Governed by Bush Schools and Bush Spirits!

On the other hand, it is very clear that the Secree Society is the Ancient Well of the Secree in general, and the Mendes in particular. Therefore, we should focus all of our investigative attention on the "Content of the Well," Bush Schools and Bush Spirits, or to say Secret Societies.

Then, we will see Grandpa's conclusion about the Secree having an Outlaw Society, from the point of view of the way Afro-Americans think of certain social conduct. And at the same time, see how a secret society government works, and the purpose it serves.

However, before we get into secret societies in general, Grandpa thinks one of the functions of Poro secret society government, male puberty ritual, should be looked at in some detail; which will also give us some insight into the spiritual-cultural side of the Mende Society as a whole.

Secree Religion
(Poro Bush School and Puberty Ritual)

First, we need some background. We will use the names of you GrandKids, for example, DionDi, Marcus, Tyree, Michael, and Orchester III; and say they are all puberty age. Now to complete our background, we need a description and location of the school and more important, a cast of Poro Bush Spirits and School Officials. We will begin with the Poro Bush School.

The school is located on the Sacred Grounds of Poro Society, called Poro Bush; consisting of some 3 or 4 acres of forest land located about 5 miles outside of town away from any paths or roads where people travel.

Poro Bush is located in the middle of tall trees and thick underbrush, which gives it the appearance and feeling of being isolated deep in some mysterious jungle hundreds of miles from any community. Thus is why it is called Poro Bush land.

In the center of this Bush land is a cleared area about a block square, where the Founder and other high Poro Officials are buried. They are buried in a standing position, symbolizing their Upright Manhood, and 4 large stones mark their graves.

It is here at these Sacred Stones, that prayer is offered to the Ancestor Spirits of Poro. This is also where the most important ceremonies, including the final graduation are performed. Only two officials are allowed near these sacred stones, the Poro Chief Priest, and the Chief Priestess.

For this reason, Poro Bush is considered Sacred, and only authorized persons are allowed; the 20 odd Elder Teachers, Counselors, and Administrators of the Poro Government, and of course a number of Students.

There is only one path that leads from town to Poro Bush. This path has a gate at its entrance, with three other gates along its way which are guarded by armed Warriors.

The further side of the first gate is called the "Sacred way," which is full of twist and turns with all kinds of traps and frightening images along its way.

It is here in Poro Bush where the male puberty ritual takes place; and for this occasion a temporary village is built for the boys to live there for up to 4 years, and in some cases even longer.

During this time, the boys are not allowed any outside visitors. The word Poro means, "Our Father's Law," or "Our Father's Knowledge;" and the school has 10 grades. The puberty ritual is only the first grade.

On the other hand, the Poro Bush Spirit ritual activities are performed by 6 Masqueraders symbolizing the 6 spirits of Poro. Or, we should say, a Major Spirit and His 5 Spirit Assistants who form the Spiritual Action Arm of Poro Government, they are as follows:

GBENI, the Chief Spirit: symbolizing the Spirit of the Knowledge of Manhood.

NGAFGOTI, symbolizing the Spirit of Soul and Chosen Destiny.

YAVEI, symbolizing Fatherhood and Family relations.

FOBAI, symbolizing economics.

DAGBADAII, symbolizing Law and Order in Society.

And WUJEI, Spokesman, symbolizing the Original Ancestor who stole the knowledge of Manhood.

However, we are only interested at this point in the Spirit of Knowledge of the Nature of Manhood; called GBENI, who is symbolized by a Mask worn by a Senior Elder Masquerader. But it is the Mask itself, and the cloths of the Masquerader that will tell us the most about this Spirit.

The GBENI Masquerader costume, not counting the Mask, consists of cloth and leather, but most of all, leopard skins which symbolized the Approach and Attitude of Manhood.

The Masquerader also has a special Poro Horn. It is made out of a cow horn. The pointed end has been pierced, covered with lizard skin, and a hole through which the Masquerader blows has been cut through the skin. A harsh nasal sound is produced, and this is the Voice of Knowledge of Manhood.

The major point we want to make is that, this Spirit, Gbeni, has the same status as a God. Meaning, it is served by a Priest and Priestess, Priest Sowa and Priestess Mabole (Mabole is the only woman official in Poro society).

This also means that GBENI is one of the Gods of Society Religion. And of course, there is Gbeni's impersonator who has a non-Masquerader ritual role as well. He is called, "keeper of Poro Horn" (voice). These three Officials are the key to Poro Puberty ritual activities.

Their position is that of spokesperson between the young boys, and the Spirits of Manhood, GBENI and His Assistants, plus, the Spirit of the first male Ancestor (who stole the knowledge in the first place).

This means that Poro puberty ritual has two spiritual forces, dealt with as one; the Spirit of the knowledge of manhood and, the spirits of Ancestors who have reached the highest level of Manhood symbolized by the Mask and 4 sacred stones. All of which are tied together through the performances of a Priest, Priestess, and a number of Masqueraders.

This leads us to the conclusion that the SECREES have a spiritual relationship with knowledge, period; or to say, they worship knowledge.

Now to complete our background; although Poro Manhood Society Government deals with lots of Manhood issues, our interest is in GBENI's role in the male puberty ritual activities; the actual process of the transformation from Childhood to Manhood.

This brings us to the spiritual idea behind these ritual ceremonies. From a spiritual point of view, GBENI is to kill and eat the boys (take them out of the community). And they are to remain in His stomach (bush school) for at least 1 to 4 years.

They will be molded, shaped, and formed spiritually and physically (taught and worked) by GBENI's knowledge until they are fully qualified to be Upstanding Men of Society.

Meanwhile, as far as the community is concerned, the boys are dead. Thus is the spiritual idea of Poro puberty ritual.

Now, against this background, we will re-introduce our major characters, DionDi, Tyree, Marcus, Michael, and Orchester III, the stars of the upcoming show. We will follow them through Poro School; and keep in mind, we are saying that they are all the same age, 12 or 13 years old, and are to remain in school for 4 years.

All of their young life, the 'Boys' have heard stories about how their fathers and uncles had reached the highest level of manhood in the Poro School. Therefore, the Boys are excited about the idea of becoming a man.

In fact, all of the men are excited about their sons, nephews and cousins "making the big step" into manhood. For this meant, "New men were to be born into male society." Although the spotlight of attention is on the boys, it is the Poro Elders who are the generator of the spotlight.

On the one hand, this is where the beauty of the Poro School comes into focus, the Poro Elders are really the Grandparents of the 'Boys', which makes their students their grandchildren.

This means, it is the Grandparent Generation teaching their Grandchildren Generation about the facts of life; and there is no greater bond than between African Grandparents and their Grandchildren.

On the other hand, the Elders have the responsibility of molding the 'Boys into a pattern that fits Society's needs. For the Elders know, for a people to survive in the Land of Secret Societies, its men must have a tough body and a strong mind.

In addition, they believe that hardship experiences are the best teacher. It is not a school that teaches Warriorship, the Warriors have their own secret school society; Poro School is heavy into defensive warfare.

Because the Elders know that if they fail in their teaching, being surrounded by Outlaw War Towns, their whole Town Society will be destroyed. This is a big responsibility, and the Elders take it very seriously, although the town people are in a festival mood.

It is the end of a successful harvesting season, last of November early December; and now with all of their food binds filled with food, they can look forward to the dry season, November to May. Which is the time for serious trading, and maybe a little warfare and other fun activities until late April.

Meanwhile, the 'Boys' little egos are riding high with all of the special attention and advice they are receiving, and especially by their expectation of becoming men.

Finally the big day arrives, this is announced by the men going around town shouting "We will dance tonight."

At this time, the men are really fired-up, and this makes for their biggest celebration. Wine and food are prepared and the men are dressed in their best; but why are the men so excited? This excitement is generated by the expectation of the appearance of their Ultimate Male Spiritual Symbol, GBENI, symbolizing the Articles of Faith of the God of Manhood,

1. A Man must know and believe in himself, family, and community, physically and spiritually.

2. A Man must know how to demand respect, and give respect where due.

3. A Man must know the art of the man-woman relationship.

4. A Man must know how to raise a farm, and a family.

5. A Man must know how to fight; and have the heart of a warrior.

6. A Man must know how to make and manage money.

7. A Man must know how to manage the affairs of his family, community and society.

This is the knowledge that all of the men hold close to their heart and mind. So naturally the appearance of GBENI is a great event for men, because they think of themselves as living examples of GBENI's articles of faith.

Therefore, celebrating GBENI is a way of celebrating what they are, their own manhood; for all of them are graduates of GBENI's stomach (Poro school).

The celebration is a men-only affair. Women and children, including the 'Boys' are at home out of sight. The men have the town square to themselves, and this is where the event is to take place.

The first Masquerader to arrive is Wujei (symbolizing the original Ancestor who stole the knowledge) with his attendants. The broom holder sweeps the road in front of where Wujei arrives. Drummers, horn players, and the musical-stick players; all of which are the smart Poro boys of past graduations are next to arrive.

All the while, Wujei is dancing the story of his ancient deed, and His followers are singing of the coming of other Spirits. Wujei's appearance is followed by those of Ngafagoti, Yauei, Fobai and Dagbadaii; each with their attendants and musicians dancing to the singing of their followers.

Last but not least, GBENI dances into town (wearing the mask shown), making harsh nasal sounds (Poro horn) like someone groaning with His large group of Attendants and musicians dancing the dance of Manhood.

While GBENI is dancing, some of His attendants go from house to house selecting the 'Boys' to be initiated. He takes them to the bush school Sacred Path, where they are turned over to an old Elder who is waiting for them.

At this point, a miracle happens. GBENI disappears, all that is left is His voice fading in the distance. However, the other Spirits (Masqueraders) remain in town the remaining of the day and all night as the major stars of the great celebration that follows GBENI's visit. But we are concerned with the 'Boys' most of all.

The 'Boys,' are not a part of this celebration. We find them at the first gate on the sacred way (path) leading to Poro Sacred Grounds. This gate, like all of the gates, are made of inter-laced vines and sticks, but so constructed that it doesn't look like it a person can walk through. There is also an armed guard posted at all times.

The old Elder walks through the gate as if by magic, and the boys follow. Now the boys are on the "Sacred Way," which is where they begin their first Poro experiences.

The Sacred Way is a twisting and turning path which leads from Town into the deep bush. It is not clearly marked. Only the old Elder knows the way, and he is acting like he is lost most of the time. The trip along this path is the first stage of their puberty ritual.

Along the route, the old Elder is following. The Poro Officials have placed all kinds of menacing things. There are tripping things, tearing things, choking things, frightening things, and terrible things along the way. This to the Boys is an invisible path, dark and gloomy, in tall underbrush higher than a man's head.

For example, there is a big vine carved just like a python snake, clay models of leopards, lions, and other man-eating animals that look real if you are not too close to them. And the old Elders are careful not to let the boys see them to well.

Then there are the Poro Officials that are following them, but out of view, making noises like wild animals about to attack, and other noises like a man being attacked. Meanwhile the Old Elder is going this way, that way, sometimes going in a big circle and giving a good impression that he is lost and in fear. Every once in a while they come to another gate that they pass through as if by magic.

This give us an idea of the creative thought and wisdom the Elders bring to their job. As we said, the Elders take their job very serious. The trip takes some 6 to 7 hours, although where they are going is no more than 6 or 7 miles from town. By this time, even the strongest of the "Boys," are terrorized, lost, and totally confused when finally they reach the last gate.

Here, they find the Official "Keeper of the Poro Horn," who puts a number of questions to the boys. For example to DionDi, "Could you uproot a full grown palm tree with your hands?" DionDi answers "yes."

After a number of impossible questions, all of which DionDi, according to the advice given by the men earlier, answers "yes;" he is passed through. This continues until all of the Boys are passed through; they are now on Poro Sacred Grounds.

From a symbolic ritual point of view, the Sacred Way, and impossible questions, symbolize the state of childhood lost and confused.

The old Elder then led the boys to a certain sacred tree, under which are the 4 sacred stones where there are a number of Poro Officials. Old Sowa 'The Teacher', and older graduates, and musicians are singing songs of welcome, followed by inspirational songs about the glories of manhood. How a man has to be tough and strong, and not be a crybaby.

After which, when the old Elder thinks the boys courage is pumped up high enough, he has them stand in a circle around three officials where they are to be circumcised. More important, from a spiritual point of view, they receive the marks of the Spirit of GBENI. The music and singing continue at an even higher intensity, especially by the "Keeper of the Poro Sacred Horn."

Two officials hold each boy, in his turn, while a third circumcised them. And at the same time, 4 semi-deep cuts are made on the back of the left shoulder, and the wounds are treated with a special medicine to heal the cuts in the form of a tattoo.

Although the boys are not supposed to cry, at this point they are not punished if they do. Anyway, the music is so loud that nobody can hear them. These shoulder cuts symbolize marks left by GBENI's Spirit when chewing the boys up before He swallowed them; the boys clothes are used to clean up the blood.

Finally, the boys are given a special herb to chew, and some snuff-like powder to sniff, which gives them a dizzy feeling; symbolically, this kills the spirit, mind, and body of childhood. The boys are now symbolically in the spiritual stomach of GBENI.

Their bloody clothes are sent to their family, and it is announced in town that the boys are dead. Now that the boys are ritually in the spiritual stomach of GBENI. They are under the direct care and direction of GBENI's Chief Priest and Teacher, Sowa. To some extent, they are also under the direction of the Chief Priestess and Teacher, Mabole, who has an independent role to play.

First off, we must say something about Priest Sowa, the Director and Teacher. He is a man that worships at the shrine of Manhood Knowledge, GBENI.

This means that Priest Sowa and his counseling Elders know all of the manhood knowledge that was stolen by the original Ancestor from NGEWO, the God of Knowledge.

But up and above that, Priest Sowa knows the ritual of transformation from childhood mind and body, to a manhood mind and body; and in the process, he establishes a relationship between the boys and GBENI. The whole thing was set-up when the boys were on the trip along the Sacred Path before they were put under Priest Sowa's authority. The path made their minds putty to be molded so to speak.

As we mentioned, a temporary village is already built not far from the Shrine of the four Sacred Stones. Let's say that there are 35 boys. This means that the village would consist of 7 huts with 5 boys per hut. A little distance away is a big house for the Officials, Elders and Teachers, and a house for Mabole who is the only female in the little village.

This is where the boys are to spend the next 4 years without any contact with their families or anybody else from the outside world.

In fact, the borders of the sacred grounds are patrolled by Warriors to make sure Priest Sowa and the 'Boys' are not disturbed in any way. Only the Elders, the older graduates, and special teachers are allowed to come and go.

Now lets see how Priest Sowa deals with his responsibilities. As was mentioned, Poro officials believe that hardship is the best teacher.

The circumcision and symbolic markings are complete, and it is now early evening. The welcoming ceremony and manhood songs continue until late, and the boys are tired and sleepy.

Finally, they are led to their huts which only contain five sleeping mats each. They are given dry covering (like blankets) being that it gets real chilly at night; and they settle in for a good nights sleep, their last for a long while.

The next morning when the boys wake up, they find the Medicine man there to see how their wounds are coming along, and hear and treat any other medical problems.

After breakfast the boys are put to work getting firewood, water, etc, etc., and generally kept busy doing odd jobs for the Officials. This goes on until about 7:00 o'clock when the boys are given their supper and a dose of motherly comfort from Priestess Mabole.

After which, there is drumming and songs and stories about the great leaders, heroes, and the foundering of the Mende Nation. Also all about old Lockjaw and company, and the experiences they had.

About 10:00 p.m. the Boys are given bed covering which has been put in water and is dripping wet. This is going to be a long cold night for the boys. An hour after they had settled in, it got very dark because the moon had gone down behind the trees, and everything was real quiet. Then all of a sudden, they hear strong loud sounds around their huts, howling sounds like Evil Spirits on the move.

Then the deliberate poorly made walls of the huts began to shake and rattle as if the Evil Spirits were trying to break in on the boys. Tearing out big holes through which strange images could be half-seen; those horrible howling Evil Spirit sounds continued for the longest time.

Naturally the boys were terrified. Some were crying, others calling for their mothers all hurled together in the center of their huts. Even DionDi, who had handled things pretty well up to this point broke down crying for his mother.

Finally, Sowa comes out of his house shouting and pretending to drive the Evil Spirits away, and things quiet down some, except for the boys. Sowa gathered the fearful and cold boys together to sing manhood songs until morning. Thus the boys get the first in a long line of lessons in dealing with fear of the unknown.

Once the sun comes up, the boys are put to work repairing their huts. About 11:00 o'clock, Priestess Mabole calls the boys for breakfast and a good dose of motherly affection, which lifts the Boys spirit to a degree.

After breakfast, under Priest Sowa's direction, the boys are to finish rebuilding their huts. After which they built a new place for the chickens, and a pen for the goats near their huts, and generally fix-up their little village.

Although they are allowed rest periods, they are worked to their limits. This goes on until about 7:00 p.m. when they are given their supper.

Again, after supper, there are stories about different Ancestors, and the things they did or did not do, especially about Old Killer Mende when they were living near the Upper Niger River, which the boys love.

Again, they are given wet blankets and sent to bed to spend another cold night. Sowa lets them sleep for a few hours, and the Evil Spirits return. Everything is damaged like before, and Sowa drives them away; and the boys sing manhood songs until sunrise. This goes on for quite some time. After supper and encouragement from Priestess Mabole, again they hear long hero stories about history of the young Mende Nation; without any explanation of what is going on.

The Boys are determined to hang tough; especially since they are punished if they cry and complain, or act like a crybaby. As we mentioned, Priest Sowa is very serious about his job; but then there was always good old Mabole to lift the Boy's spirit.

Finally, Sowa begins talking to the boys about Evil Spirits. Telling them that these were Spirits of Evil Towns who were driven by jealousy and Greed. And their goal was to destroy their village and take the Boys to some strange place where bad things happen.

But he explained, and although he was able to save them up to this point, he was not so sure he would be home all the time. Therefore, the boys had to learn to defend themselves. Then he began telling them how Spirits operate and their weaknesses.

They were told that evil Spirits only attacked when people were asleep, and the only thing they feared was the Poro special yell (Sowa would shout a special 'Poro war cry' when he drove them away).

So the first thing they had to learn was the special Poro war cry. The next thing the boys had to do, for defense, was build a ritual wall (fence) around their village using special sticks linked together with vines, and only one gate.

Then, they must clear away the bush some distance around the outside of the wall. Once this is accomplished, they must have a guard on duty at the gate all night long.

If the Spirits appear, he must make the special Poro yell and drive them away for a while. At this point the boys are ready to try anything.

Needless to say, Sowa worked the boys to their limits all day long for the following week. But at the end of the day, there was always the Mabole suppers, followed by fascinating stories of history at night.

Sowa gaged their work progress to be finished on the seventh day; at which time they, Sowa and the boys, made sacrifices at the Shrine of the 4 Sacred Stones, and to GBENI, after which Sowa blessed the ritual wall. That night, the Evil Spirit came and was driven off by the boys. Thus is their first in a long line of lessons, that knowledge defeats fears of the unknown.

Meanwhile in the last two weeks, Sowa had been looking the boys over for signs of leadership qualities. So after their first month the boy's workload is reduced, and a little government is formed. Sowa's next goal is to organize the boys into a little male society. The boys are to operate as a unit and supervise themselves, with Sowa more of an observer.

Although they still did lots of odd jobs for the officials in the morning, they now spent the afternoons in competitive sports like wrestling, racing, etc, etc. Plus, crafts like building traps, and bow and arrows for hunting small animals and birds for Priestess Mabole's cook pot. But most important, they begin learning to govern themselves in the evening with their own court system.

In the beginning, the boys only enforce the rules of the school; for instances, boys are not supposed to be a crybaby, obey all officials at once, and must show respect to all officials, especially Mabole. Also they must do their job well, not fight without just cause, and no stealing from anyone on the sacred grounds.

If there has been a problem, like one boy stealing something from another; in the evening the boys assemble their court of law and call the two boys to appear.

The proceedings follow the same pattern as grown-up courts. Witnesses are called, and everything must be proven. If the accused boy is found guilty, he is punished. On the other hand, if he is found innocent, the boy making the charge is punished for false accusation.

But then, if an official sees a rule broken in sight of a boy leader, and he doesn't take any action, this boys government member is also punished.

Old Priest Sowa doesn't take punishment lightly; we are talking about, what Grandpa calls, being given a good whipping, and being talked to real rough.

As part of this boys government, Sowa also appoints a War Chief, and the boys begin training to become defensive warriors.

This pattern continues for the next 2 to 3 months, the last of December to the middle of March. By this time the boys are not only tough minded and in good physical condition, they are taking on a rough outline of an independent society.

Although the boys are showing signs of self-discipline as a unit, and their little government is working to some extent, they are still heavily supervised by Sowa and different teachers. For example, there is an official, or at least a War Captain teaching them the art of defensive warfare.

On the other hand, although they occasionally kill small game, do a little fishing, and find some edible wild fruits and vegetables near their village; their families provide the vast majority of their food.

Sowa's next goal is for them to become completely independent economically. Meaning that they must produce all of their food. So about the middle of March, the boys are given a few chickens and goats, and begin to prepare to make a real farm.

In making a farm, the boys are under the direction of an old Elder, 'Bigcrop,' known for his successful farming methods; and he is as serious as Sowa. However, he does not have to drive the boys, their first farm is a source of great pride.

Every generation of Poro boys are graded and remembered by their first village, farm, and every generation takes great pride in trying to do better than what they have heard about what was accomplished by the last generation.

On the other side, we have old Bigcrop, who wants to teach his group of boys to be better farmers than his Ancestor Poro farm teachers, so there is a lot of personal pride involved on his side too.

This makes the approach of farming like a football game; the boys are the players, Old Bigcrop the coach, Sowa is the team owner, and the Ancestor generation are the opponents.

Plus, being a good farmer, according to Mende beliefs, is a big part of Manhood.

So in this respect, old Bigcrop knows as much about his job as Sowa does about his. His approach is that a person must know what he is doing, and especially why he is doing it.

Therefore, although old Bigcrop goes into great detail in explaining to the boys what kinds of soil they need, it is up to them to choose the actual site for their farm; this they do with great enthusiasm.

Once the land is selected, a sacrifice is made on the site to the Ancestors that founded these Poro Sacred Grounds. After a prayer by Sowa in the name of GBENI, a challenge is made to the spirit of the last Poro generation to a contest.

The Shrine, in this case, is a special wet-stone used to keep farm tools sharp, especially the machete and short-handle hoe. This wet-stone has been on Poro grounds for generations. It is the same one that the Founder used. Now the game (work) begins.

The task of clearing a site for farming starts with an attack, using machetes on the underbrush of vines and shrubs. The men will cut down any big trees later. This is fun for the boys, and Bigcrop teaches them to work in rhythm to drum beats and work songs about how great their farm is going to be and the things their generation will accomplish in life.

Everyday for the next 2 or 3 weeks, the boys go to work at 6am singing generation songs, and return for breakfast about 10 or 11 am to rest for a while. Then work until about 7pm when they have supper. In the evening, they are taught about spiritual defensive warfare. In fact, the evil Spirits still return, especially if Sowa finds the guard either not at his post or asleep on the job.

Once the trees and underbrush are cut down, they are left to dry in the hot tropical sun for a month just before the rains start in early May. At which time the dried bush is burned, which leaves the clearing covered with a layer of ashes to serve the purpose of fertilizer.

Meanwhile the boys get a month of rest from farm work. For the most part this time is spent learning about physical warfare by the war Captain in the day time. And in the evening they are taught about the art of spiritual warfare.

Finally, after the bush is burnt and the first rain comes, which softens the soil, the boys go to work with short-handle hoes, breaking up the soil. At the same time, planting dry land rice seeds which is their major crop, along with other plants like cavassa, yams, and certain vegetables. They cover the seeds and pull weeds at the same time; under the close supervision of old Bigcrop. But once the planting is done, then real warfare begins.

In growing a farm in the bush, there are three major enemies one must confront head on, birds, small plant eating animals, and especially weeds. From planting season to harvesting season, the boys spend almost every day on their farm fighting with the heart of a warrior.

Old Bigcrop only comes around every once in a while, and then only to take the boys into the surrounding bush identifying edible fruits and vegetables. This is a big part of farming, knowing what plants are good to eat and the nature of their growth.

Otherwise, the boys spend their time in open warfare with farm enemies, which comes in waves. For example, during planting and until the seeds begin to grow, the big enemy is birds who seem to have one goal in life, eat all the seeds before they even get a chance to grow.

This means that for 3 or 4 weeks, or until the seeds grow into small plants, the boys are out in the field all day long fighting birds of all descriptions. The boys sleep when the birds sleep, and get up in the morning at the same time as they do. As weapons, they have piles of rocks and sticks in different parts of the field.

We can just imagine 35 boys running over a 2 acre clearing, shouting and running with their slings and bow and arrows doing battle with some very determined birds. Although this is a battle that is not new for them, this is something that the boys have been helping their parents do all of their young life. But still they have to be on the job every minute of the day.

This is followed by waves of small animals that feel that it is their natural right to eat every young plant in sight. So the boy's battle continues throughout the growth of their crops. Even when the rice begins to produce grain, the animals and birds are still a big problem.

Don't mention the weeds. For some reason weeds grow twice as fast as crop plants the world over. However, the boys still find time to do lot of hunting, fishing, and gathering wild fruits and vegetables for Mabole's cooking pots. One of the good things about living in a rain forest is that a large number of foods grow wild year round.

When we mention warfare, we don't just mean physical fighting, we mean being taught the belief that a man must fight for what he wants, and be able to defend what he already has.

Nor do we mean that spiritual warfare is just about Evil Spirits. If we recall with the Aja, spiritual warfare is the art of trickeration (The Trickster God), which is still a way of fighting for what you want; take note, its all about what you want.

This is the foundation of the Mende's beliefs about Manhood. So we can see where Sowa and the elders are coming from, and their approach to instill this belief in the minds of the boys is rock solid.

They are giving the boys the experiences of fighting hard for what they want, their village, and especially their farm. During this time, the boys are raising chickens and a goat that they have to protect.

Finally, harvesting time comes around, and under the direction of old Bigcrop, the farm is a big success. The boys have much more than they could consume themselves. Their barns are overflowing; which calls for a big celebration in the little village.

All of the Town Officials, including the War Chief and Officials from other schools attend the festivities giving lots of praises to the success of the little society, village and farm.

There is lots of drumming and singing by the boys. Then comes the big sacrificial meal. The goat and some chickens are killed. There is wild game, and all of the fruits and vegetables that you could name. All produced by the boys; showing their new economic independence. Thus concludes the first year of Poro School. Or to say, this concludes the first year in the stomach of GBENI!

As begins, Sowa has the boys celebrate the New Year by setting fire to their village. Only the little buildings like barns and the ritual wall (fence) are allowed to remain. The boys spend the night sleeping on the ground in the open, and the next day they must get busy.

For the next 2 or 3 weeks the boys work all day, every day, rebuilding their village, still inside the ritual wall, directed by the old War Captain. During this time each boy must build a good strong hut for himself, along with a goat and chicken pen.

By the last half of December, the boys now have a village of 35 huts built close to each other with a maze of trails between them for defensive reason, on the advice of the old War Captain.

This makes the little village just like a real town with its defensive walls, and each boy sleeps in his own hut. Now we get to the second stage of the Boy's education.

Well Fellow Detectives we have finally come to the stage where Old Priest Sowa gets to the heart of his job as "Chief Teacher" of Poro.

He must now teach the Boys the highest values of Society, or to say, the 'Philosophy-of-Life' based on the 'Moral Code of Society;' in the form of 'Proverbs.'

However, he must not only teach these Society values, he also has to teach the Boys how to 'Think,' using these values as 'Thinking Tools,' in the form of 'Question-stories.'

Now we come to your Aunt Elaine's questions concerning higher education. When talking about education in the chapter on the Aja, we were focused on their ideas of 'the Seven Cycles of Life,' which we will call elementary school system. In the case of the Secree, we are talking about cultural education system we will call high school; thus is the Major focus of Poro and Sande bush schools.

Up to this point Priest Sowa has been building a strong body of practical knowledge. Now he is concerned with building a strong mind in the Boys. And for him this is the fun part of his job, training the Boys to 'think for themselves' in a manner that 'assures' them 'personal freedom and self-confidence within themselves.'

First, Priest Sowa teaches the boys the Boys that there is a natural logical order of Society in stories like the following;

Priest Sowa: "A Boy went down to the river on the same day that he was born, a hunter came and fired his gun, and the boy asked what he was shooting at. The hunter said he was shooting at the mosquitoes that were eating his wife's cassava.

The boy said that the hunter was upsetting the proper order of things by shooting a gun at mosquitoes. The hunter said that the boy was doing so (upsetting the natural order of things) by bathing himself on the day he was born.

They took their argument to the Chief, who heard their case and then announced that his mouth was locked up in a room and that his wives had taken the key away. The boy and hunter accused the Chief of upsetting things.

They looked for someone else to settle their argument, and stated their case to a palm wine taper. He heard them, and then said that one day he fell from a palm tree and broke into pieces, and then went into town to get someone to carry the pieces home. They accused him of upsetting things, and they are still arguing as to which was the most to blame."

This kind of story is followed by Priest Sowa teaching the values and moral codes, which constitute the natural logical order of things in Society; of which he defines, and they are to memorize and discuss in the form of Proverbs. There are hundreds of proverbs. However we will only present a few in each of the areas of Society, as follows.

1. "When you go into some village, the songs which the children sing, which the old folk once sang and left behind to them."

2. "When a child knows how to wash his hands clean, he and elders partake of food together." (Meaning when a child learns proper respect, right conduct, he can partake of old people's knowledge).

3. "The mouth of an old man or woman is better than any good luck charm."

4. "When your mother is poor, you do not leave her and go and make some else your mother."

5. "When you follow behind your father, you learn to walk like him."

6. "A wife is like a blanket; when you cover yourself with it, it irritates you, and yet if you cast it away you feel cold."

7. "One who is looking for a wife does not go around saying bad things about women."

8. "No one ties up a wisdom-bag, takes it and puts it away in a box, and comes and stands in the marketplace and says 'Explain the matter to me'."

9. "Ancient things remain in the ears."

10. "One falsehood spoils a thousand truths."

11. "It is the fool whose things are taken and sold back to him."

12. "It is the fool's sheep that breaks loose twice."

13. "What is bad luck for one man is good luck for another."

14. "When an old thing belonging to one person gets into the hands of another, it becomes a new thing for him."

15. "When one stands on another's shoulders, then he sees over the whole market."

16. "One man's road does not go far without meeting another's."

17. "If no one had gone and no one had come, what should we have done to find out if the road was safe."

18. "There is nothing that hurts like shame."

19. "When you place your tongue in pawn, you cannot redeem it."

20. "If you are in debt to your soul, and have not paid it, it gets angry with you."

21. "All destinies are not alike."

22. "When death camps over against a homestead, the medicine of the Medicine man is no good."

23. "Death is not a sleeping-room that can be entered and come out of again."

24. "When a Chief is going to compel you to do something, he does so by the authority of the people."

25. "The family tree is not cut."

During these discussions, Priest Sowa begins talking to the boys as young men deserving respect, by insisting that they express their opinion as forceful as they can. And at the same time, giving respect to their opinion in ways that correct any mistakes they might have made. In other words, he builds up their little intellectual minds. This should be very interesting, training a mind in cultural values of a society.

For another example, Priest Sowa tells the Boys a question-story like the following;

Priest Sowa: "Three men drove their sons from home because one knew nothing, another was a fool, and the third was stupid.

These three sons met in another village where the Chief sent one to find string, another to catch fish, and the third to gather baobab fruit; but they returned empty-handed.

The first said that he could not find any string to tie his bundle of string. The second said that thirst had prevented him from bringing his basket of fish, because he could not find any water. The third said that he had climbed the baobab tree and had put his hand on the fruit to see if it was ripe, but when he descended and threw the stick, it had failed to knock the fruit down. Which of the three was the biggest fool?"

DionDi: "If a man has a bundle of string and can't find any to tie the bundle he is the biggest fool!"

Tyree: "If a man catches fish out of water and can't find any water to drink he is the biggest fool!"

Marcus: "If a man climbs a tree and touches fruit, and not get it while there he is the biggest fool!"

Michael: "I think the one that could not find string and the one that couldn't find water are the two biggest fools!"

Orchester III: "I think that the three sons, together, are the biggest fools in the world!"

We should note that the Boys are forced to think about why they came to their conclusion. But, and this is a big 'but,' there is no way they can prove their conclusions. And this opens a big debate among themselves.

The above gives an example of how a question story is designed to make the boys think. And in this case, think about how not to be a fool; but there is no answer to the question as to which of the three sons is the biggest fool.

On the other hand, Priest Sowa also wants to make the Boy's minds strong, and to do this, he teaches them to make 'hard choices' and 'pay the price,' for instance in the following story:

Priest Sowa: "If you, your wife, your mother, and your mother-in-law were attacked by wild animals, and all of you escaped to a river full of crocodiles and found a canoe that held only three people, which do you, leave behind to be killed by the animals?"

If you leave your mother, your father, brothers, and sisters will hate you; if you leave your wife, your children will hate you; if you leave your mother-in-law, your wife will hate you; what would you do?"

Here the Boys are taught that there are hard choices in life, and still there is no satisfactory answer. However the Boys still must relate their answer to Society values. To further demonstrate what we mean, we will quote a number of these stories, and you Grandkids tell Grandpa how you would answer.

Priest Sowa: "A swindler put a quarter of a bar of salt in a bag and set off to sell it as a full load of salt. Another swindler took a strip of cotton to sell as a full load of cloth. When they met, the first said that in his country women had to go naked because there was no cloth. The second said that in his country it was salt that was lacking. They exchanged loads and parted, each thinking he had cheated the other, but when they reached home both cried, 'he robbed me!" Which is the biggest thief?"

Priest Sowa: "Long ago men and animals lived together in the same village. One day a leopard ate a baby boy, and his mother went crying to the Chief. The leopard denied its guilt, saying the boy was lost in the forest. An ape said it had seen the boy running toward the river. But a dog said it had been in the woman's house eating a bone and saw the leopard eat the boy.

The chief pronounced the sentence. The leopard was banned from the village, and men, aided by dogs, would try to kill it and its children. It was war to the death. The ape, which had also lied, was banned from the village, and could enter only when tied by the neck. It was to live in the trees and be mocked by all the animals, and men would make clothing from its skin.

The dog, because it had not defended the woman, was made the slave of man and ordered to guard women in their houses. Was the Chief right to punish the leopard, the ape, and the dog? Which one was happiest with its sentence?

Priest Sowa: "One man said that he had seen two birds fighting; the first bird swallowed the second, and then the second swallowed the first.

Another said that he had seen a man who had cut off his own head and who had it in his mouth, eating it.

A third man said that he had seen a woman carrying a house, a farm, and all of her possessions on her head. When he asked her where she was going, she said she had heard that a man had cut off his own head and had it in his mouth, eating it, so she had left the town in fear. Which told the biggest story?"

Priest Sowa: "A fisherman confronted a Bush Spirit that had been stealing from his fish-traps, but it escaped leaving behind its clothes, bag, and knife. With his two brothers, he returned the Spirit's possessions but demanded a payment for the stolen fish.

The eldest brother chose a knife that always gave him plenty of palm wine. The youngest chose a rope at the end of which he found a new cow each morning. The fisherman chose a purse in which there was always plenty of money. Now, which one made the best choice?"

This pattern, the boys learning intellectual exercises from Sowa, continues for the next 3 years. However, in the second year, planting season and some very special knowledge is introduced to the boys. Special in the sense that puberty years are a time when boy's imagination turns to fantasies about girls and sex, and this knowledge is about the man-woman relationship.

But to really see how the man-woman relationship is to fit into Sowa's goals, lets review where he is coming from, and what has been accomplished up to this point.

The Secree believe that a man must have certain knowledge before he can become a functional part of their unique Society. The act of instilling this knowledge transforms the boys from childhood to manhood, physically and spiritually, based on the spiritual knowledge of GBENI.

And we saw the boys learn about farms, towns, defensive warfare, and especially proverbs and question-stories. All symbolizing the values in Society they will follow in their adulthood. Including how to relate to womanhood with honor and respect, symbolized by the presence of Priestess Mabole. But, in the puberty years, one of the most important transformations takes place sexually, and this is where the man-woman relationship fits into the picture.

On the other hand, why did Sowa teach the boys to build a village and farm, including how to serve and protect them? As a space to live and raise a family! But what is a family? A man-woman relationship that has produced children sexually.

So naturally, Sowa's next goal is to instill in the boys mind knowledge about women and sexual relations, and especially the art of raising a family. For the rough outline of the boys little society to be complete, and before it can grow, they must have knowledge of family and personal freedom, and the whole thing tied together with knowledge of the man-woman relationship.

The nature of the man-woman relationship is not only the dynamic force that creates the family, it is also what gives style and substances to society as a whole; being as a society is only a collection of extended families. This means that the man-woman relationship is the key to understanding the Mende's society as a whole, and covers a much wider area than just sex.

However, to deal with young teenage boys who have nothing but sex on their minds calls for a special kind of teacher that can override the boy's strong sex drives. And also instill knowledge of a wider area of male and female relations, for example, the knowledge of the relationship between manhood and womanhood in Society.

And at the same time, teach the boys the nature and purpose of the role of their sex drives in manhood, family and society, and how personal freedom fits in the picture of all three. To do this job Sowa chooses a special teacher.

The Poro Elders most qualified to accomplish this task is 'Old Lionpaw,' the Medicine Man who specializes in male sexuality and the Games People play in Life, especially in the man-woman relationship.

Now we must introduce Old Lionpaw, and Lionique, his first wife. For they are the key to our understanding of the Mende's society. And, why Grandpa came to the conclusion that the Mende's Society, and its lifestyle, is by nature, what Afro-Americans call, 'Street Life.'

Old Lionpaw is in his 70's, has 12 wives, 35 children, and close to 100 grand and great grandchildren. His homestead is the ideal in peace and harmony. He is a Medicine Man, and his reputation is one of great respect for hundreds of miles in all directions.

If we recall, the Articles of Faith, according to the Mende beliefs, medicine is a method of using knowledge to deal with spiritual and physical problems on an individual as well as social level.

In this sense, to one degree or another, every man and woman in society must know something about the art of medicine-as-knowledge, or know someone who does; and old Lionpaw is a Master of the Art.

This means that his knowledge of relationships goes far beyond those of just men and women; it covers an area from personal health to society's lifestyle.

Anyway, as we mentioned, old Lionpaw is over 70 years old, and he has taught a number of Poro generation of boys; but this is his final group. He is to retire in three years, this has him both concerned and excited.

He is concerned because every teacher is looking for the one student that shows signs of greatness. He has taught some boys that have grown into great men.

However, like his Ancestor Teachers of the man-woman relationship and the art of medicine before him, Old Lionpaw wants to be remembered as the teacher of at least one Super Great Man of Society.

On the other hand, Old Lionpaw is very excited because he thinks he sees the qualities of greatness he had been looking for in not one, but five boys, DionDi, Tyree, Marcus, Michael, and Orchester III.

On the other side, Old Lionpaw's first wife, Lionique, who is the teacher of the man-woman relationship and medicine in Sande School (womanhood school), is also excited. Because she also has five girls, Tiffany, Rachel, Omni, Nikki, and Maya, and she sees signs of greatness in all of them to become Super Great Women of Society.

The point being is that Lionpaw and Lionique work together to form the ideals in the relationship between manhood and womanhood in the form of man-woman relationships.

The boys begin Poro, and girls begin Sande schools at the same time, although they do not see each other for 4 years.

However, we will get into Lionique, the girls, and the Sande School of Womanhood later. For now we are interested in Lionpaw, the boys, and Poro School, and the planting and growing season in their second year. Now that we see where old Lionpaw is coming from, we need only to look at three reasons Lionpaw began teaching in the planting season.

The first reason is that it is easy to explain farm work in terms of relations with women and family. The farm is the woman-wife, the boys are the man-husband, farming activities is the man-woman relationship, and the harvest is the children.

The second reason is that planting season (the spring of the year) is also when the majority of animals, birds and plants begin their sexual activities and raising families. For example, Lionpaw will explain why the male bird performs a singing and dancing ritual before the female bird, which leads to the explanation that all animals and plants have special knowledge of the male and female relations.

The third reason is that he can take the boys into the bush (forest) and teach them about Knowledge Spirits (Bush Spirit) related to plants and animals sexuality; just like GBENI is a Knowledge Spirit related to Manhood.

Knowledge Spirits are more active in the planting season. It is a good setting to explain how all forms of life's Ancient Ancestors stole special knowledge about life. The Spirit of that Knowledge is what animals worship.

For instance, the bird ritual we mentioned; and this is what a medicine Man seeks; to establish relations with all of these Knowledge Spirits, learn what they know, and use that knowledge to benefit his Society. And at the same time, Lionpaw demonstrates what he means by having the boys look for, and gather, medicine plants for small health problems, like colds, fevers, headaches, etc., which every man should know.

And also tell the story of how certain Medicine Men, for example, met a Knowledge Spirit of a certain tree and learned that the bark of that tree, made into a tea, would cure someone with a headache. So we can see why the farming season is a good setting to learn about sex and medicine, and the relations between the two.

Although Old Lionpaw does a lot of teaching on the farm and in the bush in the day-time, two or three days a week, his goal is to give the boys a clear sight of the overall picture of sexuality and the flow of life, and how male sexuality fits into that picture; in a teacher-student format.

However, this is more of a background to deal with his major subject, which takes place in the boy's village in the evening; after supper, in a different format than is used in his daytime teaching. Here he holds man-to-man open discussions based on the questions the boys have about any subject that concerns them.

These questions mostly, but not always, follow two patterns, how to act like men, and especially, how to get along with women, or to say, male lifestyle and sexual relations; and always end in discussions about the boy-girl relationship.

This means that we Detectives will now focus all of our investigative attention on these evening-time questions and discussions. Here, the boys ambitions are put on display in a manner that Old Lionpaw can build a knowledge base for them to reach their personal and social potential.

This is especially true with the 'Boys' that show signs of greatness in whatever their Chosen Destiny may be; all of which is shown by the nature of their questions.

Now we can just imagine that this is the most enjoyable time for Lionpaw and the boys, with Old Lionpaw sitting around a fire in the little village square, surrounded by young boys who are made to feel that they are free to ask any questions that come to their mind.

They have an old man that, as far as they are concerned, has all of the knowledge in the world, and a strong desire and purpose to give them answers they can use. This is mixed in with some boys trying to show off by answering other boy's questions and have Lionpaw agree with them.

Then, some boys start getting so fired-up that the discussions last far into the night; with Old Lionpaw observing every word with a smile on his face, correcting and urging them on and enjoying every minute of it.

With all of the above in mind, along with our conclusion about Outlaw Society, we will focus our investigative attention on the boy's questions and Lionpaw's answers.

Naturally during this time period there would be hundreds of questions and answers involving all of the boys. However, we will only focus on the questions and answers between the 'Boys' we named and Old Lionpaw.

All the Boys: "Why do they call you Lionpaw?"

Old Lionpaw: "This is because all Africans base their man-woman relationship on the way a Lion family is organized, one male Lion with a number of female Lions; and I am a master at this type of relationship."

DionDi: "I know that sex is about having babies, but how does this sex-drive thing work?"

Old Lionpaw: "Male sex drives are always a reaction to female sex drives, and female sex drives are related to giving birth.

For instance, the male bird and their singing and dancing is related to the female being ready to reproduce. This means that male sexual desires originate with the female.

She gives a sex signal to the male she wants to father her children, and low and behold, all of a sudden, he has a powerful desire to have sex. No matter what else he may have been doing or thinking about. In this sense, females control male sex drives.

This is a very important point to keep in mind when beginning a man-woman relationship, because women are master artists at faking sex signals, and this allows women to use and abuse men. Or to say, put men in a trick-bag; the Trick being a male that is out of control, and the woman in control sexually, all caused by sexually reacting to a fake sex signal."

Tyree: "If women naturally control men sexually, how do men protect themselves from 'fake sex signals?"

Old Lionpaw: "By having the knowledge of what a woman is looking for in a man, and being smart enough to recognize fake sex signals.

The key is to know that when a woman presents herself to a man, and if she is serious, she is choosing the qualities in him she wants for her children. But just as important, the knowledge she sees in his mind, and the creative ways he uses his knowledge in his life (his lifestyle).

This means that a male sexual signal is creative knowledge about living life, and if it is strong enough, it will naturally control female sex drives. She will feel secure in giving birth. This means security in giving birth which controls a woman sex drives.

On the other hand, men can also send fake sex signals; by faking creative knowledge, and putting a woman in a trick-bag. The trick is creating a fake lifestyle, and the woman is sexually reacting to a lie about what the man stands for in life; creative lying. These are the only two ways, and extent, a woman's sex drive can be controlled.

Marcus: "I have heard it said that a 'Man must be a Man' in the man woman relationship, what does this mean sexually?

Old Lionpaw: "A man has two inner forces fighting for control of his focus in life, one sitting on his shoulders (his mind) and the other, hanging between his legs (his penis). One is designed to fulfill a personal chosen destiny, and the other, out of control.

The question becomes, which of these forces are to be the master of the man while involved in a man-woman relationship? If he allows his penis to lead him through life, he is what we call a Boy-man or Trick, or to say he has no self-control, being as a woman naturally control men sex drives.

On the other hand, the man that allows his mind to lead him through life is a Man-man; he has the knowledge to turn that situation around, and indirectly control female sex drives. The most important results of this are that, the one that controls the sex drives is the one that manages the affairs of the man-woman relationship, and the family it produces."

Michael: "I need to know how this management thing works."

Old Lionpaw: "The first step in management is for the man to exercise his right to choose a destiny for his family, and this takes place between a man and his first girl friend who is to become his first wife.

Management's success or failure depends on the nature of the relationship between you and your first wife, and in this area, you can have problems you wouldn't believe.

Men have never, and never will, really understand women, so do not waste your time trying; women have secrets just like man.

The key is to understand manhood, yourself, by knowing what you want and make the rules to make it come into reality and except nothing less. This is the case with life as well as managing the affairs of a man-woman relationship. The key word is to know what you want, period. So to answer your question about managing the affairs, the answer is let knowledge of human nature do the managing for you.

Orchester III: "If this is the case, how does one get into a 'good' man-woman relationship?"

Old Lionpaw: "From the things you are now experiencing, you can see, by nature, even before puberty, about 10 or 12 years old, boys and girls begin seeking a mate, symbolized by fantasies motivated by a strong sex rush. This is also the time that they begin day-dreaming about their future lifestyle, Chosen Destiny, and the things they want to accomplish, but especially the mate they want to share their dream.

From this time, and throughout puberty years, sex is just about the only thing on their minds, and sex-signals are running wild all over the place.

Therefore, what you have is a lot of teenagers playing childish sex games, which is also a process of learning about their sex drives. And more important, looking for the man or woman to fit the image they already have in their minds.

It is on this basis that a man and woman choose their mate. But it is not as simple as it sounds. They still have to get a good understanding, and in the process, get to know if the person chosen has the qualities of their dream-image.

This means that when a woman acts like she is serious about choosing you for her lifetime mate, this is the time for you and the woman to talk about what you want and how you are going to get it.

It is during these talks that each other's qualities are exposed, and a good understanding of where each one is coming from is reached, and the actual 'harmony of Spirit' takes place.

Forget about sex, that will come later, understanding comes first. However, it is in the process of getting an understanding where you run into the games people play, and you will have problems you won't believe."

DionDi: "Tell me about the 'problems with your first wife you won't believe?"

Old Lionpaw: These problems are not limited to, but are mostly concerned with, the fact that to manage the affairs of your relation with your first wife you must be a master game player. Even if you and her are serious. Because that is what you will be confronted with everyday of your life. And in most cases, in a game, somebody wins and somebody loses.

The game goes this way, in the case of the woman, "he is not exactly what I am looking for, but I can change him with sex (known in black America as being pussy whipped)." And in the case of men, "she is not all I want, but my mind is stronger than hers and I can turn her around."

In both cases, each are being compared to a fantasy person, and neither tells the other what he or she is really thinking.

This is the major cause of most problems in a man-woman relationship; people trying to make other people into something they are not destined to be. Which leads to the man and woman fighting against the soul of the other; a fight neither can really win, is the biggest, and most painful, problems in men and women relating to each other.

Tyree: "As I see it, man-woman consists of a tug-of-war as to who can mold the other into their fantasy image."

Old Lionpaw: "Tug-of-war is another aspect of the same problem. This means that one wants to dominate the other, and from this position of strength; they can mold the other into what they want.

To answer that question, there is another point that must be taken into consideration. Knowledge comes from the penis of men, and wisdom comes from women's womb. And whereas men have a secret school about knowledge of manhood, women have a secret school about knowledge of womanhood.

However, there is not a man in Sande School like Priestess Mabole is in Poro, therefore, men don't know as much about womens wisdom as women know about men's knowledge. So do not ask me about wisdom-of-the-womb. I can only say that knowledge and wisdom are the God and Goddess of Society.

The question becomes, what is the relationship between knowledge and wisdom? As far as tug-of-war is concerned in an ideal man-woman relationship, the only competition is to see if the man can take his knowledge to a level higher than his woman can take her wisdom. In this respect, they really pull and push each other to their highest potential.

Marcus: "What is this knowledge-wisdom relation thing?"

Old Lionpaw: "The nature of the relationship between knowledge and wisdom is one of total inter-dependency. One cannot exist without the other. Nor can one grow without the other. So is the case with the man-woman relationship, this means that the relationship must be one of great respect.

For example, when a woman chooses that man for his knowledge, and a man chooses that woman for her wisdom, instead of a comparison to a childhood fantasy, this means that they will have an ideal relationship, just as our ancient Ancestors intended. This is what is called "having a good understanding!"

Michael: "So you are saying that an ideal man-woman relationship is really a relationship between knowledge and wisdom, and the two are inter-dependent, how does personal freedom fit into the picture?"

Old Lionpaw: "Knowledge and Wisdom are Personal Freedom. In other words, knowledge is the foundation of personal freedom for men, as wisdom is for women. The question becomes, freedom for what? For an example, on a personal level, every choice a man makes in life is based on the knowledge in his mind, the freedom to make your life into what you want from life, a reality in your life.

This is where the creative use of knowledge comes into play; freedom to follow your mind is the highest level of Personal freedom and creativity. And where the creative use of wisdom also comes into play; freedom to follow wisdom of the womb is the highest level of Personal Freedom. Because knowledge is the foundation of a man, and wisdom is the foundation of a woman.

On the other hand, the creative use of knowledge and wisdom, in creating realities, is the qualification of Gods and Goddesses. And this means that in your case, seeking knowledge is the first step to becoming a God in Society. In this sense, personal freedom is the backbone of our Society as well as the ideal man-woman relationship."

Orchester III: "So what is the role of the family in this mix?

Old Lionpaw: "A Family is the natural results of a "good understanding" between "knowledge and wisdom." Which is a creative act in itself, symbolized by children. However, sexuality covers a much wider area of life than just producing children. A family is a series of powerful relationships.

Let's take Orchester III for example, he exists because his family exists, and his family exists because he exists. So the relationship between him and his family, the one that produced him as well as the one he will produce in the future, is one of inter-dependency for existence.

This means that a family is held together by a combination of relationships that have their roots in the knowledge and wisdom of the man-woman relationship. For lack of a better word, we will call these, penis and womb relations. Penis and womb relations not only produce children, but also consists of father, mother, and sisters and brothers relations. They also consists of grandmother-father, uncles-Aunts and cousins in your mother and father's family.

So what do we have? Mother family, father family, and the family you will produce in the future which will add still another family to the mix, your future wife's family; all added together equals Your Family.

This means that a family is a web of relationships extending from the original penis-womb relationship, the original Ancestors of the Mendes. In this respect, the whole of the Mende Society is your Family. Thus is the wider area of sexuality.

DionDi: "Then how does this managing the affairs of the family-society thing work?"

Old Lionpaw: "As I mentioned, penis and womb relations extends throughout society as the bond that holds it together, and at the same time, have the same dynamic nature of the man-woman relationship. Therefore, family and society is managed in the same manner as the man-woman relationship, using knowledge and wisdom of the nature of relationships, and more importantly, the knowledge of human nature, you, as your management tools.

In this sense, managing our self, your family, and society is one and the same thing; but there are also differences, especially in regard to society as a whole. And this is related to the competition between the males in society.

Here the question becomes, who is the best manager of the affairs of their family. The best of these managers are chosen to be leaders in Poro. And Poro manages the affairs of society as a whole; with the help of Sande.

This is the games males play, and to survive you must be a Super Player; and to be a Super Player in Society, you must understand the relationship between knowledge and wisdom."

This gives us an idea of the kinds of things Old Lionpaw teaches the boys about relationships.

However to throw more light on his major subject, the relationship between men (knowledge) and women (wisdom), from a male ritual point of view, we will move up to their fourth year in Poro, and their graduation.

Recall when the boys entered Poro school there was a ritual in which GBENI (the Spirit of Knowledge) symbolically swallowed the boys, and their time in school were thought of as being in His stomach.

Their graduation is a continuation of that ritual, and means that the graduation ritual is thought of as the boy's rebirth into Society as men. And at the same time, should show us how much Mende males respect womanhood (wisdom).

Poro Graduation Ceremony consists of 3 rituals which involve GBENI (the Spirit of manhood Knowledge), Old Sowa (Chief Priest of Gbeni), and Mabole (Chief Priestess of GBENI and the only female member of Poro). Then there are the Boys (new men of Society), The Shrine of the 4 Sacred Stones, (Poro Ancestors) and the towns male population (Male Society). And includes festival celebrations of the Town population (Society Itself). In other words, Graduation is male Society's most important spiritual event.

Like before, the entrance to Poro graduation is also announced by the Elders of the Town going around saying, "we will dance tomorrow," and the whole town takes on a festival attitude, especially the men.

The following afternoon, GBENI makes His appearance in town surrounded by the boys. This is an all male affair. The women and children remain at home, and the men dance the "dance of manhood" until early evening.

At which time, GBENI and the boys return to their Bush School carrying gifts from the Parents, consisting of rice, a rooster, and a small container of palm oil for each boy. Upon their return, the first ritual is performed.

As with all graduation ceremony rituals, the first is performed at the Shrine of the 4 Sacred Stones.

Here, after a prayer to Poro Ancestors, Sowa takes up the roosters one at a time. Their heads are placed on a large rock and smashed with another rock as he says, "secrecy", and the boys answer, "forever".

Sowa then says, "this is what will happen to you (your head will be smashed) if you tell Poro secrets to non-Poro members, male or female."

After which, the roosters, rice, and palm oil are cooked as a sacrificial meal and eaten by all present, including Poro Ancestors as witnesses of the "vow of secrecy", then the boys return to their village.

About a week later, GBENI and the boys make another visit to town. There is another all male dance. Only this time the boy's Parents cook a big sacrificial meal for them to take back for the second ritual before the Shrine of the 4 Sacred Stones.

And again, after prayer to the Poro Ancestors, Sowa has the boys repeat their "vows of secrecy." These first two "vows of secrecy" rituals with Sowa and the boys are only to prepare them for the major graduation ritual. This involves GBENI, Sowa, Mabole, and the boys, before the Shrine of the 4 Sacred Stones. This is a 2-day affair.

The first day is a busy one. Further contributions of food are collected from the Parents. The boys destroy everything they used during their stay in school, so as not to be seen by the women. Their clothes are packed into a bundle and tied fast, which will represent GBENI's stomach.

GBENI is said to be reluctant to deliver the boys he has eaten and to whom he is expected to give birth, one by one. Therfore, force has to be used upon him, and members strike him in the stomach (bundle of clothes).

As night approaches, old members flock in from all over. At about 9 pm, a big dance is staged in town. At first, only GBENI and the men take part (the boys remain in their village), but after a while, GBENI goes to rest in His house and women freely join in the dance, which goes on until daybreak.

Then, about 4 am, like a woman in labor, GBENI returns groaning and sighing mournfully. His spokesman explains that GBENI is giving birth. The women clap their hands and the men reproach Him for detaining their children so long. They threaten to beat Him out of the town, unless he delivers them immediately, and pretend to be angry with Him.

Then, the bundle of boy's clothes (symbolizing GBENI's stomach) is dragged around town while others beat it with clubs. At each blow given, GBENI moans and leans against various objects, such as trees. The men with large wooden hooks pull anything he rested against down. Roads are blocked with branches; all to prevent GBENI from leaving before producing the boys.

Meanwhile for the boys in their village, this is a night of fear. They have been warned to keep awake lest they dream of GBENI. This would cause them to die in their sleep, and the idea is impressed on them throughout the day. Their parents send them kola nuts and a large quantity of rice in order to ward off sleep. At dawn however, GBENI disappears from town and returns to the Shrine of the 4 Sacred Stone.

As soon as GBENI returns to Poro Sacred grounds, the boys are taken to the Shrine of the 4 Sacred Stones and everything in their village, including their huts are burned on the spot. This means that the final graduation ritual is about to begin.

Each boy is now told the final secrets He has to learn about Poro, and he takes his final vow of secrecy. The boys are lined up in a semi-circle before the Sacred Stones. Moss and thread are wound round the boy's toes, so that they are all tied together in a continuous chain. On their heads they wear caps of moss and leaves of a certain sacred tree.

Mabole (Chief Priestess) stands in the middle, facing the Sacred Stones. She invokes GBENI and their behalf, and prays that each new member may be as strongly attached to Poro as the thread and moss that now binds them together. She asks that they may be productive of many children when they have wives.

"These children we are pulling from GBENI today, let nothing harm them. Let them not fall from palm trees and make their bodies strong. Give them knowledge to look after their children; let them hold themselves in a good way; let them show themselves to be men!"

As Mabole speaks, she dips a white chicken into a medicine composed of sacred leaves and water, and sprinkles the boys with it. Each boy holds out his tongue in turn, and Mabole places some grains of rice on it in order to test his future. Holding up the chicken, she says, "If this boy has a bad future before him, do not pick the grains."

The chicken is killed, as in other ceremonies, by smashing its head, and the boys are sprinkled with its blood. At the order to rise, they jump up joyfully, and cut away and throw behind them the moss and thread which bounded them together. They are now full members of Poro; but their heads must be shaved bare of boyish hair.

While this is being done, Mabole prepares the sacrificial meal. When it is ready, Sowa rolls the rice, chicken meat, and palm-oil prepared into lumps, placing each piece on Mabole's foot. Then one by one, the boys bend down with their hands behind their backs to take the food.

She raises her foot three times to the boy's mouth saying, "Secrecy," to which he answers, "forever." At the fourth time, he picks up the lump of food with his mouth, and while he chews it, the ceremony of swearing him in takes place. He is told that he will be choked by the rice if he reveals any Poro secrets.

When this is over, the boys are given a general blessing with the remaining medicine water before being taken to a stream for baptism; the final ritual in the transformation from Boyhood to Manhood.

Each boy is taken in turn, one man holding his feet and another his neck and he is lowered into the water. This is repeated four times and then the boy is given his new set of clothes.

The boys dress in these and wear a head-tie over their shaven heads; and they are given a new name, which is a symbol of their new entrance into manhood.

When everyone is ready, the boys then march in procession to town under a large cloth. Their bodies have been smeared with burned palm oil to give them a particularly fresh appearance.

Parents, kinsfolk, and the community as a whole come out to meet them, and the boys are led to the town Barri (Poro town meeting place), which has been specially prepared to lodge them. Gifts are brought out to them, and they remain there for four days, feasting and being treated like little Gods.

Before they are finally discharged on the fourth day, as many pots of palm-wine as there are boys are taken to the Shrine of the 4 Sacred Stones for the farewell; the wine is for Sowa and Mabole.

As Mabole takes up a pot of wine, the boy who has contributed it, comes forward and kneels, facing the Sacred Stones. Mabole prays for him, a small libation is poured on the ground, and Sowa pulls off the head-tie.

The initiation of the new member is now entirely complete. And when all has been finally dealt with in this manner, Poro Puberty School itself is declared over.

This is a very interesting graduation ritual. Especially the role of Mabole, who symbolizes the mid-wife to the ritual birth, as well as symbolizing the respect the Boys are to have for the wisdom of womanhood.

Grandpa's conclusion is that when the Mendes use the term "wisdom", it has the same meaning as when Afro-Americans use the term "mother-wit." However, no matter which term we use, it means "a source of knowledge that males need and do not have."

As we mentioned, sexuality covers a much wider area than just the sex drive, in the sense of the major role Mabole has in manhood ritual is spiritual sex by nature.

And it is in the context of this wider area of sexuality that we must not only look at the relationship between Mabole and the boys in the ritual, but also the relationship between manhood and womanhood in Society.

Let Grandpa put it another way, there is certain knowledge that comes from the experiences of being a man, and there is certain wisdom that comes from the experiences of being a woman.

These experiences of knowledge and wisdom are different from each other (being male and female by nature), and at the same time, need each other in order to give birth to a Society from a spiritual sex point of view. In other words, the Mendes believe that male and female minds have a sexual relationship that gives birth to a spiritual Society. This is what Old Lionpaw impressed on the boys.

Now, as far as the Poro puberty ritual itself is concerned, from start to finish, it clearly shows that they teach the boys a Spiritual Approach to Practical Knowledge.

Now if we take bright young minds like the Boys, after 4 years under Old Sowa, Lionpaw, Mabole, and a number of other Teachers, we will begin to see the nature of the role male sexuality plays in their personal life as well as Society as a whole.

But most of all, he will see their future role in male society as one of personal freedom and self-expression as a means of, functioning in, and being a part of male society's reality.

This tells us a lot about the male side of the Mende's Society. If we keep in mind that males manage the affairs of Society, for example, it shows that, among themselves, males are highly competitive in "who is to dominate who in mind games."

And at the same time, we should keep in mind that Poro is one of the Secret Society Governing Mende male Societies throughout the Boy's lifetime, and male puberty is only one of its functions.

Meanwhile, if the males in a Society think and act, and teach their male children to function from this point of view; the question becomes, how do the females in Society think and act, and teach their female children to function in harmony with males?

Or is it the other way around? Are male's approach and attitude really seeking a means to be in harmony with females? Grandpa thinks so, and to find this relationship, we must take a look at the Sande Secret Society; or to say, see what girls are taught in Sande puberty ritual about their role in Society.

Secree Religion
(Sande Bush School and Puberty Ritual)

The name Sande means Sisterhood. As far as organization is concerned, Sande and Poro have a lot in common. After all, both deal with molding the male and female sides of the same thing, society; and both are independent society governments.

Only Sande does not have male members (like Mabole is a female member of Poro); other than that Sande places much more emphasis of female unity that Poro places of male unity.

This means that Sande is governed by women Elders who ritually worship a "Spirit of Womanhood" in the form of a "Masquerader" wearing a "Sacred Mask." Sande also had "Sacred Grounds" deep in the forest where the girls remain for 3 years (compared to 4 years for the boys).

There are 3 Sacred Stone Markings on the graves of Ancestor Sande leaders buried in standing positions; symbolizing the Shrine to "upright women of society." And too, one of the major functions of Sande, as an independent "female government," is to "transform young girls into women of society."

Finally, Sande officials, like Poro officials, are teaching the "facts of life" to their grand and great granddaughters; and if anything, Sande Elders take their job even more serious then Poro officials.

Again, like Poro, there is a big all-woman festival celebration, while the men and children stay at home, when the "Spirit of Womanhood" comes to get the girls, and take them to the Sacred Grounds. Upon entering Sande School, the girls also go through the ritual of getting special tattoo marks made on their left shoulder as a symbol of being swallowed by the Spirit of Wisdom.

Up to this point, the boy and girl puberty ritual follows the same pattern. However, the girls don't get into things like building and protecting villages (their little village is built by men before school begins); nor do they make big farms, although they do make gardens of spices and some vegetables.

But the biggest difference between boy and girl puberty rituals, are the things they are taught, or to say, the difference between manhood knowledge and womanhood wisdom, and their roles in Society. This brings us to the Officials of Sande and their responsibility.

The Chief Official in Sande, Majo, is "High Priestess" of the "Spirit of Womanhood". Teaching the Sisterhood of Women, as the Owners of Society is the major responsibility of Majo and Her Assistant Priestess.

On the other hand, talking about the Sande puberty ritual, and the "Womanhood," puts Grandpa in a difficult position. Not only is there not a lot of solid evidence, but even this small amount is just about impossible for a man to understand and interpreted in any detail.

This being the case, even though the Girls are taught a lot about 'giving birth,' 'raising babies,' and childhood diseases, Grandpa will only present the evidence we have in the areas of the spiritual transformation from childhood to womanhood. And what the Girls are taught about Sisterhood, the man-woman relationship, and let my Granddaughters and their Mothers make sense of the evidence.

For example, Grandpa believes that the following story concerns something taught by mothers to their daughters be complete before a girl can make the transition from childhood to womanhood. But Grandpa doesn't have a clue to what it means, what do you think? The story is as follows.

Priest Majo: "There was once a woman who cooked beer for the Ancestors, strained it, set it aside (for the second boiling), and went to the river (to get water).

After (she had gone) her children began to drink, and one of them, as she was going to drink, took a calabash to do so; Smash went the calabash! She had broken it, and when their mother came back and saw the calabash, the sight of it blinded her eyes in darkness (she was angry).

She sat down the water-pot quickly on its stand and fetched a switch, beat the girl, and drove her away saying that she must sew up the broken calabash. Because of this the girl took her way and went off to the midst of the tall grass land and sang;

"My mother cooked her Ancestor's beer;
This child toddled along to get some to drink;
That child toddled along to get some to drink;
I also hastened along to fetch some to drink
Our father's food calabash, it did break;
It must be sewn up with a leopard's skin thong,
And with hyenas skin thong,
And with witch's veins;
There is no leopard's skin near by, near by;
There is no hyena's skin near by, near by;
You witch's vines, there are also none, near by."

A leopard (appeared, took the calabash and) sewed it for her. Next she came (to a place where there were) a hyena. He also took (the calabash) from her, and sewed it and gave it back to her.

She next came to where there was an old witch-woman, and she took the veins of witches and sewed it for her, and she (the witch) said, 'this is how you must go home. When you come to clean water, you must not go in that; but water which is muddy, go down into that.'

Of a truth, the girl, when she reached (the water) did as she was told; she left the good water, but descended into the bad water, and emerged with bangles and beads (riches) and with body shimmering wagegege (a sound). When she reached home and her mother saw the girl she shook at seeing her again (was still angry).

Another wife of the same husband, also saw the first girl riches, rose up all in a hurry, boiled beer, re-boiled it, set it down, and instructed her girl. Saying, 'you, after I have gone out, break the food calabash belonging to your father."

She (the second mother) went off to the river. The girl came and broke the calabash and sat waiting for her mother to return. She came back, reached the homestead, and began shouting, 'who broke this calabash?' She took a switch and whipped the girl, and drove her out of the yard. The girl cried and went into the middle of the long grass and began to sing;

My mother cooked the Ancestor's beer;
This child quickly came to drink;
Another child quickly came to fetch and drink;
I too came quickly to fetch and drink;
Our father's food calabash did break;
It must be sewn with a leopard's skin thong;
Sewn with a hyena's skin thong;
Sewn with the vines of you witches;
A leopard's skin thong is not near by, near by;

A hyena's skin thong is not near by, near by;
Veins of you witches are not near by, near by;
My mother approach and hear, my mother.

A leopard took (the Calabash) from her and sewed it. A hyena took it from her and sewed it. Witches took it and sewed it. An old woman said, 'when you reach water which is good, do not descend into the clear water, but the water which is bad, go down into it.'

The girl argued, saying; 'why, when I see good water, should I go down into the mud?' So she went down into the clear water and came out again with snails on her body, sticking to her. When she reaches home her mother grew tired of picking them off, and hurt her body until it was all sore."

As was mentioned, Grandpa does not know how to interpret these kinds of stories, and there are hundreds of them. Nevertheless, after saying that, I concluded that it has something to do with the transition from girlhood to womanhood. And the process has something to do with teaching the wisdom of womanhood.

And at the same time, establish a woman to woman relationship between the girl and her mother, based on the 'equality of sisterhood in the ownership of Society,' under the authority that it is women who gives birth to the society of mankind. And this fact is their title of ownership. But like Grandpa mentioned, don't put much faith in this conclusion, maybe you 'Girls' would understand it better.

Grandpa bases this on the known evidence that the Mendes and the People living in the land of Secret Societies, the Secree, take "Sisterhood" even further than the Igbo. And this is saying a lot, since Sisterhood is a big thing with all African women.

This means that to the Secree, sisterhood is the nature of womanhood, or to say, they believe the two are one and the same thing. And this is one of the major things Priestess Majo must impress on the girl's ideas of womanhood.

This brings us to another group of stories that Grandpa does not really understand, but I do believe that they are related to sisterhood, even though I cannot tell how; these stories Grandpa calls women and lioness stories.

The connection Grandpa makes is the fact that Africans base their man-woman relationship on the organization of the Lion Family, one male lion and a number of female lions.

However, it is the Lioness' relationship to each other, a strong bond of sisterhood, that I think is the focus of the following stories.

Meanwhile, you must keep in mind that Grandpa could be out of line; this may also be a case where a woman could better understand.

To make this case are three stories of women, lioness, and their children, that seem to be a variation of the same theme.

Priestess Majo: "A woman gave birth in the forest near a cave in which a lioness gave birth to a female cub. The boy and the cub met, played together, and learned to love each other.

The lioness killed the Boy's mother, but the cub refuses to eat her flesh. The boy killed the lioness and lived in the cave with her cub.

When they grew up, the boy went to town and fell in love with the Chief's daughter; the young lioness helped him to marry her.

When the boy sent his bride to spend the night with her mother, she suspected that he had a lover. One night she returned and found him in bed with the lioness.

She reported this to her father, the Chief, and he sent his warriors, who killed the lioness. The boy killed himself, and his wife killed herself."

The second story is as follows:

Priestess Majo: "A woman gave birth to a son in a cave. A lioness came to the cave and gave birth to a lion cub. The woman hid in the back of the cave and went for food when the lioness did, and the boy and the cub became friends and played together.

The lioness killed the woman, but the cub refused to eat her flesh and promised to feed the boy and avenge the woman's death.

After months had passed, the young lion killed its mother and then provided food for the boy's circumcision (puberty ritual).

The boy fell in love with the Chief's daughter, and the lion helped him to marry her. The boy, his wife, and the lion lived happily together ever after."

And, this brings us to the third story.

Priest Majo: "A woman gave birth in the forest and left her son there. A leopard with her cubs raised him, and when he grew up, the leopards stole clothes for him.

Later it left him near a town where he settled a quarrel and was proclaimed Chief. When the leopards were about to die, it came to bid him farewell.

He begged it to stay, but it ran away and died in the forest. The boy followed, flung himself on its body, and died also."

Again Grandpa must mention that I really don't know how to interpret these kinds of stories. On the other hand, to teach this Unity in the Sisterhood, Priestess Majo tells them question-stories that are easy to understand, the power of unity in the community, for example;

Priestess Majo: "Ear, Mouth, Eyes, and Hand went to look for wild fruit. Ear heard the birds in the fruit tree; Eyes saw the fruit tree; Mouth told the limbs. Foot ran to the tree, and Hand picked the fruit. Each claimed the fruit. To whom does the fruit belong?"

Priestess Majo: "A woman locked her house, went away for three years and returned to find all her possessions safe. Thieves had tried to break in, but the Door Latch was strong and had held.

A reward was claimed by the Latch for keeping the thieves out, by the Door because without it the Latch could not keep out thieves, by the Wall because without it the Latch and Door could do nothing, by the House Post because it supported the Roof, by the Roof because it covered the house and all its parts and contents, and by the Liana (rope like vine) that tied the members of the house together. They quarreled and asked the Chiefs to settle their case. Which has the right to the reward?"

Priestess Majo: "Rain, Blacksmith, and Farmer were friends, and each had a daughter. The three girls were friends and farmed together, but one day they fought over the division of their rice.

One said that her father had provided their seed. Another said her father had made their hoes. The third said that her father had made the rain. The three men heard the argument and took back the rice seeds, the hoes, and the rain, each claiming that his daughter was right. Do you agree?"

It is easy to see that these stories teach the value of unity, or to say, the value of giving value to each part of Women Society.

At this point, to better see the relationship between manhood and womanhood in Society as a whole, we will focus our attention on what the girls were taught about sexuality and the man-woman relationship (or being a Wife).

This brings Majo's Chief Assistant Priestess, Lionique (the first wife of old Lionpaw) and her favorite students, Tiffany, Rachel, Omni, Nikki and Maya into the picture. Like we mentioned, the old Priestess Lionique sees greatness in the 'Girls, and for this reason is very interested in their future.

She begins her teaching by telling the girls a question-story, like the following;

Old Lionique: "Turtle Dove was a young girl who was good at fishing, cooking, and dancing. When the time came for her to marry, she had three lovers.

The first, called Chimpanzee, was big and strong. He had already killed two elephants, and all the women ran after him.

The second, called Arrow of the forest, was small and slender. He was always gay and singing, the best dancer you could find. He ran after all the girls, knew well how to talk with them, and had children in several villages.

The third was called Toadstool. The day he was born, his mother had cooked a large dish of mushrooms in which a poisonous one was found, and his father died. He did not hunt or fish, but he brought much game and fish because he was a great medicine man, and knew how to cure sickness. He had blood in the corner of his eye, one tooth stuck out of his mouth, one shoulder was higher than the other, and he never looked others in the face. Each of the young men claimed Turtle Dove as his wife. To whom should she be married?"

Old Lionique: "The Right Hand said to its Wife, the Left Hand, 'I will not give you any more meat. You never kill any animals.' The Left Hand replied that then the Right Hand would have to butcher meat, cut vegetables, chop firewood, weave baskets, and carry game by itself. The Right Hand tried and tried but had to leave its meat to rot in the forest. Finally the Right Hand asked the Left Hand to help, and they worked together again. The case was heard and the verdict was given that the Left Hand had won the argument. But that the Right Hand had come off better because it had admitted its inability to do without the help of the Left Hand; and had asked for its assistance."

Meanwhile, the 'Girls', like most girls their age, have nothing but sex on their minds and are very concerned about dealing with "their sex drive thing".

Tiffany: "What is this thing called sex drives?"

Old Lionique: "Now we must take a look at the old Mende Proverb, "Women Own the World, and Men manage the World's Affairs. Sex drives are related to this Ownership of the World.

On the other hand, Female Sexuality is in two parts, "the Wisdom of the sex drives" and "the wisdom of nurturing." Giving birth, and sustaining life, is the nature of Ownership of the world. Sex drives are the first step of the process. We will deal with sex drives from this point of view.

Long ago, our Most Ancient Ancestors lived in a Cave with NGEWO and NDOI, and you have heard the story of how Mankind (males and females) stole something from NGEWO and NDOI.

Well, where as man stole "knowledge of the Penis", women stole "wisdom of the womb."

The word 'womb' means a combination of things, not only does it contain eggs (the substances of life), but it also contains the wisdom needed to provide a space for a baby to develop. Nurture the baby for nine months, and give birth to a brand new person. In this respect, the womb is the pathway to life.

However, this whole process is dependent on the fulfillment of sex drives (male and female) which brings the egg-of-wisdom and sperm-of-knowledge together in the first place.

This is what your sex drives are related to, and means, to understand sex drives you must have the experiences of a woman who has given birth.

Now giving birth is the process of bringing into reality two things, a body and a spirit. And in our definition, both are a process that takes place over a period of about 12 years, from conception to puberty; which is a growth process, and this is where nurturing comes into the picture.

Rachel: "How do women nurture the Spirit of a baby?"

Old Lionique: "Nurturing consists of an 'understanding' of, and 'providing', the things a baby needs to realize its potentiality, and maturity.

In other words, nurturing sustains the developing of a baby, physically and spiritually, until society takes over. This is when he or she enters Sande and Poro Puberty Bush Schools, which is still another way of nurturing and giving birth, and nurturing is the foundation of Wisdom of the Womb.

A mother is a baby's first teacher of 'Moral Values of Society', and Moral Values is the Substance of the Spirit; or to say, moral values is the food the spirit-mind needs to grow and develop spiritually. Moreover, mothers nurture the baby's spirit with moral values and, the source of moral values is wisdom of the womb. So we can say mothers nurture the spirit with the Wisdom of the Womb.

And this is not the end of it. Being as women own the womb, it follows that they own the things the womb produces Having sex, the sex act itself, and giving birth, are the beginning and end of the sex drive. This also means that all of Society comes from the womb, and it is in this since we say, though birth-and-nurturing-rights, women own the baby, the family, and Society.

Omni: "How do men fit into the process?"

Old Lionique: "Wisdom of the Womb is the source of sex drives (as we defined the term) and Birth (as we define the term). It then becomes clear that this gives women not only the ultimate power over society's existence, but also, through nurturing, the means by which Society lives and grows.

However, nurturing is not only what makes a thing grow; it also has a big influence in what a thing is to grow into. In this respect it is the woman that make the man what he is, especially in the man-woman relationship. The woman owns the man as she does every thing else in Society, manhood also needs nurturing to grow.

Therefore, in the final sense, Wisdom of the Womb is an understanding of the spiritual world of Creative Sexuality; of this, men know very little, meaning he is not cause for concern."

Nikki: "What about the problems men cause in the man-woman relationship?"

Old Lionique: "Although men manage the affairs of women, we are the High Priestess of Sexuality, and the man-woman relationship is a product of sexuality. Meaning, women create all sexual relations; men do not know enough to cause sexual relation problems.

There is always a woman in control of how a man relates to a woman, especially his mother. This means, to deal with a man is to deal with another woman's nurturing influence. And if there is a problem, you must deal with it from this point of view.

If you see a relationship filled with problems, the woman either doesn't want the man, or she is dumb. This is especially the case if she is a 'first wife;' men do not have a say in the matter."

As with the so-called man-woman problems, most of the time it is having fun in the games people play in the man-woman relationship, which has gotten out of hand.

However, the serious problems between men and women are when women think men are managing the affairs of their family and society in a manner that causes them and their Ancient Ancestress to feel Shamed instead of busting with Pride. This is the ultimate source of problems between manhood and womanhood in Society as a whole.

Maya: "Why do men have many wives, and women only have one husband, and how does wisdom of the womb and sisterhood fit together?"

Old Lionique: "They say God created the World and all therein, but it was the "Art of a Goddess" that gave reality to life. This means that it is women that gave reality to Society, and we nurture it, in a way that it will be something we are proud of say, 'This belong to Us!"

We also created a code of morals as standards to measure our "Proud-ness," not only in the way we raise our sons, but most important, the men we marry.

For example, Women divided themselves between the men that are the strongest in the area of "Upright husbands", fatherhood, businessmen, blacksmiths, hunters, medicine men, farmers, and all kinds of artist, especially musicians. As many women as possible want to have children by these men, for these are the qualities we want in Society.

This is our responsibility passed down from our Ancestress from the beginning of time. The "Creative Process" by which this takes place is "Wisdom of the Womb."

And from this point of view, we can say that wisdom of the womb is the driving force in our sisterhood, and 'Creating Societies" (and nations) is our ultimate goal."

While we are mentioning things that are taught in Sande where there is little evidence to back us up, Grandpa is basing conclusions on the role women play in Society where there is lots of evidence.

The fact that the Girls are kept in a Secret Bush School for three years with Old Women Elders, without the Girls seeing their mothers in that time period. Add to that, the Old Women Elder's stated goal is to teach the girls their role in the family and society.

Then we must come to the conclusion that when we see the women in society, we are seeing the results of what the Girls are taught in Sande. Especially when we see the power sisterhood has in Society; and there is lots of evidence to back us up in this regard.

After saying all of that we will now move up in time, three years later, to the Girl's Graduation ceremonies.

The day before graduation the parents of the Girls send the things needed for the ritual side of the final ceremonies, including clothes. This is a very serious time for the Girls and Officials, as we mention, each graduating class is in competition with the last class, the class of their mothers, which means there is a deep pride involved.

Early the next day, well before the sun comes up and it is still dark, in the light of torches, the Girls are taken to the Sacred Stream where they undress to be baptized. While Priestess Majo makes a prayer like the following:

"We wash you from all uncleanness of the past; we cleanse you of the errors and mistakes of child hood; from now you follow a new path; follow that path to the end."

All the girl's clothes are buried on the bank of the stream as they are led naked to the Sacred Tree. Under which is the Three Sacred Stone Shrine on the Grave of Sande Ancestress, where a sacrifice is made and Priest Majo prays, first speaking for the Girls as follows:

"We come unto you, our ancestors, who begot us; we come unto you with this present; receive what is your own; eat this gift of ours; call your companions, ancient and honorable as yourselves, and give them their due positions.

You, our ancestors, first in our thoughts because greatest of all we know, we come to you for blessing; rejoice with your companions, but in your rejoicing forget not those who bring this gift; we give you honor, give us benediction."

Priest Majo now speaks for the Ancestress, saying to the Girls:
"Respect female sexuality.
Respect and obey the Elders.
Respect and obey your mother and father.
Respect Birth-rights of Womanhood.
Respect Courage.
Respect Sympathy.
Respect Womanliness.
Respect Co-operation.
Stealing is undignified; if you want a thing, ask for it; if it is refused, go without it.

There are no rules between man and wife, but there is understanding; honor them.

To tell lies to another woman member of society is to pronounce yourself outside the membership of Sisterhood. Never meddle in other people's quarrels."

Next the Girls are led, still naked, to their bush house where every thing they used in the last three years is burned or buried, including their house. Then they dress in their new clothes for the upcoming 'Coming out Celebration.'

Getting dressed is a ceremony into itself, although there is no ritual involved, the Girls are getting ready to put themselves on display before Society, and they want to look their best.

With this in mind, the Girls dress themselves with ropes of tightly twisted cloth and threaded cowries shells around their waist with tiny bells attached, from which a skirt is fashioned with silk handkerchiefs pleated like ribbons.

Their braided hair is pile high and ornamented by black seeds like grapes and silver and brass ornaments, molded into a shape resembling the crest of a roman helmet. Coming well over the middle of the forehead and extending backward into the nape of the neck.

Their bodies are oiled down with a special oil fragrant with camwood dust, looking like polished ebony; and decorated with silver charms, plaques, armlets, and leg bangles that clash musically as they walk. Now they are ready for their processions into Society, their 'Coming out Celebration' in town.

The Procession is led by Na-Sin ka Sande (the Voice of Sande Womanhood), symbolized by a masked masquerader; and behind which is Majo and other Sande high Officials and their women drummers.

They are followed by the Girls walking in order of seniority, with a guardian on either side of each holding up canopies of country cloth. There are also drummers interspersed amongst the girls all along the line; they are known as the 'Resurrected Ones.'

The Girls march into town with their faces expressionless, showing no emotions. In the crowd their parents recognize their daughters in the procession, and boys and girls point out their sisters and excitedly call out their names.

But not a face among the Girls lights up with recognition, not a muscle moves to express delight, for these 'Resurrected Ones' are not supposed to know anything of their childhood life, including relatives or friends.

Upon entering the marketplace, Priestess Majo introduces the 'Resurrected Ones' to their families. They pretend not to know their parents, their brothers and sisters, relatives, friends, and former acquaintances.

The look of the town, its houses, roads, trees, spaces, have been forgotten. They have to be introduced to it all again, be given explanations for it, and be told what it is and what it is for.

For example, 'This is your father, that path leads to the river where you will get your water, we call this a calabash, and you will use it for drinking purposes,' and so on.

Following this, the Girls dance around the marketplace with baskets in which family and friends have put presents. Then there is a big family and society reunion feast and dance.

The Girls spend the night in a special Girl's House, where they are treated like Royal Ones or Young Goddesses for the next two weeks. There they receive many more presents; then they return to their family homestead and regular life.

An important point we must always keep in mind is, Poro and Sande mold the men and women of Society through their puberty rituals. Also regulate their conduct after they have entered Society, with their own court system.

In other words, Poro and Sande have the power to enforce the social and spiritual rules of manhood and womanhood on everybody in Society from the age of puberty throughout old age.

This makes them permanent independent governments of Society as far as manhood and womanhood are concerned. The major point is that Poro and Sande are Secret Societies, which govern Society.

As we mentioned, the Mende Society has many parts, at least 5, and Poro and Sande only govern two of those parts. The parts based on knowledge and wisdom of the nature of Men and Women in Society; which is the foundation of their Society.

Therefore, to complete our rough outline of the "Society" of the "People of the land of Secret Societies," we must further investigate our conclusions on the position of the 5 governing secret societies in Society as a whole.

Recall NGEWO's Knowledge was divided between all the animals (including mankind) and plants. The people have a system or method to collect and store this Knowledge. This is where secret societies come into the picture. So we must look at the remaining 3 governing Secret Societies, Humui, Njayei, and Kpa in their role of 'Priest Healers' of the spiritual and physical health and welfare of Society.

Secree Religion

(Priest-Healers and Health care)

Unlike Poro and Sande, where the Chief Teachers are Priest and Priestess, as well as health care providers; Humui, Njayei, and Kpa are Schools ran by Healers (Doctors), called Priest Healers or Medicine Men and Women whose major focus is disease on one level or another.

And from this point of view, whereas Poro and Sande is concerned with producing Men and Women for Society; Humui, Njayei and Kpa are concerned with the Health of the Sex, Mind, and Body of the Men and Women of Society; or to say they deal with the Mental and Physical illnesses of Society.

To begin, we will define two Mende terms when speaking about knowledge, "It came to me in a Dream," and "I learned this from a Bush Spirit."

The Mende believe that when the mind is engaged in "analytical thinking" they call this "Dreams," and the new knowledge that results from this thinking is called Knowledge of Bush Spirits.

However, we intend to show that from a practical point of view, the Mende use this Intelligence to base their Knowledge on Discovery and Experimentation from Observation of Nature.

Next, we must translate spiritual terms into science terms. Recall that all Africans believe that everything has a spirit. Therefore, illness has a spirit: For When a Mende doctor is studying the elements of a medicine plant, he thinks in terms of these elements as spirits that will have a positive or negative effect on the spirit or elements of a given illness.

This means, the African Healer's thoughts are in spiritual terms, but in reality, his action and re-actions are practical and to some extent, what we would call scientific. In other words, the doctor uses spiritual terms to think and talk about what we call a scientific approach to medicine. Here we get into the use of words. 'Words' are not things, they are 'names' for 'things'; and in this sense, things are not words.

So in this case, the word spiritual, and science have the same meaning; so what is meaning? The things words refer to other than the word itself.

In our case, the words are referring to the intelligence of analytical thinking based on 'discovery' made from 'observation' and 'experimentation.'

This creates understanding=knowledge as symbolized by the Bush Spirits, the logic (intelligence) of which is found in the African World View.

Now let's look at the word Discovery. If we recall in Secree Religious Beliefs, NGWE divided his Knowledge between the life-forms He created by the use of names (words), human beings, cows, monkeys, etc, etc.

This meant that human beings were left in the position, if they wanted His Knowledge, of discovering it in all life-forms. However, in order to make these discoveries, they must observe and Experiment with these other life-forms. The results of which they stored in the form of ritual words symbolized by Bush Spirits.

Finally, this brings us to the best of all examples of this logic of discovery, observation and experimentation (intelligence) we keep mentioning; the so called Medicine Men and Women. However grandpa doesn't think 'Medicine Man' is the right term to use when talking about African ideas about health and disease; it would seem that 'Priest Healer' is more to the point.

However, if we recall, we mentioned, in the African Traditional Worldview, mankind exists on three levels, Individual, Family, and Society-Community, as well as in two dimensions, the physical and the spiritual.

And because of this, throughout Africa, health and disease are also inter-related with social behavior and moral conduct, therefore, the source of health and illness lies beyond that which can only be felt, seen, and touched.

In other words, the Priest Healers job is to heal the spiritual and physical wounds of individuals, and families, as well as Society as a whole; called 'Holistic Health care.

'Now when we mention Holistic Health care, and Priest Healers, this automatically means that 'Priest Healers' must deal with 'disease' on all levels.

First, we must define the word 'disease as the Secree would use the term. According to Secree thinking, there are evil forces, the Sons and Daughters of Jealousy and Greed, sufficient to account for all of the evil, tragedies, and misfortunes in life. All of which are thought of as disease.

In addition, their attacks on a person take various forms, resulting in sickness, disaster, sorrow, or death. Therefore, disease is an attack by a spirit upon one's spirit, and it is overcome by knowledge-medicine whose spirit is stronger than the spirit of the disease.

The Secree believe that every misfortune, like every piece of good fortune, involves two questions. "How did it happen?" And "why did it happen?" The "how' is answered by using common sense of observation, it is the "why" that calls for experimentation.

Therefore, when a person becomes ill and home remedies fail to work, a cure, or in time of disaster, he turns to the Priest Healer. From whom he trusts to find the root causes of the misfortune before the necessary physical or spiritual medicine is prescribed.

Take into consideration that the Secree live in a tropical rain forest, which consists of thousands of exotic tropical plants and animals, and each of which has a spirit that has the potential of a positive or negative effect on mankind, as food or medicine.

As well as an understanding of the nature of the spirit and body of mankind, and, the morals and ethics which is the constitution of Society, we can begin to see the area in which the Priest Healer fits into the picture of health care.

Now, with Holistic health care, our definition of Dreams and Bush Spirits, and our translation of scientific and spiritual terms is to give us direction; with Disease and Priest Healers, as our background. We will turn our attention to the remaining three Bush Schools governing Mende Society, Humui, Njayei, and Kpa. Who, unlike Poro and Sande who are concerned with giving birth to Society; these three schools consist of Priest Healers who are concerned with the Health of Society; from a Sexual, Mind, and Body point of view.

This means that the Mendes believe humankind has three different major areas of illness; the sexual, the mental, and the physical.

Which are the three dimensions of the focus on medical health as far as the Traditional African Priest Healers (Medicine Man and Woman) are concerned as the Healers of Society when it becomes sick on any level.

Secree Religion
(Humui Bush School)

Humui is very interesting in the sense that its Bush Spirit is the Spirit of the Knowledge of Society sexual moral code as well as their sexual physical health and beyond, including in the Man-Woman relationship.

Like Poro and Sande, Humui is a Secret Society and has their Sacred Grounds in the Forest. And like Sande, all the High Officials are Women Elders, in fact, it is a Humui Priestess who teaches the girls in Sande the mysteries of Birth. Only for the most part, their job is to care and nurture the spiritual and physical Sexual Health of Society as a whole.

This means that they have the Spiritual Authority to Enforce Sexual Moral Laws on the Individual, Family and Society. Laws handed down by the 'Spirit of Sexuality,' symbolized by a Bush Spirit, whose shrine is located at the Graves of Ancestor Priestess on their Sacred Grounds.

Without going into great detail about their organization, we will just look at some of the moral laws they enforced. It is a violation of Humui's rules for men to have sex with;

1 His own mother, or mother's mother.

2 His own daughter, or granddaughter.

3 His own sister or half sister.

4 The daughter of his brother or sister.

5 The daughters of his brother or sister's children.

6 His wife's sisters, or their daughters and granddaughters.

7 The daughters of his wife's brother, or their daughters.

8 The sister or close kin of any woman he has had sex.

9 Any woman with whom his brother or half-brother had had sex.

10 Any woman that breast-feeds him when a baby.

11 Any first or second cousin on his mother's or father's side of his family.

12 Have sex with a woman in the forest.

13 Have sex with a girl below the age of puberty.

14 Have sex with another man's wife.

15 Have sex with a woman having her period.

16 Have sex in public.

17 Have sex with a woman whose last baby is less than two years old.

And the list goes on; With the exception of the young girl below the age of puberty, the women is guilty as well as the man.

Even though the man and the woman are guilty in the above situations, the woman is punished more than the man is, the thing that makes their acts immoral is that it is showing disrespect to female sexuality, Wisdom of the Womb.

And from that point of view, it is a far more serious thing for women to show disrespect for the Wisdom of the Womb, than men. However, both are violating the laws of Humui; and the old Women Officials do not take this lightly, especially as far as the woman is concerned.

The man and woman are brought before the Humui Council of Elder women. An important point to keep in mind is that they must join the Humui Secret Society before they can be treated.

This consists of being baptized with sacred leaves and holy water to spiritually purify their sexuality and respect for the wisdom of the womb; plus they must pay a large fine, the woman's fine is larger than the man.

This women's respect for female sexuality is shown by a long list of rules that cover a range from how to 'sit and walk', to how, and where to perform the 'sex act. As well as care for the young children that sex produces. From this point of view, we see that Humui is concerned with the purification of a violation of a moral code of sexuality.

On the other hand, Humui is involved with the medical side of sex, for example, sexual hygiene and disease, and just as important, they are generally women who specialize in all maternity needs. They can prescribe medicines for childless couples after the necessary spiritual requirements are met. During antenatal, prenatal, and postnatal periods, they are very helpful.

They also specialize in other types of women's and children's medical needs. They help women in menopause and young girls with painful menstruation, or with abortion in some cases.

In fact, Humui's sacred grounds serve as a kind of hospital in this respect, and small children may be taken there for treatment. They combine the work of a gynecologist and a pediatrician, and are skilled in family medicine generally. However, we will investigate Humui physical medical Healers under another title, the training of Healers (doctors).

Now we will turn our attention to the Njayei Bush School who deals with the mental health and well being of Society.

Secree Religion
(Njayei Bush School)

As we mentioned, the Njayei Secret Society is concerned with the mental health and well-being of Society, specializing in mental illness, but also including all forms of cultural art like entertaining Society.

This means we, as a back ground, need some insight into one of the major keys to African Traditional Religious Worship, "Spiritual Possession," especially as related to the role of the Priest Healers of the Mind. But what is spiritual possession as we use the terms?

Africans believe that the Spirit of a God, Goddess, the Dead, or another living person, can make a temporary or permanent home in the bodies of living men or women. These men or women are spoken as being "possessed."

They speak in a voice not their own, and they act in a manner alien to their natural character. Also, they are said to utter prophesies and to display knowledge which they could not normally have acquired, and in fact, do not consciously possess in their normal condition.

This means, Spiritual Possession, on which we touched on with the Aja, is one of the Key Articles of Faith that control, and mold, African Traditional Religion into a Living Spiritual Experience; in the sense that the Priest or Priestess must have a personal experience of a God or Goddess and communicate that experience to the people.

For example, like some Black Baptist Woman after a moving sermon by her Pastor will say, "I feel the presence of God in my heart," meaning that God have possessed her heart.

For still another example, Grandpa's mother, your Great Grandmother Bertha, taught him to "go off alone and pray to God to come into my soul."

For a final example, Grandpa has seen one person dominate another to the point of being in total control of what the other person thinks and feels, for instance, by a Witch.

Although Grandpa did not have any of these experiences, the point being is that Africans and Afro-Americans believe that people can be possessed by a spirit other than their own.

In these cases through a ritual, a person can invoke a spirit to take possession of his or her mind.

In fact we can go so far as to say, a religion cannot be "A Religion", without spiritual possession. For instance, in order to become a Christian, one must become possessed by the Spirit of Christ. Moslems are the same way, to become a part of their religion, one must become possessed by the Spirit of Allah.

This extends to the cases of China and India's religion of Buddha and Hindu, and includes all of the other religions in the world, anyway the ones that Grandpa has investigated. Thus is the meaning of spiritual possession as we use the terms.

Of all the Priest', the ones belonging to the Njayei Secret Society make our point even clearer, they have discovered a unique method, in the Art of Spiritual Possession, of dealing with mental illness.

Therefore, the Njayei Priest Healers define mental illness as a break in the harmony in a person's mind in the relationships between his Individual Self, Family Self, and his Community Self. Its all a matter of harmony in the relationships of the holy trinity in a Person Mind's Worldview.

Like Poro, Sande, and Humui, Njayei Bush School is located in the forest. On which there is a shrine consisting of three sacred stones on the graves of Njayei Ancestor Elders, related to the Spirit of the Mind symbolized by a Masquerader; however the Officials are both men and women.

And like Humui, the Njayei sacred grounds are used as a hospital, only in their case for the mentally ill.

With this as a back ground, we can now introduce the Njayei Priest Healer who invokes the spirit of someone with mental illness to possess him or her.

In this way the Priest Healer can experience the problem first hand, and therefore, use the knowledge from his or her experience of the problem to work out the solution. This is an example of what we meant in the 'Secree's Article of Faith that Knowledge is Medicine that can Cure.'

To demonstrate what we mean, we will take a look at the qualification, and training, in the Art of dealing with mental illness that a person needs to become a Njayei Priest Healer.

The first and foremost qualification for becoming a Njayei Priest Healer, is for one to become mentally ill and become cured, either they figure it out for themselves or with the help of a Priest Healer.

The point being, a person must have 'experienced an illness' and 'experienced the cure' for the illness.

Only then is he qualified to become a student in Njayei Bush School. He is thought of as "being possess by the Spirit of the Mind, and is set apart to serve the Bush Spirit of the Mind for the benefit of the community."

In other words, being as he has 'some' knowledge of the mind, he automatically is qualified to be trained to use all of the knowledge held secret in the Njayei Secret Society.

Keep in mind that he already has the experiences of being mentally ill and being cured. We will now take a look at how a student is trained to become a Njayei Priest Healer.

First off, the training takes at least 3 to 4 years, and the student is to remain on the sacred grounds of Njayei all of this time. During this period, the student is expected to keep strict sexual and food rules. He may not have sexual relationship even if he is married.

The Njayei Officials take their job very serious. If its rules are broken, the student is punished. Sacrifices may be offered to appease the Spirit of the Mind, and the student may have to begin his training all over again.

The first year is taken up with purification rituals. The student is baptized with various mixtures of sacred leaves and holy water sacred to 'Spirit of the Mind.'

These leaves strengthen his joints, especially his ankles, for dancing (as we will see later, dancing is a major part of becoming spiritually possessed); others are for invoking possession of the 'Spirit.'

He washes his eyes and ears with herbs that help him to see the normally unseen and to hear the normally unheard.

Special plants from the grave of the Njayei Ancestors are used for contact with these Ancestors. The student's hair, which has sacred meaning, is left uncut and unkempt; this gives him a wild look.

However, no secret knowledge is given to him at this stage until he is found to have the fortitude to withstand the mental pressures of the job.

The second year, the student is taught the knowledge known to the Njayei society, and during this period he is forbidden to drink strong drinks. He must refrain from quarreling, or any disgraceful acts. He should not use the name of the society to curse anyone. He should avoid all forms of legal involvement. He should not go out alone at night. He must not touch a dead body, or have contact with a menstruating woman. In other words, he must remain purified while learning the secret knowledge of the mind.

The third year is spent learning, and using, the art of spiritual possession, also learning the plants that have a medicine effect on the mind; and especially in the use of a special kind of divination.

The Njayei believe each category of mental illness is symbolized by a color, for instance, red, yellow, blue, green, etc, etc.

Therefore, a big part of training consists of putting a number of colored pebbles into a basket, and the student must pick the colored pebble for each illness the Teacher names.

This is the method the student will later use to make a diagnosis when examining a future patient. At this time, the Priest Healer presents the patient with such a basket of stones. And the patient picks the color of the pebble which fits how he or she feels, which gives the Priest Healer an idea of the nature of the problem.

Now to understand the nature of the training of our student, this is in two parts. First, we must recall that the student is either a man or woman that has become mentally ill for some reason, and experienced a cured of him or her self.

And it is the experience that the Njayei Elders use to teach him how to cure people with other mental problems. Second, for the full three years, the student is taught the Art of becoming spiritually possessed by the spirit of living people with mental problems.

But for our interest, we will move up in time to get more insight into the nature of spiritual possession. We will describe the final ritual ceremony of induction as a full Priest Healer; consisting of a full Possession of the student by the 'Spirit of the Mind of certain Njayei Ancestors.'

Now to graduate, as we saw, a student must learn a lot of things. But above everything else, the student must know the art of becoming spiritually possessed by rhythmic dancing to the drumming, singing, clapping, and crowd excitement; something like an old Black Baptist Church service.

Only the focus is on the Student Dancer, who when becomes spiritually possessed, will deliver sermons and prophecies, in what Afro-Americans call 'inspirational teaching.'

Grandpa has seen hundreds of spiritual possessions, which take place in hundreds of Black Churches every Sunday. And one of the major things that takes place is that the 'Possessed One' speaks in tongues (unknown languages), and all of the evidence shows that the same thing happens in Africa.

For this reason, when the Student Dances, the Chief Priest of the Spirit of the Mind attends him, and translates what the Student is saying.

The graduation ritual takes place under a special tree, under which the Shrine of 3 Sacred Stones are placed on the graves of the Njayei Ancestors. On the one hand, this is a serious ritual process involving the major Njayei Officials.

While on the other hand, this is a great festival celebration, with music and drumming with the relatives of the student, people from his village, and the general Njayei membership in the role of spectators. In a cleared space encircled by the crowd, the Student begins to dance. Now we will give an African description of a 'possessed state.'

"When the Spirit begins to show itself in him, a dramatic physical transformation takes place. In a standing position, he staggers, appears to lose his balance, begins to sway, and may fall onto the ground or into the arms of attendants or bystanders.

His entire body begins to vibrate, His hands are rigid at his sides or stretched out above. His feet are planted widely apart and he may lurch back and forth from toe to heel. The vibration increases in intensity, somewhat resembling the convulsions of a seizure state.

At the same time, he emits deep grunts and groans. His jaw begins to protrude, his lips pout and turn down sharply at the corners. His eyes dilate and stare fixedly ahead or into the sky.

His particular gait and dance as well as his speech, gestures, and mannerisms are directed by the possessing spirit; and he begins to speak in tongues.

However the linguist (Chief Priest and Teacher), who is usually a man, through his years of experience is able to interpret the Student's words.

The manner of ending possession is varied; most of the time he spins rapidly while standing in one place and suddenly falls into the arms of his attendants.

The attendants rush to take him away from the crowd, and he is given some water or palm wine. In a few moments he regains command of himself and the possession is over. In most cases, he cannot recall what happened, or what was said."

After this final ceremony, the student is now a full Priest Healer and qualified to deal with most mental illnesses. Everybody marches into his home village amidst drumming and singing where he will begin serving his role as a Mind Doctor.

However, we must point out that a Njayei Priest is in a very dangerous position, because there are some mental illnesses beyond a cure. And if by chance he becomes possessed by this type spirit, he may not be able to return to his 'right mind.'

Just imagine, spending the rest of your life, living with a crazy man's mind in your head controlling every thing you do. And you are in the position of watching yourself doing things against your will; and no other Priest Healer can help you.

On the other hand the Njayei Priest Healer deals with witchcraft, which is even more dangerous than dealing with mental illness. Because Witches themselves have as much knowledge about how the mind works as Priest Healers. This is why sometimes Priest Healers are called Witch Doctors.

This gives us some idea of the Mende's approach to dealing with mental illness. Although we did not go into to much detail, at least it was enough that we can begin to see the kinds of challenges that the Priest Healer takes in dealing with mental illness as well as Witchcraft.

It is a case of him and the illness meeting head-on in a direct confrontation, we can begin to see their approach and attitude toward mental health care.

Secree Religion
(Kpa Bush School)

Now we come to the Priest Healer that fits our idea of a general medical Doctor; the Leaders of the Kpa Bush School; the Secree called the "Leaf People or Medicine Men and Women."

Recall, the Secree live in a tropical rain forest, which consist of thousands of exotic tropical plants and animals. Each of which has the potential of a positive or negative effect on the human body and spirit as food and medicine.

This is where the Kpa Priest Healer fits into the healthcare picture. Through discovery, experimentation and observation, they study the relationship between humankind and nature (especially the nature of plants and animals called Bush Spirits).

On the one hand, we must not lose sight that the Kpa Bush School is also a government in Society. Which means they have authority to enforce and make rules about medicine as well as what food is good to eat.

And naturally the Kpa Bush School is organized like Poro, Sande, Humui, and Njayei, with their Masqueraders, Ancestors and Sacred Stones. All of which are based on Sacred Knowledge held in Secret and located in the Forest; only they specialize in major physical health care problems.

While on the other hand, Kpa Bush School is really a number of schools combined into one, we will call departments of study.

For example, there is the Priest Healers that specialize in broken bones; while others are concerned with poisonous snakebites, and still others treat fevers, headaches, or stomach problems, and so on.

Each department consists of a group having a secret body of knowledge. However, all is taught on Kpa Sacred Grounds. But we don't mean to imply that the departments don't overlap at times.

In this sense, the Kpa School is more like a general medical school. And like Njayei, to become qualified to join Kpa one must have had a illness and found a cure with some exceptions, especially the department dealing with poison snake bites.

Now to demonstrate what we mean that Kpa Priest Healers, through discovery, experimentation, and observation, fit into the picture in the case of health care and African Traditional Worldview. But also, the Secree's religious beliefs concerning how NGWE divided all of His knowledge between all of the life forms He Created.

Now there can be no doubt, from lots of solid evidence that, all Africans, and naturally this includes the Secree and Kpa Priest Healers, knew how to cure a large number of what we call major physical medical problems. As far as we are concerned, the question becomes, how did they get the knowledge?

Up to this point we came to the conclusion that their major tools were discovery, experimentation, and observation from a practical point of view based on the intelligence of their world view.

For example, if a man gets sick, he looks for a cure in Bush Spirits of animals and plants. However, to show the relationship between intelligence and health care, we will not go into great detail of "how" the Kpa Priest Healer deals with major physical medical problems.

We will only focus on the subject of the intellectual approach and attitude, or logic that leads him to a successful cure.

As we mentioned, the Kpa Bush School consists of a number of departments, to take a look at their approach, we will begin with the department, and Priest Healers, that specialize in poisonous snake bites; known as Ba Kona.

Although the West Africa Forest areas have many species of dangerous snakes, not all of them present a big threat to people. Those that give people problems, like hanging around people's farms and villages and other places people congregate, generally do not fear people. The most dangerous ones are the "Saw-Scale Viper," "Spitting Cobra," and the "Green Mamba."

The question becomes, how to solve this problem? To deal with this problem, and other poisonous snake problems, was the function of the organization of Priest Healers known as the Ba Kona Society, and we will call, the "Snake Doctors."

Now to return to our example of the game of Wari, with the Yoruba's while we have the Snake Doctors on one side of the board, we must take a look at the players on the other side, the three Snakes we mentioned.

However, the Green Mamba is not only one of the most poisonous snakes in Africa, but they are also short-tempered and do not fear man, and will attack without being provoked.

Plus, they are the master fighters of the snake world and are very aggressive, and sometimes hang around villages and peoples houses. When confronted, they will kill as many as 5 or 6 people at one time.

Now to get some insight into the Snake Doctors, we must see how the Green Mamba fits into their rituals; and things taught in their school about poison snakes in general.

The qualification to become a Snake Doctor, unlike the other areas of illness, does not mean that a student has been bitten by a poison snake and learned to cure himself. A snake's poison works to fast for that to be possible.

This knowledge is the direct results of analytical thinking based on discovery, experimentation, and observation. Also from studying the effects of plants on snakes and humans. Thus is the job of the Snake Doctor. Here, we are talking about solving a problem, snakes on one side, and the Snake Doctors on the other.

On the other hand, we are also interested in the ritual, or spiritual side of this intelligence we keep mentioning. So we will begin with the Snake Doctor's spiritual relations with his knowledge of how to deal with poison snakes.

This means, for example, with the Akan we were focused on the subject of the ritual symbolism of ideas and reality of Society as related to the King. From that point of view, we will now look at the ritual symbolism of knowledge and health care of Society as related to the Snake Doctors.

For this reason, we will take a much more detailed look at the Priest Healers called Snake Doctors than we will of the other Kpa Priest Healers.

First we will describe some of the ritual objects kept in a special box by the "Gba Ku" (Chief Snake Doctor) used for the ritual of induction of a new student into the secret knowledge the Snake Doctors;

1. Home made brass needle.
2. Cotton thread.
3. Small mask.
4. A quartz crystal.
5. A brass ring.
6. Two iron rings, tied together.
7. Two animal horns fill with a special medicine.
8. And a special mat, about six feet square, with four cowries sewn into a cross (road) pattern in each corner.

Students who have a desire to become Snake Doctors, for whatever reasons, he or she makes an application to the Gba Ku (Chief Snake Doctor) with a sum of money. Like throughout Africa, everybody gets paid, and if he is accepted, a date is set for the ritual introduction ceremony.

The Snake Doctor's Shrine is located on Kpa's sacred grounds, and on the appointed day. The student is brought to the shrine house by one of Gba Ku's assistants.

Before entering, the student is given the follow instructions; the student is to enter the shrine house backwards, the left foot the first to cross the doorway

He is told that he will see a mat inside on which he is to sit. He is warned to touch nothing until he has seen a needle sticking in the edge of the mat. He must pull this needle and its thread through, and hand it to the Gba Ku with his left hand. And that every thing related to the upcoming ritual should be done with the left hand.

Meanwhile in the shrine house, Gba Ku and his assistants have prepared to receive the student by emptying the ritual property box onto the square mat. The needle made of brass and threaded with cotton thread has already been stuck into the border of the mat and left with the point sticking out.

The student, following the instructions enters backward, left foot first, and seats himself on the mat where the Gba Ku and his chief assistant are already seated.

Gba Ku asks him what he came for, he answers "to join the Ba Kona society."

Then Gba Ku says, "Do you really want to join?"

He answers, "Yes."

Now Gba Ku and his assistants show the student the things spread out on the mat, handing them to him, always using the left hand, but he does not accept nor touch them; indicating he doesn't know what they mean.

After a few minutes, the Student catches hold of the point of the needle that was stuck under the border of the mat, pulls it through, handling it to Gba Ku. Then the two iron rings, tied together are taken from the collection of ritual objects on the mat and handed back and forth from the Gba Ku and the student four times.

Now the snake whose bite is most feared in the green mamba because it will attack without warning, striking from a tree or on the ground; whose poison is deadly.

For this reason the threaded needle is called "The Green Mamba," (and the student pulling it through, symbolizes the catching of the mamba).

As we mentioned, the other objects on the mat are a small "mask" (symbolizing the spirit of the green mamba), a quartz crystal (symbolizing the soul of the Green mamba), the two iron rings tied together (symbolizing the knowledge of the green mamba) and, "two horns filled with black medicine" (symbolizing the two fangs of the green mamba filled with poison).

Finally, the box and its contents symbolize the "Head of the Green Mamba." The student swears on the "Head" never to tell any outsider what goes on in the Ba Kona society. This ends the first stage of the ritual ceremony.

Next, the Gba Ku, his assistants, and the student go into the forest. The bearer of the Head (box) is a young girl who is a member, and no one except the Gba Ku and his chief assistant may speak to her. During the procession, no other person may touch the box except the Gba Ku, who alone is permitted to open it.

In the forest, a ritual meal is prepared and all eat together. For this meal each two men must bring a chicken, some rice, palm oil, and salt. No one may taste the meal during preparation, which is seasoned with shoots of Kma ti (Albizzia Zygia) and Guo (Desmodium ascendent).

No one may eat first before the other. So Gba ku puts a little bit of rice and meat into the left hand of each man, and puts some into the box containing the ritual objects. At a given signal each eats his bit of food.

After the sacrificial meal, the ritual assistants gather a number of pieces of plants, leaves, vines, and roots of which we will give the African as well as the (science names),

Lu gai (Rutaceous tree)

Kping keko fu (Mezoneurum sp)
Da (Acacia)
Tene gene (Dichrostachys glomerata)
Si sue (Uncaria Talbotii)
Tui (Rhynchosia sp)
Tue Sao (Leptoderris fasciculata)
Zo Kpai bele (Tetracera potatoria)
Gene zolo (Combretum grandiflorum)
Gongo kala (Hybophrynium Braunianum)
To (Baphia sp)
Gui go (Baphia sp)
Gei yidi (Erythrina altissima)
Ge (Bombax sp)
Zu fili ko (Gouania longipetala)
To fo gene (Gardenia Abbockutac)
Gbili sai wele (Entada scelerata)
Fai la (Manniophyton africanum)
Pipi (Scleria Barteri and Vogelii)

All are calcined (parched into a powder) in a pot, beaten to a black powder in a mortar brought along for the purpose, and mixed with red palm oil.

This medicine called "Ti le (poison that kills snakes)," is put into an animal horn furnished by the student. Leaves of Wana (Mareya spicaata) are beaten up with white clay, and a little is put in the horn, before it is filled with the calcined (powdered) mixture.

The "Ti la" is used to smear on the legs if going into the forest. It is said to kill a snake if rubbed on its head. Even handling a snake after the snake doctor has recently had "Ti la" on his hands will harm the snake.

Even if he is bitten by a poisonous snake, the "Ti La" paralyzes the snake's poison gland muscles and he cannot eject his poison, plus, coming into contact with "Ti La" will kill the snake. But once the snake smells the Ti la, he is not going to attack in the first place.

This means that the Snake Doctors take a competitive approach and attitude towards poisonous snakes. The snake creates a poison that kills man, and the Snake Doctors created a poison that kills snakes.

A horn of this "Ti la," decorated with several bracelets is carried by each Snake Doctor. One bracelet goes through a hole in the big end of the horn.

The other bracelets are linked into this one like keys on a key ring. After enough "Ti la" has been made to fill a horn for the Student, and to renew the supply of older members, the procession forms to return to the Shrine House.

Everyone must enter the Shrine house left foot first. When the box is once more in its place, the Gba Ku takes a piece of the vine Ka nai la (Synclisia sp), brought for the purpose, and makes it an armlet of three or four coils. This is wrapped with black or blue dyed cotton thread, and rubbed with "Ti la."

The new student Snake Doctor wears this above the elbow. He also swallows a few drops of juice squeezed from the same vine.

Finally the Gba Ku tells the Student the by-laws of the Ba Kona Society;

1. A Snake Doctor always uses the left hand in shaking hands with a fellow member.

2. He does everything while in the Shrine house with the left hand.

3. He is to always enter the Shrine house with the left foot first, but he does not enter backwards any more.

4. He must sit cross-legged with the left foot in front.

5. The password to the Shrine house is to call the doorkeeper by his title "Ya Zia," and to tell him to move the snake so one can come in. This "snake" is a noose of vine or string on the floor, just inside the door, arranged to catch the foot of anyone who is not aware of it.

6. When anyone asks the student to show him the snake, the answer is to point out the plaited side of the mat-border.

7. The plain side of the border is called, "outside" or "uninitiated person."

8. To the question, "Where are the snake people?" the answer is to point to the group of cowries shells sewed on each corner of the mat.

9. When asked. "Where is the snake's mat?" the answer is to point out a leaf of to a yei (Smilax Kraussiana).

We can see, that the Snake Doctors take an "eye for a eye" kind of approach. But as far as we are concerned, the question becomes, how did the Snake Doctors create a poison that would kill a snake, or beat the snake at his own game so to speak?

Our conclusion is that the Snake Doctors found this knowledge through observation, experimentation, and discovery of snakes and plants; which symbolizes the intelligence we keep mentioning.

To get a clearer picture of what we mean, we will take a look at the things the new student must learn about plants, snakes, and snake bites, before he becomes a qualified Snake Doctor.

First the student must familiarize himself with snakes and their habits, and learn to handle them without danger. In other words, he must learn to catch and tame any kind of poisonous snake, except the spitting Cobra.

But includes the very dangerous Green Mamba, Gabon Viper, Saw-Scale Viper to name a few, with out removing the snakes fangs or poison. But to do this, he must learn about certain plants and their effects on snakes. All of which he learns by observing the Gba Ku.

Before going to catch snakes, Gba Ku and the student take the leaves of a climbing fern, gbidi woa or da-vo (Ageratum conyzoides), and rubs them to a pulp between the hands. And smears it all over their arms, the smell of which totally confuses snakes.

This allows them to reach into holes, and drag them out by the tails, tap them on the head two or three times, then pick them up by the neck.

The taming of snakes is accomplished by the use of leaves of the plant sei (Microdesmis puberula), chewed up and spit onto the snake's head, or put on by a quick tap on the head.

This substance makes the snake "high" like "downers." Snakes when treated with "sei" can be handled freely, and played with as though they were not dangerous snakes at all. They do not hiss or make any attempt to escape.

After they are tamed, it is not necessary to put this sei on their heads. Instead, they take the succulent base of a leaf of ze wele ko (Piper guineense) vine, chew it up, and squeeze the juice from the pulp in the snake's mouth, held open by an assistant; which neutralizes or weakens the snake's poison to some extent.

There is also an art in handling a snake. A tamed snake is picked up gently by the middle, without squeezing, but by sliding a hand under a coil as easily as possible. They can be twined around the Snake Doctor's neck, can be bath, etc, etc. This allows the Snake Doctors to study snakes as long as he wants.

On the other hand, some snakes are to be caught without any attempt to preserve them alive and unharmed, especially the Green Mamba who spends most of his time in trees. In these cases, Gba Ku "parch" the leaves of wana (Marcya spicata) and mix them with red palm oil.

This "medicine" is put in any convenient horn. And when a Green Mamba is seen in a tree, the Snake Doctor takes some of this "medicine" and rubs it around the trunk of the tree.

Before the snake will crawl pass the medicine, he will jump from the tree and is easily killed. If there is no stick handy to kill it with, he rubs the wana mixture on both hands, grabs the snake by the tail, and beats it against the ground.

Throughout the Student's training, tame poisonous snakes are kept in the Shrine House in a box whose bottom is covered with the leaves of Toa yei (Smilax Kraussiana) for the Snake's mat. Where they are fed and given water and otherwise cared for.

Now we should again recall the Mende's beliefs about "NGWE" and the "Cave of Life;" where each life form was given a name and certain knowledge.

The training of Snake Doctors gives us some insight into how the Secree's, through experimentation, discovery, and observation learn and use the knowledge of other life forms to benefit Society.

There is complex substances that make up snake poison. Include; (1) nerve effecting elements (nevrotoxin). 2) Blood affecting elements (haemotoxin). (3) Digestive agents; or (4) a combination of the 3. Divided between two families of snakes, "Elapid family" includes the "Green Mamba," and the "Viperidae family" which includes the "Saw-Scale Viper."

The "Green Mamba:" There is often a period of 1 to 2 hours after the bite when there are no dramatic symptoms or evidence of serious poisoning. After which the drooping of the eyelids gives the victim a sleepy or doped expression. Followed by difficulty in swallowing and speaking, drooling of saliva, weakness, gasping for breath and irregularity of heart beat. Which indicates a deadly attack on a persons nervous system; however, there is no pain involved.

The "Saw-Scale Viper:" The poison of the Vipers contain the largest number of different poisoning agents. Which include those that destroy the lining of blood vessels, those that destroy red blood corpuscles, those that destroy white blood corpuscles and tissue cells, those that cause clotting within the vessels and those that prevent blood clotting. Finally digestive elements, that can become gangrenous and cause limbs to be amputated; all of which are very painful, including the bite itself.

On the other hand, while taming and handling snakes, even master snake handlers, Gba Ku, will make a mistake and are bitten.

However, if any tame snake bites, kept by a Gba Ku, it is considered a serious business. For it is thought that the snake has won the game; and it does happen from time to time, especially with young Doctors.

Therefore, early in training, and one of the major focuses of Ba Kona, the student learns to deal with snake bites. Although the Snake Doctors used the age-old method of making a cut into the bite, and sucking out the poison, the medicine they use is related to the kind of snake involved.

And it is these medicines that interest us at this point. For we must keep in mind that the Snake Doctors believe that when a snake bites a man, the effects are not only the poison in his body, but there is also a effect the man's spirit. Which means the medicine must treat both, as well as protect the Doctor.

This means that the treatments for snakebites differ according to the kind of snake, as though each snake bite was a different disease. However, there are a few medicines that will do some good for any kind of snake bite, and for the more dangerous snakes there are several treatments.

If the kind of snake is not known, the Snake Doctor takes a few bud leaves of wana (Mareya spicata), chews them, and holding the chewed up leaf in his mouth, sucks the wound and spits out the poison.

He then takes more of the same leaves, crushes them, and puts the mass on the wound. This is to protect the spirit of the man from that of the snake.

A strip of wana bark is then used to make a tourniquet, and tied above the wound, not too tight, but tight enough to constrict blood vessels.

The tender bud leaves of a young palm tree (elacis guineensis) are crushed and applied to the bite of any snake to relieve the pain. The latex of bo-fie-ko (carpodinus sp) is also used on the wound as a first-aid remedy.

The snake whose bite is most feared is the Green Mamba, there are consequently several plants used specifically against it.

However the most used, after applying a tourniquet, the Snake Doctor pulls out the tender bud leaves of an oil palm (Elaeis guincensis), chews up the soft heart end, and with this in his mouth sucks out the poison.

After repeating this treatment twice, the bud leaves of gbana na (tetracera, either potatoria or leiocarpa) are beaten up with a little white clay and rubbed on the wound.

This shows that the Student must learn a lot about snakes and plants. However, this is as far as we will go into snakebites, as far as treatment is concerned. Because our major goal is the approach and attitude the Snake Doctor takes toward the threat the snakes present to the welfare of the health of Society.

And our point being, this is the same approach and attitude all Kpa Doctors take in the treatment of disease whatever their specialty. The disease is thought of as the Snake Doctor thinks of, and relate to snakes, spiritually and physically.

Secree Religion
(Conclusion)

Our conclusion was that there are five bush schools, "Poro, Sande, Humui, Njayei, and Kpa;" (Wunde, the warrior school, is not included at this point). These five Bush Schools not only deal with the social side of society, they also perform rituals related to Society Religion.

It is these five governments, working in harmony with each other that govern the social conduct and spiritual attitude of the Mende Society.

Collectively, they handle general education in the sense of social and vocational training, and indoctrination of spiritual attitudes; regulate sexual conducts and, supervise political and economical affairs.

Plus they operate social services, ranging from medical treatment, to forms of entertainment and recreation.

Like Poro and Sande, the three remaining bush schools are also based on a body of "bush knowledge" of their own, symbolized by a "Spirit of Knowledge" in the form of a "Masquerader" wearing a "Sacred Mask."

If Poro and Sande are the Mother and Father of Society, then these three schools are the Uncles and Aunts of Society. Together, they create and maintain Society. The point being that, as far as ritual worship is concerned, all of these "Bush Schools" worship a "Bush Spirit", and the "Ancestors" of their school.

And being, as we saw for example in Poro and Sande, the only form of ritual worship the children are taught, and the Elders are concerned with, is related to the "Spirit of Manhood Knowledge" and the "Spirit of Womanhood Wisdom."

So what do we have as far as Society Religion is concerned, we have five Secret Society Bush Spirits and Ancestors, as the subject of ritual worship, and the source of moral law. First, we must define what we mean by Society Religion and Moral Law.

If we recall, with the Yoruba, the Akan, the Ajax, and the Igbos, the source of moral law comes directly from the God and Goddess of life. For example with the Igbo, moral law came from The Earth Goddess.

However, with the Mendes, the sources of moral laws come from "Bush Spirits of Stolen Knowledge and Ancestor Priest." And it is these five Bush Spirits, and Priest Ancestors that are the source of moral law. For example, like Christ and His Disciples are the source of moral law in Christian Religion.

This means that Bush Spirits and Ancestor Priest are not only the source of moral law, but also the only source of spiritual forgiveness for the violation of moral laws.

This also means that Bush Spirits and Ancestor Priest are the Gods and Goddesses of a religion that everybody in Society believes in, and this makes it a Society Religion. And most important, this means that Bush Spirits and Ancestor Priest serve the same purpose as the Gods and Goddesses.

Now we will take a look at how Secret Society Bush Spirits and Ancestor Priest function as the foundation of a Religion and Source of Moral laws.

In this sense, the Mendes have two sources of moral laws, one from Bush Spirits and Ancestor Priest, and the other, from Most Ancient Ancestors.

Recall the Most ancient Ancestors are the Great Redeemers of Mankind, and Bush Spirits are the Spirit of the Knowledge of the Nature of Mankind and life itself.

The violation of moral laws is what Afro-Americans call "Sin", and the Mendes call "Kaye" (in the case of Bush Spirits) and "Koto" (in the case of Most Ancient Ancestors). All of which causes "Spiritual Sickness" or "Moral shame" from which one must be "Spiritually Cleansed" or "Spiritually Purified."

However, as far as Society Religion is concerned, we are more interested in the Moral Laws of Bush Spirits. For example, like the Poro Bush Spirit of Manhood Knowledge, GBENI, who is worshipped at the Shrine of Sacred Stones located at the graves of Ancestor Priests and Priestesses.

This includes the "Moral Laws" of not only Poro Bush Spirit, but also the Bush Spirits of Sande, Humui, Njayei, and Kpa.

But does not include Wunde, War chief and Warrior, Secret Society Bush Spirit. Who does not make any laws and is concerned only with enforcing the laws of the five schools; like police officers.

Therefore, we must conclude that the Mende Society is organized around a religion of its own, based on Knowledge and wisdom, symbolized by Bush Spirit, who is the God and Goddess of their Society.

So from what we have learned about what the Mende teach their children, and the fact that people only ritually worship and teach their children their highest values, we must come to the conclusion that the "Highest Values the in the Mende Society is Knowledge and Wisdom as related to the laws of the jungle."

On the other hand, being as the Mendes think of NGEWO and NDOI as the God and Goddess of Knowledge and Wisdom, any worship of Knowledge and Wisdom, even if indirectly, is worship of NGEWO and NDOI directly.

So we cannot say that the Mendes do not worship the God and Goddess of Creation, only that they have a complicated way of going about it. However, all of this goes even further to show that Knowledge and Wisdom are their Highest Values.

Now, as to the nature of Secret Societies, the evidence shows that the attitude of Secret Societies is a "Spiritual approach to communicating and understanding Practical Knowledge and Wisdom for the benefit of Society.

For example, the Poro ritual teaches the boys practical things like building and protecting their little village from a spiritual as well as a physical point of view. This is the case with making a farm, the man-woman relationship, and raising a family.

We can also reach the conclusion that the idea of a "Spiritual approach to Practical Knowledge and Wisdom" is the key to understanding "Secret Society's" role in "Society as a whole."

They create and maintain Society in the same manner as a man and woman create and raise a family. This is why Poro, Sande, Humoi, Njayei, and Kpa are called the Mother, Father, Aunts, and Uncles of Society.

On the other hand, the "Spirit of Knowledge and Wisdom" of each of these "Secret Societies" is the only God-like-Spirits that are ritually worshipped by members of Society.

Therefore, we must conclude that these "Spirits" are the "Gods and Goddesses" of Society and therefore, are the bases of a "Society Religion." Because, besides the "Ancestors as the Redeemers of Mankind," they are the only "Spirits" that are the subject of "Ritual Worship." Thus is the nature of the Mende Society.

We must keep in mind that the Mendes are only an example of all of the "Nations" that make up the "People in the Land of Secret Societies," we call "The Secree."

And up to this point, to some degree, we have established the Mende's highest values, and therefore the highest values of the Secree in general, being as all of them are governed to be secret societies.

And at the same time, we have shown the role of Secret Societies to be that of "Spiritual and Social Governments of Society;" which is another thing all of the Secree Nations have in common.

Therefore, we must come to the conclusion that the "Trinity of Highest Values of all Secree is Knowledge, Wisdom, and Secrecy."

Other Books by
Orchester (Hip-hop Grandpa) Benjamin Family

Grandpa! Tell us a Story/
Drinking from Ancient Wells

**The Story of the Game Black people Play/Trilogy
Book One: The Game's Soul**
ISBN 978-0-9773421-1-2 $24.95
Book Two: the Game's Mind
ISBN 978-0-9773421-8-1 $24.95
Book Three: The Game's Heart
ISBN 978-0-9773421-6-7 $24.95

**Questions of Black Salvation/
The Black History and African Soul Story
ISBN 978-0-9773421-3-6 $9.95**

**The AfroSacredStar Story/
Ancient West African Spirituality
ISBN 978-0-9773421-9-8 $34.95**

Order online www.Amazon.com
Or
Order with the publisher at www.SoulViewWorld.com
using PayPal